WEST'S LAW SCHOOL ADVISORY BOARD

LAW AND HEALTH CARE QUALITY, PATIENT SAFETY, AND MEDICAL LIABILITY

Seventh Edition

■ ■ ■

By

Barry R. Furrow
Professor of Law and Director, Health Law Program
Drexel University

Thomas L. Greaney
Chester A. Myers Professor of Law and
Co–Director, Center for Health Law Studies
Saint Louis University School of Law

Sandra H. Johnson
Professor Emerita of Law and Health Care Ethics
Center for Health Law Studies
Saint Louis University School of Law

Timothy Stoltzfus Jost
Robert L. Willett Family Professor of Law
Washington and Lee University

Robert L. Schwartz
Senior Visiting Professor
University of California Hastings College of the Law
Weihofen Professor of Law Emeritus
University of New Mexico

AMERICAN CASEBOOK SERIES®

WEST®

Mat #41238530

610 Opperman Drive
St. Paul, MN 55123
1-800-313-9378

Printed in the United States of America

ISBN: 978–0–314–27990–3

Dedication

To Donna Jo, Elena, Michael, Nicholas, Eva, Robert, Hayden, Aspen, and Grey

B.R.F.

To Nancy, T.J., and Kati

T.L.G.

To Bob, Emily, Kathleen, Colin, Nicholas, Zachary, and Abigail

S.H.J.

To Ruth, Jacob, Micah, David, Felix, and Emily

T.S.J.

To Jane, Mirra, and Elana

R.L.S.

This book is also dedicated to the memory of Nancy Rhoden and Jay Healey, great teachers, wonderful colleagues and warm friends.

PREFACE

This seventh edition of this casebook marks the twenty–sixth anniversary of our text, first published in 1987. Since that first edition, no part of the American landscape has changed more than the American health care system. The system has been stressed by demographic changes, buffeted by the winds of political change, and utterly transformed by social and economic developments. The formal structure of the business of health care was a small part of the subject of health law when we published our first edition; it is now the subject of entire graduate programs. The for–profit commercial sector of the health care economy sounded like a lamb twenty–five years ago; now it roars like a lion. Until a few years ago virtually no one attained elective office because of her position on issues related to health care; now health care reform is the most politically controversial issue in America. Indeed, we repeatedly delayed bringing out a seventh edition because of the uncertain fate of health care reform, threatened first by a Supreme Court case and then by the 2012 elections.

Derived from the comprehensive material contained in the seminal casebook, *Health Law: Cases, Materials, and Problems*, this text incorporates current case law, statutes, and regulations in conjunction with insightful notes and hypothetical problems to provide a sophisticated, up–to–date inquiry into the field. Concern over the quality of health care has been a central issue for health reform for decades, and the tools used to enhance the quality of care have seen a remarkable development over the past several years. Patient safety has now become a new focus of both government regulators and private organizations concerned with health care quality. The Affordable Care Act itself incorporates many significant patient safety reforms, and this text accounts for those changes as well.

Law and Health Care Quality, Patient Safety, and Medical Liability is uniquely broad enough to be used in courses outside of law schools while sufficiently detailed to provide meaningful instruction to future health law practitioners. By presenting nuanced notes and examples, this book offers realistic situations for students to begin grappling with problems similar to those they may encounter in practice.

In addition to this text, the seventh edition of the comprehensive *Health Law* casebook has been issued in three other versions. The paperback abridged version of the complete casebook offers a survey of the field in about half the length of the comprehensive casebook. *Bioethics: Health Care Law and Ethics* presents the chapters addressing bioethics issues that occur most commonly in the health care setting. It contains chapters on end–of–life decision making, including medically assisted death; reproduction; genetics; organ transplantation; determination of death; regulation of research; and public health. It also includes an additional chapter introducing students to underlying theories and approaches to ethical analysis in the health care setting. *The Law of Health Care Organization and Finance* presents an in–depth treatment of issues of concern to the business of health care. It contains chapters on structural issues in health care organizations, including substantial materials on accountable care organizations, on corporate governance, and on tax exemption; fraud and abuse; antitrust; Medicare and Medicaid payment and eligibility; duties to provide care; professional licensure; institutional quality control regulation; and staff privileges, employment, and contracting.

Each of these casebooks is designed to be a teachable book. We are grateful for the many comments and helpful suggestions that health law teachers across the United States (and from elsewhere, too) have made to help us improve this new edition. We attempt to present all sides of policy issues, not to evangelize for any political, economic or social agenda of our own. This task is made easier, undoubtedly, by the diverse views on virtually all policy issues that the several different authors of this casebook bring to this endeavor. A large number of very well respected health law teachers have contributed a great deal to this and previous editions by making suggestions, reviewing problems, or encouraging our more thorough investigation of a wide range of health law subjects. We are especially grateful to Charles Baron, Eugene Basanta, David Bennahum, Robert Berenson, Kathleen Boozang, Don Chalmers, Ellen Wright Clayton, Judith Daar, Dena Davis, Arthur Derse, Kelly Dineen, Ileana Dominguez–Urban, Stewart Duban, Barbara Evans, Margaret Farrell, Rob Field, David Frankford, Michael Gerhart, Joan McIver Gibson, Susan Goldberg, Jesse Goldner, Andrew Grubb, Sarah Hooper, Jaime King, Art LaFrance, Diane Hoffmann, Jill Horwitz, Amy Jaeger, Eleanor Kinney, Thomasine Kushner, Pam Lambert, Theodore LeBlang, Antoinette Sedillo Lopez, Lawrence Singer, Joan Krause, Leslie Mansfield, Thomas Mayo, Maxwell Mehlman, Alan Meisel, Vicki Michel, Frances Miller, John Munich, David Orentlicher, Elizabeth Pendo, Vernellia Randall, Ben Rich, Arnold Rosoff, Karen Rothenberg, Mark Rothstein, Sallie Sanford, Giles Scofield, Jeff Sconyers, Charity Scott, Ross Silverman, Loane Skene, George Smith, Roy Spece, Jr., Carol Suzuki, Michael Vitiello, Sidney Watson, Lois Weithorn, Ellen Wertheimer, William Winslade, and Susan M. Wolf for the benefit of their wisdom and experience.

We wish to thank those who provided support for our research and the preparation of the manuscript, including the Frances Lewis Law Center, the Robert L. Willett family, Carrie Snow, Patrick Pedano, Yamini Laks, Erica Cohen, Laura Spencer, Melanie Rankin, Chelsea Averill, Autumn Berge, Theresa Vertucci Hacsi, Nicole Hamberger, Rebecca Kreiner, Nicole Moskowitz, Monica Smith, Vera Mencer, David Knoespel, Brittany Rainey, James Kovacs, David Fuchs, and James Bailey. We all have special appreciation for the exceptional work done by Mary Ann Jauer and Cheryl Cooper at Saint Louis University, and for the tremendous publication assistance provided by Pamela Siege Chandler, Louis Higgins, James Cahoy, Greg Olson, Pat Sparks, and Jennifer Schlagel of West Academic Publishing. Finally, we wish to thank our deans, Roger Dennis, Michael Wolff, Barbara Bergman, Frank Wu, and Nora Demleitner.

It has been a splendid opportunity to work on this casebook. It has been a constant challenge to find a way to teach cutting edge issues influencing our health care system—at times before the courts or legislatures have given us much legal material for our casebook. Each time we have done a new edition, there have been developments that we find difficult to assess as to whether they will become more significant during the lifespan of the edition or are simply blips. It is always difficult to delete materials that required much labor and still remain quite relevant but that have been eclipsed in importance by others, and the length of each succeeding edition attests to our challenge. Finally, we do not write this casebook for our classes alone, but rather for yours as well. We enjoy teaching, and we hope that comes through to the students and teachers who use this book.

A note on editorial style: Ellipses in the text of the quoted material indicate an omission of material within the quoted paragraph. Centered ellipses indicate the omission of a paragraph or more; the first line following centered ellipses may not be the first line of the next paragraph, and the last line preceding centered ellipses may not be the last line of the preceding paragraph. Brackets indicate the omission of a citation without the omission of other materials. There is no acknowledgment of omitted footnotes. To the extent it is possible, the style of this casebook is consistent with the principle that legal writing form should follow function, and the function of this text is to help students understand health law.

BARRY R. FURROW
THOMAS L. GREANEY
SANDRA H. JOHNSON
TIMOTHY S. JOST
ROBERT L. SCHWARTZ

April 2013

ACKNOWLEDGMENTS

Devers, Kelly and Robert Berenson, Can Accountable Care Organizations Improve the Value of Health Care by Solving the Cost and Quality Quandries?, Copyright 2009, The Urban Institute. Reprinted with permission.

Davis, Karen, Cathy Schoen, and Kristof Stremikis, Mirror, Mirror on the Wall: How the Performance of the U.S. Health Care System Compares Internationally 2010 Update (New York: The Commonwealth Fund, June 2010), http://www.commonwealthfund.org/Publications/Fund–Reports/2010/Jun/Mirror–Mirror–Update.aspx. Used with permission.

Donabedian, Avedis, The Definition of Quality and Approaches to its Assessment, 1st ed., 4–6, 7, 13, 14, 27, 79–84, 102, 119 (Health Administration Press, Ann Arbor, MI, 1980). Reprinted from Avedis Donabedian, The Definition of Quality and Approaches to its Assessment, in Explorations in Quality Assessment and Monitoring, Volume 1. Copyright 1980. Reprinted with permission.

Enthoven, Alain, Health Plan: The Only Practical Solution to the Soaring Costs of Health Care 1–12 (1980). Copyright 1980 Alain Enthoven. Reprinted with permission.

Hacker, Jacob S., and Theodore R. Marmor, How Not to Think About "Managed Care," 32 University of Michigan Journal of Law Reform 661 (1999). Copyright University of Michigan Journal of Law Reform. Used with permission.

Leape, Lucian L., Error in Medicine, 272 JAMA 1851 (1994). Copyright 1994, American Medical Association. Reprinted with permission of the American Medical Association.

SUMMARY OF CONTENTS

TABLE OF CONTENTS

TABLE OF CASES

The principal cases are in bold type.

Cases

LAW AND HEALTH CARE QUALITY, PATIENT SAFETY, AND MEDICAL LIABILITY

Seventh Edition

CHAPTER 1

COST, QUALITY, ACCESS, AND CHOICE

■ ■ ■

I. INTRODUCTION

Cost, quality, access, and choice are the chief concerns of the health care system and the central themes of these materials. The four operate in a dynamic and complex relationship. It is easy, for example, to assume that increasing quality or access must naturally increase costs. One might assume that increasing the required staff–to–patient ratio in health care facilities increases the costs of care. The same assumption may be made about the impact on health care costs caused by increasing the numbers of individuals eligible or the range of services covered by Medicaid or Medicare, our public programs for covering the elderly, disabled, and poor. In each of these examples, however, it is possible that total cost actually is lowered by avoiding facility–generated injuries or infections or by providing timely care that avoids extraordinary costs incurred as a medical condition or disease moves to later stages untreated. In other situations, however, enhancing one value truly may diminish another. Preserving individual choice through maintaining the private health insurance system, for example, most likely increases costs overall, but perhaps the increase in cost is justified.

Of course, the analysis of the impact of particular legal and policy decisions on cost, quality, access, and choice is not entirely a dispassionate, rational, empirically–based calculation. Political strength, economic power, and culture and tradition all influence how we view the relative advantages and disadvantages of particular proposals and how we ultimately design our systems. In addition, gains and losses are not shared equally, so advocates may represent particular interests.

The recent health reform debates put a powerful spotlight on concerns over access, cost, quality, and choice. Public understanding of the Patient Protection and Affordable Care Act (ACA) centers on the tentative adoption of the principle that providing access to some form of basic medical care is important to the health and flourishing of society as a whole. Access to care is the banner headline for the ACA, even as that principle faces continued opposition. The vehicles chosen for achieving this goal rest on a second principle so embedded in our culture that forward progress was probably impossible without honoring it. That value is individual choice, and it is reflected in the oft–stated mantra expressed in the campaign to gain public support for the ACA: "No one will make you change your coverage; if you like it, you can keep it." In addition, the question of individual choice, and its apparent conflict with increasing access, took center stage in the battles over the Constitutionality of the ACA.

The ACA certainly responded to concerns about access and choice, but it is attempting to do much more in refashioning the health care delivery and payment systems. The goal is to develop a system that provides quality health care to more people at lower cost. It is ambitious.

II. REGULATION OR COMPETITION?

Concerns over cost, quality, access, and choice dominate health care policymaking. The ultimate goal may be clear: we want a health care system that delivers quality care at lower cost for more people but preserves appropriate choice for the individual. How we get there is anything but clear. One of the essential strategies is the selection of the most effective tools for influencing health care providers and the system toward making decisions that will improve care and lower cost. This section addresses a central debate over whether government regulation or private market competition, or some combination of the two, is the best tool for achieving our desired outcome.

Health care is sometimes referred to as a "regulated industry." To be sure, numerous aspects of hospital, physician, and health insurance markets are subject to state and federal controls. As we will see, a wide spectrum of regulations affect health care payment and delivery: physician licensure, accreditation of hospitals and other health facilities, supervision of provider behavior by government payers, regulation of insurance industry practices, and certificate of need regulation requiring governmental approval to open or add to health care facilities, to name just a few. Moreover, because federal, state, and local governments purchase an enormous share, perhaps as much as 45%, of all of health care services, their influence over the industry is obviously substantial.

Despite the pervasiveness of regulation, market competition is a key feature of the American health care system. Indeed, a major theme of government policy over the last thirty years has been to rely more on market competition rather than regulation, even in sectors in which the government is the payer such as Medicare and Medicaid. In fact, much of health care regulation is aimed at strengthening the impact of competition, and many laws you will study in the coming weeks are explicitly designed to improve the performance of the market. Examples of these market–improving devices include encouraging the spread of HMOs and insurance products that promote consumer choice; removing regulatory barriers to competition through aggressive antitrust enforcement; regulating health insurance to encourage transparency and consumer choice; and limiting providers' ability to take advantage of their trusted position as agents to engage in self–referral practices or accept kickbacks. Of course, some government regulation supplements or replaces the market.

Why does government regulate any industry or economic enterprise? The most common justification is that the industry in question is subject to "market imperfections" that result in suboptimal performance for consumers. Economists invariably begin discussions of health care with a list of market and regulatory failures that pervade the financing and delivery of health care services. Market imperfections, including imperfect agency relations, information gaps and asymmetry, moral hazard, and monopoly are widely recognized shortcomings that undermine consumer welfare in commercial markets for health care products and services. Nobel laureate Kenneth J. Arrow's path–breaking analysis summarized the potential consequences of these distortions from an economic standpoint:

> The failure of one or more of the competitive preconditions has as its most immediate and obvious consequence a reduction in welfare below that obtainable from existing resources and technology.

Kenneth J. Arrow, Uncertainty and the Welfare Economics of Medical Care, 53 Am. Econ. Rev. 941 (1963).

Several of these market failures merit special attention. First, asymmetries in information, especially between patients and providers, and uncertainty as to diagnosis, treatment, and outcome are critical to understanding the health care marketplace. Because of the technical nature of medical information and the complexity of diagnoses and treatment alternatives, patients and third–party payers find it difficult to evaluate the cost and quality of health services. Indeed, the considerable uncertainty that attends medical treatment makes judgments on causation (and hence costs and benefits of the treatment) difficult. In addition, information is asymmetrically distributed among providers, patients, and payers. This characteristic may permit physicians to "induce demand" for their services or make referrals based on their own economic interest. At a minimum it makes the information consumers need to shop in their own best interest hard to acquire. Even on the most basic level, it is nearly impossible for consumers to learn the exact price for services in advance. See Paul Starr, Law and the Fog of Health Care: Complexity and Uncertainty in the Struggle over Health Policy, ___ St. Louis U. J. Health L. & Pol'y ___ (2013).

Second, agency relationships, which pervade health markets, are highly influential in health care transactions. Most people "purchase" health care services with the assistance of multiple agents—their employers, the plans or insurers chosen by their employers, and, most significantly, the physicians who guide their choices. In many instances, these intermediaries are "imperfect agents"—they are subject to conflicts of interest or they do not fully understand the needs of their consumers or patients.

Third, health insurance markets exhibit conditions that give rise to market failures. "Moral hazard," for example, refers to the overuse of medical care resulting from the fact that insurance lowers the cost of each purchase for insured individuals. This can result in inefficiency due to overuse of some services. In addition, insurers have a strong incentive to engage in favorable risk selection—seeking a healthy cohort of beneficiaries—which can cause the entire industry to spiral to inefficient performance.

Finally (although this does not exhaust the list of imperfections in health markets), an important requirement of a competitive market is the presence of multiple buyers and sellers and ease of entry for new competitors. In health care, the markets for hospital services, physician specialty services, and commercial insurance are highly concentrated. Moreover a large number of regulatory barriers such as certificate of need, licensure, and scope of practice laws inhibit entry into hospital and physician services markets.

Appreciation of these characteristics helps explain why government regulation is needed in the health care sector. For example, uncertainty and information asymmetries underlie the need for physician licensure and much regulation of insurance. Imperfect agency justifies the need for regulating physician referrals and prohibiting kickbacks. Problems endemic to insurance explain the need for laws encouraging formation of large pools of insured and preventing risk selection as well as antitrust laws and regulations designed to facilitate entry of new competition work to prevent or offset the effects of monopoly power.

At the same time it should be understood that many of these regulations also help make market competition work more efficiently. In fact, the role of government regulation in improving the market illustrates an important principle. Rather than viewing health policy as facing dichotomous choices—competition or regulation—it is more accurate to see the two as potentially complementary. See Kristen Madison, Regulating Health Care Quality in an Information Age, 40 U.C.Davis L.J. 1577 (2007) (employing a tricotomy of market–displacing, market–facilitating, and market–channeling regulations to analyze regulatory responses to information failures in health care). For a comprehensive examination of regulation in health care, see Robert I. Field, Health Care Regulation in America: Complexity, Confrontation and Compromise (2007). Indeed it can be argued that much of the landmark health reform law, the Affordable Care Act, is designed to improve competitiveness of markets by imposing a host of regulations. See Thomas L. Greaney, The Affordable Care

Act and Competition Policy: Antidote or Placebo? 89 Or. L. Rev. 811 (2011).

QUESTIONS

How would you decide whether competition or regulation (more precisely perhaps, what type of regulation) best responds to the reality of the practice of medicine and health care delivery? Consider the following three perspectives:

1. Alain Enthoven, an economist who is best known as one of the early proponents of "managed competition" and the development of HMOs, authored a seminal analysis of the potential for competition in health care markets. A core part of his analysis was debunking a number of commonly held assumptions about health care and replacing those with more sophisticated, accurate, and complex understandings. Alain Enthoven, in Health Plan: The Only Practical Solution to the Soaring Costs of Health Care (1980). Among his examples are:

> *"The doctor should be able to know what condition the patient has, be able to answer patient's questions precisely, and prescribe the right treatment."* Instead, he points out that "there is a great deal of *uncertainty* in each step of medical care. Doctors are confronted with patients who have symptoms and syndromes, not labels with their diseases."
>
> *"For each medical condition, there is a 'best' treatment. It is up to the doctor to know about that treatment and to use it. Anything else is unnecessary surgery, waste, fraud, or underservice."* In reality, Enthoven argues, for many medical conditions "there are *several possible treatments*, each of which is legitimate and associated with different benefits, risks, and costs"
>
> *"Medicine is an exact science. Unlike 50 or 100 years ago, there is now a firm scientific base for what the doctor does. Standard treatments are supported by scientific proof of efficacy."* To the contrary, he states that "medicine remains more of an art than a science" and although "it uses and applies scientific knowledge . . . the application of this knowledge is a matter of judgment."
>
> *"Medical care consists of standard products that can be described precisely and measured meaningfully in standard units such as "in-patient days", "outpatient visits", or "doctor office visits".* Enthoven does not believe medical services are subject to easy categorization: "In fact, medical care is usually anything but a standard product. Much of it is a uniquely personal interaction between two people. The elements of personal trust and confidence are an integral part of the process."

Dr. Atul Gawande, a prolific commenter on health policy matters, described his training as a surgical resident. Complications: A Surgeon's Notes on an Imperfect Science (2002). A major theme of the book is his discovery of the prevalence of uncertainty in the practice of medicine:

> We look for medicine to be an orderly field of knowledge and procedure. But it is not. It is an imperfect science, an enterprise of constantly changing knowledge, uncertain information, fallible individuals, and at the same time lives on the line. There is science in what we do, yes, but also habit, intuition, and sometimes plain old guessing. The gap between what we know and what we aim for persists. And this gap complicates everything we do.

What do these considerations teach about the obstacles to effective regulation? For example, what problems do they suggest for regulations designed to assure that health systems provide high quality care? What issues arise with respect to the efforts of managed care organizations to enhance their competitive position by adopting cost–efficient practice protocols?

2. Thomas Rice and Bruce Vladeck articulate the traditional assumptions of the competitive model concerning conditions that allow a competitive market to operate. They posit the following preconditions for robust markets:

> Not only do consumers have access to good information about alternatives, but they are able to use it to make rational, cost–effective choices that will optimize their best interests.
>
> Moreover, consumers are endowed with predetermined tastes and preferences that are immutable—subject to the pressures neither of advertisers nor of their peers. In short, they know what they want.
>
> Providers do not possess market power.
>
> Providers do not influence consumers' decisions, over and above their role as hired, perfect experts or agents.

Bruce C. Vladeck and Thomas Rice, Market Failure and the Failure of Discourse: Facing Up to the Power of Sellers, 28 Health Affairs 1305 (2009).

How well does the market for medical care and health care services measure up against Rice and Vladeck's criteria? Can you match up Enthoven's description of the nature of medical care with these criteria for functional markets? Rice and Vladeck argue that where these and other classic economic assumptions are not met, "reliance on the marketplace is likely to lead to outcomes that are not in society's best interest." So, does that mean that government regulation necessarily will lead to better outcomes? What sorts of regulation might help improve the market in health care?

3. The "system" we have for delivering health care services is hardly systematic. Instead, services are offered in fragmented and inefficient segments, as any patient who has dealt with even a relatively simple episode

understands. With physicians practicing primarily in solo practices or small groups and group practices often not coordinating across specialty lines or with inpatient facilities, care delivery is extraordinarily uncoordinated and episodic. See generally The Fragmentation of U.S. Health Care: Causes and Solutions (Einer R. Elhauge, ed., 2010). Fragmentation causes serious deficiencies in quality through uncoordinated care and discontinuity of care that leads to misdiagnosis and duplicative testing, among other problems. Fragmented delivery also produces markets that impair effective bargaining and comparative shopping. See Thomas L. Greaney, Competition Policy and Organizational Fragmentation in Health Care, 71 U. Pitt. L. Rev. 217, 229 (2009). The absence of vertical integration (for example, integration between physician services offered in clinical offices and hospital services) frustrates the capacity of managed care, or any payer, to negotiate for cost–effective bundles of services. In hospital markets, most patients delegate choice to their physicians but do not internalize the hospitals' costs and are insensitive to costs of care that they do not bear directly. In this context, hospitals benefit more by competing for physician affiliation though various forms of nonprice competition than by economizing for the benefit of efficient contracting.

Regulation and government payment policies, which strongly influence the practices and norms in the private sector, also bear significant responsibility for market inefficiencies in health care. Most notably, the longstanding reliance on fee–for–service methods of payment has spawned an ethos of provider payment that rewards volume rather than selectivity and efficiency. Fee–for–service payment also creates a disincentive for providers to consider cost–benefit tradeoffs of particular interventions. See Uwe E. Reinhardt, Can Efficiency in Health Care Be Left to the Market?, 26 J. Health Pol. Pol'y & L. 967 (2001).

Is the fragmentation of the health care system a problem that can be fixed? How would you fix it? If you could create one regulation that would have a significant impact, what might it be? Could you instead stimulate competition among providers to improve the situation? How might that happen? Can you do anything as a consumer of services? What if you were a payer?

III. WHAT IS ILLNESS?

We all have an operational definition of health and sickness. I know when I am depressed, have a broken leg, a headache or a hangover. In these circumstances I consider myself to be in ill health because I am not functioning as well as I usually do, even though I may lack a scientific medical explanation of my malaise. But am I in poor health because my arteries are gradually becoming clogged, a process that probably began when I was a teenager? Am I sick or in poor health if I am obese, or addicted to alcohol or drugs, or becoming very old and enfeebled, or struggling with my sexual identity?

We need some definition of health in order to assess the quality of care needed to promote or restore it. A malpractice suit or medical quality audit depends on an ability to distinguish a bad from a good medical care outcome. An understanding of the nature of sickness and health is required to determine what health care society should provide the poor and how much society ought to spend on health care. Should Medicaid (a federal/state health care program for the poor) or a commercial insurer, for example, cover in vitro fertilization or abortions? If the state of being old becomes a state of sickness, does it mean that sickness must be "cured" at public expense? Finally, the definition of health raises questions of autonomy, responsibility and personhood. Should health be defined by the doctor as scientist or the patient as person, or both? Is the drunkard or serial killer diseased or sinning or both or neither?

The Constitution of the World Health Organization defines health as "[a] state of complete physical, mental and social well–being and not merely the absence of disease or infirmity." When did you last feel that way? Can health ever be achieved under this definition, or is everyone always in a state of ill health? How much can physicians and hospitals contribute to health under this definition? A further provision of the WHO Constitution provides that "Governments have a responsibility for the health of their peoples which can be fulfilled only by the provision of adequate health and social measures." What are the political ramifications of these principles?

Health can be viewed in a more limited sense as the performance by each part of the body of its "natural" function. Definitions in terms of biological functioning tend to be more descriptive and less value–laden. As Englehardt writes, "The notion required for an analysis of health is not that of a good man or a good shark, but that of a good specimen of a human being or shark." H. Tristam Englehardt, "The Concepts of Health and Disease," in Concepts of Health and Disease 552 (Arthur Caplan, H. Tristam Engelhardt, and James McCartney, eds. 1981) (hereafter Concepts).

Boorse compares health to the mechanical condition of a car, which can be described as good because it conforms to the designers' specifications, even though the design is flawed. Disease is then a biological malfunction, a deviation from the biological norm of natural function. Illness can be defined as a subset of disease. Boorse writes:

> An illness must be, first, a reasonably *serious* disease with incapacitating effects that make it undesirable. A shaving cut or mild athlete's foot cannot be called an illness, nor could one call in sick on the basis of a single dental cavity, though all these conditions are diseases. Secondly, to call a disease an illness is to view its owner as deserving special treatment and diminished moral accountability * * *. Where we do not make the appropriate nor-

> mative judgments or activate the social institutions, no amount of disease will lead us to use the term "ill." * * *
>
> There are, then, two senses of "health". In one sense it is a theoretical notion, the opposite of "disease." In another sense it is a practical or mixed ethical notion, the opposite of "illness."

Christopher Boorse, "On the Distinction between Disease and Illness," in Concepts, *supra* at 553.

Illness is thus a socially constructed deviance. Something more than a mere biological abnormality is needed. To be ill is to have deviant characteristics for which the sick role is appropriate. The sick role, as Parsons has described it, exempts one from normal social responsibilities and removes individual responsibility. See Talcott Parsons, The Social System (1951). Our choice of words reflects this: an alcoholic is sick; a drunkard is not.

A sick person can be assisted by treatment defined by the medical model. He becomes a patient, an object of medical attention by a doctor. The doctor has the right and the ability to label someone ill, to determine whether the lump on a patient's skin is a blister, a wart or a cancer. The doctor can thus decide whether a patient is culpable or not, disabled or malingering. Illness also enjoins the physician to action to restore the patient to health.

Illness thus has many ramifications. First, it affects the individual. It relieves responsibility. The sick person need not report for work at 8:00; the post–traumatic stress syndrome or premenstrual syndrome victim may be declared not guilty of an assault. Sickness means loss of control. The mild pain may have disproportionate effects on the individual who sees it as the harbinger of cancer or a brain tumor. The physician can restore control by providing a rational explanation for the experience of impairment. Illness costs the patient money, in lost time and in medical expenses. And someone receives that money for trying to treat that patient's illness.

Our understanding of illness also affects society. Defining a condition as an illness to be aggressively treated, rather than as a natural condition of life to be accepted and tolerated, has significant economic effects. Medical care is an object of economic choice, a good that many perceive to be different from other goods, with greater, sometimes immeasurable value. Some people are willing to pay far more for medical care than they would for other goods, or, more typically, to procure insurance that will deliver them from ever having to face the choice of paying for health care and abandoning all else. Society may also feel a special obligation to pay for the medical expenses of those who need treatment but lack resources to pay for it.

KATSKEE V. BLUE CROSS/BLUE SHIELD OF NEBRASKA

Supreme Court of Nebraska, 1994.
245 Neb. 808, 515 N.W.2d 645.

WHITE, JUSTICE.

This appeal arises from a summary judgment issued by the Douglas County District Court dismissing appellant Sindie Katskee's action for breach of contract. This action concerns the determination of what constitutes an illness within the meaning of a health insurance policy issued by appellee, Blue Cross/Blue Shield of Nebraska. We reverse the decision of the district court and remand the cause for further proceedings.

In January 1990, upon the recommendation of her gynecologist, Dr. Larry E. Roffman, appellant consulted with Dr. Henry T. Lynch regarding her family's history of breast and ovarian cancer, and particularly her health in relation to such a history. After examining appellant and investigating her family's medical history, Dr. Lynch diagnosed her as suffering from a genetic condition known as breast–ovarian carcinoma syndrome. Dr. Lynch then recommended that appellant have a total abdominal hysterectomy and bilateral salpingo–oophorectomy, which involves the removal of the uterus, the ovaries, and the fallopian tubes. Dr. Roffman concurred in Dr. Lynch's diagnosis and agreed that the recommended surgery was the most medically appropriate treatment available.

After considering the diagnosis and recommended treatment, appellant decided to have the surgery. In preparation for the surgery, appellant filed a claim with Blue Cross/Blue Shield. Both Drs. Lynch and Roffman wrote to Blue Cross/Blue Shield and explained the diagnosis and their basis for recommending the surgery. Initially, Blue Cross/Blue Shield sent a letter to appellant and indicated that it might pay for the surgery. Two weeks before the surgery, Dr. Roger Mason, the chief medical officer for Blue Cross/Blue Shield, wrote to appellant and stated that Blue Cross/Blue Shield would not cover the cost of the surgery. Nonetheless, appellant had the surgery in November 1990.

Appellant filed this action for breach of contract, seeking to recover $6,022.57 in costs associated with the surgery. Blue Cross/Blue Shield filed a motion for summary judgment. The district court granted the motion. It found that there was no genuine issue of material fact and that the policy did not cover appellant's surgery. Specifically, the court stated that (1) appellant did not suffer from cancer, and although her high–risk condition warranted the surgery, it was not covered by the policy; (2) appellant did not have a bodily illness or disease which was covered by the policy; and (3) under the terms of the policy, Blue Cross/Blue Shield reserved the right to determine what is medically necessary. Appellant filed a notice of appeal to the Nebraska Court of Appeals, and on our motion, we removed the case to the Nebraska Supreme Court.

Appellant contends that the district court erred in finding that no genuine issue of material fact existed and granting summary judgment in favor of appellee.

* * *

Blue Cross/Blue Shield contends that appellant's costs are not covered by the insurance policy. The policy provides coverage for services which are medically necessary. The policy defines "medically necessary" as follows: The services, procedures, drugs, supplies or Durable Medical Equipment provided by the Physician, Hospital or other health care provider, in the diagnosis or treatment of the Covered Person's Illness, Injury, or Pregnancy, which are: 1. Appropriate for the symptoms and diagnosis of the patient's Illness, Injury or Pregnancy; and 2. Provided in the most appropriate setting and at the most appropriate level of services[;] and 3. Consistent with the standards of good medical practice in the medical community of the State of Nebraska; and 4. Not provided primarily for the convenience of any of the following: a. the Covered Person; b. the Physician; c. the Covered Person's family; d. any other person or health care provider; and 5. Not considered to be unnecessarily repetitive when performed in combination with other diagnoses or treatment procedures. We shall determine whether services provided are Medically Necessary. Services will not automatically be considered Medically Necessary because they have been ordered or provided by a Physician. (Emphasis supplied.) Blue Cross/Blue Shield denied coverage because it concluded that appellant's condition does not constitute an illness, and thus the treatment she received was not medically necessary. Blue Cross/Blue Shield has not raised any other basis for its denial, and we therefore will limit our consideration to whether appellant's condition constituted an illness within the meaning of the policy.

The policy broadly defines "illness" as a "bodily disorder or disease." The policy does not provide definitions for either bodily disorder or disease.

An insurance policy is to be construed as any other contract to give effect to the parties' intentions at the time the contract was made. When the terms of the contract are clear, a court may not resort to rules of construction, and the terms are to be accorded their plain and ordinary meaning as the ordinary or reasonable person would understand them. In such a case, a court shall seek to ascertain the intention of the parties from the plain language of the policy. [ ]

Whether a policy is ambiguous is a matter of law for the court to determine. If a court finds that the policy is ambiguous, then the court may employ rules of construction and look beyond the language of the policy to ascertain the intention of the parties. A general principle of construction, which we have applied to ambiguous insurance policies, holds that an ambiguous policy will be construed in favor of the insured. However, we will not read an ambiguity into policy language which is plain and unambiguous in order to construe it against the insurer. [ ]

When interpreting the plain meaning of the terms of an insurance policy, we have stated that the " ' "natural and obvious meaning of the provisions in a policy is to be adopted in preference to a fanciful, curious, or hidden meaning." ' "[ ] We have further stated that " '[w]hile for the purpose of judicial decision dictionary definitions often are not controlling, they are at least persuasive that meanings which they do not embrace are not common.' "[ ]

Applying these principles, our interpretation of the language of the terms employed in the policy is guided by definitions found in dictionaries, and additionally by judicial opinions rendered by other courts which have considered the meaning of these terms. Webster's Third New International Dictionary, Unabridged 648 (1981), defines disease as an impairment of the normal state of the living animal or plant body or of any of its components that interrupts or modifies the performance of the vital functions, being a response to environmental factors . . . to specific infective agents . . . to inherent defects of the organism (as various genetic anomalies), or to combinations of these factors: Sickness, Illness. The same dictionary defines disorder as "a derangement of function: an abnormal physical or mental condition: Sickness, Ailment, Malady." [ ]

These lay definitions are consistent with the general definitions provided in Dorland's Illustrated Medical Dictionary (27th ed. 1988). Dorland's defines disease as any deviation from or interruption of the normal structure or function of any part, organ, or system . . . of the body that is manifested by a characteristic set of symptoms and signs and whose etiology [theory of origin or cause], pathology [origin or cause], and prognosis may be known or unknown. [ ] Dorland's defines disorder as "a derangement or abnormality of function; a morbid physical or mental state." [ ]

* * *

[The court looked at similar definitional disputes in other jurisdictions, noting that hemophilia, aneurysms, and chronic alcoholism had been held to be diseases or illnesses under insurance policies.]

We find that the language used in the policy at issue in the present case is not reasonably susceptible of differing interpretations and thus not ambiguous. The plain and ordinary meaning of the terms "bodily disorder" and "disease," as they are used in the policy to define illness, encompasses any abnormal condition of the body or its components of such a degree that in its natural progression would be expected to be problematic; a deviation from the healthy or normal state affecting the functions or tissues of the body; an inherent defect of the body; or a morbid physical or mental state which deviates from or interrupts the normal structure or function of any part, organ, or system of the body and which is manifested by a characteristic set of symptoms and signs.

The issue then becomes whether appellant's condition—breast–ovarian carcinoma syndrome—constitutes an illness.

Blue Cross/Blue Shield argues that appellant did not suffer from an illness because she did not have cancer. Blue Cross/Blue Shield characterizes appellant's condition only as a "predisposition to an illness (cancer)" and fails to address whether the condition itself constitutes an illness. This failure is traceable to Dr. Mason's denial of appellant's claim. Despite acknowledging his inexperience and lack of knowledge about this specialized area of cancer research, Dr. Mason denied appellant's claim without consulting any medical literature or research regarding breast–ovarian carcinoma syndrome. Moreover, Dr. Mason made the decision without submitting appellant's claim for consideration to a claim review committee. The only basis for the denial was the claim filed by appellant, the letters sent by Drs. Lynch and Roffman, and the insurance policy. Despite his lack of information regarding the nature and severity of appellant's condition, Dr. Mason felt qualified to decide that appellant did not suffer from an illness.

Appellant's condition was diagnosed as breast–ovarian carcinoma syndrome. To adequately determine whether the syndrome constitutes an illness, we must first understand the nature of the syndrome.

The record on summary judgment includes the depositions of Drs. Lynch, Roffman, and Mason. In his deposition, Dr. Lynch provided a thorough discussion of this syndrome. In light of Dr. Lynch's extensive research and clinical experience in this particular area of medicine, we consider his discussion extremely helpful in our understanding of the syndrome.

According to Dr. Lynch, some forms of cancer occur on a hereditary basis. Breast and ovarian cancer are such forms of cancer which may occur on a hereditary basis. It is our understanding that the hereditary occurrence of this form of cancer is related to the genetic makeup of the woman. In this regard, the genetic deviation has conferred changes which are manifest in the individual's body and at some time become capable of being diagnosed.

At the time that he gave his deposition, Dr. Lynch explained that the state of medical research was such that detecting and diagnosing the syndrome was achieved by tracing the occurrences of hereditary cancer throughout the patient's family. Dr. Lynch stated that at the time of appellant's diagnosis, no conclusive physical test existed which would demonstrate the presence of the condition. However, Dr. Lynch stated that this area of research is progressing toward the development of a more determinative method of identifying and tracing a particular gene throughout a particular family, thus providing a physical method of diagnosing the condition.

Women diagnosed with the syndrome have at least a 50–percent chance of developing breast and/or ovarian cancer, whereas unaffected women have only a 1.4–percent risk of developing breast or ovarian cancer. In addition to the genetic deviation, the family history, and the significant risks associated with this condition, the diagnosis also may encompass symptoms of anxiety and stress, which some women experience because of their knowledge of the substantial likelihood of developing cancer.

The procedures for detecting the onset of ovarian cancer are ineffective. Generally, by the time ovarian cancer is capable of being detected, it has already developed to a very advanced stage, making treatment relatively unsuccessful. Drs. Lynch and Roffman agreed that the standard of care for treating women with breast carcinoma syndrome ordinarily involves surveillance methods. However, for women at an inordinately high risk for ovarian cancer, such as appellant, the standard of care may require radical surgery which involves the removal of the uterus, ovaries, and fallopian tubes.

Dr. Lynch explained that the surgery is labeled "prophylactic" and that the surgery is prophylactic as to the prevention of the onset of cancer. Dr. Lynch also stated that appellant's condition itself is the result of a genetic deviation from the normal, healthy state and that the recommended surgery treats that condition by eliminating or significantly reducing the presence of the condition and its likely development.

Blue Cross/Blue Shield has not proffered any evidence disputing the premise that the origin of this condition is in the genetic makeup of the individual and that in its natural development it is likely to produce devastating results. Although handicapped by his limited knowledge of the syndrome, Dr. Mason did not dispute the nature of the syndrome as explained by Dr. Lynch and supported by Dr. Roffman, nor did Dr. Mason dispute the fact that the surgery falls within the standard of care for many women afflicted with this syndrome.

In light of the plain and ordinary meaning of the terms "illness," "bodily disorder," and "disease," we find that appellant's condition constitutes an illness within the meaning of the policy. Appellant's condition is a deviation from what is considered a normal, healthy physical state or structure. The abnormality or deviation from a normal state arises, in part, from the genetic makeup of the woman. The existence of this unhealthy state results in the woman's being at substantial risk of developing cancer. The recommended surgery is intended to correct that morbid state by reducing or eliminating that risk.

Although appellant's condition was not detectable by physical evidence or a physical examination, it does not necessarily follow that appellant does not suffer from an illness. The record establishes that a woman who suffers from breast–ovarian carcinoma syndrome does have a physical state which significantly deviates from the physical state of a normal, healthy woman. Specifically, appellant suffered from a different or abnormal genetic constitution which, when combined with a particular family history of hereditary cancer, significantly increases the risk of a devastating outcome.

We are mindful that not every condition which itself constitutes a predisposition to another illness is necessarily an illness within the meaning of an insurance policy. There exists a fine distinction between such conditions * * *.

* * *

The issue raised in Fuglsang [ ] was whether the disease from which the plaintiff suffered constituted a preexisting condition which was excluded from coverage by the terms of the policy. Blue Cross/Blue Shield relies on the following rule from Fuglsang as a definition of "disease": A disease, condition, or illness exists within the meaning of a health insurance policy excluding preexisting conditions only at such time as the disease, condition, or illness is manifest or active or when there is a distinct symptom or condition from which one learned in medicine can with reasonable accuracy diagnose the disease. [ ]

This statement concerns when an illness exists, not whether the condition itself is an illness. If the condition is not a disease or illness, it would be unnecessary to apply the above rule to determine whether the condition was a preexisting illness. In the present case, Blue Cross/Blue Shield maintains that the condition is not even an illness.

Even assuming arguendo that the rule announced in Fuglsang is a definition of "disease," "illness," and "condition," the inherent problems with the argument put forth by Blue Cross/Blue Shield undermine its reliance on that rule. Blue Cross/Blue Shield emphasizes the fact that appellant was never diagnosed with cancer and therefore, according to Blue Cross/Blue Shield, appellant did not have an illness because cancer was not active or manifest. Appellant concedes that she did not have cancer prior to her surgery. The issue is whether the condition she did have was an illness. Blue Cross/Blue Shield further argues that "[n]o disease or illness is 'manifest or active' and there is no 'distinct symptom or condition' from which Dr. Lynch or Dr. Roffman could diagnose a disease." We stated above that lack of a physical test to detect the presence of an illness does not necessarily indicate that the person does not have an illness.

When the condition at issue—breast–ovarian carcinoma syndrome—is inserted into the formula provided by the Fuglsang rule, the condition would constitute an "illness" as Blue Cross/Blue Shield defines the term. The formula is whether the breast–ovarian carcinoma syndrome was manifest or active, or whether there was a distinct symptom or condition from which one learned in medicine could with reasonable accuracy diagnose the disease. The record establishes that the syndrome was manifest, at least in part, from the genetic deviation, and evident from the family medical history. The condition was such that one learned in medicine, Dr. Lynch, could with a reasonable degree of accuracy diagnose it. Blue Cross/Blue Shield does not dispute the nature of the syndrome, the method of diagnosis, or the accuracy of the diagnosis.

In the present case, the medical evidence regarding the nature of breast–ovarian carcinoma syndrome persuades us that appellant suffered from a bodily disorder or disease and, thus, suffered from an illness as defined by the insurance policy. Blue Cross/Blue Shield, therefore, is not entitled to judgment as a matter of law. Moreover, we find that appellant's condition did constitute an illness within the meaning of the policy. We reverse the decision of the district court and remand the cause for further proceedings. [ ]

NOTES AND QUESTIONS

1. Why did the court hold that Katskee was ill when she had no symptoms and no cancer? Can we have a variable definition of illness? For example, could Katskee be ill for purposes of payment for the surgery but not ill for purposes of pre–existing condition exclusions or excusal from work? What about treatment for high blood pressure or arteriosclerosis? The medications to prevent heart attacks are expensive, and are typically covered by health insurance plans. .

Why would Blue Cross resist covering this treatment for this problem?

2. The syndrome in *Katskee*, if it materializes, is a medical problem for which the patient bears no responsibility. A more difficult problem area in defining "disease" involves those conditions or syndromes within some control by the individual. Consider for example alcoholism as a "disease". What difference does such a label make? What characteristics of alcohol consumption justify the label "disease"? See H. Thomas Milhorn, The Diagnosis of Alcoholism, AFP 175 (June 1988) (". . . alcoholism can be defined as the continuation of drinking when it would be in the patient's best interest to stop.") See Traynor v. Turnage, 485 U.S. 535, 108 S.Ct. 1372, 99 L.Ed.2d 618 (1988) (considering alcoholism as attributable to "willful misconduct" under Veterans' Administration rules). See also Herbert Fingarette, Heavy Drinking: The Myth of Alcoholism as a Disease (1988); contra, see George Vaillant, The Natural History of Alcoholism (1983).

3. What other emerging clinical "syndromes" or diseases can you think of that raise troubling problems for the medical model of disease? How about anorexia? Obesity? Battered wife syndrome? Restless leg syndrome? Parental

alienation syndrome? What forces have led to the proliferation of these new syndromes or diseases?

4. Disputes over insurance coverage of treatments are the most common legal battleground over the meanings of "disease" and "treatment". Other legal contexts however also give rise to definitional battles, such as the Internal Revenue Code and taxpayer claims that their medical expenses should be allowable deductions. In O'Donnbhain v. Commissioner of Internal Revenue, 134 T.C. 34 (2010), the IRS determined a deficiency in petitioner's Federal income tax. The issue was whether the petitioner could deduct as a medical care expense amounts paid in 2001 for hormone therapy, sex reassignment surgery, and breast augmentation surgery that she contended she incurred to treat her gender identity disorder, totaling over $60,000. None of petitioner's expenses were covered by insurance or other sources of reimbursement. Rhiannon G. O'Donnabhain (petitioner) was born a genetic male with unambiguous male genitalia. She was, however, uncomfortable as a male from childhood and she first wore women's clothing secretly around age 10. Her gender discomfort increased as a teenager, and she continued to dress in women's clothing secretly. After completing university and military service, she married, but the marriage ended finally after more than 20 years. After separating from her spouse in 1992, petitioner's feelings that she wanted to be female intensified and grew more persistent. Her discomfort with her male gender and her strong desire to be female intensified, and she sought a psychotherapist to address them. She found a therapist who specialized in gender identity disorder (GID), and had twenty individual therapy sessions with the therapist, who then concluded that petitioner needed treatment. The court recounted the therapist's diagnostic description of the petitioner as follows:

> Petitioner was a transsexual suffering from severe gender identity disorder (GID), a condition listed in the Diagnostic and Statistical Manual of Mental Disorders (4th ed.2000 text revision) (DSM–IV–TR), published by the American Psychiatric Association. The DSM–IV–TR states that a diagnosis of GID is indicated where an individual exhibits (1) a strong and persistent desire to be, or belief that he or she is, the other sex; (2) persistent discomfort with his or her anatomical sex, including a preoccupation with getting rid of primary or secondary sex characteristics; (3) an absence of any physical intersex (hermaphroditic) condition, and (4) clinically significant distress or impairment in social, occupational, or other important areas of functioning as a result of the discomfort arising from the perceived incongruence between anatomical sex and perceived gender identity.

The standard of care, described by the Tax Court,

> [consisted] of (1) hormonal sex reassignment; i.e., the administration of cross–gender hormones to effect changes in physical appearance to more closely resemble the opposite sex; (2) the "real–life" ex-

> perience (wherein the individual undertakes a trial period of living full time in society as a member of the opposite sex); and (3) sex reassignment surgery, consisting of genital sex reassignment and/or nongenital sex reassignment * * *. These standards also required the recommendation of a licensed psychotherapist for these treatments, with evidence of transsexualism for a period of at least 2 years.
>
> Petitioner underwent hormone therapy, and followed these treatments with "real–life" experience, presenting in public as a female on a full–time basis, including at work. While this made petitioner feel better, her anxiety as a result of having male genitalia persisted. The therapist concluded that sex reassignment therapy was therapeutically desirable, given petitioner's anxiety, and helped petitioner arrange the surgery. Petitioner then underwent sex reassignment surgery in 2001. Her surgeon performed procedures that included surgical removal of the penis and testicles and creation of a vaginal space using genital skin and tissue, designed to create female genitalia both in appearance and in function, capable of sexual arousal and intercourse. He also performed breast augmentation surgery and subsequent surgery on petitioner's face to "feminize her facial features".

The court noted that

> * * * since the inception of the medical expense deduction, the definition of deductible "medical care" has had two prongs. The first prong covers amounts paid for the "diagnosis, cure, mitigation, treatment, or prevention of disease" and the second prong covers amounts paid "for the purpose of affecting any structure or function of the body."

The court undertook a careful analysis of the meaning of "disease," and concluded:

> " * * *GID is a "disease" within the meaning of section 213 [of the Internal Revenue Code]. * * * In view of (1) GID's widely recognized status in diagnostic and psychiatric reference texts as a legitimate diagnosis, (2) the seriousness of the condition as described in learned treatises in evidence and as acknowledged by all three experts in this case; (3) the severity of petitioner's impairment as found by the mental health professionals who examined her; (4) the consensus in the U.S. Courts of Appeal that GID constitutes a serious medical need for purposes [prison medical care], we conclude and hold that GID is a "disease" for purposes of section 213.

After a dictionary–based definitional analysis of "treat", the court found in favor of the petitioner. The therapy and surgery were accepted treatments of GID; they have positive results according to psychiatric experts, so they alleviate suffering within the definitions of treatment. The court continued: "We therefore conclude and hold that petitioner's hormone therapy and sex reassignment surgery "[treated] * * * disease" within the meaning of section 213(d)(9)(B) and accordingly are not "cosmetic surgery" as defined in that section." The court finally held that the surgery was medically necessary. The court rejected petitioner's deduction for breast augmentation surgery, since she failed to show that her surgery treated GID, finding it was "cosmetic surgery" and not deductible.

How does the Tax Court determine that O'Donnbhain's condition is a "disease"? Is GID treatment distinguishable from psychiatric treatments for depression or schizophrenia? The use of hormones, which have side effects, is certainly similar to the use of drugs in psychotherapy, which sometimes work moderately well but with side effects. The surgical removal of healthy body parts on the other hand does not resemble other medical therapies for treating diseases, does it? Would the *Katskee* court's definition of disease apply to this case?

Critics of GID therapy contend that it is an example of a personal problem that has been medicalized. What do they mean by that? Can you think of any good examples of a medicalized problem? See Lauren Herman, A Non–Medicalized Medical Deduction? O'Donnabhain v. Commissioner & the I.R.S.'s Understanding of Transgender Medical Care, 35 Harv. J. L. & Gender 487 (2012) (noting that a diagnosis of GID is required before a deduction is possible, which has the effect of medicalizing a person's personal choice).

PROBLEM: THE COUPLE'S ILLNESS

You represent Thomas and Jill Henderson, a couple embroiled in a dispute with their health insurance plan over coverage of infertility treatments. The Hendersons have been having trouble getting pregnant. Thomas has a low sperm count and motility, while Jill has irregular ovulation. They have undergone infertility treatment successfully in the past and have one child. They again sought further treatment, in order to have a second child. A simple insemination procedure failed. The health and disability group benefit plan of Thomas's employer, Clarion, paid their health benefits for this procedure.

They were then advised to try a more complex and expensive procedure, called Protocol I, which involved treating Thomas' sperm to improve its motility. Drug therapy was prescribed for Jill to induce ovulation. Semen was then taken from Thomas, and put through an albumin gradient to improve its mobility. The semen was then reduced to a small pellet size and injected directly into the uterine cavity at the time of ovulation.

The Hendersons underwent Protocol I and submitted a bill to Clarion, which refused to pay it. Clarion cited a provision in its plan, Article VI, section 6.7, which provided:

> If a covered individual incurs outpatient expenses relating to injury or illness, those expenses charged, including but not limited to, of-

> fice calls and for diagnostic services such as laboratory, x–ray, electrocardiography, therapy or injections, are covered expenses under the provisions of [the plan].

Under section 2.24 of the plan, "illness" was defined as "any sickness occurring to a covered individual which does not arise out of or in the course of employment for wage or profit." Clarion denied the Hendersons' claim on the grounds that the medical services were not performed because of any illness of Jill or Thomas, as required under section 6.7. No provisions in the plan specifically excluded fertilization treatments like Protocol I.

What arguments can you make on behalf of the Hendersons that their situation is an "illness"? What arguments can you make for the insurance company that it is not?

IV. FROM DEFINING QUALITY TO REGULATING PATIENT SAFETY

Lawyers are involved with quality of health care issues through a variety of routes. They file, or defend against, malpractice suits when a patient is injured during the course of medical treatment. They handle medical staff privileges cases that frequently turn on the quality of the staff doctor's performance. They represent the government in administering programs that aim to cut the cost of health care and improve its quality as well as providers who must adjust to these programs. They contest insurer refusals to pay claims, or represent insurers who don't want to pay for poor quality or unproven treatments.

A. THE NATURE OF QUALITY IN MEDICINE

The Institute of Medicine has developed a definition that is a useful starting point:

> * * * quality of care is the degree to which health services for individuals and populations increase the likelihood of desired health outcomes and are consistent with current professional knowledge. Institute of Medicine, Medicare: A Strategy for Quality Assurance, Vol. I, 20 (K. Lohr, Ed.1990).

Unnecessary care that causes harm is poor in quality, since unnecessary harm is not counterbalanced by any expectation of benefit. How about care that is unnecessary yet harmless, like over–the–counter medicines that contain no therapeutic ingredients? Or medical interventions that have no proven value? Such care also fails a quality test, because it yields no benefits, wastes resources, and indicates poor judgment or ignorance on the part of the practitioner. See Riser v. American Medical International, Inc., 620 So.2d 372 (La.App. 5th Cir., 1993), where the doctor performed a femoral arteriogram on the patient, who suffered a stroke and died. The court found that the physician had breached the standard of care by subjecting the patient to a technology that he should reasonably have known would be of "no practical benefit to the patient".

Much of American medical practice does not improve health. In controlled trials, many cherished practices have been found unhelpful and even harmful. Treatments effective for one indication are frequently extended to other indications where effectiveness data do not exist. See, e.g., William B. Borden et al., Patterns and Intensity of Medical Therapy in Patients Undergoing Percutaneous Coronary Intervention, 305 JAMA 1882, 1886 (2011).

Higher quality care may cost more, raising the question of cost–effectiveness. Or it might be obtained for less money, cutting out ineffective services. Or quality care may be less expensive. See Charles Andel, et al., The Economics of Health Care Quality and Medical Errors, 39 J Health Care Finance 39, 48 (2012), contending that quality care "is better, more efficient, and by definition, less wasteful. It is the right care, at the right time, every time. It should mean that far fewer patients are harmed or injured." See also Peter S. Hussey, et al., The Association Between Health Care Quality and Cost: A Systematic Review, 158 Ann. Int. Med. 27 (2013) (concluding that "the association between cost and quality is small to moderate, regardless of whether the direction is positive or negative. Future studies should focus on what types of spending are most effective in improving quality and what types of spending represent waste.")

Should patient engagement in her care be part of an expanded definition of quality medical care? This shared decision making model of the doctor–patient relationship certainly maximizes patient autonomy. See Chapter 4 for a discussion of major developments in "shared decision making" models of informed patient consent.

How do cost considerations fit into this individualized definition of quality? If the patient has no insurance and probably cannot pay for an expensive surgical procedure, or if the patient decides to forego a treatment after making his or her own cost tradeoffs, how should the doctor respond? Must the doctor be satisfied with giving the patient less medical care than would be possible and would in fact help the patient?

Even in a society with comprehensive social benefits, such as a national health insurance program, costs must be considered by the practitioner, who is still constrained by the resources available for health care. The doctor as citizen must choose whether to help the patient as much as possible, with the taxpayers absorbing the costs; or to stop short of giving the individual the maximum help. See the *Wickline* and *Murray* cases in Chapter 5 for a discussion of these tensions.

The distribution of benefits within a population is another important dimension of quality. Patients' insurance status significantly affects the procedures they receive to treat various medical problems. Lack of insurance can reduce the length of one's life: mortality studies suggest a reduction in the uninsured's mortality as high as 20% to 25%. The uninsured receive fewer preventive and diagnostic services, tend to be more severely ill when diagnosed, and receive less therapeutic care. Other literature suggests that improving health status from fair or poor to very good or excellent would increase both work effort and annual earnings by approximately 15% to 20%. Jack Hadley, Sicker and Poorer—The Consequences of Being Uninsured: A Review of the Research on the Relationship between Health Insurance, Medical Care Use, Health, Work, and Income, 60 The Urban Institute Medical Care Research and Review, 2 suppl, 3S–75S (2003).

1. Medical Practice Variation

The phenomenon of medical practice variation highlights the role of uncertainty in the setting of medical standards. John Wennberg, whose studies in this area are often cited, has analyzed states and regions within states for variation in surgical and other practices:

> [I]n Maine by the time women reach seventy years of age in one hospital market the likelihood they have undergone a hysterectomy is 20 percent while in another market it is 70 percent. In Iowa, the chances that male residents who reach age eighty–five have undergone prostatectomy range from a low of 15 percent to a high of more than 60 percent in different hospital markets. In Vermont the probability that resident children will undergo a tonsillectomy has ranged from a low of 8 percent in one hospital market to a high of nearly 70 percent in another.

John E. Wennberg, Dealing with Medical Practice Variations: A Proposal for Action, 3 Health Affairs 6, 9 (1984).

Wennberg is one of the creators of the *Dartmouth Atlas*, which uses Medicare data to track medical practice variation over the country, by procedure. Physician variation in treatment approaches is greatest with aging–related conditions, where the outcomes of conservative treatment are unknown. Procedures least subject to variation are those for which there is a professional consensus on the preferred place or style of treatment. Wennberg gives the example of patient time in intensive care units in the last six months of life in selected teaching hospitals. The number of days ranged from 11.4 at UCLA Medical Center to as low as 2.8 at Massachusetts General Hospital.

Wennberg's studies of medical practice variation are based on studies of three categories of care: effective care, preference–sensitive care, and supply–sensitive care.

(1) "Effective Care": interventions that are viewed as medically necessary on the basis of clinical outcomes evidence and for which the benefits so outweigh the risks that virtually all patients with medical need should receive them.

(2) "Preference–sensitive Care": treatments, such as discretionary surgery, for which there are two or more valid treatment alternatives, and the choice of treatment involves tradeoffs that should be based on patients' preferences. Variation in such care is typified by elective surgeries, such as hip fracture, knee replacement, or back surgery. Surgeons in adjoining counties in Florida, for example, may operate at very different levels for the same condition and patient.

(3) "Supply–sensitive Care": services such as physician visits, referrals to specialists, hospitalizations, and stays in intensive care units involved in the medical (non–surgical) management of disease. In Medicare, the large majority of these services are for patients with chronic illness.

Wennberg concluded that "system" causes of unwarranted variation include misuse of preference–sensitive care; poor communication between the doctor and patient regarding the risks and benefits of alternative treatments; patient dependency on a physician's opinion in sorting out preferences; inadequate evaluation of (evolving) treatment theory; and the effects of our health care finance system that rewards procedures, not time spent with patients or the quality of decision making.

See generally John E. Wennberg, Variation in Use of Medicare Services Among Regions and Selected Academic Medical Centers: Is More Better?, Commonwealth Fund Pub. No. 874, at 4 (Dec. 2005) (noting "striking regional variations in the proportion of early stage breast cancer patients who undergo lumpectomy" and identifying "idiosyncratic practice style" as the "major source of such widely varying discretionary surgery rates"). For a graphic depiction of the variation, see John E. Wennberg, Understanding Practice Patterns: A Focus on What the Quality Movement Can Do to Reduce Unwarranted Variations. The Institute for Healthcare Improvement), Orlando, Fl. (2005). See also John E. Wennberg, et al., Evaluating The Efficiency Of California Providers In Caring For Patients With Chronic Illnesses, Health Affairs (November 16, 2005) Web Exclusive 10.1377. See also Lars Noah, Medicine's Epistemology: Mapping the Haphazard Diffusion of Knowledge in the Biomedical Community, 44 Ariz. L. Rev. 373, 382 (2002) (recognizing physicians' traditional reliance on personal experience and anecdotal information).

The attitudes of individual doctors influence the range of variation where consensus is lacking. Wennberg has termed this the "practice style factor." This style can exert its influence in the absence of scientific information on outcomes; in other cases it may be unrelated to controversies. Physicians in some hospital markets practice medicine in ways that have extremely adverse implications for the cost of care, motivated perhaps by reasons of their own or their patients' convenience, or because of individualist interpretations of the requirements for defensive medicine. See John E. Wennberg, The Paradox of Appropriate Care, 258 J.A.M.A. 2568 (1987). See generally John Eisenberg, Doctors' Decisions and the Cost of Medical Care (1986).

Some critics have contended that medical practice variation is overstated by Wennberg. Economic disparities in regional populations, not physician practice patterns, may drive health care utilization and therefore health care spending. Poorer people are demonstrably sicker and cost more to treat than do more economically stable people by a large margin. Therefore, the key to lowering health care costs is to reduce poverty and increase wealth. See e.g. Louise Sheiner, Why the Geographic Variation in Health Care Spending Can't Tell Us Much about the Efficiency or Quality of our Health Care System, Federal Reserve Board of Governors, December 20, 2012 ("This paper examines the geographic variation in Medicare and non–Medicare health spending and finds little support for the view that most of the variation is attributable to differences in practice styles. Instead, I find that socioeconomic factors that affect the need for medical care, as well as interactions between the Medicare system, Medicaid, and private health spending, can account for most of the variation in Medicare health spending.") For responses to these criticisms, see Reflections on Variation, Dartmouth Atlas of Health Care.

Several approaches to quality improvement can be pursued. We can rely on the traditional forces of professional ethics and socialization. We can expand the role of the marketplace, using dissemination of quality information to consumers and buyers of health, on the theory that prudent buyers will reject lower quality providers. See discussion of regulation and competition in Section II, above. We can improve the current modes of self–regulation of the medical profession and the industry, which include accreditation, medical staff privileges, and medical licensing actions. The process by which a patient sues for malpractice can be improved. And the government, as a primary source of financing for much health care in the United States, can intervene, setting standards and demanding better processes and outcomes. We will examine each of these methods of quality improvement in later sections and chapters.

2. Quality and the Patient Protection and Affordable Care Act of 2010

The ACA has an astonishing variety of provisions aimed at improving the quality of the U.S. health care system, reducing errors, and generally promoting patient safety. These provisions include new centers, demonstration projects, and funding awards for a wide range of quality improvement projects.

The ACA has a variety of quality definitions and measurements. Quality is defined in Section 3013 of the ACA as "a standard for measuring the performance and improvement of population health or of health plans, providers of services, and other clinicians in the delivery of health care services."

Section 3013 contains a range of useful benchmarks for defining quality. Good quality care is care that improves patient health outcomes and their functional status. It provides management and coordination of care across episodes of care and care transitions across providers, settings, and plans. It makes patients part of the decision making process through a variety of tools. It uses health information technology effectively. The care provided must be safe, effective, patient–centered, patient satisfying, appropriate, timely, efficient, and innovative. The ACA also has a strong focus on population health, and one of its quality tests is whether care given promotes "the equity of health services and health disparities across health disparity populations [ ] and geographic areas." ACA, section 3013, subsections A through J.

Other programs such as payment bundling, section 3023, use more specific tests for quality improvement or shortcomings: patient functional status improvement; reduction in the rates of avoidable hospital readmissions; rates of discharge to the community; rates of admission to an emergency room after a hospitalization; incidence of health care acquired infections; efficiency measures; measures of patient–centeredness of care; and patient perception of care.

Quality improvement is central to the ACA. Section 3501 mandates the Director of the Center for Quality Improvement Programs to "identify, develop, evaluate, disseminate, and provide training in innovative methodologies and strategies for quality improvement practices in the delivery of health care services that represent best practices in health care quality, safety, and value" in collaboration with other Federal agencies.

The Center for Quality Improvement and Patient Safety of the Agency for Healthcare Research and Quality sets quality priorities. These include improving health outcomes, efficiency, and patient–centeredness of health care for all populations; identifying areas that can be rapidly improved; addressing gaps in information about outcomes; improving Federal payment policy to improve quality and efficiency; addressing patients with high–cost chronic diseases; improving research and dissemination of strategies and best practices to improve patient safety and reduce medical errors, preventable admissions and readmissions, and health care infections; and reducing health disparities.

The Center's research goals include, among others, reducing preventable morbidity, mortality, and associated costs of morbidity and mortality by building capacity for patient safety research; supporting the discovery of processes for the reliable, safe, efficient, and responsive delivery of health care, taking into account discoveries from clinical research and comparative effectiveness research; allowing communication of research findings and translating evidence into practice recommendations that are adaptable to a variety of settings; analyzing reports from patient safety reporting systems and patient safety organizations, and developing responses; reviewing existing practices and how to improve them; and examining how to measure and evaluate the progress of quality and patient safety activities.

Excess readmissions are presumed to indicate lower quality care by hospitals. The ACA creates the Hospital Readmission Reduction Program. Section 3025 ties excess readmissions (however defined) to a reduction in Medicare payments that would otherwise be made to that hospital. Information on all patient readmission rates shall be made available on the CMS Hospital Compare website in a form and manner determined appropriate by the Secretary. The Secretary may also make other information determined appropriate available on such website.

The ACA directs the Secretary of HHS to develop provider–level outcome measures for hospitals and physicians, as well as other providers. Section 10303. Such measures will include at least ten outcome measurements for acute and chronic diseases, including the five most prevalent and resource–intensive conditions, within two years; and for primary and preventative care, ten measurements for distinct populations, within three years.

Section 3021 establishes a new Center for Medicare and Medicaid Innovation (CMI) within the Centers for Medicare & Medicaid Services (CMS). The purpose of the Center will be to research, develop, test, and expand innovative payment and delivery arrangements to improve the quality and reduce the cost of care provided to patients in each program. Dedicated funding is provided to allow for testing of models that require benefits not currently covered by Medicare. The expectation is that successful models would then be expanded nationally.

The goals of the models to be researched and tested include promoting payment and practice reform, including patient–centered medical homes and models that move toward comprehensive payment or salary payment; direct contracting with groups of providers, through risk–based or salary–based payments; care coordination; patient decision making support tools; hospital care using specialists linked by electronic monitoring at integrated systems; and payments to Healthcare Innovation Zones. The Medicare Shared Savings Program (Section 3022) creates Accountable Care Organizations (ACOs).

NOTES AND QUESTIONS

1. The ACA presents a confusing, sometimes overlapping and inconsistent, approach to patient quality and improvements to patient safety. It is a grab bag of existing health policy ideas about what quality means, how to measure it, reduce uncertainty, and then maximize health care quality. What are the strategies that the ACA employs to generate new outcomes data and best practices information, from a regulatory perspective? Consider the range of regulatory tools that you can find in the various provisions that will serve the ends of quality as you read through the casebook. Who is likely to seek the grants that the federal government makes available in these provisions? Is this morass of provisions really just a disguise for what will ultimately be a top–down national health system? Or is it a design that promotes maximum flexibility and the ability of a system to evolve through consensus and buy–in by all parties?

2. Many of the payment strategies are just a more aggressive expansion of Medicare payment reforms now in place. Will providers respond positively to these incentive–based devices to promote quality and standardization? What kinds of strategies might you expect from providers, as they push back against both the pressures toward standardization, and the intensified linkage of payment to performance?

3. Tools are already available to improve clinical performance. One obvious example is checklists. See generally Atul Gawande, Annals of Medicine: The Checklist, *The New Yorker* (December 10, 2007). Gawande writes about the tension between the model of expert audacity (the doctor as medical hero) and the model of regimentation, drawn from management of complex systems. He notes that in the ICU you have a very sick patient who requires that hundreds of things are done right, every day, to keep him alive. He argues that checklists have tremendous advantages in the complex world of the ICU. First, they help with memory recall. Second, they make clear and explicit the "the minimum, expected steps in complex processes." Even experienced providers don't always understand the critical important of some precautions, such as the use of antacid medication for ventilated patients. In Gawande's words, "[c]hecklists established a higher standard of baseline performance." He continues:

> We have the means to make some of the most complex and dangerous work we do—in surgery, emergency care, and I.C.U. medicine more effective than we ever thought possible. But the prospect pushes against the traditional culture of medicine, with its central belief that in situations of high risk and complexity what you want is a kind of expert audacity—the right stuff, again. Checklists and standard operating procedures feel like exactly the opposite, and that's what rankles many people.

PROBLEM: DEFINING "QUALITY"

The ACA has several provisions that attempt to define quality, primarily by listing quality measures, as noted above. As CEO of a large multi–hospital system, you are developing standards for quality to improve patient safety at the thirty–five hospitals in your system. The hospitals range from small inner–city hospitals to large tertiary care hospitals. Review the various quality measures described in the ACA. How will you begin to prioritize these measures for your system? What other elements of the ACA will guide your decisions about what measures to focus on?

PROBLEM: BATTLING STANDARDS I

As the CEO of the large integrated health system described in the previous problem, you are well aware that cardiac care is an important and profitable component of patient care. You have recently begun a study of cardiac care in your system, with particular attention to the treatment of heart patients with clogged arteries. Cardiologists routinely use stents for stable coronary artery disease (CAD). In angioplasties, doctors guide a narrow tube through a blood vessel near the groin up toward the heart, inflate a tiny balloon to flatten blockages, and insert a stent to keep arteries propped open. The procedure costs about $20,000, based on average Medicare reimbursement for doctor and hospital fees, and generally requires an overnight hospital stay. You are aware of the COURAGE study, a major research study in 2007 that concluded that intensive drug treatment in non–emergency patients with chest pain (aspirin, beta blockers, and statins) worked as well as angioplasty in preventing heart attacks, improving survival and relieving discomfort in the long run. In a seven–year follow–up, the study found that the outcomes were the same for stents and drug therapies.

The use of stents by cardiologists in your system hospitals has continued at about the same level in 2011 as in 2007, in spite of their much higher costs and identical outcomes. You would like to change the practice patterns of the cardiologists in your system. How should you proceed? What kind of approach do you advise to deal with the problem of variation in practice approaches in cardiology? What ideas do you have to reduce such conflicts and to guide providers into the best practices? Given the structure of most hospitals, how will you orchestrate a unified approach to cardiology practice? Are you likely to be conflicted about this choice, given the likelihood of substantial hospital revenue from interventions like angioplasty?

What mechanisms might be used to resolve such possible conflicts among best practices, comparative effectiveness research findings, practice guidelines, and other standards of ACA? To what extent do variations inherent in medical practice styles confound such research? And what about the confounding effects of variations in patients, physician and support teams, and available resources? See William B. Borden et al., Patterns and Intensity of Medical Therapy in Patients Undergoing Percutaneous Coronary Intervention, 305 J.A.M.A. 1882 (2010), reporting that fewer than half of patients undergoing percutaneous coronary intervention (PCI) are receiving optimal medical therapy (OMT), despite the guideline–based recommendations to maximize OMT and the clinical logic of doing so before PCI.

B. EVIDENCE–BASED MEDICINE (EBM) AND COMPARATIVE EFFECTIVENESS RESEARCH (CER)

Evidence–based medicine (EBM) has been defined as "the conscientious, explicit, and judicious use of current best evidence in making decisions about the care of individual patients." David L. Sackett et al., Evidence–Based Medicine: What It Is and What It Isn't, 312 Brit. Med. J. 71, 71 (1996). EBM incorporates clinical expertise and patient values as well, but the emphasis is on the use of current best evidence. EBM assumes that the physician will keep up with and incorporate the best evidence into his practice in advance of the development of a clinical practice guideline. See generally Carter Williams, Evidence–Based Medicine in the Law Beyond Clinical Practice Guidelines: What Effect Will EBM Have on the Standard of Care? 61 Wash. & Lee L. Rev. 479 (2004).

Comparative effectiveness research (CER) is a natural outgrowth of EBM. It is a major component of current federal health policy. This "effectiveness initiative" in modern medicine is based on three premises. First, many current medical practices either are ineffective or could be replaced with less expensive substitutes. Wennberg's medical practice variation studies support this premise to a large extent.

Second, physicians often select more expensive treatments because of bias, fear of litigation, or financial incentives. Physician defensive medical practices like unnecessary tests, motivated by fear of litigation, supports this premise. So do payment incentives like fee–for–service medicine, where the more a physician does, the more she gets paid.

Third, patients would often choose different options from those recommended by their physicians if they had better information about treatment risks, benefits, and costs. The burgeoning literature on shared decision making and the use of decision aids supports this idea that patient choices might often lead to conservative treatment or no treatment at all. See Chapter 4.

The goal of evidence–based medicine and comparative effectiveness research is to narrow variation in medical practice by developing guidelines and best practices for clinicians. *See* David Eddy, Evidence–Based Medicine: A Unified Approach, 24 Health Affairs 9 (2005); Alan M. Garber, Evidence–Based Guidelines As a Foundation For Performance Incentives, 24 Health Affairs 174 (2005); M.C. Weinstein & J.A. Skinner, Comparative Effectiveness and Health Care Spending: Implications for Reform, 326 NEJM 460 (2010).

The federal government has a range of CER programs that predate the ACA. The Federal Coordinating Council for Comparative Effectiveness Research was created and funded by the American Recovery and Reinvestment Act of 2009 (ARRA) to promote optimum coordination of comparative effectiveness research conducted or supported by federal departments and agencies. The Council in its first report defines comparative effectiveness research:

> * * *the conduct and synthesis of research comparing the benefits and harms of different interventions and strategies to prevent, diagnose, treat and monitor health conditions in "real world" settings. The purpose of this research is to improve health outcomes by developing and disseminating evidence–based information to patients, clinicians, and other decision–makers, responding to their expressed needs, about which interventions are most effective for which patients under specific circumstances.

See Federal Coordinating Council for Comparative Effectiveness Research, Report to the President and the Congress 5, June 30, 2009.

The ACA continues the strong emphasis in federal health policy on comparative effectiveness research. Section 6301 of the ACA defines "comparative clinical effectiveness research" to mean research evaluating and comparing health outcomes and the clinical effectiveness, risks, and benefits of two or more medical treatments, services, and items. These include "health care interventions, protocols for treatment, care management, and delivery, procedures, medical devices, diagnostic tools, pharmaceuticals (including drugs and biologics), integrative health practices, and any other strategies or items being used in the treatment, management, and diagnosis of, or prevention of illness or injury in, individuals."

The ACA created several entities to further CER. The primary new entity is a nonprofit corporation, the Patient–Centered Outcomes Research Institute (PCORI). The Institute's purpose is:

> * * * to assist patients, clinicians, purchasers, and policymakers in making informed health decisions by advancing the quality and relevance of evidence concerning the manner in which diseases, disorders, and other health conditions can effectively and appropriately be prevented, diagnosed, treated, monitored, and managed through research and evidence synthesis that considers variations in patient subpopulations, and the dissemination of research findings with respect to the relative health outcomes, clinical effectiveness, and appropriateness of the medical treatments, services, and other items.

For a full list of federal programs, see National Information Center on Health Services Research and Health Technology (NICHSR), Comparative Effectiveness Research.

Critics of comparative effectiveness research note several problems with the enterprise, primarily the difficulties inherent in clinical adoption of research findings as to what works. They note that historically, medical practices are very slow to change in the face of new scientific evidence about what works. Timbie et al. list five sources of resistance to the adoption of research findings: "* * * financial incentives, such as fee–for–service payment, that may militate against the adoption of new clinical practices; ambiguity of study results that hamper decision making; cognitive biases in the interpretation of new information; failure of the research to address the needs of end users; and limited use of decision support by patients and clinicians." See Justin W. Timbie et al., Five Reasons That Many Comparative Effectiveness Studies Fail To Change Patient Care And Clinical Practice, 31 Health Affairs 2168 (2012) (The authors offer a note of optimism: "Policies that encourage the development of consensus objectives, methods, and evidentiary standards before studies get under way and that provide strong incentives for patients and providers to use resources efficiently may help overcome at least some of these barriers and enable comparative effectiveness results to alter medical practice more quickly.")

See also Eleanor D. Kinney, Comparative Effectiveness Research under the Patient Protection and Affordable Care Act: Can New Bottles Accommodate Old Wine? 37 Am. J. Law & Med. 522 (2011) (providing an excellent history of comparative effectiveness research and a detailed discussion of the Patient–Centered Outcomes Research Institute, and its potential strengths and problems.); Richard S. Saver, Health Care Reform's Wild Card: The Uncertain Effectiveness of Comparative Effectiveness Research, 159 U. Pa. L. Rev. 2147 (2011) (discussing the limitations of CER as rolled out under the ACA, and concluding that "to even begin fulfilling some of its promise, CER must be deployed under better starting conditions. This means paying a great deal more attention to how physicians, the critical gatekeepers, will likely respond and directly confronting the serious risks of physician tune–out and indifference.")

C. THE PROBLEM OF MEDICAL ERROR

1. Adverse Events: Definition and Scope

Injury caused by doctors and health care institutions, or iatrogenesis, is the inverse of quality medicine. The literature on adverse events is growing rapidly as the patient safety movement begins to permeate federal health policies. What is an adverse event?

The Institute of Medicine developed working definitions of "adverse event" and "medical error" in *To Err Is Human.* The IOM defined an adverse event as "an injury caused by medical management rather than the underlying condition of the patient," and a medical error as "the failure of a planned action to be completed as intended . . . or the use of a wrong plan to achieve an aim. . . . " Institute of Med., To Err Is Human: Building a Safer Health System 28 (Linda T. Kohn, et al., eds., 2000) [hereinafter, IOM Report].

The U.S. Agency for Healthcare Research and Quality (AHRQ) defines an adverse event as "Any negative or unwanted effect from any drug, device, or medical test," essentially the same as the IOM's definition. AHRQ cites the following examples of adverse events: "pneumothorax from central venous catheter placement," "anaphylaxis to penicillin," "postoperative wound infection," and "hospital–acquired delirium (or 'sundowning') in elderly patients."

The law has historically focused on physician "error." Until recently, malpractice cases were brought against the treating physician and not his institution because of a variety of legal rules that shielded the hospital. State licensing boards brought disciplinary actions against the individual errant doctor. Staff privileges cases involved the individual doctor's qualifications. The narrow focus on individual error facilitated a clear definition of "bad medicine." Bad medicine was what bad doctors did. The "bad apples" were doctors whose incompetence was obvious.

The larger problem of quality in medical care must also address systemic failures, poor administrative design for review of health care, inadequacies in training of physicians, and the nature of practice incentives. The concept of "error" often misses the point of quality improvement, which requires a look at many other facets of health care delivery. See Chapter 6.

2. The Extent of Medical Misadventures

PATIENTS, DOCTORS, AND LAWYERS: MEDICAL INJURY, MALPRACTICE LITIGATION, AND PATIENT COMPENSATION IN NEW YORK

The Report of the Harvard Medical Practice.
Study to the State of New York (1990).

[The Harvard Medical Practice Study in New York looked at the incidence of injuries resulting from medical interventions (adverse events) beginning with a sample of more than 31,000 New York hospital records drawn from the study year 1984. The review was conducted by medical record administrators and nurses in the screening phase, and by board certified physicians for the physician–review phase.]

* * *

We analyzed 30,121 (96%) of the 31,429 records selected for the study sample. After preliminary screening, physicians reviewed 7,743 records, from which a total of 1,133 adverse events were identified that occurred as a result of medical management in the hospital or required hospitalization for treatment. Of this group, 280 were judged to result from negligent care. Weighting these figures according to the sample plan, we estimated the incidence of adverse events for hospitalizations in New York in 1984 to be 3.7%, or a total of 98,609. Of these, 27.6%, 27,179 cases, or 1.0% of all hospital discharges, were due to negligence.

* * *

The majority of adverse events (57%) resulted in minimal and transient disability, but 14% of patients died at least in part as a result of their adverse event, and in another 9% the resultant disability lasted longer than 6 months. Based on these figures, we estimated that about 2,500 cases of permanent total disability resulted from medical injury in New York hospitals in 1984. Further, we found evidence that medical injury contributed at least in part to the deaths of more than 13,000 patients in that year. Many of the deaths occurred in patients who had greatly shortened life expectancies from their underlying diseases, however. Negligent adverse events resulted, overall, in greater disability than did non–negligent events and were associated with 51% of all deaths from medical injury.

Risk Factors

The risk of sustaining an adverse event increased with age. When rates were standardized for DRG [diagnosis–related group] level, persons over 65 years had twice the chance of sustaining an adverse event of those in the 16–44 years group. Newborns had half the adverse event rate of the 16–44 years group. The percent of adverse events resulting from negligence was increased in elderly patients. We found no gender differences in adverse event or negligence rates. Although the rates were higher in the self–pay group than in the insured categories, the differences were not significant. Blacks had higher rates of adverse events and adverse events resulting from negligence, but these differences overall were not significant. However, higher rates of adverse events and negligent events were found in hospitals that served a higher proportion of minority patients. At hospitals that cared for a mix of white and minority patients, blacks and whites had nearly identical rates.

Adverse event rates varied 10–fold between individual hospitals, when standardized for age and DRG level. Although standardized adverse event and negligence rates for small hospitals (fewer than 8,000 discharges/year) were less than for larger hospitals, these differences were not significant. Hospital ownership (private, non–profit, or government) also was not associated with significantly different rates of adverse events. The fraction of adverse events due to negligence in government hospitals was 50% higher than in non–profit institutions, however, and three times that in proprietary hospitals. These differences were significant. The standardized rate of adverse events in upstate, non–MSA hospitals was one–third that of upstate metropolitan hospitals and less than one–fourth that in New York City. These differences were highly significant. The percent of adverse events due to negligence was not significantly different across regions. Non–teaching hospitals had half the adverse event rates of university or affiliated teaching hospitals, but university teaching hospitals had rates of negligence that were less than half those of the non–teaching or affiliated hospitals.

The Nature of Adverse Events

Nearly half (47%) of all adverse events occurred in patients undergoing surgery, but the percent caused by negligence was lower than for non–surgical adverse events (17% vs 37%). Adverse events resulting from errors in diagnosis and in non–invasive treatment were judged to be due to negligence in over three–fourths of patients. Falls were considered due to negligence in 45% of instances.

The high rate of adverse events in patients over 65 years occurred in three categories: non–technical postoperative complications, complications of non–invasive therapy, and falls. A larger proportion of adverse events in younger patients was due to surgical failures. The operating room was the site of management for the highest fraction of adverse events, but relatively few of these were negligent. On the other hand, most (70%) adverse events in the emergency room resulted from negligence.

The most common type of error resulting in an adverse event was that involved in performing a procedure, but diagnostic errors and prevention errors were more likely to be judged negligent, and to result in serious disability.

The more severe the degree of negligence the greater the likelihood of resultant serious disability (moderate impairment with recovery taking more than six months), permanent disability, or death).

Litigation data

We estimated that the incidence of malpractice claims filed by patients for the study year was between 2,967 and 3,888. Using these figures, together with the projected statewide number of injuries from medical negligence during the same period, we estimated that eight times as many patients suffered an injury from negligence as filed a malpractice claim in New York State. About 16 times as many patients suffered an injury from negligence as received compensation from the tort liability system.

* * *

NOTES AND QUESTIONS

1. The Harvard Study was designed to produce empirical data to better inform the debate about reform of the tort system, including no–fault re-

forms. Do the findings of the study, as to level of patient injury attributable to medical error, surprise you? The Study is generally acknowledged as one of the first to take an epidemiological approach to medical errors. It has also been criticized on a number of grounds. See generally Tom Baker, Reconsidering the Harvard Medical Practice Study Conclusions about the Validity of Medical Malpractice Claims, 33 J. L., Med. & Ethics 501 (2005). The IOM Report extrapolated from the Harvard Study to predict almost 100,000 patient deaths annually due to medical errors. IOM Report 26–27.

2. A second study, the Utah–Colorado Medical Practice Study (UCMPS), found that adverse events connected to surgery accounted for about half (44.9%) of adverse events across both states, with only 16.9% of the surgical adverse events involving negligence. Drug related adverse events comprised the second most prevalent group. The authors concluded that the UCMPS produced results similar to the earlier New York Harvard Study. That is, three to four percent of hospitalizations give rise to adverse events. David M. Studdert, et al., Beyond Dead Reckoning: Measures of Medical Injury Burden, Malpractice Litigation, and Alternative Compensation Models from Utah and Colorado, 33 Ind. L. Rev. 1643, 1662 (2000).

3. More recent studies have confirmed that adverse events occur at even higher levels than previously thought. The Office of the Inspector General found that 13.5% of Medicare hospital admissions suffered an adverse event, with an equal percentage experiencing temporary harm. U.S. Dep't of Health & Human Servs., Office of Inspector Gen., Adverse Events in Hospitals: National Incidence Among Medicare Beneficiaries, at i–ii (2010). Another study, using newer methodologies for discovering adverse events, concluded that patients suffer adverse events in one–third of all admissions. David C. Classen et al., 'Global Trigger Tool' Shows that Adverse Events in Hospitals May Be Ten Times Greater than Previously Measured, 30 Health Affairs 581, 581 (2011).

4. While the Harvard data were based on hospital records, studies analyzing the actual incidence of negligent events in hospital wards found that many injuries were not reported in hospital records as required—especially when the main person responsible for the error was a senior physician. Lori Andrews, Studying Medical Error In Situ: Implications for Malpractice Law and Policy, 54 DePaul L. Rev. 357 (2005).

5. Most malpractice claims do involve medical errors, and those claims that lack evidence of error are usually denied compensation. David M. Studdert et al., Claims, Errors, and Compensation Payments in Medical Malpractice Litigation, 354 N.E.J.M. 2024 (2006).

6. Errors in office–based surgery are a significant problem, as surgical procedures have migrated from hospitals to surgicenters and physician offices. One study of surgical procedures performed in doctors' offices and ambulatory surgery centers in Florida found that there was a 10–fold increased risk of adverse events and death in the office setting. See Hector Vila, et al.,

Comparative Outcomes Analysis of Procedures Performed in Physician Offices and Ambulatory Surgery Centers, 138 Arch.Surg. 991 (2003).

D. THE PATIENT SAFETY MOVEMENT

LUCIAN L. LEAPE, ERROR IN MEDICINE

272 JAMA 1851 (1994).

* * *

Why Is the Error Rate in the Practice of Medicine So High?

Physicians, nurses, and pharmacists are trained to be careful and to function at a high level of proficiency. Indeed, they probably are among the most careful professionals in our society. It is curious, therefore, that high error rates have not stimulated more concern and efforts at error prevention. One reason may be a lack of awareness of the severity of the problem. Hospital–acquired injuries are not reported in the newspapers like jumbo–jet crashes, for the simple reason that they occur one at a time in 5000 different locations across the country. Although error rates are substantial, serious injuries due to errors are not part of the everyday experience of physicians or nurses, but are perceived as isolated and unusual events—"outliers." Second, most errors do no harm. Either they are intercepted or the patient's defenses prevent injury. (Few children die from a single misdiagnosed or mistreated urinary infection, for example.)

But the most important reason physicians and nurses have not developed more effective methods of error prevention is that they have a great deal of difficulty in dealing with human error when it does occur. The reasons are to be found in the culture of medical practice.

Physicians are socialized in medical school and residency to strive for error–free practice. There is a powerful emphasis on perfection, both in diagnosis and treatment. In everyday hospital practice, the message is equally clear: mistakes are unacceptable. Physicians are expected to function without error, an expectation that physicians translate into the need to be infallible. One result is that physicians, not unlike test pilots, come to view an error as a failure of character—you weren't careful enough, you didn't try hard enough. This kind of thinking lies behind a common reaction by physicians: "How can there be an error without negligence?"

Cultivating a norm of high standards is, of course, highly desirable. It is the counterpart of another fundamental goal of medical education: developing the physician's sense of responsibility for the patient. If you are responsible for everything that happens to the patient, it follows that you are responsible for any errors that occur. While the logic may be sound, the conclusion is absurd, because physicians do not have the power to control all aspects of patient care. Nonetheless, the sense of duty to perform faultlessly is strongly internalized.

Role models in medical education reinforce the concept of infallibility. The young physician's teachers are largely specialists, experts in their fields, and authorities. Authorities are not supposed to err. It has been suggested that this need to be infallible creates a strong pressure to intellectual dishonesty, to cover up mistakes rather than to admit them. The organization of medical practice, particularly in the hospital, perpetuates these norms. Errors are rarely admitted or discussed among physicians in private practice. Physicians typically feel, not without reason, that admission of error will lead to censure or increased surveillance or, worse, that their colleagues will regard them as incompetent or careless. Far better to conceal a mistake or, if that is impossible, to try to shift the blame to another, even the patient.

Yet physicians are emotionally devastated by serious mistakes that harm or kill patients. Almost every physician who cares for patients has had that experience, usually more than once. The emotional impact is often profound, typically a mixture of fear, guilt, anger, embarrassment, and humiliation. However, as Christensen et al. note, physicians are typically isolated by their emotional responses; seldom is there a process to evaluate the circumstances of a mistake and to provide support and emotional healing for the fallible physician. Wu et al. found that only half of house officers discussed their most significant mistakes with attending physicians.

Thus, although the individual may learn from a mistake and change practice patterns accordingly, the adjustment often takes place in a vacuum. Lessons learned are shared privately, if at all, and external objective evaluation of what went wrong often does not occur. As Hilfiker points out, "We see the horror of our own mistakes, yet we are given no permission to deal with their enormous emotional impact. . . . The medical profession simply has no place for its mistakes."

Finally, the realities of the malpractice threat provide strong incentives against disclosure or investigation of mistakes. Even a minor error can place the physician's entire career in jeopardy if it results in a serious bad outcome. It is hardly surprising that a physician might hesitate to reveal an error to either the patient or hospital authorities or to expose a colleague to similar devastation for a single mistake.

The paradox is that although the standard of medical practice is perfection—error-free patient care—all physicians recognize that mistakes are inevitable. Most would like to examine their mistakes and learn from them. From an emotional standpoint, they need the support and understanding of their colleagues and patients when they make mistakes. Yet, they are denied both insight and support by misguided concepts of infallibility and by fear: fear of embarrassment by colleagues, fear of patient reaction, and fear of litigation. Although the notion of infallibility fails the reality test, the fears are well grounded.

The Medical Approach to Error Prevention

Efforts at error prevention in medicine have characteristically followed what might be called the perfectibility model: if physicians and nurses could be properly trained and motivated, then they would make no mistakes. The methods used to achieve this goal are training and punishment. Training is directed toward teaching people to do the right thing. In nursing, rigid adherence to protocols is emphasized. In medicine, the emphasis is less on rules and more on knowledge.

Punishment is through social opprobrium or peer disapproval. The professional cultures of medicine and nursing typically use blame to encourage proper performance. Errors are regarded as someone's fault, caused by a lack of sufficient attention or, worse, lack of caring enough to make sure you are correct. Punishment for egregious (negligent) errors is primarily (and capriciously) meted out through the malpractice tort litigation system.

Students of error and human performance reject this formulation. While the proximal error leading to an accident is, in fact, usually a 'human error,' the causes of that error are often well beyond the individual's control. All humans err frequently. Systems that rely on error–free performance are doomed to fail.

The medical approach to error prevention is also reactive. Errors are usually discovered only when there is an incident—an untoward effect or injury to the patient. Corrective measures are then directed toward preventing a recurrence of a similar error, often by attempting to prevent that individual from making a repeat error. Seldom are underlying causes explored.

For example, if a nurse gives a medication to the wrong patient, a typical response would be exhortation or training in double–checking the identity of both patient and drug before administration. Although it might be noted that the nurse was distracted because of an unusually large case load, it is unlikely that serious attention would be given to evaluating overall work assignments or to determining if large caseloads have contributed to other kinds of errors.

It is even less likely that questions would be raised about the wisdom of a system for dispensing medications in which safety is contingent on inspection by an individual at the end point of use. Reliance on inspection as a mechanism of quality control was discredited long ago in industry. A simple procedure, such as the use of bar coding like that used at supermarket checkout counters, would probably be more effective in this situation. More imaginative solutions could easily be found—if it were recognized that both systems and individuals contribute to the problem.

It seems clear, and it is the thesis of this article, that if physicians, nurses, pharmacists, and administrators are to succeed in reducing errors in hospital care, they will need to fundamentally change the way they think about errors and why they occur. Fortunately, a great deal has been learned about error prevention in other disciplines, information that is relevant to the hospital practice of medicine.

* * *

Prevention of Accidents

* * *

The primary objective of system design for safety is to make it difficult for individuals to err. But it is also important to recognize that errors will inevitably occur and plan for their recovery. Ideally, the system will automatically correct errors when they occur. If that is impossible, mechanisms should be in place to at least detect errors in time for corrective action. Therefore, in addition to designing the work environment to minimize psychological precursors, designers should provide feedback through instruments that provide monitoring functions and build in buffers and redundancy. Buffers are design features that automatically correct for human or mechanical errors. Redundancy is duplication (sometimes triplication or quadruplication) of critical mechanisms and instruments, so that a failure does not result in loss of the function.

Another important system design feature is designing tasks to minimize errors. Norman has recommended a set of principles that have general applicability. Tasks should be simplified to minimize the load on the weakest aspects of cognition: short–term memory, planning, and problem solving. The power of constraints should be exploited. One way to do this is with "forcing functions," which make it impossible to act without meeting a precondition (such as the inability to release the parking gear of a car unless the brake pedal is depressed). Standardization of procedures, displays, and layouts reduces error by reinforcing the pattern recognition that humans do well. Finally, where possible, operations should be easily reversible or difficult to perform when they are not reversible.

Training must include, in addition to the usual emphasis on application of knowledge and following procedures, a consideration of safety issues. These issues include understanding the rationale for procedures as well as how errors can occur at various stages, their possible consequences, and instruction in methods for avoidance of errors. Finally, it must be acknowledged that injuries can result from behavioral problems that may be seen in impaired physicians or incompetent physicians despite well–designed systems; methods for identifying and correcting egregious behaviors are also needed.

The Aviation Model

The practice of hospital medicine has been compared, usually unfavorably, to the aviation industry, also a highly complicated and risky enterprise but one that seems far safer. Indeed, there seem to be many similarities. As Allnutt observed,

> Both pilots and doctors are carefully selected, highly trained professionals who are usually determined to maintain high standards, both externally and internally imposed, whilst performing difficult tasks in life–threatening environments. Both use high technology equipment and function as key members of a team of specialists . . . both exercise high level cognitive skills in a most complex domain about which much is known, but where much remains to be discovered.

While the comparison is apt, there are also important differences between aviation and medicine, not the least of which is a substantial measure of uncertainty due to the number and variety of disease states, as well as the unpredictability of the human organism. Nonetheless, there is much physicians and nurses could learn from aviation.

* * *

There are strong incentives for making flying safe. Pilots, of course, are highly motivated. Unlike physicians, their lives are on the line as well as those of their passengers. But, airlines and airplane manufacturers also have strong incentives to provide safe flight. Business decreases after a large crash, and if a certain model of aircraft crashes repeatedly, the manufacturer will be discredited. The lawsuits that inevitably follow a crash can harm both reputation and profitability.

Designing for safety has led to a number of unique characteristics of aviation that could, with suitable modification, prove useful in improving hospital safety.

First, in terms of system design, aircraft designers assume that errors and failures are inevitable and design systems to "absorb" them, building in multiple buffers, automation, and redundancy. * * *

Second, procedures are standardized to the maximum extent possible. Specific protocols must be followed for trip planning, operations, and maintenance. Pilots go through a checklist before each takeoff. Required maintenance is specified in detail and must be performed on a regular (by flight hours) basis.

Third, the training, examination, and certification process is highly developed and rigidly, as well as frequently, enforced. Airline pilots take proficiency examinations every 6 months. Much of the content of examinations is directly concerned with procedures to enhance safety.

Pilots function well within this rigorously controlled system, although not flawlessly. For example, one study of cockpit crews observed that human errors or instrument malfunctions occurred on the average of one every 4 minutes during an overseas flight. Each event was promptly recognized and corrected with no untoward effects. Pilots also willingly submit to an external authority, the air traffic controller, when within the constrained air and ground space at a busy airport.

Finally, safety in aviation has been institutionalized. * * *. The FAA recognized long ago that pilots seldom reported an error if it led to disciplinary action. Accordingly, in 1975 the FAA established a confidential reporting system for safety infractions, the Air Safety Reporting System (ASRS). If pilots, controllers, or others promptly report a dangerous situation, such as a near–miss midair collision, they will not be penalized. This program dramatically increased reporting, so that unsafe conditions at airports, communication problems, and traffic control inadequacies are now promptly communicated. Analysis of these reports and subsequent investigations appear as a regular feature in several pilots' magazines. The ASRS receives more than 5000 notifications each year.

The Medical Model

By contrast, accident prevention has not been a primary focus of the practice of hospital medicine. It is not that errors are ignored. Mortality and morbidity conferences, incident reports, risk management activities, and quality assurance committees abound. But, as noted previously, these activities focus on incidents and individuals. When errors are examined, a problem–solving approach is usually used: the cause of the error is identified and corrected. Root causes, the underlying systems failures, are rarely sought. System designers do not assume that errors and failures are inevitable and design systems to prevent or absorb them. There are, of course, exceptions. Implementation of unit dosing, for example, markedly reduced medication dosing errors by eliminating the need for the nurse to measure out each dose. * * *.

Second, standardization and task design vary widely. In the operating room, it has been refined to a high art. In patient care units, much more could be done, particularly to minimize reliance on short–term memory, one of the weakest aspects of cognition. On–time and correct delivery of medications, for example, is often contingent on a busy nurse remembering to do so, a nurse who is responsible for four or five patients at once and is repeatedly interrupted, a classic set up for a "loss–of–activation" error.

On the other hand, education and training in medicine and nursing far exceed that in aviation, both in breadth of content and in duration, and few professions compare with medicine in terms of the extent of continuing education. Although certification is essentially universal, including the recent introduction of periodic recertification, the idea of periodically testing performance has never been accepted. Thus, we place great emphasis on education and training, but shy away from demonstrating that it makes a difference.

Finally, unlike aviation, safety in medicine has never been institutionalized, in the sense of being a major focus of hospital medical activities. Investigation of accidents is often superficial, unless a malpractice action is likely; noninjurious error (a "near miss") is rarely examined at all. Incident reports are frequently perceived as punitive instruments. As a result, they are often not filed, and when they are, they almost invariably focus on the individual's misconduct.

One medical model is an exception and has proved quite successful in reducing accidents due to errors: anesthesia. Perhaps in part because the effects of serious anesthetic errors are potentially so dramatic—death or brain damage—and perhaps in part because the errors are frequently transparently clear and knowable to all, anesthesiologists have greatly emphasized safety. The success of these efforts has been dramatic. Whereas mortality from anesthesia was one in 10,000 to 20,000 just a decade or so ago, it is now estimated at less than one in 200,000. Anesthesiologists have led the medical profession in recognizing system factors as causes of errors, in designing fail–safe systems, and in training to avoid errors.

Systems Changes to Reduce Hospital Injuries

Can the lessons from cognitive psychology and human factors research that have been successful in accident prevention in aviation and other industries be applied to the practice of hospital medicine? There is every reason to think they could be. Hospitals, physicians, nurses, and pharmacists who wish to reduce errors could start by considering how cognition and error mechanisms apply to the practice of hospital medicine. Specifically, they can examine their care delivery systems in terms of the systems' ability to discover, prevent, and absorb errors and for the presence of psychological precursors.

Discovery of Errors

The first step in error prevention is to define the problem. Efficient, routine identification of errors needs to be part of hospital practice, as does routine investigation of all errors that cause injuries. The emphasis is on "routine." Only when errors are accepted as an inevitable, although manageable, part of everyday practice will it be possible for hospital personnel to shift from a punitive to a creative frame of mind that seeks out and identifies the underlying system failures.

Data collecting and investigatory activities are expensive, but so are the consequences of errors. Evidence from industry indicates that the savings from reduction of errors and accidents more than make up for the costs of data collection and investigation. * * *.

Prevention of Errors

Many health care delivery systems could be redesigned to significantly reduce the likelihood of error. Some obvious mechanisms that can be used are as follows:

Reduced Reliance on Memory.—Work should be designed to minimize the requirements for human functions that are known to be particularly fallible, such as short–term memory and vigilance (prolonged attention). * * * Checklists, protocols, and computerized decision aids could be used more widely. * * *.

Improved Information Access.—Creative ways need to be developed for making information more readily available: displaying it where it is needed, when it is needed, and in a form that permits easy access. Computerization of the medical record, for example, would greatly facilitate bedside display of patient information, including tests and medications.

Error Proofing.—Where possible, critical tasks should be structured so that errors cannot be made. The use of "forcing functions" is helpful. For example, if a computerized system is used for medication orders, it can be designed so that a physician cannot enter an order for a lethal overdose of a drug or prescribe a medication to which a patient is known to be allergic.

Standardization.—One of the most effective means of reducing error is standardizing processes wherever possible. The advantages, in efficiency as well as in error reduction, of standardizing drug doses and times of administration are obvious. Is it really acceptable to ask nurses to follow six different "K–scales" (directions for how much potassium to give according to patient serum potassium levels) solely to satisfy different physician prescribing patterns? Other candidates for standardization include information displays, methods for common practices (such as surgical dressings), and the geographic location of equipment and supplies in a patient care unit. There is something bizarre, and really quite inexcusable, about "code" situations in hospitals where house staff and other personnel responding to a cardiac arrest waste precious seconds searching for resuscitation equipment simply because it is kept in a different location on each patient care unit.

Training.—Instruction of physicians, nurses, and pharmacists in procedures or problem solving should include greater emphasis on possible errors and how to prevent them. * * *.

Absorption of Errors

Because it is impossible to prevent all error, buffers should be built into each system so that errors are absorbed before they can cause harm to patients. At minimum, systems should be designed so that errors can be identified in time to be intercepted. The drug delivery systems in most hospitals do this to some degree already. Nurses and pharmacists often identify errors in physician drug orders and prevent improper administration to the patient. As hospitals move to computerized records and ordering systems, more of these types of interceptions can be incorporated into the computer programs. * * *.

Psychological Precursors

Finally, explicit attention should be given to work schedules, division of responsibilities, task descriptions, and other details of working arrangements where improper managerial decisions can produce psychological precursors such as time pressures and fatigue that create an unsafe environment. While the influence of the stresses of everyday life on human behavior cannot be eliminated, stresses caused by a faulty work environment can be. Elimination of fear and the creation of a supportive working environment are other potent means of preventing errors.

Institutionalization of Safety

Although the idea of a national hospital safety board that would investigate every accident is neither practical nor necessary, at the hospital level such activities should occur. Existing hospital risk management activities could be broadened to include all potentially injurious errors and deepened to seek out underlying system failures. Providing immunity, as in the FAA ASRS system, might be a good first step. At the national level, the Joint Commission on Accreditation of Healthcare Organizations should be involved in discussions regarding the institutionalization of safety. Other specialty societies might well follow the lead of the anesthesiologists in developing safety standards and require their instruction to be part of residency training.

Leape's analysis laid the foundation for a new federal focus on patient safety, which was then launched in 1999 by the first in a series of Institute of Medicine publications dealing with medical errors.

TO ERR IS HUMAN: BUILDING A SAFER HEALTH SYSTEM

Institute of Medicine, 2000.

Executive Summary

* * *

When extrapolated to the over 33.6 million admissions to U.S. hospitals in 1997, the results of the study in Colorado and Utah imply that at least 44,000 Americans die each year as a result of medical errors. The results of the New York Study suggest the number may be as high as 98,000. Even when using the lower estimate, deaths due to medical errors exceed the number attributable to the 8th leading cause of death. More people die in a given year as result of medical errors than from motor vehicle accidents (43,458), breast cancer (42,297), or AIDS (16,516).

Total national costs (lost income, lost household production, disability and health care costs) of preventable adverse events (medical errors resulting in injury) are estimated to be between $17 billion and $29 billion, of which health care costs represent over one half.

In terms of lives lost, patient safety is as important an issue as worker safety. Every year, over 6,000 Americans die from workplace injuries. Medication errors alone, occurring either in or out of the hospital, are estimated to account for over 7,000 deaths annually.

Medication–related errors occur frequently in hospitals and although not all result in actual harm, those that do, are costly. One recent study conducted at two prestigious teaching hospitals, found that about two out of every 100 admissions experienced a preventable adverse drug event, resulting in average increased hospital costs of $4,700 per admission or about $2.8 million annually for a 700 bed teach hospital. If these findings are generalizable, the increased hospital costs alone of preventable adverse drug events affecting inpatients are about $2 billion for the nation as a whole.

These figures offer only a very modest estimate of the magnitude of the problem since hospital patients represent only a small proportion of the total population at risk, and direct hospital costs are only a fraction of total costs. More care and increasingly complex care is provided in ambulatory settings. Outpatient surgical centers, physical offices and clinics serve thousands of patients daily. Home care requires patients and their families to use complicated equipment and perform follow–up care. Retail pharmacies play a major role in filling prescriptions for patients and educating them about their use. Other institutional settings, such as nursing homes, provide a broad array of services to vulnerable populations. Although many of the available studies have focused on the hospital setting, medical errors present a problem in any setting, not just hospitals.

Errors are also costly in terms of opportunity costs. Dollars spent on having to repeat diagnostic tests or counteract adverse drug events are dollars unavailable for other purposes. Purchasers and patients pay for errors when insurance costs and copayments are inflated by services that would not have been necessary had proper care been provided. It is impossible for the nation to achieve the greatest value possible from the hundreds of millions of dollars spent on medical care if the care contains errors.

But not all the costs can be directly measured. Errors are also costly in terms of loss of trust in the system by patients and diminished satisfaction by both patients and health professionals. Patients who experienced a longer hospital stay or disability as a result of errors pay with physical and psychological discomfort. Health care professionals pay with loss of morale and frustration at not being able to provide the best care possible. Employers and society, in general, pay in terms of lost worker productivity, reduced school attendance by children, and lower levels of population health status.

Yet silence surrounds this issue. For the most part, consumers believe they are protected. Media coverage has been limited to reporting of anecdotal cases. Licensure and accreditation confer, in the eyes of the public, a "Good Housekeeping Seal of Approval." Yet, licensing and accreditation processes have focused only limited attention on the issue, and even these minimal efforts have confronted some resistance from health care organizations and providers. Providers also perceive the medical liability systems as a serious impediment to systematic efforts to uncover and learn from errors.

The decentralized and fragmented nature of the health care delivery system (some would say "nonsystem") also contributes to unsafe conditions for patients, and serves as an impediment to efforts to improve safety. Even within hospitals and large medical groups, there are rigidly–defined areas of specialization and influence. For example, when patients see multiple providers in different settings, none of whom have access to complete information, it is easier for something to go wrong than when care is better coordinated. At the same time, the provision of care to patients by a collection of loosely affiliated organizations and providers makes it difficult to implement improved clinical information systems capable of providing timely access to complete patient information. Unsafe care is one of the prices we pay for not having organized systems of care with clear lines of accountability.

* * *

In this report, safety is defined as freedom from accidental injury. This definition recognizes that this is the primary safety goal from the patient's perspective. Error is defined as the failure of a planned action to be completed as intended or the use of a wrong plan to achieve an aim. According to noted expert James Reason, errors depend on two kinds of failures: either the correct action does not proceed as intended (an error of execution) or the original intended action is not correct (an error of planning). Errors can happen in all stages in the process of care, from diagnosis, to treatment, to preventive care.

Not all errors result in harm. Errors that do result in injury are sometimes called preventable adverse events. An adverse event is an injury resulting from a medical intervention, or in other words, it is not due to the underlying condition of the patient. While all adverse events result from medical management, not all are preventable (i.e., not all are attributable to errors). For example, if a patient has surgery and dies from pneumonia he or she got postoperatively, it is an adverse event. If analysis of the case reveals that the patient got pneumonia because of poor hand washing or instrument cleaning techniques by staff, the adverse event was preventable (attributable to an error of execution). But the analysis may conclude that no error occurred and the patient would be presumed to have had a difficult surgery and recovery (not a preventable adverse event).

* * *

Recommendations

* * *

The recommendations contained in this report lay out a four–tiered approach:

- establishing a national focus to create leadership, research, tools and protocols to enhance the knowledge base about safety;
- identifying and learning from errors through immediate and strong mandatory reporting efforts, as well as the encouragement of voluntary efforts, both with the aim of making sure the system continues to be made safer for patients;
- raising standards and expectations for improvements in safety through the actions of oversight organizations, group purchasers, and professional groups; and
- creating safety systems inside health care organizations through the implementation of safe practices at the delivery level. This level is the ultimate target of all the recommendations.

NOTES AND QUESTIONS

1. The IOM Report on error in medicine caused an upheaval in health care. It was, in the words of one commentator, " * * * the single most important spur to the development of patient safety, catapulting it into public and political awareness and galvanizing political and professional will at the highest levels in the United States." Charles Vincent, Patient Safety 25 (Wiley–Blackwell, 2d ed. 2010) (2006). See Lucian L. Leape and Donald M. Berwick, Five Years After To Err Is Human: What Have We Learned? 293 JAMA 2384 (2005).

2. The Report turned a critical eye on health care systems as a primary source of many adverse events. What are the implications of a focus on system errors? Does the physician as a virtuoso disappear from the model of the health care system as we move toward a model of organizations that that deliver care, rather than physicians that treat patients? Do we care if we reduce the level of patient injuries from adverse events to a significantly lower level?

3. If we focus on system errors and system excellence, what happens to the traditional tort suit that starts with physician error? If errors are preventable by attention to the overall organization, then physicians should no longer be viewed as at "fault" when a patient is injured. What about medical licensing? The merits of discipline for physician errors should be reconsidered, if most errors are due to failures of an organization to provide resources, support, or other structures. What about differential pay for physicians in different practice areas? As health care is integrated and outcomes used to evaluate the overall benefits to a population of patients, why should we pay differentials that reflect the older model of the physician as craftsperson or artist? Perhaps this new model suggests a salary approach to compensation, with bonuses at best for compliance with institutional norms. Or should pervasive federal regulation of safety be developed, along the lines of the regulation of workplace safety through OSHA?

PROBLEM: WHY OPERATE?

Bonnie Bowser, eighty–two years old, fell and severely injured her elbow. She was examined at the Emergency Department of the Miraculous Regional Health System and diagnosed with a fractured olecranon process, and referred to an orthopedic surgeon. The surgeon who examined Mrs. Bowser scheduled her for corrective surgery the next day. He noted in his examination that she had a past medical history of hypertension, diabetes mellitus, two myocardial infarctions with quadruple bypass surgery, and a cerebrovascular accident affecting her left side. She was taking several medications including Lasix (a diuretic), Vasotec (for treatment of hypertension and symptomatic congestive heart failure), Klotrix (potassium supplement), and Glyburide (for the treatment of hyperglycemia related to diabetes). He noted that she smoked an average of one pack of cigarettes per day; that she had abnormal chest x–rays, suggesting congestive heart failure; an EKG that indicated ischemic heart disease; and signs of edema, indicating congestive heart failure. She was a high risk candidate for any kind of surgery. After the anesthesia was administered, she deteriorated rapidly, had cardiopulmonary failure and stroke, and died a few days later from complications of the stroke. The anesthesia was the cause of her death, as she was severely "medically compromised" and an elbow operation did not justify the obvious risks. Bonnie had consented to the operation. Her health insurance paid for the procedure. The hospital allowed the operation to proceed.

What do you propose to reduce this kind of risk to patients, as Vice–President and General Counsel of the System?

What system–wide rules will you propose to avoid a repetition of such cases, as the head of your state's Department of Health?

As a congressman from your state, what legislation might you propose?

For a general overview of the patient safety provisions of the ACA, and programs that now operate in tandem with the Act, see generally Barry R.

Furrow, Regulating Patient Safety: The Patient Protection and Affordable Care Act, 159 U. Pa. L. Rev. 101 (2011).

E. REGULATING TO REDUCE MEDICAL ADVERSE EVENTS

1. Patient Safety and the Affordable Care Act

The ACA has an astonishing variety of provisions aimed at improving the quality of the U.S. health care system, reducing errors, and generally promoting patient safety. These provisions include new centers, demonstration projects, and funding awards for a wide range of quality improvement projects.

Patient safety strategies can be summed up in six major regulatory categories:

(1) *Standardizing Good Medical Practices.* The ACA aims to reduce medical practice variation by promoting best practices, practice guidelines, and research on what works, as noted above.

(2) *Tracking Adverse Events in Hospitals.* Policies mandating adverse event data as to infections, readmissions, and other adverse events are coming online, since both health care providers and regulators need data in order to select the most serious problem areas for repair.

(3) *Disclosing Provider Performance.* Disclosure of adverse events can occur at three levels: (a) induced disclosure of hospital adverse events and "near misses" to state regulators and quasi–regulators like the Joint Commission; (b) disclosure by the provider of adverse events to patients; and (c) publication of performance data about relative risks by private/public agents, designed for purchaser use.

(4) *Reforming Payment Systems.* These strategies include creating a range of financial incentives for providers to promote safety, through "pay for performance" initiatives, including bonuses and docking reimbursement for failures to meet minimum standards as well as using insurance exchanges to promote quality and safety improvements. (b) disclosure by the provider of adverse events to patients; and (c) publication of performance data about relative risks by private/public agents, designed for purchaser use.

(5) *Coordinating and Integrating Care.* This strategy is the largest and most innovative category of federal health care reform, which promotes several new models for integrating health care delivery in the fragmented U.S. system.

6) *Expanding Provider Responsibility.* This strategy includes implementing legislative requirements for disclosure, such as the requirement of "decision aids" in the ACA, changing tort liability rules through new doc-

trines, expanding damage remedies, and developing alternative dispute resolution approaches that focus on health care organizations as systems. See Chapter 6.

2. Error Tracking and System Improvements

The Institute of Medicine reports, beginning with To Err Is Human, focused attention on medical systems and the level of errors they produced. Hospitals and other providers were asked to respond by developing error tracking systems and strategies for improvement including disclosure of both errors and so–called "near misses," events that could have resulted in patient injury but were detected in time. This is not a new idea; as early as 1858 Florence Nightingale developed the use of statistical methodology to show the effects of unsanitary conditions in military field hospitals. Her approach laid the groundwork for standard statistical approaches for hospitals. Florence Nightingale, Notes on Matters Affecting the Health, Efficiency and Hospital Administration of the British Army (1858). See also John Maindonald and Alice M. Richardson, This Passionate Study: A Dialogue with Florence Nightingale, 12 J. Stat. Ed. (2004).

The idea of tracking errors in hospitals is also not new. The first systematic approach was developed by Dr. Ernest Codman, a Boston doctor who wanted hospitals and doctors to track their practices and evaluate outcomes of their patients, an ideal he developed around 1920. To Codman, patient harm due to infections or unnecessary or inappropriate operations was a hospital "waste product". His work laid the foundation for the Joint Commission, which has slowly moved toward a more outcome–based accreditation system. See Virgina A. Sharpe and Alan I. Faden, Medical Harm: Historical, Conceptual, and Ethical Dimensions of Iatrogenic Illness 31 (1998).

Discovering and reporting adverse events is essential to system approaches, but it has been a concern for health care providers, who are afraid that disclosure of an error will come to plaintiff lawyers' attention. Voluntary reporting of mistakes has been argued to be the preferable approach to uncovering errors and correcting them. States that have mandatory reporting requirements for errors have found that underreporting is too often the norm. But the fact that underreporting occurs does not mean that performance cannot be improved. The reasons for such poor performance are several. Mandatory systems lack support from physicians, who are worried about liability, damage to reputation, and the hassle factor of any reporting system. Brian Liang, Promoting Patient Safety Through Reducing Medical Error, 22 J.L.Med & Ethics 564 (2002).

a. Sentinel Events and the Joint Commission

The Joint Commission is a private accreditor, granted authority by federal and state governments to accredit hospitals. See Chapter 3. The Joint Commission Sentinel Event Policy has adopted the view of medical errors of the Institute of Medicine report To Err is Human.

SENTINEL EVENT POLICY AND PROCEDURES

December 6, 2012.

In support of its mission to continuously improve the safety and quality of health care provided to the public, the Joint Commission reviews organizations' activities in response to sentinel events in its accreditation process, including all full accreditation surveys and random unannounced surveys and, as appropriate, for–cause surveys.

- A sentinel event is an unexpected occurrence involving death or serious physical or psychological injury, or the risk thereof. Serious injury specifically includes loss of limb or function. The phrase "or the risk thereof" includes any process variation for which a recurrence would carry a significant chance of a serious adverse outcome.
- Such events are called "sentinel" because they signal the need for immediate investigation and response.
- The terms "sentinel event" and "medical error" are not synonymous; not all sentinel events occur because of an error and not all errors result in sentinel events.

NOTES AND QUESTIONS

1. Hospitals may report serious events to the Joint Commission, and if they do not and the Joint Commission learns of the events from a third party, the hospital must conduct an analysis of the root cause or risk loss of accreditation. Loss of accreditation is rarely exercised, however.

2. The Joint Commission is a private accreditation organization, and its primary weapon for hospital improvement is the threat that accreditation will be revoked, or the hospital placed on the "Accreditation Watch List". Given the infrequency of revocation of hospital accreditation, how does the Joint Commission have a significant effect on hospital behavior? It does not mandate the reporting of its serious adverse events to the Joint Commission, although it does mandate a "root cause analysis" and will check during accreditation inspections to make sure that such analyses have been done.

3. What are the limits of a private entity in getting hospitals to be serious about adverse events? The entity can withdraw accredited status, which means the federal Medicare program will no longer allow the hospital to remain in the program and receive Medicare reimbursement. This nuclear op-

tion however means that it is almost never exercised, leaving the Joint Commission tools that include reporting requirements and embarrassment.

b. Reporting Hospital Adverse Events: Hospital–Acquired Conditions and "Never Events"

The regulatory response to the 1999 Institute of Medicine study—identifying medical errors as a leading cause of illness and death in the United States—branched in several directions. Given the complexity of our state–federal system, and the mix of private accreditation and standard–setting bodies, as well as the rapid maturation of the Center for Medicare & Medicaid Services (CMS) as a quality regulator, adverse event regulation took several steps.

First, the National Quality Forum ("NQF"), a not–for–profit organization "created to develop and implement a national strategy for health care quality measurement and reporting," identified 28 serious preventable conditions, including events such as wrong–site and wrong–patient surgeries, foreign object retention post surgery, and discharge of an infant to the wrong person. These were initially termed "never events," and later renamed "serious reportable events".

Second, state regulators saw the value of the list of adverse events, given the recognized impartiality of the NQF and the obvious nature of the harms described by "never events." Twenty odd states created their own reporting systems based on the events. This was a major regulatory step forward, forcing hospitals to disclose adverse outcomes on the list to the state department responsible, with the goal of improving their operations. Such reporting allows for systematic recording and tracking of errors, for purpose of analysis of patterns of adverse events, feedback to hospitals, and in some states, information for consumers as to the relative performance of hospitals and other providers.

Minnesota was the first state to adopt the approach in 2003, now calling these conditions "serious adverse health events", requiring hospitals and now ambulatory surgical centers, to report whenever a serious adverse health event occurs and to conduct a thorough analysis of the reasons for the event. See Adverse Health Events in Minnesota, Ninth Annual Public Report, January 2013. Under the Minnesota Adverse Health Care Events Reporting Law, hospitals and surgical centers are required to submit a report to the Minnesota Department of Health (MDH) whenever one of 28 serious reportable events occurs. The reports include details of the event, as well as a summary of the most important causes or contributing factors for the event (called a root cause analysis) and the corrective action plan that will be put in place to prevent a repeat of the event. The MDH is directed to review all reported events, root cause analyses, and corrective action plans, and provide direction to reporting facilities to ensure that the actions they take will be effective in preventing future harm.

Third, large businesses wanted quality metrics to use in reducing the costs of employee health care plans and in improving the quality of that care. The Leapfrog Group, a group of private companies that purchased health care for their employees, saw the Never Events list as a first step toward specific quality improvement based on clear adverse events. The Leapfrog Group was created for the purpose of focusing on health care quality improvement and affordability, and many private insurers have used this list in an attempt to improve quality and health care affordability. By late 2006, The Leapfrog Group developed a policy for hospitals to handle Never Events that some hospitals have adopted. The Leapfrog policy required issuing an apology to the patient and family involved in the event, reporting the event to an accrediting agency such as the Joint Commission, performing a root cause analysis per the accrediting agency's instruction, and waiving all costs directly related to the event.

NOTES AND QUESTIONS

1. Consider the nature of the regulatory incentives described above. Does a reporting obligation change hospital corporate behavior? There are no sanctions involved—no penalties, either civil or criminal; no obvious financial impact. Why would a hospital report honestly its full range of adverse events when there is little risk in not doing so? What about the Leapfrog approach? If corporate purchasers adopt the adverse event approach, what can they do to get health care providers that serve their employees to do? What incentives can such parties offer and what penalties can they impose?

2. It costs money to generate and mine data, produce useful feedback and finally implement new quality measures. Computer software is needed, new personnel must be hired or retrained, and an institution would like to be able to recapture those costs from its payers or through greater efficiencies that increase its margins. But perverse incentives dominate, and poor care is reimbursed at the same level as high quality care. Use of market power through purchasing to increase consumer and purchaser knowledge about providers has been one attempted solution to poor quality care. The Leapfrog Group is the most visible current example of this manifestation. Leapfrog members are encouraged to refer patients to hospitals with the best survival odds, staff intensive care units with doctors having credentials in critical care, and use error prevention software to prescribe medications. See Leapfrog Initiatives to Drive Great Leaps in Patient Safety (2002).

3. Federal Reimbursement Strategies

a. Federal Adoption of "Hospital–Acquired Conditions" Reimbursement Penalties

The federal government began to rethink its approach to reimbursing adverse events under the federal Medicare program, with the Deficit Reduction Act of 2005 (DRA) the first step in a new regulatory approach. The DRA requires the Secretary of the U.S. Department of Health and Human Services (DHHS) to identify at least two reasonably preventable high–cost conditions that result in higher payment when they occur in a patient as a secondary diagnosis. The Act anticipated that identifying such conditions would promote both efficiency and quality in patient care.

When the Centers for Medicare & Medicaid Services (CMS) issued a Final Rule in 2007, it excluded payment for several hospital–acquired conditions (HACs) if these conditions occurred during a Medicare beneficiary's inpatient stay. The CMS Final Rule for the 2009 Inpatient Prospective Payment System (IPPS) then expanded the exclusions for HACs. These actions clearly reflected the earlier initiatives of both NQF and Leapfrog. This regulatory approach used Medicare reimbursement to force these hospitals to internalize the costs of certain Never Events or hospital–acquired conditions (HACs)—conditions that were high volume, involved higher payment, and could be easily prevented. This was a significant change in regulatory incentives for hospitals receiving Medicare payments. These hospital–acquired conditions are no longer reimbursed at the normal rate for the costs of treatment, as they are presumptively preventable patient charges.

For a useful history of the origins of the federal policy involving hospital–acquired conditions, see CMS Rules for Hospital–Acquired Conditions Pose Challenges and Opportunities, The Q. J. for Health Care Practice & Risk Man. 13 (Fall 2010).

Another example of a regulatory reimbursement strategy has been the Hospital Readmission Reduction Program, created by section 3025 of the ACA. This program ties excess readmissions to a reduction in Medicare payments that would otherwise be made to that hospital. Information on all patient readmission rates are made available on the CMS Hospital Compare website.

NOTES AND QUESTIONS

1. Treatment costs induced by errors and adverse events are usually either covered by insurance or absorbed by patients, families, insurers, employers and state and private disability and income–support programs. This means that the adverse outcomes are externalized to other payors and not internalized by providers best able to reduce these hazards or prevent them. The added costs of a failed intervention caused either by error or by a failure

to use an effective approach include added acute care costs, lost income, lost household production, and extra pain. As Leape and Berwick note,

> [P]ayers often subsidize unsafe care quite well, although unknowingly. In most industries, defects cost money and generate warranty claims. In health care, perversely, under most forms of payment, health care professionals receive a premium for a defective product; physicians and hospitals can bill for the additional services that are needed when patients are injured by their mistakes.

Lucian L. Leape and Donald M. Berwick, Five Years After To Err Is Human: What Have We Learned? 293 JAMA 2384, 2388 (2005).

Only tort suits have traditionally imposed these excess costs on the hospital or provider that was responsible for the patient's injury. See generally Barry R. Furrow, Adverse Events and Patient Injury: Coupling Detection, Disclosure, and Compensation, 46 New Eng. L. Rev. 437 (2012)

2. How potent is the regulatory weapon that CMS threatens for failures of hospitals to meet their new standards? What more do you need to know to judge its potential force on hospital safety planning? If you represent a hospital, what will you advise hospitals to do to achieve compliance and retain their Medicare status? Imagine you are a Vice–President for Safety and Quality in a large hospital system in several states. Your regulatory environment now must include not only Medicare reimbursement policy, but also each state's approach to serious adverse events and possible individual contract constraints imposed by large corporate purchasers of your health care. Does this complicate your life? How do you approach the problem of adverse events in terms of your internal compliance approach to patient safety?

b. Federal Quality Incentive Strategies

The CMS/Premier Hospital Quality Incentive Demonstration (HQID) was a major federal initiative over six years to test out the effect of value–based purchasing on quality of care. Thirty standardized well accepted care measures are used to get hospital to raise their quality of care, and CMS has claimed that overall quality has been raised by an average of 18.6 percent over six years. It offered a range of incentive payments, including a Top Performance Aware for the top 20% of hospitals; an Improvement Award that gives additional incentive payments; and an Attainment Award incentive payment for hospitals that attain or exceed the median level composite quality score (CQS) benchmark from two years prior.

4. Disclosure of Errors to Patients

Adverse event reporting is often coupled with disclosure of classes of bad outcomes to patients and their families. This disclosure idea developed as the result of a program begun by a Veterans Administration hospital, and has been adopted by the VA system.

DISCLOSURE OF ADVERSE EVENTS TO PATIENTS

October 2, 2012 VHA HANDBOOK 1004.08.

* * *

3. Definitions.

* * *

d. Disclosure of Adverse Events * * * refers to the forthright and empathetic discussion of clinically–significant facts between providers or other VHA personnel and patients or their personal representatives about the occurrence of a harmful adverse event, or an adverse event that could result in harm in the foreseeable future. VA recognizes three types of adverse event disclosure. * * *

(1) Clinical Disclosure of Adverse Events. Clinical disclosure of adverse events is a process by which the patient's clinician informs the patient or the patient's personal representative, as part of routine clinical care, that a harmful or potentially harmful adverse event has occurred during the patient's care. * * *.

(2) Institutional Disclosure of Adverse Events. Institutional disclosure of adverse events (sometimes referred to as "administrative disclosure") is a formal process by which facility leader(s) together with clinicians and others, as appropriate, inform the patient or the patient's personal representative that an adverse event has occurred during the patient's care that resulted in, or is reasonably expected to result in, death or serious injury, and provide specific information about the patient's rights and recourse.

* * *

5. Adverse Events That Warrant Disclosure

a. Disclosure is warranted for harmful or potentially–harmful adverse events, defined broadly to include:

(1) Adverse events that cause death or disability, lead to prolonged hospitalization, require life–sustaining intervention or intervention to prevent impairment or damage (or that are reasonably expected to result in death or serious and/or permanent disability), or that are "sentinel events" as defined by [the Joint Commission].

(2) Adverse events that have had, or are reasonably expected to have, an effect on the patient that is perceptible to either the patient or the health care team. For example, if a patient is mistakenly given a dose of a diuretic (a medication that dramatically increases urine output), disclosure is required because a perceptible effect has, or is anticipated to occur.

(3) Adverse events that precipitate a change in the patient's care. For example, a medication error that necessitates extra blood tests, extra hospital days, or follow–up visits that would otherwise not be required, or a surgical procedure that necessitates further (corrective) surgery.

(4) Adverse events with a clinically–significant risk of serious future health consequences to patients, even if the likelihood of that risk is small. For example, a known, accidental exposure of a patient to "ionizing radiation," "a toxin," "an organism," or "infectious entity" associated with a rare, but recognized serious short–term or long–term effect (e.g., blood borne pathogen infection or increased incidence of cancer). * * *

(5) Any event that requires an unexpected treatment or procedure to be initiated without the patient's consent (e.g., if an event occurs while a patient is under anesthesia, necessitating a deviation from the procedure the patient expected). Patients have a fundamental right to be informed about what is done to them and why.

b. Where adverse events occur that have a potential to affect, or may have already affected multiple patients at one or more VHA facilities, the process for large–scale disclosure must be followed * * *.

c. Disclosure of adverse events other than those that fall under the previous descriptions is optional and at the discretion of the providers involved. Cases need to be considered individually and in relation to the specific circumstances.

d. Disclosure of "close calls" to patients is discretionary, but is advisable at times, such as when the patient or family become aware that something out of the ordinary has occurred.

(1) For example, a nurse sets up a patient for a blood transfusion and, discovering that the patient is about to receive the wrong unit of blood, abruptly stops the transfusion just before the blood enters the patient's vein. The patient deserves an explanation, even if this is not considered a clinical disclosure of an adverse event.

(2) Although the disclosure of a close call to the patient is optional, reporting close calls is required.

* * *

6. Communicating Adverse Events

a. The process for disclosing an adverse event depends on the nature and circumstances of the event. VA recognizes three types of adverse event disclosure: clinical disclosure of adverse events, institutional disclosure of adverse events, and large–scale disclosure of adverse events.

b. The process of adverse event disclosure is not necessarily a singular event but may involve a series of conversations. For example, as more information is learned in a particular case, a clinical disclosure may need to be followed by an institutional disclosure, which itself may involve multiple conversations. In some cases, the disclosure process may ultimately involve all three types of disclosure.

c. Whenever a potential harm is disclosed to a patient, it may be necessary, after an investigation has been conducted, to follow up with the patient to inform the patient whether the potential harm that was initially disclosed did or did not, in fact, occur (e.g., a patient who is initially told that the patient may have been exposed to a blood–borne virus as a result of improperly sterilized equipment, must be informed of investigation results that would have a significant impact on the patient's health or wellbeing).

* * *

8. Institutional Disclosure of Adverse Events

a. Institutional disclosure of adverse events [as defined above]. Serious injury may include significant or permanent disability, injury that leads to prolonged hospitalization, injury requiring life–sustaining intervention, or intervention to prevent impairment or damage, including, for example "sentinel events" as defined by [the Joint Commission]. Such adverse events require institutional disclosure regardless of whether they resulted from an error.

(1) When an adverse event has resulted in or is reasonably expected to result in death or serious injury, an institutional disclosure must be performed regardless of when the event is discovered. This disclosure is required even if clinical disclosure has already occurred. If an initial clinical disclosure has been made, it is important to determine what role, if any, the treating clinician(s) will play in the institutional disclosure process, as well as in the ongoing care of the patient.

(2) Institutional disclosure must be initiated as soon as reasonably possible and generally within 72 hours. This timeframe does not apply to adverse events that are only recognized after the associated episode of care (e.g., through investigation of a sentinel event, a routine quality review, or a look–back). Under such circumstances, if the adverse event has resulted in or is reasonably expected to result in death or serious injury, institutional disclosure is required, but disclosure may be delayed to allow for a thorough investigation of the facts provided.

b. Institutional disclosure of adverse events needs to take place after organizational leaders (e.g., the Facility Director, Chief of Staff, Associate Director for Patient Care Services, members of the treatment team, and/or others as appropriate), have conferred with Regional Counsel and have determined what is to be communicated, by whom, and how.

c. When initiating an institutional disclosure, institutional leaders invite the patient or personal representative to meet. * * *.

d. Institutional disclosure ideally needs to be made face–to–face with the patient or the patient's personal representative, unless it is neither possible nor practical. * * *.

e. If the patient is not capable of understanding either the situation or the information provided in a disclosure, and does not have a personal representative * * *, the facility must make the institutional disclosure to a family member involved in the patient's care, if available. * * *

f. A request made in advance of the discussion by a patient or personal representative to bring an attorney must be honored, but may influence the choice of participants on behalf of the institution.

g. Institutional disclosure of adverse events must include:

(1) An expression of concern and an apology, including an explanation of the facts to the extent that they are known.

(2) An outline of treatment options, if appropriate.

(3) Arrangements for a second opinion, additional monitoring, expediting clinical consultations, bereavement support, or whatever might be appropriate depending on the circumstances and within the constraints of VA's statutory and regulatory authority.

(4) Contact information regarding designated staff who are to respond to questions regarding the disclosed information or clinical sequelae associated with the adverse event.

(5) Notification that the patient or personal representative has the option of obtaining outside medical or legal advice for further guidance.

(6) Offering information about potential compensation under 38 U.S.C. § 1151 and the Federal Tort Claims Act where the patient is a Veteran or under the Federal Tort Claims Act where the patient is a non–Veteran. * * *

NOTES AND QUESTIONS

1. What do you think motivated the development of such a remarkable policy? What problems if any do you see with the VA policy?

2. Pennsylvania created a Patient Safety Authority that mandates reports to the Authority by hospitals of all "serious events". Fines may be levied for failures to report, and the statute provides for whistleblower protections among other things. Pennsylvania also adopted a patient notification requirement if a patient is affected by a serious event. The statute provides:

> A medical facility through an appropriate designee shall provide written notification to a patient affected by a serious event or, with the consent of the patient, to an available family member or designee, within seven days of the occurrence or discovery of a serious event. * * *

3. The patient notification requirements of Pennsylvania and the Veterans Administration raise the risk that patients will become aware of adverse events that they might not otherwise have discovered. Will the incidence of malpractice claims increase? Or will disclosure and an apology reduce litigation?

Patient disclosure requirements have the potential to not only reduce medical errors but also the frequency of malpractice litigation, if done well. There is evidence that disclosure and apology is desired by patients, and it may even serve to reduce patient inclinations to sue for malpractice when they have experience a bad outcome. See Thomas H. Gallagher, et al., Disclosing Harmful Medical Errors to Patients, 356 N. Eng. J. Med. 2713 (2007) (discusses the movement by regulators, hospitals and accreditors to develop standards for communication with patients after harmful errors have occurred); Thomas H. Gallagher et al., Patients' and Physicians' Attitudes Regarding the Disclosure of Medical Errors, 289 J.A.M.A. 1001 (2003) (finding that patients are troubled by the unwillingness of physicians to discuss the cause and future prevention of medical errors); Audrey S. Wang, and Daniel B. Eisen, Surgical Complications: Disclosing Adverse Events and Medical Errors, 68 J. Am. Acad. Dermatol. 144 (2013) (discussing the nature of disclosure of clinical error in practice and some of the factual and ethical complications in deciding when and what to disclose). The *Sorry Works! Coalition* has been heavily involved in promoting the benefits of an apology approach.

4. The National Quality Forum (NQF) has added standards for disclosure of unanticipated outcomes to its list of safe practices. The "3Rs" program at COPIC, a liability insurer directed by physicians in Colorado has also been held out as a model of disclosure. COPIC insures approximately 6000 physicians and is the largest insurer in Colorado. In 2000, the company developed a program designed to facilitate transparent communication about injuries and expedite compensation in selected circumstances. We will consider such programs again when we consider liability reform in Chapter 6.

PROBLEM: DISCLOSING ERRORS

You represent St. Jude Hospital in Pennsylvania, which has implemented a new error management policy in light of the new Joint Commission, CMS, and Pennsylvania rules. How should the hospital handle the following medical misadventures?

1. Joseph Banes entered the hospital for surgery on a cervical disk to relieve his chronic back pain. During the surgery a nerve was severed at the base of his spine, causing severe pain and limitations in mobility in his left leg and foot. The injury is likely to be permanent. This is a rare risk of lower back surgery generally, but in this case the surgeon made a slip of the scalpel and cut the nerve. Your investigation reveals that the surgeon and the nurses in the operating room were aware of the surgical error. What steps should the hospital take to comply with Joint Commission sentinel event requirements? The VA rules? The Pennsylvania state requirements?

2. Sally Thomas, a 45–year–old woman with a history of abdominal pain, was found lying on the floor of her home in severe pain. She was taken to the emergency room of St. Jude, admitted for diagnosis, and tested to determine the source of the problem. After several days of diagnostic uncertainty, the physicians considered an exploratory laparoscopy, suspecting an abnormality in her small intestine. Before surgery an anesthesiologist inserted a central venous catheter (central line) in Sally. She then underwent surgery, and her right fallopian tube and ovary were removed because of infection. She was taken to the Post Anesthesia Care Unit (PACU) with the central line still in place. A surgical resident who had assisted during the surgery wrote out post–operative orders. These orders included a portable chest x–ray to be taken in the PACU. The purpose of the chest x–ray was to check the placement of the central line. The x–ray was completed by approximately 1:45 p.m. Sally continued to have pain, and was given pain medications. Finally the x–ray, taken four hours earlier, was checked and it revealed that the central line was inserted incorrectly, and the tip went into the pericardial sac of Thomas' heart. The doctors successfully resuscitated her. She recovered after a week in the hospital, narrowly escaping a cardiac tamponade, in which her heart would have been crushed by fluid pressure, leading to cardiac arrest. What steps do you advise the hospital to take?

3. Wilhelm Gross entered St. Jude to have surgery on his left leg to repair an artery. The surgical team prepped Wilhelm, preparing his right leg for the procedure. Minutes before the surgeon was to make the first incision, nurse Jost noticed on the chart that the procedure was to be done on his left leg. The team then prepped the correct leg and the operation went smoothly. What reporting obligations does the hospital have?

5. Shopping for Quality: Information for Consumers

In the American consumer culture, information is king. It is therefore plausible that shopping for quality by the consumers of health care makes sense: employers certainly take advantage of Leapfrog data and standards to measure the productivity and quality of providers serving their employees; managed care plans presumably want the best providers in their networks; and consumers want to know as much as possible about their doctors and hospitals. Or so the argument goes.

Section 3015 of the ACA provides for performance websites. Performance websites shall make available to the public "performance information summarizing data on quality measures. Such information shall be tailored to respond to the differing needs of hospitals and other institutional health care providers, physicians and other clinicians, patients, consumers, researchers, policymakers, States, and other stakeholders, as the Secretary may specify." This performance information, to be available on a public website, "shall include information regarding clinical conditions to the extent such information is available, and the information shall, where appropriate, be provider–specific and sufficiently disaggregated and specific to meet the needs of patients with different clinical conditions."

The ACA provides for a range of information to facilitate shopping for health care providers. Comparison websites existed prior to the ACA, most notably *Hospital Compare* and *Nursing Home Compare*. The *Hospital Compare* website now includes data on the rate of hospital–based infections, as required by the ACA. The ACA institutes several new sites to complement these. The ACA creates a *Physician Compare* website based on the model of the *Hospital Compare*. This new website will contain information on physician performance that allowing the public to compare physicians on performance measures, including measures collected under the Physician Quality Reporting Initiative; assessments of patient health outcomes and the functional status of patients; continuity and coordination of care and care transitions, including episodes of care and risk–adjusted resource use; efficiency; patient experience and patient, caregiver, and family engagement; safety, effectiveness, and timeliness of care.

The Office of Communication and Knowledge Transfer at AHRQ will broadly disseminate the research findings that are published by the Patient Centered Outcomes Research Institute and other agencies that are relevant to comparative clinical effectiveness research. The Office is creating informational tools that organize and disseminate research findings for physicians, health care providers, patients, payers, and policy makers. The Office will also develop a publicly available resource database that collects and contains government–funded evidence and research from public, private, not–for profit, and academic sources.

Should consumers shop on the basis of evidence of higher quality care? Will they? Can consumer choice be based on different levels of care, representing different levels of resources? The hope of consumer choice advocates is that the proliferation of information about quality will promote improvements in quality as consumer demand selects higher quality providers.

Can we expect individual consumers to shop for their care on the basis of quality? A Rand review of health care report cards, provider profiles, and consumer reports concluded that few are influenced by this information. RAND Health, Report Cards for Health Care: Is Anyone Checking Them? Research Highlights (2002) (In a review of earlier RAND studies, finding that neither consumers nor physicians pay much attention to comparative performance data, but health provider organizations do.)

Is the public simply discounting this information, on the theory that health information is usually aimed to sell a product? In a media environment full of advertising pretending to be scientific, and where medical journals get fooled, even the most intelligent laymen may not easily distinguish hype from information they need. It may also be that quality information—presented in terms of what a patient might reasonably expect—might create a new set of pressures on providers to guarantee their work. One recent study concluded that ". . . there is limited evidence that public report cards improve quality through this mechanism, and there is some evidence that they paradoxically reduce quality." R.M.Werner and D.A. Asch, The Unintended Consequences of Publicly Reporting Quality Information, 293 J.A.M.A. 1239 (2005). See also Mark A. Hall and Carl E. Schneider, Patients as Consumers: Courts, Contracts, and the New Medical Marketplace, 106 Mich. L. Rev. 643 (2008).

Informed consumerism is harder than it looks, and it may be that generating more information will have little effect on quality. Patients may not use the information, and employers are likely to disregard it. Is the drive toward quality information for consumer use a strategy to shift from government oversight to a strong market approach? Supporters of free market approaches often argue that consumers should be allowed to suffer the consequences of their bad choices. Does this also relieve government regulatory agencies from developing tough rules to govern an unruly and complex health care system? See Chapter 4 for a discussion of information and consumers and Section III, above, for discussion of competition and regulation.

For an excellent overview of the elements of patient safety regulation, see generally Michelle M. Mello, et al., Fostering Rational Regulation of Patient Safety, J. Health Pol., Pol., and Law 30 J. Health Pol., Pol'y & L. 375 (2005).

CHAPTER 2

QUALITY CONTROL REGULATION: LICENSING HEALTH CARE PROFESSIONALS

■ ■ ■

I. INTRODUCTION

Structure of the Licensure System

State law controls the licensure of health care professionals under the state's police power. State licensing statutes govern entry into the licensed professions; regulate the health care services that licensed professionals may provide; and prohibit unlicensed persons from providing services reserved for the licensed professions. The system also monitors the quality of care provided by licensees and penalizes or removes incompetent practitioners from practice.

Health professional licensure in the United States is commonly described as a system of professional self–regulation because the entities, often called "boards," which implement the applicable statutes are generally dominated by members of the licensed profession and often rely on customary practice of the professions for standards. The boards, however, operate formally as state administrative agencies; usually include lay members to represent a consumer perspective; are governed by procedures and standards set in the state's licensing statute and administrative procedures act; and are subject to judicial review in both their adjudicatory and rulemaking decisions. The concept of professional licensure and discipline as professional self–regulation has weakened over time, but the licensed professions retain significant influence over the decisions of the boards.

Although the central legal framework for licensure and discipline is a matter of state law, there is a federal overlay. Licensure is subject to federal (and state) Constitutional requirements of procedural and substantive due process and equal protection. Certain federal statutes, including antidiscrimination laws such as the Americans with Disabilities Act, apply to licensure boards as well, although there are Constitutional limits on their application.

Licensure is only one component of the quality control array in health care, which includes malpractice and negligence litigation, institutional licensure, private accreditation, hospital credentialing, public information disclosure requirements, and public and private payment and reimbursement standards. Each of these is covered elsewhere in this casebook.

Quality, Access, Cost, and Choice

The overarching concerns treated throughout this casebook—quality, cost, access, and choice—are all at stake in the licensure and disciplinary system. Using specific examples from the materials that follow: Do the boards contribute to the quality of care available to patients if they aggressively pursue physicians prescribing controlled substances for chronic pain, or do they drive physicians away from treating such patients and thus decrease access to treatment? If nurse practitioners provide care more cheaply than doctors, are licensure restrictions on their scope of practice worth the increased cost of care? Does the common prohibition against the provision of birthing assistance by professional midwives produce higher quality outcomes for mothers and babies? And, even if this were so, is the potential gain worth the cost in terms of access to prenatal care or individual choice of attendant or site for childbirth? How does the licensure system accommodate innovation, either in terms of particular treatments or in terms of health care delivery? Who should decide whether to employ a treatment, medication, or intervention rejected by the majority of practitioners—individual health care professionals and their patients or the state boards?

In all of these questions, the core issues are whether the prohibitions and restrictions imposed by licensure and discipline serve the public good or established professional interests and whether the state health professions boards are the best tool for achieving desirable goals of patient safety and accessible care. This debate over the performance and ultimate cost and benefit of professional licensure and discipline is an old one, dating back to the emergence of the health professions boards. For an historical perspective on the dominance of licensure by allopathic physicians, see Paul Starr, The Social Transformation of American Medicine (1982).

Pressures for Change in Licensure and Discipline

Professional domination of licensure has long been a source of criticism of board performance. See, e.g., Carl F. Ameringer, State Medical Boards and the Politics of Public Protection (1999). The boards' heavy reliance on the participation of their licensees advances the public interest by bringing expertise to the evaluation of professionals' competency and behavior. In this era of more intense competition among a broader range of health care professionals, however, this reliance creates substantial opportunities for anticompetitive conduct facilitated by the authority of the board.

The traditional rationale for health care quality regulation is the lack of information available to consumers to make their own risk–benefit balance in choosing providers as well as the limited capacity of patients to evaluate the information that is available. As health care data become cheaper and more accessible, health care quality regulation will be challenged. Kristin Madison, for example, speculates that more robust health databanks will lead to contradictory claims that greater direct consumer access to quality information reduces the need for state medical boards and that the boards should take a greater role in actively monitoring quality as data improves. Kristin Madison, Regulating Health Care Quality in an Information Age, 40 U.C. Davis L.Rev. 1577 (2007). See also, Timothy S. Jost, Oversight of the Quality of Medical Care: Regulation, Management or the Market, 37 Ariz. L. Rev. 825 (1995); William M. Sage, Regulating through Information: Disclosure Laws and American Healthcare, 99 Colum. L. Rev. 1701 (1999).

Licensure boards currently reflect the traditional way that we know what appropriate care is; i.e., the customary practice of the majority of practitioners with some reliance on a rather spotty and non–clinically relevant body of studies. The Affordable Care Act (ACA) pushes stronger reliance on scientific evidence of effectiveness and outcomes as the gold measure for quality. (See Chapter 1.) If the hopes for this shift toward scientific evidence are realized, it will have implications for enforcement and standard setting by the health professions boards.

The ACA also fosters expanded roles for nurses and physician assistants as the health care system is reorganized to emphasize continuity of care, accessible preventive care, and management of chronic illness at a lower cost. The activities of the licensure boards in restricting the work of these professionals are coming under increased scrutiny.

Chapter Roadmap

This chapter begins with the standard setting and adjudicative functions of the boards in responding to claims that individual physicians have provided substandard medical care to patients. The chapter then continues working with the challenge of setting regulatory standards for medical care but in the context of licensees offering complementary and alternative medicine. Finally, the chapter examines the border–patrolling functions of the various health professions boards in two areas: the provision of services by unlicensed providers and the scope of practice of non–physician licensed health care professionals.

II. DISCIPLINE

IN RE WILLIAMS

Supreme Court of Ohio, 1991.
60 Ohio St.3d 85, 573 N.E.2d 638.

Syllabus by the Court

* * *

* * * Between 1983 and 1986, Dr. Williams prescribed Biphetamine or Obetrol for fifty patients as part of a weight control treatment regimen. [Both drugs are controlled substances.]

On November 17, 1986, appellant, the Ohio State Medical Board ("board"), promulgated Ohio Adm.Code 4731–11–03(B), which prohibited the use of [drugs such as Biphetamine and Obetrol] for purposes of weight control. Dr. Williams ceased prescribing Biphetamine and Obetrol for weight control upon becoming aware of the rule.

By letter dated March 12, 1987, the board charged Dr. Williams with violating R.C. 4731.22(B)[2] by prescribing these stimulants without "reasonable care," and thereby failing to conform to minimal standards of medical practice. The crux of the board's charge was that Dr. Williams had departed from accepted standards of care by using these drugs as a long–term, rather than a short–term, treatment.

A hearing was held before a board examiner. The parties stipulated to the accuracy of the medical records of the patients in question, which detailed the use of Biphetamine and Obetrol for periods ranging from nearly seven months to several years. The board also introduced into evidence the Physician's Desk Reference entries for Biphetamine and Obetrol, which recommend that these drugs be used for only "a few weeks" in the treatment of obesity. The board presented no testimony or other evidence of the applicable standard of care.

Dr. Williams presented expert testimony from Dr. John P. Morgan, the director of the pharmacology program at the City University of New

---

[2] R.C. 4731.22(B) provides in pertinent part:

"The board, pursuant to an adjudicatory hearing.... shall, to the extent permitted by law,.... [discipline] the holder of a certificate [to practice medicine] for one or more of the following reasons:

....

"(2) Failure to use reasonable care, discrimination in the administration of drugs, or failure to employ acceptable scientific methods in the selection of drugs or other modalities for treatment of disease;

"(3) Selling, prescribing, giving away, or administering drugs for other than legal and legitimate therapeutic purposes....

....

"(6) A departure from, or the failure to conform to, minimal standards of care.... [.]"

York Medical School, and Dr. Eljorn Don Nelson, an associate professor of clinical pharmacology at the University of Cincinnati College of Medicine. These experts stated that there are two schools of thought in the medical community concerning the use of stimulants for weight control. The so–called "majority" view holds that stimulants should only be used for short periods, if at all, in weight control programs. The "minority" view holds that the long–term use of stimulants is proper in the context of a supervised physician–patient relationship. Both experts testified that, though they themselves supported the "majority" view, Dr. Williams's application of the "minority" protocol was not substandard medical practice.

The hearing examiner found that Dr. Williams's practices violated R.C. 4731.22(B). The examiner recommended subjecting Dr. Williams to a three–year monitored probation period. The board modified the penalty, imposing a one–year suspension of Dr. Williams's license followed by a five–year probationary period, during which he would be unable to prescribe or dispense controlled substances.

Dr. Williams appealed to the Court of Common Pleas of Franklin County pursuant to R.C. 119.12. The court found that the board's order was ". . . not supported by reliable, probative and substantial evidence and . . . [was] not in accordance with law." The court of appeals affirmed.

HERBERT R. BROWN, JUSTICE.

In an appeal from an administrative agency, a reviewing court is bound to uphold the agency's order if it is ". . . supported by reliable, probative, and substantial evidence and is in accordance with law. . . . "[ ]. In the instant case, we must determine if the common pleas court erred by finding that the board's order was not supported by sufficient evidence. For the reasons which follow, we conclude that it did not and affirm the judgment of the court below.

In its arguments to this court, the board contends that Arlen v. Ohio State Medical Bd. (1980), 61 Ohio St.2d 168, 15 O.O.3d 190, 399 N.E.2d 1251, is dispositive. In *Arlen*, the physician was disciplined because he had written prescriptions for controlled substances to a person who the physician knew was redistributing the drugs to others, a practice prohibited by R.C. 3719.06(A). The physician appealed on the ground that the board failed to present expert testimony that such prescribing practices fell below a reasonable standard of care.

We held that the board is not required in every case to present expert testimony on the acceptable standard of medical practice before it can find that a physician's conduct falls below this standard. We noted that the usual purpose of expert testimony is to assist the trier of facts in understanding "issues that require scientific or specialized knowledge or experience beyond the scope of common occurrences. . . . "[ ] The board was then made up of ten (now twelve) persons, eight of whom are licensed physicians. [ ] Thus, a majority of board members are themselves experts in the medical field who already possess the specialized knowledge needed to determine the acceptable standard of general medical practice.

While the board need not, in every case, present expert testimony to support a charge against an accused physician, the charge must be supported by some reliable, probative and substantial evidence. It is here that the case against Dr. Williams fails, as it is very different from *Arlen*.

Arlen involved a physician who dispensed controlled substances in a manner that not only fell below the acceptable standard of medical practice, but also violated the applicable statute governing prescription and dispensing of these drugs. In contrast, Dr. Williams dispensed controlled substances in what was, at the time, a legally permitted manner, albeit one which was disfavored by many in the medical community. The only evidence in the record on this issue was the testimony of Dr. Williams's expert witnesses that his use of controlled substances in weight control programs did not fall below the acceptable standard of medical practice. While the board has broad discretion to resolve evidentiary conflicts [ ] and determine the weight to be given expert testimony [ ], it cannot convert its own disagreement with an expert's opinion into affirmative evidence of a contrary proposition where the issue is one on which medical experts are divided and there is no statute or rule governing the situation.

It should be noted, however, that where the General Assembly has prohibited a particular medical practice by statute, or where the board has done so through its rulemaking authority, the existence of a body of expert opinion supporting that practice would not excuse a violation. Thus, if Dr. Williams had continued to prescribe Biphetamine or Obetrol for weight control after the promulgation of Ohio Adm.Code 4731–11–03(B), this would be a violation of R.C. 4731.22(B)(3), and the existence of the "minority" view supporting the use of these substances for weight control would provide him no defense. Under those facts, *Arlen* would be dispositive. Here, however, there is insufficient evidence, expert or otherwise, to support the charges against Dr. Williams. Were the board's decision to be affirmed on the facts in this record, it would mean that a doctor would have no access to meaningful review of the board's decision. The board, though a majority of its members have special knowledge, is not entitled to exercise such unbridled discretion.

WRIGHT, JUSTICE, dissenting.

The message we send to the medical community's regulators with today's decision is one, I daresay, we would never countenance for their counterparts in the legal community. We are telling those charged with policing the medical profession that their expertise as to what constitutes the acceptable standard of medical practice is not enough to overcome the assertion that challenged conduct does not violate a state statute. * * *

HOOVER V. THE AGENCY FOR HEALTH CARE ADMINISTRATION

District Court of Appeal of Florida, 1996.
676 So.2d 1380.

JORGENSON, JUDGE.

Dr. Katherine Anne Hoover, a board–certified physician in internal medicine, appeals a final order of the Board of Medicine penalizing her and restricting her license to practice medicine in the State of Florida. We reverse because the board has once again engaged in the uniformly rejected practice of overzealously supplanting a hearing officer's valid findings of fact regarding a doctor's prescription practices with its own opinion in a case founded on a woefully inadequate quantum of evidence.

In March 1994, the Department of Business and Professional Regulation (predecessor in these proceedings to the Agency for Health Care Administration) filed an administrative complaint alleging that Dr. Hoover (1) inappropriately and excessively prescribed various . . . controlled substances to seven of her patients and (2) provided care of those patients that fell below that level of care, skill, and treatment which is recognized by a reasonably prudent similar physician as being acceptable under similar conditions and circumstances; in violation of sections 458.331(1)(q) and (t), Florida Statutes, respectively. All seven of the patients had been treated by Dr. Hoover for intractable pain arising from various non–cancerous diseases or ailments.

Dr. Hoover disputed the allegations of the administrative complaint and requested a formal hearing. * * *

The agency presented the testimony of two physicians as experts. Neither had examined any of the patients or their medical records. The sole basis for the opinions of the agency physicians was computer printouts from pharmacies in Key West where the doctor's patients had filled their prescriptions. These printouts indicated only the quantity of each drug filled for each patient, occasionally referring to a simplified diagnosis. Both of these physicians practiced internal medicine and neither specialized in the care of chronic pain. In fact, both doctors testified that they did not treat but referred their chronic pain patients to pain management clinics. The hearing officer found that this was a common practice among physicians—perhaps to avoid prosecutions like this case.[5] Both doctors "candidly testified that without being provided with copies of the medical records for those patients they could not evaluate Respond-

[5] Referral to a pain management clinic was not an option for Dr. Hoover's indigent Key West resident patients.

ent's diagnoses or what alternative modalities were attempted or what testing was done to support the use of the medication chosen by Respondent to treat those patients." Despite this paucity of evidence, lack of familiarity, and seeming lack of expertise, the agency's physicians testified at the hearing that the doctor had prescribed excessive, perhaps lethal amounts of narcotics, and had practiced below the standard of care.

Dr. Hoover testified in great detail concerning the condition of each of the patients, her diagnoses and courses of treatment, alternatives attempted, the patients' need for medication, the uniformly improved function of the patients with the amount of medication prescribed, and her frequency of writing prescriptions to allow her close monitoring of the patients. She presented corroborating physician testimony regarding the appropriateness of the particular medications and the amounts prescribed and her office–setting response to the patients' requests for relief from intractable pain.

Following post–hearing submissions, the hearing officer issued her recommended order finding that the agency had failed to meet its burden of proof on all charges. The hearing officer concluded, for instance, "Petitioner failed to provide its experts with adequate information to show the necessary similar conditions and circumstances upon which they could render opinions that showed clearly and convincingly that Respondent failed to meet the standard of care required of her in her treatment of the patients in question."

The agency filed exceptions to the recommended findings of fact and conclusions of law as to five of the seven patients. The board of medicine accepted all the agency's exceptions, amended the findings of fact in accordance with the agency's suggestions, and found the doctor in violation of sections 458.331(1)(q) and (t), Florida Statutes. The board imposed the penalty recommended by the agency: a reprimand, a $4,000 administrative fine, continuing medical education on prescribing abusable drugs, and two years probation. This appeal follows.

For each of the five patients, the hearing officer found the prescribing practices of Doctor Hoover to be appropriate. This was based upon (1) the doctor's testimony regarding the specific care given, (2) the corroborating testimony of her physician witness, and (3) the fact that the doctor's prescriptions did not exceed the federal guidelines for treatment of intractable pain in cancer patients, though none of the five patients were diagnosed as suffering from cancer.

The board rejected these findings as not based on competent substantial evidence. As particular reasons, the board adopted the arguments of the agency's exceptions to the recommended order that (1) the hearing officer's findings were erroneously based on irrelevant federal guidelines, and (2) the agency's physicians had testified that the doctor's prescription pattern was below the standard of care and outside the practice of medicine. * * *

First, the board mischaracterizes the hearing officer's reference to the federal guidelines. The board reasoned in its final order that "[t]he record reflects that the federal guidelines relied upon by the Hearing Officer for this finding were designed for cancer patients and [the five patients at issue were] not being treated for cancer." It is true, as the hearing officer noted,

"Respondent presented expert evidence that there is a set of guidelines which have been issued for the use of Schedule II controlled substances to treat intractable pain and that although those guidelines were established to guide physicians in treating cancer patients, those are the only guidelines available at this time. Utilizing those guidelines, because they exist, the amount of medication prescribed by Respondent to the patients in question was not excessive or inappropriate."

In so finding, however, the hearing officer did not, as the board suggests, rely solely upon the federal guidelines in its ruling that the doctor's prescribing practices were not excessive. Rather, the federal guidelines merely buttressed fact findings that were independently supported by the hearing officer's determination of the persuasiveness and credibility of the physician witnesses on each side. For example, though he admitted he had not even reviewed the federal guidelines, one of the agency physicians asserted that the amounts prescribed constituted a "tremendous number of pills" and that the doses involved would be lethal. That Dr. Hoover's prescriptions fell within the guidelines for chronic–pained cancer patients may properly be considered to refute this assertion. Such a use of the federal guidelines was relevant and reasonable.

Second, Dr. Hoover testified in great detail concerning her treatment of each patient, the patient's progress under the medication she prescribed, and that the treatment was within the standard of care and practice of medicine. The hearing officer, as arbiter of credibility, was entitled to believe what the doctor and her physician expert opined. [ ] The agency's witnesses' ultimate conclusions do not strip the hearing officer's reliance upon Dr. Hoover of its competence and substantiality. The hearing officer was entitled to give Dr. Hoover's testimony greater weight than that of the agency's witnesses, who did not examine these patients or regularly engage in the treatment of intractable pain.

[T]he hearing officer explicitly recognized that the 1994 [Florida] intractable pain law was not in effect at the time of Dr. Hoover's alleged infractions but cited it for a permissible purpose—to rebut any claim that there is a strong public policy mandate in favor of the board's draconian policy of policing pain prescription practice. [ ] * * *

Reversed.

NOTE: STATE AND FEDERAL REGULATION OF PRESCRIBING PRACTICES

Both *Williams* and *Hoover* involve disciplinary action by a state medical board based on a physician's prescribing practices. Prescribing is also regulated by the Food and Drug Administration (FDA) and the Drug Enforcement Administration (DEA), two powerful federal agencies. Public and private payers (including Medicare, Medicaid, and private insurers) also influence prescribing through coverage and payment policies.

In our federal system, the regulation of the practice of medicine traditionally has belonged to the states through the police power. Congress did not intend that either the FDA or the DEA engage in the regulation of the *legitimate* practice of medicine. The boundary between the agencies' statutory authority and the restraint on their regulation of medical practice is blurry, however, as it is nearly impossible to regulate prescribing without regulating the practice of medicine in some way. Still, the boundary has some force as a rhetorical device and policy consideration in disputes claiming overreaching, especially by the DEA. See Lars Noah, Ambivalent Commitments to Federalism in Controlling the Practice of Medicine, 53 U. Kan. L. Rev. 149 (2004).

The FDA has the authority to approve and monitor the safety of drugs and devices; and this certainly makes the FDA an important gatekeeper of access to drugs. Once a drug is approved for prescribing, however, the FDA does not have the authority to restrict physicians in their prescribing of the drug for particular purposes. Thus, once a drug is approved for a particular purpose (e.g., for the treatment of a particular sort of cancer), a physician may prescribe the drug for other purposes (e.g., for the treatment of another type of cancer). Prescribing drugs for a different purpose, in a higher or lower dose, or for a different population (e.g., children) than those for which the FDA approved the medication is called "off–label" prescribing. Off–label prescribing is common and necessary in the practice of medicine and may become the standard of care in particular circumstances. See Chapter 5. Off–label prescribing raises issues of medical judgment, evidence–based medicine, the relations between pharmaceutical firms and prescribing physicians, and standard setting by medical licensure boards as in *Hoover* and *Williams*. See, e.g., Sandra H. Johnson, Polluting Medical Judgment? False Assumptions in the Pursuit of False Claims Regarding Off–Label Prescribing, 9 Minn. J. L. Sci. Tech. 61 (2008).

The DEA more directly regulates prescribing practices through its authority under the Controlled Substances Act (CSA). 21 U.S.C. § 801. Under the CSA, the federal government governs the production and distribution of drugs that have the potential for abuse or addiction. Such drugs are categorized as controlled substances and placed on a "schedule" that rates a drug by its abuse potential from Schedule V (the lowest potential) to Schedules I and II (the highest potential). Schedule I drugs, including heroin and marijuana, are those that are viewed as having a very high potential for abuse and no therapeutic benefit. Doctors may not prescribe Schedule I drugs.

Doctors must have a permit issued by the DEA to prescribe drugs on Schedules II through V. The DEA may revoke a permit or pursue criminal action against physicians whose prescription or distribution of these drugs falls outside of the DEA's view of legitimate medical practice. In recent years, DEA policies have conflicted directly with state health policy on several fronts.

One of the areas of conflict between federal and state law and policy is the legalization of marijuana for medical use. Several states have enacted legislation to allow physicians or patients access to marijuana for the treatment of medical conditions. See, e.g., Cal. Health & Saf. Code § 11362.5. Under the Bush administration, the federal government actively opposed such efforts by aggressively enforcing federal prohibitions under the CSA, stimulating significant Constitutional challenges to federal authority. In Gonzales v. Raich, 545 U.S. 1, 125 S.Ct. 2195, 162 L.Ed.2d 1 (2005), the Supreme Court rejected the argument that the CSA exceeded the federal government's authority under the Commerce Clause. During the course of the litigation over federal authority, the Ninth Circuit held that physicians had a First Amendment right to discuss medical marijuana with their patients in the face of federal threats to prosecute doctors who did so. Conant v. Walters, 309 F.3d 629 (9th Cir. 2002), *cert. denied,* 540 U.S. 946, 124 S.Ct. 387, 157 L.Ed.2d 276 (2003). The Obama administration has relied on prosecutorial discretion to reduce the level of enforcement in states legalizing marijuana for medical use, although the federal government has continued some prosecutions. Adam Nagourney, In California, It's U.S. vs. State Over Marijuana, N.Y.Times, A1, 1/13/2013. The move to legalize marijuana, including beyond medical use, continues with the states taking a variety of strategies from outright legalization for personal use (by Colorado and Washington by ballot in 2012) to removing penalties for possession of small amounts. See generally, Symposium: The Road to Legitimizing Marijuana: What Benefit at What Cost?, 43 McGeorge L. Rev. 1 (2012).

Federal and state health policy has also been in conflict over prescribing of controlled substances for the treatment of patients in pain. At the time of the *Hoover* case, there was strong evidence that medical boards had not adjusted their standards to reflect medical evidence that supported the use of opioids for treatment over the long term and in higher doses than had been customary. This meant that doctors who treated their patients' chronic pain effectively were at risk of disciplinary action while those doctors who provided inadequate treatment faced no legal risk at all. In an attempt to balance legal risks, nearly half of the states enacted legislation generally referred to as "intractable pain treatment acts" which limit state agencies in taking action against physicians in certain circumstances, as discussed in the notes below. The Federation of State Medical Boards also adopted a model policy that specifically recognizes that opioids are essential to the treatment of pain and that state medical boards should be equally concerned about the neglect of pain as they are about prescribing abuse. FSMB, Model Policy for the Use of Controlled Substances for the Treatment of Pain (2004). In contrast, the DEA continued to pursue a more aggressive stance against prescribers of controlled substances for pain management. The National Association of Attorneys General expressed concern that as state medical boards took steps to ensure access to pain treatment, the DEA was moving to criminalize physician prescribing, commenting that "the state and federal policies are diverging with respect to the relative emphasis on ensuring the availability of prescription pain medications to those who need them." Conflict between state and federal policy on this issue continues. There is also evidence that state prosecutions of physicians prescribing pain medication may be increasing as well. On criminal prosecutions of physicians, see Diane E. Hoffmann, Treating Pain v. Reducing Drug Diversion and Abuse: Recalibrating the Balance in Our Drug Control Laws and Policies, 1 St. Louis U. J. Health & Pol'y 231 (2008).

The Affordable Care Act (ACA) established an Interagency Pain Research Coordinating Committee to coordinate federal research efforts and directed the Secretary of HHS to provide grants and contracts with health professions schools, hospices, and other entities to improve education and practice in caring for patients in pain. In response to an ACA mandate, the IOM issued a report documenting the impact of pain on public health (over 100 million persons in America are in chronic pain and costs for medical care and lost productivity exceed $560 billion annually) and making recommendation to improve pain treatment and expand research. IOM, Relieving Pain in America: A Blueprint for Transforming Prevention, Care, Education, and Research (2011).

NOTES AND QUESTIONS

1. The Ohio State Medical Board promulgated an administrative rule, cited in *Williams*, requiring that physicians meet the majority standard of practice regarding the prescription of controlled substances. Should licensure boards establish standards of practice or practice guidelines that prefer one approach over another; or should they simply recognize the full range of medical practices, including minority views? Would your answer depend on whether the board was acting in a rulemaking or in an adjudicatory role? Should they consider requiring physicians to inform their patients that the particular recommended treatment is not accepted by the majority of physicians and then allow patients to decide what course of treatment to follow? Do *Williams* and *Hoover* present identical issues in that regard? Do *Williams* and *Hoover* present special challenges because the medications may have a risk of use or diversion for nontherapeutic uses? How should state boards account for the gatekeeper role of physicians in such cases? Where does concern for the public health lie in such cases?

2. If almost all members of the medical board are physicians, what is at the heart of the dispute over expert testimony in *Williams*? On what basis did the Florida court reject the testimony of the agency's experts in *Hoover*?

3. The court in *Hoover* implies that disciplinary actions by a state medical board against individual physicians have an effect on other physi-

cians' practices. Beyond penalizing or removing the "bad apple" from practice, this is actually a core objective of professional discipline. In the case of treatment for pain, however, this deterrence has been called the "Chilling Effect" because the threat of legal sanction seems to lead doctors to avoid legitimate and effective treatments. Judge Kozinski of the Ninth Circuit, quoting an expert on this point, observes:

> Physicians are particularly easily deterred by the threat of governmental investigation and/or sanction from engaging in conduct that is entirely lawful and medically appropriate. .* * * [A] physician's practice is particularly dependent upon the physician's maintaining a reputation of unimpeachable integrity. A physician's career can be effectively destroyed merely by the fact that a governmental body has investigated his or her practice * * *. Concurring Opinion in Conant v. Walters, 309 F.3d 629 (9th Cir. 2002), *cert. denied,* 540 U.S. 946 (2003).

If physicians provide inadequate care because of their fear of legal entanglement, what are the implications for medical boards that want to encourage quality care? Physicians dread being investigated, and avoid occasions that might trigger investigation, because of the high cost of legal representation and the emotional stress. Should the standards for beginning an investigation be higher because of this impact? Or, does the public health demand active investigations whenever physician prescribing appears questionable? Can anything be done in the investigatory process that could diminish the unintended consequence of driving doctors away from treating chronic pain patients? See Sandra H. Johnson, Regulating Physician Behavior: Taking Doctors' "Bad Law" Claims Seriously, 53 St. Louis U. L.J. 973 (2009).

4. The Florida statute referenced in *Hoover* provides:

> Notwithstanding any other provision of law, a physician may prescribe or administer any controlled substance to a person for the treatment of intractable pain, provided the physician does so in accordance with the level of care, skill, and treatment recognized by a reasonable prudent physician under similar conditions and circumstances.

This statute follows a pattern that is familiar in statutes regulating a particular treatment. It is intended to allow or encourage a specific practice (through a form of safe harbor) while at the same time retaining significant authority for discipline in particular cases. How well does this statute satisfy these two goals? For example, would this statute provide adequate protection to physicians such as Dr. Hoover? Does it provide the medical board with enough authority? Should it be more specific in carving out a safe harbor for the treatment? Is it appropriate for legislatures to enact statutes concerning permissible medical practices, or should they leave that to rulemaking by the licensure boards?

5. Rates of serious disciplinary action vary considerably among the states. In 2011, for example, South Carolina had the lowest rate of 1.33/1,000 doctors, and Wyoming had the highest at 6.79/1,000. Public Citizen's Health Research Group, Ranking of the Rate of State Medical Boards' Serious Disciplinary Actions, 2009–2011 (2012). The report notes the five–fold difference between the "best and worst state disciplinary boards." How would you measure whether the number of disciplinary actions in your state was too many, too few, or just right? The report notes that the "remarkable variability," in the absence of evidence of substantial variation in physician quality or behavior among the states, can only be explained by the effectiveness of the state boards. See also, discussion in the Note on the National Practitioner Data Bank, below. A study of disciplinary actions levied between 1994 and 2002 concludes that somewhere between 25% and 30% of actions were taken for incompetence or negligence or other quality concerns, but that it is difficult to identify the reasons for action using available data. Darren Grant & Kelly C. Alfred, Sanctions and Recidivism: An Evaluation of Physician Discipline by State Medical Boards, 32 J. Health Pol. Pol'y & L. 867 (2007). This study also found a high repeat rate among physicians disciplined. Of those physicians receiving a "medium or severe" sanction in one period (1994–1998), 20% were sanctioned at least once again in the second period (1999–2004). For an empirical study relating rates of actions to infrastructure, including size of budget, size of board, and membership composition, see Marc Law & Zeynep Hansen, Medical Licensing Board Characteristics and Physician Discipline, 35 J. Health Pol. Pol'y & L. 63 (2010).

6. Most states have programs that provide rehabilitative, non–punitive interventions for impaired nurses, doctors, and other health professionals. The rehabilitative approach to impairment naturally emerges from the recent emphasis on chemical dependency as an illness. It also responds to perceived concerns that a punitive disciplinary approach pushes impaired health care providers undercover, risking greater injury to the public. It is hoped that the availability of a program of non–punitive rehabilitation encourages a higher rate of reporting and self–reporting of impaired physicians.

Constitutional due process requires that discipline for behavior, including the use of drugs and alcohol, must demonstrate a nexus between the behavior and the ability to practice medicine. See, e.g., Watson v. Superior Court, 176 Cal. App.4th 1407, 98 Cal. Rptr.3d 715 (Cal. App. 2009), regarding alcohol abuse. See, Nadia Sawicki, Character, Competence, and the Principles of Medical Discipline, 13 J. Health L. & Pol'y 285 (2010).

Should voluntary enrollment in an impaired professional program be confidential, or should the program be required to notify the board of the enrollment? Should boards allow impaired professionals to choose a rehabilitative program with discipline stayed and then expunged upon successful completion? Physicians who are disciplined for impairment due to drug or alcohol abuse are more likely to have their licenses restored than those disciplined for other reasons, but they are also more likely to be subject to repeat disciplinary action. Matthew C.Holtman, Disciplinary Careers of Drug–Impaired

Physicians, 64 Soc.Sci.Med. 543 (2007). Should physicians who are abusing alcohol or drugs or who are participating in a state–sanctioned rehabilitation program be required to inform their patients? Would this better protect the public? See W.Va. Code § 30–3–9, providing for confidentiality.

7. Telemedicine has become commonplace and offers increased access to medical care and potential cost reductions, for example by remote consultation on imaging by specialists. The practice has raised a host of issues. It tests the state–based structure of medical licensure, and a central issue is whether a physician must be licensed within the state where the patient is. Diane Hoffmann & Virginia Rowthorn, Legal Impediments to the Diffusion of Telemedicine (Symposium Issue on Telemedicine), 14 J. Health Care L. & Pol'y 1 (2011); Michael Young & Rachel Alexander, Recognizing the Nature of American Medical Practice: An Argument for Adopting Federal Medical Licensure, 13 DePaul J. Health Care L. 145 (2010); Carl F. Ameringer, State–Based Licensure of Telemedicine: The Need for Uniformity but not a National Scheme, 14 J. Health Care L. & Pol'y 55 (2011). State statutes have taken a variety of approaches ranging from the very restrictive to the very open. See, e.g., Smith v. Laboratory Corp. of America, 2010 WL 5464770 (W.D.Wash. 2010), involving a physician in Washington providing remote review of biopsies for patients in Idaho, contrasting the approach of Washington and Idaho.. Internet–only pharmacies that offer one–stop service for patients who fill out an online medical questionnaire and have a prescription written by a physician working for the pharmacy have raised serious concerns, especially when controlled substances are prescribed. The physicians involved may be violating licensure requirements for prescribing. See generally, Regina A. Bailey, The Legal, Financial, and Ethical Implications of Online Medical Consultations, 16 J. Tech. L. & Pol'y 53 (2011).

8. Title II of the federal Americans with Disabilities Act applies to licensure and discipline by the professional licensure boards of the States. See, e.g., Colorado State Bd. of Med. Examiners v. Ogin, 56 P.3d 1233 (Colo. Ct. App. 2002). See also The Yuri N. Walker, Impact of the Americans with Disabilities Act on Licensure Considerations Involving Mentally Impaired Medical and Legal Professionals, 25 J. Legal Med. 441 (2004), concluding that the ADA does not seriously constrict the ability of the boards to enforce licensure requirements. There has been significant litigation (including two Supreme Court cases) over the issue of whether the states are immune under the Eleventh Amendment from Title II ADA money damages claims, and the application of that analysis to claims against state medical boards for disciplinary action is complex. See, e.g., Guttman v. Khalsa, 669 F.3d 1101 (10th Cir. 2012), holding that state is immune.

NOTE: THE NATIONAL PRACTITIONER DATA BANK

Congress established the National Practitioner Data Bank (NPDB) in part to create an effective system for preventing doctors with disciplinary history in one state from moving to another and practicing until detected, if ever. 42 U.S.C. §§ 11101–11152. State disciplinary and licensure boards are required to report certain disciplinary actions against physicians. Hospitals and other entities engaging in peer review processes are required to report adverse actions as well. Licensure boards have access to the Data Bank to check on licensees, and hospitals must check the Data Bank for physicians applying for staff privileges and periodically for physicians who hold staff privileges. See discussion in Chapter 9. The ACA directed HHS to fold its collection of data concerning adverse actions for fraud and abuse (the Healthcare Integrity and Protection Data Bank (HIPDB)) into the NPDB. See HHS Proposed Rule, 77 Fed. Reg. 9138 (Feb. 15, 2012). Practitioners have access to their own records in the NPDB except for the reports made through the HIPDB as access could compromise ongoing criminal investigations. 76 Fed. Reg. 9295 (Feb. 17, 2011).

The public is not allowed access to information on individual practitioners in the Data Bank although access to deidentified information is permitted. For a short time in 2011, HHS closed this access to the data in the NPDB when it discovered that users could identify particular physicians when the reports were combined with other publicly available information. HHS has since reopened the public use files, but now requires users to sign an agreement not to combine the NPDB data with other information to identify specific physicians. 20 Health Law Reptr.1695 (2011). For arguments for and against public access, see Kristen Baczynski, Do You Know Who Your Physician Is?: Placing Physician Information on the Internet, 87 Iowa L. Rev. 1303 (2002); Laura A. Chernitsky, Constitutional Arguments in Favor of Modifying the HCQIA to Allow the Dissemination of Information to Healthcare Consumers, 63 Wash. & Lee L. Rev. 737 (2006).

Following the lead of Massachusetts, most states have established publicly accessible websites where they post physician profiles. The Massachusetts site posts background information on the physician (such as education, specialties, insurance plans) as well as malpractice claims paid, hospital credentialing actions, criminal convictions, and board disciplinary actions. Mass. Bd. of Reg. in Med., On–Line Physician Profile Site. Should these sites expand to include complaints filed with the medical board? Malpractice suits filed? Deselection by health plans? See Szold v. Med. Bd. of California, 127 Cal.App.4th 591, 25 Cal.Rptr.3d 665 (Ct. App. 2005), interpreting statute requiring posting of disciplinary actions. If an open book on physicians is created, at what point could it replace the disciplinary system? See discussion in Chapters 1 and 3 for more on public dissemination of quality data.

Review of data from the National Practitioner Data Bank revealed that only 45% of doctors with an NPDB report of adverse privileges actions or malpractice settlements also had a report of a disciplinary action by the state medical board. Alan Levine et al., State Medical Boards Fail to Discipline Doctors with Hospital Actions against Them, Public Citizen (2011). Most state boards reported that they had been aware of the reports against specific physicians in all but the rarest of cases, but that their board's investigation had concluded that the circumstances did not warrant disciplinary action in the specific cases at issue. Medical boards in a couple of states, however, responded that they were not aware of the reports of adverse action against a good number of their licensees. 20 Health Law Reptr. 1615 (2011). Should malpractice payments necessarily lead to licensure penalties? Consider the following Problem.

PROBLEM: THREE STRIKES AND YOU'RE OUT?

Medical boards report that disciplinary actions for substandard care or incompetency are the most difficult in terms of requirements of time, expert witnesses, legal representation, and expense. Although some studies point out the vagaries of the malpractice litigation system, studies are consistent on one point: the filing of a malpractice claim against a physician, even if no payment is made on the claim, is predictive of future malpractice claims. See, e.g., Randall R. Bovbjerg & Kenneth R. Petronis, The Relationship between Physicians' Malpractice Claims History and Later Claims: Does the Past Predict the Future? 272 JAMA 1421(1994).

Some states are beginning to integrate malpractice actions into their disciplinary processes. Almost all states require that liability insurance carriers report paid claims to the board, and some states require reporting of claims filed. Approximately 70% of the reports to the NPDB are of malpractice payouts. A study, however, found that only 33% of doctors who had paid out on ten or more malpractice claims were disciplined by their state boards. Public Citizen, The Great Medical Malpractice Hoax: NPDB Data Continue to Show Medical Liability System Produces Rational Outcomes (2007). Some states require investigation of physicians with multiple malpractice settlements or judgments. See, e.g., Mich. Comp.Laws Ann. § 333.16231.

In 2004, Florida voters approved by an overwhelming majority the following amendment to the state constitution:

> (a) No person who has been found to have committed three or more incidents of medical malpractice shall be licensed. * * *
>
> (b)(1) The phrase "medical malpractice" means the failure to practice medicine * * * with that level of care, skill, and treatment recognized in general law related to health care providers' licensure. * * *
>
> (b)(2) The phrase "found to have committed" means that the malpractice has been found in a final judgment of a court of law, final administrative agency decision, or decision of binding arbitration.

Thereafter, the Florida legislature codified the amendment in the medical licensure statute but added the following provision:

> [T]he board shall not license or continue to license a medical doctor found to have committed repeated medical malpractice [defined as three or more incidents], the finding of which was based upon clear and convincing evidence. In order to rely on an incident of medical malpractice to determine whether a license must be denied or re-

> voked under this section, if the facts supporting the finding of the incident of medical malpractice were determined on a standard less stringent than clear and convincing evidence, the board shall review the record of the case and determine whether the finding would be supported under a standard of clear and convincing evidence.

Did the legislature significantly alter the impact of the amendment? Why might they have made this change? See Roy Spece & John Marchalonis, Sound Constitutional Analysis, Moral Principle, and Wise Policy Judgment Require A Clear and Convincing Evidence Standard of Proof in Physician Disciplinary Proceedings, 3 Ind. Health L. Rev. 107 (2006), recognizing that two–thirds of states require the lower preponderance of the evidence standard; Advisory Opinion to the Attorney General Re Public Protection From Repeated Medical Malpractice, 880 So.2d 667 (Fla. 2004), in which the court reviewed the proposed amendment; Dinah Stein, Florida's "Three Strikes" Legislation: A Defense Perspective, 29 Trial Advocacy Q. 22 (2010).

Assume that your state's licensure statute provides only that disciplinary action may be taken when a physician has engaged in:

> Any conduct or practice which is or might be harmful or dangerous to the mental or physical health of a patient or the public; or incompetency, gross negligence or repeated negligence in the performance of the functions or duties of any profession licensed or regulated by this chapter. For the purposes of this subdivision, "repeated negligence" means the failure, on more than one occasion, to use that degree of skill and learning ordinarily used under the same or similar circumstances by the member of the applicant's or licensee's profession.

Does the medical board have the authority under this provision to issue a rule or adopt a policy that it will sanction a doctor with final judgments of malpractice in three or more cases? A doctor with ten or more malpractice claims made? Should the board adopt such a rule? Or, would you argue that there should always be hearing before discipline?

III. COMPLEMENTARY AND ALTERNATIVE MEDICINE

> Complementary and alternative medicine (CAM) is a broad domain of resources that encompasses health systems, modalities, and practices and their accompanying theories and beliefs, other than those intrinsic to the dominant health system of a particular society or culture in a given historical period. CAM includes such resources perceived by their users as associated with positive health outcomes. Boundaries within CAM and between the CAM domain and the domain of the dominant system are not

always sharp or fixed. IOM, Complementary and Alternative Medicine in the United States (2005).

The National Institutes of Health, National Center for Complementary and Alternative Medicine (NCCAM) defines CAM as health services that "are not presently considered to be part of conventional medicine," and goes on to list four domains (whole medical systems, such as homeopathy; mind–body medicine, including music; energy medicine, including therapeutic touch; and bioelectromagnetic–based therapies, such as pulsed fields).

The IOM report notes that all proposed definitions of CAM were "imprecise, ambiguous, or otherwise subject to misinterpretation." Both the IOM and the NCCAM definitions are deficient as they use a negative to define CAM—it is unconventional. Furthermore, they define CAM in relation to allopathic medicine and do not communicate the integration and coherence of CAM systems standing alone.

Even though limited, they capture the fluid sense of what is conventional and what is alternative as well as the vastness of what might be considered complementary and alternative (or integrative) medicine. These medically oriented definitions, however, reflect the current legal framework for CAM.

State professional licensure boards become involved in CAM in three ways. First, licensed doctors (or nurses, dentists, and so on) may utilize CAM therapies, integrating them within conventional medicine. See IOM, Integrative Medicine and the Health of the Public: A Summary of the February 2009 Summit (2009), including discussion of integrating "evidence–based interventions or practices derived from ancient folk practices, cultural–specific sources, contemporary product development, or crafted from a blend of these" with allopathic approaches. Integrating CAM approaches, however, will attract the attention of the licensure board if the practice violates licensure standards for acceptable or appropriate treatment. That issue is addressed in this section. In addition, licensure boards may take action against unlicensed CAM practitioners for violating the state's prohibition against the unlicensed practice of a licensed health care profession, as discussed in Section IV. Finally, where CAM providers are licensed, they will be subject to restrictions on their scope of practice, as discussed in Section V of this chapter.

The IOM adopted the following "ethical commitments" to guide its work in regard to CAM: a social commitment to public welfare; a commitment to protect patients and the public; respect for patient autonomy; recognition of medical pluralism; and public accountability. As you study the materials that follow, consider whether these values work as a guide for decisions by the licensure boards. Do all of the values lead to the same conclusion in each case?

IN RE GUESS

Supreme Court of North Carolina, 1990.
327 N.C. 46, 393 S.E.2d 833.

MITCHELL, JUSTICE.

* * *

The facts of this case are essentially uncontested. The record evidence tends to show that Dr. George Albert Guess is a licensed physician practicing family medicine in Asheville. In his practice, Guess regularly administers homeopathic medical treatments to his patients. Homeopathy has been defined as:

A system of therapy developed by Samuel Hahnermann on the theory that large doses of a certain drug given to a healthy person will produce certain conditions which, when occurring spontaneously as symptoms of a disease, are relieved by the same drug in small doses. This [is] . . . a sort of "fighting fire with fire" therapy. [ ] [Both the NCCAM and the Society of Homeopaths provide more detailed descriptions of homeopathy on their websites.]

* * *

[T]he Board charged Dr. Guess with unprofessional conduct [ ] specifically based upon his practice of homeopathy. * * *

Following notice, a hearing was held by the Board on the charge against Dr. Guess. The hearing evidence chiefly consisted of testimony by a number of physicians. Several physicians licensed to practice in North Carolina testified that homeopathy was not an acceptable and prevailing system of medical practice in North Carolina. In fact, there was evidence indicating that Guess is the only homeopath openly practicing in the State. Guess presented evidence that homeopathy is a recognized system of practice in at least three other states and many foreign countries. There was no evidence that Guess' homeopathic treatment had ever harmed a patient, and there was anecdotal evidence that Guess' homeopathic remedies had provided relief to several patients who were apparently unable to obtain relief through allopathic medicine.

Following its hearing, the Board revoked Dr. Guess' license to practice medicine in North Carolina, based upon findings and conclusions that Guess' practice of homeopathy "departs from and does not conform to the standards of acceptable and prevailing medical practice in this State," thus constituting unprofessional conduct as defined and prohibited by N.C.G.S. § 90–14(a)(6). The Board, however, stayed the revocation of Guess' license for so long as he refrained from practicing homeopathy.

Guess appealed the Board's decision to the Superior Court. * * * After review, the Superior Court * * * reversed and vacated the Board's decision. The Superior Court found and concluded that Guess' substantial rights had been violated because the Board's findings, conclusions and decision were "not supported by competent, material and substantial evidence and [were] arbitrary and capricious."

[T]he Court of Appeals rejected the Superior Court's reasoning to the effect that the Board's findings, conclusions and decision were not supported by competent evidence. [ ] The Court of Appeals, nonetheless, affirmed the Superior Court's order reversing the Board's decision,

> because the Board neither charged nor found that Dr. Guess' departures from approved and prevailing medical practice either endangered or harmed his patients or the public, and in our opinion the revocation of a physician's license to practice his profession in this state must be based upon conduct that is detrimental to the public; it cannot be based upon conduct that is merely different from that of other practitioners.

We granted the Board's Petition for Discretionary Review, and now reverse the Court of Appeals.

The statute central to the resolution of this case provides in relevant part:

> § 90–14. Revocation, suspension, annulment or denial of license.
>
> (a) The Board shall have the power to deny, annul, suspend, or revoke a license . . . issued by the Board to any person who has been found by the Board to have committed any of the following acts or conduct, or for any of the following reasons:
>
> . . . .
>
> (6) Unprofessional conduct, including, but not limited to, any departure from, or the failure to conform to, the standards of acceptable and prevailing medical practice, or the ethics of the medical profession, irrespective of whether or not a patient is injured thereby. . . .
> [ ]

The Court of Appeals concluded that in exercising the police power, the legislature may properly act only to protect the public from harm. Therefore, the Court of Appeals reasoned that, in order to be a valid exercise of the police power, the statute must be construed as giving the Board authority to prohibit or punish the action of a physician only when it can be shown that the particular action in question poses a danger of harm to the patient or the public. Specifically, the Court of Appeals held that:

> Before a physician's license to practice his profession in this state can be lawfully revoked under G.S. 90–14(a)(6) for practices contrary to acceptable and prevailing medical practice that it

must also appear that the deviation complained of posed some threat of harm to either the physician's patients or the public.

The Board argues, and we agree, that the Court of Appeals erred in construing the statute to add a requirement that each particular practice prohibited by the statute must pose an actual threat of harm. Our analysis begins with a basic constitutional principle: the General Assembly, in exercising the state's police power, may legislate to protect the public health, safety and general welfare. [ ] When a statute is challenged as being beyond the scope of the police power, the statute will be upheld unless it has no rational relationship to such a legitimate public purpose. [ ]

[R]egulation of the medical profession is plainly related to the legitimate public purpose of protecting the public health and safety. [ ] State regulation of the medical profession has long been recognized as a legitimate exercise of the police power. As the Supreme Court of the United States [in Dent v. West Virginia, 129 U.S. 114, 98 S.Ct. 231, 32 L.Ed. 623 (1889)] has pointed out:

> The power of the State to provide for the general welfare of its people authorizes it to prescribe all such regulations as in its judgment will secure or tend to secure them against the consequences of ignorance and incapacity as well as of deception and fraud ..... The nature and extent of the qualifications required must depend primarily upon the judgments of the States as to their necessity. . . .
>
> Few professions require more careful preparation by one who seeks to enter it than that of medicine. It has to deal with all those subtle and mysterious influences upon which health and life depend. . . . Reliance must be placed upon the assurance given by his license, issued by an authority competent to judge in that respect, that he possesses the requisite tions. . . . The same reasons which control in imposing conditions, upon compliance with which the physician is allowed to practice in the first instance, may call for further conditions as new modes of treating disease are discovered, or a more thorough acquaintance is obtained of the remedial properties of vegetable and mineral substances, or a more accurate knowledge is acquired of the human system and of the agencies by which it is affected.

The provision of the statute in question here is reasonably related to the public health. We conclude that the legislature reasonably believed that a general risk of endangering the public is inherent in any practices which fail to conform to the standards of "acceptable and prevailing" medical practice in North Carolina. We further conclude that the legislative intent was to prohibit any practice departing from acceptable and prevailing medical standards without regard to whether the particular practice itself could be shown to endanger the public. * * * Therefore, the statute is a valid exercise of the police power.

* * *

Certain aspects of regulating the medical profession plainly require expertise beyond that of a layman. Our legislature recognized that need for expertise when it created a Board of Medical Examiners composed of seven licensed physicians and one additional member. * * * The statutory phrase "standards of acceptable and prevailing medical practice" is sufficiently specific to provide the Board—comprised overwhelmingly of expert physicians—with the "adequate guiding standards" necessary to support the legislature's delegation of authority.

The statute in question is a valid regulation which generally tends to secure the public health, safety, and general welfare, and the legislature has permissibly delegated certain regulatory functions connected with that valid exercise of the police power to the Board. There is no requirement, however, that every action taken by the Board specifically identify or address a particular injury or danger to any individual or to the public. It is enough that the statute is a valid exercise of the police power for the public health and general welfare, so long as the Board's action is in compliance with the statute. The Court of Appeals thus erred in requiring a showing of potential harm from the particular practices engaged in by Dr. Guess as a prerequisite to Board action, and for that reason the Court of Appeals' decision is reversed.

* * *

Findings by the Board of Medical Examiners, if supported by competent evidence, may not be disturbed by a reviewing court. * * * The Board's findings leading to its decision were based upon competent, material and substantial evidence regarding what constitutes "acceptable and prevailing" standards of medical practice in North Carolina. No more was required. Guess' evidence concerning the efficacy of homeopathy and its use outside North Carolina simply was not relevant to the issue before the Board.

Dr. Guess also contends that the Board's decision was arbitrary and capricious and, therefore, must be reversed. He argues that the Board's arbitrariness is revealed in its "selective" application of the statute against him. He seems to contend that if the Board is to take valid action against him, it must also investigate and sanction every physician who is the "first" to utilize any "new" or "rediscovered" medical procedure. We disagree. The Board properly adhered to its statutory notice and hearing requirements, and its decision was amply supported by uncontroverted competent, material and substantial evidence. We detect no evidence of arbitrariness or capriciousness.

Dr. Guess strenuously argues that many countries and at least three states recognize the legitimacy of homeopathy. While some physicians may value the homeopathic system of practice, it seems that others consider homeopathy an outmoded and ineffective system of practice. This conflict, however interesting, simply is irrelevant here in light of the uncontroverted evidence and the Board's findings and conclusion that homeopathy is not currently an "acceptable and prevailing" system of medical practice in North Carolina.

While questions as to the efficacy of homeopathy and whether its practice should be allowed in North Carolina may be open to valid debate among members of the medical profession, the courts are not the proper forum for that debate. The legislature may one day choose to recognize the homeopathic system of treatment, or homeopathy may evolve by proper experimentation and research to the point of being recognized by the medical profession as an acceptable and prevailing form of medical practice in our state; such choices, however, are not for the courts to make.

* * * The Board argues, and we agree within our admittedly limited scope of medical knowledge, that preventing the practice of homeopathy will not restrict the development and acceptance of new and beneficial medical practices. Instead, the development and acceptance of such new practices simply must be achieved by "acceptable and prevailing" methods of medical research, experimentation, testing, and approval by the appropriate regulatory or professional bodies.

* * *

REVERSED and REMANDED.

NOTES AND QUESTIONS

1. After the *Guess* decision, the North Carolina legislature amended the grounds for discipline to limit the section under which Dr. Guess was penalized:

> The Board shall not revoke the license of or deny a license to a person solely because of that person's practice of a therapy that is experimental, nontraditional, or that departs from acceptable and prevailing medical practices unless, by competent evidence, the Board can establish that the treatment has a safety risk greater than the prevailing treatment or that the treatment is generally ineffective. N.C. Gen. Stat. 90–14(a)(6).

How would the North Carolina board prove that the alternative treatment is less safe than prevailing practice where there may be little evidence that the current practice is safe? Many argue that CAM is not amenable to scientific method in testing effectiveness. See discussion in Julie Stone & Joan Matthews, Complementary Medicine and the Law (1996), arguing that while some alternative or complementary practices have a technological base and are subject to the same type of verification as allopathic medicine, other practices are not amenable to such testing; and, therefore, conventional quality–control regulation is inadequate. See also, IOM Report, *supra*, recommending that "the same principles and standards of evidence of treatment effectiveness apply to all treatments" but offering "innovative" methods for testing effectiveness.

2. The North Carolina statute is one example of statutory approaches adopted by a good number of state legislatures to accommodate the use of CAM by licensed physicians. (For a similar statute, see Ga. § 43–34–38.) Other states have taken a practice–by–practice approach in statutes that specifically authorize licensed physicians to provide particular CAM interventions such as acupuncture. Some states require that licensed physicians who practice certain forms of CAM hold a separate state license or registration to do so, although this departs from the nearly universal form of medical licensure which grants physicians a general medical license and does not require separate licensure for medical specialties. See, for example, Haw. Rev. Stat. § 436–E. In a third CAM–friendly approach, some state statutes now require that CAM practitioners be represented on the medical board. See, e.g., N.Y. Public Health Law § 230. On regulation of CAM generally, see Michael H. Cohen, Complementary and Alternative Medicine: Legal Boundaries and Regulatory Perspectives (1998); Michael Ruggio & Lauren DeSantis–Then, Complementary and Alternative Medicine: Longstanding Legal Obstacles to Cutting Edge Treatment, 2 J. Health & Life Sci. L. 137 (2009).

3. While the traditional licensed health care professionals are increasingly incorporating CAM into their standard medical and nursing practices, practitioners offering solely alternative health care services without conventional medical or nursing training or licensure are a very significant arm of the movement toward CAM. In fact, a dominant strain in the CAM movement would argue that only alternative providers can offer such services effectively and authentically. Some states license practitioners of particular CAM therapies. See, e.g., Ariz. Rev. Stat. § 32–1521 and Alaska Stat. § 08.45.030 (licensing naturopaths); Nev. Rev. Stat. § 630A.155 (licensing homeopaths); Cal. Bus. & Prof. Code § 4935 (licensing acupuncturists).

4. Courts give deference to legislative choices in these matters, as you saw in *Guess*. For a discussion of Constitutional claims of choice of provider, claims that typically fail, see Section III, below. See also, Michael S. Goldstein, The Persistence and Resurgence of Medical Pluralism, 29 J. Health Pol. Pol'y & L. 925 (2004); The Role of Complementary and Alternative Medicine: Accommodating Pluralism (Daniel Callahan ed., 2002).

PROBLEM: THE DOCTOR AND . . . CAM?

Dr. McDonagh, D.O., is a licensed physician who employs chelation therapy in treating atherosclerosis. The FDA has approved chelation therapy only for the removal of heavy metals from the body. It has neither approved nor prohibited the use of chelation therapy for any other condition, and so Dr. McDonagh's use is "off–label." (See the discussion of off–label prescribing in Section I, above.) The American College for the Advancement of Medicine (an organization of about 1,000 members) has developed protocols for the use of chelation therapy, which McDonagh follows. The American Medical Association, however, has adopted a position statement that controlled studies illustrate that there is no scientific documentation that the therapy is effective in treating cardiovascular disease and that the therapy should be considered "an experimental process with no proven efficacy."

The state medical board charged Dr. McDonagh with endangering the health of patients through the inappropriate use of chelation therapy. Dr. McDonagh denied that his treatments endangered his patients He noted that prior to receiving chelation therapy, his patients signed a consent form clearly stating that the treatment was not approved by the FDA, the AMA, or other recognized medical organizations for the treatment of vascular disease. Dr. McDonagh encouraged patients to follow a diet and exercise plan, and did not discourage patients from seeing other physicians, including specialists.

Both the board and Dr. McDonagh presented expert testimony at the hearing held by the state's administrative hearings commission. The board's experts, all cardiovascular specialists who do not use chelation therapy, testified that the treatment does not meet the medical standard of care and that no self–respecting M.D. or D.O. would use it. McDonagh's experts testified that anecdotal evidence indicates that the therapy benefits some patients with cardiovascular disease, although controlled studies indicated no benefit; and that Dr. McDonagh met the standard of care used by those physicians willing to provide patients with this therapy. The commission upheld the board's discipline of Dr. McDonagh.

1. You are the judge of the court to which McDonagh has appealed. Assume first that the case is to be decided under the following statutory provision:

> Grounds for disciplinary action include the failure, on more than one occasion, of a licensee to use that degree of skill and learning ordinarily used under the same or similar circumstances by competent members of the profession.

Do you overturn or uphold the action against Dr. McDonagh and why? Assume now that the case is to be decided under the North Carolina statute excerpted in Note 1, above. Is the result different?

2. After this case, assume that the state medical board adopted the following rule:

> The board declares the use of chelation therapy to be of no medical value except for those uses approved by the FDA. The board, however, shall not seek disciplinary action against a licensee based solely upon a non-approved use of chelation therapy if the patient has signed a consent form, approved by the board, that clearly describes that the therapy is

nonapproved and of no efficacy. (Based on 20 CSR 2150–2.165, adopted by the Missouri Board of Healing Arts in 2001.)

Compare this rule to the following, adopted by the Kentucky board:

> Physicians may incorporate non–validated treatments if the research results are very promising, if the physician believes that a particular patient may benefit, if the risk of harm is very low, and if the physician adheres to the conventions that govern the doctrine of informed consent for non–validated treatment.

If you were an attorney for the board, what guidance would you give them in preparing their case for disciplinary action under each rule? Which of the two rules do you prefer, if either, and why? See also, The Federation of State Medical Boards Model Guidelines for the Use of Complementary and Alternative Therapies in Medical Practices (2002), which address CAM and mainstream medicine together and apply process standards, such as medical evaluation and informed consent, equally to both.

The facts in this Problem are drawn from State Board of Registration for the Healing Arts v. McDonagh, 123 S.W.3d 146 (Mo. 2003).

IV. UNLICENSED PROVIDERS

In this section, we focus on the practitioner who does not have a license. The state medical board has the primary responsibility for enforcing the prohibition against the unauthorized practice of medicine by unlicensed providers. This prohibition is enforced by criminal sanctions against the unlicensed practitioner and license revocation or criminal sanctions against any physician who aids and abets the unlicensed practitioner. The board responsible for licensure and discipline for nursing has parallel authority to pursue unlicensed practitioners charged with engaging in the unauthorized practice of nursing. The issue of the scope of practice of licensed health care professionals is taken up in Section V of this chapter.

PROBLEM: MAKING ROOM FOR ALTERNATIVE PRACTITIONERS

Cal. Bus. & Prof. Code § 2052

[A]ny person who practices or attempts to practice, or who advertises or holds himself or herself out as practicing, any system or mode of treating the sick or afflicted in this state, or who diagnoses, treats, operates for, or prescribes for any ailment, blemish, deformity, disease, disfigurement, disorder, injury, or other physical or mental condition of any person, without having at the time of so doing a valid, unrevoked, or unsuspended certificate as provided in this chapter or without being authorized to perform the act pursuant to a certificate obtained in accordance with some other provision of law is guilty of a public offense, punishable by [a fine or imprisonment or both].

Cal. Bus. & Prof. Code § 2053.5

[A] person who complies with the requirements of Section 2053.6 shall not be in violation of Section 2052 unless that person does any of the following:

(1) Conducts surgery or any other procedure on another person that punctures the skin or harmfully invades the body; (2) Administers or prescribes X–ray radiation * * * (3) Prescribes or administers legend drugs or controlled substances * * * (4) Recommends the discontinuance of legend drugs or controlled substances prescribed by an appropriately licensed practitioner (5) Willfully diagnoses and treats a physical or mental condition of any person under circumstances or conditions that cause or create a risk of great bodily harm, serious physical or mental illness, or death (6) Sets fractures (7) Treats lacerations or abrasions through electrotherapy (8) Holds out, states, indicates, advertises, or implies to a client or prospective client that he or she is a physician, a surgeon, or a physician and surgeon.

Cal. Bus. & Prof. Code § 2053.6

(a) A person who provides services pursuant to Section 2053.5 that are not unlawful under Section * * * 2052, shall, prior to providing those services, do the following:

(1) Disclose to the client in a written statement [and obtain a written acknowledgement from the patient that he or she received this information] using plain language the following information:

(A) That he or she is not a licensed physician.

(B) That the treatment is alternative or complementary to healing arts services licensed by the state.

(C) That the services to be provided are not licensed by the state.

(D) The nature of the services to be provided.

(E) The theory of treatment upon which the services are based.

(F) His or her educational, training, experience, and other qualifications regarding the services to be provided.

In enacting this legislation, the California legislature included a statement that its intent was "to allow access * * * to complementary and alternative health care practitioners who are not providing services that require medical training and credentialing?" How would these provisions apply to homeopaths? To practitioners of healing touch? To personal trainers? Assume that your state is considering the same legislation. Would you amend specific provisions or recommend a different approach entirely? Would you prefer that the state establish a licensure system for alternative providers? See Michael H. Cohen, Complementary and Alternative Medicine: Legal Boundaries and Regulatory Perspectives (1998), recommending licensure; John Lunstroth, Voluntary Self–Regulation of Complementary and Alternative Medicine Practitioners, 70 Alb. L. Rev. 209 (2006), arguing in favor of unlicensed practice.

How would these statutes apply to midwifery? See the following case.

STATE BOARD OF NURSING AND STATE BOARD OF HEALING ARTS V. RUEBKE

Supreme Court of Kansas, 1996.
259 Kan. 599, 913 P.2d 142.

LARSON, JUSTICE:

The State Board of Healing Arts (Healing Arts) and the State Board of Nursing (Nursing) appeal the trial court's denial of a temporary injunction by which the Boards had sought to stop E. Michelle Ruebke, a practicing lay midwife, from continuing her alleged practice of medicine and nursing.

* * *

Factual Background

* * *

The hearing on the temporary injunction revealed that Ruebke acts as a lay midwife comprehensively assisting pregnant women with prenatal care, delivery, and post–partum care. She is president of the Kansas Midwives Association and follows its promulgated standards, which include a risk screening assessment based upon family medical history; establishing prenatal care plans, including monthly visitations; examinations and assistance in birth; and post–partum care. She works with supervising physicians who are made aware of her mode of practice and who are available for consultation and perform many of the medical tests incident to pregnancy.

* * *

Dr. Debra L. Messamore, an obstetrician/gynecologist, testified she had reviewed the Kansas Midwives Association standards of care and opined those standards were similar to the assessments incident to her practice as an OB/GYN. Dr. Messamore concluded that in her judgment the prenatal assessments made by Ruebke were obstetrical diagnoses.

Dr. Messamore testified that the prescriptions Ruebke has women obtain from their physicians are used in obstetrics to produce uterine contractions. She further testified the Kansas Midwives Association standard of care relating to post–delivery conditions of the mother and baby involved obstetrical judgments. She reviewed the birth records of [one] birth and testified that obstetrical or medical judgments were reflected. [She admitted] that many procedures at issue could be performed by a nurse rather than a physician. * * * She also stated her opinion that so defined obstetrics as a branch of medicine or surgery.

Ginger Breedlove, a Kansas certified advanced registered nurse practitioner and nurse–midwife, testified on behalf of Nursing. She reviewed the records [of two births] and testified nursing functions were involved. She admitted she could not tell from the records who had engaged in certain practices and that taking notes, giving enemas, and administering oxygen is often done by people who are not nurses, although education, experience, and minimum competency are required.

* * * The court held that provisions of both acts were unconstitutionally vague, Ruebke's midwifery practices did not and were not intended to come within the healing arts act or the nursing act, and her activities fell within exceptions to the two acts even if the acts did apply and were constitutional.

The factual findings, highly summarized, were that Ruebke had not been shown to hold herself out as anything other than a lay midwife; has routinely used and consulted with supervising physicians; was not shown to administer any prescription drugs; was not shown to do any suturing or episiotomies, make cervical or vaginal lacerations, or diagnose blood type; and had engaged only in activities routinely and properly done by people who are not physicians.

Regulatory History of Midwifery

One of the specific statutory provisions we deal with, K.S.A. 65–2802(a), defines the healing arts as follows:

> The healing arts include any system, treatment, operation, diagnosis, prescription, or practice for the ascertainment, cure, relief, palliation, adjustment, or correction of any human disease, ailment, deformity, or injury, and includes specifically but not by way of limitation the practice of medicine and surgery; the practice of osteopathic medicine and surgery; and the practice of chiropractic.

K.S.A. 65–2869 specifically provides that for the purpose of the healing arts act, the following persons shall be deemed to be engaged in the practice of medicine and surgery:

> (a) Persons who publicly profess to be physicians or surgeons, or publicly profess to assume the duties incident to the practice of medicine or surgery or any of their branches.
>
> (b) Persons who prescribe, recommend or furnish medicine or drugs, or perform any surgical operation of whatever nature by the use of

any surgical instrument, procedure, equipment or mechanical device for the diagnosis, cure or relief of any wounds, fractures, bodily injury, infirmity, disease, physical or mental illness or psychological disorder, of human beings.

* * *

[M]idwifery belonged to women from Biblical times through the Middle Ages. However, subsequent to the Middle Ages, women healers were often barred from universities and precluded from obtaining medical training or degrees. With the rise of barber–surgeon guilds, women were banned from using surgical instruments.

When midwives immigrated to America, they occupied positions of great prestige. Some communities licensed midwives and others did not. This continued until the end of the 19th century. In the 19th and 20th centuries, medical practice became more standardized. Economically and socially well–placed doctors pressed for more restrictive licensing laws and for penalties against those who violated them. [One commentator] suggests that licensure was a market control device; midwives were depriving new obstetricians of the opportunity for training; and elimination of midwifery would allow the science of obstetrics to grow into a mature medical specialty.

There is a notable absence of anything in the history of Kansas healing arts regulation illustrating any attempt to specifically target midwives. In 1870, the Kansas Legislature adopted its first restriction on the practice of medicine. * * *

[T]here can be little doubt that in 1870 Kansas, particularly in rural areas, there were not enough educated physicians available to deliver all of the children born in the state. In fact, until 1910 approximately 50 percent of births in this country were midwife assisted. [ ]

* * *

Although obstetricians held themselves out as a medical specialty in the United States as early as 1868, midwives were not seen as engaged in the practice of obstetrics, nor was obstetrics universally viewed as being a branch of medicine. In 1901, North Carolina recognized obstetricians as engaged in the practice of medicine but women midwives, as a separate discipline, were exempted from the licensure act. [ ] * * *

Although many states in the early 1900s passed laws relating to midwifery, Kansas has never expressly addressed the legality of the practice. In 1915 [ ] this court implied that a woman with considerable midwife experience was qualified to testify as an expert witness in a malpractice case against an osteopath for allegedly negligently delivering the plaintiff's child.

* * *

The 1978 Kansas Legislature created a new classification of nurses, Advanced Registered Nurse Practitioner (ARNP). [ ] One classification of ARNP is certified nurse midwives. Although the regulations permitting the practice of certified nurse midwives might be argued to show additional legislative intent to prohibit the practice of lay midwives, this argument has been rejected elsewhere. [ ]

In 1978, Kansas Attorney General opinion No. 78–164 suggested that the practice of midwifery is a violation of the healing arts act. * * * Although potentially persuasive, such an opinion is not binding on us.

Most probably in response to the 1978 Attorney General opinion, a 1978 legislative interim committee undertook a study of a proposal to recognize and regulate the practice of lay midwifery. However, the committee reached no conclusion.

* * *

A 1986 review of the laws of every state found that lay midwifery was specifically statutorily permitted, subject to licensing or regulation, in 25 jurisdictions. Twelve states, including Kansas, had no legislation governing or prohibiting lay midwifery directly or by direct implication. Several states recognized both lay and nurse midwives. Some issued new licensing only for nurse midwives, while others regulated and recognized both, often as separate professions, subject to separate standards and restrictions. [ ]

* * *

In April 1993, the Board of Healing Arts released Policy Statement No. 93–02, in which the Board stated it reaffirmed its previous position of August 18, 1984, that

> [m]idwifery is the practice of medicine and surgery and any practice thereof by individuals not regulated by the Kansas State Board of Nursing or under the supervision of or by order of or referral from a licensed medical or osteopathic doctor constitutes the unlicensed practice of medicine and surgery.

* * *

This historical background brings us to the question of whether the healing arts act is unconstitutionally vague. * * *

* * *

[A] statute "is vague and violates due process if it prohibits conduct in terms so vague that a person of common intelligence cannot understand what conduct is prohibited, and it fails to adequately guard against arbitrary and discriminatory enforcement." [ ] A statute which requires specific intent is more likely to withstand a vagueness challenge than one, like that here, which imposes strict liability. [ ]

* * *

We have held that the interpretation of a statute given by an administrative agency within its area of expertise is entitled to deference, although final construction of a statute always rests with courts. [ ] * * *

We do, of course, attempt wherever possible to construe a statute as constitutional [ ]. * * *

* * *

The definition of healing arts uses terms that have an ordinary, definite, and ascertainable meaning. The trial court's conclusion that "disease, ailment, deformity or injury" are not commonly used words with settled meanings cannot be justified.

* * *

* * * Although we hold the act not to be unconstitutionally vague, we also hold the definitional provisions do not cover midwifery. In their ordinary usage the terms in K.S.A. 65–2802(a) used to define healing arts clearly and unequivocally focus exclusively on pathologies (i.e., diseases) and abnormal human conditions (i.e., ailments, deformities, or injuries). Pregnancy and childbirth are neither pathologies nor abnormalities.

* * *

Healing Arts argues that the "practice of medicine" includes the practice of obstetrics. It reasons, in turn, that obstetrics includes the practices traditionally performed by midwives. From this, it concludes midwifery is the practice of medicine.

However, equating midwifery with obstetrics, and thus with the practice of medicine, ignores the historical reality, discussed above, that midwives and obstetricians coexisted for many years quite separately. From the time of our statehood, the relationship between obstetricians and midwives changed from that of harmonious coexistence, cooperation, and collaboration, to open market competition and hostility. [ ]

* * *

To even the most casual observer of the history of assistance to childbirth, it is clear that over the course of this century the medical profession has extended its reach so deeply into the area of birthing as to almost completely occupy the field. The introduction of medical advances to the childbirth process drew women to physicians to assist during the birth of their children. Yet, this widespread preference for physicians as birth attendants hardly mandates the conclusion that only physicians may assist with births.

* * * The fact that a person with medical training provides services in competition with someone with no medical degree does not transform the latter's practices into the practice of medicine.

* * *

Although we hold the practice of midwifery is not itself the practice of the healing arts under our statutory scheme, our conclusions should not be interpreted to mean that a midwife may engage in any activity whatsoever with regard to a pregnant woman merely by virtue of her pregnancy. * * *

* * * However, we need not decide the precise boundaries of what a midwife may do without engaging in the practice of the healing arts because, in the case before us, Ruebke was found to have worked under the supervision of physicians who were familiar with her practices and authorized her actions. Any of Ruebke's actions that were established at trial, which might otherwise have been the practice of the healing arts, were exempt from the healing arts act because she had worked under the supervision of such physicians.

K.S.A. 65–2872 exempts certain activities from the licensure requirements of the healing arts act. In relevant part it provides:

> The practice of the healing arts shall not be construed to include the following persons:
>
> (g) Persons whose professional services are performed under the supervision or by order of or referral from a practitioner who is licensed under this act.

* * *

In light of the uncontested factual findings of the trial court, which were supported by competent evidence in the record, we agree with the trial court that the exception to the healing arts act recognized by K.S.A. 65–2872(g) applies to any of Ruebke's midwifery activities which might otherwise be considered the practice of the healing arts under K.S.A. 65–2802(a) and K.S.A. 65–2869.

* * *

As we have held, the legislature has never specifically acted with the intent to restrict or regulate the traditional practice of lay midwifery. Nevertheless, Nursing argues such birth assistants must be licensed nurses before they may render aid to pregnant women. In oral argument, Nursing conceded much of its argument would be muted were we to hold, as we do above, that the practice of midwifery is not the practice of the healing arts and thus not part of a medical regimen.

* * *

The practice of nursing is defined [in the Kansas nurse practice act] by reference to the practitioner's substantial specialized knowledge in areas of the biological, physical, and behavioral sciences and educational preparation within the field of the healing arts. Ruebke claims no specialized scientific knowledge, but rather readily admits she has no formal education beyond high school. Her assistance is valued not because it is the application of a firm and rarified grasp of scientific theory, but because, like generations of midwives before, she has practical experience assisting in childbirth.

Moreover, "nursing" deals with "persons who are experiencing changes in the normal health processes." As these words are commonly understood, pregnancy and childbirth do not constitute changes in the normal health process, but the continuation of it.

* * * As we have held, the practice of lay midwifery has, throughout the history of the regulation of nursing, been separate and distinct from the practice of the healing arts, to which nursing is so closely joined. While we have no doubt of the legislature's power to place lay midwifery under the authority of the State Board of Nursing, the legislature has not done so.

We find no legislative intent manifested in the language of the nursing act clearly illustrating the purpose of including the historically separate practice of midwifery within the practice of nursing. [ ] Assistance in childbirth rendered by one whose practical experience with birthing provides comfort to the mother is not nursing under the nursing act, such that licensure is required.

Affirmed in part and reversed in part.

NOTES AND QUESTIONS

1. Should the Kansas Supreme Court have analyzed research on the quality and safety of services provided by nurse midwives as compared to lay (also called traditional, direct–entry, or professional) midwives? If it did so, would the court have been usurping the role of the legislature or simply trying to interpret an ambiguous statute? The Kansas statute on certified nurse midwives describes substantial educational requirements for the provision of nurse midwife services. The court concluded, however, that formal education is unnecessary and that practical experience can be valued as highly. If it would amend its statutes, should the legislature provide for minimal educational requirements for persons assisting in childbirth? Should that education adopt an obstetrical model, a nursing model, or a midwifery model for childbirth? Should the legislature require supervision by a licensed physician? See

Sara K. Hayden, The Business of Birth: Obstacles Facing Low–Income Women in Choosing Midwifery Care after the Licensed Midwifery Practice Act of 1993, 19 Berkeley Women's L. J. 257 (2004), addressing the requirement of direct physician supervision.

2. Although a wide variety of health care services and providers have been subject to prosecution for the unauthorized practice of medicine, the realm of assistance at childbirth has been a particularly contentious area. Doctors, nurses, nurse–midwives, physician assistants, and lay midwives have all exerted a claim to participation in assisting in childbirth. Courts have adopted many approaches to analyzing whether services provided in assistance at childbirth constitute the unauthorized practice of medicine as defined in the relevant statutes. See, e.g., Cal. Bus. & Prof. Code § 2052, above. Some courts have examined individual actions that may be performed during childbirth. For example, in Leigh v. Board of Reg. in Nursing, 395 Mass. 670, 481 N.E.2d 1347 (1985), the court distinguished "ordinary assistance in the normal cases of childbirth" from that in which a lay midwife used "obstetrical instruments" and "printed prescriptions or formulas," and concluded that the former does not constitute the practice of medicine while the latter does. In People v. Jihan, 127 Ill.2d 379, 130 Ill.Dec. 422, 537 N.E.2d 751 (1989), the court distinguished "assisting" at birth from "delivering" the child. Statutes authorizing childbirth services by traditional midwives also set boundaries on their practice and may exclude, for example, use of any surgical instrument or assisting childbirth "by artificial or mechanical means." See, e.g., Minn. Stat. Ann. § 147D.03. Does dividing childbirth assistance into discrete activities reflect and adequately address health and safety concerns?

3. *Ruebke* illustrates that professional midwifery confronts the unauthorized practice prohibitions of both nursing and medicine. In Sherman v. Cryns, 203 Ill.2d 264, 271 Ill.Dec. 881, 786 N.E.2d 139 (2003), the court held that the state had successfully established a prima facie case against a lay midwife for practicing nursing without a license. The court distinguished its case from *Ruebke* on the basis of the broad definition of professional nursing in the Illinois statute (which was quite similar to that of the statute in *Sermchief* in the next Section, below). The Illinois statute specifically provided for licensure for certified nurse midwives but was silent on the question of lay midwifery. See also, Hunter v. State, 110 Md.App. 144, 676 A.2d 968 (Ct. Spec. App. 1996), concluding that the legislative history of certification of nurse midwives (similar to the Kansas provisions cited in *Ruebke)* required the conclusion that the statute permitted only registered nurses certified by the board as nurse midwives to provide midwifery services; Albini v. Conn. Med. Examining Bd., 2011 WL 1566994 (Superior Ct. Conn.), applying *Ruebke.*

4. A number of states recognize lay or direct–entry midwifery by statute. See, e.g., Or. Rev. Stat. 687.405. See also Sarah Anne Stover, Born by the Woman, Caught by the Midwife: The Case for Legalizing Direct–Entry Midwifery in All Fifty States, 21 Health Matrix 307 (2011), reporting that 41

states permit direct–entry midwifery, most by statute, and 9 states specifically prohibit the practice by statute, regulation, or case law. Several states have incorporated certification by the North American Registry of Midwives within their standards for recognition of lay midwives. See, e.g., Minn. § 47D.01; Utah Code 1953 § 58–77–302. Several articles provide a more detailed history of the waxing and waning of direct–entry or professional midwifery as well as the emergence of nurse–midwifery. See, e.g., Stacey A. Tovino, American Midwifery Litigation and State Legislative Preferences for Physician–Controlled Childbirth, 11 Cardozo Women's L. J. 61 (2004), addressing class, race, and gender conflicts in the law on childbirth assistance; Katherine Beckett & Bruce Hoffman, Challenging Medicine: Law, Resistance, and the Cultural Politics of Childbirth, 39 Law & Soc'y Rev. 125 (2005), analyzing sources of influence in legislatures and in litigation on behalf of lay midwifery; Rebecca Spence, Abandoning Women to their Rights: What Happens When Feminist Jurisprudence Ignores Birthing Rights?, 19 Cardozo J. L. & Gender 75 (2012).

5. The court in *Ruebke* ultimately concludes that the midwife was operating within a common exception to the prohibition against the unauthorized practice of medicine by working under the supervision of a physician. But see Marion OB/GYN v. State Med. Bd., 137 Ohio App.3d 522, 739 N.E.2d 15 (Ct. App. 2000) in which the court held that delivering infants was beyond the scope of practice allowed a physician assistant although state law allowed licensed nurses to practice midwifery. See the discussion of physician assistants and delegation in Section V, below.

6. Claims of a Constitutional right to choice of provider of health care services consistently fail even when made in the context of the woman's right to privacy in reproductive decision making and the lack of empirical evidence of better childbirth outcomes with commonly used obstetrical technology. See, e.g., Lange–Kessler v. Department of Educ., 109 F.3d 137 (2d Cir.1997); Hunter v. State, 110 Md.App. 144, 676 A.2d 968 (Ct. Spec. App. 1996). See Lisa C. Ikemoto, The Code of Perfect Pregnancy: At the Intersection of the Ideology of Motherhood, the Practice of Defaulting to Science, and the Interventionist Mindset of Law, 53 Ohio St. L. J. 1205 (1992); Amy F. Cohen, The Midwifery Stalemate and Childbirth Choice: Recognizing Mothers–to–Be as the Best Late Pregnancy Decisionmakers, 80 Ind. L. J. 849 (2005). On home births, see Alexis Chmell, Home Sweet Home, 33 J. Leg. Med. 137 (2012). See, also, People v. Rogers, 249 Mich.App. 77, 641 N.W.2d 595 (Ct. App. 2001), holding that penalty against non–M.D. practicing naturopathy did not violate the doctor's First Amendment rights as penalty was for conduct, not speech.

7. *Ruebke* is in the overwhelming majority in refusing to declare the medical practice or nursing practice act void for vagueness in their application to unlicensed service providers. See, e.g., Weyandt v. State, 35 S.W.3d 144 (Tex.Ct. App. 2000); Sherman v. Cryns, *supra*. But see, Miller v. Medical Ass'n of Georgia, 262 Ga. 605, 423 S.E.2d 664 (Ga. 1992).

V. SCOPE OF PRACTICE REGULATION

All of the policy concerns in health reform converge at the point of scope of practice (SOP) regulation. Physician–directed medical care is giving way to a team approach as a core characteristic of health care delivery and as a formal requirement for medical homes and other forms of health care delivery. A stronger emphasis on preventive care, on primary care, and on chronic disease management all point to critical and greatly expanded roles for advanced nurse practitioners (ANPs) and physician assistants (PAs). The great concern over the shortage of primary care physicians to meet these goals is also fostering a push to expand practice opportunities for these midlevel practitioners. Tine Hansen–Turton et al., Nurse Practitioners in Primary Care, 82 Temple L. Rev. 1235 (2010); Daniel Marino, Overextended: The Role of the Independent Nurse Practitioner Practice in Addressing Problems with Affordability of U.S. Primary Care, 20 Annals Health L. Advance Directive 12 (2011); Thomas R. McLean, The Schizophrenia of Physician Extender Utilization, 20 Annals of Health Law (2011).

The Affordable Care Act provides significant support for health care workforce development directed toward advanced practice nursing and other non–physician health professionals. Perhaps even more importantly, several of the health care delivery models supported by the ACA—including the medical home, the Nurse–Managed Health Clinic, and the Independence at Home Medical Practice—mandate a team approach to care with very significant practice and leadership roles for ANPs and PAs. Still, the ACA defers to state law on the permissible scope of practice of these practitioners.

Licensed nonphysician health care providers cannot legally practice medicine, but practices that fall within their own licensure (for example, as a nurse or a physician assistant) are not considered the practice of medicine. A nurse who is providing services authorized under the nurse practice act would not be practicing medicine while an unlicensed practitioner providing the same services would be guilty of the unauthorized practice of medicine or nursing. If a nurse engages in practices that exceed those authorized in the nurse practice act, however, that nurse would be guilty of exceeding the authorized scope of practice of the profession of nursing as well as violating the prohibition against the unauthorized practice of medicine.

Scope of practice regulation focuses on boundary setting between professions and attempts to separate medicine from nursing from other health care disciplines. In doing so, it faces an inherent difficulty, as you saw in *Ruebke*. To the extent that SOP regulation depends on identifying discrete activities that "belong" to each profession, it applies a notion that reflects neither the overlapping competencies of health care professionals nor the nature of diagnosis and treatment.

SERMCHIEF V. GONZALES

Supreme Court of Missouri, 1983.
660 S.W.2d 683.

WELLIVER, JUDGE.

This is a petition for a declaratory judgment and injunction brought by two nurses and five physicians[1] employed by the East Missouri Action Agency (Agency) wherein the plaintiff–appellants ask the Court to declare that the practices of the Agency nurses are authorized under the nursing law of this state, § 335.016.8, RSMo 1978 and that such practices do not constitute the unauthorized practice of medicine under Chapter 334 relating to the Missouri State Board of Registration For the Healing Arts (Board). * * * The holding below was against appellants who make direct appeal to this Court alleging that the validity of the statutes is involved. [ ]. * * *

I

The facts are simple and for the most part undisputed. The Agency is a federally tax exempt Missouri not–for–profit corporation that maintains offices in Cape Girardeau (main office), Flat River, Ironton, and Fredericktown. The Agency provides medical services to the general public in fields of family planning, obstetrics and gynecology. The services are provided to an area that includes the counties of Bollinger, Cape Girardeau, Perry, St. Francis, Ste. Genevieve, Madison, Iron and Washington. Some thirty–five hundred persons utilized these services during the year prior to trial. The Agency is funded from federal grants, Medicaid reimbursements and patient fees. The programs are directed toward the lower income segment of the population. Similar programs exist both statewide and nationwide.

Appellant nurses Solari and Burgess are duly licensed professional nurses in Missouri pursuant to the provisions of Chapter 335 and are employed by the Agency. Both nurses have had post–graduate special training in the field of obstetrics and gynecology. Appellant physicians are also employees of the Agency and duly licensed to practice medicine (the healing arts) pursuant to Chapter 334. Respondents are the members and the executive secretary of the Missouri State Board of Registration for the Healing Arts (Board) * * *.

The services routinely provided by the nurses and complained of by the Board included, among others, the taking of history; breast and pelvic examinations; laboratory testing of Papanicolaou (PAP) smears, gonor-

[1] The physicians are joined for the reason that they are charged with aiding and abetting the unauthorized practice of medicine by the nurses.

rhea cultures, and blood serology; the providing of and giving of information about oral contraceptives, condoms, and intrauterine devices (IUD); the dispensing of certain designated medications; and counseling services and community education. If the nurses determined the possibility of a condition designated in the standing orders or protocols that would contraindicate the use of contraceptives until further examination and evaluation, they would refer the patients to one of the Agency physicians. No act by either nurse is alleged to have caused injury or damage to any person. All acts by the nurses were done pursuant to written standing orders and protocols signed by appellant physicians. The standing orders and protocols were directed to specifically named nurses and were not identical for all nurses.

The Board threatened to order the appellant nurses and physicians to show cause why the nurses should not be found guilty of the unauthorized practice of medicine and the physicians guilty of aiding and abetting such unauthorized practice. Appellants sought Court relief in this proceeding.

* * *

III

The statutes involved are:

It shall be unlawful for any person not now a registered physician within the meaning of the law to practice medicine or surgery in any of its departments, or to profess to cure and attempt to treat the sick and others afflicted with bodily or mental infirmities, or engage in the practice of midwifery in this state, except as herein provided.

Section 334.010.

This Chapter does not apply . . . *to nurses licensed and lawfully practicing their profession within the provisions of chapter 335, RSMo;* . . .

Section 334.155, RSMo Supp.1982 (emphasis added).

Definitions.—As used in sections 335.011 to 335.096, unless the context clearly requires otherwise, the following words and terms shall have the meanings indicated:

* * *

(8) "Professional nursing" is the performance for compensation of any act which requires substantial specialized education, judgment and skill based on knowledge and application of principles derived from the biological, physical, social and nursing sciences, including, but not limited to:

(a) Responsibility for the teaching of health care and the prevention of illness to the patient and his family; or

(b) Assessment, nursing diagnosis, nursing care, and counsel of persons who are ill, injured or experiencing alterations in normal health processes; or

(c) The administration of medications and treatments as prescribed by a person licensed in this state to prescribe such medications and treatments; or

(d) The coordination and assistance in the delivery of a plan of health care with all members of the health team; or

(e) The teaching and supervision of other persons in the performance of any of the foregoing.

Section 335.016.8(a)–(e).

At the time of enactment of the Nursing Practice Act of 1975, the following statutes were repealed:

2. A person practices professional nursing who for compensation or personal profit performs, *under the supervision and direction of a practitioner authorized to sign birth and death certificates,* any professional services requiring the application of principles of the biological, physical or social sciences and nursing skills in the care of the sick, in the prevention of disease or in the conservation of health.

Section 335.010.2, RSMo 1969 (emphasis added).

Nothing contained in this chapter shall be construed as conferring any authority on any person to practice medicine or osteopathy or to undertake the treatment or cure of disease.

Section 335.190, RSMo 1969.

The parties on both sides request that in construing these statutes we define and draw that thin and elusive line that separates the practice of medicine and the practice of professional nursing in modern day delivery of health services. A response to this invitation, in our opinion, would result in an avalanche of both medical and nursing malpractice suits alleging infringement of that line and would hinder rather than help with the delivery of health services to the general public. Our consideration will be limited to the narrow question of whether the acts of these nurses were permissible under § 335.016.8 or were prohibited by Chapter 334.

* * *

The legislature substantially revised the law affecting the nursing profession with enactment of the Nursing Practice Act of 1975. Perhaps the most significant feature of the Act was the redefinition of the term "professional nursing," which appears in § 335.016.8. Even a facile reading of that section reveals a manifest legislative desire to expand the scope of authorized nursing practices. Every witness at trial testified that the new definition of professional nursing is a broader definition than that in the former statute. A comparison with the prior definition vividly demonstrates this fact. Most apparent is the elimination of the requirement that a physician directly supervise nursing functions. Equally significant is the legislature's formulation of an open–ended definition of professional nursing. The earlier statute limited nursing practice to "services . . . in the care of the sick, in the prevention of disease or in the conservation of health." § 335.010.2, RSMo 1969. The 1975 Act not only describes a much broader spectrum of nursing functions, it qualifies this description with the phrase "including, but not limited to." We believe this phrase evidences an intent to avoid statutory constraints on the evolution of new functions for nurses delivering health services. Under § 335.016.8, a nurse may be permitted to assume responsibilities heretofore not considered to be within the field of professional nursing so long as those responsibilities are consistent with her or his "specialized education, judgment and skill based on knowledge and application of principles derived from the biological, physical, social and nursing sciences." § 335.016.8.

The acts of the nurses herein clearly fall within this legislative standard. All acts were performed pursuant to standing orders and protocols approved by physicians. Physician prepared standing orders and protocols for nurses and other paramedical personnel were so well established and accepted at the time of the adoption of the statute that the legislature could not have been unaware of the use of such practices. We see nothing in the statute purporting to limit or restrict their continued use.

Respondents made no challenge of the nurses' level of training or the degree of their skill. They challenge only the legal right of the nurses to undertake these acts. We believe the acts of the nurses are precisely the types of acts the legislature contemplated when it granted nurses the right to make assessments and nursing diagnoses. There can be no question that a nurse undertakes only a nursing diagnosis, as opposed to a medical diagnosis, when she or he finds or fails to find symptoms described by physicians in standing orders and protocols for the purpose of administering courses of treatment prescribed by the physician in such orders and protocols.

The Court believes that it is significant that while at least forty states have modernized and expanded their nursing practice laws during the past fifteen years neither counsel nor the Court have discovered any case challenging nurses' authority to act as the nurses herein acted.

* * * The hallmark of the professional is knowing the limits of one's professional knowledge. The nurse, either upon reaching the limit of her or his knowledge or upon reaching the limits prescribed for the nurse by the physician's standing orders and protocols, should refer the patient to the physician. There is no evidence that the assessments and diagnoses made by the nurses in this case exceeded such limits.

* * *

Having found that the nurses' acts were authorized by § 335.016.8, it follows that such acts do not constitute the unlawful practice of medicine for the reason that § 334.155 makes the provisions of Chapter 334 inapplicable "to nurses licensed and lawfully practicing their profession within the provisions of Chapter 335 RSMo."

This cause is reversed and remanded with instructions to enter judgment consistent with this opinion.

NOTES AND QUESTIONS

1. The nurse practice act in *Sermchief* contains an open–ended definition of the practice of nursing. If the board of nursing had issued regulations embracing the plaintiffs' practice within the authorized practice of nursing, under what standard would the court review such regulations if challenged? Would the regulation of the board of nursing prevent the board of medicine from proceeding against the nurses? In most such disputes, the key legal question is whether the board's rule is consistent with the state statute governing the specific practice or is otherwise arbitrary. For example, the Missouri Supreme Court reviewed a letter issued by the state medical board warning doctors that permitting CRNAs to perform a particular intervention would be a delegation to an unqualified individual and would, therefore, violate the state medical practice act and result in sanctions against the doctor. The Court relied on *Sermchief* and the state nursing practice act to hold that the state board of nursing held the authority to define the SOP of nurse anesthetists and that the state medical board lacked authority to restrict physicians in working with nurses. The nursing practice act permitted the two boards to issue joint rules, however. Mo. Assoc. of Nurse Anesthetists v. State Bd. of Registration, 343 S.W.3d 348 (Mo. 2011). See also Tex. Bd. of Chiropractic Examiners v. Tex. Med. Ass'n, 375 S.W.3d 464 (Tex.App. 2012).

2. Scope of practice regulation provides an arena for interprofessional conflicts, often expressed in requirements that the midlevel practitioner practice only within a defined relationship with a licensed physician. State statutes and regulations often require either physician supervision at a particular intensity or formal collaboration with a licensed physician as a condition of practice. Whether rooted in concerns over quality or preserving the competitive or economic advantage of physicians, such requirements have a significant effect on the function and impact of ANPs and PAs. See note 6 below and IOM, The Future of Nursing: Leading Change, Advancing Health (2011), criticizing restrictive SOP regulation as diminishing access to care.

3. ANPs (including nurse midwives, nurse anesthetists, and other specialist nurse practitioners) view themselves as operating from a nursing model of health care and acting as independent practitioners who collaborate with physicians. The relationship described in *Sermchief* illustrates one form of collaborative practice. Some advanced practice nursing statutes require a nurse practitioner, generally applicable to named nurse practitioner special-

ists, to practice under the supervision of a physician. See e.g., Cal. Bus. & Prof. Code § 2746.5(b) (certificate authorizes nurse–midwife to practice nurse–midwifery "under the supervision of a licensed physician and surgeon who has current practice or training in obstetrics"). Others recognize advanced practice nursing in collaboration with licensed physicians. See e.g., Mo. Ann. Stat. § 334.104, enacted after *Sermchief*, authorizing collaborative practice arrangements in the form of written agreements, protocols or standing orders, but describing the prescriptive authority of the nurse practitioner as delegated. Some describe the advanced nursing practice without reference to the participation of a supervisory or collaborative physician. For a review of state requirements, see Lauren E. Battaglia, Supervision and Collaboration Requirements: The Vulnerability of Nurse Practitioners and Its Implications for Retail Health, 87 Wash. U. L. Rev. 1127 (2010); Pearson Report 2011.

4. Physician assistants have a different self–adopted professional identity than do nurses. Rather than viewing themselves as independent practitioners, PAs view themselves as working as physician delegates. Physician assistants first practiced under general delegation exceptions included in medical practice acts. General delegation exceptions in medical practice acts tend to be quite broad, as you saw in *Ruebke*. States vary in the standards and methods they use to assure that delegation to physician assistants is appropriate and supervision is adequate. It is reasonable to assume that all general delegation statutory provisions include at least implied requirements that the physician assistant have adequate training and competency for the specific practice and that the supervising physician likewise have the competency to oversee the practice. Some states take an individualized approach and require the physician assistant or supervising physician to submit particular details about the specific position for review by an agency. See e.g., Md. Code Ann., Health Occ. § 15–302(d). Some limit the number of physician assistants a doctor may supervise. See e.g., Ohio Rev. Code Ann. § 4730.21. Other states simply define "supervision," with great variations among the states. See e.g., Mo. Ann. Stat. § 334.735(10), defining supervision as "control exercised over a physician assistant working within the same facility as the supervising physician sixty–six percent of the time a physician assistant provides patient care, except a physician assistant may make follow–up patient examinations in hospitals, nursing homes, patient homes, and correctional facilities, each such examination being reviewed, approved and signed by the supervising physician."

5. Authority to prescribe medication has been a major issue in debates over the appropriate scope of practice of nurses and physician assistants. Most states authorize prescribing by ANPs and many for PAs. Some state statutes set particular limits on prescribing. See, e.g., Cal. Bus. & Prof. Code § 2836.1(d), requiring physician supervision for the furnishing of drugs or devices by nurse practitioner; Cal. Bus. & Prof. Code § 3502.1, setting specific requirements for PAs. Some licensed health care professions, such as dentistry, commonly have prescribing authority, but others do not. Prescribing au-

thority for licensed, doctorally trained psychologists, for example, has been particularly controversial. Patrick Yeagle, Prescription War Escalates, IllinoisTimes (10/11/12), reporting on legislative fight over prescribing authority for psychologists; Julia Johnson, Whether States Should Create Prescription Power for Psychologists, 33 Law & Psychol. Rev. 167 (2009). For a very good delineation of legal boundaries, including prescribing, and the practice of nurses, PAs, and CAM practitioners, see Joy L. Delman, The Use and Misuse of Physician Extenders, 24 J. Legal Med. 249 (2003).

6. The Federal Trade Commission has long been active in contesting what it views as anticompetitive scope–of–practice regulation by health professions boards. It has brought cease–and–desist actions against state health profession boards for engaging in unfair competition in violation of the Federal Trade Commission Act in establishing restrictive scope–of–practice standards. See, for example, North Carolina Board of Dental Examiners v. FTC, 768 F.Supp.2d 818 (E.D.N.C. 2011). It also has regularly sent letters of support or concern to state government agencies and legislatures acting to expand or limit scope of practice. In a letter urging the Texas legislature to adopt legislation removing restrictions on the SOP of ANPs, the FTC argued:

> * * * [ANP] care is generally less expensive [and is reimbursed at lower rates by Medicaid and Medicare]. * * * [The proposed statutes could reduce that cost further because] supervision and delegation requirements create administrative costs for [ANPs], and these costs would be reduced * * *. To the extent that [both bills] would increase the deployment of [ANPs] in a variety of health care delivery settings and thereby widen the range of choices available to consumers, [they] are also likely to spur innovation in health care delivery and increase the competition to provide basic health care services. * * * For example, [ANP–staffed] clinics generally offer weekend and evening hours, which provides greater flexibility for patients, and may provide competitive incentives for other types of clinics to offer extended hours as well. * * * [P]articular health care procedures may require specialized training or heightened supervision if they are to be safely administered. There does not appear to be any evidence, however, that the safety of care provided by [ANPs] varies according to differences in physician supervision or scope of practice requirements. * * * Available evidence suggests that [ANPs] generally are safe providers of health care services when they provide services consistent with their training. * * * [I]ncreased [ANP] care may even be associated with improved outcomes for particular disease indications or patient populations. FTC Letter to Texas State Senators (May 11, 2011).

7. Payment policies have a significant effect on the de facto scope of practice of advanced practice nonphysician health care providers. For example, current Medicare standards require that nurse anesthesists (CRNAs) be supervised by a physician as a condition of Medicare reimbursement for their services. States are allowed to opt out of this particular provision, however,

and California recently joined over a dozen other states in opting out, paving the way for reimbursement of CRNA services pursuant to physician orders rather than under physician supervision. Two California medical associations contested the state's decision, but the appeals court held that the California statute on scope of practice for CRNAs allows for the practice. California Society of Anesthesiologists v. Superior Court, 204 Cal.App.4th 390, 138 Cal.Rptr.3d 745 (Cal. App. 2012).

PROBLEM: PHYSICIANS, PHYSICIAN ASSISTANTS, AND NURSES

Drs. Allison Jones and Emily Johnson have a practice in Jerrold, which is located in south St. Louis County. Both Drs. Jones and Johnson are board–certified internists with a rather broad family practice. They would like to expand their practice to Jackson County, a primarily rural area about seventy miles south of Jerrold. They are especially interested in Tesson, a town of approximately 6,000 that is centrally located among the four or five small towns in the area. They are interested in Tesson because it has a small community hospital and is located close to the interstate highway. They also believe the town is underserved by physicians. There is no pediatrician in Tesson, although there is one thirty miles away. The town has one internist. It has no obstetricians, although Joan Mayo, a certified nurse midwife, has an office in a small town about eighteen miles distant from Tesson.

Ms. Mayo has been providing childbirth, family planning, and other women's health services. She has an agreement with an obstetrician in Jerrold through which protocols and standing orders for her practice were established and are maintained. She can consult with this OB by phone at any time, and they make it a practice to meet once a month to discuss Ms. Mayo's patients. Ms. Mayo refers patients who require special services to this OB or to the internist in Tesson. Ms. Mayo has clinical privileges for childbirth services at the community hospital, although her patients must be admitted by the internist.

Mariah Ellis works as a physician assistant in the Jones/Johnson office in Jerrold. She is not separately licensed, but the doctors are impressed with her handling of routine patients. In most cases, Ms. Ellis examines the patient, decides on a course of treatment and prescribes medication using blank prescription slips that are signed by the doctors. In more difficult cases, she asks for advice from one of the doctors. There is high patient satisfaction with her work.

Drs. Jones and Johnson would like to open an office in Tesson and employ a physician assistant and a pediatric nurse practitioner to staff the office full–time. Either Dr. Jones or Dr. Johnson would have office hours at that office once a week. They are also interested in establishing an affiliation with Ms. Mayo because they see room for growth in that area. They hope to serve the needs of Tesson by establishing active obstetrical and pediatric practices working with the pediatric nurse practitioner and Ms. Mayo.

For their Tesson office, they would like to find a physician assistant with extensive experience in trauma so that the assistant could care for the high incidence of farming and hunting injuries expected in that area. This PA, then, would complement the doctors' own skills as the doctors have had little experience with such injuries.

A. Drs. Jones and Johnson have come to you for advice concerning their plans for a new Tesson office. They have many questions, including whether their plans are consistent with the laws regulating practice in Allstate. Please specify how they might comply with the law while maintaining a lower cost practice. If for some reason the Board decides to take action against them, what is the likelihood of the physicians' success in challenging the Board's action?

B. Is Ms. Mayo's current practice permitted under the Allstate statutes? If Drs. Jones and Johnson acquired her practice, how should they structure their relationship in regard to the cases she takes, when she must refer patients, and their supervision of her work? Is Ms. Ellis's work as a physician assistant permitted under the Allstate statutes?

C. As noted in the introduction to this section, the ACA creates a number of delivery organizations that anticipate expanded practice by ANPs and PAs. Do the Allstate statutes measure up to the goals of increasing access to lower cost quality care?

Allstate Nurse Practice Act and Medical Practice Act

These two Allstate statutes are identical to the Missouri statutes in *Sermchief*, above.

Allstate Stat. § 2746.5.

The practice of nurse–midwifery constitutes the furthering or undertaking by any certified person, under the supervision of a licensed physician and surgeon who has current practice or training in obstetrics, to assist a woman in childbirth so long as progress meets criteria accepted as normal. All complications shall be referred to a physician immediately. The practice of nurse–midwifery does not include the assisting of childbirth by any artificial, forcible, or mechanical means. As used in this article, "supervision" shall not be construed to require the physical presence of the supervising physician. A nurse–midwife is not authorized to practice medicine and surgery by the provisions of this chapter.

Allstate Stat. § 147A.18

(a) A supervising physician may delegate to a physician assistant who is registered with the board, certified by the National Commission on Certification of Physician Assistants, and who is under the supervising physician's supervision, the authority to prescribe, dispense, and administer prescription drugs, medical devices, and controlled substances subject to the requirements in this section.

(b) The delegation must be appropriate to the physician assistant's practice and within the scope of the physician assistant's training. Supervising physicians shall retrospectively review, on a daily basis, the prescribing, dispensing, and administering of prescription and controlled drugs and medical devices by physician assistants. During each daily review, the supervising physician shall document by signature and date that the prescriptive, administering, and dispensing practice of the physician assistant has been reviewed.

Allstate § 334.104

1. Collaborative practice arrangements shall be in the form of written agreements, jointly agreed–upon protocols, or standing orders for the delivery of health care services. Collaborative practice arrangements may delegate to an advanced practice registered nurse the authority to administer or dispense drugs and provide treatment as long as the delivery of such health care services is within the scope of practice of the nurse and is consistent with that nurse's skill, training and competence.

2. The written collaborative practice arrangement shall contain at least the following provisions:

A requirement that there shall be posted at every office where the advanced practice registered nurse is authorized to prescribe, in collaboration with a physician, a prominently displayed disclosure statement informing patients that they may be seen by an advanced practice registered nurse and have the right to see the collaborating physician;

The manner of collaboration between the collaborating physician and the advanced practice registered nurse, including how the collaborating physician and the advanced practice registered nurse will:

(a) Engage in collaborative practice consistent with each professional's skill, training, education, and competence; (b) Maintain geographic proximity; and (c) Provide coverage during absence, incapacity, infirmity, or emergency by the collaborating physician;

A description of the advanced practice registered nurse's controlled substance prescriptive authority in collaboration with the physician, including a list of the controlled substances the physician authorizes the nurse to prescribe and documentation that it is consistent with each professional's education, knowledge, skill, and competence;

A description of the time and manner of the collaborating physician's review of the advanced practice registered nurse's delivery of health care services. The description shall include provisions that the advanced practice registered nurse shall submit a minimum of ten percent of the charts documenting the advanced practice registered nurse's delivery of health care services to the collaborating physician for review by the collaborating physician, or any other physician designated in the collaborative practice arrangement, every fourteen days.

PROBLEM: RETAIL CLINICS

A national pharmacy chain wants to open health clinics in several of their stores in your state. These health clinics would handle non–emergency cases, such as health screenings, vaccinations, and testing and treatment for a range of common infections, such as urinary tract infections and strep throat testing. Prices for services would be posted, and the clinics would be open for weekend and evening hours. The clinics would be staffed by ANPs and PAs with referral to hospitals and consultation with cooperative physicians in the area, as needed. The development of these "limited service clinics" is generating some controversy.

As the state's Attorney General, you represent both the medical board and the board of nursing, which are in conflict over these clinics. Like almost all states, your state doesn't have a statute regulating retail clinics. In the absence of a specific statute, the boards must rely on their current SOP statutes. In light of the conflict between the boards and among other stakeholders, you have decided to give negotiated rulemaking a try. This would involve gathering stakeholders to engage in assisting the boards in developing rules or regulations applicable to the clinics. Who has a stake in regulatory standards applicable to the scope of practice of nursing or physician assistants in this setting such that they would be involved in the negotiation process? What positions do you expect to be taken by the stakeholders you have identified? Where does the public interest lie?

Based on your experience with this exercise, do you believe that the ACA should have established a national standard for scope–of–practice regulation rather than relying on the states? (Assume that the federal government would have authority to do so through its spending authority.)

For more on retail clinics, see Kristin Schleiter, Retail Medical Clinics: Increasing Access to Low Cost Medical Care Amongst a Developing Legal Environment, 19 Annals Health L. 527 (2010); Lauren Battaglia, Supervision and Collaboration Requirements: The Vulnerability of Nurse Practitioners and Its Implications for Retail Health, 87 Wash. U. L. Rev. 1127 (2010).

CHAPTER 3

QUALITY CONTROL REGULATION OF HEALTH CARE INSTITUTIONS

■ ■ ■

I. INTRODUCTION

Patient safety and well–being are directly dependent on the quality of health care institutions as much as on the quality of the individual patient's doctor or nurse or therapist. The range of institutional factors that can pose a danger to patients extends from building design, maintenance, and sanitation through health information technology and management; from fiscal soundness through the selection, training, and monitoring of the individuals directly providing care; from staffing levels through food service. The patient safety movement (discussed in Chapter 1), in fact, focuses on the quality of systems within health care organizations rather than on the behaviors of individual caregivers standing alone.

For most consumer goods and services, the market plays a significant role in setting an acceptable level of quality. State and federal governments are making efforts to strengthen the influence of the market over the quality of health care facilities. Most of these efforts have focused on collecting and posting quality data to allow consumers to select among facilities and to encourage facilities to take action to improve their performance on reportable factors. See Chapter 1.

Significant barriers to the working of the market around quality, such as a persistent lack of relevant, timely, and accurate information on quality measures; inability to evaluate available information; and decision making processes that place the choice of facility in the hands of someone other than the patient, still diminish the impact of consumer markets in health care. In the face of market failure, state and federal governments often use a "command–and–control" system of licensure or certification through which the government sets standards, monitors for compliance, and imposes sanctions for violations. The debate over whether the market or direct governmental regulation of performance is most effective in improving the quality of health care institutions has raged for decades. See Chapter 1.

State and federal governments are not the only players in the quality arena, of course. Private nonprofit organizations offer voluntary accreditation processes through which facilities can measure their compliance against standards established by their own segment of the industry. Facilities themselves also engage in internal quality assurance and quality improvement efforts, as a result of governmental mandate, accreditation standards, or risk of liability. Private tort and related litigation can create pressure for improvement. Finally, professionals working in health care facilities have ethical and legal obligations of their own to assure the quality of the organizations in which they care for patients.

These public and private mechanisms do not work the same across the wide variety of health care organizations and facilities that offer services to patients. The question of the appropriate mix of quality control mechanisms, therefore, does not produce a one–size–fits–all answer. Consider the following section.

II. CONTEXT

The materials in this chapter focus primarily on nursing home care, a critically important and growing segment of our nation's health care sector. There are approximately 16,000 nursing homes in the United States with nearly 1.5 million people residing within them. CDC, Data Highlights from 2004 National Nursing Home Survey (2012). Nearly 3 million people receive care in a nursing home at some point during the year. CMS, 2012 Nursing Home Action Plan. In addition, the Affordable Care Act's (ACA) focus on coordination of care and payment restrictions on hospital readmissions both elevate the importance of nursing homes as an integral part of the health care system. See Vincent Mor et al., The Revolving Door of Rehospitalization from Skilled Nursing Facilities, 29 Health Affairs 57 (2010).

Nursing homes are subject to a high degree of public quality control regulation by both federal and state governments, especially as compared to hospitals. The contrast between nursing homes and hospitals provides a framework for understanding the factors that determine under what circumstances particular forms of quality control efforts, whether reliant on the market or on government enforcement, are likely to be more or less effective.

A. DIFFERENCES BETWEEN HOSPITALS AND NURSING HOMES

Hospitals and nursing homes are quite distinctive organizations even though they both provide medical and nursing care for patients/residents. They differ in their patient population; their scope of services; the composition of their staffing; and other internal organizational characteristics. They are also subject to different external pressures.

Differences in Patient Population and Scope of Services

Part of what makes nursing homes unique in the health care system is their responsibility for the complete and total environment of their residents, typically over a very long time. Their involvement with the daily life of residents usually includes assistance in activities of daily living (ADLs), including bathing, dressing, toileting, and eating. Over a third of residents are totally dependent in toileting, for example, and 98% need assistance in at least one ADL. The majority of residents of a nursing home typically have resided in the facility for more than a year: approximately 20% of nursing home residents will stay for 6 months or less, but 30% stay 1–3 years and 12% stay for over 5 years. Nearly half of nursing home residents are over 85 years in age.

Nursing home residents typically bear multiple serious, chronic, and intractable medical conditions. With the increasing utilization of home care and assisted living, however, the average nursing home patient is much sicker than those of past decades. Their physical frailty often requires rigorous and sophisticated care. Younger people who are severely disabled or mentally ill also reside in nursing homes; and regulations addressing their needs are attracting more enforcement effort as well.

The choice of nursing home is unlike the choice of other consumer goods or even the selection of a doctor or a hospital. The selection of a nursing home generally is made under duress, often upon discharge from an unexpected hospitalization; with uncertainty as to the individual's prognosis which in turn influences whether the admission will be a short–stay rehabilitation admission or a longer term or permanent admission; and by an individual other than the patient/resident themselves often using persuasion or coercion to make the placement even when the patient/resident is competent. See, e.g., Deborah Stone, Shopping for Long–Term Care, 23 Health Affairs 191 (2004). Once serious considerations (such as level of care, proximity to family due to potential lengthy stay, and whether the nursing home will accept Medicaid payments upon admission or once personal funds are exhausted) are accounted for, the remaining choice can be quite slim. Finally, the ability of a resident to transfer from a facility providing unsatisfactory services is limited as well due to the physical and mental frailty of the resident.

Differences in Organizational Structure

While hospitals developed in the United States as charitable institutions often under the direction of religious organizations, nursing homes developed originally as "mom–and–pop" enterprises, in which individuals boarded elderly persons in private homes. After the advent of Medicare and Medicaid, nursing homes attracted substantial activity from investors and were viewed primarily as real estate investments. Even today, most nursing homes are for–profit (61%), while most hospitals are not–for–profit. National for–profit chains own the majority of the for–profit nursing home industry. Studies of nursing homes have found consistently that nonprofit facilities offer higher quality care. M.P. Hilmer, Nursing Home Profit Status and Quality of Care: Is There Any Evidence of an Association?, 62 Med. Care Res. Rev. 139 (2005), reviewing studies published in 1990–2002. See also Charles Duhigg, At Many Homes, More Profit and Less Nursing, N.Y.Times 11 (Sept. 23, 2007), reporting on citations against investor–owned facilities.

Physicians are still largely absent from daily medical care in nursing homes, and professional nurses act primarily as administrators rather than direct care providers. Thus, nursing homes lack the history and embedded custom that strengthen internal professional peer review processes in hospitals. Further, hospitals have long subjected themselves to accreditation by the Joint Commission, while private accreditation of nursing homes is not as well established or influential. See discussion in Section IV, below.

In contrast to the hospital market, the demand for nursing home care exceeds available beds although demand may be ebbing somewhat in the face of more alternatives, such as assisted living facilities. Certificate of need programs in the majority of states restrict the number of nursing homes in a particular area on the theory that more beds will raise health care costs. David C. Grabowski, Medicaid Reimbursement and the Quality of Nursing Home Care, 20 J. Health Econ. 549 (2001). Low supply and excess demand, however, have been associated with lower quality perhaps because of weak competition or because enforcement efforts are constrained by the lack of alternatives for continuing care of the residents. John V. Jacobi, Competition Law's Role in Health Care Quality, 11 Ann. Health L. 45 (2002).

Medicaid pays for nearly one million of the 1.5 million nursing home residents. Medicaid is generally the only source of public payment for long–term stays as Medicare covers very limited nursing home services, focusing on shorter stays for rehabilitation only. Because nursing home care consumes the bulk of the Medicaid dollar and Medicaid is the largest spending item in state budgets, Medicaid payment levels for nursing homes are contentious and many argue that they are inadequate. Research on whether increases in payment levels improve the quality of nursing home care, however, has produced mixed results. See, e.g., David C. Grabowski et al., Medicaid Payment and Risk–Adjusted Nursing Home Quality Measures, 23 Health Affairs 243 (2004), concluding that higher payment levels were associated with lower incidence of pressure sores and use of restraints but not with improvements in pain management; GAO, Nursing Homes: Quality of Care More Related to Staffing than Spending (2002). But see, Brietta Clark, Medicaid Access, Rate Setting and Payment Suits: How the Obama Administration is Undermining its Own Health Reform Goals, 55 How. L.J. 771 (2012).

Differences in the Impact of Private Litigation over Quality

Hospitals are subject to frequent and substantial lawsuits for injuries to patients. In contrast, the characteristics of the nursing home population generally limit their ability to bring suit themselves for harms suffered as a result of poor care or abuse. Causation may be difficult to prove. Physical injuries in very frail elderly persons may be caused either by ordinary touching or by poor care or abuse. Mental impairment makes many nursing home residents poor witnesses. Limited remaining life spans and disabilities minimize legally recognizable damages. They do not suffer lost wages, and medical costs for treatment of injuries generally will be covered by Medicaid or Medicare.

The incidence and success of private lawsuits against these facilities have increased significantly in some regions of the country, however, particularly in Florida and Texas. Some cases have produced very large verdicts, but these are rare. See review of data in Michael L. Rustad, Heart of Stone: What Is Revealed About the Attitude of Compassionate Conservatives Toward Nursing Home Practices, Tort Reform, and Noneconomic Damages, 35 New Mex. L. Rev. 337 (2005). Even in states where private litigation has grown, the litigation is concentrated in just a few facilities. See, Toby S. Edelman, An Advocate's Response to Professor Sage, 9 J. Health Care L. & Pol'y 291 (2006).

Litigation against nursing homes has raised concerns that such damage awards might divert resources for care, although this is not identified as an issue with hospital liability. Jennifer L. Troyer & Herbert G. Thompson, The Impact of Litigation on Nursing Home Quality, 29 J. Health Pol., Pol'y & L. 11 (2004). In a provision reflecting this attitude, a plaintiff receiving an award of punitive damages against a nursing home in Florida is required to pay half to the Quality of Long–Term Care Facility Improvement Trust Fund. F.S.A. § 400.0238.

Many states enacted legislation some years ago to encourage, through enhanced damages and attorney's fees, nursing home patients to pursue private remedies as a means of enforcing regulatory standards. Many states have since amended these statutes, limiting damages and attorney's fees or subjecting such claims to limitations included in general tort reform legislative packages. See discussion in Ellen J. Scott, Punitive Damages in Lawsuits Against Nursing Homes, 23 J. Legal Med. 115 (2002).

Finally, nursing homes frequently include binding arbitration clauses in admission agreements. These clauses are enforceable if they meet the standards applicable to binding arbitration generally, although significant concerns regarding agreement to the clause and other issues can arise in the nursing home context. See Marmet Health Care Center, Inc. v. Brown, 132 S.Ct. 1201 (2012), relying on the Federal Arbitration Act (FAA) in reversing decision of West Virginia Supreme Court that binding arbitration clauses in nursing home admission agreements categorically violated public policy and were unenforceable. But see, Brown v. Genesis Healthcare Corp., 729 S.E.2d 217 (W.Va. 2012), holding the same clauses to be unenforceable under common law unconscionability applicable to all contracts and, therefore, not preempted by the FAA.

PROBLEM: DESIGNING MARKET–DRIVEN QUALITY INITIATIVES FOR NURSING HOMES

You are on the staff of a newly elected U.S. Congresswoman who is interested in improving the quality of nursing homes. She has asked you to prepare a justification for legislation that would take a market–based, consumer–choice approach rather than a government–driven regulatory approach. Over the past several years, federal and state governments have increased mandates for the collection and disclosure of data concerning the performance of health care facilities, including both hospitals and nursing homes. The theory of these efforts is that they will create incentives for quality improvement by enhancing market choices by consumers (or proxy decision makers such as family, case managers, and discharge planners) and by better informing facilities themselves of their comparative performance. See discussion in Chapter 1.

Check out Nursing Home Compare, the report card on nursing homes for consumers established by CMS in 1998, redesigned in 2012. http://www.medicare.gov/NursingHomeCompare. The Affordable Care Act required CMS to improve the site by adding additional information, including staff turnover rates; complaints; and whether the facility is for–profit, nonprofit, governmental, or religiously affiliated. The ACA also requires the states to develop their own sites for nursing home consumers.

The data on Nursing Home Compare begin with a five–star rating system for nursing homes on four factors: overall rating, health inspections, staffing, and quality ratings. The number of stars tends not to be consistent over the four elements, however. You'll see facilities, for example, with two stars (below average) for overall rating and four stars (above average) for quality. The site also provides a lot more information, including citations from the most recent inspection and staffing levels compared to state and national averages. Use this tool to compare up to three nursing homes, and then provide the Congresswoman with an evaluation. Is the information useful? Understandable? Is it timely? Reasonably accurate? (See Bryn Mawr Care. v. Sebelius, 2012 WL 4481924 (N.D.Ill.), holding that the facility has no right to a hearing on star rating where HHS mistakenly gave it two stars instead of four and failed to correct the mistake for two years.) Is there other information you would like to know? How does this form of web–based report card compare with those you use to select hotels?

Does the rationale in favor of report cards apply equally well to nursing homes as to hospitals? Include in your report an analysis of the relative strengths and weaknesses of the various internal and external forces that influence the quality or the accountability of nursing homes as compared to hospitals. Grade each force according to its comparative strength. Pay close attention to the market for nursing home care as opposed to hospital care. Consider, for example, supply issues; the process of selection; and the rate of turnover of customers for nursing homes and for hospitals. Does your accounting support a shift in reliance from government quality control systems toward consumer–choice approaches?

For an in–depth examination of nursing home regulation and public reporting, see Edward Miller & Vincent Mor, Balancing Regulatory Controls and Incentives: Toward Smarter and More Transparent Oversight in Long–Term Care, 33 J. Health Pol. Pol'y & L. 249 (2008). See also, David G. Stevenson, Is a Public Reporting Approach Appropriate for Nursing Home Care?, 31 J. Health Pol. Pol'y & L. 773 (2006), comparing impact on hospitals with that on nursing homes; Rachel Werner et al., Public Reporting Drove Quality Gains at Nursing Homes, 29 Health Affairs 1706 (2010), reporting small changes; Rachel Werner & R. Tamara Konetzka, Advancing Nursing Home Quality through Quality Improvement Itself, 10 Health Affairs 1877 (2010), noting that nursing home report cards ignore quality of life issues and use only narrow measures of care.

B. DEFINING QUALITY

What constitutes quality in health care? Avedis Donabedian, using the management of a specific episode of illness by a physician as the model, identifies three components on which the quality of care can be measured: the technical, the interpersonal, and amenities. He defines the technical as "the application of the science and technology of medicine, and of the other health sciences, to the management" of the patient's health issue. He defines the interpersonal as "the social and psychological interaction between client and practitioner." Finally, he categorizes as amenities "the more intimate aspects of the settings in which care is provided," although he notes that these may be integral to the care itself. The Definition of Quality and Approaches to Its Assessment (Vol. 1) (1980).

Is each of Donabedian's three factors equally important, or might one take precedence over the others? Might it depend on the context and goals of care? Would you expect that a definition of quality care might differ as between emergency room care and nursing home care?

What is the role of the patient (or "resident," in the case of nursing homes) and her values in the delivery of medical care? Donabedian concludes that quality care is

> that kind of care which is expected to maximize an inclusive measure of patient welfare, after one has taken account of the balance of expected gains and losses that attend the process of care in all its parts.

In what Donabedian called an "absolutist" medical view, the doctor best balances the benefits and risks of care; and other factors, including "the patient's expectations and valuations" are regarded as impeding or facilitating quality care. The alternative view, called "individualized" by Donabedian, holds that if advancing the patient's welfare is paramount, then "it is inevitable that the patient must share with the practitioner" the work of defining the goals of care and the evaluation of comparative risks and benefits.

Patient participation in weighing risks and benefits is familiar from informed consent for medical treatment. The same process is also quite relevant to measures of institutional quality. In fact, the movement for "patient–centered care," captured in parts of the Affordable Care Act, aims at shifting institutional measures of quality away from universal or patient–neutral standards toward standards that more directly account for patients' and residents' choices and values. (See Section III.B., below.) See also, Kristin Madison, Patients as Regulators?, 31 J. Legal Med. 9 (2010); Lois Shepherd & Mark Hall, Patient–Centered Health Law and Ethics (Symposium), 45 Wake Forest L. Rev. 1427 (2010).

C. ASSESSING QUALITY

Once again, Donabedian provides a classic analysis of the work of quality assessment:

> [T]here are three major approaches to quality assessment: "structure," "process," and "outcome." This three–fold approach is possible because there is a fundamental functional relationship among the three elements, which can be shown schematically as follows:
>
> Structure→Process→Outcome

This means that structural characteristics of the settings in which care takes place have a propensity to influence the process of care so that its quality is diminished or enhanced. Similarly, changes in the process of care, including variations in its quality, will influence the effect of care on health status, broadly defined. The Definition of Quality and Approaches to Its Assessment, Vol. 1 (1980) 84.

Donabedian defines structural standards for care as "the human, physical, and financial resources that are needed to provide . . . care." Structural standards for quality perhaps are the easiest to implement, and for this reason much of quality control regulation in the past has focused on this approach. Personnel, equipment, and buildings can be counted or described; internal regulations and staff organization measured against specific criteria; and budgets critiqued. Quantifiable and concrete structural standards are particularly useful in contentious enforcement systems because there is less concern with the human factor, or variability, in the inspection process. Unfortunately, structural standards don't measure whether the care is actually any good, only that the tools required for good care are present.

Process standards relate directly to the activities that take place in the delivery of care. For example, are orders for medication written properly; are they filled and delivered to patients accurately? Are caregivers washing their hands? Is the intervention the one accepted as appropriate for that medical condition? Donabedian favored process standards because they relate directly to what happens in care. In that way, they are more direct than structural standards.

The current wave of quality control efforts, however, is quite firmly shifting the emphasis to outcomes standards. The ACA launched several initiatives to research and implement outcomes standards for health care providers. For example, the Act established the Center for Quality Improvement and Patient Safety, which will develop research for development of standards, and the Patient–Centered Outcomes Research Institute. The ACA also required HHS to develop outcome measurements for hospitals, physicians, and other providers for the treatment of particular conditions. In addition, payment systems are increasingly orienting around performance as measured by certain outcomes. See discussion in Chapter 1.

In an important way, outcomes standards offset a critical weakness in process standards for health care; i.e., that a good deal of medical care is not grounded firmly in evidence, but rather relies on professional custom and consensus. Donabedian notes that "the use of prevalent norms as a basis for judging quality may, therefore, encourage dogmatism and perpetuate error." Outcomes instead measure the actual improvement or decline in the patient's health status. See Barry R. Furrow, Regulating Patient Safety: The Patient Protection and Affordable Care Act, 159 U.Pa. L. R. 1727 (2011). See also, the discussion of restraints in Section III.B., below. Outcome measures also have their problems, however: the onset, duration, and extent of desired outcomes are often hard to specify; it is often hard to credit a good outcome to a specific intervention; and the outcome is often known too late to affect practice.

At times, convenience outweighs significance, and outcomes measurements can focus on items that are easily measurable but less important to quality care. At the same time, attaching outcomes to consequences, even if only public disclosure, drives organizational effort toward the outcomes that will be measured, whether or not these are the most important. See Werner & Konetzka, above, criticizing nursing home report cards for using outcomes measures that are too narrow. Furthermore, the measurement of outcomes must be sensitive to variations other than quality that may determine outcomes. Consider mortality rates among hospitals, which HHS gathers and releases to the public. What variables need to be controlled if this outcome measure is to reflect comparative quality among hospitals?

The maturing of health informatics provides rich opportunities for studying the outcomes of care. Data mining is potentially a powerful new addition to quality monitoring, moving beyond tracking a particular patient to a satellite view of an entire patient population over time. Using pattern recognition algorithms, data mining can be set to search databases to investigate particular problems. It can spot trends in infections using infection surveillance results, or it can be used in a broad search strategy to mine for hidden problems, trends or other patterns that are fixable. For example, a Florida hospital, using data mining software, found that pneumonia patients who were not given medication immediately upon admission suffered significantly worse outcomes than those who were. Another facility discovered that patients with cardiovascular disease were not always prescribed beta–blockers because the discharge process did not include a crucial step to ensure the prescription was ordered, and that an easy solution was to change work processes. See generally, Barry R. Furrow, Data Mining and Substandard Medical Practice: The Difference between Privacy, Secrecy and Hidden Defects, 51 Vill. L. Rev. 803 (2006).

In its 2012 Action Plan for Nursing Homes, CMS incorporates a "Three–Part Aim" for improving health care: "Improving the individual experience of care; improving the health of populations; and reducing the per capita cost of care for populations." Does the Donabedian taxonomy measure health of populations? Should it? Do Donabedian's measures of quality relate to cost? Should standard setting for quality account for cost? Can it not do so?

III. REGULATORY PROCESS

A. NURSING HOMES: LICENSURE AND MEDICARE/MEDICAID CERTIFICATION

Nursing homes that wish to receive payment for services to Medicare or Medicaid beneficiaries must be licensed by the state and must meet federal standards in order to be certified to enter into a provider agreement with those programs. Medicare and Medicaid standards apply to every resident in the facility, however, and not only to beneficiaries. If a nursing facility chooses not to participate in Medicare or Medicaid, however, it will be subject only to state licensure requirements. Only approximately one–tenth of 1% of nursing homes does not participate in either Medicare or Medicaid.

Until the late 1980s, the federal agency responsible for Medicare and Medicaid certification (now the Centers for Medicare & Medicaid Services

(CMS) in HHS) largely deferred to the state licensure systems to set standards and monitor quality. With federal nursing home reform in 1987 (the federal Nursing Home Reform Act), however, the federal government established standards and methods for the inspection and sanctions process to be used to enforce Medicare and Medicaid requirements, although it continues to rely substantially on the states for on–site inspections. State licensure standards and inspection processes at this point largely parallel the Medicare and Medicaid certification system, but can differ.

B. STANDARD SETTING, INSPECTION, AND SANCTIONS

The regulatory process—whether licensure or Medicare/Medicaid certification—involves three functions: standard setting; inspection (known as "survey" in nursing home regulation); and sanctions. For a comprehensive empirical and bibliographic analysis of the history and current status of federal nursing home regulation, see Philip Aka et al., Political Factors and Enforcement of the Nursing Home Regulatory Regime, 24 J. L. & Health 1 (2011).

1. Standard Setting

IN RE THE ESTATE OF MICHAEL PATRICK SMITH V. HECKLER

United States Court of Appeals, Tenth Circuit, 1984.
747 F.2d 583.

MCKAY, CIRCUIT JUDGE:

Plaintiffs * * * alleged that the Secretary of Health and Human Services (Secretary) has a statutory duty under Title XIX of the Social Security Act, 42 U.S.C.A. §§ 1396–1396n * * * to develop and implement a system of nursing home review and enforcement designed to ensure that Medicaid recipients residing in Medicaid–certified nursing homes actually receive the optimal medical and psychosocial care that they are entitled to under the Act. The plaintiffs contended that the enforcement system developed by the Secretary is "facility–oriented," not "patient–oriented" and thereby fails to meet the statutory mandate. The district court found that although a patient care or "patient–oriented" management system is feasible, the Secretary does not have a duty to introduce and require the use of such a system. [ ]

The primary issue on appeal is whether the trial court erred in finding that the Secretary does not have a statutory duty to develop and implement a system of nursing home review and enforcement, which focuses on and ensures high quality patient care. * * *

Background

[P]laintiffs instituted the lawsuit in an effort to improve the deplorable conditions at many nursing homes. They presented evidence of the lack of adequate medical care and of the widespread knowledge that care is inadequate. Indeed, the district court concluded that care and life in some nursing homes is so bad that the homes "could be characterized as orphanages for the aged." [ ]

* * *

The Medicaid Act

An understanding of the Medicaid Act (the Act) is essential to understand plaintiffs' contentions. The purpose of the Act is to enable the federal government to assist states in providing medical assistance to "aged, blind or disabled individuals, whose income and resources are insufficient to meet the costs of necessary medical services, and ... rehabilitation and other services to help such ... individuals to attain or retain capabilities for independence or self care." [ ] To receive funding, a state must submit to the Secretary and have approved by the Secretary, a plan for medical assistance, which meets the requirements of [the Act].

* * * A state seeking plan approval must establish or designate a single state agency to administer or supervise administration of the state plan, [ ], and must provide reports and information as the Secretary may require. [ ] Further, the state agency is responsible for establishing and maintaining health standards for institutions where the recipients of the medical assistance under the plan receive care or services. [ ] The plan must include descriptions of the standards and methods the state will use to assure that medical or remedial care services provided to the recipients "are of high quality." [ ]

The state plan must also provide "for a regular program of medical review ... of each patient's need for skilled nursing facility care ..., a written plan of care, and, where applicable, a plan of rehabilitation prior to admission to a skilled nursing facility. ... " [ ] Further, the plan must provide for periodic inspections by medical review teams of:

> (i) the care being provided in such nursing facilities ... to persons receiving assistance under the State plan; (ii) with respect to each of the patients receiving such care, the adequacy of the services available in particular nursing facilities ... to meet the current health needs and promote the maximum physical well–being of patients receiving care in such facilities ...; (iii) the necessity and desirability of continued placement of such patients in such nursing facilities ...; and (iv) the feasibility of meeting their health care needs through alternative institutional or noninstitutional services. [ ]

The state plan must provide that any skilled nursing facility receiving payment comply with [the Act]. . . . The key requirement for purposes of this lawsuit is that a skilled nursing facility must meet "such other conditions relating to the health and safety of individuals who are furnished services in such institution or relating to the physical facilities thereof as the Secretary may find necessary. . . ." [ ]

The state plan must provide for the appropriate state agency to establish a plan, consistent with regulations prescribed by the Secretary, for professional health personnel to review the appropriateness and quality of care and services furnished to Medicaid recipients. [ ] The appropriate state agency must determine on an ongoing basis whether participating institutions meet the requirements for continued participation in the Medicaid program. [ ] While the state has the initial responsibility for determining whether institutions are meeting the conditions of participation, [the Act] gives the Secretary the authority to "look behind" the state's determination of facility compliance, and make an independent and binding determination of whether institutions meet the requirements for participation in the state Medicaid plan. Thus, the state is responsible for conducting the review of facilities to determine whether they comply with the state plan. In conducting the review, however, the states must use federal standards, forms, methods, and procedures. * * *

Implementing Regulations

* * * Congress gave the Secretary a general mandate to promulgate rules and regulations necessary to the efficient administration of the functions with which the Secretary is charged by the Act. [ ] Pursuant to this mandate the Secretary has promulgated standards for the care to be provided by skilled nursing facilities and intermediate care facilities. [ ] * * *

The Secretary has established a procedure for determining whether state plans comply with the standards set out in the regulations. This enforcement mechanism is known as the "survey/certification" inspection system. Under this system, the states conduct reviews of nursing homes pursuant to [the Act]. The Secretary then determines, on the basis of the survey results, whether the nursing home surveyed is eligible for certification and, thus, eligible for Medicaid funds. The states must use federal standards, forms, methods, and procedures in conducting the survey. [ ] At issue in this case is the form SSA–1569, [ ], which the Secretary requires the states to use to show that the nursing homes participating in Medicaid under an approved state plan meet the conditions of participation contained in the Act and the regulations. Plaintiffs contend that the form is "facility–oriented," in that it focuses on the theoretical capability of the facility to provide high quality care, rather than "patient–oriented," which would focus on the care actually provided. * * *

The Plaintiffs' Claims

* * *

The plaintiffs do not challenge the substantive medical standards, or "conditions of participation," which have been adopted by the Secretary and which states must satisfy to have their plans approved. [ ] Rather, plaintiffs challenge the enforcement mechanism the Secretary has established. The plaintiffs contend that the federal forms, form SSA–1569 in particular, which states are required to use, evaluate only the physical facilities and theoretical capability to render quality care. The surveys assess the care provided almost totally on the basis of the records, documentation, and written policies of the facility being reviewed. [ ] Further, out of the 541 questions contained in the Secretary's form SSA–1569 which must be answered by state survey and certification inspection teams, only 30 are "even marginally related to patient care or might require any patient observation. . . ." [ ] Plaintiffs contend that the enforcement mechanism's focus on the facility, rather than on the care actually provided in the facility, results only in "paper compliance" with the substantive standards of the Act. Thus, plaintiffs contend, the Secretary has violated her statutory duty to assure that federal Medicaid monies are paid only to facilities, which meet the substantive standards of the Act—facilities which actually provide high quality medical, rehabilitative, and psychosocial care to resident Medicaid recipients.

The District Court's Holding

[T]he district court found the type of patient care management system advocated by plaintiffs clearly feasible and characterized the current enforcement system as "facility–oriented." [ ] However, the court concluded that the failure to implement and require the use of a "patient–oriented" system is not a violation of the Secretary's statutory duty. * * *

* * *

The Secretary's Duty

* * * The Secretary of Health and Human Services has a duty to establish a system to adequately inform herself as to whether the facilities receiving federal money are satisfying the requirements of the Act, including providing high quality patient care. This duty to be adequately informed is not only a duty to be informed at the time a facility is originally certified, but is a duty of continued supervision.

Nothing in the Medicaid Act indicates that Congress intended the physical facilities to be the end product. Rather, the purpose of the Act is to provide medical assistance and rehabilitative services. [ ] The Act repeatedly focuses on the care to be provided, with facilities being only part of that care. For example, the Act provides that health standards are to be developed and maintained [ ], and that states must inform the Secretary what methods they will use to assure high quality care. [ ] In addition to the "adequacy of the services available," the periodic inspections must address "the care being provided" in nursing facilities. [ ] State plans must provide review of the "appropriateness and quality of care and services furnished," [ ], and do so on an ongoing basis. [ ]

* * * The Secretary, not the states, determines which facilities are eligible for federal funds. [ ] While participation in the program is voluntary, states who choose to participate must comply with federal statutory requirements. [ ] The inspections may be conducted by the states, but the Secretary approves or disapproves the state's plan for review. Further, the inspections must be made with federal forms, procedures, and methods.

It would be anomalous to hold that the Secretary has a duty to determine whether a state plan meets the standards of the Act while holding that the Secretary can certify facilities without informing herself as to whether the facilities actually perform the functions required by the state plan. The Secretary has a duty to ensure more than paper compliance. * * *

* * *

* * * Congress gave the Secretary authority to promulgate regulations to achieve the functions with which she is charged. The "look–behind" provision and its legislative history clearly show that Congress intended the Secretary to be responsible for assuring that federal Medicaid money is given only to those institutions that actually comply with Medicaid requirements. The Act's requirements include providing high quality medical care and rehabilitative services. In fact, the quality of the care provided to the aged is the focus of the Act. Being charged with this function, we must conclude that a failure to promulgate regulations that allow the Secretary to remain informed, on a continuing basis, as to whether facilities receiving federal money are meeting the requirements of the Act, is an abdication of the Secretary's duty. * * *

* * * Having determined that the purpose and the focus of the Act is to provide high quality medical care, we conclude that by promulgating a facility oriented enforcement system the Secretary has failed to follow that focus and such failure is arbitrary and capricious. [ ]

Reversed and Remanded.

NOTES AND QUESTIONS

1. The plaintiffs in *Smith* were concerned that federal standards at the time measured only the facility's "theoretical capability to render quality care" and that the items covered in the inspection of facilities were "facility oriented." How does this relate to the Donabedian triad for assessing quality, described in Section II.C, above? Which of the three types of standards are

subject to criticism for measuring only the capacity for quality care? Are those types of standards irrelevant or merely inadequate? How does the conflict over standards in *Smith* relate to the ACA's emphasis on "patient–centered care" and outcomes?

2. After *Smith*, Congress commissioned the Institute of Medicine to conduct a study of nursing home regulation. See Improving the Quality of Care in Nursing Homes (1986). The report significantly influenced the subsequent federal Nursing Home Reform Act (NHRA), commonly also referred to as OBRA 1987, which still provides the core of federal regulation of nursing homes. The NHRA delivered a comprehensive and significant change in federal standards, surveillance methods, and enforcement. It shifted the standards toward focusing on the actual care received by residents and included in the inspection/survey process a requirement that the survey team actually interview a number of residents. The standard–setting effort continues almost thirty years later, however, and has progressed through several subsequent reforms. As you read through the notes below, ask yourself: Why can't regulators get this right? Are there competing values at stake? Is there new knowledge that requires change? Does the industry have too much influence on standards? Consider the Problem: Setting Standards for Staffing, below.

3. The Affordable Care Act provided for grants to nursing homes that are developing and engaged in best practices in the mode of the "culture change movement." The culture change movement developed from the approach to measuring and inspecting for quality advocated in *Smith* and adopted in the NHRA in 1987. Mary Jane Koren, Person–Centered Care for Nursing Home Residents: The Culture–Change Movement, 29 Health Affairs 312 (2010), describing the NHRA as "a sweeping set of nursing home reforms that required facilities to provide individualized, or 'person–centered' care." Advocates of culture change support the following principles: resident direction and choices; homelike atmosphere; bonds between caregivers and residents; staff empowerment; collaborative decision making; and an internal quality improvement process. Approximately one–third of facilities report having adopted at least some of these practices and another third reported that they intend to do so. Do the culture change principles relate to the quality of care under Donabedian's definition? The Affordable Care Act included the Nursing Home Transparency and Improvement Act (NHTIA in Sections 6101–6121), which enhanced public reporting of quality; required improved intrafacility quality processes; and provided new procedures for civil fines, among other changes.

4. Federal standards in the NHRA intended to reduce the use of physical and chemical restraints represented not only a regulatory change but a fundamental shift in the foundation of a customary practice. Prior to the mid 1980s, physically restraining a nursing home resident was viewed as protective of the patient by preventing falls. It was also believed that a nursing home would be liable for injuries due to falls if it did not restrain patients. Research in the field radically changed that view. The then–new standards on restraints responded to medical and legal research proving that physical

restraints counterintuitively caused injuries rather than protecting patients; and that nursing homes indeed faced liability risks for falls, but that the cases did not support the use of restraints as a preventive measure. See, for example, Julie A. Braun & Elizabeth A. Capezuti, The Legal and Medical Aspects of Physical Restraints and Bed Siderails and Their Relationship to Falls and Fall–Related Injuries in Nursing Homes, 4 DePaul J. of Health Care Law 1 (2000); Sandra H. Johnson, The Fear of Liability and the Use of Restraints in Nursing Homes, 18 Law, Med. & Health Care 263 (1990). The move against restraints in nursing homes eventually made its way to hospital standards. 71 Fed. Reg. 71378 (Dec. 8, 2006). The Department of Justice Civil Rights Division now investigates the inappropriate use of physical and chemical restraints in nursing homes as a violation of the civil rights of residents under the Civil Rights of Institutional Persons Act. 42 U.S.C. § 1997. See also the Problem: Residents' Rights, below.

5. The CMS Nursing Home Quality Initiative (NHQI) identifies quality measurements (QMs) for nursing homes, using data collected in the Minimum Data Set (an instrument requiring each facility to collect and report standardized data on each resident). For long–stay residents, the QMs are the percentage of residents with infections, pain, pressure sores (with residents allocated into low–risk and high–risk groups), physical restraints, and loss of ability in basic daily tasks. Data on the QMs are posted on the Nursing Home Compare website and may eventually be used to change the reimbursement system to value–based payments. If you were an administrator of a nursing home and wanted to improve your performance on these outcome measures, you might increase or reorganize staff effort or other resources. This is the whole point of outcome measures, right? Outcome measures at times create perverse incentives, however. For example, if the QM relating to assistance in basic daily tasks excludes from the count patients who are terminally ill but does not exclude patients who have Alzheimer's disease or have suffered a debilitating stroke in which the natural progression may be losses in self–care, it may encourage facilities to avoid admitting particular types of residents. Jennifer L. Hilliard, The Nursing Home Quality Initiative, 26 J. Legal. Med. 41 (2005); Steven Clauser & Arlene Bierman, Significance of Functional Status Data for Payment and Quality, 24 Health Care Fin. Rev. 1 (2003).

6. When the Secretary finally issued final regulations to implement a new survey system as ordered by the court in *Smith,* she refused to include the survey instrument itself in the regulations: "[T]he new forms and instructions are not set forth in these regulations, and any future changes will be implemented through general instructions, without further changes in these regulations. This allows flexibility to revise and improve the survey process as experience is gained." 51 Fed.Reg. 21550 (June 13, 1986). What else does this allow the agency to do? The federal district court rejected the final rules because they did not include the survey instruments or instructions and held the Secretary in contempt of court. Smith v. Bowen, 675 F.Supp. 586 (D.Colo. 1987). What is the significance of the "survey instrument" if the regulations

meet the requirements of the court? See the Guidance to Surveyors in the Problem: Residents' Rights, below.

7. The court's opinion in *Smith* describes the allocation of authority in the federal–state Medicaid quality control program. Exactly which functions are allocated to the state and which to the federal government? Is the federal–state effort duplicative and inefficient? Should Congress consider requiring that nursing facilities receiving Medicaid or Medicare dollars merely be licensed by the state? What is the justification for the federal role in this situation? For further discussion of federal–state relations, see Senator Charles Grassley, The Resurrection of Nursing Home Reform: A Historical Account of the Recent Revival of the Quality of Care Standards for Long–Term Care Facilities Established in the Omnibus Reconciliation Act of 1987, 7 Elder L.J. 267 (1999); William Gromley & Christine Boccuti, HCFA and the States: Politics and Intergovernmental Leverage, 26 J. Health Pol. Pol'y and L. 557 (2001).

PROBLEM: SETTING STANDARDS FOR STAFFING

Staff–to–resident and nurse–to–resident ratio is a structural standard that has been viewed as a key indicator of quality in nursing homes and hospitals. See, e.g., GAO, Nursing Homes: Quality of Care More Related to Staffing than Spending (2002); Theresamarie Mantese et al., Nurse Staffing, Legislative Alternatives and Health Care Policy, 9 DePaul J. Health Care L. 1171 (2006).

A few states have established mandatory staffing ratios. See, e.g., Del. Code Ann. Tit. 16, § 1162; Cal. Health & Safety Code § 1276.5. The California statute requires a minimum of 3.2 hours of nursing (defined as care by nurses' aides and orderlies as well as registered nurses, but with a weighted rate for RNs) per day per nursing home resident. See Shuts v. Covenant Holdco LLC, 208 Cal.App.4th 609, 145 Cal.Rptr.3d 709 (Cal.App., 2012), holding that a class action against a nursing home chain for violation of required staffing can proceed.

CMS includes staffing data on its Nursing Home Compare website. The ACA did not change staffing levels currently required of nursing homes, but it did add requirements for training in dementia care and abuse prevention for nurses' aides and changed the methodology for capturing facility data on staffing.

A recent development at CMS illustrates how other standards may impact staffing levels. CMS has targeted reduction of nursing home use of antipsychotics (which are viewed as chemical restraints as medications used to control behavior) in its 2012 Nursing Home Action Plan. CMS is advising facilities that consistent staff assignments, increased opportunities for exercise or time outdoors, monitoring and managing pain, and planning and providing individualized activities will reduce reliance on antipsychotic medication.

Assume that you are an attorney working for CMS or the state licensing agency; or for the American Health Care Association (representing for–profit nursing homes); or for an advocacy group representing nursing home residents; or a Tea Party candidate for state office. Formulate your organization's position on staffing requirements.

Should CMS increase the required nurse staffing levels for nursing homes, or do you think posting staffing ratios on Nursing Home Compare will allow the market to drive up staffing? Is it better to focus on staffing ratios or on care outcomes? For example, the CMS initiative on antipsychotics uses an outcome measure, and facilities may find that they need to increase the number or training of staff to achieve that outcome. Should the standards abandon staffing levels as an independent criterion? The Joint Commission (see Section IV, below) revised its staffing standards for hospitals and nursing homes in 2010 in response to industry arguments that complying with the standards consumed resources and failed to produce better outcomes. If outcomes are the better measure, does requiring posting of staffing levels mislead the public in choosing a facility? Increased staffing is likely to raise costs, but should it also raise payment levels by Medicare and Medicaid? What data would you like to see if increased rates are to be considered? Are there other stakeholders who should be at the table if cost to Medicare and Medicaid becomes an issue? See Edward Miller et al., Improving Direct–Care Compensation in Nursing Homes: Medicaid Wage Pass–Through Adoption, 1999–2004, 37 J. Health Pol. Pol'y & L. 469 (2012), studying how political party of state governor influenced support for increased rates for labor costs.

PROBLEM: RESIDENTS' RIGHTS

Assume that you are the attorney for Pine Acres Nursing Home, located in an older section of the city. The administrator has approached you regarding problems with certain patients. One patient, Francis Scott, aged 88, has been a resident of the facility for a few months. Mr. Scott's mental and physical condition has been deteriorating slowly for several years and much more rapidly in the past six months. His family placed him in the nursing home because they wanted him to be safe. They were concerned because he had often left his apartment and become totally lost on the way back. Mr. Scott's family always promptly pays the monthly fee. Mr. Scott is angry about the placement, tends to be rude to staff, and insists on walking through the hallways and around the fenced–in grounds of the facility on his own. He has always been an early riser and likes to take his shower at the crack of dawn. He refuses to be assisted in showering by a nurses' aide. In addition, his friends from the neighborhood like to visit. They like to play pinochle when they come, and they usually bring a six–pack.

Another patient, Emma Kaitz, has fallen twice, apparently while trying to get out of bed. The staff is very concerned that she will be hurt. The physician who is medical director of the facility will write an order for restraints "as needed" for any resident upon the request of the director of nursing. Mrs. Kaitz's daughter is willing to try whatever the doctor advises. The staff have begun using "soft restraints" (cloth straps on her wrists) tied to the bedrails, but Mrs. Kaitz becomes agitated and cries. She says she feels like a dog when they tie her up. Other times they just use the bedrails alone. When she becomes agitated, she is given a sedative to help her relax, but it also tends to make her appear confused. To avoid the agitation as much as possible during the day, they have been able to position her wheelchair so that she can't get out by herself. She stops trying after a while and becomes so relaxed she nods off.

The administrator wants to know what he can do. What would you advise this administrator? Can he restrict the visiting hours for Mr. Scott? Can he require Mr. Scott to be assisted in the shower? Can Mr. Scott be transferred or discharged? Is the facility providing quality care for Mrs. Kaitz? How should an inspector treat Mr. Scott's and Mrs. Kaitz's complaints? What does your nursing home client expect of you here? What role should you play in regard to quality of care standards?

Can the residents sue the facility for violation of the regulations? See Grammer v. John J. Kane Regional Centers—Glen Hazel, 570 F.3d 520 (3d Cir. 2009), cert. den. 130 S.Ct. 1524 (2010), finding that the federal statute is "replete with rights–creating language;" that the resident was the intended beneficiary of the statute; and that Congress intended to create a private right of action. But see, Hawkins v. County of Brent, 800 F.Supp.2d 1162 (D. Colo. 2011), holding that the statute does not create an implied private right of action and commenting that *Grammer* is inconsistent with Supreme Court precedent. As described in Section II.A. above, however, a number of states have statutes giving residents a private right of action to enforce the state's nursing home licensure standards, which generally are quite similar to the federal standards. Of course, the resident could sue for malpractice or negligence if they could prove that the federal standards reflect the standard of care. How do you assess the actual risk that Mrs. Kaitz or Mr. Scott will file suit? On the lack of self help remedies for inappropriate transfer or discharge, see William Pipal, You Don't Have to Go Home But You Can't Stay Here: The Current State of Federal Nursing Home Involuntary Discharge Laws, 20 Elder L. J. 235 (2012).

The text that follows includes excerpts from the Residents' Rights section of the Medicaid statute; the regulation on the use of physical restraints; and the interpretive guidelines on physical restraints provided to surveyors for the inspection of Medicaid facilities.

42 U.S.C.A. § 1396r

(b)(1) QUALITY OF LIFE.—

(A) IN GENERAL.—A nursing facility must care for its residents in such a manner and in such an environment as will promote maintenance or enhancement of the quality of life of each resident.

* * *

(c) REQUIREMENTS RELATING TO RESIDENTS' RIGHTS—

(1) GENERAL RIGHTS.—

(A) SPECIFIED RIGHTS.—A nursing facility must protect and promote the rights of each resident, including each of the following rights:

(i) FREE CHOICE.—The right to choose a personal attending physician, to be fully informed in advance about care and treatment that may affect the resident's well–being, and (except with respect to a resident adjudged incompetent) to participate in planning care and treatment or changes in care and treatment.

(ii) FREE FROM RESTRAINTS.—The right to be free from physical or mental abuse, corporal punishment, involuntary seclusion, and any physical or chemical restraints imposed for purposes of discipline or convenience and not required to treat the resident's medical symptoms. Restraints may only be imposed—

(I) to ensure the physical safety of the resident or other residents, and

(II) only upon the written order of a physician that specifies the duration and circumstances under which the restraints are to be used (except in emergency circumstances specified by the Secretary until such an order could reasonably be obtained).

(iii) PRIVACY.—The right to privacy with regard to accommodations, medical treatment, written and telephonic communications, visits, and meetings of family and of resident groups. [Does not require private rooms.]

(v) ACCOMMODATION OF NEEDS.—The right—

(I) to reside and receive services with reasonable accommodations of individual needs and preferences, except where the health or safety of the individual or other residents would be endangered, and

(II) to receive notice before the room or roommate of the resident in the facility is changed.

* * *

(viii) PARTICIPATION IN OTHER ACTIVITIES.—The right of the resident to participate in social, religious, and community activities that do not interfere with the rights of other residents in the facility.

* * *

(D) USE OF PSYCHOPHARMACOLOGIC DRUGS.

Psychopharmacologic drugs may be administered only on the orders of a physician and only as part of a plan (included in the written plan of care * * *) designed to eliminate or modify the symptoms for which the drugs are prescribed and only if, at least annually an independent, external consultant reviews the appropriateness of the drug plan of each resident receiving such drugs.

(2) TRANSFER AND DISCHARGE RIGHTS.—

(A) IN GENERAL.—A nursing facility must permit each resident to remain in the facility and must not transfer or discharge the resident from the facility unless—

(i) the transfer or discharge is necessary to meet the resident's welfare and the resident's welfare cannot be met in the facility;

(ii) the transfer or discharge is appropriate because the resident's health has improved sufficiently so the resident no longer needs the services provided by the facility;

(iii) the safety of individuals in the facility is endangered;

(iv) the health of individuals in the facility would otherwise be endangered;

(v) the resident has failed, after reasonable and appropriate notice, to pay * * * for a stay at the facility; or

(vi) the facility ceases to operate. [The ACA added new requirements for facilities that are closing. 42 U.S.C.A. § 1320a–7j(h).]

* * *

(B) PRE–TRANSFER AND PRE–DISCHARGE NOTICE.—

(i) IN GENERAL.—Before effecting a transfer or discharge of a resident, a nursing facility must—

(I) notify the resident (and, if known, an immediate family member of the resident or legal representative) of the transfer or discharge and the reasons therefore,

(II) record the reasons in the resident's clinical record * * * and

(III) include in the notice the items described in clause (iii), [concerning appeal of transfer].

(ii) TIMING OF NOTICE.—The notice under clause (i)(I) must be made at least 30 days in advance of the resident's transfer or discharge except—

(I) in a case described in clause (iii) or (iv) of subparagraph (A);

(II) in a case described in clause (ii) of subparagraph (A), where the resident's health improves sufficiently to allow a more immediate transfer or discharge;

(III) in a case described in clause (i) of subparagraph (A), where a more immediate transfer or discharge is necessitated by the resident's urgent medical needs; or

(IV) in a case where a resident has not resided in the facility for 30 days.

In the case of such exceptions, notice must be given as many days before the date of the transfer or discharge as is practicable. [The statute also requires the state to establish a hearing process for transfers and discharges contested by the resident or surrogate. The ACA added required notice to the State with a plan for relocation of residents and a potential fine against noncompliant administrator.]

(3) ACCESS AND VISITATION RIGHTS.—A nursing facility must—

(A) permit immediate access to any resident by any representative of the Secretary, by any representative of the State, by an ombudsman * * * , or by the resident's individual physician;

(B) permit immediate access to a resident, subject to the resident's right to deny or withdraw consent at any time, by immediate family or other relatives of the resident;

(C) permit immediate access to a resident, subject to reasonable restrictions and the resident's right to deny or withdraw consent at any time, by others who are visiting with the consent of the resident;

(D) permit reasonable access to a resident by any entity or individual that provides health, social, legal, or other services to the resident, subject to the resident's right to deny or withdraw consent at any time; and

(E) permit representatives of the State ombudsman * * * , with the permission of the resident (or the resident's legal representative) and consistent with State law, to examine a resident's clinical records.

(4) EQUAL ACCESS TO QUALITY CARE.—

A nursing facility must establish and maintain identical policies and practices regarding transfer, discharge and the provision of services * * * for all individuals regardless of source of payment.

42 C.F.R. § 483.13(a)

Restraints. The resident has the right to be free from any physical or chemical restraints imposed for purposes of discipline or convenience, and not required to treat the resident's medical symptoms.

GUIDANCE TO SURVEYORS—LONG TERM CARE FACILITIES

CMS State Operations Manual, Appendix PP, § 483.13(a) (Jan. 7, 2011)

* * *

"Convenience" is defined as any action taken by the facility to control a resident's behavior or manage a resident's behavior with a lesser amount of effort by the facility and not in the resident's best interest.

Restraints may not be used for staff convenience. However, if the resident needs emergency care, restraints may be used for brief periods to permit medical treatment to proceed unless the facility has a notice indicating that the resident has previously made a valid refusal of the treatment in question. If a resident's unanticipated violent or aggressive behavior places him/her or others in imminent danger, the resident does not have the right to refuse the use of restraints. In this situation, the use of restraints is a measure of last resort to protect the safety of the resident or others and must not extend beyond the immediate episode. * * *

"Physical Restraints" are defined as any manual method or physical or mechanical device, material, or equipment attached or adjacent to the resident's body that the individual cannot remove easily which restricts freedom of movement or normal access to one's body.

"Physical restraints" include, but are not limited to, leg restraints, arm restraints, hand mitts, soft ties or vests, lap cushions, and lap trays the resident cannot remove easily. Also included as restraints are facility practices that meet the definition of a restraint, such as:

- Using side rails that keep a resident from voluntarily getting out of bed;
- Tucking in or using velcro to hold a sheet, fabric, or clothing tightly so that a resident's movement is restricted;
- Using devices in conjunction with a chair, such as trays, tables, bars or belts, that the resident can not remove easily, that prevent the resident from rising;
- Placing a resident in a chair that prevents a resident from rising; and placing a chair or bed so close to a wall that the wall prevents the resident from rising out of the chair or voluntarily getting out of bed.

* * *

The same device may have the effect of restraining one individual but not another, depending on the individual resident's condition and circumstances. For example, partial rails may assist one resident to enter and exit the bed independently while acting as a restraint for another.

* * *

* * * The resident's subjective symptoms may not be used as the sole basis for using a restraint. Before a resident is restrained, the facility must determine the presence of a specific medical symptom that would require the use of restraints, and how the use of restraints would treat the medical symptom, protect the resident's safety, and assist the resident in attaining or maintaining his or her highest practicable level of physical and psychosocial well–being.

* * * While there must be a physician's order reflecting the presence of a medical symptom, CMS will hold the facility ultimately accountable for the appropriateness of that determination. The physician's order alone is not sufficient to warrant the use of the restraint. * * *

In order for the resident to be fully informed, the facility must explain, in the context of the individual resident's condition and circumstances, the potential risks and benefits of all options under consideration including using a restraint, not using a restraint, and alternatives to restraint use. * * * In addition, the facility must also explain the potential negative outcomes of restraint use which include, but are not limited to, declines in the resident's physical functioning (e.g., ability to ambulate) and muscle condition, contractures, increased incidence of infections and development of pressure sores/ulcers, delirium, agitation, and incontinence. * * * Restraints have been found in some cases to increase the incidence of falls or head trauma due to falls and other accidents (e.g., strangulation, entrapment). Finally, residents who are restrained may face a loss of autonomy, dignity and self respect, and may show symptoms of withdrawal, depression, or reduced social contact. * * *

In the case of a resident who is incapable of making a decision, the legal surrogate or representative may exercise this right based on the same information that would have been provided to the resident. [ ] However, the legal surrogate or representative cannot give permission to use restraints for the sake of discipline or staff convenience or when the restraint is not necessary to treat the resident's medical symptoms. * * *

2. Survey and Inspection

An effective quality–control regulatory system requires an effective inspection (survey) process that, with an acceptable degree of accuracy, detects and documents violations of standards. Providers tend to believe that nursing home surveyors are overly aggressive; resident advocates, that they are too lax. Several studies have concluded that state and federal surveys seriously understate deficiencies, failing to cite for deficiencies or categorizing cited deficiencies as less serious than they are. See, e.g., GAO, Continued Attention is Needed to Improve Quality of Care in Small but Significant Share of Homes (May 2007). See Edward Miller & Vincent Mor, Balancing Regulatory Controls and Incentives: Toward Smarter and More Transparent Oversight in Long–Term Care, 33 J. Health Pol. Pol'y & L. 249 (2008), for a detailed analysis of the limitations of the current inspection system.

Studies have consistently concluded that there is wide variation among the states in terms of the number of citations. Does this variation reflect the quality of facilities or of inspection processes? What role should the courts play in the question of surveyor discretion or inconsistency? Should the survey standards be more rigid, or more flexible?

Surveyors may have difficulty with patient–focused and outcome–oriented survey techniques. In particular, researchers have reported that surveyors hesitate to cite facilities because they may be uncomfortable with the sophisticated level of assessment required for a citation on an outcome standard and may instead opt to cite the facility for less serious but more easily documented violations. Michael J. Stoil, Surveyors Stymied by Survey Criteria, Researchers Find, 43 Nursing Homes 58 (1994).. What might steer surveyors toward more quantifiable citations and away from problems on which there might be more room for disagreement?

CMS requires more frequent surveys of facilities that are substantially in noncompliance with federal standards. The ACA codifies this practice and requires surveys of "Special Focus Facilities" (SFF) at least every six months. 42 U.S.C. § 1395i–3(f)(8). A 2010 GAO report on the SFF program showed that it produced improvement in the majority of SFF facilities. Special Focus Facilities Are Often Improving, but CMS's Program Could be Strengthened.

The ACA also enhances the complaint filing and investigation system in long–term care. It requires that Nursing Home Compare and the state websites include a standardized complaint form with instructions on how to file complaints and a description of the process that is used to resolve them. States are required to establish a complaint resolution process that tracks complaints, determines the severity of the complaint to set priority for investigation, and sets deadlines for notifying complainants of the outcome. 42 U.S.C. § 1395i–3(i) and 1320a–7j(f).

What relationship should the surveyor establish with the facility? Is the surveyor a consultant or advisor? Should the surveyor offer suggestions for improvement? Should the surveyor commend the facility on noted improvements or other indicators of quality identified during the inspection? For a critique of the enforcement–oriented survey process, see John Braithwaite et al., Regulating Aged Care: Ritualism and The New Pyramid (2007).

3. Sanctions

FAIRFAX NURSING HOME, INC. V. U.S. DEP'T OF HEALTH & HUMAN SERVICES

United States Court of Appeals for the Seventh Circuit, 2002.
300 F.3d 835, cert. den., 537 U.S. 1111, 123 S.Ct. 901, 154 L.Ed.2d 784 (2003).

RIPPLE, CIRCUIT JUDGE.

* * * Fairfax was assessed a civil monetary penalty ("CMP") by the Center for Medicare and Medicaid Services ("CMS") because of its failure to comply substantially with Medicare regulations governing the care of respirator–dependent nursing home residents. Fairfax appealed to the Department Appeals Board of the Department of Health and Human Services ("HHS"); after a hearing before an Administrative Law Judge, both the ALJ and the Appellate Division affirmed the CMP. * * * Fairfax appeals that decision to this court. * * *

I

Background

Fairfax is a skilled nursing facility ("SNF"), [ ] participating in Medicare and Medicaid (collectively "Medicare") as a provider. Regulation of SNFs is committed to the Center for Medicare and Medicare Services, formerly known as the Health Care Financing Administration ("HCFA"), and to state agencies with whom the Secretary of Health and Human

Services has contracted. [ ] The primary method of regulation is by unannounced surveys of SNFs, conducted in this case by surveyors of the Illinois Department of Public Health ("IDPH"). [ ] These surveys are conducted at least once every 15 months. [ ] If the state survey finds violations of Medicare regulations, the state may recommend penalties to CMS. The civil monetary penalty imposed here was based on an IDPH recommendation.

On December 20, 1996, R10, a ventilator–dependent resident at Fairfax, suffered respiratory distress and required emergency care. Respiratory therapists administered oxygen directly to R10, and one therapist turned off R10's ventilator because the alarm was sounding. Once R10 was stabilized, the therapists left, but neglected to turn the ventilator back on. As a result, R10 died. Prompted by this incident, Fairfax began to develop a policy for the care of ventilator–dependent residents. That policy was completed in February 1997 and was implemented in early March of that year. * * *

On March 2, 1997, R126 was observed to have a low oxygen saturation level, an elevated pulse and temperature, and to be breathing rapidly. These signs indicated that the resident was having respiratory difficulties. R126's physician was called; he ordered a chest x–ray and gave several other instructions. However, contrary to Fairfax's policy, R126's medical chart did not reflect whether these orders were carried out. R126 died shortly thereafter.

On March 5, 1997, R127 was found with low oxygen saturation and mottled extremities. Fairfax staff failed to make a complete assessment, took no vital signs, made no follow–up assessments and did not notify a physician. On March 7, R127 was found cyanotic and required five minutes of ambu–bagging. Nurses charted four follow–up notes, but only observed R127's color and oxygen saturation and took no other vital signs. Also on March 7, during the 7 a.m. to 3 p.m. shift, three episodes of respiratory distress were noted, each of which required ambu–bagging. No physician was called. On March 10, R127's skin was observed turning blue, but there was no record of treatment for respiratory distress and no vital signs or assessments were charted. On March 21, R127 had another episode, this time with mottled legs, shaking and a dangerously low oxygen saturation. The physician was present; R127 was ambu–bagged and administered Valium. There was no complete assessment and no follow–up. On March 25, R127 was found to have a severe infection and died on March 27.

On March 23, 1997, R83 was found nonresponsive with low oxygen saturation, low blood pressure, an elevated pulse rate and a low respiratory rate. R83 was ambu–bagged, and the treating physician was called. The first noted follow–up was an hour later and 2–1/2 hours passed before R83 was monitored again.

On April 2, 1997, a state surveyor observed a Fairfax employee fail to use sterile procedures while performing tracheostomy care on R6 and R11. * * *

* * *

After a survey on April 8, 1997, IDPH surveyors determined that Fairfax's actions and omissions posed "immediate jeopardy" to the health and safety of its residents. Specifically, Fairfax had violated 42 C.F.R. § 483.25(k), which pertains in part to the special care of ventilator–dependent residents. CMS concurred and notified Fairfax by a letter dated May 7, 1997, that CMS was imposing a CMP of $3,050 per day for a 105–day period, from December 20, 1996, through April 3, 1997, during which Fairfax was not in substantial compliance with HHS regulations governing the care of ventilator–dependent residents. * * *

* * * The ALJ found that all but one of the surveyors' reported violations constituted a risk to patients at the immediate jeopardy level. The ALJ emphasized the repeated monitoring failures and the threat those failures posed to the residents. The ALJ found that "there is not only a prima facie case of noncompliance here, but the preponderance of the evidence is that Petitioner was not complying substantially" with the regulations governing the proper care of vent–dependent residents. Finally, the ALJ found that the amount of the CMP was reasonable.

* * *

We first address Fairfax's argument that the ALJ employed the incorrect legal standard. The regulations set up two basic categories of conduct for which CMPs may be imposed. [ ] The upper range, permitting CMPs of $3,050 per day to $10,000 per day, is reserved for deficiencies that constitute immediate jeopardy to a resident or, under some circumstances, repeated deficiencies. [ ] By contrast, the lower range of CMPs, which begin at $50 per day and run to $3,000 per day, is reserved for "deficiencies that do not constitute immediate jeopardy, but either caused actual harm or have the potential for causing more than minimal harm." [ ] "Immediate jeopardy" is defined as "a situation in which the provider's noncompliance with one or more requirements of participation has caused, or is likely to cause, serious injury, harm, impairment, or death to a resident." [ ]

Fairfax emphasizes the ALJ's use of the term "potential" to describe the probability of harm in several of the ALJ's findings. It submits that the ALJ's use of this terminology establishes that the deficiencies in question were deserving of "lower range" penalties. We take each in turn.

[T]he ALJ found that "Petitioner was woefully inadequate in the treatment and care of R126. . . . Such conduct caused or was likely to cause serious injury, harm, impairment or death to the resident." The

ALJ found that "[t]he record presents a picture of a lackadaisical staff, rather than a staff aggressively treating a pneumonia that was further aggravating the resident's already compromised health." The ALJ clearly was aware of the proper standard for immediate jeopardy and applied it correctly.

* * * The ALJ found that [the] monitoring failure [of R127] "had the potential for serious injury, harm, impairment, or death to the resident and constitutes immediate jeopardy." * * * Again, the ALJ's discussion of this finding demonstrates that he was well aware of the proper standard and applied it correctly. The ALJ devoted four pages of his opinion to discussing the treatment of R127, and addressed the specific risks posed to the resident by Fairfax's failure to monitor R127 after several respiratory episodes in close succession. He closes his analysis with a finding that the failures of the staff to assess properly and monitor the patient, as well as the failure to call the treating physician, "exposed the resident to risk of serious injury, harm, impairment, or death."

* * *

* * * The ALJ's conclusion with respect to R83 makes manifestly clear that there was no misunderstanding of the applicable standard: "That R83 survived Petitioner's incompetent care and treatment does not excuse the fact that he was placed at risk of serious injury, harm, impairment, or death." * * * In similar language, the ALJ concluded that patients R6 and R11 were "placed at serious risk of injury, harm, impairment or death" from the "deficient tracheostomy" care that they received.

* * * Fairly read, his "bottom line" is that a respiratory patient in Fairfax during the time in question was in continuous jeopardy of serious injury or death because of the systemic incapacity of the facility to render the necessary care to sustain life and avoid serious injury. * * *

* * *

We also believe that the HHS' decision is supported by substantial evidence. The state surveyors documented numerous instances of Fairfax's failure to care adequately for its respirator–dependent residents. The common thread running through most of these omissions is Fairfax's repeated lack of follow–up and monitoring after a resident experienced respiratory distress. * * * The record firmly supports HHS' determination that a state of immediate jeopardy to resident health existed at Fairfax from December 20, 1996, until April 3, 1997.

NOTES AND QUESTIONS

1. Should CMS have terminated Fairfax's certification and provider agreement? Was the less severe sanction more appropriate? Will the care of the

remaining residents be compromised because of the fine? The fine was accumulated on a daily basis, so on what evidence does the court conclude that Fairfax was noncompliant during the entire period? Apply the statute in the Problem: Restful Manor, below, to the situation at Fairfax.

In Vencor Nursing Ctrs. v. Shalala, 63 F. Supp.2d 1 (D.D.C. 1999), the court described the rationale for intermediate sanctions:

> In enacting the enforcement provisions to the Medicare and Medicaid Acts [in OBRA 1987], Congress expressly wished to expand the panoply of remedies available to HHS. [ ]. Committee reports noted with concern the "yo–yo" phenomenon in which noncomplying facilities temporarily correct their deficiencies before an on–site survey and then quickly lapse into noncompliance until the next review. [ ]. [T]he new version of the statute ameliorates this problem by giving HHS a set of intermediate sanctions to choose from rather than the extreme choices of termination or no sanction. There is no indication in the legislative history that Congress wished to limit HHS's ability to terminate a persistently noncompliant facility. [ ]. In fact, the recurring theme emerging from the legislative history is that the new provisions would grant HHS remedial powers in addition to those already available. [ ].

2. If a facility is cited for but then corrects a deficiency, should it still be penalized for that violation? What arguments would support an emphasis on correction rather than punishment? What would argue against? An OIG report noted that 23 of the 30 facilities that exceeded the statutory timeline for correction actually came into compliance 17 days after the statutory deadline. Nursing Home Enforcement: Application of Mandatory Remedies (May 2006). Would this prove that CMS's choice to forego termination was the right decision after all? The GAO also reported patterns of merely temporary compliance and repetitive violations while noting that the number of sanctions decreased significantly from 2000–2005. GAO, Nursing Homes: Efforts to Strengthen Federal Enforcement Have Not Deterred Some Homes from Repeatedly Harming Residents (Mar. 2006).

3. The Accountable Care Act modified the federal civil monetary penalty sanction. CMS's final rule under this section allows for cutting a fine by 50% if the facility self–reported the violation within 10 days of the date on which the facility became aware of the situation and before inspection or citation by a government agency or complaint to an agency by any individual. In addition, the facility must have taken prompt action to correct the matter, and the facility must waive its right to a hearing. This option is not available for the most serious violations or for repeated violations. There has always been controversy regarding whether any sanction should be levied if the facility actually corrects the violation in a timely fashion. Reducing the amount, rather than waiving it entirely, and requiring that the nursing home have reported the violation before citation would seem to be an effective compromise solution to that controversy. The final rule creates other controversies,

however. For example, some parties argue that a self–reported violation should not trigger a fine at all, while CMS argues that a self–report is such an admission of violation that no hearing should be allowed prior to sanction.

The Act also created an opportunity for facilities to contest a fine through an independent informal dispute resolution process and provides that a daily fine shall not be levied for the days during which that procedure is occurring. In its final rule, CMS has interpreted this provision to mean that the fines are not to be collected during the resolution process but that the daily fines will continue to accrue. CMS requires that the facility bear the cost of the independent informal dispute resolution process through a user fee. 76 Fed. Reg. 15106 (Mar. 18, 2011).

The states can use the funds collected through the Medicaid civil monetary penalties to support particular quality improvement initiatives. See CMS Letter to State Survey Agencies, Dec. 16, 2011, describing approval process for use of funds.

4. An OIG report on CMS's implementation of mandatory statutory sanctions, *supra* note 2, found that the agency failed to terminate the provider agreement in 30 out of 55 cases in which the facility remained out of compliance (on those specific citations) past the six–month deadline for reaching compliance or had an unabated condition that presented immediate jeopardy to the health and safety of the residents for more than 23 days. CMS also failed to deny payment for new admissions to 28% of the over 700 facilities that remained out of compliance for over 3 months after citation, as required by statute. CMS reported to the OIG that it did not intend to make any changes to its policies or practices:

> While the law requires that mandatory actions occur at specified times and under specific circumstances, it also contemplates that sanctions will be used to motivate improvements and lasting corrections. Where these expectations may be in conflict, we seek to resolve the conflict with the solution that best protects the well–being of the resident. Nursing Homes that Merit Punishment Not Terminated, Federal Review Finds, 15 Health L. Reptr. 628 (2006).

Is this statement persuasive? Could a nursing home residents' advocacy group bring a *Smith v. Heckler* action against CMS for violation of the federal statute? See, California Advocates for Nursing Home Reform v. California Dept. of Health Services, 2006 WL 2829865 (Cal. Super. 2006), granting writ of mandamus on claim that Department failed to investigate complaints filed with the Department against nursing homes.

5. State and federal health care fraud agencies have stepped up their actions against nursing homes. These agencies prosecute on the basis that deficiencies in the quality of care amount to fraud against the government because the facilities failed to deliver what the government paid for. See, e.g., United States v. Villaspring Health Care Ctr., 2011 WL 6337455 (E.D. Ky.).

6. In *Fairfax*, the nursing home challenged the imposition of a sanction by the federal Medicare agency. If the agency had found the facility to be out of compliance, but had not levied or had rescinded a sanction, the nursing home ordinarily does not have the right to a hearing on the finding of noncompliance. Ruqalijah A. Yearby, A Right to No Meaningful Review under the Due Process Clause: The Aftermath of Judicial Deference to the Federal Administrative Agencies, 16 Health Matrix 773 (2006). Under the Special Focus Facilities program (discussed in Section III.B.2, above) and with the posting of citations on Nursing Home Compare, however, the consequences of a citation even without sanction are significant and possibly may warrant a right to a hearing on citations even in the absence of sanctions. See, e.g., Golden Living Center–Grand Island Lakeview v. Sebelius, 2012 WL 2685001 (D.Neb.), holding that a facility had a right to a hearing on citation because of the risk that it could be identified as a Special Focus Facility as a result. But see discussion of appeals of Nursing Home Compare ratings in Section II.A., above.

PROBLEM: RESTFUL MANOR

Restful Manor is a skilled nursing facility licensed by the state and operating in its largest city. It has 117 residents, all of whom are elderly. Only twenty percent of the residents are ambulatory. Until eighteen months ago, the home had a good record of compliance with state nursing home standards. The facility has begun to have problems with compliance, although it still consistently has corrected violations or has submitted an acceptable plan of correction. The facility has also experienced some financial difficulties recently.

The most recent inspection of the facility took place four months ago. At that time, the facility was out of compliance with several standards relating to quality of meals, cleanliness of the kitchen, and maintenance of patients' medical records. The facility also had some staffing problems. Other problems included the lack of a qualified dietitian and a high, though borderline acceptable, rate of errors in the administration of medications by the nurses. As a result of this inspection report, the facility was required to submit a written plan of correction in which it agreed to remedy the violations. The next on–site inspection was scheduled to take place within six to eight weeks to check on progress in correcting the violations.

Prior to that inspection, however, an investigative news team from a local television station visited the facility with a hidden camera. The news team posed as potential out–of–town buyers interested in the facility. The visit revealed several patients who were soiled and unattended and several others who were restrained in wheelchairs. A recorded conversation with the Director of Nursing indicated that there was one nurses' aide for every ten patients, which the D.O.N. thought was probably "not enough to do a good job for some of these patients." When asked about these incidents, the owner attributed these "temporary" problems to financial constraints and to his inability to hire a good administrator who was willing to work within a reasonable budget.

The news team showed portions of the videotape on the nightly news. Three days later it followed up with a report that one of the ambulatory, mentally–impaired patients at the facility had wandered out of the building. A passerby had found the patient walking aimlessly along the main thoroughfare near the facility and called the police. The state agency felt pressured to respond. It conducted an unannounced inspection two days after the latest news report. The surveyor conducting this inspection cited the facility for violations of several regulations including the following:

1. Each resident should receive adequate skin care that supports his or her health and well being and avoids decubitus ulcers (bed sores). (The surveyor found that the facility was not turning or positioning bed–bound patients in the manner that is advised for avoidance of ulcers. The facility also lacked supportive supplies, such as certain kinds of pads, ordinarily used to reduce the incidence of ulcers. At the time of the inspection, however, two patients had minor incipient pressure sores. The surveyor believes, but could not confirm, that another patient had been transferred to the hospital eight months ago for serious bedsores.)

2. The facility must assure that a resident who did not present mental or psychosocial adjustment difficulties at admission does not display patterns of decreased social interaction or increased withdrawal, angry or depressive behaviors, unless the residents' clinical condition demonstrates that such a pattern was unavoidable. (The surveyor identifies several residents who report boredom, lethargy, loss of appetite, and feelings of uselessness and who complain of a lack of interesting things to do. Their medical records do not indicate any clinical diagnosis that would explain their psychosocial states.)

3. The facility shall provide a nursing staff that is appropriately trained and adequate in number to care for the residents of the facility. (The surveyor wrote in his report that the facility provided one nurses' aide for every ten patients and that this was "inadequate in light of the dependency of the residents.")

4. The facility shall employ a certified dietitian. (The surveyor noted that "the facility currently does not employ a certified dietitian, but in the exit conference the owner reported that he has been trying to hire one for the last three months.")

5. The nurses of the facility shall administer ordered medications safely and adequately. An error rate in excess of 5% in the administration of medication is unacceptable and shall constitute a viola-

tion of this standard. (The surveyor reported an error rate of 5% in one sample medications pass and an error rate of 4.9% in another.)

Even though the facility is currently in violation of several standards, families of Restful Manor's patients have rallied to the facility's support. They believe the care is good despite the problems cited. The Department disagrees.

The Department of Health expects litigation as a result of any enforcement action it takes in this case. It has come to the office of the state's Attorney General for advice. The Director of the Department wants to be aggressive in this case in part because the poor condition of the facility has become public knowledge. She believes that the agency's effectiveness has been challenged and that the facility is seriously deficient and heading for more problems.

Several students should serve as the assistant A.G. who has been assigned to this case. Please advise the Department on the course of action they should follow in this instance. Other students should serve in the role of attorneys representing the facility. Please identify any defenses available to the facility, your strategy, and the course the dispute is likely to take. The state statute (an edited version of the federal statute) is excerpted below.

Having worked through these provisions, what recommendations for change would you make to the legislature, both as to enforcement mechanisms and as to the standards?

488.404. Factors to be considered in selecting remedies

(b) To determine the seriousness of the deficiency, the State must consider at least the following factors:

(1) Whether a facility's deficiencies constitute—

(i) No actual harm with a potential for minimal harm; (ii) No actual harm with a potential for more than minimal harm, but not immediate jeopardy; (iii) Actual harm that is not immediate jeopardy; or (iv) Immediate jeopardy to resident health or safety.

(2) Whether the deficiencies—

(i) Are isolated; (ii) Constitute a pattern; or (iii) Are widespread.

(c) Following the initial assessment, the State may consider other factors, which may include, but are not limited to the following:

(1) The relationship of the one deficiency to other deficiencies resulting in noncompliance.

(2) The facility's prior history of noncompliance in general and specifically with reference to the cited deficiencies.

488.408. Selection of remedies

(a) In this section, remedies are grouped into categories and applied to deficiencies according to how serious the noncompliance is.

(c)(1) Category 1 remedies include the following:

(i) Directed plan of correction.

(ii) State monitoring.

(iii) Directed in–service training.

(2) The State must apply one or more of the remedies in Category 1 when there—

(i) Are isolated deficiencies that constitute no actual harm with a potential for more than minimal harm but not immediate jeopardy; or (ii) Is a pattern of deficiencies that constitutes no actual harm with a potential for more than minimal harm but not immediate jeopardy.

(3) Except when the facility is in substantial compliance, the State may apply one or more of the remedies in Category 1 to any deficiency.

(d)(1) Category 2 remedies include the following

(i) Denial of payment for new admissions.

(iii) Civil money penalties of $50–$3,000 per day.

(iv) Civil money penalty of $1,000–$10,000 per instance of noncompliance.

(2) The State must apply one or more of the remedies in Category 2 when there are—

(i) Widespread deficiencies that constitute no actual harm with a potential for more than minimal harm but not immediate jeopardy; or (ii) One or more deficiencies that constitute actual harm that is not immediate jeopardy.

(3) The State may apply one or more of the remedies in Category 2 to any deficiency except when—

(i) The facility is in substantial compliance; or (ii) The State imposes a civil money penalty for a deficiency that constitutes immediate jeopardy, the penalty must be in the upper range of penalty amounts.

(e)(1) Category 3 remedies include the following:

(i) Temporary management.

(ii) Immediate licensure revocation.

(iii) Civil money penalties of $50–$3,000 per day.

(iv) Civil money penalty of $1,000–$10,000 per instance of noncompliance.

(2) When there are one or more deficiencies that constitute immediate jeopardy to resident health or safety—

(i) The State must do one or both of the following;

(A) Impose temporary management; or

(B) Revoke the facility license;

(ii) The State may impose a civil money penalty of $3,050–$10,000 per day or $1,000–$10,000 per instance of noncompliance, in addition to imposing temporary management.

(3) When there are widespread deficiencies that constitute actual harm that is not immediate jeopardy, the State may impose temporary management, in addition to Category 2 remedies.

488.410. Action when there is immediate jeopardy

(a) If there is immediate jeopardy to resident health or safety, the State must either revoke the facility license within 23 calendar days of the last date of the survey or appoint a temporary manager to remove the immediate jeopardy . . .

(b) The State may also impose other remedies, as appropriate.

(d) The State must provide for the safe and orderly transfer of residents when the facility is terminated.

488.412. Action when there is no immediate jeopardy

(a) If a facility's deficiencies do not pose immediate jeopardy to residents' health or safety, and the facility is not in substantial compliance, the State may revoke the facility's license agreement or may allow the facility to continue to participate for no longer than 6 months from the last day of the survey if—

(1) The State survey agency finds that it is more appropriate to impose alternative remedies than to terminate the facility's provider agreement;

(2) The facility has submitted an approved plan and timetable for corrective action.

488.415. Temporary management

(a) Temporary management means the temporary appointment by the State of a substitute facility manager or administrator with authority to hire, terminate or reassign staff, obligate facility funds, alter facility procedures, and manage the facility to correct deficiencies identified in the facility's operation.

NOTE: CMS QUALITY IMPROVEMENT INITIATIVES

The Affordable Care Act increased the emphasis on internal quality processes within nursing homes, adopting some structures that have been commonplace in hospitals for some time. For example, the Act requires nursing homes to establish an internal compliance and ethics program. Although this process will be guided by standards from the Office of Inspector General of HHS, which prosecutes fraud and abuse in health care, the focus of the nursing home committees is to be compliance as it relates to the quality of care provided in the facility. 42 U.S.C. § 1320a–7j (b).

The Act also required CMS to extend the Medicare Quality Assessment and Performance Improvement Program (QAPI) requirement to nursing homes. 42 U.S.C. § 1320a–7j (c). A nursing home's internal QAPI program is to emphasize a data–driven, systems–oriented approach to quality of care and patient safety. QAPI programs generally require a facility to use data to identify, prioritize, and demonstrate improvement in outcomes, processes of care, patient satisfaction, facility operations, and other performance indicators. In 2011, CMS funded a demonstration project in 17 nursing homes to test the implementation of QAPI in nursing homes. QAPI programs have been a Medicare condition of participation for several types of facilities, including hospitals, for some time.

CMS contracts with a private, expert organization in each state to serve as a Quality Improvement Organization (QIO). The contractual statement of work for the QIOs includes reviewing individual beneficiary complaints, but also includes leadership of particular quality improvement strategies using a consultative approach. QIOs are currently working with nursing homes and Medicare beneficiaries to reduce the incidence of pressure sores. On quality improvement, see Rachel Werner & R. Tamara Konetzka, Advancing Nursing Home Quality through Quality Improvement Itself, 29 Health Affairs 81 (2010).

IV. PRIVATE ACCREDITATION OF HEALTH CARE FACILITIES

Private accreditation is a nongovernmental, voluntary activity typically conducted by not–for–profit associations. The Joint Commission and the National Committee on Quality Assurance (NCQA) are two of the leading organizations in the accreditation of health care entities. You can review the scope of their activities and new developments through their websites.

As a voluntary process, accreditation may be viewed as a private communicative device, providing the accredited health care entity with a seal of approval—a method for communicating in shorthand that it meets standards established by an external organization. See, Clark C. Havighurst, Foreword: The Place of Private Accrediting Among the Instruments of Government, 57 L. & Contemp. Probs. 1 (1994). In practice, however, there is a much closer marriage between some private accreditation programs and government regulation of health care facilities. This is especially true of the Joint Commission hospital accreditation program.

Both state and federal governments rely to a great extent on accreditation in their hospital licensure and Medicare/Medicaid hospital certification programs. Most states have incorporated the Commission's accreditation program into their hospital licensure standards. See e.g., Tex. Health & Safety Code § 222.024, exempting Joint Commission accredited hospitals from annual licensure inspection. Under the Medicare statute, Joint Commission accredited hospitals are "deemed" to have met requirements for Medicare certification. Although the Secretary retains a look–behind authority, the Joint Commission substitutes for the routine surveillance process.

Originally, the acceptance of accreditation by the Medicare program was designed to entice an adequate number of hospitals to participate in the then–new Medicare program. That original rationale has dissipated as hospitals have become much more dependent on Medicare payments. At the same time, the federal government's reliance on private accreditation as a substitute for routine government surveillance has expanded considerably beyond the original hospital setting and now extends to clinical laboratories and home health care, among others.

What might explain this extensive reliance on private organizations for public regulation? Some argue that private accreditation more effectively encourages voluntary compliance and avoids some of the prosecutorial environment of a government–conducted inspection program. Furthermore, and perhaps more pragmatically, deemed status allows the government to shift the cost of the inspection process because accredited facilities pay for the costs of accreditation, including the site visit.

In 1981, the Reagan Administration proposed extending deemed status to nursing homes accredited by the Joint Commission. This proposal was opposed vigorously by consumer advocates and was withdrawn with the effect that deemed status for Medicare certification still does not extend to nursing homes. Should nursing homes be treated differently, and arguably more restrictively, than other Medicare providers on the question of deemed status?

CMS has become more directly engaged in the Joint Commission's standards for hospital accreditation as a result of the 2008 Medicare Improvements for Patients and Providers Act, which removed permanent deemed status for the Commission's hospital accreditation program and required the Commission to reapply periodically for that status. The Commission has been required to reapply for deemed status for its other accreditation programs for some time.

How does the private accreditation process compare to public regulation? Private accreditation programs traditionally have engaged in practices that encourage voluntary subscription to the accreditation program. For example, accreditation programs often perform only announced site visits and keep negative evaluations confidential, at least until the accreditation itself is reduced or not renewed. Standards established by accreditation programs, which are often dominated by professionals in the industry rather than consumer groups, may differ from those set by a process that arguably fosters broader public participation. With the Joint Commission accrediting program for hospitals, in particular, governance and policymaking are dominated by physician organization members such as the AMA. The Joint Commission accreditation survey is explicitly consultative in nature. The Joint Commission, however, began performing some of its inspections on an unannounced basis in spring 2006.

The Joint Commission has had a tremendous influence on the operation of hospitals. The Joint Commission, for example, established the framework for staff privileges and credentialing in hospitals, as described in Chapter 9, and continues to be an important arena for change in those processes, including its recent focus on disruptive health care professionals and requirement of continuous review of outcomes for physicians with privileges. The Joint Commission's embrace of the patient safety movement, described in Chapter 1, certainly furthered diffusion of the movements principles into hospitals. The Joint Commission's "Sentinel Event" initiative, for example, encouraged facilities to report errors and root cause analyses for the benefit of systemic change in areas such as wrong–site surgery and medication errors and has spawned a number of refinements over the years. (See Chapters 1 and 6 for discussion of sentinel event policies.) In a survey identifying the most powerful influences on hospitals' adoption of patient safety initiatives, hospital administrators reported that the Joint Commission was the key factor and that their patient safety programs were linked specifically to its patient safety standards and goals. Kelly J. Devers et al., What is Driving Hospitals' Patient–Safety Efforts?, 23 Health Affairs 103 (2004). But see, Charles Andel et al., The Economics of Health Care Quality and Medical Errors, 39 J. Health Care Fin. 39 (2012), documenting that hospital adoption of patient safety and outcomes approaches to quality improvement has not met expectations.

For a history of the Joint Commission and a broad review of legal issues related to private accreditation, see Timothy S. Jost, The Joint Commission on Accreditation of Hospitals: Private Regulation of Health Care and the Public Interest, 24 B.C.L.Rev. 835 (1983). For a discussion of the relation between private accreditation and public regulation, see Jody Freeman, The Private Role in Public Governance, 75 N.Y.U. L.Rev. 543 (2000); Gillian Metzger, Privatization as Delegation, 103 Col. L. Rev. 1367 (2003), discussing claims of state action in relation to accreditation. More recently, scholars have begun to view private efforts, such as accreditation, and public regulatory efforts as a "new governance" framework for achieving a variety of goals in health care, including the goal of quality vigilance. See, e.g., Louise G. Trubek, New Governance and Soft Law in Health Care Reform, 3 Ind. Health L. Rev. 139 (2006). On delegation of governmental functions to private organizations generally but including the Joint Commission, see Harold Krent, The Private Performing the Public: Delimiting Delegations to Private Parties, 65 U. Miami L. Rev. 507 (2011).

CHAPTER 4

THE PROFESSIONAL–PATIENT RELATIONSHIP

■ ■ ■

I. INTRODUCTION

The focus of legal duties and ethical analysis begins with the individual physician, or other health care professional, who has primary responsibility for seeing the patient, diagnosing the problem, and prescribing the treatment. Health care today however is delivered in a variety of settings—hospitals, ambulatory care clinics, nursing homes, and doctors' offices. And the institutional framework for such care, in terms of its financing, support, and obligations, may encompass medical staffs, managed care organizations, partnerships, and institutional employers. It may also have an impact on legal obligations, especially as the duty of the physician to the patient may be extended to the organization (or not) and as organizational controls impact the capacity of the physician to meet his or her obligations to the patient.

This chapter considers the formation of the physician–patient relationship and a range of other obligations that the law imposes on physicians and other health care professionals. Professional liability, discussed in Chapter 5, focuses upon a breach of duty of care owed by the physician to a particular patient.

ESQUIVEL V. WATTERS

Court of Appeals of Kansas, 2007.
154 P.3d 1184.

Michelle and Jesse Esquivel, the parents of Jadon Esquivel, appeal the district court's entry of summary judgment in favor of Dr. Aaron T. Watters and the South Central Kansas Regional Medical Center (SCKRMC) in these survivor and wrongful death actions which arose from Jadon's death several weeks following his birth.

Upon learning she was pregnant, Michelle Esquivel obtained obstetric counseling from the Ark City Clinic. A clinic worker gave Michelle a certificate from SCKRMC for a free gender determination sonogram. Michelle went to SCKRMC for her free sonogram on November 15, 2001. Prior to the sonogram being performed, Michelle signed a document entitled "Consent to Procedure to Determine Sex of Unborn Baby." The consent form stated in relevant part:

> "2. The purpose of the procedure is to attempt to determine the sex of my unborn baby and I acknowledge there is no guarantee or assurance that an accurate determination can be made by this procedure.
>
> "I further acknowledge that this procedure is not to determine any fetal abnormality or any other complication of pregnancy and is not considered a diagnostic examination for any medical purpose other than to attempt to determine the sex of my unborn baby.
>
> "3. To induce Medical Center to perform this procedure the undersigned hereby waives and releases South Central Kansas Regional Medical Center, its officers, employees, agents, and affiliates from any and all claims, costs, liabilities, expenses, judgments, attorney fees, court costs, causes of action and compensation whatsoever arising out of the foregoing described procedure."

David Hazlett, an SCKRMC technician, performed the sonogram and noted that Michelle's baby's bowel was outside of his body, a condition known as gastroschisis. Hazlett did not inform Michelle of this irregularity because he is not a doctor and not qualified or licensed to make a medical diagnosis. Hazlett was unable to determine the baby's gender because of the gastroschisis. Nevertheless he took sonogram pictures which he sent to a radiologist at the Ark City Clinic. The radiologist refused to look at them because the sonogram was only for gender determination and not for diagnosis.

Hazlett also reported the irregularity to Watters, Michelle's obstetrician. Hazlett did not send any of the sonogram pictures to Watters. He sent no written report to Watters. Watters made no note of Hazlett's oral report in Michelle's medical chart. However, he directed his nurse to call Michelle. Watters' nurse made 11 attempts to contact Michelle by telephone over the next 10 days. On November 26, 2001, a man the nurse believed to be Jesse Esquivel answered the phone. The nurse told him to tell Michelle to call Watters' office. Michelle missed her prenatal appointment scheduled for that day. She next saw Watters on January 4, 2002. Since Watters had forgotten Hazlett's oral report of the abnormal sonogram and there was nothing in Michelle's chart to remind him, he failed to discuss it with her. When he saw Michelle again a month later, he again forgot to inform her of the abnormal sonogram.

On February 8, 2002, Michelle became ill and went to SCKRMC for treatment. Jadon was born by emergency caesarean section the next day.

Neither Michelle nor Jesse nor the medical staff who delivered Jadon was aware that Jadon had gastroschisis until he was born.

Jadon was transferred to Wesley Medical Center (WMC) in Wichita on the day he was born. Dr. Phillip J. Knight performed surgery on Jadon that day. His examination of Jadon disclosed that almost all of Jadon's bowel had been dead for weeks prior to his birth. Since there was no hope that Jadon could survive without his bowel, Jadon was sent home with his parents on February 20, 2002, and placed on palliative care. Jadon died at home on March 3, 2002.

Michelle and Jesse commenced this action against Watters, the Ark City Clinic, and SCKRMC. The district court granted summary judgment to the Ark City Clinic, whose radiologist refused to examine Michelle's sonogram. That ruling is not a subject of this appeal.

The district court granted summary judgment in favor of Watters based upon the failure of plaintiffs to present expert testimony that Watters deviated from the applicable standard of care and the lack of proximate cause between Watters' failure to notify Michelle of the abnormal sonogram and Jadon's postnatal suffering and death. The court also granted summary judgment in favor of SCKRMC based upon its conclusions that SCKRMC did not owe Michelle and Jesse the duty upon which they based their claims, and their claims were barred by the release signed by Michelle before the sonogram.

Michelle and Jesse appeal the district court's entry of summary judgment in favor of Watters and SCKRMC.

* * *

[The court's discussion of the standard of care is omitted.]

1. Duty

The district court found that SCKRMC's undertaking was limited to performing a sonogram to determine the gender of Michelle's baby, which it did in a non–negligent manner. Thus, the court reasoned, having performed the sonogram in a careful manner, SCKRMC had no further duty to Michelle and was not obligated to inform her about anything other than Jadon's gender.

Our analysis of this essential element of Michelle and Jesse's causes of action is a rather disheartening exercise. As a society we expect of ourselves a certain level of looking out for the welfare of others. This is an attribute which society encourages rather than discourages. We would expect this urge to be particularly strong in the hearts of those who choose to enter the medical and health care community. However, the transition from a societal expectation to a legal duty is often determined by public policy considerations which are not within the purview of an intermediate appellate court such as ours. Consequently, we turn to the case law for guidance.

Whether a legal duty exists is a question of law over which this court exercises de novo review. [ ] In the context of a medical negligence claim, the existence of a doctor–patient relationship is crucial to the recognition of a legal duty. * * *. We recognize the distinction between a doctor–patient relationship which is fiduciary in nature, [ ] and a hospital–patient relationship which is not [ ]. Nevertheless, the doctor–patient cases are instructive.

[The Court discussed Smith v. Welch and Doss v. Manfredi. The cases involved independent medical examinations conducted as part of personal injury actions. In neither case was a traditional doctor–patient relationship recognized by the courts. [ ] Absent such a duty, the physician is under no legal obligation to discover and disclose problems in the person under examination.]

* * *

In the case now before us, no patient–healthcare provider relationship existed between Michelle and SCKRMC. Webster's II New College Dictionary 1174 (2001), defines "treatment" as "medical application of remedies so as to effect a cure." SCKRMC did not undertake to advise Michelle regarding, or to treat Michelle for, any disease, illness, or medical condition. It undertook only to determine the gender of her baby. Thus, SCKRMC only owed Michelle the duty to perform the sonogram in a non–negligent manner, and no negligence in the performance of the sonogram is alleged. Summary judgment based upon the lack of a duty was appropriate.

[The court's discussion of the release and waiver in the consent form signed by the plaintiff is omitted.].

Affirmed.

NOTES AND QUESTIONS

1. Expert testimony in the case indicated that the standard of care would have required no different management of the pregnancy or the birth. In that case, what damage did the plaintiff suffer? How would you articulate her damage? How would early discovery of the condition have been beneficial to Michelle? Consider the time line of events—the free sonogram was performed on November 15, and the fetus was delivered by caesarean section on February 9, at 38 weeks, almost three months later.

Should the Ark City Clinic have been dismissed from the suit? Michelle went to the clinic for counseling, after all, and all their radiologist had to do was look at the sonogram to spot the problem with the fetus. And what is the relationship of the Clinic to the hospital? Is this free coupon part of a marketing strategy to bring patients to the hospital? If the coupon promises results, does this create a reliance interest in the coupon holder?

2. A physician–patient relationship is usually a prerequisite to a professional malpractice suit against a doctor, as the court in *Esquivel* observes. However, courts have disagreed about the nature of a duty to notify even in the absence of the physician–patient contract. One approach is found in Webb v. T.D., 287 Mont. 68, 951 P.2d 1008 (1997), where the court articulated a duty on physicians retained by third parties to do independent medical examinations:

> 1. to exercise ordinary care to discover those conditions which pose an imminent danger to the examinee's physical or mental well–being and take reasonable steps to communicate to the examinee the presence of any such condition;
>
> 2. to exercise ordinary care to assure that when he or she advises an examinee about her condition following an independent examination, the advice comports with the standard of care for the health care provider's profession.

3. The court in *Esquivel* is troubled by the failures of health care providers in the case. How should the law recognize a higher "fiduciary" duty on the part of health care providers to a person not yet a "contractual" patient, in a case such as this?

Once the physician–patient relationship is established, the law in fact imposes a higher level of duty on physicians. The language of fiduciary law is often used to describe special obligations that one person owes to another. Restatement (Third) of Agency, § 1.01 Agency defines agency as " * * * the fiduciary relationship that arises when one person (a "principal") manifests assent to another person (an "agent") that the agent shall act on the principal's behalf and subject to the principal's control, and the agent manifests assent or otherwise consents so to act."

Justice Cardozo has described the fiduciary obligation as follows: "Many forms of conduct permissible in a workaday world for those acting at arm's length, are forbidden to those bound by fiduciary ties. A trustee is held to something stricter than the morals of the market place. Not honesty alone, but the punctilio of an honor the most sensitive, is then the standard of behavior." Meinhard v. Salmon, 249 N.Y. 458, 164 N.E. 545, 546 (1928).

A fiduciary obligation in medicine means that the physician focuses exclusively on the patient's health; the patient assumes the doctor's single–minded devotion to him; and the doctor–patient relationship is expected to be free of conflict. One ethicist defines a health care fiduciary as "someone who commits to becoming and remaining scientifically and clinically competent, acts primarily to protect and promote the interests of the patient and keeps self–interest systematically secondary, and maintains and passes on medicine as a public trust for current and future physicians and patients." Laurence B. McCullough, A Primer on Bioethics (2nd Edition 2006). Is this a workable standard for physicians? Is this an appropriate standard? What about resource limitations, public health concerns about populations, and other patients. See generally Theodore W. Ruger, Can a Patient–Centered Ethics Be Other–Regarding? Should It Be? 45 Wake Forest L. Rev. 1013 (2010) (asking whether a patient–centered focus is a good model).

4. Trust has been proposed as a unifying theme in analyzing medical ethics, professionalism, and the doctor–patient relationship generally. In the words of Mark Hall, "[t]rust is the core, defining characteristic of the doctor–patient relationship—the 'glue' that holds the relationship together and makes it possible. Preserving, justifying, and enhancing trust is a prominent objective in health care law and public policy and is the fundamental goal of much of medical ethics." Mark Hall, Law, Medicine, and Trust, 55 Stan. L. Rev. 463, 470–71 (2002). For a contrary position, see M. Gregg Bloche, Trust and Betrayal in the Medical Marketplace, 55 Stan. L. Rev. 919 (2003).

Is trust a useful unifying principle in analyzing the variety of legal approaches to physicians and institutional providers generally? We don't completely trust our doctors. They are expensively well–trained, having given up close to a decade or more of their productive years in demanding medical study; they are professionals, socialized into high ethical standards; they are paid to look after the patients' best interests. Yet we don't trust them completely because of situational pressures that may at times corrupt or at least tempt them: doctors work for economic and other gains, as we all do; they are weak at times, prey to needs and pressures not aligned with those of their patients; and they are under tremendous pressures—from patients, insurers, their own needs, other doctors, drug companies. Conflicts of interest run through the physician–patient relationship. One function of legal rules is to manage or reduce these conflicts of interest.

II. THE CONTRACT BETWEEN PATIENT AND PHYSICIAN

WHITE V. HARRIS

Supreme Court of Vermont, 2011.
190 Vt. 647, 36 A.3d 203, 2011 Vt 115.

Present: REIBER, C.J., DOOLEY, JOHNSON and SKOGLUND, JJ.

ENTRY ORDER

Plaintiffs appeal from a superior court order granting summary judgment to defendant Fletcher Allen Health Care, Inc. in this wrongful death action alleging medical malpractice. This case arises from the suicide of plaintiffs' fourteen–year–old daughter. Plaintiffs sued defendant, which employed a psychiatrist who was briefly involved with decedent's case through a telepsychiatry research study. Plaintiffs argue that summary judgment was improperly granted on the issue of the duty owed to decedent by the psychiatrist. We agree, and thus reverse and remand for additional proceedings.

The record indicates the following. Decedent suffered from ongoing mental health problems. On the recommendation of her case manager, she consulted with defendant's psychiatrist through a telepsychiatry research study he was conducting. As part of the study, plaintiffs and decedent completed pre–assessment documentation, and they participated in a one–time, ninety–minute video–conference session with the psychiatrist in August 2006. Following the session, the participants completed a questionnaire about their reaction to using telemedicine. The psychiatrist later completed a consultation evaluation that described decedent and the history of her present illness; it also provided the doctor's diagnostic impression of decedent and set forth recommendations for an initial treatment plan. The evaluation specifically stated that, consistent with the telepsychiatry research protocol, no follow–up services would be provided, and no medication prescriptions would be directly provided by the doctor. The report further explained that the recommended treatment plan was to be weighed by decedent's treatment team, including her primary care physician, for possible implementation. After sending his evaluation, the psychiatrist had no further interaction with plaintiffs, decedent, or any member of her treatment team.

On June 10, 2007, decedent committed suicide. An autopsy report indicated that she died from the combined effects of ingesting Propoxyphene, opiates, and Citalopram. The psychiatrist had not prescribed or recommended any of these medications.

In June 2009, plaintiffs filed an amended complaint, alleging that defendant, among eight doctors and medical care providers, treated decedent in a manner that "fell below the standard of care required of reasonably skillful, careful, and prudent professionals," and that decedent died as a proximate result. Defendant moved for summary judgment in December 2009, asserting that its doctor had no duty to decedent when she committed suicide because there was no doctor–patient relationship. Alternatively, defendant argued that any such relationship was formally terminated in writing following their one–time interaction. Defendant acknowledged that if the trial court found that a duty existed, its motion would be premature. The trial court also recognized that the motion came at an early stage in the proceedings, but reasoned that if no duty existed, then no additional discovery to show a breach of that duty would be necessary. Ultimately, the trial court agreed that the psychiatrist's contact with decedent was "so minimal as to not establish a physician–patient relationship," and consequently found that no duty existed at the time of decedent's death. Even assuming that a doctor–patient relationship was established, the court concluded that it was terminated following the video–conference and, thus, any duty was extinguished by termination of the relationship and no duty existed at the time of decedent's death. The court thus granted defendant's summary judgment motion. This appeal followed.

Plaintiffs argue that the court erred in finding that the doctor owed no duty to decedent. They maintain that the doctor had a duty to exercise reasonable care to protect decedent from the danger she posed to herself, and that the doctor did not effectively terminate the doctor–patient relationship prior to decedent's death.

* * *

We agree that a duty applies to the service provided. The doctor had a duty of due care in his professional contact with decedent, which was not extinguished by the ministerial act of termination of their professional relationship. [ ] We have defined duty as "an expression of the sum total of those considerations of policy which lead the law to say that the plaintiff is entitled to protection." [ ] In assessing whether a duty exists, "[t]he question is whether the relationship of the parties was such that the defendant was under an obligation to use some care to avoid or prevent injury to the plaintiff." In their analysis of circumstances similar to those here, other courts have considered these factors:

> whether the doctor was in a unique position to prevent harm, the burden of preventing harm, whether the plaintiff relied upon the doctor's diagnosis or interpretation, the closeness of the connection between the defendant's conduct and the injury suffered, the degree of certainty that the plaintiff has or will suffer harm, the skill or special reputation of the actors, and public policy. [ ].

The facts here disclose a consultation of limited duration. Decedent and her mother signed an informed consent form, and the doctor stated in writing that the scope of his services was limited. At the same time, however, there is no dispute that the doctor performed a psychiatric evaluation of decedent, following which the doctor offered recommendations for decedent's treatment. And the record reveals the parties' expectation that the doctor would aid in decedent's treatment through his expertise, regardless of the mechanism of doctor–patient contact. In requesting a consultation with the doctor, decedent's treatment team specifically sought recommendations about decedent's medication, particularly given the increase in decedent's angry and aggressive behavior and self–mutilation. They also sought the doctor's diagnostic impression and recommendations about the role that Attention–Deficit Hyperactivity Disorder might play in decedent's behavior. While decedent's medical records may not have been provided to the doctor, the doctor was provided with a very recent medical evaluation of decedent performed by another doctor, which was supplemented by additional information about decedent from decedent's treatment team. This included information that decedent had a history of depressive behavior and had recently exhibited an increase in angry, aggressive behavior, along with more frequent cutting behavior. All of this information bears on the scope of the professional relationship from which defendant's duty arose and it helps to frame the applicable standard of care. We find it sufficient to support the existence of a duty here.

A professional consultation may arise in many different circumstances. Defendant's involvement here was limited, but that does not mean it was nonexistent. It may be analogized to cases in which a doctor is asked to perform an *independent medical examination* (IME) [italics supplied] of a patient as part of a legal investigation or an insurance claim. As in the current case, an IME doctor usually does not see a patient again or maintain an ongoing relationship with the patient; rather he or she performs a limited analysis of the patient's condition that is provided to a third party. [ ] Many courts addressing IME cases have concluded that an IME creates a doctor–patient relationship that "imposes fewer duties on the examining physician than does a traditional physician–patient relationship," but "still requires that the examiner conduct the examination in such a way as not to cause harm." [ ]

Here, the relationship between doctor and patient was even more direct than a third–party–retained IME doctor. The defendant became involved on referral from decedent's treatment team and reported to them his findings and recommendations after evaluation. We hold that the ninety–minute consultation performed in this case created a doctor–patient relationship. We acknowledge that the telepsychiatry research study conducted by the doctor provided no treatment component directly to decedent, other than recommendations to her treatment team. However, through this consultation, a limited doctor–patient relationship was established, and we conclude that a duty of due care applies. Through this consultation, defendant's doctor assumed a duty to act in a manner consistent with the applicable standard of care so as not to harm decedent through the consultation services provided.

Defendant argues that submission of the psychiatrist's consultation evaluation to decedent's treatment team terminated any doctor–patient relationship that ever existed, and defendant equates the ending of this relationship with the termination of any "further duty to the patient."[2]

[2] Defendant contends that plaintiffs failed to properly preserve their arguments pertaining to termination of the doctor-patient relationship, claiming that "[p]laintiffs here did not . . . argue that the doctor-patient relationship—if any ever existed—between [defendant] and [decedent] was not terminated in exactly the manner [defendant] contended it was." To some extent, defendant appears to conflate the issue of whether a doctor-patient relationship existed with whether defendant had a continuing responsibility for the quality of care provided to decedent. We agree that defendant had no ongoing duty to provide care for decedent after the psychiatrist's consultation ended. This does not affect, however, whether defendant can be held liable for any alleged breach of the psychiatrist's duty to meet the required standard of care during the course of the telepsychiatry research study. While plaintiffs may not have specifically addressed defendant's argument about the termination clause in the psychiatrist's consultation evaluation, whether or not the doctor-patient relationship was terminated is not dispositive.

We hold, however, that even if doctor–patient contact had ended, this does not terminate the doctor's responsibility for the consequences of any lapses in his duty to provide services consistent with the applicable standard of care for the consultation. Under 12 V.S.A. § 1908(1), a doctor must exercise "the degree of care ordinarily exercised by a reasonably skillful, careful, and prudent health care professional engaged in a similar practice under the same or similar circumstances." A doctor may be liable for malpractice if "as a proximate result of . . . the failure to exercise this degree of care the plaintiff suffered injuries that would not otherwise have been incurred." [ ]. Under this statute, whether or not a doctor has ceased treating a patient is irrelevant to whether he or she may be held liable for injuries resulting from his or her failure to exercise the proper degree of care *while treating* the patient. It is the doctor's responsibility for the services provided that is significant here, and not simply the duration of the doctor–patient relationship itself.

On these facts, however, the scope of defendant's duty and the standard of care cannot yet be determined. In evaluating the standard of care, we must not conflate the existence of a duty with the appropriate standard of care, an issue that takes us beyond the limited facts in the record before us and was not properly raised below. [ ] Prosser explains that in negligence cases, the duty is always the same–to conform to the legal standard of reasonable conduct in light of the apparent risk. What the defendant must do, or must not do, is a question of the standard of conduct required to satisfy the duty." [ ]

As the *McCarver* court observed, "[t]he standard of care imposes on those with special skills or training . . . the higher obligation to act in light of that skill, training, or knowledge." [ ] Thus, in *McCarver,* the court found that the doctor in question had "assumed a duty to conform to the legal standard of care for one with his skill, training, and knowledge," but concluded that the question of "what is necessary to satisfy the standard will depend upon the facts of each case." *Id.* We do not yet know plaintiffs' position on the standard of care in this case, i.e., what a "reasonably skillful, careful, and prudent health care professional" would have done under similar circumstances, or how any alleged breach of this standard was the proximate cause of harm to decedent. [ ].

The issue of standard of care was not raised by defendant in its motion for summary judgment, nor decided by the trial court. It is not the role of this Court to set that standard or to evaluate whether it was breached at this stage of the proceedings. Expert testimony is required. [ ]

This is a lawsuit in its formative stages. The motion for summary judgment was filed six months after the complaint was filed and raised the sole question of the duty of care of this consulting doctor. The remaining elements of plaintiffs' claim have not yet been fully developed, and defendant did not move for summary judgment on these elements. [ ],

Given our conclusion that a duty exists, we reverse and remand for additional proceedings.

Reversed and remanded.

NOTES AND QUESTIONS

1. When a physician treating a patient consults by telephone or otherwise with another physician, some courts are reluctant to find a doctor–patient relationship created by such a conversation. The concern is that such informal conferences will be deterred by the fear of liability. See Reynolds v. Decatur Memorial Hosp., 277 Ill.App.3d 80, 214 Ill.Dec. 44, 49, 660 N.E.2d 235, 240 (1996) ("It would have a chilling effect upon practice of medicine. It would stifle communication, education and professional association, all to the detriment of the patient.") Others find a duty in such a consultation. See e.g. Diggs v. Arizona Cardiologists, Ltd., 198 Ariz. 198, 8 P.3d 386 (2000), where just being the on–call physician is not sufficient in many states to create the physician–patient relationship.

By contrast, *White* involves telepsychiatry and a real therapeutic encounter, with patient expectations. Web based psychiatry in particular has been expanding. See Lucas Mearian, Web–Based Counseling—Telepsychiatry—Is Taking Off, Computerworld, February 9, 2012. ("In many instances, telepsychiatry is a necessity, not just a convenience for doctors and patients. Patients are often located in regions with no private psychiatric practices or where hospitals don't employ staff psychiatrists.")

The relationship in *White* had ended, but the court noted that there was the possibility of ". . . lapses in his duty to provide services consistent with the applicable standard of care for the consultation." What does the court mean by this?

2. The physician–patient relationship can be considered initially as a contractual one. Physicians in private practice may contract for their services as they see fit, and retain substantial control over the extent of their contact with patients. Physicians may limit their specialty, their scope of practice, their geographic area, and the hours and conditions under which they will see patients. They have no obligation to offer services that a patient may require that are outside their competence and training; or services outside the scope of the original physician–patient agreement, in which the physician has limited the contract to a type of procedure, to an office visit, or to consultation only. They may transfer responsibility by referring patients to other specialists. They may refuse to enter into a contract with a patient, or to treat patients, even under emergency conditions. See discussion in Chapter 7. When a patient goes to a doctor's office with a particular problem, he is offering to enter into a contract with the physician. When the physician engages with the patient, for example through a conversation, an examination, or perhaps through the physician's staff, she accepts the offer and an implied contract is created. The physician is free to reject the offer and send the patient away, relieving herself of any duty to that patient.

Once the physician–patient relationship has been created, physicians are subject to an obligation of "continuing attention." See Ricks v. Budge, in Chapter 7. Refusal to continue to treat a patient is abandonment, and it also may be malpractice. See, e.g., Tierney v. University of Michigan Regents, 257 Mich.App. 681, 669 N.W.2d 575 (2003) (treating gynecologist withdrew from treating plaintiff after she filed suit against another member of the medical group). Termination of the physician–patient relationship, once created, is subject in some jurisdictions to a "continuous treatment" rule to determine when the statute of limitations is tolled. Treatment obligations cease if the physician can do nothing more for the patient. See Jewson v. Mayo Clinic, 691 F.2d 405 (8th Cir.1982).

An express written contract is rarely drafted for specific physician–patient interactions. An implied contract is usually the basis of the relationship between a physician and a patient. A physician who talks with a patient by telephone may be held to have an implied contractual obligation to that patient. Bienz v. Central Suffolk Hospital, 163 A.D.2d 269, 557 N.Y.S.2d 139 (1990). Likewise, a physician, such as a pathologist, who renders services to a patient but has not contracted with him, is nonetheless bound by certain implied contractual obligations. When the physician evaluates information provided by a nurse and makes a medical decision as to a patient's status, a doctor–patient relationship may be established. Wheeler v. Yettie Kersting Memorial Hospital, 866 S.W.2d 32 (Tex.App.1993). Merely scheduling an appointment is not by itself sufficient to create a relationship. Jackson v. Isaac, 76 S.W.3d 177 (Tex.App. 2002).

There was a written agreement in *White* in the form of the written consent that laid out limits on what the defendant physician was undertaking. Why didn't the court enforce that agreement? Is the question really a procedural one; i.e., this is a summary judgment motion, not a full examination of the facts? Or, should the courts not enforce limited agreements?

3. The apparent voluntariness of the physician–patient relationship and its reciprocity, i.e., a fee for a service, or consideration, make the relationship look like a traditional contract. In other ways, however, the analogy to a contract is limited. First, the terms of the contract are largely fixed in advance of any bargaining, by standard or customary practices that the physician must follow at the risk of liability for malpractice. The exact nature of the work to be done by the physician is usually vaguely defined at best. The relationship seems closer to quasi–contract, where we impute to both the physician and the patient standard intentions and reasonable expectations. See Robert Goodin, Protecting the Vulnerable 63, 64–65 (1985).

Courts also often look outside the parameters of contract law analysis in judging the obligations of a physician to treat a patient. The courts stress that the physician's obligation to his patient, while having its origins in contract, is governed also by fiduciary obligations and other public considerations "inseparable from the nature and exercise of his calling * * *." Norton v. Hamilton, 92 Ga.App. 727, 89 S.E.2d 809, 812 (1955). See Section III, below.

Third, professionals are constrained in their ability to withdraw from their contracts by caselaw defining patient abandonment. A doctor who withdraws from the physician–patient relationship before a cure is achieved or the patient is transferred to the care of another may be liable for abandonment. To escape liability, the physician must give the patient time to find alternative care. See Cole v. Marshall Medical Center, 2007 WL 1576391 (Cal.App. 3 Dist. 2007).

A. PHYSICIAN CONTRACTS WITH THIRD PARTIES

Most physicians are part of managed care networks and therefore have a contractual relationship with the plan that requires them to treat subscribers. In Hand v. Tavera, 864 S.W.2d 678 (Ct.App. Texas 1993), the plaintiff went to the emergency room complaining of a headache. Dr. Tavera was the doctor responsible for authorizing admissions, and he sent Hand home and said he should be treated as an outpatient. Hand had a stroke. Dr. Tavera defended on the grounds that no physician–patient relationship existed.

The court disagreed, concluding that "[t]he contract between Humana and Southwest Medical Group (which employed Tavera) obligated its doctors to treat Humana enrollees as they would treat their other patients:"

The contract specified as follows:

> PHYSICIAN agrees to provide or arrange for covered health care services for ENROLLEES in accordance with Attachment B. [Attachment B specifies various physician responsibilities, including "emergency care of a covered ENROLLEE who has been assigned to PHYSICIAN."]
>
> * * *
>
> PHYSICIAN agrees to provide ENROLLEES with medical services which are within the normal scope of PHYSICIAN's medical practice. These services shall be made available to ENROLLEES without discrimination and in the same manner as provided to PHYSICIAN's other patients. PHYSICIAN agrees to provide medical services to ENROLLEES in accordance with the prevailing practices and standards of the profession and community.

The court concluded that the contract created a doctor–patient relationship:

> Hand paid premiums to Humana to purchase medical care in advance of need; Humana met its obligation to Hand and its other enrollees by employing Tavera's group to treat them; and Tavera's medical group agreed to treat Humana enrollees in ex-

change for the fees received from Humana. In effect, Hand had paid in advance for the services of the Humana plan doctor on duty that night, who happened to be Tavera, and the physician–patient relationship existed. We hold that when the health–care plan's insured shows up at a participating hospital emergency room, and the plan's doctor on call is consulted about treatment or admission, there is a physician–patient relationship between the doctor and the insured.

NOTES AND QUESTIONS

1. Physicians who practice in organizations must provide health care within the limits of the health plan coverage or their employment contracts with the institution. In such a case, the contact between the physician and the patient is preceded by an express contract spelling out the details of the relationship. Physicians who are members of a hospital's medical staff have duties created by medical staff privilege by–laws; physicians who are part of health maintenance organizations have a duty to treat plan members as a result of their contractual obligation to the HMO. In these situations, the express contract is between the physician and the health plan, and the subscriber and the plan, with an implied contract between the subscriber and the treating physician.

2. A physician who has staff privileges at a hospital also agrees to abide by hospital by–laws and policies, including requirements that certain physicians be on–call as needed. According to most courts that have considered the issue, the physician's agreement with the hospital extends to the patient. Physicians on call to treat emergency patients are under a duty to treat patients. See discussion of common law duties of on–call physicians in Section II of Chapter 7 and statutory obligations under EMTALA in Section III.A. of the same chapter.

B. SPECIFIC CONTRACT PROMISES

KAPLAN V. MAYO CLINIC

8th Circuit, 2011.
653 F.3d 720.

ARNOLD, CIRCUIT JUDGE.

Elliot and Jeanne Kaplan, husband and wife, filed suit against Mayo Clinic Rochester, Inc., other Mayo entities (referred to collectively as Mayo), and Mayo doctors David Nagorney and Lawrence Burgart, making a number of claims arising out of Mr. Kaplan's erroneous diagnosis of pancreatic cancer and his surgery based on that diagnosis. The district court granted summary judgment in favor of Dr. Nagorney, and the case proceeded to trial against the other defendants on claims of breach of contract and negligent failure to diagnose. At the close of the Kaplans' case–

in–chief, the district court granted judgment as a matter of law (JAML) against them on their breach–of–contract claim. The jury then returned a verdict for Mayo and Dr. Burgart on the plaintiffs' claim for negligent failure to diagnose, and the district court entered judgment on that verdict.

The Kaplans appeal the judgments in favor of Mayo and Dr. Burgart on their negligent–failure–to–diagnose and contract claims. We affirm the judgment on the claim for negligent failure to diagnose and the judgment in favor of Dr. Burgart on the contract claim, but we vacate the judgment in favor of Mayo on the contract claim and remand for further proceedings.

I.

After Mr. Kaplan complained of severe abdominal pain, he was taken from his home to a nearby hospital in a suburb of Kansas City, Missouri. Dr. John Dunlap, his long–time family physician, ordered a CT scan, which showed that Mr. Kaplan's pancreas was enlarged and that a "mass could not be excluded." (The pancreas is a large organ behind the stomach and close to the beginning of the small intestine.) Based on a needle biopsy that the hospital performed at Dr. Dunlap's request, a pathologist at the hospital prepared a report stating, "Ductal carcinoma is favored as being the changes noted in the ducts. There was agreement with two other members of the department." Dr. Dunlap told the Kaplans about the report and referred Mr. Kaplan to Mayo and, specifically, to Dr. Nagorney, a Mayo surgeon. Dr. Dunlap also wrote to Dr. Nagorney, asking him to "evaluate" Mr. Kaplan for "probable ductal carcinoma of the head of the pancreas and for consideration of resective surgery." When Mr. Kaplan called to ask Dr. Nagorney to treat him, he told the doctor that he had "concerns" about the cancer diagnosis and that his father, who was the chief of cardiology at a Los Angeles hospital, had described the diagnosis as "pretty weak."

Dr. Nagorney agreed to treat Mr. Kaplan and asked him for the hospital records and the biopsy slides that the pathologists had examined. After the hospital removed tissue by inserting a needle into Mr. Kaplan's pancreas, the tissue was embedded in paraffin wax that was formed into a block; the hospital then used thin slices of the block to make the slides that the pathologist examined. After the slides arrived at Mayo, Dr. Burgart reviewed them and provided a written "diagnosis": "Pancreas, head, needle biopsy. Infiltrating grade 2 (of four) adenocarcinoma." In accordance with Dr. Burgart's custom, he had another Mayo pathologist, Dr. Thomas Smyrk, review the slides without knowing Dr. Burgart's diagnosis; Dr. Smyrk also diagnosed pancreatic cancer.

Dr. Nagorney reviewed Dr. Burgart's report before the Kaplans arrived at Mayo. When the Kaplans came to his office, Dr. Nagorney immediately told them that Mr. Kaplan had pancreatic cancer, that it was deadly and aggressive, and that he (Dr. Nagorney) could do surgery the next morning. He recommended the so–called "Whipple procedure," which entails removing part of the pancreas and stomach, as well as the duodenum; he performed the procedure on Mr. Kaplan three days later. But after Dr. Burgart and other Mayo pathologists examined the excised pancreatic tissue, they concluded that Mr. Kaplan had never had cancer at all. The pathology report stated that the tissue had features of pancreatitis. The Kaplans first brought suit in Missouri state court against the Kansas City medical care providers, as well as the defendants in this case. After the state court dismissed the Mayo defendants for lack of personal jurisdiction, the Kaplans brought the present action.

[At trial, the parties presented conflicting expert testimony as to whether the biopsy slides that Dr. Burgart relied on supported his diagnosis of pancreatic cancer; on the harms suffered by Mr. Kaplan caused by the Whipple procedure; and as to whether Dr. Nagorney had promised the plaintiffs that he would do an intraoperative biopsy to determine whether Mr. Kaplan had cancer and abandon the procedure if the biopsy showed that he did not.]

* * *

II.

[The Court rejected Kaplans' evidentiary claims—that photographs and documents referring to insurance were improperly admitted into evidence and that the omission of an expert's name from jury instructions was plain error.]

III.

The Kaplans also maintain that the district court erred in granting JAML to Mayo and Dr. Burgart on their contract claim. We review the grant of JAML *de novo* and will affirm only if "no reasonable jury" could have found in favor of the nonmoving party. [ ]

To make out a claim for breach of contract, the plaintiffs had to show the formation of the contract, the defendants' breach, and resulting damages.[ ] The district court concluded that the Kaplans' claim merely restated a medical negligence claim as a breach of contract, and held that the Kaplans therefore required expert testimony to show that Dr. Nagorney failed to meet the appropriate standard of care by not performing an intraoperative biopsy and that this failure caused Mr. Kaplan to undergo the Whipple surgery. [ ] We disagree.

In their amended complaint, the Kaplans alleged that after Mr. Kaplan told Dr. Nagorney that he was concerned about the accuracy of the cancer diagnosis, Dr. Nagorney, individually and on behalf of Mayo, made a "definitive agreement" with Mr. Kaplan that Dr. Nagorney and his Mayo colleagues "would insure that Mayo's pathology diagnosis would be exhaustive and precise," and that, as consideration, Mr. Kaplan authorized Dr. Nagorney and his colleagues to perform the Whipple procedure and paid them for that surgery. The plaintiffs further alleged that Dr. Nagorney breached the agreement by failing to tell his colleagues about Mr. Kaplan's concerns, failing to "insist that Mayo perform its own biopsy, or create it's [sic] own slides" from the tissue removed during the needle biopsy, and failing to "take any of the other steps that Mr. Kaplan was told that Dr. Nagorney and Mayo would take to insure that the diagnosis of his condition was correct."

* * *

We view the evidence in a light favorable to the Kaplans, as the context requires. When the Kaplans arrived at Mayo, Dr. Nagorney immediately told them that Mr. Kaplan had cancer. Mr. Kaplan responded by asking the doctor whether he was sure of the diagnosis. Dr. Nagorney said that he had no doubt that Mr. Kaplan had cancer because a Mayo pathologist, who was one of the best in the world, if not the best, had unequivocally diagnosed him with it. After Dr. Nagorney explained the Whipple procedure to the Kaplans, Mr. Kaplan asked him if they could verify that he had cancer after they opened him up for surgery. Dr. Nagorney said that they would do a biopsy of the "mass . . . to verify that it's cancer," and that "if they didn't find cancer, they'd just close [Mr. Kaplan] up and send [him] home." Dr. Nagorney outlined three possibilities to the Kaplans: In the third one, if the biopsy they performed showed no cancer, they would close him up. But Dr. Nagorney did not perform an intraoperative biopsy of Mr. Kaplan's pancreatic tissue to verify that he had cancer.

It is true that Dr. Nagorney testified that he had not promised to do such a biopsy. He testified that, "unfortunately," there was no intraoperative (or preoperative) procedure that could have confirmed Dr. Burgart's cancer diagnosis and that the only way to find out that Mr. Kaplan did not actually have cancer was to "proceed with the operation" (apparently the Whipple procedure). But this testimony merely raises factual questions for the jury as to whether there was an agreement. Dr. Nagorney acknowledged, moreover, that he had performed intraoperative biopsies of the pancreas in the past to determine whether to proceed with a Whipple surgery and that other surgeons still followed that protocol. This evidence lends some credibility to the testimony that Dr. Nagorney promised to do the procedure in this case (perhaps to ease Mr. Kaplan's ongoing concerns about the accuracy of the diagnosis).

Dr. Nagorney's testimony also shows that it was commonplace for him to perform intraoperative biopsies during pancreatic cancer surgery. When he saw something "suspicious," he would send a piece of the tissue to the pathologist, who would report the result over a loudspeaker within ten minutes. In Mr. Kaplan's case, Dr. Nagorney had three pieces of tissue checked for cancer before doing the Whipple procedure. If the pathologist had found that cancer had spread to any of these areas, Dr. Nagorney said he would have stopped the operation. As he always did before closing, Dr. Nagorney had the pathologist examine the tissue removed during Mr. Kaplan's Whipple procedure for so–called "clean margins," *i.e.*, healthy tissue surrounding the excised cancer. Clean margins indicate that the surgeon has removed all the cancer, and, if the margins were not clean, Dr. Nagorney would remove additional tissue. Though he did not perform the promised biopsy, he repeatedly had the pathologist check for cancer during Mr. Kaplan's surgery.

The testimony of the Kaplans and Dr. Nagorney was quite evidently more than sufficient to support a finding of the formation of a contract, and the breach is undisputed. To prove damages, the plaintiffs would first have had to offer evidence to support a finding that the intraoperative biopsy results would have been negative for cancer. We think that they did that: It's undisputed that Mr. Kaplan did not have cancer, and the defendants presented evidence that, although a biopsy sometimes appears to show cancer where there is none, that occurs rarely. In addition, the intraoperative biopsy of pancreatic tissue removed during the Whipple showed no cancer. We therefore believe that a jury could reasonably find that, had Dr. Nagorney done the promised procedure, it would have shown that Mr. Kaplan did not have cancer.

[The court found that Dr. Nagorney would not have performed the Whipple procedure if the promised biopsy was negative. The plaintiffs testified that he told them he would not proceed with the Whipple procedure if he could not verify the cancer diagnosis through the intraopoerative biopsy.]

* * * [T]he evidence would support a finding that Dr. Nagorney would not have done the Whipple procedure in the face of an intraoperative biopsy that showed no cancer. Dr. Nagorney admitted at trial that Mr. Kaplan did not need the Whipple procedure, and we believe that the plaintiffs provided sufficient evidence of economic damages resulting from that procedure—though the amount was greatly disputed—to meet the final requirement for making out their contract claim.

[The Court noted that under Minnesota law, "expert testimony is not necessary to establish matters that lie within the general knowledge of lay people."[ ]] No such testimony is necessary in this perfectly ordinary, garden–variety contract claim. The claim is straightforward and does not depend, for instance, on a showing that the defendants violated a standard of care that Minnesota doctors are required to adhere to. Here, the plaintiffs' claim is simply that a physician promised to perform a certain procedure and did not do it, resulting in damages to them. The plaintiffs therefore offered sufficient evidence in their case–in–chief to support a breach–of–contract claim against Mayo without offering the testimony of an expert.

VI.

We reverse the grant of JAML to Mayo on the Kaplans' claim for breach of contract and remand for further proceedings. We affirm the judgment in favor of Dr. Burgart on the contract claim and the judgment for Mayo and Dr. Burgart on the Kaplans' claim for negligent failure to diagnose.

NOTES AND QUESTIONS

1. What is the scope of the contract? Was it simply that Mayo's pathology diagnosis would be "exhaustive and precise"? Is this a specific enough term to create a contract promise?

2. A contract claim may have several advantages for the plaintiff. The statute of limitations is typically longer than for a tort action. The plaintiff need not establish the medical standard of care and thus may not need to present expert testimony. A contract claim may be viable even when the doctor has made the proper risk disclosure, satisfying the requirements of the tort doctrine of informed consent. Finally, a contract claim offers a remedy to the plaintiff who underwent the procedure because of the enticements of the physician, including economic damages for the contract breach.

3. Physicians may expressly contract with a patient for a specific result on rare occasions. Stewart v. Rudner, 349 Mich. 459, 84 N.W.2d 816, 822–23 (1957) (couple contracted with physician to have wife's child delivered by Caesarian section, as she had had two stillbirths and was worried about normal vaginal delivery; the court held that "a doctor and his patient * * * have the same general liberty to contract with respect to their relationship as other parties entering into consensual relationship with one another, and a breach thereof will give rise to a cause of action."). Courts will sometimes allow parol evidence to fill in the terms of these contracts, where the patient has signed other consent forms. Murray v. University of Penn. Hospital, 340 Pa.Super. 401, 490 A.2d 839 (1985) (court allowed parol evidence to show the existence of an oral agreement to guarantee the prevention of future pregnancies by a tubal ligation).

4. An actionable breach of an express warranty may be found where the doctor promises a particular result which fails to occur. See Mills v. Pate, 225 S.W.3d 277 (Court of Appeals of Texas—El Paso, 2006). The plaintiff Ms. Mills wanted to have liposuction. She consulted with Dr. Pate, and told him she wanted to "remove the fat bulges she had on her abdomen, hips, and thighs." He said that the little bulges and sags in her skin would be removed by the liposuction process. Dr. Pate told her she was going to be beautiful after having liposuction, which to her meant smooth skin and no "pooches." The procedure did not go well, and she had bagging on her left thigh, rippling and

a bulge on her left abdomen, a bulge on her right thigh, and her hips were "disproportionate". She sued for a breach of express warranty claim, among other counts. The court held that "there is some evidence that Dr. Pate's particular representations were actionable as an express warranty claim in that his representations did not conform to the character and quality of the services promised, they formed the basis of the parties' bargain for the first surgery, and injury resulted to Ms. Mills." The court noted that the defendant could raise a Statute of Frauds defense as an affirmative defense, but this was not an element of Ms. Pate's case. The Statute of Frauds specifically requires that for agreements guaranteeing therapeutic results to be enforceable, they must be in writing and signed. See, e.g., West's Ann.Ind.Code 16–915–1–4.

C. EXCULPATORY CLAUSES

TUNKL V. REGENTS OF UNIV. OF CALIFORNIA

Supreme Court of California, 1963.
60 Cal.2d 92, 32 Cal.Rptr. 33, 383 P.2d 441.

TOBRINER, JUSTICE.

This case concerns the validity of a release from liability for future negligence imposed as a condition for admission to a charitable research hospital. For the reasons we hereinafter specify, we have concluded that an agreement between a hospital and an entering patient affects the public interest and that, in consequence, the exculpatory provision included within it must be invalid under Civil Code section 1668.

Hugo Tunkl brought this action to recover damages for personal injuries alleged to have resulted from the negligence of two physicians in the employ of the University of California Los Angeles Medical Center, a hospital operated and maintained by the Regents of the University of California as a nonprofit charitable institution. Mr. Tunkl died after suit was brought, and his surviving wife, as executrix, was substituted as plaintiff.

The University of California at Los Angeles Medical Center admitted Tunkl as a patient on June 11, 1956. The Regents maintain the hospital for the primary purpose of aiding and developing a program of research and education in the field of medicine; patients are selected and admitted if the study and treatment of their condition would tend to achieve these purposes. Upon his entry to the hospital, Tunkl signed a document setting forth certain "Conditions of Admission." The crucial condition number six reads as follows: "RELEASE: The hospital is a nonprofit, charitable institution. In consideration of the hospital and allied services to be rendered and the rates charged therefor, the patient or his legal representative agrees to and hereby releases The Regents of the University of California, and the hospital from any and all liability for the negligent or wrongful acts or omissions of its employees, if the hospital has used due care in selecting its employees."

Plaintiff stipulated that the hospital had selected its employees with due care. The trial court ordered that the issue of the validity of the exculpatory clause be first submitted to the jury and that, if the jury found that the provision did not bind plaintiff, a second jury try the issue of alleged malpractice. When, on the preliminary issue, the jury returned a verdict sustaining the validity of the executed release, the court entered judgment in favor of the Regents.[1] Plaintiff appeals from the judgment.

We shall first set out the basis for our prime ruling that the exculpatory provision of the hospital's contract fell under the proscription of Civil Code section 1668; we then dispose of two answering arguments of defendant.

We begin with the dictate of the relevant Civil Code section 1668. The section states: "All contracts which have for their object, directly or indirectly, to exempt anyone from responsibility for his own fraud, or willful injury to the person or property of another, or violation of law, whether willful or negligent, are against the policy of the law."

* * *

In one respect, as we have said, the decisions are uniform. The cases have consistently held that the exculpatory provision may stand only if it does not involve "the public interest."

what is public interest?

* * *

If, then, the exculpatory clause which affects the public interest cannot stand, we must ascertain those factors or characteristics which constitute the public interest. * * *

* * * It concerns a business of a type generally thought suitable for public regulation. The party seeking exculpation is engaged in performing a service of great importance to the public, which is often a matter of practical necessity for some members of the public. The party holds himself out as willing to perform this service for any member of the public who seeks it, or at least for any member coming within certain established standards. As a result of the essential nature of the service, in the economic setting of the transaction, the party invoking exculpation possesses a decisive advantage of bargaining strength against any member of the public who seeks his services. In exercising a superior bargaining power the party confronts the public with a standardized adhesion contract of exculpation, and makes no provision whereby a purchaser may

1 Plaintiff at the time of signing the release was in great pain, under sedation, and probably unable to read. At trial plaintiff contended that the release was invalid, asserting that a release does not bind the releasor if at the time of its execution he suffered from so weak a mental condition that he was unable to comprehend the effect of his act. [ ]

pay additional reasonable fees and obtain protection against negligence. Finally, as a result of the transaction, the person or property of the purchaser is placed under the control of the seller, subject to the risk of carelessness by the seller or his agents.

* * *

In the light of the decisions, we think that the hospital–patient contract clearly falls within the category of agreements affecting the public interest. To meet that test, the agreement need only fulfill some of the characteristics above outlined; here, the relationship fulfills all of them. Thus the contract of exculpation involves an institution suitable for, and a subject of, public regulation. [ ] That the services of the hospital to those members of the public who are in special need of the particular skill of its staff and facilities constitute a practical and crucial necessity is hardly open to question.

The hospital, likewise, holds itself out as willing to perform its services for those members of the public who qualify for its research and training facilities. While it is true that the hospital is selective as to the patients it will accept, such selectivity does not negate its public aspect or the public interest in it. The hospital is selective only in the sense that it accepts from the public at large certain types of cases which qualify for the research and training in which it specializes. But the hospital does hold itself out to the public as an institution which performs such services for those members of the public who can qualify for them.

In insisting that the patient accept the provision of waiver in the contract, the hospital certainly exercises a decisive advantage in bargaining. The would–be patient is in no position to reject the proffered agreement, to bargain with the hospital, or in lieu of agreement to find another hospital. The admission room of a hospital contains no bargaining table where, as in a private business transaction, the parties can debate the terms of their contract. As a result, we cannot but conclude that the instant agreement manifested the characteristics of the so–called adhesion contract. Finally, when the patient signed the contract, he completely placed himself in the control of the hospital; he subjected himself to the risk of its carelessness.

* * *

We turn to a consideration of the * * * arguments urged by defendant to save the exemptive clause. Defendant contends that while the public interest may possibly invalidate the exculpatory provision as to the paying patient, it certainly cannot do so as to the charitable one. * * *

* * *

In substance defendant here asks us to modify our decision in *Malloy*, which removed the charitable immunity; defendant urges that otherwise the funds of the research hospital may be deflected from the real objective of the extension of medical knowledge to the payment of claims for alleged negligence. Since a research hospital necessarily entails surgery and treatment in which fixed standards of care may not yet be evolved, defendant says the hospital should in this situation be excused from such care. But the answer lies in the fact that possible plaintiffs must *prove negligence;* the standards of care will themselves reflect the research nature of the treatment; the hospital will not become an insurer or guarantor of the patient's recovery. To exempt the hospital completely from any standard of due care is to grant it immunity by the side–door method of a contractual clause exacted of the patient. We cannot reconcile that technique with the teaching of *Malloy.*

* * *

The judgment is reversed.

NOTES AND QUESTIONS

1. Written waivers of the right to sue are typically upheld in settings other than health care, if the waiver of negligence is clearly described, the activity is a voluntary one, the waiver freely given by a party who understands what he is giving up, and there is not a serious imbalance of bargaining power. Courts view such waivers as a valid exercise of the freedom of contract. See generally Jaffe v. Pallotta Teamworks, 276 F. Supp.2d 102 (D.C.D.C. 2003) (upholding waiver by a runner in an AIDS charity event, a voluntary activity).

2. The *Tunkl* context is a special case of a charitable teaching hospital. Why does the court view this context as special? In other health care situations other than emergencies, why shouldn't a patient be able to waive the right to sue in exchange for lower cost or free treatment? See *Esquivel*, above, and discussion of consumer–driven health care, below. Is there something special about medical care in general, or *Tunkl*'s situation in particular, that makes such a choice by a patient suspect? Do the court's arguments convince you as to the reasons for invalidating such attempts by health care institutions to limit their liability? Short of a complete waiver of a right to sue, how else might hospitals or doctors protect themselves? Can a patient be asked to waive the right to sue for punitive damages? Could the parties agree on liquidated damages? Could the parties agree that an action would be brought in the local state court? Could treatment be conditioned on the patient submitting any malpractice claim to an administrative body, or to arbitration? Should the patient's source of payment determine whether an exculpatory agreement should be enforced?

California has continued to follow *Tunkl*'s analysis. See, e.g Health Net of California, Inc. v. Department of Health Services (2003) 113 Cal.App.4th 224, 6 Cal.Rptr.3d 235 (2003) (exculpatory clause related to managed health care for Medi–Cal beneficiaries).

Other courts have ~~also~~ rejected exculpatory agreements under a Tunkl–influenced analysis. See, e.g., Vodopest v. MacGregor, 128 Wash.2d 840, 913 P.2d 779, 783 (1996) (invalidating, under Washington law, a release related to medical research). One exception that has been found to be acceptable is an exculpatory agreement for treatments involving experimental procedures as the patient's last hope for survival. See Colton v. New York Hospital, 98 Misc.2d 957, 414 N.Y.S.2d 866 (1979). See also, 42 CFR § 46.116, governing research funded by HHS: "No informed consent, whether oral or written, may include any exculpatory language through which the subject or the representative is made to waive or appear to waive any of the subject's legal rights, or releases or appears to release the investigator, the sponsor, the institution or its agents from liability for negligence."

SHORTER V. DRURY

Supreme Court of Washington, 1985.
103 Wash.2d 645, 695 P.2d 116.

DOLLIVER, JUSTICE.

This is an appeal from a wrongful death medical malpractice action arising out of the bleeding death of a hospital patient who, for religious reasons, refused a blood transfusion. Plaintiff, the deceased's husband and personal representative, appeals the trial court's judgment on the verdict in which the jury reduced plaintiff's wrongful death damages by 75 percent based on an assumption of risk by the Shorters that Mrs. Shorter would die from bleeding. The defendant doctor appeals the judgment alleging that a plaintiff–signed hospital release form completely barred the wrongful death action. Alternatively, defendant asks that we affirm the trial court's judgment on the verdict. Defendant does not appeal the special verdict in which the jury found the defendant negligent.

The deceased, Doreen Shorter, was a Jehovah's Witness, as is her surviving husband, Elmer Shorter. Jehovah's Witnesses are prohibited by their religious doctrine from receiving blood transfusions.

Doreen Shorter became pregnant late in the summer of 1979. In October of 1979, she consulted with the defendant, Dr. Robert E. Drury, a family practitioner. Dr. Drury diagnosed Mrs. Shorter as having had a "missed abortion". A missed abortion occurs when the fetus dies and the uterus fails to discharge it.

When a fetus dies, it is medically prudent to evacuate the uterus in order to guard against infection. To cleanse the uterus, Dr. Shorter recommended a "dilation and curettage" (D and C). There are three alternative ways to perform this operation. The first is with a curette, a metal instrument which has a sharp–edged hoop on the end of it. The second, commonly used in an abortion, involves the use of a suction device. The third alternative is by use of vaginal suppositories containing prostaglandin, a chemical that causes artificial labor contractions. Dr. Drury chose to use curettes.

Although the D and C is a routine medical procedure there is a risk of bleeding. Each of the three principal methods for performing the D and C presented, to a varying degree, the risk of bleeding. The record below reflects that the curette method which Dr. Drury selected posed the highest degree of puncture–caused bleeding risk due to the sharpness of the instrument. The record also reflects, however, that no matter how the D and C is performed, there is always the possibility of blood loss.

Dr. Drury described the D and C procedure to Mr. and Mrs. Shorter. He advised her there was a possibility of bleeding and perforation of the uterus. Dr. Drury did not discuss any alternate methods in which the D and C may be performed. Examination of Mr. Shorter at trial revealed he was aware that the D and C posed the possibility, albeit remote, of internal bleeding.

The day before she was scheduled to receive the D and C from Dr. Drury, Mrs. Shorter sought a second opinion from Dr. Alan Ott. Mrs. Shorter advised Dr. Ott of Dr. Drury's intention to perform the D and C. She told Dr. Ott she was a Jehovah's Witness. Although he confirmed the D and C was the appropriate treatment, Dr. Ott did not discuss with Mrs. Shorter the particular method which should be used to perform it. He did, however, advise Mrs. Shorter that "she could certainly bleed during the procedure" and at trial confirmed she was aware of that possibility. Dr. Ott testified Mrs. Shorter responded to his warning by saying "she had faith in the Lord and that things would work out. * * * "

At approximately 6 a.m. on November 30, Mrs. Shorter was accompanied by her husband to Everett General Hospital. At the hospital the Shorters signed [a consent form that included the following language]: "I hereby release the hospital, its personnel, and the attending physician from any responsibility whatever for unfavorable reactions or any untoward results due to my refusal to permit the use of blood or its derivatives and I fully understand the possible consequences of such refusal on my part."

The operation did not go smoothly. Approximately 1 hour after surgery, Mrs. Shorter began to bleed internally and go into shock. Emergency exploratory surgery conducted by other surgeons revealed Dr. Drury had severely lacerated Mrs. Shorter's uterus when he was probing with the curette.

Mrs. Shorter began to bleed profusely. She continued to refuse to authorize a transfusion despite repeated warnings by the doctors she would likely die due to blood loss. Mrs. Shorter was coherent at the time she refused to accept blood. While the surgeons repaired Mrs. Shorter's perforated uterus and abdomen, Dr. Drury and several other doctors pleaded with Mr. Shorter to permit them to transfuse blood into Mrs. Shorter. He likewise refused. Mrs. Shorter bled to death. Doctors for both parties agreed a transfusion in substantial probability would have saved Doreen Shorter's life.

Mr. Shorter thereafter brought this wrongful death action alleging Dr. Drury's negligence proximately caused Mrs. Shorter's death; the complaint did not allege a survival cause of action. The release was admitted into evidence over plaintiff's objection. Plaintiff took exception to jury instructions numbered 13 and 13A which dealt with assumption of the risk.

The jury found Dr. Drury negligent and that his negligence was "a proximate cause of the death of Doreen Shorter". Damages were found to be $412,000. The jury determined, however, that Mr. and/or Mrs. Shorter "knowingly and voluntarily" assumed the risk of bleeding to death and attributed 75 percent of the fault for her death to her and her husband's refusal to authorize or accept a blood transfusion. Plaintiff was awarded judgment of $103,000. Both parties moved for judgment notwithstanding the verdict. The trial court denied both motions. Plaintiff appealed and defendant cross–appealed to the Court of Appeals, which certified the case pursuant to RCW 2.06.030(d).

The three issues before us concern the admissibility of the "Refusal to Permit Blood Transfusion" (refusal); whether assumption of the risk is a valid defense and if so, whether there is sufficient evidence for the jury to have found the risk was assumed by the Shorters; and whether the submission of the issue of assumption of the risk to the jury violated the free exercise clause of the First Amendment. The finding of negligence by Dr. Drury is not appealed by defendant.

I

Plaintiff argues the purpose of the refusal was only to release the defendant doctor from liability for not transfusing blood into Mrs. Shorter had she required blood during the course of a nonnegligently performed operation. He further asserts the refusal as it applies to the present case violates public policy since it would release Dr. Drury from the consequences of his negligence.

Defendant concedes a survival action filed on behalf of Mrs. Shorter for her negligently inflicted injuries would not be barred by the refusal since enforcement would violate public policy. Defendant argues, however, the refusal does not release the doctor for his negligence but only for the consequences arising out of Mrs. Shorter's voluntary refusal to accept blood, which in this case was death.

While the rule announced by this court is that contracts against liability for negligence are valid except in those cases where the public interest is involved [ ], the refusal does not address the negligence of Dr.

Drury. This being so it cannot be considered as a release from liability for negligence. * * *

Plaintiff categorizes the refusal as an all or nothing instrument. He claims that if it is a release of liability for negligence it is void as against public policy and if it is a release of liability where a transfusion is required because of nonnegligent treatment then it is irrelevant. We have already stated the document cannot be considered as a release from liability for negligence. The document is more, however, than a simple declaration that the signer would refuse blood only if there was no negligence by Dr. Drury. * * *

We find the refusal to be valid. There was sufficient evidence for the jury to find it was not signed unwittingly but rather voluntarily. * * *

We also hold the release was not against public policy. We emphasize again the release did not exculpate Dr. Drury from his negligence in performing the surgery. Rather, it was an agreement that Mrs. Shorter should receive no blood or blood derivatives. The cases cited by defendant, [including Tunkl, above] all refer to exculpatory clauses which release a physician or hospital from all liability for negligence. The Shorters specifically accepted the risk which might flow from a refusal to accept blood. Given the particular problems faced when a patient on religious grounds refuses to permit necessary or advisable blood transfusions, we believe the use of a release such as signed here is appropriate. [ ] Requiring physicians or hospitals to obtain a court order would be cumbersome and impractical. * * * [ ] The alternative of physicians or hospitals refusing to care for Jehovah's Witnesses is repugnant in a society which attempts to make medical care available to all its members.

We believe the procedure used here, the voluntary execution of a document protecting the physician and hospital and the patient is an appropriate alternative and not contrary to the public interest.

If the refusal is held valid, defendant asserts it acts as a complete bar to plaintiff's wrongful death claim. We disagree. While Mrs. Shorter accepted the consequences resulting from a refusal to receive a blood transfusion, she did not accept the consequences of Dr. Drury's negligence which was, as the jury found, a proximate cause of Mrs. Shorter's death. Defendant was not released from his negligence. We next consider the impact of the doctrine of assumption of the risk on this negligence.

II

[In Part II the court considered assumption of the risk as a defense.]

* * * Defendant argues, and we agree, that the Shorters could be found by the jury to have assumed the risk of death from an operation which had to be performed without blood transfusions and where blood could not be administered under any circumstances including where the

doctor made what would otherwise have been correctable surgical mistake. The risk of death from a failure to receive a transfusion to which the Shorters exposed themselves was created by, and must be allocated to, the Shorters themselves.

* * *

III

[The court in Part III rejected the argument that the submission of the issue of assumption of the risk to the jury violated the free exercise clause of the First Amendment, since no state action was present.]

* * *

Affirmed.

NOTES AND QUESTIONS

1. Consider the relative risks of the different approaches to a missed abortion. Did the treating physician properly take into account the risk factors presented by a Jehovah's Witness patient? Is a religious or personal belief of this sort part of the presenting characteristics of a patient, requiring adjustment of the treatment approach?

2. Jehovah's Witnesses rarely sue physicians who respect their decisions not to receive blood. A decision to vitiate the partial release in *Shorter* might have discouraged surgeons from agreeing to treat Jehovah's Witnesses consistent with their religious beliefs.

The refusal by Jehovah's Witnesses to accept blood transfusions has its origins in their interpretation of the Bible. They have prepared brochures for health care professionals that explain these beliefs, stating that they will sign consent forms that relieve doctors of any responsibility for possible adverse consequences of blood refusal. See the website of the Associated Jehovah's Witnesses for Reform on Blood for an example of cards that reflect the Church's blood policies. Advance directive statutes typically provide immunity for complying with a directive meeting the statutory standards.

3. *Shorter* offers a defense of a partial waiver, under a special set of circumstances. The issue is important for two reasons. First, providers would like to limit their liability exposure in order to keep malpractice premiums under control. Second, economists and other reformers of the tort system advocate the use of contracts that allocate risk by agreement.

4. California has a binding arbitration provision in MICRA (Medical Injury Compensation Reform Act) and it is estimated that about ten percent of medical malpractice disputes go to binding arbitration. See Michael F. Cannon, CATO Handbook for Policymakers (7th Edition), Chapter 15, Health Care Regulation.

What objections might be raised to such forms of binding arbitration imposed by contract? See discussion of enforceability of arbitration agreements, including application of the Federal Arbitration Act, in Chapter 3.

Several states have adopted contract approaches, such as elective arbitration contracts that allow the provider and the patient to change the forum for resolving the dispute. Some states do not mandate the referral of medical malpractice claims to arbitration, but instead authorize health care providers to include arbitration clauses in their contracts, so long as an agreement to arbitrate is not a condition of service. The patient must have a right to rescind within 90 days. See for example Colo. Rev. Stat. Ann. § 13–64–403. See generally Carol A. Crocca, Arbitration of Medical Malpractice Claims, 24 A.L.R.5th 1.

PROBLEM: ARBITRATING DISASTER

Rhoda Cumin went to the Gladstone Clinic in Las Vegas, Nevada to get a prescription for an oral contraceptive. Her medical history put her at a higher risk of a stroke from use of birth control pills. She did not know this, but her medical records and history would have alerted an obstetrician to the risk. She obtained a prescription for the pills, and began taking them. Six months later she suffered a cerebral incident that left her partially paralyzed. Her lifetime medical expenses, including physical therapy, lost earning capacity, and pain suffering, could be as much as $ 10 million.

Ms. Cumin has asked you to handle her suit against the clinic. Your investigation determines that the clinic was negligent in prescribing the contraceptive in light of Ms. Cumin's history. You file a negligence action. The clinic then moves to stay the lawsuit pending arbitration, and for a court order to compel arbitration. Its affidavit states that the clinic requires all patients to sign an arbitration agreement before receiving treatment. This agreement requires two things: first, it provides that all disputes must be submitted to binding arbitration and that the parties expressly waive their right to a trial. Second, it puts a cap of $250,000 on the patient's right to recover.. The clinic's standard procedure is to have the receptionist hand the patient the agreement along with two information sheets, informing her that any questions will be answered. The patient must sign the agreement before receiving treatment; the physician signs later. If the patient refuses to sign, the clinic refuses treatment. The agreement, signed by your client, is attached to the affidavit.

Ms. Cumin tells you that she does not remember either signing the agreement or having it explained to her, and you file an affidavit to that effect. Prepare a memorandum of law in support of your motion in opposition to arbitration.

PROBLEM: MEDIATING DISASTER

Rhoda Cumin suffered a cerebral incident as a result of her use of birth control pills (see previous problem). She was admitted to Gladstone Urban

Hospital, a major teaching hospital in the State of Sympathy. At the time of admission, she was presented for her signature a mediation clause which stated:

> I agree that any claim which may arise out of the care provided to me by the physicians, nurses and other health care providers at the Gladstone Urban Hospital or any of its affiliates shall be governed by the law of the State of Sympathy. I also agree that before any lawsuit is filed for damages arising out of or related to the care provided to me, I must attempt to resolve any claim through mediation. Mediation is a process through which a neutral third person tries to help settle claims. I do not waive my right to file a lawsuit if the mediation process fails to resolve my claim. I further agree that any mediation or court proceeding must take place in the State of Sympathy. This agreement is binding on me and any individual or entity making claim on my behalf.

She signed the mediation clause. During the course of her treatment, she suffered a serious medical error during treatment for her stroke, which left her partially paralyzed. Gladstone is aware that this was a preventable adverse event, the result of a combination of surgical, charting, and nursing errors.

You represent Gladstone. How will you design mediation? What approach will you take to the mediation discussions? What goals do you have in mind on behalf of the Hospital?

III. INFORMED CONSENT: THE PHYSICIAN'S OBLIGATION

A. ORIGINS OF THE INFORMED CONSENT DOCTRINE

Informed consent has developed out of strong judicial deference toward individual autonomy, reflecting a belief that an individual has a right to be free from nonconsensual interference with his or her person, and a basic moral principle that it is wrong to force another to act against his or her will. This principle was articulated in the medical context by Justice Cardozo in Schloendorff v. Society of New York Hospital, 211 N.Y. 125, 105 N.E. 92 (1914): "Every human being of adult years and sound mind has a right to determine what shall be done with his own body . . . ".

Informed consent doctrine has guided medical decision making by setting boundaries for the doctor–patient relationship and is one of the forces altering the attitudes of a new generation of doctors toward their patients. Informed consent is a foundation for federal regulations on human experimentation, and the touchstone for end–of–life decision making. The consent forms that health care institutions require all patients to sign upon admission and before various procedures are performed are the most concrete manifestations of the doctrine.

Professor Alexander Capron has argued that the doctrine can serve six salutary functions. Informed consent can:

1) protect individual autonomy;

2) protect the patient's status as a human being;

3) avoid fraud or duress;

4) encourage doctors to carefully consider their decisions;

5) foster rational decision–making by the patient; and

6) involve the public generally in medicine.

Alexander Capron, Informed Consent in Catastrophic Disease Research and Treatment, 123 U.Penn.L.Rev. 340, 365–76 (1974).

Current research suggests that patient health outcomes may in fact improve if patients are fully involved in understanding their treatments and their illness, and in managing their own treatments to a greater extent. We are moving beyond informed consent to a more robust model of "patient engagement" and "activation." As one study argues, "[t]he assumption is that if individual patients made more informed health care choices, were better able to manage their own conditions, and adopted healthier lifestyles, their health care costs would be lessened." The quality of care is also expected to improve when patients are engaged in their own care.

See generally Judith H. Hibbard, Jessica Greene, and Valerie Overton, Patients With Lower Activation Associated With Higher Costs: Delivery Systems Should Know Their Patients' 'Scores', 32 Health Affairs 216 (2013). See also Yves Longtin et. al., Patient Participation: Current Knowledge and Applicability to Patient Safety, 85 Mayo Clin. Proc. 53 (2010) ("By participating in the decision–making process, the patient exercises his or her most fundamental rights. * * * Like any consumer, the patient may demand quality services. By continuously evaluating the service and sometimes lodging complaints toward it, the patient–consumer can improve the health care system."); Angela Coulter, Suzanne Parsons and Janet Askham, WHO Policy Brief: Where Are the Patients in Decision–Making About Their Own Care? (arguing that "[p]atients can play a distinct role in protecting their health, choosing appropriate treatments for episodes of ill health and managing chronic disease. Considerable evidence suggests that patient engagement can improve their experience and satisfaction and also can be effective clinically and economically.")

This is not just a policy debate. Patient engagement and shared decisionmaking are two central components of both Stage 2 meaningful use requirements and the Medicare Shared Savings Program. Medical Homes discussions also emphasize patient engagement as crucial to quality, and the Accountable Care Organization regulations spend a great deal of time on the importance of patient engagement. See Centers for Medicare & Medicaid Services, Medicare Program; Medicare Shared Savings Program: Accountable Care Organizations, 425.106, Shared governance (discussing the promotion of patient engagement.)

Informed consent has been an unnatural graft onto medical practice. Jay Katz, The Silent World of Doctor and Patient 1 (1984). The judicial development of informed consent into a distinct doctrine can be roughly divided into three periods, according to Katz. During the first period, up to the mid–twentieth century, courts built upon the law of battery and required little more than disclosure by doctors of their proposed treatment. The second period saw an emerging judicial policy that doctors should disclose the alternatives to a proposed treatment and their risks, as well as of risks of the proposed treatment itself. The third period, from 1972 to the present, has seen legislative retrenchment and judicial inertia. See also Peter H. Schuck, Rethinking Informed Consent, 103 Yale L.J. 899, 900–05 (1994) (describing the rise of the informed–consent doctrine after 1957).

During the first period of doctrinal development, the doctrine of battery provided the theoretical underpinnings for a cause of action. The doctrine of battery protects a patient's physical integrity from harmful contacts and her personal dignity from unwanted bodily contact, requiring a showing only that the patient was not informed of the very nature of the medical touching, typically a surgical procedure. Physical injury is not necessary. When a surgeon, in the course of surgery, removes or operates upon an organ other than the one he and the patient discussed, a battery action lies. The most obvious medical battery cases, e.g., where a surgeon amputates the wrong leg, can be readily brought as a negligence case.

The procedural and other advantages of a battery–based action tip the scales substantially in the favor of the patient. First, the focus is on the patient's right to be free from a touching different from that to which she consented. The physician has few defenses to a battery. Second, the plaintiff need not prove through expert testimony what the standard of care was; the proof is only that the particular physician failed to explain to the patient the nature and character of the particular procedure. Third, to prove causation, the plaintiff need only show that an nonconsensual touching occurred.

As you read the cases in this section, ask how far the courts have gone toward permitting patients to control treatment decisions that affect them. Consider also what a plaintiff must show to make out an informed consent case in various jurisdictions. Finally, ask if any other processes are likely to serve the purposes of informed consent more efficiently, and with less adverse effect on the doctor–patient relationship. Has the law improved the doctor–patient relationship?

B. THE LEGAL FRAMEWORK OF INFORMED CONSENT

1. Negligence as a Basis for Recovery

CANTERBURY V. SPENCE

United States Court of Appeals, District of Columbia Circuit, 1972.
464 F.2d 772.

SPOTTSWOOD W. ROBINSON, III, CIRCUIT JUDGE:

This appeal is from a judgment entered in the District Court on verdicts directed for the two appellees at the conclusion of plaintiff–appellant Canterbury's case in chief. His action sought damages for personal injuries allegedly sustained as a result of an operation negligently performed by appellee Spence, a negligent failure by Dr. Spence to disclose a risk of serious disability inherent in the operation, and negligent post–operative care by appellee Washington Hospital Center. On close examination of the record, we find evidence which required submission of these issues to the jury. We accordingly reverse the judgment as to each appellee and remand the case to the District Court for a new trial.

I

The record we review tells a depressing tale. A youth troubled only by back pain submitted to an operation without being informed of a risk of paralysis incidental thereto. A day after the operation he fell from his hospital bed after having been left without assistance while voiding. A few hours after the fall, the lower half of his body was paralyzed, and he had to be operated on again. Despite extensive medical care, he has never been what he was before. Instead of the back pain, even years later, he hobbled about on crutches, a victim of paralysis of the bowels and urinary incontinence. In a very real sense this lawsuit is an understandable search for reasons.

At the time of the events which gave rise to this litigation, appellant was nineteen years of age, a clerk–typist employed by the Federal Bureau of Investigation. In December, 1958, he began to experience severe pain between his shoulder blades. He consulted two general practitioners, but the medications they prescribed failed to eliminate the pain. Thereafter, appellant secured an appointment with Dr. Spence, who is a neurosurgeon.

Dr. Spence examined appellant in his office at some length but found nothing amiss. On Dr. Spence's advice appellant was x–rayed, but the films did not identify any abnormality. Dr. Spence then recommended that appellant undergo a myelogram—a procedure in which dye is injected into the spinal column and traced to find evidence of disease or other disorder—at the Washington Hospital Center.

Appellant entered the hospital on February 4, 1959. The myelogram revealed a "filling defect" in the region of the fourth thoracic vertebra. Since a myelogram often does no more than pinpoint the location of an aberration, surgery may be necessary to discover the cause. Dr. Spence told appellant that he would have to undergo a laminectomy—the excision of the posterior arch of the vertebra—to correct what he suspected was a ruptured disc. Appellant did not raise any objection to the proposed operation nor did he probe into its exact nature.

Appellant explained to Dr. Spence that his mother was a widow of slender financial means living in Cyclone, West Virginia, and that she could be reached through a neighbor's telephone. Appellant called his mother the day after the myelogram was performed and, failing to contact her, left Dr. Spence's telephone number with the neighbor. When Mrs. Canterbury returned the call, Dr. Spence told her that the surgery was occasioned by a suspected ruptured disc. Mrs. Canterbury then asked if the recommended operation was serious and Dr. Spence replied "not any more than any other operation." He added that he knew Mrs. Canterbury was not well off and that her presence in Washington would not be necessary. The testimony is contradictory as to whether during the course of the conversation Mrs. Canterbury expressed her consent to the operation. Appellant himself apparently did not converse again with Dr. Spence prior to the operation.

Dr. Spence performed the laminectomy on February 11 at the Washington Hospital Center. Mrs. Canterbury traveled to Washington, arriving on that date but after the operation was over, and signed a consent form at the hospital. The laminectomy revealed several anomalies: a spinal cord that was swollen and unable to pulsate, an accumulation of large tortuous and dilated veins, and a complete absence of epidural fat which normally surrounds the spine. A thin hypodermic needle was inserted into the spinal cord to aspirate any cysts which might have been present, but no fluid emerged. In suturing the wound, Dr. Spence attempted to relieve the pressure on the spinal cord by enlarging the dura—the outer protective wall of the spinal cord—at the area of swelling.

For approximately the first day after the operation appellant recuperated normally, but then suffered a fall and an almost immediate setback. Since there is some conflict as to precisely when or why appellant fell, we reconstruct the events from the evidence most favorable to him. Dr. Spence left orders that appellant was to remain in bed during the process of voiding. These orders were changed to direct that voiding be done out of bed, and the jury could find that the change was made by hospital personnel. Just prior to the fall, appellant summoned a nurse and was given a receptacle for use in voiding, but was then left unattended. Appellant testified that during the course of the endeavor he slipped off the side of the bed, and that there was no one to assist him, or side rail to prevent the fall.

Several hours later, appellant began to complain that he could not move his legs and that he was having trouble breathing; paralysis seems to have been virtually total from the waist down. Dr. Spence was notified on the night of February 12, and he rushed to the hospital. Mrs. Canterbury signed another consent form and appellant was again taken into the operating room. The surgical wound was reopened and Dr. Spence created a gusset to allow the spinal cord greater room in which to pulsate.

Appellant's control over his muscles improved somewhat after the second operation but he was unable to void properly. As a result of this condition, he came under the care of a urologist while still in the hospital. In April, following a cystoscopic examination, appellant was operated on for removal of bladder stones, and in May was released from the hospital. He reentered the hospital the following August for a 10–day period, apparently because of his urologic problems. For several years after his discharge he was under the care of several specialists, and at all times was under the care of a urologist. At the time of the trial in April, 1968, appellant required crutches to walk, still suffered from urinal incontinence and paralysis of the bowels, and wore a penile clamp.

In November, 1959 on Dr. Spence's recommendation, appellant was transferred by the F.B.I. to Miami where he could get more swimming and exercise. Appellant worked three years for the F.B.I. in Miami, Los Angeles and Houston, resigning finally in June, 1962. From then until the time of the trial, he held a number of jobs, but had constant trouble finding work because he needed to remain seated and close to a bathroom. The damages appellant claims include extensive pain and suffering, medical expenses, and loss of earnings.

II

* * *

At the close of appellant's case in chief, each defendant moved for a directed verdict and the trial judge granted both motions. The basis of the ruling, he explained, was that appellant had failed to produce any medical evidence indicating negligence on Dr. Spence's part in diagnosing appellant's malady or in performing the laminectomy; that there was no proof that Dr. Spence's treatment was responsible for appellant's disabilities; and that notwithstanding some evidence to show negligent post–operative care, an absence of medical testimony to show causality precluded submission of the case against the hospital to the jury. The judge did not allude specifically to the alleged breach of duty by Dr. Spence to divulge the possible consequences of the laminectomy.

We reverse. The testimony of appellant and his mother that Dr. Spence did not reveal the risk of paralysis from the laminectomy made out a prima facie case of violation of the physician's duty to disclose which Dr. Spence's explanation did not negate as a matter of law. * * *

III

* * *

* * * True consent to what happens to one's self is the informed exercise of a choice, and that entails an opportunity to evaluate knowledgeably the options available and the risks attendant upon each. The average patient has little or no understanding of the medical arts, and ordinarily has only his physician to whom he can look for enlightenment with which to reach an intelligent decision. From these almost axiomatic considerations springs the need, and in turn the requirement, of a reasonable divulgence by physician to patient to make such a decision possible.

A physician is under a duty to treat his patient skillfully but proficiency in diagnosis and therapy is not the full measure of his responsibility. The cases demonstrate that the physician is under an obligation to communicate specific information to the patient when the exigencies of reasonable care call for it. Due care may require a physician perceiving symptoms of bodily abnormality to alert the patient to the condition. It may call upon the physician confronting an ailment which does not respond to his ministrations to inform the patient thereof. It may command the physician to instruct the patient as to any limitations to be presently observed for his own welfare, and as to any precautionary therapy he should seek in the future. It may oblige the physician to advise the patient of the need for or desirability of any alternative treatment promising greater benefit than that being pursued. Just as plainly, due care normally demands that the physician warn the patient of any risks to his well–being which contemplated therapy may involve.

The context in which the duty of risk–disclosure arises is invariably the occasion for decision as to whether a particular treatment procedure is to be undertaken. To the physician, whose training enables a self–satisfying evaluation, the answer may seem clear, but it is the prerogative of the patient, not the physician, to determine for himself the direction in which his interests seem to lie. To enable the patient to chart his course understandably, some familiarity with the therapeutic alternatives and their hazards becomes essential.

A reasonable revelation in these respects is not only a necessity but, as we see it, is as much a matter of the physician's duty. It is a duty to warn of the dangers lurking in the proposed treatment, and that is surely a facet of due care. It is, too, a duty to impart information which the patient has every right to expect. The patient's reliance upon the physician is a trust of the kind which traditionally has exacted obligations beyond those associated with arms–length transactions. His dependence upon the physician for information affecting his well–being, in terms of contemplated treatment, is well–nigh abject. As earlier noted, long before the instant litigation arose, courts had recognized that the physician had the responsibility of satisfying the vital informational needs of the patient. More recently, we ourselves have found "in the fiducial qualities of [the physician–patient] relationship the physician's duty to reveal to the patient that which in his best interests it is important that he should know." We now find, as a part of the physician's overall obligation to the patient, a similar duty of reasonable disclosure of the choices with respect to proposed therapy and the dangers inherently and potentially involved.

* * *

IV

Duty to disclose has gained recognition in a large number of American jurisdictions, but more largely on a different rationale. The majority of courts dealing with the problem have made the duty depend on whether it was the custom of physicians practicing in the community to make the particular disclosure to the patient. If so, the physician may be held liable for an unreasonable and injurious failure to divulge, but there can be no recovery unless the omission forsakes a practice prevalent in the profession. We agree that the physician's noncompliance with a professional custom to reveal, like any other departure from prevailing medical practice, may give rise to liability to the patient. We do not agree that the patient's cause of action is dependent upon the existence and nonperformance of a relevant professional tradition.

There are, in our view, formidable obstacles to acceptance of the notion that the physician's obligation to disclose is either germinated or limited by medical practice. To begin with, the reality of any discernible custom reflecting a professional concensus [sic] on communication of option and risk information to patients is open to serious doubt. We sense the danger that what in fact is no custom at all may be taken as an affirmative custom to maintain silence, and that physician–witnesses to the so–called custom may state merely their personal opinions as to what they or others would do under given conditions. We cannot gloss over the inconsistency between reliance on a general practice respecting divulgence and, on the other hand, realization that the myriad of variables among patients makes each case so different that its omission can rationally be justified only by the effect of its individual circumstances. Nor can we ignore the fact that to bind the disclosure obligation to medical usage is to arrogate the decision on revelation to the physician alone. Respect for the patient's right of self–determination on particular therapy demands a standard set by law for physicians rather than one which physicians may or may not impose upon themselves.

* * * The caliber of the performance exacted by the reasonable–care standard varies between the professional and non–professional worlds, and so also the role of professional custom. * * *

* * *

The majority rule, moreover, is at war with our prior holdings that a showing of medical practice, however probative, does not fix the standard governing recovery for medical malpractice. Prevailing medical practice, we have maintained, has evidentiary value in determinations as to what the specific criteria measuring challenged professional conduct are and whether they have been met, but does not itself define the standard. That has been our position in treatment cases, where the physician's performance is ordinarily to be adjudicated by the special medical standard of due care. We see no logic in a different rule for nondisclosure cases, where the governing standard is much more largely divorced from professional considerations. And surely in nondisclosure cases the factfinder is not invariably functioning in an area of such technical complexity that it must be bound to medical custom as an inexorable application of the community standard of reasonable care.

Thus we distinguished, for purposes of duty to disclose, the special– and general–standard aspects of the physician–patient relationship. When medical judgment enters the picture and for that reason the special standard controls, prevailing medical practice must be given its just due. In all other instances, however, the general standard exacting ordinary care applies, and that standard is set by law. In sum, the physician's duty to disclose is governed by the same legal principles applicable to others in comparable situations, with modifications only to the extent that medical judgment enters the picture. We hold that the standard measuring performance of that duty by physicians, as by others, is conduct which is reasonable under the circumstances.

V

Once the circumstances give rise to a duty on the physician's part to inform his patient, the next inquiry is the scope of the disclosure the physician is legally obliged to make. The courts have frequently confronted this problem but no uniform standard defining the adequacy of the divulgence emerges from the decisions. Some have said "full" disclosure, a norm we are unwilling to adopt literally. It seems obviously prohibitive and unrealistic to expect physicians to discuss with their patients every risk of proposed treatment—no matter how small or remote—and generally unnecessary from the patient's viewpoint as well. Indeed, the cases speaking in terms of "full" disclosure appear to envision something less than total disclosure, leaving unanswered the question of just how much.

The larger number of courts, as might be expected, have applied tests framed with reference to prevailing fashion within the medical profession.

* * * We have explored this rather considerable body of law but are unprepared to follow it. The duty to disclose, we have reasoned, arises from phenomena apart from medical custom and practice. The latter, we think, should no more establish the scope of the duty than its existence. Any definition of scope in terms purely of a professional standard is at odds with the patient's prerogative to decide on projected therapy himself. That prerogative, we have said, is at the very foundation of the duty to disclose, and both the patient's right to know and the physician's correlative obligation to tell him are diluted to the extent that its compass is dictated by the medical profession.

In our view, the patient's right of self–decision shapes the boundaries of the duty to reveal. That right can be effectively exercised only if the patient possesses enough information to enable an intelligent choice. The scope of the physician's communications to the patient, then, must be measured by the patient's need, and that need is the information material to the decision. Thus the test for determining whether a particular peril must be divulged is its materiality to the patient's decision: all risks potentially affecting the decision must be unmasked. And to safeguard the patient's interest in achieving his own determination on treatment, the law must itself set the standard for adequate disclosure.

Optimally for the patient, exposure of a risk would be mandatory whenever the patient would deem it significant to his decision, either singly or in combination with other risks. Such a requirement, however, would summon the physician to second–guess the patient, whose ideas on materiality could hardly be known to the physician. That would make an undue demand upon medical practitioners, whose conduct, like that of others, is to be measured in terms of reasonableness. Consonantly with orthodox negligence doctrine, the physician's liability for nondisclosure is to be determined on the basis of foresight, not hindsight; no less than any other aspect of negligence, the issue on nondisclosure must be approached from the viewpoint of the reasonableness of the physician's divulgence in terms of what he knows or should know to be the patient's informational needs. If, but only if, the fact–finder can say that the physician's communication was unreasonably inadequate is an imposition of liability legally or morally justified.

Of necessity, the content of the disclosure rests in the first instance with the physician. Ordinarily it is only he who is in position to identify particular dangers; always he must make a judgment, in terms of materiality, as to whether and to what extent revelation to the patient is called for. He cannot know with complete exactitude what the patient would consider important to his decision, but on the basis of his medical training and experience he can sense how the average, reasonable patient expectably would react. Indeed, with knowledge of, or ability to learn, his patient's background and current condition, he is in a position superior to that of most others—attorneys, for example—who are called upon to make judgments on pain of liability in damages for unreasonable miscalculation.

From these considerations we derive the breadth of the disclosure of risks legally to be required. The scope of the standard is not subjective as to either the physician or the patient; it remains objective with due regard for the patient's informational needs and with suitable leeway for the physician's situation. In broad outline, we agree that "[a] risk is thus material when a reasonable person, in what the physician knows or should know to be the patient's position, would be likely to attach significance to the risk or cluster of risks in deciding whether or not to forego the proposed therapy."

The topics importantly demanding a communication of information are the inherent and potential hazards of the proposed treatment, the alternatives to that treatment, if any, and the results likely if the patient remains untreated. The factors contributing significance to the dangerousness of a medical technique are, of course, the incidence of injury and the degree of the harm threatened. A very small chance of death or serious disablement may well be significant; a potential disability which dramatically outweighs the potential benefit of the therapy or the detriments of the existing malady may summon discussion with the patient.

There is no bright line separating the significant from the insignificant; the answer in any case must abide a rule of reason. Some dangers—infection, for example—are inherent in any operation; there is no obligation to communicate those of which persons of average sophistication are aware. Even more clearly, the physician bears no responsibility for discussion of hazards the patient has already discovered, or those having no apparent materiality to patients' decision on therapy. The disclosure doctrine, like others marking lines between permissible and impermissible behavior in medical practice, is in essence a requirement of conduct prudent under the circumstances. Whenever nondisclosure of particular risk information is open to debate by reasonable–minded men, the issue is for the finder of the facts.

NOTES AND QUESTIONS

1. Imagine you are a trial judge in the District Court of the District of Columbia circuit. What will you extract from *Canterbury* as a clear and precise statement of the law of informed consent? How will you craft jury instructions on the evaluation of a physician's disclosure? Can you criticize Judge Robinson's logic? His statement of the standard? For the backstory on this case, see Alan Meisel, Canterbury v. Spence: The Inadvertant Landmark Case in Health Law & Bioethics Cases in Context, Sandra H. Johnson, et al. (eds.) (2009).

2. A slight majority of courts has adopted the professional disclosure standard, measuring the duty to disclose by the standard of the reasonable medical practitioner similarly situated. Expert testimony is required to establish the content of a reasonable disclosure. The *Canterbury* rule, using the "reasonable patient" as the measure of the scope of disclosure, has won over several states in the last few years. Some states have adopted tort reform legislation that imposes the professional disclosure standard. See Eady v. Lansford, 351 Ark. 249, 92 S.W.3d 57 (2002); Walls v. Shreck, 265 Neb. 683, 658 N.W.2d 686 (2003). King and Moulton conclude that twenty five states have the physician–based standard, two a hybrid standard, and the rest a patient–based standard. Jaime Staples King and Benjamin Moulton, Rethinking Informed Consent: The Case for Shared Medical Decisionmaking, 32 Am. J. Law & Med. 429, 493–501 (2006) (Appendix).

What justifies the professional standard? Jurisdictions that follow the professional standard ordinarily require the plaintiff to offer medical testimony to establish 1) that a reasonable medical practitioner in the same or similar community would make this disclosure, and 2) that the defendant did not comply with this community standard. Fuller v. Starnes, 268 Ark. 476, 597 S.W.2d 88 (1980). Expert testimony is essential, since determination of what information needs to be disclosed is viewed as a medical question.

3. Judge Robinson suggests that the *Canterbury* standard is nothing more than the uniform application of the negligence principle to medical practice. However, the negligence principle normally evaluates the conduct of a reasonable actor—not the expectations of a reasonable victim. The values served by the doctrine—patient autonomy and dignity—are unrelated to the values served by the doctrine of negligence. Informed consent really serves the values we otherwise identify with the doctrine of battery. It is ironic that a doctrine developed to foster and recognize individual choice should be measured by an objective standard.

4. The effect of a patient–oriented disclosure standard is to ease the plaintiff's burden of proof, because the trier of fact could find that a doctor acted unreasonably in failing to disclose, in spite of unrebutted expert medical testimony to the contrary. The question of whether a physician disclosed risks that a reasonable person would find material is for the trier of fact, and technical expertise is not required. Pedersen v. Vahidy, 209 Conn. 510, 552 A.2d 419 (1989). Expert testimony is still needed, however, to clarify the treatments and their probabilities of risks. Cross v. Trapp, 170 W.Va. 459, 294 S.E.2d 446, 455 (1982).

5. The doctor must consider disclosure of a variety of factors:

a. Diagnosis. This includes the medical steps preceding diagnosis, including tests and their alternatives.

b. Nature and purpose of the proposed treatment.

c. Risks of the treatment. The threshold of disclosure, as the *Canterbury* court suggests, varies with the product of the probability and the severity of the risk. Thus a five percent risk of lengthened recuperation might be ignored, while a one percent risk of paralysis, as in *Canterbury* or an even smaller risk of death, should be disclosed. Cobbs v. Grant, 8 Cal.3d 229, 104 Cal.Rptr. 505, 502 P.2d 1 (1972). The risk, even if small, may be significant to the particular plaintiff because of unique health considerations. Hartke v. McKelway, 707 F.2d 1544, 1549 (D.C.Cir.1983).

The difference between a temporary and permanent risk can be critical: even the mention in a consent form of the general risk, characterized as temporary when it could be permanent, will be insufficient to constitute full disclosure. See, e.g., Johnson v. Brandy, 1995 WL 29230 (Ohio App.1995) (risk of scalp numbness after scalp–reduction surgery for baldness not described as permanent risk, but only temporary; consent form held to be inadequate disclosure).

Where a drug or injectable substance is part of treatment, a patient is entitled to know whether that drug or substance has been tested or approved by Federal authorities such as the Food and Drug Administration. Gaston v. Hunter, 121 Ariz. 33, 588 P.2d 326 (App.1978) (investigational procedure must be disclosed). See the *Richardson* case in Chapter 5, *infra*.

d. Treatment alternatives. Doctors should disclose those alternatives that are generally acknowledged within the medical community as feasible, Martin v. Richards, 192 Wis.2d 156, 531 N.W.2d 70, 78 (1995), their risks and consequences, and their probability of success. Even if the alternative is more hazardous, some courts have held that it should be disclosed. Logan v. Greenwich Hospital Association, 191 Conn. 282, 465 A.2d 294 (1983).

A physician must disclose medical information even if the procedure is noninvasive, because forgoing aggressive treatments in order to wait and observe a patient may entail significant risks. Martin v. Richards, 192 Wis.2d 156, 531 N.W.2d 70, 79 (1995) (physician failed to disclose to parents the risks of intracranial bleeding and the need for a CT scan or transfer to another facility in that case).

If the alternative is not a legitimate treatment option, it need not be disclosed to the patient. See Morris v. Ferriss, 669 So.2d 1316 (La.App. 4 Cir.1996) (physician did not have to advise patient that psychiatric treatment was an alternative treatment for epileptic partial complex seizures because it was not accepted as feasible).

e. Consequences of patient refusal of tests or treatments. How about offering a patient a test that may prevent a life–threatening outcome, and having the patient refuse the test? Must the doctor explain the consequences of such refusal? The California Supreme Court has held that "[i]f the physician knows or should know of a patient's unique concerns or lack of familiarity with medical procedures, this may expand the scope of required disclosure". Truman v. Thomas, 27 Cal.3d 285, 165 Cal.Rptr. 308, 611 P.2d 902 (1980).

f. Disclosing the tradeoffs of treatment versus watchful waiting. In a health care environment of cost–effective care, conservative practice is the goal—doing nothing and "watchful waiting" are desirable clinical approaches to patient care. A physician may have a duty to advise a patient of the option of choosing no treatment at all. Wecker v. Amend, 22 Kan.App.2d 498, 918 P.2d 658 (1996).

6. More than half of the states have enacted legislation dealing with informed consent, largely in response to various "malpractice crises" in their states. The statutes take a variety of forms, from specific to general, but they all share the common thread of moving the informed consent standard toward greater deference to medical judgment. Given the current state and national mood of legislative limitations on common law tort remedies, it may be expected that the common law of informed consent will continue to be affected by legislative action. A consent form, or other written documentation of the patient's verbal consent, is treated in many states as presumptively valid consent to the treatment at issue, with the burden on the patient to rebut the presumption. See Jaime Staples King & Benjamin W. Moulton, *supra*, note 2, for a fifty–state review of the law of informed consent.

2. Decision Aids and Informed Consent

John Wennberg and others have long argued for the use of decision aids to help patients decide whether or not to have procedures that Wennberg calls "preference–based"—such as prostate surgery or treatments for heart disease. John E. Wennberg & Philip G. Peters, Unwanted Variations in the Quality of Health Care: Can the Law Help Medicine Provide a Remedy/Remedies?, 37 Wake Forest L. Rev. 925,925–941 (2002). See discussion of Wennberg's work on medical practice variation and lack of evidence of efficacy of many medical procedures in Chapter 1, *supra*.

Decision aids (DAs) are decision support tools that provide patients with detailed and specific information on options and outcomes, help them clarify their values, and guide them through the decision making process. See, e.g., Elie A. Akl, et al., A Decision Aid for COPD Patients Considering Inhaled Steroid Therapy: Development and Before and After Pilot Testing, 15 BMC Med. Inform. Dec. Mak. 7 (2007).

The process by which such decision aids are used by the provider and the patient has come to be called "shared medical decision–making." Shared decision making is defined by King and Moulton as "a process in which the physician shares with the patient all relevant risk and benefit information on all treatment alternatives and the patient shares with the physician all relevant personal information that might make one treatment or side effect more or less tolerable than others. Then, both parties use this information to come to a mutual medical decision." Jaime Staples King and Benjamin Moulton, Rethinking Informed Consent: The Case for Shared Medical Decisionmaking, 32 Am. J. Law & Med. 429, 431 (2006). Numerous studies indicate that when decision aids (such as brochures,

DVDs, or online tools) are available to patients and they have the opportunity to participate in medical decision–making with their physician, the patient–physician dialogue and patient well–being both improves. See generally the website of the Foundation for Informed Medical Decisionmaking; Michael J. Barry, Health Decision Aids To Facilitate Shared Decision Making in Office Practice, 136 Annals Internal Med. 127, 127 (2002); website of the Center for Informed Patient Shared Decision Making, Decision Aid Library, Dartmouth–Hitchcock.

The Affordable Care Act adopts the use of decision aids for preference–sensitive care in section 3506. Preference–sensitive care is defined as follows:

> medical care for which the clinical evidence does not clearly support one treatment option such that the appropriate course of treatment depends on the values of the patient or the preferences of the patient, caregivers or authorized representatives regarding the benefits, harms and scientific evidence for each treatment option, the use of such care should depend on the informed patient choice among clinically appropriate treatment options.

Section 3501 of the ACA adopts the patient decision aid concept, as described above, and develops a regulatory approach for implementing shared decision aids. The stated purpose is to facilitate collaboration between patients and caregivers in decisionmaking, provide information on trade–offs among treatment options, and incorporate ". . . patient preferences and values into the medical plan."

Section 3506 requires the Secretary of HHS to contract with an independent entity to develop consensus–based standards for such aids and to develop a certification process for such patient decision aids for use in federal health programs and by other interested parties. This entity will, under (2)(A), ". . . synthesize evidence and convene a broad range of experts and key stakeholders to develop and identify consensus–based standards to evaluate patient decision aids for preference sensitive care." Subsection (B) then requires that such aids be endorsed by the entity through a certification process. The Secretary will, in collaboration with other federal agencies, disseminate these aids and develop information and training for providers in their use.

Shared Decisionmaking Resource Centers will be created under the ACA, funded "to provide technical assistance to providers and to develop and disseminate best practices and other information to support and accelerate adoption, implementation, and effective use of patient decision aids and shared decisionmaking by providers." The idea is to present current clinical evidence about the risks and benefits of treatment options in an age–appropriate way, with sensitivity to different cultural and educational backgrounds.

The certification process for approving decision aids under the ACA has not yet been funded. However, some states are adopting them, and health care organizations have also been disseminating such aids. See King and Moulton, *supra*.

NOTES AND QUESTIONS

1. Section 3501 of the ACA appears to federalize the informed consent process for a certain category of medical problems, so–called "preference sensitive care," without saying so. It proposes a federal requirement for certain procedures on top of the common law of informed consent. Why did Congress think that this particular type of care was sufficiently important to require the development of federal decision aids? Take a look at the list of decision aids described in the Dartmouth website above and consider what treatments might be eligible for such aids.

Nothing in Section 3501 really "mandates" the use of such decision aids. There are no sanctions mentioned. However, given the size of the Medicare program and its role in setting practice standards in many cases by default, it would appear that decision aids will gradually start to be adopted with or without an explicit mandate. See for example the use of decision aids by Group Health Cooperative in Seattle, Washington. Group Health introduced the aids for patients with hip and knee arthritis who faced elective surgeries. See David Arterburn, et al., Introducing Decision Aids at Group Health was Linked to Sharply Lower Hip and Knee Surgery Rates and Cost, 31 Health Affairs 2094 (2012) (The authors concluded that ". . . our findings provide further evidence to support the view that the implementation of patient decision aids for some preference sensitive health conditions may both reduce the rates of elective surgery and lower costs in a setting that integrates health care and coverage.")

2. Why does section 3501 offer such decision aids only for a certain category of care? Will not all treatment decisions benefit from an evidence–based set of tools to help patients decide at a minimum between treatment and no treatment?

3. Section 3501 requires certification of decision aids. The certification process is found in many areas of the law, for example employment certification, such as for perioperative nursing; or LEED certification for "green" buildings. Certification validates a status or a product as meeting an understood standard of performance or reliability. Why did section 3501 choose this approach? Are there other approaches you might suggest for validating a model of informed disclosure, such as accrediting organizations like the Foundation for Informed Medical Decision Making, or the Center for Informed Choice at Dartmouth as approved issuers of decision aids? (See discussion of accreditation in Chapter 3.) Or allowing a group to "grade" the aids, much as the ECRI Institute now "grades" practice guidelines under contract with HHS? See National Guideline Clearinghouse. Are the endorsements of the National Quality Forum (a non–profit organization) more or less

trustworthy than a certification? Or is the issue simply whether or not the organization itself is seen as reliable in its development and testing of standards?

4. Washington State already has amended its informed consent statute to fund demonstration projects and to incorporate decision aids into state informed consent law. The provisions of the ACA do not describe how the burden of proof might be altered, if at all, by requirements that such aids be used. Washington State requires that such aids be used, once developed and certified. Rev. Code Wash § 7.70.060 creates a presumption of informed consent if a practitioner uses decision aids, and the presumption can only be rebutted by clear and convincing evidence.

5. For a critical perspective on mandated disclosures in health care and other domains, see generally Omri Ben Shahar and Carl E. Schneider, The Failure of Mandated Disclosure, 159 U.Pa.L.Rev. 647 (2011), noting that doctors fail to disclose full information, forms are poorly written, and patients fail to understand or remember even clearly described choices. Their bottom line: "Patients prefer not to make medical decisions, and the sicker and older they are, the less they wish to do so." Is their criticism equally applicable to decision aids and the procedures they explain? If you can distinguish among treatments, explain your distinctions.

PROBLEM: ESTABLISHING THE CENTERS

Golden University (through its Center for Outcomes Research and its Center for Health Communications) intends to apply for federal grants to develop shared decision making aids and to be a Shared Decision Making Resource Center. Omniscient, a subsidiary of insurer United Medical Care (UMC), also intends to apply for both grant opportunities.

Assume that you are drafting the request for proposals for these federal grant programs and that you have some discretion in setting the parameters.

Should Omniscient be eligible for these grants? Would you limit the opportunity to tax–exempt organizations only? If so, would you be concerned if Omniscient changes its relationship to UMC such that Omniscient becomes a tax–exempt organization funded largely by UMC? How would you view a grant in which Golden University will partner with an insurer to require that providers contracting with the insurer will use the aids?

The Act prioritizes "preference sensitive care," but are there more specific priorities that should be set in the grant making process? What would those be? If you were establishing a weighting system for evaluating the significance of particular decisions, how would you weigh the following: "preference sensitive" treatments that risk harm to patients; the incidence of the particular treatment decision; cost; impact on populations defined by race, gender, age, or economic class; and others you may add? Should the grants focus on decisions relating to screening tests, such as mammography and the prostate specific antigen test, because those tests are gateways to more expensive diagnostic testing and interventions with attendant risks?

PROBLEM: STATE LEGISLATION

Your state legislature is considering legislation that would provide that any physician that uses a patient decision aid, certified through the process described in the ACA, will be immune from suit under state informed consent law. You are counsel to the Governor, and she has asked you to brief her on what she should expect should the bill reach her desk. What stakeholders or interests do you expect will be contacting the Governor, and what positions will they be taking? Would you advocate that she veto the bill? What amendments might you propose to improve the legislation?

Should Congress instead choose to preempt state informed consent law and provide the same immunity? Does it have the constitutional authority to do so? Does it make any difference to you in your role as counsel whether the immunity proceeds from federal or state law?

3. Disclosure of Physician–Specific Risk Information

Section 10331 of the ACA adopts a model of disclosure of provider performance information to consumers, creating a *Physician Compare* Internet website based on the model of the *Hospital Compare* site now in operation. This website will contain information on physician performance that will allow the public to compare physician performance on quality and patient experience measures with respect to physicians enrolled in the Medicare program.

Such information under ACA will include:

(A) measures collected under the Physician Quality Reporting Initiative;

(B) an assessment of patient health outcomes and the functional status of patients;

(C) an assessment of the continuity and coordination of care and care transitions, including episodes of care and risk–adjusted resource use;

(D) an assessment of efficiency;

(E) an assessment of patient experience and patient, caregiver, and family engagement;

(F) an assessment of the safety, effectiveness, and timeliness of care; and

(G) other information as determined appropriate by the Secretary [of HHS].

Physicians will be able to review their results before they are publicly reported, and the Secretary of HHS is admonished to ensure that the data is statistically valid and reliable, including risk adjustment mechanisms; that it provides "a robust and accurate portrayal of a physician's performance"; that it provides "a more accurate portrayal of physician performance"; that appropriate attribution of care can be done when multiple physicians and other providers are involved in care; that "timely statistical performance feedback" is provided; and that Centers for Medicare & Medicaid Services (CMS) has computer and data systems capable of supporting "valid, reliable, and accurate public reporting activities authorized under this section."

Such an Internet comparison site assumes that consumers will access the site and use it to make choices among providers. Section 10331 goes one step further by providing financial incentives to patients to choose high quality providers. Subsection (h) provides that the Secretary may establish a demonstration program, not later than January 1, 2019, to provide financial incentives to Medicare beneficiaries who are furnished services by high quality physicians, as determined by the Secretary based on factors in subparagraphs (A) through (G) of subsection (a)(2).

These provisions of the ACA reinforce a consumerist movement in health, giving patients information about health care risks and costs to maximize their choice. Kristen Madison defines consumerism as "individual choice within a health care marketplace characterized by the exchange of money for health care services for health care good or services." See Kristin Madison, Patients as Regulators? Patients' Evolving Influence over Health Care Delivery, 31 J. Legal Med. 9, 15 (2010).

Consumers rely on information from many different sources, particularly websites. This consumerist approach moves the patient from a passive recipient of medical advice to an aggressive shopper seeking information to satisfy her preferences for treatments, risks, and costs. Sources of information include existing web–based sites such as WebMD®, health care report cards issued by private and public organizations, and a range of government–run websites including *PhysicianCompare*, *HospitalCompare*, and *HomeHealthCompare*. See discussion of Nursing Home Compare in Chapter 3, *supra*.

CMS has added infection rate comparisons among hospitals to the consumer shopping list. Medicare is now reporting three sets of patient safety measures on the *Hospital Com*pare website:

- The Serious Complications and Deaths measures, developed by the Agency for Healthcare Research and Quality (AHRQ), provide information about how likely it is that patients will suffer from preventable complications and deaths while in the hospital.
- The Hospital Acquired Conditions measures show how often patients got certain serious conditions while in the hospital that might have been prevented if the hospital followed procedures based on best practices and scientific evidence.

- The Healthcare Associated Infection measures are developed by Centers for Disease Control and Prevention (CDC) and collected through the National Healthcare Safety Network. They provide information on infections, many of which are preventable, that occur while the patient is in the hospital. These infections can be related to devices, such as central lines and urinary catheters, or spread from patient to patient after contact with an infected person or surface.

Does this emergent consumerism, which the ACA reinforces, have problems? Some critics argue that it turns patients into consumers and healthcare into a business, risking a more predatory "buyer beware" world. But isn't the health care marketplace already a "buyer beware" environment where more information can only help consumers to control their risks? It has been argued that the mere production and publication of such data is enough to motivate providers to improve their statistics, to improve their reputation and competitiveness.

Consumerism assumes that most patients have the ability to be active consumers. The fault in this assumption is that patients are most likely to engage the health care system—when they are ill, dependent, and weak. Shopping is the last thing on their minds. For a skeptical analysis of consumers as shoppers, see Mark A. Hall and Carl E. Schneider, Patients As Consumers: Courts, Contracts, and the New Medical Marketplace, 106 Mich. L. Rev. 643 (2008).

PROBLEM: CONTENT FOR PHYSICIAN COMPARE

The Secretary has discretion to add information to the *Physician Compare* site beyond what is required in the ACA. Should the Secretary include disciplinary information provided by the state medical boards? If so, should it include complaints and investigations as well as final disciplinary actions? Should the Secretary include information on denial, limitation, or revocation of staff privileges? Should the *Physician Compare* website include malpractice filings, settlements, or judgments? In other words, should the Secretary incorporate the information that is now collected in the National Practitioner Data Bank (NPDB) which is not open to the public? (See discussion of the NPDB in Chapter 2.) Was the failure to mention the NPDB simply a legislative oversight? Or is the ACA quietly deemphasizing the NPDB?

JOHNSON V. KOKEMOOR

Supreme Court of Wisconsin, 1996.
199 Wis.2d 615, 545 N.W.2d 495.

SHIRLEY S. ABRAHAMSON, JUSTICE.

* * *

Donna Johnson (the plaintiff) brought an action against Dr. Richard Kokemoor (the defendant) alleging his failure to obtain her informed consent to surgery as required by Wis. Stat. § 448.30 (1993–94). The jury found that the defendant failed to adequately inform the plaintiff regarding the risks associated with her surgery. The jury also found that a reasonable person in the plaintiff's position would have refused to consent to surgery by the defendant if she had been fully informed of its attendant risks and advantages.

This case presents the issue of whether the circuit court erred in admitting evidence that the defendant, in undertaking his duty to obtain the plaintiff's informed consent before operating to clip an aneurysm, failed (1) to divulge the extent of his experience in performing this type of operation; (2) to compare the morbidity and mortality rates[5] for this type of surgery among experienced surgeons and inexperienced surgeons like himself; and (3) to refer the plaintiff to a tertiary care center staffed by physicians more experienced in performing the same surgery. The admissibility of such physician–specific evidence in a case involving the doctrine of informed consent raises an issue of first impression in this court and is an issue with which appellate courts have had little experience.

* * *

I.

* * *

On the advice of her family physician, the plaintiff underwent a CT scan to determine the cause of her headaches. Following the scan, the family physician referred the plaintiff to the defendant, a neurosurgeon in the Chippewa Falls area. The defendant diagnosed an enlarging aneurysm at the rear of the plaintiff's brain and recommended surgery to clip the aneurysm. The defendant performed the surgery in October of 1990.

The defendant clipped the aneurysm, rendering the surgery a technical success. But as a consequence of the surgery, the plaintiff, who had no neurological impairments prior to surgery, was rendered an incomplete quadriplegic. She remains unable to walk or to control her bowel and bladder movements. Furthermore, her vision, speech and upper body coordination are partially impaired.

---

[5] As used by the parties and in this opinion, morbidity and mortality rates refer to the prospect that surgery may result in serious impairment or death.

At trial, the plaintiff introduced evidence that the defendant overstated the urgency of her need for surgery and overstated his experience with performing the particular type of aneurysm surgery which she required. According to testimony introduced during the plaintiff's case in chief, when the plaintiff questioned the defendant regarding his experience, he replied that he had performed the surgery she required "several" times; asked what he meant by "several," the defendant said "dozens" and "lots of times."

In fact, however, the defendant had relatively limited experience with aneurysm surgery. He had performed thirty aneurysm surgeries during residency, but all of them involved anterior circulation aneurysms. According to the plaintiff's experts, operations performed to clip anterior circulation aneurysms are significantly less complex than those necessary to clip posterior circulation aneurysms such as the plaintiff's. Following residency, the defendant had performed aneurysm surgery on six patients with a total of nine aneurysms. He had operated on basilar bifurcation aneurysms only twice and had never operated on a large basilar bifurcation aneurysm such as the plaintiff's aneurysm.[11]

* * *

Finally, the plaintiff introduced into evidence testimony and exhibits stating that a reasonable physician in the defendant's position would have advised the plaintiff of the availability of more experienced surgeons and would have referred her to them. The plaintiff also introduced evidence stating that patients with basilar aneurysms should be referred to tertiary care centers—such as the Mayo Clinic, only 90 miles away—which contain the proper neurological intensive care unit and microsurgical facilities and which are staffed by neurosurgeons with the requisite training and experience to perform basilar bifurcation aneurysm surgeries.

* * *

The defendant's expert witnesses testified that the defendant's recommendation of surgery was appropriate, that this type of surgery is regularly undertaken in a community hospital setting, and that the risks attending anterior and posterior circulation aneurysm surgeries are comparable. * * * The defendant's expert witnesses also testified that when queried by a patient regarding their experience, they would divulge the extent of that experience and its relation to the experience of other physicians performing similar operations.

[11] The defendant testified that he had failed to inform the plaintiff that he was not and never had been board certified in neurosurgery and that he was not a subspecialist in aneurysm surgery.

II.

[In Part II The court discussed Wisconsin's approach to informed consent, essentially the *Canterbury* position. The court noted that significant potential risks must be disclosed, as part of all information material to a patient's decision.]

* * *

IV.

[In Part IV, the court considered whether a physician's experience with a procedure should be considered by the trier of fact. It held that information as to such experience could be important to the plaintiff's decision as to whether to proceed with a medical procedure.]

In this case, the plaintiff introduced ample evidence that had a reasonable person in her position been aware of the defendant's relative lack of experience in performing basilar bifurcation aneurysm surgery, that person would not have undergone surgery with him. According to the record the plaintiff had made inquiry of the defendant's experience with surgery like hers. In response to her direct question about his experience he said that he had operated on aneurysms comparable to her aneurysm "dozens" of times. The plaintiff also introduced evidence that surgery on basilar bifurcation aneurysms is more difficult than any other type of aneurysm surgery and among the most difficult in all of neurosurgery. We conclude that the circuit court did not erroneously exercise its discretion in admitting evidence regarding the defendant's lack of experience and the difficulty of the proposed procedure. A reasonable person in the plaintiff's position would have considered such information material in making an intelligent and informed decision about the surgery.

* * *

V.

* * * The defendant * * * objects to comparative risk statistics purporting to estimate and compare the morbidity and mortality rates when the surgery at issue is performed, respectively, by a physician of limited experience such as the defendant and by the acknowledged masters in the field. Expert testimony introduced by the plaintiff indicated that the morbidity and mortality rate expected when a surgeon with the defendant's experience performed the surgery would be significantly higher than the rate expected when a more experienced physician performed the same surgery.

* * *

* * * The plaintiff * * * introduced evidence that the defendant estimated the risk of death or serious impairment associated with her surgery at two percent. At trial, however, the defendant conceded that be-

cause of his relative lack of experience, he could not hope to match the ten–and–seven–tenths percent morbidity and mortality rate reported for large basilar bifurcation aneurysm surgery by very experienced surgeons.

The defendant also admitted at trial that he had not shared with the plaintiff information from articles he reviewed prior to surgery. These articles established that even the most accomplished posterior circulation aneurysm surgeons reported morbidity and mortality rates of fifteen percent for basilar bifurcation aneurysms. Furthermore, the plaintiff introduced expert testimony indicating that the estimated morbidity and mortality rate one might expect when a physician with the defendant's relatively limited experience performed the surgery would be close to thirty percent.

Had a reasonable person in the plaintiff's position been made aware that being operated upon by the defendant significantly increased the risk one would have faced in the hands of another surgeon performing the same operation, that person might well have elected to forego surgery with the defendant. * * *

* * * When different physicians have substantially different success rates, whether surgery is performed by one rather than another represents a choice between "alternate, viable medical modes of treatment" under § 448.30.

For example, while there may be a general risk of ten percent that a particular surgical procedure will result in paralysis or death, that risk may climb to forty percent when the particular procedure is performed by a relatively inexperienced surgeon. It defies logic to interpret this statute as requiring that the first, almost meaningless statistic be divulged to a patient while the second, far more relevant statistic should not be. Under * * * Wis.Stat. § 448.30, the second statistic would be material to the patient's exercise of an intelligent and informed consent regarding treatment options. A circuit court may in its discretion conclude that the second statistic is admissible.

The doctrine of informed consent requires disclosure of "all of the viable alternatives and risks of the treatment proposed" which would be material to a patient's decision. [ ] We therefore conclude that when different physicians have substantially different success rates with the same procedure and a reasonable person in the patient's position would consider such information material, the circuit court may admit this statistical evidence. [ ]

We caution, as did the court of appeals, that our decision will not always require physicians to give patients comparative risk evidence in statistical terms to obtain informed consent. [The court notes in a footnote that comparative risk data can itself be unreliable, citing articles noting deficiencies in statistical design or collection methods.] Rather, we hold that evidence of the morbidity and mortality outcomes of different physicians was admissible under the circumstances of this case.

In keeping with the fact–driven and context–specific application of informed consent doctrine, questions regarding whether statistics are sufficiently material to a patient's decision to be admissible and sufficiently reliable to be non–prejudicial are best resolved on a case–by–case basis. The fundamental issue in an informed consent case is less a question of how a physician chooses to explain the panoply of treatment options and risks necessary to a patient's informed consent than a question of assessing whether a patient has been advised that such options and risks exist.

As the court of appeals observed, in this case it was the defendant himself who elected to explain the risks confronting the plaintiff in statistical terms. He did this because, as he stated at trial, "numbers giv[e] some perspective to the framework of the very real, immediate, human threat that is involved with this condition." Because the defendant elected to explain the risks confronting the plaintiff in statistical terms, it stands to reason that in her effort to demonstrate how the defendant's numbers dramatically understated the risks of her surgery, the plaintiff would seek to introduce other statistical evidence. Such evidence was integral to her claim that the defendant's nondisclosure denied her the ability to exercise informed consent.

VI.

The defendant also asserts that the circuit court erred as a matter of law in allowing the plaintiff to introduce expert testimony that because of the difficulties associated with operating on the plaintiff's aneurysm, the defendant should have referred her to a tertiary care center containing a proper neurological intensive care unit, more extensive microsurgical facilities and more experienced surgeons. While evidence that a physician should have referred a patient elsewhere may support an action alleging negligent treatment, argues the defendant, it has no place in an informed consent action.

* * *

When faced with an allegation that a physician breached a duty of informed consent, the pertinent inquiry concerns what information a reasonable person in the patient's position would have considered material to an exercise of intelligent and informed consent. [ ] Under the facts and circumstances presented by this case, the circuit court could declare, in the exercise of its discretion, that evidence of referral would have been material to the ability of a reasonable person in the plaintiff's position to render informed consent.

The plaintiff's medical experts testified that given the nature and difficulty of the surgery at issue, the plaintiff could not make an intelligent decision or give an informed consent without being made aware that surgery in a tertiary facility would have decreased the risk she faced. One of the plaintiff's experts, Dr. Haring J.W. Nauta, stated that "it's not fair not to bring up the subject of referral to another center when the problem is as difficult to treat" as the plaintiff's aneurysm was. Another of the plaintiff's experts, Dr. Robert Narotzky, testified that the defendant's "very limited" experience with aneurysm surgery rendered reasonable a referral to "someone with a lot more experience in dealing with this kind of problem." * * *

Articles from the medical literature introduced by the plaintiff also stated categorically that the surgery at issue should be performed at a tertiary care center while being "excluded" from the community setting because of "the limited surgical experience" and lack of proper equipment and facilities available in such hospitals.

* * * Hence under the materiality standard [ ], we conclude that the circuit court properly exercised its discretion in admitting evidence that the defendant should have advised the plaintiff of the possibility of undergoing surgery at a tertiary care facility.

The defendant asserts that the plaintiff knew she could go elsewhere. This claim is both true and beside the point. Credible evidence in this case demonstrates that the plaintiff chose not to go elsewhere because the defendant gave her the impression that her surgery was routine and that it therefore made no difference who performed it. The pertinent inquiry, then, is not whether a reasonable person in the plaintiff's position would have known generally that she might have surgery elsewhere, but rather whether such a person would have chosen to have surgery elsewhere had the defendant adequately disclosed the comparable risks attending surgery performed by him and surgery performed at a tertiary care facility such as the Mayo Clinic, only 90 miles away.

* * *

Moreover, we have already concluded that comparative risk data distinguishing the defendant's morbidity and mortality rate from the rate of more experienced physicians was properly before the jury. A close link exists between such data and the propriety of referring a patient elsewhere. A physician who discloses that other physicians might have lower morbidity and mortality rates when performing the same procedure will presumably have access to information regarding who some of those physicians are. When the duty to share comparative risk data is material to a patient's exercise of informed consent, an ensuing referral elsewhere will often represent no more than a modest and logical next step. [ ]

* * *

For the reasons set forth, we conclude that the circuit court did not erroneously exercise its discretion in admitting the evidence at issue, and accordingly, we reverse the decision of the court of appeals and remand the cause to the circuit court for further proceedings consistent with this opinion.

NOTES AND QUESTIONS

1. Do you see any problems with the duty to disclose articulated in *Kokemoor*? Can a surgeon manage to disguise poor results or repackage the data to confuse the patient? Or is this likely to represent the future, in which patients peruse batting averages before choosing their providers? Is there anything wrong with a consumer–driven model of medicine? Physician experience does matter, in terms of volume of cases handled. Selywn O. Rogers, et al., Relation of Surgeon and Hospital Volume to Processes and Outcomes of Colorectal Cancer Surgery, 244 Annals Surg. 1003 (2006) (greater surgeon and hospital volumes associated with improved outcomes for patients undergoing surgery for colorectal cancer); Richard J. Veerapen, Informed Consent: Physician Inexperience is a Material Risk for Patients, 35 J. Law, Med & Ethics 478, 481–82 (2007), ("*actual* risk of bowel injury may indeed be much higher in the hands of a practitioner who has had little unsupervised experience with the operation as compared to the risk in the hands of a more experienced surgeon.")

2. In *Kokemoor,* accurate physician–specific information was material because it was evidence of the proposed treatment's greater risk. In a later Wisconsin case, Prissel v. Physicians Insurance Company of Wisconsin, Inc, 269 Wis.2d 541, 674 N.W.2d 680 (Wis.App. 2003), the plaintiff argued that information on restrictions on the physician's surgeries—he was prohibited from performing any operation without another senior cardiovascular surgeon as his assistant—was relevant and material, as was the fact that the surgeon would be performing the plaintiff's operation with only a physician assistant. The court noted that the evidence was "devoid of evidence of alternate viable medical modes of treatment or mortality or morbidity rates;" the court found that "Prissel offered no evidence showing that cardiovascular surgeons have substantially different success rates when operating with another surgeon to assist than when operating with a physician's assistant. There was no evidence that had another surgeon assisted, rather than a physician's assistant, the morbidity or mortality rate would have been significantly lower. There was no evidence that another experienced cardiovascular surgeon was available to perform the surgery or that another cardiovascular surgeon was available to assist."

3. Most courts resist requirements that specific percentages of risks be disclosed, arguing that medicine is an inexact science. Recall how *Kokemoor* handled the issue of the relevance of statistics generally. See also Whiteside v. Lukson, 89 Wash.App. 109, 947 P.2d 1263 (1997). But see Hales v. Pittman, 118 Ariz. 305, 576 P.2d 493 (1978) (discussing the battery count of the plaintiff's complaint, the court proposed that the doctor should disclose

both the general statistical success rate for a given procedure and his particular experience with that procedure.).

4. Courts continue to tread carefully in the thickets of mandated physician disclosure of experience and qualifications. If the patient asks questions specifically about these issues, a physician who equivocates may risk liability, as *Kokemoor* demonstrates. In Willis v. Bender, 596 F.3d 1244 (10th Circuit 2010), the defendant Bender, a general surgeon, perforated Marcy Willis' small bowel while performing a laparoscopic surgery to remove her gallbladder. Willis had asked Dr. Bender several questions before deciding to proceed, including whether he had ever been sued, had had problems with his medical license, and the extent of his experience and track record with the laparoscopic procedure. The court observed that "Bender had in fact been sued several times, including by a family of a patient who had died after undergoing [the same procedure] performed by Bender in 2001." The court framed the issue as "not whether Bender had a duty under Wyoming's informed consent law to voluntarily disclose physician–specific information but rather whether he had a duty to truthfully answer Willis' physician–specific questions."

After reviewing the caselaw in other states, the court concluded:

> We only predict the Wyoming Supreme Court would allow an informed consent claim where a physician lies to a patient as to *physician–specific* information *in direct response to a patient's questions concerning the same* in the course of obtaining the patient's consent and the questions seek *concrete verifiable facts,* not the doctor's subjective opinion or judgment as to the quality of his performance or abilities.

See also Howard v. University Medicine & Dentistry of New Jersey, 172 N.J. 537, 800 A.2d 73 (2002), where the court left open the questions of whether a physician might have a duty to disclosure his credentials accurately. Plaintiff had gone to see a surgeon about his back problems. The procedure went badly. Plaintiff's suit claimed in part that the defendant had misrepresented both his credentials and his experience in doing the procedure he proposed. The court held that the Plaintiff might claim lack of informed consent because of the false answers allegedly given by the surgeon, but left open the question as to whether a physician might have an affirmative duty to disclose the information in question.

5. See Chapter 6 for a discussion of the use of comparative outcomes data for credentialing for hospital staff privileges.

PROBLEM: DISCLOSING PHYSICIAN RISKS

1. Dr. Patterson, a cardiac surgeon, misrepresents to his patient Tom Jones the number of times he had done a procedure, telling him he had performed it sixty when he had done it nine times. He gives this erroneous information in response to Tom's question to him about his experience. Should

this be sufficient to allow an informed consent action to proceed? Why or why not? What about other claims, such as fraud?

2. Dr. Ratler, an orthopedic surgeon in his late fifties, has begun to notice that his skill level—his vision and his fine motor skills—is diminishing. He examines his patients' records over the past three years, and discovers that his patient statistics are worsening, such that the odds of an iatrogenic injury at the hands of Ratler have increased from 1 in 1,000 to 1 in 750. His overall record is still excellent, much better than an orthopedic surgeon just coming out of a residency program. Should he disclose to his patients that he is beginning to suffer the inevitable results of aging? Or just that his success rate is a certain percentage?

3. Boosier City Memorial Hospital has a staff surgeon, Dr. Williams, who is an alcoholic. He is an excellent surgeon when he is not impaired by drinking. But because he is a chronic alcoholic, it is hard to predict when he may be impaired. Should Dr. Williams be required to disclose to patients that he is an alcoholic, so they can choose whether to continue with him? (See discussion of impaired physicians and licensure in Chapter 2.)

4. Disclosure of Statistical Mortality Information

Patients with diseases such as cancer usually face a reduced life expectancy even with the best medical treatment. Such patients would presumably like to know as much as possible about their life expectancy for a variety of reasons—estate planning, goodbyes to family and friends, and fortifying themselves to face death for personal and religious reasons. Must the doctor inform the patient of his life expectancy based on statistical tables?

ARATO V. AVEDON

Supreme Court of California, 1993.
5 Cal.4th 1172, 23 Cal.Rptr.2d 131, 858 P.2d 598.

ARABIAN, JUSTICE.

A physician's duty to disclose to a patient information material to the decision whether to undergo treatment is the central constituent of the legal doctrine known as "informed consent." In this case, we review the ruling of a divided Court of Appeal that, in recommending a course of chemotherapy and radiation treatment to a patient suffering from a virulent form of cancer, the treating physicians breached their duty to obtain the patient's informed consent by failing to disclose his statistical life expectancy.

* * *

I

A

Miklos Arato was a successful 42–year–old electrical contractor and part–time real estate developer when, early in 1980, his internist diagnosed a failing kidney. On July 21, 1980, in the course of surgery to remove the kidney, the operating surgeon detected a tumor on the "tail" or distal portion of Mr. Arato's pancreas. After Mrs. Arato gave her consent, portions of the pancreas were resected, or removed, along with the spleen and the diseased kidney. A follow–up pathological examination of the resected pancreatic tissue confirmed a malignancy. Concerned that the cancer could recur and might have infiltrated adjacent organs, Mr. Arato's surgeon referred him to a group of oncology practitioners for follow–up treatment.

During his initial visit to the oncologists, Mr. Arato filled out a multipage questionnaire routinely given new patients. Among the some 150 questions asked was whether patients "wish[ed] to be told the truth about [their] condition" or whether they wanted the physician to "bear the burden" for them. Mr. Arato checked the box indicating that he wished to be told the truth.

The oncologists discussed with Mr. and Mrs. Arato the advisability of a course of chemotherapy known as "F.A.M.," a treatment employing a combination of drugs which, when used in conjunction with radiation therapy, had shown promise in treating pancreatic cancer in experimental trials. The nature of the discussions between Mr. and Mrs. Arato and the treating physicians, and in particular the scope of the disclosures made to the patient by his doctors, was the subject of conflicting testimony at trial. By their own admission, however, neither the operating surgeon nor the treating oncologists specifically disclosed to the patient or his wife the high statistical mortality rate associated with pancreatic cancer.

Mr. Arato's oncologists determined that a course of F.A.M. chemotherapy was indicated for several reasons. According to their testimony, the high statistical mortality of pancreatic cancer is in part a function of what is by far the most common diagnostic scenario—the discovery of the malignancy well after it has metastasized to distant sites, spreading throughout the patient's body. As noted, in Mr. Arato's case, the tumor was comparatively localized, having been discovered in the tail of the pancreas by chance in the course of surgery to remove the diseased kidney.

Related to the "silent" character of pancreatic cancer is the fact that detection in such an advanced state usually means that the tumor cannot as a practical matter be removed, contributing to the high mortality rate. In Mr. Arato's case, however, the operating surgeon determined that it was possible to excise cleanly the tumorous portion of the pancreas and to leave a margin of about one–half centimeter around the surgical site, a margin that appeared clinically to be clear of cancer cells. Third, the mortality rate is somewhat lower, according to defense testimony, for pancreatic tumors located in the distal part of the organ than for those found in the main body. Finally, then–recent experimental studies on the use of F.A.M. chemotherapy in conjunction with therapeutic radiation treatments had shown promising response rates—on the order of several months of extended life—among pancreatic cancer patients.

Mr. Arato's treating physicians justified not disclosing statistical life expectancy data to their patient on disparate grounds. According to the testimony of his surgeon, Mr. Arato had exhibited great anxiety over his condition, so much so that his surgeon determined that it would have been medically inappropriate to disclose specific mortality rates. The patient's oncologists had a somewhat different explanation. As Dr. Melvin Avedon, his chief oncologist, put it, he believed that cancer patients in Mr. Arato's position "wanted to be told the truth, but did not want a cold shower." Along with the other treating physicians, Dr. Avedon testified that in his opinion the direct and specific disclosure of extremely high mortality rates for malignancies such as pancreatic cancer might effectively deprive a patient of any hope of cure, a medically inadvisable state. Moreover, all of the treating physicians testified that statistical life expectancy data had little predictive value when applied to a particular patient with individualized symptoms, medical history, character traits and other variables.

According to the physicians' testimony, Mr. and Mrs. Arato were told at the outset of the treatment that most victims of pancreatic cancer die of the disease, that Mr. Arato was at "serious" or "great" risk of a recurrence and that, should the cancer return, his condition would be judged incurable. This information was given to the patient and his wife in the context of a series of verbal and behavioral cues designed to invite the patient or family member to follow up with more direct and difficult questions. Such follow–up questions, on the order of "how long do I have to live?," would have signaled to his doctors, according to Dr. Avedon's testimony, the patient's desire and ability to confront the fact of imminent mortality. In the judgment of his chief oncologist, Mr. Arato, although keenly interested in the clinical significance of the most minute symptom, studiously avoided confronting these ultimate issues; according to his doctors, neither Mr. Arato nor his wife ever asked for information concerning his life expectancy in more than 70 visits over a period of a year. Believing that they had disclosed information sufficient to enable him to make an informed decision whether to undergo chemotherapy, Mr. Arato's doctors concluded that their patient had as much information regarding his condition and prognosis as he wished.

Dr. Avedon also testified that he told Mr. Arato that the effectiveness of F.A.M. therapy was unproven in cases such as his, described its principal adverse side effects, and noted that one of the patient's options was not to undergo the treatment. In the event, Mr. Arato consented to the proposed course of chemotherapy and radiation, treatments that are prolonged, difficult and painful for cancer patients. Unfortunately, the treatment proved ineffective in arresting the spread of the malignancy. Although clinical tests showed him to be free of cancer in the several months following the beginning of the F.A.M. treatments, beginning in late March and into April of 1981, the clinical signs took an adverse turn.[1] By late April, the doctors were convinced by the results of additional tests that the cancer had returned and was spreading. They advised the patient of their suspicions and discontinued chemotherapy. On July 25, 1981, a year and four days following surgery, Mr. Arato succumbed to the effects of pancreatic cancer.

B

Not long after his death, Mr. Arato's wife and two children brought this suit against the physicians who had treated their husband and father in his last days, including the surgeon who performed the pancreas resection and the oncologists who had recommended and administered the chemotherapy/radiation treatment. As presented to the jury, the gist of the lawsuit was the claim that in discussing with their patient the advisability of undergoing a course of chemotherapy and radiation, Mr. Arato's doctors had failed to disclose adequately the shortcomings of the proposed treatment in light of the diagnosis, and thus had failed to obtain the patient's informed consent. Specifically, plaintiffs contended that the doctors were aware that, because early detection is difficult and rare, pancreatic cancer is an especially virulent malignancy, one in which only 5 to 10 percent of those afflicted live for as long as five years, and that given the practically incurable nature of the disease, there was little chance Mr. Arato would live more than a short while, even if the proposed treatment proved effective.

Such mortality information, the complaint alleged—especially the statistical morbidity rate of pancreatic cancer—was material to Mr. Arato's decision whether to undergo postoperative treatment; had he known the bleak truth concerning his life expectancy, he would not have undergone the rigors of an unproven therapy, but would have chosen to live out

[1] Around this time—on March 12, 1981, according to the record—an article appeared in the Los Angeles Times stating that only 1 percent of males and 2 percent of females diagnosed as having pancreatic cancer live for five years. According to his wife's testimony, Mr. Arato read the Times article and brought it to the attention of his oncologists. One of his oncologists confirmed such a discussion but denied that he told Mr. Arato that the statistics did not apply to his case, as Mrs. Arato testified. Mr. Arato continued to undergo chemotherapy treatment after reading the article and evidently made no changes in his estate planning or business and real estate affairs.

his last days at peace with his wife and children, and arranging his business affairs. Instead, the complaint asserted, in the false hope that radiation and chemotherapy treatments could effect a cure—a hope born of the negligent failure of his physicians to disclose the probability of an early death—Mr. Arato failed to order his affairs in contemplation of his death, an omission that, according to the complaint, led eventually to the failure of his contracting business and to substantial real estate and tax losses following his death.

As the trial neared its conclusion and the court prepared to charge the jury, plaintiffs requested that several special instructions be given relating to the nature and scope of the physician's duty of disclosure. Two proffered instructions in particular are pertinent to this appeal. In the first, plaintiffs asked the trial court to instruct the jury that "A physician has a fiduciary duty to a patient to make a full and fair disclosure to the patient of all facts which materially affect the patient's rights and interests." The second instruction sought by plaintiffs stated that "The scope of the physician's duty to disclose is measured by the amount of knowledge a patient needs in order to make an informed choice. All information material to the patient's decision should be given."

The trial judge declined to give the jury either of the two instructions sought by plaintiffs. * * *

After concluding its deliberations, the jury returned two special verdicts—on a form approved by plaintiffs' counsel—finding that none of the defendants was negligent in the "medical management" of Mr. Arato, and that defendants "disclosed to Mr. Arato all relevant information which would have enabled him to make an informed decision regarding the proposed treatment to be rendered him." Plaintiffs appealed from the judgment entered on the defense verdict, contending that the trial court erred in refusing to give the jury the special instructions requested by them. As noted, a divided Court of Appeal reversed the judgment of the trial court, and ordered a new trial. We granted defendants' ensuing petition for review and now reverse the judgment of the Court of Appeal.

C

[The court in section C discusses the Court of Appeal decision, which required that Mr. Arato's doctors disclose numerical life expectancy information so that he could reduce the risks of financial loss; and found that the trial court instructions were defective in several regards].

II

A

[The court discusses Cobbs v. Grant at length, and the duty it imposed on a treating physician "of reasonable disclosure of the available choices with respect to proposed therapy and of the dangers inherently and potentially involved in each." [ ] It also considered both Truman v. Thomas and Moore v. Board of Regents, and their refinement of California's informed consent law.]

B

* * *

* * * The principal question we must address is whether our holding in Cobbs v. Grant, [ ] * * * accurately conveys to juries the legal standard under which they assess the evidence in determining the adequacy of the disclosures made by physician to patient in a particular case or whether, as the Court of Appeal here appeared to conclude, the standard instruction should be revised to mandate specific disclosures such as patient life expectancy as revealed by mortality statistics.

In our view, one of the merits of the [instruction used by the lower court] is its recognition of the importance of the overall medical context that juries ought to take into account in deciding whether a challenged disclosure was reasonably sufficient to convey to the patient information material to an informed treatment decision. The contexts and clinical settings in which physician and patient interact and exchange information material to therapeutic decisions are so multifarious, the informational needs and degree of dependency of individual patients so various, and the professional relationship itself such an intimate and irreducibly judgment–laden one, that we believe it is unwise to require as a matter of law that a particular species of information be disclosed. . . . [ ]

* * *

This sensitivity to context seems all the more appropriate in the case of life expectancy projections for cancer patients based on statistical samples. Without exception, the testimony of every physician–witness at trial confirmed what is evident even to a nonprofessional: statistical morbidity values derived from the experience of population groups are inherently unreliable and offer little assurance regarding the fate of the individual patient; indeed, to assume that such data are conclusive in themselves smacks of a refusal to explore treatment alternatives and the medical abdication of the patient's well–being. Certainly the jury here heard evidence of articulable grounds for the conclusion that the particular features of Mr. Arato's case distinguished it from the typical population of pancreatic cancer sufferers and their dismal statistical probabilities—a fact plaintiffs impliedly acknowledged at trial in conceding that the oncologic referral of Mr. Arato and ensuing chemotherapy were not in themselves medically negligent.

* * *

Rather than mandate the disclosure of specific information as a matter of law, the better rule is to instruct the jury that a physician is under a legal duty to disclose to the patient all material information—that is, "information which the physician knows or should know would be regarded as significant by a reasonable person in the patient's position when deciding to accept or reject a recommended medical procedure"—needed to make an informed decision regarding a proposed treatment. That, of course, is * * * the instruction given in this case. Having been properly instructed, the jury returned a defense verdict—on a form approved by plaintiffs' counsel—specifically finding that defendants had "disclosed to Mr. Arato all relevant information which would have enabled him to make an informed decision regarding the proposed treatment to be rendered him."

We decline to intrude further, either on the subtleties of the physician–patient relationship or in the resolution of claims that the physician's duty of disclosure was breached, by requiring the disclosure of information that may or may not be indicated in a given treatment context. Instead, we leave the ultimate judgment as to the factual adequacy of a challenged disclosure to the venerable American jury, operating under legal instructions such as those given here and subject to the persuasive force of trial advocacy.

Here, the evidence was more than sufficient to support the jury's finding that defendants had reasonably disclosed to Mr. Arato information material to his decision whether to undergo the proposed chemotherapy/radiation treatment. There was testimony that Mr. and Mrs. Arato were informed that cancer of the pancreas is usually fatal; of the substantial risk of recurrence, an event that would mean his illness was incurable; of the unproven nature of the F.A.M. treatments and their principal side effects; and of the option of forgoing such treatments. Mr. Arato's doctors also testified that they could not with confidence predict how long the patient might live, notwithstanding statistical mortality tables.

In addition, the jury heard testimony regarding the patient's apparent avoidance of issues bearing upon mortality; Mrs. Arato's testimony that his physicians had assured her husband that he was "clear" of cancer; and the couple's common expectation that he had been "cured," only to learn, suddenly and unexpectedly, that the case was hopeless and life measurable in weeks. The informed consent instructions given the jury to assess this evidence were an accurate statement of the law, and the Court of Appeal in effect invaded the province of the trier of fact in overturning a fairly litigated verdict.[ ]

C

In addition to their claim that his physicians were required to disclose statistical life expectancy data to Mr. Arato to enable him to reach an informed treatment decision, plaintiffs also contend that defendants should have disclosed such data because it was material to the patient's nonmedical interests, that is, Mr. Arato's business and investment affairs and the potential adverse impact of his death upon them. In support of this proposition, plaintiffs rely on the following statement * * *[ ]: "As fiduciaries it was the duty of defendants [physicians] to make a full and fair disclosure to plaintiff of all facts which materially affected his rights and interests." Plaintiffs contend that since Mr. Arato's contracting and real estate affairs would suffer if he failed to make timely changes in estate planning in contemplation of imminent death, and since these matters are among "his rights and interests," his physicians were under a legal duty to disclose all material facts that might affect them, including statistical life expectancy information. We reject the claim as one founded on a premise that is not recognized in California.

The short answer to plaintiffs' claim is our statement in *Moore* [ ] that a "physician is not the patient's financial adviser."[ ] From its inception, the rationale behind the disclosure requirement implementing the doctrine of informed consent has been to protect the patient's freedom to "exercise . . . control over [one's] own body" by directing the course of medical treatment.[ ] We recently noted that "the principle of self–determination . . . embraces all aspects of medical decisionmaking by the competent adult. . . . "[ ] Although an aspect of personal autonomy, the conditions for the exercise of the patient's right of self–decision presuppose a therapeutic focus * * *. The fact that a physician has "fiducial" obligations * * * which * * * prohibit misrepresenting the nature of the patient's medical condition, does not mean that he or she is under a duty, the scope of which is undefined, to disclose every contingency that might affect the patient's nonmedical "rights and interests." Because plaintiffs' open–ended proposed instruction—that the physician's duty embraces the "disclosure * * * of all facts which materially affect the patient's rights and interests"—failed to reflect the therapeutic limitation inherent in the doctrine of informed consent, it would have been error for the trial judge to give it to the jury.

Finally, plaintiffs make much of the fact that in his initial visit to Dr. Avedon's office, Mr. Arato indicated in a lengthy form he was requested to complete that he "wish[ed] to be told the truth about [his] condition." In effect, they contend that as a result of Mr. Arato's affirmative answer, defendants had an absolute duty to make specific life expectancy disclosures to him. Whether the patient has filled out a questionnaire indicating that he or she wishes to be told the "truth" about his or her condition or not, however, a physician is under a legal duty to obtain the patient's informed consent to any recommended treatment. Although a patient may validly waive the right to be informed, we do not see how a request to be told the "truth" in itself heightens the duty of disclosure imposed on physicians as a matter of law.

III.

[The court finally considered the role of expert testimony in informed consent cases. The trial court had allowed two medical experts to testify that the standard of practice was not to disclose to pancreatic cancer patients specific life expectancy data unless the patient specifically requested such information; and defendants met the standard by not disclosing such information to Arato under the circumstances. Plaintiff's experts disagreed. The court held that expert testimony in an informed consent case, while serving a limited and subsidiary role, is appropriate where adequacy of disclosure turns on the standard of practice within a medical specialty.]

Conclusion

The judgment of the Court of Appeal is reversed and the cause is remanded with directions to affirm the judgment of the trial court.

NOTES AND QUESTIONS

1. The California Supreme Court says it is simply applying the *Cobbs* analysis to the facts of the *Arato* case. It refuses to impose any requirement that a physician disclose to the patient his life expectancy. Why? Is it a desire to leave the lay jury some "wiggle" room, empowering it as the trier of fact? Or a desire to give physicians the flexibility to avoid difficult disclosures? Is life expectancy data so inherently untrustworthy that patients should not be told? There is evidence that doctors generally fail to convey statistical data on survival rates to cancer patients, and may refuse to give up to 25 percent of their patients accurate estimates as to survival. See, e.g., Elizabeth B. Lamont and Nicholas A. Christakis, Prognostic Disclosure to Patients with Cancer near the End of Life, 134 Annals Intern. Med. 1096 (2001).

2. Consider the following cancer survival comparisons:

Estimates of Relative Survival Rates, By Cancer Site

	5 year	10 year	15 year	20 year
Prostate	98.8	95.2	87.1	81.1
Rectum	62.6	55.2	51.8	49.2
Stomach	23.8	19.4	19.0	14.9
Pancreas	4.0	3.0	2.7	2.7

This is an abbreviated chart, taken from Hermann Brenner, Long–term Survival Rates of Cancer Patients Achieved By the End of the 20th century:

A Period Analysis, 360 The Lancet 1131 (2002); as reinterpreted by Edward Tufte, Cancer survival rates: tables, graphics, and PP (October 28, 2002).

Does this change your thinking about the correctness of *Arato*?

3. Does *Arato* in effect expand the defense of "therapeutic privilege", giving professional standards undue weight in both the instructions and the expert testimony? If a patient has a cancer that is often lethal in a short time, how much more terrifying is specific knowledge as to life expectancy? Oncologists generally are reluctant to discuss prognosis in order to preserve patient hope. One study found that "oncologists vary the amount of prognostic information given to patients depending on patients' levels of hope, the presence of unrealistic expectations, and responses to earlier efforts to disclose prognostic information". Elisa J. Gordon and Christopher K. Daugherty, "Hitting You Over the Head": Oncologists' Disclosure of Prognosis to Advanced Cancer Patients, 17 Bioethics 142 (2003).

4. To what extent should a health care provider's informational power expand its obligations to protect a patient's financial interests? A middle–aged patient, facing imminent death, might pursue several alternatives to protect assets for his or her family. He or she might declare personal bankruptcy to wipe out debts, might undertake estate planning to protect assets for the family, might restructure a small business to bring in new administrators, etc. *Arato* seems to blame the plaintiff for not asking, letting the physicians off the hook. Should we let them off so easily? Physicians historically had to discuss treatment costs with patients. In the early days of fee–for–service medicine, patients had to choose between expensive treatments and their other needs, since insurance was not readily available. Today, patients seeking organ transplantation or experimental therapies need to know about their insurance coverage or the availability of Medicaid or other government sources. Both the hospital and treating physician have some role in helping a patient sort out payment sources and costs. Would you be willing to make providing this information an ethical obligation if not a legal duty? Or, would you want to prohibit a discussion of cost?

5. Courts have generally refused to find a hospital or physician negligent for failing to advise patients that they were eligible for government funding. See, e.g., Mraz v. Taft, 85 Ohio App.3d 200, 619 N.E.2d 483 (1993) (neither hospital nor nursing home had any duty to advise husband that he qualified for Medicaid). Nor is a physician liable for the financial consequences of a misdiagnosis, for example a patient's cancellation of a life insurance policy upon being erroneously informed that he did not have cancer. See Blacher v. Garlett, 857 P.2d 566, 568 (Colo.App. Div.III 1993). But see the discussion in Chapter 5 of the *Wickline* and *Wilson* cases.

PROBLEM: INFORMATION OVERLOAD

You have been asked by one of your clients, the Gladstone Women's Clinic, to draft some guidelines to help staff physicians handle disclosures to patients who are reluctant to discuss risks of tests or procedures or who are uninsured and therefore careful about medical costs. What are the safe outer limits of physician silence about diagnostic options and their risks? What is best for the patient therapeutically? Consider new techniques of genetic diagnosis performed on adults to see if they might be carriers of the gene for Huntington's disease, cystic fibrosis, manic–depressive illness and other neurological disorders. The purpose of these tests is to assess whether the patient will develop a particular condition. However, the presence of particular genetic structures and the development of clinically relevant disease is not straightforward for diseases such as heart disease, hypertension, mental illness, or cancer. An abnormal gene may not result in clinical disease. In Huntington's chorea, for example, the time of onset varies from early childhood to the seventies. Thus, a patient needs to know a great deal about the likelihood of a disease developing before a positive test result indicating the presence of a genetic marker for a disease becomes useful.

The very existence of techniques for prenatal diagnosis also produces stress in potential parents. Negative results give relief, alleviating anxiety that the very existence of the tests created. The tests' availability "sharpens what might otherwise be low–level, diffuse concerns that surface only, as one woman put it, 'on bad days,' and turns them into real and dreaded possibilities." Aliza Kolker, Advances in Prenatal Diagnosis: Social–Psychological and Policy Issues, 5 Intl.J.Tech.Assess. in Health Care 601, 608 (1989). Consider the controversy over regular mammograms, and the consensus recommendation to avoid annual mammograms if no specific risk factors are present. See David Gorksi, The Mammography Wars Heat Up Again, Science Based Medicine (2012); for background, see Gail R. Wilensky, The Mammography Guidelines and Evidence–Based Medicine, Health Affairs Blog (2010).

Consider the kinds of tests that might be available to women who come to the clinic:

1. Pap Smears and mammograms to detect cancer;

2. Amniocentesis, chorionic villus sampling (CVS) and ultrasound imaging for evaluating fetal development and health;

3. HIV tests to look for the possibility of the AIDS virus in a woman who may want to get pregnant;

4. Genetic diagnostic technologies used to assess whether a patient will develop a given condition such as breast cancer; or whether her children will develop Huntington's disease, cystic fibrosis or other diseases for which the mother may have genetic markers.

5. Disclosure of Financial Conflicts of Interest

MOORE V. REGENTS OF THE UNIVERSITY OF CALIFORNIA

Supreme Court of California, 1990.
51 Cal.3d 120, 271 Cal.Rptr. 146, 793 P.2d 479.

[The plaintiff John Moore underwent treatment for hairy–cell leukemia at the Medical Center of the University of California at Los Angeles (UCLA Medical Center). The defendants were Dr. David Golde, the attending physician; the Regents of the University of California, who own and operate the university; Shirley Quan, a researcher at the University; Genetics Institute; and Sandoz Pharmaceuticals Corporation. The Supreme Court granted review to determine whether Moore had stated a cause of action for breach of the physician's disclosure obligations and for conversion. The Court rejected the conversion cause of action.]

* * *

II. Facts

* * *

Moore first visited UCLA Medical Center on October 5, 1976, shortly after he learned that he had hairy–cell leukemia. After hospitalizing Moore and "withdr[awing] extensive amounts of blood, bone marrow aspirate, and other bodily substances," Golde confirmed that diagnosis. At this time all defendants, including Golde, were aware that "certain blood products and blood components were of great value in a number of commercial and scientific efforts" and that access to a patient whose blood contained these substances would provide "competitive, commercial, and scientific advantages."

On October 8, 1976, Golde recommended that Moore's spleen be removed. Golde informed Moore "that he had reason to fear for his life, and that the proposed splenectomy operation * * * was necessary to slow down the progress of his disease." Based upon Golde's representations, Moore signed a written consent form authorizing the splenectomy.

Before the operation, Golde and Quan "formed the intent and made arrangements to obtain portions of [Moore's] spleen following its removal" and to take them to a separate research unit. Golde gave written instructions to this effect on October 18 and 19, 1976. These research activities "were not intended to have * * * any relation to [Moore's] medical * * * care." However, neither Golde nor Quan informed Moore of their plans to conduct this research or requested his permission. Surgeons at UCLA Medical Center, whom the complaint does not name as defendants, removed Moore's spleen on October 20, 1976.

Moore returned to the UCLA Medical Center several times between November 1976 and September 1983. He did so at Golde's direction and based upon representations "that such visits were necessary and required for his health and well–being, and based upon the trust inherent in and by virtue of the physician–patient relationship. * * * " On each of these visits Golde withdrew additional samples of "blood, blood serum, skin, bone marrow aspirate, and sperm." On each occasion Moore traveled to the UCLA Medical Center from his home in Seattle because he had been told that the procedures were to be performed only there and only under Golde's direction.

"In fact, [however,] throughout the period of time that [Moore] was under [Golde's] care and treatment, * * * the defendants were actively involved in a number of activities which they concealed from [Moore]. * * * " Specifically, defendants were conducting research on Moore's cells and planned to "benefit financially and competitively * * * [by exploiting the cells] and [their] exclusive access to [the cells] by virtue of [Golde's] on–going physician–patient relationship. * * * "

Sometime before August 1979, Golde established a cell line from Moore's T–lymphocytes. On January 30, 1981, the Regents applied for a patent on the cell line, listing Golde and Quan as inventors. "[B]y virtue of an established policy * * *, [the] Regents, Golde, and Quan would share in any royalties or profits * * * arising out of [the] patent." The patent issued on March 20, 1984, naming Golde and Quan as the inventors of the cell line and the Regents as the assignee of the patent. (U.S. Patent No. 4,438,032 (Mar. 20, 1984).

The Regent's patent also covers various methods for using the cell line to produce lymphokines. Moore admits in his complaint that "the true clinical potential of each of the lymphokines * * * [is] difficult to predict, [but] * * * competing commercial firms in these relevant fields have published reports in biotechnology industry periodicals predicting a potential market of approximately $3.01 Billion Dollars by the year 1990 for a whole range of [such lymphokines]. * * * "

With the Regents' assistance, Golde negotiated agreements for commercial development of the cell line and products to be derived from it. Under an agreement with Genetics Institute, Golde "became a paid consultant" and "acquired the rights to 75,000 shares of common stock." Genetics Institute also agreed to pay Golde and the Regents "at least $330,000 over three years, including a pro–rata share of [Golde's] salary and fringe benefits, in exchange for * * * exclusive access to the materials and research performed" on the cell line and products derived from it. On June 4, 1982, Sandoz "was added to the agreement," and compensation payable to Golde and the Regents was increased by $110,000. "[T]hroughout this period, * * * Quan spent as much as 70 [percent] of her time working for [the] Regents on research" related to the cell line.

* * *

III. Discussion

A. *Breach of Fiduciary Duty and Lack of Informed Consent*

Moore repeatedly alleges that Golde failed to disclose the extent of his research and economic interests in Moore's cells before obtaining consent to the medical procedures by which the cells were extracted. These allegations, in our view, state a cause of action against Golde for invading a legally protected interest of his patient. This cause of action can properly be characterized either as the breach of a fiduciary duty to disclose facts material to the patient's consent or, alternatively, as the performance of medical procedures without first having obtained the patient's informed consent.

Our analysis begins with three well–established principles. First, "a person of adult years and in sound mind has the right, in the exercise of control over his own body, to determine whether or not to submit to lawful medical treatment." [ ] Second, "the patient's consent to treatment, to be effective, must be an informed consent." [ ] Third, in soliciting the patient's consent, a physician has a fiduciary duty to disclose all information material to the patient's decision. * * * [ ]

These principles lead to the following conclusions: (1) a physician must disclose personal interests unrelated to the patient's health, whether research or economic, that may affect the physician's professional judgment; and (2) a physician's failure to disclose such interests may give rise to a cause of action for performing medical procedures without informed consent or breach of fiduciary duty.

* * *

Indeed, the law already recognizes that a reasonable patient would want to know whether a physician has an economic interest that might affect the physician's professional judgment. [ ] The desire to protect patients from possible conflicts of interest has also motivated legislative enactments. Among these is Business and Professions Code section 654.2. Under that section, a physician may not charge a patient on behalf of, or refer a patient to, any organization in which the physician has a "significant beneficial interest, unless [the physician] first discloses in writing to the patient, that there is such an interest and advises the patient that the patient may choose any organization for the purposes of obtaining the services ordered or requested by [the physician]." [ ] Similarly, under Health and Safety Code section 24173, a physician who plans to conduct a medical experiment on a patient must, among other things, inform the patient of "[t]he name of the sponsor or funding source, if any, * * * and the organization, if any, under whose general aegis the experiment is being conducted." [ ]

It is important to note that no law prohibits a physician from conducting research in the same area in which he practices. Progress in medicine often depends upon physicians, such as those practicing at the university hospital where Moore received treatment, who conduct research while caring for their patients.

Yet a physician who treats a patient in whom he also has a research interest has potentially conflicting loyalties. This is because medical treatment decisions are made on the basis of proportionality—weighing the *benefits* to the patient against the *risks* to the patient. * * * [ ] A physician who adds his own research interests to this balance may be tempted to order a scientifically useful procedure or test that offers marginal, or no, benefits to the patient. The possibility that an interest extraneous to the patient's health has affected the physician's judgment is something that a reasonable patient would want to know in deciding whether to consent to a proposed course of treatment. It is material to the patient's decision and, thus, a prerequisite to informed consent. [ ]

Golde argues that the scientific use of cells that have already been removed cannot possibly affect the patient's medical interests. The argument is correct in one instance but not in another. If a physician has no plans to conduct research on a patient's cells at the time he recommends the medical procedure by which they are taken, then the patient's medical interests have not been impaired. In that instance the argument is correct. On the other hand, a physician who does have a preexisting research interest might, consciously or unconsciously, take that into consideration in recommending the procedure. In that instance the argument is incorrect: the physician's extraneous motivation may affect his judgment and is, thus, material to the patient's consent.

We acknowledge that there is a competing consideration. To require disclosure of research and economic interests may corrupt the patient's own judgment by distracting him from the requirements of his health. But California law does not grant physicians unlimited discretion to decide what to disclose. Instead, "it is the prerogative of the patient, not the physician, to determine for himself the direction in which he believes his interests lie." [ ] * * *

Accordingly, we hold that a physician who is seeking a patient's consent for a medical procedure must, in order to satisfy his fiduciary duty[10] and to obtain the patient's informed consent, disclose personal interests unrelated to the patient's health, whether research or economic, that may affect his medical judgment.

---

[10] In some respects the term "fiduciary" is too broad. In this context the term "fiduciary" signifies only that a physician must disclose all facts material to the patient's decision. A physician is not the patient's financial adviser. As we have already discussed, the reason why a physician must disclose possible conflicts is not because he has a duty to protect his patient's financial interests, but because certain personal interests may affect professional judgment.

1. Dr. Golde

We turn now to the allegations of Moore's third amended complaint to determine whether he has stated such a cause of action. We first discuss the adequacy of Moore's allegations against Golde, based upon the physician's disclosures prior to the splenectomy.

Moore alleges that, prior to the surgical removal of his spleen, Golde "formed the intent and made arrangements to obtain portions of his spleen following its removal from [Moore] in connection with [his] desire to have regular and continuous access to, and possession of, [Moore's] unique and rare Blood and Bodily Substances." Moore was never informed prior to the splenectomy of Golde's "prior formed intent" to obtain a portion of his spleen. In our view, these allegations adequately show that Golde had an undisclosed research interest in Moore's cells at the time he sought Moore's consent to the splenectomy. Accordingly, Moore has stated a cause of action for breach of fiduciary duty, or lack of informed consent, based upon the disclosures accompanying that medical procedure.

We next discuss the adequacy of Golde's alleged disclosures regarding the postoperative takings of blood and other samples. In this context, Moore alleges that Golde "expressly, affirmatively and impliedly represented * * * that these withdrawals of his Blood and Bodily Substances were necessary and required for his health and well–being." However, Moore also alleges that Golde actively concealed his economic interest in Moore's cells during this time period. "[D]uring each of these visits * * *, and even when [Moore] inquired as to whether there was any possible or potential commercial or financial value or significance of his Blood and Bodily Substances, or whether the defendants had discovered anything * * * which was or might be * * * related to any scientific activity resulting in commercial or financial benefits * * *, the defendants repeatedly and affirmatively represented to [Moore] that there was no commercial or financial value to his Blood and Bodily Substances * * * and in fact actively discouraged such inquiries."

Moore admits in his complaint that defendants disclosed they "were engaged in strictly academic and purely scientific medical research. * * * " However, Golde's representation that he had no financial interest in this research became false, based upon the allegations, at least by May 1979, when he "began to investigate and initiate the procedures * * * for [obtaining] a patent" on the cell line developed from Moore's cells.

In these allegations, Moore plainly asserts that Golde concealed an economic interest in the postoperative procedures. Therefore, applying the principles already discussed, the allegations state a cause of action for breach of fiduciary duty or lack of informed consent.

[The court held that the plaintiff could state a cause of action based on Dr. Golde's alleged failure to disclosure his research interest before the splenectomy. It also held that the operation had a therapeutic purpose.]

* * * Even if the splenectomy had a therapeutic purpose,[11] it does not follow that Golde had no duty to disclose his additional research and economic interests. As we have already discussed, the existence of a motivation for a medical procedure unrelated to the patient's health is a potential conflict of interest and a fact material to the patient's decision.

NOTES AND QUESTIONS

1. In *Moore,* the court explicitly uses both fiduciary duty and informed consent doctrine in order to impose an obligation on the physicians to disclose their research and economic interests. Does a claim of breach of fiduciary duty add anything to an informed consent claim? If so, what? What worries the California Supreme Court? Is it that the patient's medical interests will somehow be impaired because the physician's judgment during treatment may be corrupted by the promise of financial gain? Or is the court concerned about the patient's economic interests?

2. Does the normal treatment setting pose any comparable conflicts of interest, in which the physician's treatment decision may be affected by his financial interests in treating a particular patient? Suppose a physician examines a boy brought into the emergency room of a small community hospital after an auto accident. The boy has an injured leg and foot. The x–ray suggests a dislocated foot. The doctor can either try to reduce the dislocation in the hospital, or he can refer the boy to an orthopedic specialist in a large city a hundred miles away. If the physician chooses to treat, he gets a fee, while the referral generates no further income for him. What should the physician choose to disclose to the boy's parents? The medical risks in either approach? The economic issue that may color his judgment? See David Hilifiker, Facing Our Mistakes, 310 N.Eng.J.Med. 118, 119 (1984). See Principles of Medical Ethics of the American Medical Association § 8 (requiring doctor to seek consultation "whenever it appears that the quality of medical services may be enhanced thereby.")

3. Physicians may at times want to try a new or innovative approach to a patient's problems. What are their obligations to disclose that they are in effect "experimenting" on the patient? In Estrada v. Jaques, 70 N.C.App. 627, 321 S.E.2d 240 (1984), the surgeons treated the plaintiff for a gunshot wound to his leg. They tried a new technique, inserting a small steel coil into his weakened artery upstream from his aneurysm to cut off the flow of blood. Plaintiff signed a consent form prior to surgery. The surgery failed, and Estrada had to have his leg amputated. He argued that his consent was not "in-

[11] The record shows that the splenectomy did have a therapeutic purpose. The Regents' patent application, which the superior court and the Court of Appeal both accepted as part of the record, shows that Moore had a grossly enlarged spleen and that its excision improved his condition.

formed" since neither the surgeons nor the radiologists told him the procedure was experimental. The court held that the patient had a right to know that the embolization procedure was experimental.

> * * * With experimental procedures the "most frequent risks and hazards" will remain unknown until the procedure becomes established. If the health care provider has a duty to inform of *known* risks for *established* procedures, common sense and the purposes of the statute equally require that the health care provider inform the patient of any *uncertainty* regarding the risks associated with *experimental* procedures. This includes the experimental nature of the procedure and the *known or projected most likely risks.*

How does the court in *Estrada* define "experimental" for purposes of disclosure to patients? They mention the fact that the surgeons and radiologists were aware of only one previous operation and one article, and that the surgeons had no personal experience. Does the court have the same attitude toward such clinical experimentation as the court did in *Brook,* in Chapter 5, *infra*?

What should be disclosed to a patient about to undergo an experimental procedure? That this is the first time this team has attempted this procedure? That the literature lacks support at present for it? That the surgeons and radiologists will benefit financially or in career recognition if the procedure succeeds? Must the motivations of the team be clearly disclosed to the patient? Should the physicians' motivations even matter, so long as the patient and the physicians believe that the new procedure offers a better chance for the patient? Note that "experimental" is a term that can be used to describe any new or untested intervention, but that the federal regulations governing "research" use the latter term to describe only a subset of experimental interventions. 45 C.F.R.§ 46.102 (d) and (e).

4. Should a physician working in a managed care setting have to disclose the financial arrangements for his or her compensation? The argument is that the cost–conserving strategies of managed care (described in Chapter 6 *infra*) will alter the physician's judgment and the patient has a right to know this influence. This argument has generally been rejected by the courts. In Neade v. Portes, 193 Ill.2d 433, 250 Ill.Dec. 733, 739 N.E.2d 496 (2000), a plan physician twice refused to authorize an angiogram for a patient who was experiencing symptoms of coronary artery blockage, relying instead on a thallium stress test, and concluding that the patient did not have cardiac problems. The patient died a few days later from a massive myocardial infarction caused by coronary artery blockage.

The plaintiff alleged that he should have been informed about the Plan's Medical Incentive Fund, which set aside money that would be returned to participating physicians if not used for referrals or outside tests. The court cited Pegram v. Herdrich, 530 U.S. 211, 120 S.Ct. 2143, 147 L.Ed.2d 164 (2000):

> [T]he defense of any HMO would be that its physician did not act out of financial interest but for good medical reasons, the plausibility of which would require reference to standards of reasonable and customary medical practice in like circumstances. That, of course, is the traditional standard of the common law. [Citation.] Thus, for all practical purposes, every claim of fiduciary breach by an HMO physician making a mixed decision [about a patient's eligibility for treatment under an HMO and the appropriate treatment for the patient] would boil down to a malpractice claim, and the fiduciary standard would be nothing but the malpractice standard traditionally applied in actions against physicians. [ ]

The court then rejected the breach of fiduciary duty claim, on the ground that it added nothing to a basic negligence claim. They argued that plaintiff would end up having to show that she would have chosen differently with knowledge of the salary incentive system; that another physician would have offered the test; and that the test would have detected the plaintiff's condition.

What should a physician say? And how much would a patient have to know about the incentives that affect other physicians whom she might choose over Dr. Portes? Isn't it sufficient that a physician will always face the threat of a malpractice suit for breaching the standard of care, and this is a powerful counterforce to the subtle effects of salary incentives operating on physicians? How would you go about studying these questions?

Can you make an argument that a right to information in such cases does add something to a plaintiff's rights? Isn't this claim similar to the underlying goals of a battery–based informed consent claim? Is it in the same category as claimed rights to know about a physician's performance record, mental status, and substance abuse?

Is the court right that any meaningful disclosure of how physicians are paid should be done at the level of the managed care plan itself at the time the subscriber selects the plan? See generally Chapter 6 for a discussion of managed care regulation and liability.

5. Are physicians exposed to conflicting incentives with regard to testing patients? Consider emerging genetic diagnostic technologies. The adoption of such diagnostics by physicians will be driven by both clinical and economic motivations. Genetic testing will proliferate if third party payers reimburse such testing. Providers paid on a fee–for–service basis will adopt them if they are profitable. Malpractice fears will also cause physicians to use new tests if there is any chance of detecting a predisposition to disease. And of course some providers will want the information even if it is of marginal value.

NOTE: PHYSICIAN PAYMENT SUNSHINE ACT

The Affordable Care Act included two provisions regarding the disclosure of physician financial interests related to treatment of patients. The first creates a publicly accessible data base on industry payments made to physicians. The second requires that physicians disclose certain ownership interests to patients.

The ACA included the Physician Payment Sunshine Act (PPSA), codified at 42 U.S.C.A. § 1320a–7h (2010). The PPSA requires that manufacturers of drugs, devices, biologics, medical supplies or other items covered by Medicare or Medicaid must submit to the Secretary of HHS a list of physicians and teaching hospitals ("covered entities") to whom they have made payments or financial transfers. Reportable transfers include consulting fees, entertainment, travel (including the destination), food, honoraria, education, research, speaking or service as a faculty member, royalties, grants, or "any other" payment. The statute includes a list of exempt items, such as educational materials supplied for patients.

Any benefit or transfer that is valued at more than $10 must be reported. Exceptions include items provided for use in charity care, educational materials intended for the benefit of the patient, distributions or dividends paid on stock held in a publicly traded company, or devices loaned to the provider for a trial period not to exceed 90 days, among a few others. Manufacturers must also disclose if they have made a payment or contribution to any other party at the request of a covered entity. If a reportable transfer is made in connection with a specific product, the name or other identifier of the item must be disclosed as well.

The reporting obligation is enforced through civil monetary penalties. The data included in the reports will be available to the public, including physicians' patients, in a searchable web site, listed by name of the manufacturer and the covered entity. The Act also includes reporting requirements for distribution of drug samples by manufacturers.

HHS issued proposed rules under the Act. 76 Fed. Reg. 78742 (Dec. 19, 2011). See also Igor Gorlach, The Shaping of the Physician Payment Sunshine Rule, 40 J.L. Med. & Ethics 700 (2012); David Sclar and Gary Keilty, Sunshine and Strategy: Managing and Monitoring Compliance with PPACA's Sunshine Provisions—Evolving Legal Requirements and Operational Considerations, 24 The Health Lawyer 5, 14 (2012) (including discussion of state sunshine statutes).

The ACA also requires that certain doctors who are referring patients for certain radiology tests, including MRIs, in which the doctors have an ownership interests (self–referrals) disclose those interests to the patients. The disclosure must be in writing and must inform the patients that they may choose a different provider for that service.

C. CAUSATION COMPLEXITIES

CANTERBURY V. SPENCE

United States Court of Appeals, District of Columbia Circuit, 1972.
464 F.2d 772.

VII.

* * *

Better it is, we believe, to resolve the causality issue on an objective basis: in terms of what a prudent person in the patient's position would have decided if suitably informed of all perils bearing significance. If adequate disclosure could reasonably be expected to have caused that person to decline the treatment because of the revelation of the kind of risk or danger that resulted in harm, causation is shown, but otherwise not. The patient's testimony is relevant on that score of course but it would not threaten to dominate the findings. And since that testimony would probably be appraised congruently with the factfinder's belief in its reasonableness, the case for a wholly objective standard for passing on causation is strengthened. Such a standard would in any event ease the fact–finding process and better assure the truth as its product.

NOTES AND QUESTIONS

1. Causation can only be established if there is a link between the failure of a doctor to disclose and the patient's injury. Two tests of causation have emerged: the objective reasonable patient test and the subjective particular patient test. The former asks what a reasonable patient would have done. The latter asks what the particular patient would have done. *Canterbury* adopted the objective test, after a good deal of vacillation. The court was concerned with patient hindsight testimony that he or she would have foregone the treatment, testimony which the court feared would be "hardly * * * more than a guess, perhaps tinged by the circumstance that the uncommunicated hazard has in fact materialized." The fear is of self–serving testimony.

The risk must be "material" to a reasonable patient in the shoes of the plaintiff. Under this standard, a patient's testimony is not needed to get the issue of causation to the jury. The testimony may be admissible and relevant on causation, but not dispositive. The jury can decide without it "what a reasonable person in that position would have done." Hartke v. McKelway, 707 F.2d 1544 (D.C.Cir.1983).

Even if the plaintiff can establish that a reasonable patient would not have consented if properly informed, evidence that the plaintiff would have consented if fully informed may be presented to the jury. Bourgeois v. McDonald, 622 So.2d 684 (La.App. 4 Cir.1993).

For a critique of the objective test of causation, see Evelyn M. Tenenbaum, Revitalizing Informed Consent and Protecting Patient Autonomy: An Appeal to Abandon Objective Causation, 64 Okla. L. Rev. 697 (2012).

2. Is it easy for a jury to put themselves in the shoes of a particular plaintiff? To some extent, that is what the jury is always asked to do in tort cases, particularly as to pain and suffering awards. In that sense, therefore, the courts' rejection of the particular patient test seems unreasonable. Is, however, the jury's empathetic attempt to understand the plaintiff's pain in a personal injury case the same as the jury's collective attempt to second guess the plaintiff's decision whether or not to undergo the diagnosis or treatment proposed by the doctor?

Adoption of an objective standard on causation takes away most of what the *Canterbury* court granted as to risk disclosure. It asks the jury to put themselves in the place of a reasonable person, rather than the particular person. Is a jury likely to find causation in these cases, unless (1) the doctor was clearly negligent, so no reasonable person would have agreed to the treatment; (2) the doctor offered an experimental procedure which a person might refuse in spite of the doctor's urging; (3) the jury ignores its instructions and applies a subjective standard?

IV. CONFIDENTIALITY AND DISCLOSURE IN THE PHYSICIAN–PATIENT RELATIONSHIP

A. BREACHES OF CONFIDENTIALITY

One of the most important obligations owed by a professional to a patient is the protection of confidences revealed by the patient to the professional. State courts have developed common law rules to protect these confidences, and most states have adopted either a comprehensive medical confidentiality statute or several statutes addressing specific types of medical information. The Federal Medical Privacy Rules under HIPAA and the amendments provided by HITECH offer an elaborate protective framework for patient information. These state and federal obligations are discussed in this section.

HUMPHERS V. FIRST INTERSTATE BANK OF OREGON

Supreme Court of Oregon, In Banc, 1985.
298 Or. 706, 696 P.2d 527.

LINDE, JUSTICE.

We are called upon to decide whether plaintiff has stated a claim for damages in alleging that her former physician revealed her identity to a daughter whom she had given up for adoption.

In 1959, according to the complaint, plaintiff, then known as Ramona Elwess or by her maiden name, Ramona Jean Peek, gave birth to a daughter in St. Charles Medical Center in Bend, Oregon. She was unmarried at the time, and her physician, Dr. Harry E. Mackey, registered her in the hospital as "Mrs. Jean Smith." The next day, Ramona consented to the child's adoption by Leslie and Shirley Swarens of Bend, who named her Leslie Dawn. The hospital's medical records concerning the birth were sealed and marked to show that they were not public. Ramona subsequently remarried and raised a family. Only Ramona's mother and husband and Dr. Mackey knew about the daughter she had given up for adoption.

Twenty–one years later the daughter, now known as Dawn Kastning, wished to establish contact with her biological mother. Unable to gain access to the confidential court file of her adoption (though apparently able to locate the attending physician), Dawn sought out Dr. Mackey, and he agreed to assist in her quest. Dr. Mackey gave Dawn a letter which stated that he had registered Ramona Jean Peek at the hospital, that although he could not locate his medical records, he remembered administering diethylstilbestrol to her, and that the possible consequences of this medication made it important for Dawn to find her biological mother. The latter statements were untrue and made only to help Dawn to breach the confidentiality of the records concerning her birth and adoption. In 1982, hospital personnel, relying on Dr. Mackey's letter, allowed Dawn to make copies of plaintiff's medical records, which enabled her to locate plaintiff, now Ramona Humphers.

Ramona Humphers was not pleased. The unexpected development upset her and caused her emotional distress, worry, sleeplessness, humiliation, embarrassment, and inability to function normally. She sought damages from the estate of Dr. Mackey, who had died, by this action against defendant as the personal representative. After alleging the facts recounted above, her complaint pleads for relief on five different theories: First, that Dr. Mackey incurred liability for "outrageous conduct"; second, that his disclosure of a professional secret fell short of the care, skill and diligence employed by other physicians in the community and commanded by statute; third, that his disclosure wrongfully breached a confidential or privileged relationship; fourth, that his disclosure of confidential information was an "invasion of privacy" in the form of an "unauthorized intrusion upon plaintiff's seclusion, solitude, and private affairs;" and fifth, that his disclosures to Dawn Kastning breached a contractual obligation of secrecy. The circuit court granted defendant's motion to dismiss the complaint on the grounds that the facts fell short of each theory of relief and ordered entry of judgment for defendant. On appeal, the Court of Appeals affirmed the dismissal of the first, second, and fifth counts but reversed on the third, breach of a confidential relationship, and the fourth, invasion of privacy. [ ] We allowed review. We hold that if plaintiff has a claim, it arose from a breach by Dr. Mackey of a professional duty to keep plaintiff's secret rather than from a violation of plaintiff's privacy.

A physician's liability for disclosing confidential information about a patient is not a new problem. In common law jurisdictions it has been more discussed than litigated throughout much of this century. There are precedents for damage actions for unauthorized disclosure of facts conveyed in confidence, although we know of none involving the disclosure of an adoption. Because such claims are made against a variety of defendants besides physicians or other professional counselors, for instance against banks [ ], and because plaintiffs understandably plead alternative theories of recovery, the decisions do not always rest on a single theory.

Sometimes, defendant may have promised confidentiality expressly or by factual implication, in this case perhaps implied by registering a patient in the hospital under an assumed name. * * * [ ] A contract claim may be adequate where the breach of confidence causes financial loss, and it may gain a longer period of limitations; but contract law may deny damages for psychic or emotional injury not within the contemplation of the contracting parties, [ ] though perhaps this is no barrier when emotional security is the very object of the promised confidentiality. A contract claim is unavailable if the defendant physician was engaged by someone other than the plaintiff [ ] and it would be an awkward fiction at best if age, mental condition, or other circumstances prevent the patient from contracting; yet such a claim might be available to someone less interested than the patient, for instance her husband [ ].

Malpractice claims, based on negligence or statute, in contrast, may offer a plaintiff professional standards of conduct independent of the defendant's assent. * * * Finally, actions for intentional infliction of severe emotional distress fail when the defendant had no such intention or * * * when a defendant was not reckless or did not behave in a manner that a factfinder could find to transcend "the farthest reaches of socially tolerable behavior." [ ] Among these diverse precedents, we need only consider the counts of breach of confidential relationship and invasion of privacy on which the Court of Appeals allowed plaintiff to proceed. Plaintiff did not pursue her other theories * * * and we express no view whether the dismissal of those counts was correct.

Privacy

Although claims of a breach of privacy and of wrongful disclosure of confidential information may seem very similar in a case like the present, which involves the disclosure of an intimate personal secret, the two claims depend on different premises and cover different ground. Their common denominator is that both assert a right to control information, but they differ in important respects. Not every secret concerns personal or private information; commercial secrets are not personal, and governmental secrets are neither personal nor private. Secrecy involves intentional concealment. * * *

For our immediate purpose, the most important distinction is that only one who holds information in confidence can be charged with a breach of confidence. If an act qualifies as a tortious invasion of privacy, it theoretically could be committed by anyone. In the present case, Dr. Mackey's professional role is relevant to a claim that he breached a duty of confidentiality, but he could be charged with an invasion of plaintiff's privacy only if anyone else who told Dawn Kastning the facts of her birth without a special privilege to do so would be liable in tort for invading the privacy of her mother.

Whether "privacy" is a usable legal category has been much debated in other English–speaking jurisdictions as well as in this country, especially since its use in tort law, to claim the protection of government against intrusions by others, became entangled with its use in constitutional law, to claim protection against rather different intrusions by government. No concept in modern law has unleashed a comparable flood of commentary, its defenders arguing that "privacy" encompasses related interests of personality and autonomy, while its critics say that these interests are properly identified, evaluated, and protected below that exalted philosophical level. Indeed, at that level, a daughter's interest in her personal identity here confronts a mother's interest in guarding her own present identity by concealing their joint past. But recognition of an interest or value deserving protection states only half a case. Tort liability depends on the defendant's wrong as well as on the plaintiff's interest, or "right," unless some rule imposes strict liability. One's preferred seclusion or anonymity may be lost in many ways; the question remains who is legally bound to protect those interests at the risk of liability.

* * *

In this country, Dean William L. Prosser and his successors, noting that early debate was more "preoccupied with the question whether the right of privacy existed" than "what it would amount to if it did," concluded that invasion of privacy "is not one tort but a complex of four" * * * Prosser and Keeton, Torts 851, § 117 (5th ed. 1984). They identify the four kinds of claims grouped under the "privacy" tort as, first, appropriation of the plaintiff's name or likeness; second, unreasonable and offensive intrusion upon the seclusion of another; third, public disclosure of private facts; and fourth, publicity which places the plaintiff in a false light in the public eye. *Id.* at 851–66. [ ]

This court has not adopted all forms of the tort wholesale. * * *

* * *

* * * The Court of Appeals concluded that the complaint alleges a case of tortious intrusion upon plaintiff's seclusion, not by physical means such as uninvited entry, wiretapping, photography, or the like, but in the sense of an offensive prying into personal matters that plaintiff reasona-

bly has sought to keep private. [ ] We do not believe that the theory fits this case.

Doubtless plaintiff's interest qualifies as a "privacy" interest. That does not require the judgment of a court or a jury; it is established by the statutes that close adoption records to inspection without a court order. [ ]. * * * But as already stated, to identify an interest deserving protection does not suffice to collect damages from anyone who causes injury to that interest. Dr. Mackey helped Dawn Kastning find her biological mother, but we are not prepared to assume that Ms. Kastning became liable for invasion of privacy in seeking her out. Nor, we think, would anyone who knew the facts without an obligation of secrecy commit a tort simply by telling them to Ms. Kastning.

Dr. Mackey himself did not approach plaintiff or pry into any personal facts that he did not know; indeed, if he had written or spoken to his former patient to tell her that her daughter was eager to find her, it would be hard to describe such a communication alone as an invasion of privacy. The point of the claim against Dr. Mackey is not that he pried into a confidence but that he failed to keep one. If Dr. Mackey incurred liability for that, it must result from an obligation of confidentiality beyond any general duty of people at large not to invade one another's privacy. We therefore turn to plaintiff's claim that Dr. Mackey was liable for a breach of confidence, the third count of the complaint.

Breach of Confidence

It takes less judicial innovation to recognize this claim than the Court of Appeals thought. A number of decisions have held that unauthorized and unprivileged disclosure of confidential information obtained in a confidential relationship can give rise to tort damages. [ ] * * *.

* * *

In the case of the medical profession, courts in fact have found sources of a nonconsensual duty of confidentiality. Some have thought such a duty toward the patient implicit in the patient's statutory privilege to exclude the doctor's testimony in litigation[ ]. More directly in point are legal duties imposed as a condition of engaging in the professional practice of medicine or other occupations.

[The court noted that medical licensing statutes and professional regulations have been used as sources of a duty.]

This strikes us as the right approach to a claim of liability outside obligations undertaken expressly or implied in fact in entering a contractual relationship. [ ] The contours of the asserted duty of confidentiality are determined by a legal source external to the tort claim itself.

* * *

Because the duty of confidentiality is determined by standards outside the tort claim for its breach, so are the defenses of privilege or justification. Physicians, like members of many ordinary confidential professions and occupations, also may be legally obliged to report medical information to others for the protection of the patient, of other individuals, or of the public. *See, e.g.,* ORS 418.750 (physician's duty to report child abuse); ORS 433.003, 434.020 (duty to report certain diseases). * * * Even without such a legal obligation, there may be a privilege to disclose information for the safety of individuals or important to the public in matters of public interest. [ ] Some cases have found a physician privileged in disclosing information to a patient's spouse, [ ] or perhaps an intended spouse, [ ] In any event, defenses to a duty of confidentiality are determined in the same manner as the existence and scope of the duty itself. They necessarily will differ from one occupation to another and from time to time. A physician or other member of a regulated occupation is not to be held to a noncontractual duty of secrecy in a tort action when disclosure would not be a breach or would be privileged in direct enforcement of the underlying duty.

A physician's duty to keep medical and related information about a patient in confidence is beyond question. It is imposed by statute. ORS 677.190(5) provides for disqualifying or otherwise disciplining a physician for "wilfully or negligently divulging a professional secret." * * *

It is less obvious whether Dr. Mackey violated ORS 677.190(5) when he told Dawn Kastning what he knew of her birth. She was not, after all, a stranger to that proceeding. * * * If Ms. Kastning needed information about her natural mother for medical reasons, as Dr. Mackey pretended, the State Board of Medical Examiners likely would find the disclosure privileged against a charge under ORS 677.190(5); but the statement is alleged to have been a pretext designed to give her access to the hospital records. If only ORS 677.190(5) were involved, we do not know how the Board would judge a physician who assists at the birth of a child and decades later reveals to that person his or her parentage. But as already noted, other statutes specifically mandate the secrecy of adoption records. * * * Given these clear legal constraints, there is no privilege to disregard the professional duty imposed by ORS 677.190(5) solely in order to satisfy the curiosity of the person who was given up for adoption.

For these reasons, we agree with the Court of Appeals that plaintiff may proceed under her claim of breach of confidentiality in a confidential relationship. The decision of the Court of Appeals is reversed with respect to plaintiff's claim of invasion of privacy and affirmed with respect to her claim of breach of confidence in a confidential relationship, and the case is remanded to the circuit court for further proceedings on that claim.

NOTES AND QUESTIONS

1. What harm was the plaintiff exposed to by the disclosure of her relationship to the plaintiff? Was the doctor's action a breach of medical ethics? Should he have been sanctioned by the state medical licensing board? See discussion of interaction of ethics and licensure in Chapter 2.

2. Who uses medical information? Professional and non–professional medical staff must have access to records of patients in medical institutions for treatment purposes. Consent to such access is commonly presumed. Third party payers are the most common requestors of medical records outside the treatment setting. Access to records also is sought routinely for a variety of medical evaluation and support purposes. For example, in–house quality assurance committees, Joint Commission accreditation inspection teams, and state institutional licensure reviewers all must review medical records to assess the quality of hospital care. State public health laws require medical professionals and institutions to report a variety of medical conditions and incidents: venereal disease, contagious diseases, wounds inflicted by violence, poisonings, industrial accidents, abortions, and child abuse.

3. Access to medical records is also sought for secondary, nonmedical purposes. Law enforcement agencies, for example, often seek access to medical information. A moderate–size Chicago hospital reported that the FBI requested information about patients as often as twice a month. Attorneys seek medical records to establish disability, personal injury, or medical malpractice claims for their clients. Though they most commonly will ask for records of their own clients, they may also want to review records of other patients to establish a pattern of knowing medical abuse by a physician or the culpability of a hospital for failing to supervise a negligent practitioner. Life, health, disability, and liability insurers often seek medical information, as do employers and credit investigators. Disclosure of information from medical records may occur without a formal request. Though secondary users of medical information commonly receive information pursuant to patient record releases, they have been known to seek and compile information surreptitiously. These secondary disclosures of medical information are of great import to patients, as disclosure can result in loss of employment or denial of insurance or credit, or, at least, severe embarrassment. See generally the Preamble to the Medical Privacy Rules, *infra*.

4. What legal devices have traditionally protected the confidentiality of medical information? The physician–patient privilege comes first to mind, but in fact it plays a very limited role. First, and most important, it is only a testimonial privilege, not a general obligation to maintain confidentiality: though it may permit a doctor to refuse to disclose medical information in court, it does not require the doctor to keep information from employers or insurers. Second, it is a statutory privilege or one created through judicial rulemaking and does not exist in all jurisdictions. Third, as a privilege created by state statute, it does not apply in non–diversity federal court proceedings. Fourth, the privilege in most states is subject to many exceptions. Fi-

nally, the privilege applies only to confidential disclosures made to a physician in the course of treatment and is easily waived.

5. Several federal and state statutes protect the confidentiality of medical information. Most notable among these are amendments to the Drug Abuse and Treatment Acts and Comprehensive Alcohol Abuse and Alcoholism Prevention, Treatment, and Rehabilitation Act, 42 U.S.C.A. §§ 290dd–3, 390ee–3 (West 1982 & Supp.1986), and implementing regulations, 42 C.F.R. Part 2 (1985), which impose rigorous requirements on the disclosure of information from alcohol and drug abuse treatment programs. Some state statutes provide civil penalties for disclosure of confidential information. See Ill.Rev.Stat. ch. 91, § 815; West's Fla.Stat.Ann. § 395.018.

6. State courts have imposed liability on doctors for violating a duty of confidentiality expressed or implied in state licensure or privilege statutes. Several common law theories have also been advanced to impose liability on professionals who disclose medical information. Two of these, invasion of privacy and breach of confidential relationship, are discussed in *Humphers*.

7. Medical records often play a pivotal role in medical malpractice cases. By the time a malpractice action comes to trial memories may have dimmed as to what actually occurred at the time negligence is alleged to have taken place, leaving the medical record as the most telling evidence. Medical records, if properly authenticated, will usually be admitted under the business records exception to the hearsay rule. Because either documentation of inadequate care or inadequate documentation of care may result in liability, physicians are sometimes tempted to destroy records or to alter them to reflect the care they wish in retrospect they had rendered. There is nothing wrong with correcting records, so long as corrections are made in such a way as to leave the previous entry clearly readable and the new entry clearly identified as a corrected entry. Conscious concealment, fabrication, or falsification of records may result in an inference of awareness of guilt, Pisel v. Stamford Hospital, 180 Conn. 314, 340, 430 A.2d 1, 15 (1980), or punitive damages. It may also toll the statute of limitations. Finally, premature disposition of records could result in negligence liability, Fox v. Cohen, 84 Ill.App.3d 744, 40 Ill.Dec. 477, 406 N.E.2d 178 (1980).

PROBLEM: THE HUNT FOR PATIENT RECORDS

Two partners of a law firm, Findem and Howe, got the idea of working with a hospital to determine whether unpaid medical bills could be submitted to the Social Security Administration for payment as reimbursable disability treatment. They proposed the idea to the President of the law firm, who was also a trustee of the Warner General Hospital Health System.

The hospital agreed to search patient records and provide four pieces of patient information: name, telephone number, age, and medical condition. The patient registration forms were then furnished to the firm. The hospital agreed to pay a contingency fee to the firm for claims paid by Social Security. Patients who were possible candidates were called by the firm, on behalf of the hospital, telling them that they might be entitled to Social Security benefits that would help them pay their hospital bills. Some of the patients came in to talk with firm lawyers. A total of twelve thousand patient records were examined as part of this enterprise.

A group of angry former patients of Warner General have come to you to see what rights they have for what they feel is a violation of their privacy rights. How will you proceed? What arguments can you make on their behalf?

DOE V. MEDLANTIC HEALTH CARE GROUP, INC.

District of Columbia Court of Appeals, 2003.
814 A.2d 939.

RUIZ, ASSOCIATE JUDGE:

[A jury award to John Doe against Medlantic Health Care Group, Inc ("Medlantic") in the amount of $250,000 for breach of confidential relationship was reinstated on appeal.]

I.

Facts

In the spring of 1996, Doe held two jobs: by day he worked for a federal agency and at night he worked as a janitor for a company that contracted to clean the Department of State. Although Doe had been diagnosed with HIV in August of 1985, he had not told anyone at his janitorial job that he was HIV positive. One of Doe's co–workers in the evenings at the State Department was Tijuana Goldring, who also held a day position at the Washington Hospital Center ("WHC") as a temporary receptionist. On April 13, 1996, Doe went to WHC's emergency room suffering from severe headaches, nausea and high fever. He was discharged on April 16, 1996, but was unable to return to work for approximately two weeks because of these health problems.

On April 23, 1996, while still absent from work, Doe returned to WHC for a follow–up clinic visit after his discharge from the hospital. Knowing that Goldring worked at WHC, Doe stopped by the receptionist's desk to pay her a "courtesy call." After a brief conversation, Goldring asked him for the correct spelling of his uncommon last name because she wanted to send him a get well card. Doe testified that he did not think Goldring's request was odd and complied with the request as it was not unusual to get such a card from co–workers after having been out sick. Doe never received a card from Goldring, but did receive a card from fellow co–workers at the State Department with $50 enclosed.

Sometime in April of 1996, before Doe returned to work, Goldring told another co–worker at the State Department, Donnell Fuell, that John Doe "had that shit," meaning HIV or AIDS. When Fuell questioned her veracity, Goldring replied that it was "for real," and told Fuell she "got it from the hospital." Fuell knew that Goldring worked at WHC during the day.

Doe stipulated that within "a couple of days" of his conversation with Goldring at WHC on April 23, he learned that his co–workers at State knew of his AIDS diagnosis. On April 25, 1996, still before he returned to work, Doe went to the State Department to collect his paycheck, and he encountered co–workers Derek Nelson and Gordon Bannister outside the building. Both were laughing as Doe approached, and Nelson said to him, "Hey motherfucker, I hear you're dying of AIDS." Doe was "stunned" by this comment, but tried to cover his shock by laughing it off, saying, "Do I look like I'm dying?" before entering the building. Doe did not ask where Nelson had gotten this information, and Nelson did not tell him. As he left the building later that same day, Doe saw Fuell, who told him that Tijuana was "going around telling everybody you got AIDS." Fuell did not tell him how Goldring knew this information. Doe had never been teased by co–workers before that Friday about having AIDS, and that weekend he called Willie Jones, a co–worker and friend from the State Department, to ask if she had heard any rumors at work that he had AIDS. Jones stated she had. Doe did not ask Jones where she had heard the rumors or if Goldring was the source.

* * *

Doe testified that his time at work after April 25, was "like a living hell," as he was teased, ridiculed, pitied and scorned. Co–workers who had previously eaten with him now shunned him, and he was the object of snide remarks, stares, and unwanted attention. This included crass comments such as, Doe has "that faggot thing," and "[don't] eat [Doe's] food."

[Doe realized that Goldring was the source of the rumors about him, and he suspected that she might have seen his medical records.] * * *

The following day, on May 21, 1996, Doe called WHC and spoke with the vice president of personnel and human resources to ask if the hospital had a policy on employees who disseminate confidential medical information. Doe explained what had happened and gave Goldring's name. The vice–president said she would talk to Goldring and told Doe that this type of dissemination was against hospital policy and the laws of the District of Columbia. She referred him to the hospital's "risk management" department.

Doe filed a complaint against Medlantic and Goldring on May 20, 1997, alleging tort claims of invasion of privacy based on Goldring's disclosure and breach of confidential relationship based on WHC's negligence in permitting Goldring's access to confidential patient information. After Goldring was dismissed from the case, it proceeded to trial against Medlantic. The jury found Medlantic liable for breach of confidential relationship and awarded damages in the amount of $250,000. The jury found against Doe on the invasion of privacy claim because Goldring's disclosure was not within the scope of Goldring's employment with WHC. * * *

* * *

B. Motion for Judgment—Sufficiency of the Evidence

* * *

"The tort of breach of confidential relationship is generally described as consisting of the unconsented, unprivileged disclosure to a third party of nonpublic information that the defendant has learned within a confidential relationship."[ ] The tort arises from a duty that "attaches to nonpersonal relationships [such as hospital–patient] customarily understood to carry an obligation of confidence." [ ] This duty imposes an obligation—stricter than the reasonable person test—to "scrupulously honor the trust and confidence reposed in them because of that special relationship. . . ." [ ] It is undisputed that the jury was properly instructed on the elements of this tort.

We agree with the trial court that the evidence, viewed in the light most favorable to the plaintiff, sufficed to permit the jury to find that WHC breached its duty to "observe the utmost caution," * * *, in protecting the confidentiality of Doe's medical records. First, we reject the suggestion that expert testimony was necessary to establish the applicable standard of care in this case. In the negligence context, we have "refused to require expert testimony when the issue before the jury did not involve either a subject too technical for lay jurors to understand or the exercise of sophisticated professional judgment." [ ] The jury, as instructed, could consider the protocols that the hospital had established, which had been approved by a national hospital accreditation committee, as establishing the standard of care. The jury was specifically instructed that it could take into account whether the hospital's protocol "is or is not followed in practice" and "whether it was successful historically in preventing unauthorized disclosure." That instruction, which is not challenged by appellee, was proper here, where the evidence showed that Medlantic had failed to follow protocols it had established to safeguard its patients' medical records. [ ]

Substantial evidence was presented concerning the hospital's protocols and the routine failure of employees to comply with them. Crockett, a former medical records supervisor at WHC, and Ward, a worker for thirty–five years in the medical records department, testified as to the departures in practice from the established protocols. Crockett stated that while persons requesting medical records were supposed to give certain information, including their name, where they were calling from, and the purpose of the request for the record, in practice it did not always happen. The hospital's protocols were followed less often in the Employee Health department where Goldring worked as a receptionist. Ward similarly testified about lax enforcement of the protocols. As examples, she said that if a person called from the Employee Health department and merely gave his or her first name, that person's request for records would be processed without independent verification, and that individuals wearing a badge from a known department in the hospital could request medical records "stat" for emergencies—and be given the records without further inquiry if the need was considered urgent. Moreover, although Employee Health staff did not have authority to request charts of persons who were not hospital employees, if a person with a hospital department badge asked for a record, staff at the records control desk would accept what the person requesting the record said, without independently verifying if the record requested pertained to an employee.

Evidence was also presented showing that Goldring was a receptionist at the Employee Health department in April 1996 and that, of all Doe's co–workers, she alone could have had access to his medical records at WHC. She was identified by Fuell and others as the source of the rumors about Doe's condition, and it was she who asked for the spelling of Doe's last name, allegedly for the purpose of sending a card, which she never did. Finally, neither the log books which purportedly recorded all requests for medical records nor computer entries of such requests were produced by the hospital to show if anyone had accessed Doe's records at the relevant time. Although there was no direct evidence that the hospital's protocols were deficient or that they were breached to obtain Doe's medical records, evidence that there were significant lapses in the enforcement of the hospital's protocols to safeguard medical records, and that pointed to Goldring, a hospital employee, as the source of the unauthorized disclosure, sufficed to permit the jury to conclude that the hospital breached its duty as a fiduciary to maintain the confidentiality of Doe's medical records.

* * *

IV.

For the foregoing reasons, the trial court's entry of judgment for appellee is reversed, and the case is remanded with instructions that the jury verdict be reinstated and judgment entered in favor of appellant.

So ordered.

NOTES AND QUESTIONS

1. The states have adopted a variety of legislative and administrative approaches to confidentiality and disclosure of information regarding HIV–positivity, ARC, and AIDS status. All states now require physicians to report both HIV and AIDS cases to the state health department. Several states have

adopted statutes mandating strict confidentiality of AIDS–related information. See Cal. Health & Safety Code, § 199.21.

2. For a discussion of the disclosure of genetic information to family members, Safer v. Pack, 677 A.2d 1188 (N.J. App. 1996).

B. FEDERAL MEDICAL PRIVACY STANDARDS

Concerns about the privacy of patient medical information have intensified with the growth of both electronic recordkeeping and the Internet. The federal government studied this problem for several years before developing a highly detailed set of standards for health care providers. The HIPAA standards were effective in 2003, were amended in 2009 by the American Recovery and Reinvestment Act of 2009 (ARRA) (the Stimulus or The Recovery Act) and were amended again in 2013 by the final HIPAA Amendments.

STANDARDS FOR PRIVACY OF INDIVIDUALLY IDENTIFIABLE HEALTH INFORMATION

Department of Health and Human Services Office of the Secretary.
45 CFR Parts 160 and 164.

This regulation has three major purposes: (1) To protect and enhance the rights of consumers by providing them access to their health information and controlling the inappropriate use of that information; (2) to improve the quality of health care in the U.S. by restoring trust in the health care system among consumers, health care professionals, and the multitude of organizations and individuals committed to the delivery of care; and (3) to improve the efficiency and effectiveness of health care delivery by creating a national framework for health privacy protection that builds on efforts by states, health systems, and individual organizations and individuals.

* * *

In enacting HIPAA, Congress recognized the fact that administrative simplification cannot succeed if we do not also protect the privacy and confidentiality of personal health information. The provision of high–quality health care requires the exchange of personal, often–sensitive information between an individual and a skilled practitioner. Vital to that interaction is the patient's ability to trust that the information shared will be protected and kept confidential. Yet many patients are concerned that their information is not protected. Among the factors adding to this concern are the growth of the number of organizations involved in the provision of care and the processing of claims, the growing use of electronic information technology, increased efforts to market health care and other products to consumers, and the increasing ability to collect highly sensitive information about a person's current and future health status as a result of advances in scientific research.

Rules requiring the protection of health privacy in the United States have been enacted primarily by the states. While virtually every state has enacted one or more laws to safeguard privacy, these laws vary significantly from state to state and typically apply to only part of the health care system. Many states have adopted laws that protect the health information relating to certain health conditions such as mental illness, communicable diseases, cancer, HIV/AIDS, and other stigmatized conditions. An examination of state health privacy laws and regulations, however, found that "state laws, with a few notable exceptions, do not extend comprehensive protections to people's medical records." Many state rules fail to provide such basic protections as ensuring a patient's legal right to see a copy of his or her medical record. See Health Privacy Project, "The State of Health Privacy: An Uneven Terrain," Institute for Health Care Research and Policy, Georgetown University (July 1999) [ ] (the "Georgetown Study").

Until now, virtually no federal rules existed to protect the privacy of health information and guarantee patient access to such information. This final rule establishes, for the first time, a set of basic national privacy standards and fair information practices that provides all Americans with a basic level of protection and peace of mind that is essential to their full participation in their care. The rule sets a floor of ground rules for health care providers, health plans, and health care clearinghouses to follow, in order to protect patients and encourage them to seek needed care. The rule seeks to balance the needs of the individual with the needs of the society. It creates a framework of protection that can be strengthened by both the federal government and by states as health information systems continue to evolve.

The Office of Civil Rights, which enforces the HIPAA Privacy Rule, summarized its key provisions as promulgated in 2003.

OFFICE OF CIVIL RIGHTS, SUMMARY OF THE HIPAA PRIVACY RULE

* * *

Who Is Covered By the Privacy Rule?

The Privacy Rule, as well as all the Administrative Simplification rules, apply to health plans, health care clearinghouses, and to any health care provider who transmits health information in electronic form in connection with transactions for which the Secretary of HHS has adopted standards under HIPAA (the "covered entities"). * * * Individual and group plans that provide or pay the cost of medical care are covered entities.

* * *

Health Care Providers. Every health care provider, regardless of size, who electronically transmits health information in connection with certain transactions, is a covered entity. These transactions include claims, benefit eligibility inquiries, referral authorization requests, or other transactions for which HHS has established standards under the HIPAA Transactions Rule. Using electronic technology, such as email, does not mean a health care provider is a covered entity; the transmission must be in connection with a standard transaction. The Privacy Rule covers a health care provider whether it electronically transmits these transactions directly or uses a billing service or other third party to do so on its behalf. Health care providers include all "providers of services" (e.g., institutional providers such as hospitals) and "providers of medical or health services" (e.g., non–institutional providers such as physicians, dentists and other practitioners) as defined by Medicare, and any other person or organization that furnishes, bills, or is paid for health care.

* * *

Business Associates

Business Associate Defined. In general, a business associate is a person or organization, other than a member of a covered entity's workforce, that performs certain functions or activities on behalf of, or provides certain services to, a covered entity that involve the use or disclosure of individually identifiable health information. Business associate functions or activities on behalf of a covered entity include claims processing, data analysis, utilization review, and billing.

Business associate services to a covered entity are limited to legal, actuarial, accounting, consulting, data aggregation, management, administrative, accreditation, or financial services. However, persons or organizations are not considered business associates if their functions or services do not involve the use or disclosure of protected health information, and where any access to protected health information by such persons would be incidental, if at all. A covered entity can be the business associate of another covered entity. [Note: The definition of "business associate" is substantially expanded by the 2013 Amendments. See below.]

What Information is Protected.

Protected Health Information. The Privacy Rule protects all "individually identifiable health information" held or transmitted by a covered entity or its business associate, in any form or media, whether electronic, paper, or oral. The Privacy Rule calls this information "protected health information (PHI)."

"Individually identifiable health information" is information, including demographic data, that relates to:

- the individual's past, present or future physical or mental health or condition,
- the provision of health care to the individual, or
- the past, present, or future payment for the provision of health care to the individual,

and that identifies the individual or for which there is a reasonable basis to believe can be used to identify the individual. Individually identifiable health information includes many common identifiers (e.g., name, address, birth date, Social Security Number).

* * *

De–Identified Health Information. There are no restrictions on the use or disclosure of de–identified health information.

General Principle for Uses and Disclosures

Basic Principle. A major purpose of the Privacy Rule is to define and limit the circumstances in which an individual's protected heath information may be used or disclosed by covered entities. A covered entity may not use or disclose protected health information, except either: (1) as the Privacy Rule permits or requires; or (2) as the individual who is the subject of the information (or the individual's personal representative) authorizes in writing.

Required Disclosures. A covered entity must disclose protected health information in only two situations: (a) to individuals (or their personal representatives) specifically when they request access to, or an accounting of disclosures of, their protected health information; and (b) to HHS when it is undertaking a compliance investigation or review or enforcement action.

Permitted Uses and Disclosures.

Permitted Uses and Disclosures. A covered entity is permitted, but not required, to use and disclose protected health information, without an individual's authorization, for the following purposes or situations: (1) To the Individual [who is the subject of the information] (unless required for access or accounting of disclosures); (2) Treatment, Payment, and Health Care Operations; (3) Opportunity to Agree or Object; (4) Incident to an otherwise permitted use and disclosure; (5) Public Interest and Benefit Activities; and (6) Limited Data Set for the purposes of research, public health or health care operations. Covered entities may rely on professional ethics and best judgments in deciding which of these permissive uses and disclosures to make.

* * *

(2) **Treatment, Payment, Health Care Operations**. A covered entity may use and disclose protected health information for its own treatment, payment, and health care operations activities.

A covered entity also may disclose protected health information for the treatment activities of any health care provider, the payment activities of another covered entity and of any health care provider, or the health care operations of another covered entity involving either quality or competency assurance activities or fraud and abuse detection and compliance activities, if both covered entities have or had a relationship with the individual and the protected health information pertains to the relationship. [ ]

> **Treatment** is the provision, coordination, or management of health care and related services for an individual by one or more health care providers, including consultation between providers regarding a patient and referral of a patient by one provider to another.
>
> **Payment** encompasses activities of a health plan to obtain premiums, determine or fulfill responsibilities for coverage and provision of benefits, and furnish or obtain reimbursement for health care delivered to an individual and activities of a health care provider to obtain payment or be reimbursed for the provision of health care to an individual.
>
> **Health care operations** are any of the following activities: (a) quality assessment and improvement activities, including case management and care coordination; (b) competency assurance activities, including provider or health plan performance evaluation, credentialing, and accreditation; (c) conducting or arranging for medical reviews, audits, or legal services, including fraud and abuse detection and compliance programs; (d) specified insurance functions, such as underwriting, risk rating, and reinsuring risk; (e) business planning, development, management, and administration; and (f) business management and general administrative activities of the entity, including but not limited to: de–identifying protected health information, creating a limited data set, and certain fundraising for the benefit of the covered entity.

Most uses and disclosures of psychotherapy notes for treatment, payment, and health care operations purposes require an authorization as described below.

Obtaining "consent" (written permission from individuals to use and disclose their protected health information for treatment, payment, and health care operations) is optional under the Privacy Rule for all covered entities. The content of a consent form, and the process for obtaining consent, are at the discretion of the covered entity electing to seek consent.

(3) **Uses and Disclosures with Opportunity to Agree or Object**. Informal permission may be obtained by asking the individual outright, or by circumstances that clearly give the individual the opportunity to agree, acquiesce, or object. Where the individual is incapacitated, in an emergency situation, or not available, covered entities generally may make such uses and disclosures, if in the exercise of their professional judgment, the use or disclosure is determined to be in the best interests of the individual.

(4) **Incidental Use and Disclosure**. The Privacy Rule does not require that every risk of an incidental use or disclosure of protected health information be eliminated. A use or disclosure of this information that occurs as a result of, or as "incident to," an otherwise permitted use or disclosure is permitted as long as the covered entity has adopted reasonable safeguards as required by the Privacy Rule, and the information being shared was limited to the "minimum necessary," as required by the Privacy Rule.[ ]

(5) **Public Interest and Benefit Activities**. The Privacy Rule permits use and disclosure of protected health information, without an individual's authorization or permission, for 12 national priority purposes. These disclosures are permitted, although not required, by the Rule in recognition of the important uses made of health information outside of the health care context. Specific conditions or limitations apply to each public interest purpose, striking the balance between the individual privacy interest and the public interest need for this information.

> **Required by Law.** Covered entities may use and disclose protected health information without individual authorization as required by law (including by statute, regulation, or court orders).
>
> **Public Health Activities.** Covered entities may disclose protected health information to: (1) public health authorities authorized by law to collect or receive such information for preventing or controlling disease, injury, or disability and to public health or other government authorities authorized to receive reports of child abuse and neglect; (2) entities subject to FDA regulation regarding FDA regulated products or activities for purposes such as adverse event reporting, tracking of products, product recalls, and postmarketing surveillance; (3) individuals who may have contracted or been exposed to a communicable disease when notification is authorized by law; and (4) employers, regarding employees, when requested by employers, for information concerning a work–related illness or injury or workplace related medical surveillance, because such information is needed by the employer to comply with the Occupational Safety and

Health Administration (OSHA), the Mine Safety and Health Administration (MSHA), or similar state law.

[Other permissive disclosures may be made for example regarding victims of abuse, health oversight activities, judicial and administrative proceedings, law enforcement, research, serious threats to public safety, Workers' Compensation, and essential government functions.]

* * *

Authorized Uses and Disclosures

Authorization. A covered entity must obtain the individual's written authorization for any use or disclosure of protected health information that is not for treatment, payment or health care operations or otherwise permitted or required by the Privacy Rule. A covered entity may not condition treatment, payment, enrollment, or benefits eligibility on an individual granting an authorization, except in limited circumstances.

An authorization must be written in specific terms. It may allow use and disclosure of protected health information by the covered entity seeking the authorization, or by a third party. Examples of disclosures that would require an individual's authorization include disclosures to a life insurer for coverage purposes, disclosures to an employer of the results of a pre–employment physical or lab test, or disclosures to a pharmaceutical firm for their own marketing purposes.

All authorizations must be in plain language, and contain specific information regarding the information to be disclosed or used, the person(s) disclosing and receiving the information, expiration, right to revoke in writing, and other data. * * *

Psychotherapy Notes. A covered entity must obtain an individual's authorization to use or disclose psychotherapy notes * * *.

Marketing. Marketing is any communication about a product or service that encourages recipients to purchase or use the product or service. The Privacy Rule carves out the following health–related activities from this definition of marketing:

- Communications to describe health–related products or services, or payment for them, provided by or included in a benefit plan of the covered entity making the communication;
- Communications about participating providers in a provider or health plan network, replacement of or enhancements to a health plan, and health–related products or services available only to a health plan's enrollees that add value to, but are not part of, the benefits plan;
- Communications for treatment of the individual; and

- Communications for case management or care coordination for the individual, or to direct or recommend alternative treatments, therapies, health care providers, or care settings to the individual.

Marketing also is an arrangement between a covered entity and any other entity whereby the covered entity discloses protected health information, in exchange for direct or indirect remuneration, for the other entity to communicate about its own products or services encouraging the use or purchase of those products or services. A covered entity must obtain an authorization to use or disclose protected health information for marketing, except for face–to–face marketing communications between a covered entity and an individual, and for a covered entity's provision of promotional gifts of nominal value. No authorization is needed, however, to make a communication that falls within one of the exceptions to the marketing definition. An authorization for marketing that involves the covered entity's receipt of direct or indirect remuneration from a third party must reveal that fact.[ ]

Limiting Uses and Disclosures to the Minimum Necessary

Minimum Necessary. A central aspect of the Privacy Rule is the principle of "minimum necessary" use and disclosure. A covered entity must make reasonable efforts to use, disclose, and request only the minimum amount of protected health information needed to accomplish the intended purpose of the use, disclosure, or request. A covered entity must develop and implement policies and procedures to reasonably limit uses and disclosures to the minimum necessary. When the minimum necessary standard applies to a use or disclosure, a covered entity may not use, disclose, or request the entire medical record for a particular purpose, unless it can specifically justify the whole record as the amount reasonably needed for the purpose. [ ]

The minimum necessary requirement is not imposed in any of the following circumstances: (a) disclosure to or a request by a health care provider for treatment; (b) disclosure to an individual who is the subject of the information, or the individual's personal representative; (c) use or disclosure made pursuant to an authorization; (d) disclosure to HHS for complaint investigation, compliance review or enforcement; (e) use or disclosure that is required by law; or (f) use or disclosure required for compliance with the HIPAA Transactions Rule or other HIPAA Administrative Simplification Rules.

Access and Uses. For internal uses, a covered entity must develop and implement policies and procedures that restrict access and uses of protected health information based on the specific roles of the members of their workforce. * * *

Disclosures and Requests for Disclosures. Covered entities must establish and implement policies and procedures (which may be standard protocols) for routine, recurring disclosures, or requests for disclosures, that limits the protected health information disclosed to that which is the minimum amount reasonably necessary to achieve the purpose of the disclosure. Individual review of each disclosure is not required. For non–routine, non–recurring disclosures, or requests for disclosures that it makes, covered entities must develop criteria designed to limit disclosures to the information reasonably necessary to accomplish the purpose of the disclosure and review each of these requests individually in accordance with the established criteria.

* * *

Notice and Other Individual Rights

Privacy Practices Notice. Each covered entity, with certain exceptions, must provide a notice of its privacy practices. The Privacy Rule requires that the notice contain certain elements. The notice must describe the ways in which the covered entity may use and disclose protected health information. The notice must state the covered entity's duties to protect privacy, provide a notice of privacy practices, and abide by the terms of the current notice. The notice must describe individuals' rights including the right to complain to HHS and to the covered entity if they believe their privacy rights have been violated. The notice must include a point of contact for further information and for making complaints to the covered entity. Covered entities must act in accordance with their notices. The Rule also contains specific distribution requirements for direct treatment providers, all other health care providers, and health plans. [ ]

* * *

[The Privacy rules specify when and how the notice of privacy practices is presented to patients. It requires that a patient give a written acknowledgement of the receipt of the privacy practices notice, without specifying any particular form for the acknowledgment.]

Access. Except in certain circumstances, individuals have the right to review and obtain a copy of their protected health information in a covered entity's designated record set. The "designated record set" is that group of records maintained by or for a covered entity that is used, in whole or part, to make decisions about individuals, or that is a provider's medical and billing records about individuals or a health plan's enrollment, payment, claims adjudication, and case or medical management record systems. [Cost–based fees may be charged for copying and postage.]

* * *

Administrative Requirements

* * *

Privacy Policies and Procedures. A covered entity must develop and implement written privacy policies and procedures that are consistent with the Privacy Rule.

Privacy Personnel. A covered entity must designate a privacy official responsible for developing and implementing its privacy policies and procedures, and a contact person or contact office responsible for receiving complaints and providing individuals with information on the covered entity's privacy practices.

Workforce Training and Management. * * * A covered entity must train all workforce members on its privacy policies and procedures, as necessary and appropriate for them to carry out their functions. A covered entity must have and apply appropriate sanctions against workforce members who violate its privacy policies or the Privacy Rule.

Mitigation. A covered entity must mitigate, to the extent practicable, any harmful effect it learns was caused by use or disclosure of protected health information by its workforce or its business associates in violation of its privacy policies and procedures or the Privacy Rule.

Data Safeguards. A covered entity must maintain reasonable and appropriate administrative, technical, and physical safeguards to prevent intentional or unintentional use or disclosure of protected health information in violation of the Privacy Rule and to limit its incidental use and disclosure pursuant to otherwise permitted or required use or disclosure. * * *

* * *

Enforcement and Penalties for Noncompliance

* * *

Civil Money Penalties. [See Note on HITECH, below.]

Criminal Penalties. A person who knowingly obtains or discloses individually identifiable health information in violation of HIPAA faces a fine of $50,000 and up to one–year imprisonment. The criminal penalties increase to $100,000 and up to five years imprisonment if the wrongful conduct involves false pretenses, and to $250,000 and up to ten years imprisonment if the wrongful conduct involves the intent to sell, transfer, or use individually identifiable health information for commercial advantage, personal gain, or malicious harm. Criminal sanctions will be enforced by the Department of Justice.

* * *

NOTES AND QUESTIONS

1. The obvious benefits of computerized record–keeping have propelled medical records to a central position in health care delivery. A standardized database of patient information has the potential to promote efficiency, further competition, and allow providers to better track patient outcomes. Only a computerized record, in spite of its confidentiality dimensions, can further such goals. The Medical Privacy Standards offer considerable protection to patients; they also require substantial expenditures by providers to achieve compliance with the complex requirements.

2. Who is covered by the Medical Privacy Rules? What are "covered entities?"

3. HIPAA penalties have been substantially increased by subsequent legislation. See ***Note: 2013 Amendments to HIPAA Privacy, Security, Breach Notification, and Enforcement Rules, infra.*** Hospital medical staff are worried that they will be jailed if they inadvertently release health care information to an unauthorized person. The Office of Civil Rights (OCR) has reassured providers that they can discuss a patient's treatment among themselves. "Disclosures for treatment purposes (including requests for disclosures) between health care providers are explicitly exempted from the minimum necessary requirements."

Incidental uses and disclosures of individual identifiable health information are generally allowed when the covered entity has in place reasonable safeguards and "minimum necessary" policies and procedures to protect an individual's privacy. OCR confirmed that providers may have confidential conversations with other providers and patients even when there is a chance that they might be overheard. Nurses can speak over the phone with a patient or family member about the patient's condition. Providers may also discuss a patient's condition during training rounds at an academic medical institution.

4. Notice the substantial compliance obligations imposed on health care providers. Critics note that HIPAA standards create little more than a federal confidentiality code based around a regulatory compliance model rather than one that creates patient rights. Nicolas P. Terry and Leslie P. Francis, Ensuring the Privacy and Confidentiality of Electronic Health Records, 2007 Univ. Ill. Law. Rev. 681, 714 (2007). Terry and Francis note that the HIPAA standards focus on the process of patient consent to disclosure, not on limits to collection of data; lack any consent–to–disclosure restrictions; lack a true national standard, given the interplay between state and federal law; apply overbroad exceptions to consent such as public health; are too lax as to secondary uses of patient information; and fail to cover all medical data or users of data.

However, the creation of privacy compliance officers in hospitals, and the requirement of staff education, is surely a good thing in terms of protection of patient's medical privacy.

5. The Medical Privacy Standards quoted above in an abbreviated form give some sense of the scope and detail of the rules as originally promulgated. They have several laudatory goals. First and foremost, they aim to give consumers some control over their own health information. Health providers must inform patients about how their information is being used and to whom it is disclosed. The rules create a "disclosure history" for individuals. Most important, the release of private health information is limited by a requirement of authorization under some circumstances. Some nonroutine disclosure requires specific patient authorization. Patients may access their own health files and request correction of potentially harmful errors.

Second, the rules set boundaries on medical record use and release. The amount of information to be disclosed is restricted to the "minimum necessary" in contrast to prevailing practice of releasing a patient's entire health record even if an entity needs very specific information.

Third, the rules attempt to ensure the security of personal health information. The rules are very specific in their mandates on providers and others who might access health information. They require privacy–conscious business practices, with internal procedures and privacy officers to protect the privacy of medical records. The rules create a whole new category of compliance officer within health care institutions as a result of the mandates in the rules.

Fourth, the rules create accountability for medical record use and release, with new criminal and civil penalties for improper use or disclosure.

Fifth, the rules attempt to balance public responsibility with privacy protections, requiring that information be disclosed only limited public purposes such as public health and research. They attempt to limit disclosure of information without sacrificing public safety.

The Office of Civil Rights website provides useful information on HIPAA and its interpretation. In addition, the Health Privacy Project produces materials that critically address all aspects of HIPAA.

6. The use of electronic health records has worried physicians. Will they reduce the risk of malpractice suits or create new risks? One study found that EHRs had substantial advantages, reducing the rate of claims to about one–sixth the rate when EHRs were not used. " * * * The results of this study support the hypothesis that EHR adoption and use lead to improved quality of care and patient safety, resulting in fewer adverse events and fewer paid malpractice claims." See Anunta Virapongse et al., Electronic Health Records and Malpractice Claims in Office Practice, 168 Arch. Intern. Med. 2362 (2008).

NOTE: 2013 AMENDMENTS TO HIPAA PRIVACY, SECURITY, BREACH NOTIFICATION, AND ENFORCEMENT RULES

The 2013 Amendments to HIPAA include a number of sweeping changes to the HIPAA Rules, finalizing the 2009 changes under the ARRA. Below is a summary of some of the amendments and their effect on the Medical Privacy rule, as first amended in 2009.

Breach. The 2013 Amendments modify the definition of "breach", originally defined as an inappropriate use or disclosure of PHI involving a ***significant risk*** of financial, reputational or other harm. The 2013 Amendments now provide that an impermissible use or disclosure of PHI is ***presumed*** to be a breach, unless it can be demonstrated that there is a ***low probability*** that PHI has been compromised based upon a four–part risk assessment that considers: (1) the nature and extent of the PHI involved in the breach; (2) the unauthorized person who used the PHI or to whom the disclosure was made; (3) whether the PHI was actually acquired or viewed; and (4) the extent to which the risk to PHI has been mitigated. If the risk assessment evaluation fails to demonstrate there is a low probability that any PHI has been compromised, breach notification is required. Certain exceptions to the definition of a breach continue to apply.

Notification of a Breach. Covered entities must now notify each affected individual whose unsecured PHI has been compromised. Even if such breach is caused by a business associate, the covered entity is ultimately responsible for providing the notification (although the covered entity is free to delegate the breach response function to the business associate). Moreover, a business associate's knowledge of a breach will be imputed to a covered entity. If the breach involves more than 500 persons, the Office of Civil Rights (OCR) must be notified in accordance with instructions posted on its website. The HIPAA–covered entity bears the ultimate burden of proof to demonstrate that all notifications were given or that the impermissible use or disclosure of PHI did not constitute a breach. The covered entity must maintain supporting documentation, including documentation pertaining to the risk assessment.

Marketing Rules. The 2013 Amendments substantially modify the definition of marketing to require an authorization from an individual for the receipt of certain marketing materials for treatment or operations purposes. Patients must first approve the use of their data for marketing communications if the maker of the product or service pays for that sales pitch. This change is aimed at patient concerns about the use of their personal health information for marketing without their consent. Marketing broadly applies to any communications about a product or service that encourages a recipient to purchase or use the product or service. The definition also includes communications issued by a covered entity or business associate regarding a treatment– or operations–related product or service offered by a third party *and* the third party has compensated the covered entity or business associate for the communication.

In these situations, an individual's authorization that covers subsidized communications is required.

Exceptions to the definition of marketing communications include any communication that is made: (1) to provide refill reminders or information regarding a drug that is currently being prescribed, as long as any financial remuneration received by the covered entity is "reasonably related" to the cost related to the marketing; (2) regarding the product or service of a third party for certain treatment or operations purposes, ***except*** *where financial remuneration is involved.*

The kinds of communications covered include (1) those offered to an individual as part of treatment, or to a larger population as part of operations, regarding case management, care coordination, or alternative treatment modalities; or (2) to describe a health–related product or service, or payment for the product or service, provided by the covered entity or included in a plan of benefits—examples would be communications about network–participating providers or value–added products or services not offered by a plan such as vision plan enhancements.

When the covered entity makes the communication face–to–face or the communication consists of a promotional gift of nominal value, patient authorization is not required.

Business Associates. The *Business Associates* definition was expanded by HITECH, and the 2013 regulations continue that expansion. Individuals handling patient health information in order to perform services for an entity covered by HIPAA (doctors, hospitals, health plans) are now accountable for complying with the HIPAA Privacy and Security Rules—and this accountability extends to any subcontractors that access data to help perform those services. Business associates—and their subcontractors—are now directly liable both for violations of the Security Rule and for uses and disclosures of PHI in violation of the Privacy Rule.

Business associates also have the following responsibilities:

1. To keep records and submit compliance reports to HHS, when HHS requires such disclosure in order to investigate the business associate's compliance with HIPAA, and to cooperate with complaint investigations and compliance reviews;

2. To disclose PHI as needed by a covered entity to respond to an individual's request for an electronic copy of his/her medical record;

3. To notify the covered entity of a breach of unsecured PHI;

4. To make reasonable efforts to limit use and disclosure of PHI, and requests for PHI, to the minimum necessary;

5. To provide an accounting of disclosures; and

6. To enter into agreements with subcontractors that comply with the Privacy and Security Rules.

Copies of Patient Health Data. Patients now have the right to receive an electronic copy of their health data and to have that copy sent at their request somewhere else, for example, to a doctor, a caregiver, or a personal health record or mobile health app. Electronic copies can be received by insecure email. The final rule still allows for a sixty day turnaround on records requested, but encourages a faster response when feasible.

Payment in Cash to Avoid PHI Sharing with Health Plans. HHS responded to concerns about sharing of certain health information that might lead to economic or other negative effects on patients. "When individuals pay by cash they can instruct their provider not to share information about their treatment with their health plan." HHS News Release, January 17, 2013.

This allows patients worried about the harms they might suffer if their personal health information got back to their employers or others can now avoid any sharing of such information by paying in cash. Physicians worry however that this may mean, in the case of diseases like HIV/AIDS, that specialists will not have access to essential patient information, defeating the purpose of the electronic health record, and putting the patient at risk of inadequate care.

Civil Monetary Liability. The 2013 Amendments substantially increase the potential civil monetary fines for violations for covered entities and business associates, and establish tiers of escalating penalty amounts based on increasing degrees of culpability of violators and other responsible parties. The 2013 Amendments also reduce OCR's discretion in assessing these fines. Fines range from $100 to $50,000 per each violation, with the minimum increasing with the degree of culpability and with an annual maximum of $1,500,000.

In circumstances where discretion is available, the Secretary, in determining the amount of penalty, is required to take into account the nature of the claims and the circumstances under which they were presented, the degree of culpability, history of prior offenses, financial condition of the person presenting the claims and other matters. OCR also intends to consider factors, such as the time period during which the violations occurred; reputational harm; and the number of individuals affected.

Breaches of Health Information, or the "Wall of Shame". The Secretary must post a list of breaches of unsecured protected health information affecting 500 or more individuals. These breaches are now posted in a new, more accessible format that allows users to search and sort the posted breaches. See Breaches Affecting More Than 500 Individuals, on the HHS Health Privacy web site.

YATH V. FAIRVIEW CLINICS, N.P.

Court of Appeals, Minnesota, 2009.
767 N.W.2d 34.

OPINION

ROSS, JUDGE.

This invasion–of–privacy case involves the Internet posting of embarrassing personal information taken surreptitiously from a patient's medical file. A Fairview Cedar Ridge Clinic employee saw a personal acquaintance at the clinic and read her medical file, learning that she had a sexually transmitted disease and a new sex partner other than her husband. The employee disclosed this information to another employee, who then disclosed it to others, including the patient's estranged husband. Then someone created a MySpace.com webpage posting the information on the Internet. The patient sued the clinic and the individuals allegedly involved in the disclosure under various legal theories.

* * *

FACTS

The controversy in this case began when a clinic employee saw an acquaintance visiting a doctor and decided to nose around in the acquaintance's confidential file. Candace Yath went to a medical appointment in March 2006 at Fairview Cedar Ridge Clinic in Apple Valley. Yath told her doctor that she wanted to be tested for sexually transmitted diseases because she had a new sex partner. Navy Tek, a medical assistant who is related to Yath's husband, saw Yath at the clinic and became curious.

Tek's job gave her access to the clinic's electronic medical records. Tek decided to satisfy her curiosity by accessing Yath's medical file, knowing this would violate clinic policy. Tek learned from Yath's medical file that Yath's medical appointment was for sexually–transmitted–disease screening related to a new sex partner. She also learned that Yath had been diagnosed with a sexually transmitted disease.

Two days later, Tek sent an electronic mail message to Net Phat. Phat was related to both Tek and Yath by marriage, and she worked as a medical records coder at Fairview Ridges Hospital. In her e–mail to Phat, Tek wrote, "i gotta tell you somethin but can't do it over this. . . . i'll call you when i'm not busy. . . . but only if you promise not to say anything to anybody." Phat responded that she would not tell anyone and added, "Now I'm curious what it is . . . you will have to tell me." Three minutes later, Tek replied, "you may already know anyways. . . . i'll call you in a bit."

Tek called and told Phat that she saw Yath's record and that Yath had another sex partner. Phat wrote back to Tek, "Wow . . . I'm shocked."

She also wrote, "I look differently at my sister in law." Phat was unaware that Candace Yath and her husband, Paul, had separated.

In April 2006, Phat told her brother (Yath's now ex–husband) what Tek relayed from Yath's medical file. Paul asked Phat if she had seen Yath's file, but Phat said that she had not. Word eventually reached Candace Yath that Tek had viewed her medical file and had shared the information with Phat. Yath's grandmother called Cedar Ridge Clinic and spoke with Michelle St. Sauver, the clinic's manager. She complained that she believed that Tek had wrongfully accessed and told others the information in Yath's medical file. She also told St. Sauver that she believed Phat was involved.

Fairview investigated and learned that Tek had accessed Yath's medical file five times between March 21 and May 4, 2006. Fairview determined that Tek had no legitimate business reason to do so and that, therefore, her access was unauthorized by Fairview policy and prohibited by HIPAA. St. Sauver and a human resources worker confronted Tek on May 4. Although Tek initially denied accessing Yath's records, she recanted after St. Sauver showed her a computer usage audit. But she claimed that she had not disclosed the information to anyone.

St. Sauver also questioned Phat on May 4. Phat denied knowing anything about Yath's medical information. Neither Cedar Ridge Clinic nor Fairview Ridges Hospital, where Phat worked, investigated Phat's computer. St. Sauver and Lois Dahl, Fairview's information privacy and security director, explained that they did not search Phat's computer because Phat did not have a username or password that allowed her to access Yath's medical records at the clinic and because the clinic and hospital use different records software systems.

St. Sauver sent Tek home on May 4. Convinced that Tek had repeatedly accessed Yath's records without a legitimate business purpose, Fairview decided to fire Tek on May 10, 2006, for violating Fairview policy and HIPAA.

The next day, St. Sauver received an e–mail from Yath's grandmother accusing Tek or Phat of creating a disparaging Internet webpage at MySpace.com using the name "Rotten Candy" and posting information that Tek learned from Yath's medical file. The webpage included a photograph of Candace Yath and stated that "Rotten Candy" has a sexually transmitted disease, that she recently cheated on her husband, and that she is addicted to plastic surgery. The page listed six "friends," indicating that by then at least those six people had accessed the page.

Fairview investigated the accusations. It tried to view the webpage on either May 11 or May 12, 2006, but by then the webpage had been "removed." MySpace.com is a "blocked" website at Fairview, meaning that employees cannot access it using Fairview's internet system and that the webpage therefore could not have been created by an employee using a Fairview workplace computer. Yath and her attorneys also investigated the MySpace webpage. They discovered that the MySpace account for the webpage originated on a computer having an Internet Protocol address assigned to a business in Eagan. Tek's sister, Molyka Mao, worked at that business.

Yath sued Tek, Mao, Phat, and Fairview on a variety of theories. She sued all the defendants directly for invasion of her privacy, and all except Mao for "breach of a confidential relationship." She sued Tek, Mao, and Phat for intentional infliction of emotional distress. She sued Fairview for negligent infliction of emotional distress. She also sued all the defendants directly for violating Minnesota Statutes section 144.335, subdivision 3a(e), by disclosing information in Yath's medical file.

* * *

ANALYSIS

* * *

I

[The court rejected Yath's spoliation claim on the grounds that she presented insufficient evidence to support the claim.]

* * *

II

[Yath contested the dismissal of her invasion of privacy claim. The court upheld her claim that the temporary posting of data gleaned from her medical file on MySpace.com met the publicity requirements for a successful claim.]

* * *

Minnesota recognizes the tort of invasion of privacy on three alternative theories: intrusion of seclusion, appropriation of a name or likeness of another, and publication of private facts. [ ] Yath's invasion–of–privacy claim is based on the publication of private facts, so the claim can survive summary judgment only if the record contains evidence that (1) a defendant gave "publicity" to a matter concerning Yath's private life, (2) the publicity of the private information would be highly offensive to a reasonable person, and (3) the matter is not of legitimate concern to the public.[ ] The district court held that Yath's private information was not given "publicity" within the meaning of the tort of invasion of privacy because Yath had not proven a sufficient number of people had seen the webpage. We reach a different legal conclusion.

* * *

We hold that the publicity element of an invasion–of–privacy claim is satisfied when private information is posted on a publicly accessible Internet website.

The MySpace.com webpage that triggers Yath's claim was such a site. Access to it was not protected, as some webpages are, by a password or some other restrictive safeguard. It was a window that Yath's enemies propped open for at least 24 hours allowing any internet–connected voyeur access to private details of her life. The claim therefore survives the "publicity" challenge.

* * *

That the Internet vastly enlarges both the amount of information publicly available and the number of sources offering information does not erode the reasoning leading us to hold that posting information on a publicly accessible webpage constitutes publicity. If a late–night radio broadcast aired for a few seconds and potentially heard by a few hundred (or by no one) constitutes publicity as a matter of law, a maliciously fashioned webpage posted for one or two days and potentially read by hundreds, thousands, millions (or by no one) also constitutes publicity as a matter of law.

It is true that mass communication is no longer limited to a tiny handful of commercial purveyors and that we live with much greater access to information than the era in which the tort of invasion of privacy developed. A town crier could reach dozens, a handbill hundreds, a newspaper or radio station tens of thousands, a television station millions, and now a publicly accessible webpage can present the story of someone's private life, in this case complete with a photograph and other identifying features, to more than one billion Internet surfers worldwide. This extraordinary advancement in communication argues for, not against, a holding that the MySpace posting constitutes publicity.

* * *

We acknowledge that some public webpages might get little actual attention. But the same may be said of a card posted on the door of a residence or a poster displayed in a shop window, each of which constitutes publicity. [ ] The unrestricted MySpace.com webpage posting likewise constitutes publicity.

* * *

Because Yath failed to produce any evidence on an essential element of her claim—specifically, that any of the defendants surviving on appeal were involved in creating or sustaining the disparaging MySpace.com webpage—her invasion–of–privacy claim fails.

[The court rejects Yath's other claims: negligent infliction of emotional distress; vicarious liability of Fairview for its employees' misconduct; and a private right of action under a state statute.]

* * *

VI

[The court finally addressed Yath's argument that " * * *HIPAA supersedes or preempts any "contrary" provision of state law."]

* * * Fairview argued, and the district court agreed, that Minnesota Statutes section 144.335 is "contrary" to HIPAA because section 144.335 provides for a private cause of action for the wrongful disclosure of an individual's medical records while HIPAA does not. But just because a distinction exists does not make the Minnesota provision "contrary" to HIPAA.

A state law is "contrary" to HIPAA if a health care provider "would find it impossible to comply with both the State and federal requirements" or if the state law is "an obstacle to the accomplishment and execution of the full purposes" of HIPAA. [ ] It would not be impossible for Fairview or Phat to comply with both HIPAA and Minnesota Statutes section 144.335 because both laws, in complementary rather than contradictory fashion, discourage a person from wrongfully disclosing information from another person's health record. [ ]. The goals of the two laws are similar. Both protect the privacy of an individual's health care information. The difference in remedy is functional only, in that a HIPAA violation subjects a person to criminal penalties while section 144.335 exposes a person to compensatory damages in a civil action.[ ] Although the penalties under the two laws differ, compliance with section 144.355 does not exclude compliance with HIPAA.

Section 144.335 also is not "an obstacle to the accomplishment and execution of the full purposes" of HIPAA. The stated purpose of HIPAA is to improve the Medicare and Medicaid programs and "the efficiency and effectiveness of the health care system, by encouraging the development of a health information system through the establishment of standards and requirements for the electronic transmission of certain health information." [ ]. To accomplish that purpose, HIPAA requires entities that maintain or transmit health care information to establish safeguards "to ensure the integrity and confidentiality" of an individual's health care information and "to protect against any reasonably anticipated . . . unauthorized uses or disclosures of the information." [ ] If a person wrongfully discloses health care information, that person may be subject to criminal penalties, including fines or imprisonment. [ ] Rather than creating an "obstacle" to HIPAA, Minnesota Statutes section 144.335 supports at least one of HIPAA's goals by establishing another disincentive to wrongfully disclose a patient's health care record. We hold that Minnesota Statutes section 144.335 is not a contrary state law preempted by HIPAA.

* * *

* * * Unlike the question of whether Yath introduced evidence that any remaining defendant participated in the Internet publicity, this question of statutory construction depends on novel legal arguments that should be addressed first by the district court. We repeat that the district court did not address Yath's vicarious liability argument as applied to section 144.335, presumably because of its preemption analysis and decision. We have therefore also offered no opinion about the merits of that argument. Because we reverse the district court's preemption decision, the district court will have an opportunity on remand to address all unresolved issues related to liability under section 144.335.

DECISION

The district court did not abuse its discretion by declining to impose sanctions for Phat's alleged spoliation of evidence. Yath's claims on the theories of invasion of privacy, negligent infliction of emotional distress, respondeat superior for the intentional torts, and breach of confidential relationship fail as a matter of law. But because we conclude that HIPAA does not preempt Minnesota Statutes section 144.335, we reverse the dismissal of those claims and remand for the district court to consider the claims' unresolved issues.

Affirmed in part, reversed in part, and remanded. [The concurring opinion of JUDGE JOHNSON is omitted.]

NOTES AND QUESTIONS

1. *Yath* represents the emerging judicial approach to arguments that HIPAA preempts state medical privacy statutes. See also R.K. v. St. Mary's Medical Center, Inc., 735 S.E.2d 715, 2012 WL 5834577 (West Virginia Supreme Court of Appeal, 2012) (quoting *Yath* case at length, the court found that " * * * such state–law claims compliment HIPAA by enhancing the penalties for its violation and thereby encouraging HIPAA compliance.") Variation among state laws regarding health information privacy presents a significant hurdle for the establishment of health information exchanges (HIEs) or even the interstate exchange of patient information. See discussion of HIEs, below.

Yath also presents an interesting problem—the broadcast of confidential patient information using social media. It reveals the risks of large scale dissemination by a disgruntled person of personal health information of a hospital patient.

2. HIPAA creates a standard of care for the handling of confidential patient information, but does not create a private right of action for individuals, only criminal remedies.

A person must file a written complaint with the Secretary of Health and Human Services via the Office for Civil Rights. It is then within the Secretary's discretion to investigate the complaint. HHS may impose civil penalties ranging from $100 to $25,000. Criminal sanctions range from $50,000 to $250,000, with corresponding prison terms, enforced by the Department of Justice. However, according to the 2013 Amendments, HHS "intends to seek and promote voluntary compliance" and "will seek to resolve matters by informal means whenever possible." Therefore enforcement "will be primarily complaint driven," and civil penalties will only be imposed if the violation was willful. Such penalties will not be imposed if the failure to comply was due to reasonable cause and is corrected within 30 days from when the covered entity knew or should have known of the failure to comply. The standard is even higher for imposing criminal penalties. §§ 160.306, 160.312 (a)(1), 160.304(b), 42 U.S.C § 1320 et seq.

3. *HIPAA Standards and Private Actions*. HIPAA has been held by the federal courts not to create a private right of action, which was not altered by the 2013 Amendments. See e.g. Acara v. Banks, 470 F.3d 569, 571 (5th Cir. 2006), in which the Fifth Circuit held: "HIPAA does not contain any express language conferring private rights upon a specific class of individuals. * * * Because HIPAA specifically delegates enforcement, there is a strong indication that Congress intended to preclude private enforcement."

One state court has allowed a plaintiff to use HIPAA standards as some evidence of a standard of care for medical records privacy. In Acosta v. Byrum, 638 S.E.2d 246 (N.C. Ct. App. 2006), *Acosta* recognized HIPAA as a basis for determining the appropriate level of care in relation to the privacy of medical information. Acosta was treated by Dr. Faber, a psychiatrist. During the course of the treatment, hostility developed between Acosta and Dr. Faber's assistant, Robin Byrum. Acosta sued both Faber and Byrum, alleging that Dr. Faber allowed Byrum to use his access code to view Acosta's psychiatric records, and that Byrum disclosed this information to third parties. Acosta sued Byrum for the intentional infliction of emotional distress, and more importantly for this review, sued Farber for the negligent infliction of emotional distress. One element of the alleged negligence was Dr. Faber's action in permitting Byrum to use his password in a way that violated the HIPAA standard of privacy. Again, the trial court dismissed Acosta's action and appeal followed.

The appeals court reversed the trial court's dismissal, finding, among other conclusions, that the action was not a medical malpractice claim (which would require pre–suit expert certification) but was rather based on the administrative conduct of the psychiatrist in permitting a staff member to view a patient's record by use of the physician's access code. The court recognized that the patient's action was not a claim under HIPAA, which does not provide a private right of action; however, HIPAA may be used to establish an appropriate standard for the protection of health care information. The court, noting that the plaintiff made no independent HIPAA claim, concluded that " * * * HIPAA is inapplicable beyond providing evidence of the duty of care owed by Dr. Faber with regards to the privacy of plaintiff's medical records." *Id.* at 253. Through this mechanism, the plaintiff provided evidence of one of the necessary elements of negligence. Courts are likely to take notice of the standards and any violation of them in evaluating a negligence suit against a hospital or medical office.

One court has allowed a plaintiff's tort complaint to proceed on a negligence per se theory. See I.S. v. The Washington University, Case No. 4:11CV235SNLJ (U.S. District Court, Missouri 2011), where the federal court held that the plaintiff's claim for negligence per se was valid; HIPAA was clearly implicated in the claim, which falls within the broad class of state claims based on federal regulations brought in the state court.

4. One major liability risk created by reliance on computer record–keeping is the failure to protect such computerized patient records. Computer storage raises issues of security, privacy, and integrity of computer records. Breaches of security and unauthorized access to patient information can lead to a range of tort suits, from invasion of privacy to negligence in record maintenance. As patient records are computerized, it becomes easier to gain access to a full patient history. Patient records can be easily stored on flash drives, laptops or iPads or other media, so that access is virtually instantaneous. Computers can be hacked, and records extracted and used for a variety of criminal purposes. And they can be misplaced or stolen, a surprisingly common way in which large numbers of patient records are exposed. See generally Office of Civil Rights, Health Information Privacy, Breaches Affecting 500 or More Individuals, (listing unsecured breaches of health information; a large percentage of the breaches involve laptops or other electronic devices that were lost or stolen).

PROBLEM: LEAKING PATIENT INFORMATION

1. Dr. Jasmine is a dentist in solo practice. He submits his bills only by mail, not electronically; and he does not email his patients or use electronic media in any part of his business. He therefore does not give patients a Notice of Privacy Practices nor in any way indicate to patients what their rights are as to their dental history information. Jasmine sells his patient lists to various dental supply companies for their use in marketing. Has he violated HIPAA?

2. Goldberg goes to the medical office laboratory for a series of tests, and her physician gives her a form indicating which tests have been ordered and tells her to take the form to the lab. When she arrives at the lab, she sees a sign–in sheet and a notice advising patients to deposit the form in the open basket that sits next to the sign–in sheet. The forms lie face–up in the basket, and they show a patient's name, address, birth date, social security number,

and other demographic information, as well as the tests ordered. Is this a violation of HIPAA? If so, how can it be corrected?

3. Dr. Newman, a psychiatrist, is having dinner out with colleagues when she is paged by her answering service with an urgent message to call one of her patients. She left her cell phone at home, so she borrows the phone of one of her dinner companions to return the patient's call. The borrowed cell phone automatically maintains a log of the outgoing phone number. Can a patient whose identity is thereby revealed file a complaint against Dr. Newman?

4. During a routine blood test, Frent chats with the lab technician, Gosford, about a new football game. Gosford responds by telling an amusing story about a well known sports figure who happened to have his blood test done on the previous day by Gosford. The technician mentions the high level of steroids that the test revealed. Can the athlete sue Gosford? The laboratory? What are his options?

5. Gosford obtains her prescriptions for genital herpes treatment from XYZ pharmacies in her area. One day she receives a mailing from a pharmaceutical company advertising their herpes treatment product. The mail has piled up with other pieces on the lobby of her apartment building, and her fellow tenants can easily see the description of the product and her name on the flyer. What recourse does Gosford have?

6. Reconsider *Doe v. Medlantic Health Care Group, Inc., supra,* in light of HIPAA requirements and penalties. What if anything do the Medical Privacy Rules add to Doe's rights?

7. Reconsider **Problem: The Hunt for Patient Records** in light of HIPAA requirements and penalties. Did the hospital violate HIPAA? Did the law firm?

PROBLEM: HITECH AND HIPAA

The HITECH Act both limits access to patient information beyond that required by HIPAA and also substantially improves the enforcement mechanisms available to medical consumers. If you are general counsel to a large hospital chain, what steps will you recommend in a memorandum to all system hospitals? What are the issues you will red flag? Will you propose a redesign of the compliance mechanisms to place a stronger emphasis on patient privacy issues?

Now suppose that you are the Physician Director of a large multi–practice physician group. What are your worries now? Do you see different risks with a group practice, compared to a hospital chain?

C. PRIVACY, CONFIDENTIALITY, AND SECURITY IN HEALTH INFORMATION EXCHANGES

The Health Information Technology for Economic and Clinical Health Act (HITECH), which was part of the American Recovery and Reinvestment Act of 2009 (ARRA), provided federal grants to the states to establish statewide health information exchanges (HIEs). The goal of these health information exchanges is to magnify the gains in quality and efficiency that are expected generally from electronic medical records.

In its most basic form an HIE allows clinicians treating a patient to access necessary patient records—including lab test results, allergies, diagnoses made by others treating the patient, and so on—through a one–stop portal rather than by contacting each of the patient's health care providers individually. With a master patient index that gives each patient and each provider a unique identifier, the HIE consolidates patient health information from the patient's many health care providers into one virtual record. Of course, system–wide electronic medical records (EMRs)—for example, an EMR system adopted by a multi–hospital system and provided to affiliated health care professionals—are HIEs of a sort (sometimes called "enterprise HIEs"). HIEs also have the capacity to aggregate the data from EMRs to create very large data sets for research, monitoring, and performance–based payment.

Under the HITECH amendments to HIPAA, discussed in the previous section, the HIE itself is obliged to protect patient privacy by assuring that disclosure of and access to patient health information meets, at a minimum, HIPAA standards. As you saw in the discussion of HIPAA, HIPAA permits disclosure of personal health information without patient consent for treatment and payment purposes and, in itself, does not form an obstacle to HIEs. The aggregation of personal data and the broader access to that data that is part of the purpose of an HIE, however, both work to raise concerns about confidentiality and privacy that are more pointed than are currently attached to paper medical record systems.

State law may impose higher standards than does HIPAA for privacy and confidentiality and more restrictive standards for disclosure of personal health information. Variation among the states in this regard is extreme. Most states still have a variety of statutes that address specific types of information, such as genetic information and information relating to HIV, or specific disclosures, such as disclosure to parents of minors or to litigants or to government agencies. These statutes are quite specific in some respects and entirely ambiguous in others. Some of these statutes in some states fall within the authority of specific state agencies, so that there is an option of clarifying their application to HIE through agency rulemaking or policy guidance. Many of these statutes, however, simply establish a duty on the part of the provider and a legal claim on the part of the patient, with ambiguities to be resolved through litigation. Finally, most states have recognized a common law duty of confidentiality for medical information. The common law duty tends to be rather broadly stated in one or two state court cases but applied in very few specific circumstances.

Some states have enacted privacy or confidentiality statutes that replace this more episodic statutory pattern with a more coherent framework. Some states are hoping to propose and enact a statute specifically to govern the confidentiality and privacy issues for an HIE. Most states, however, are planning to work with their state law as it is and to use consent and contracts to assure that disclosures through the HIE comply with state law.

One of the major goals of a statewide HIE must be to assure providers that their mere participation will not subject them to legal risk for violation of their duties under these laws. Of course, the state variation could be leveled if Congress would preempt state law entirely or would pay states to voluntarily submit to federal standards for privacy of personal health information.

An HIE's consent, privacy, and confidentiality standards must inspire trust on the part of patients that the information will not be misused or distributed inappropriately. That concern extends to providers as well.

Patient trust is viewed as a significant factor in encouraging participation and has led most developing HIEs to adopt some form of consent for the exchange of clinical information for treatment purposes even though this is not required in HIPAA. State law may also require consent for the exchange of clinical information even if HIPAA doesn't. Providers currently are not required to participate in a regional or statewide HIE.

A counterweight to trust–building through individualized consent requirements, however, is the important goal of assuring a high participation rate among providers and patients. Burdensome consent policies may encumber broad participation.

For discussion of these issues, see Consumer Consent Options for Electronic Health Information Exchange: Policy Considerations and Analysis, Privacy and White Paper Series, ONC (March 2010); Tiger Team Recommendations Concerning Privacy and Security Policies and Practices (September 2010), both available on the website of the Office of the National Coordinator.

PROBLEM: CONSENT TO DISCLOSURE WITHIN AN HIE

Your state's HITECH project is developing a structure for a statewide HIE, including rules for privacy and confidentiality. The consent policies are not the only protection for patients, of course. The HIE will have policies concerning security, authorization of individuals to have access to information, authentication of the identity of persons disclosing and accessing information, an audit process for compliance, and so on. There are federal standards for authentication, authorization, and audit, which your HIE intends to adopt.

The stickier question is how the HIE should handle the issue of patient consent for disclosure of personal health information for treatment purposes.

Three options have been identified. First, the HIE could adopt HIPAA standards and allow the exchange of information for treatment and payment purposes without consent. Second, the HIE could presume that patients consent to disclosure and allow patients to opt out of the HIE. The opt–out model usually requires that providers give their patients notice of the HIE and the opportunity to refuse to participate. Opting out could be made easier or more difficult as the HIE chooses. Third, the HIE could require that patients opt in to the HIE by recording their affirmative consent. The opt in model could make the consent durable (i.e., not requiring a refresh and having no expiration date); it is likely to provide that the consent is easily revocable; and it might require only a global consent to both disclosure and access given at one point of service or on the web or, alternatively, could require consent for each provider to disclose or access information. Most states are choosing among different forms of the opt–out and opt–in models.

HITECH requires that the state use an open and transparent process to develop its HIE policies. Who are the stakeholders who should participate in making the decision concerning consent? What positions would you expect them to take? How would you expect the choice to affect the participation rate, trust in the exchange, workflow for providers, and so on? Which model do you think should be chosen?

The issue of consent is linked directly to the type of information that is included in the EMRs in the HIE. Assume that your state has several statutes that govern the confidentiality and disclosure of information relating to particularly sensitive types of health information. Statutes in your state specifically require patient "authorization" or "permission" or "written authorization" for the disclosure of genetic information, HIV status, and mental health treatment information. How would this influence your choice of the no–consent–needed, opt–out, or opt–in model? How easy would it be to exclude the restricted information, if you choose the no–consent–needed or opt–out model? Assuming that you will have the technical capacity to block particular discrete information bits, would you be able to exclude lab results of a genetic or HIV test? If your statute concerning genetic information defines that information more broadly than a DNA test, as many such statutes do, how easy will it be to exclude that information? Your statute prohibits disclosing HIV status, with certain exceptions that are quite narrow and ambiguous. What clinical information is likely to disclose HIV status? What kind of clinical information concerns mental health treatment?

So far, your HITECH project is examining only the use of personal health information for treatment purposes. Do you anticipate that you will use a uniform consent model for all the uses you may permit for the data in the exchange? Or, will you use different models for different uses? Will you require consent for access to de–identified data for research purposes, for example? For quality monitoring or quality improvement efforts? For access by insurers, or would that depend on the purpose for which they are accessing the information? Should employers have access to the HIE? Should courts be permitted to issue subpoenas requiring the HIE to open the information to plaintiffs and defendants in litigation in which a party's health is at issue? Will your HIE adopt a policy concerning whether payers—private, Medicaid, or Medicare—can require patients to consent to the payer's access to their information in the HIE as a condition of coverage?

V. DRUG DETAILING AND STATE REGULATION

Drug companies spend billions of dollars marketing their drugs, bombarding physicians with information about their products. States have responded to fears that physicians will be misled by this marketing. Vermont passed a law in 2007 aimed at limiting the ability of drug manufacturers and marketers to use prescriber–identifiable information for marketing or promoting a drug, absent prescriber consent. The State was concerned that detailing caused doctors to make decisions based on "incomplete and biased information", that physicians are too busy to research drug applications and rely on pharmaceutical representations. This overreliance, it was feared, that lead to unnecessary prescribing practices that add to health care costs unnecessarily and also put patients at risk from drug side effects.

In Sorrell v. IMS Health Inc., 131 S. Ct. 2653 (S.C. 2011), the Supreme Court considered Vermont's Prescription Confidentiality Law, which restricted the sale, disclosure, and use of pharmacy records that reveal the prescribing practices of individual doctors. This information under the statute could not be sold, disclosed by pharmacies for marketing purposes, or used for marketing by pharmaceutical manufacturers. Vermont justified this legislation by arguing that its prohibitions safeguard medical privacy and diminish the likelihood that marketing will lead to prescription decisions not in the best interests of patients or the State. The Supreme Court, however, concluded that

> [s]peech in aid of pharmaceutical marketing * * * is a form of expression protected by the Free Speech Clause of the First Amendment. As a consequence, Vermont's statute must be subjected to heightened judicial scrutiny. The law cannot satisfy that standard.

The Court described the value to a drug company of knowledge of physician prescribing patterns:

> Pharmaceutical manufacturers promote their drugs to doctors through a process called "detailing." This often involves a scheduled visit to a doctor's office to persuade the doctor to prescribe a particular pharmaceutical. Detailers bring drug samples as well as medical studies that explain the "details" and potential advantages of various prescription drugs. Interested physicians listen, ask questions, and receive followup data. Salesper-

sons can be more effective when they know the background and purchasing preferences of their clientele, and pharmaceutical salespersons are no exception. Knowledge of a physician's prescription practices—called "prescriber–identifying information"—enables a detailer better to ascertain which doctors are likely to be interested in a particular drug and how best to present a particular sales message. Detailing is an expensive undertaking, so pharmaceutical companies most often use it to promote high–profit brand–name drugs protected by patent. Once a brand–name drug's patent expires, less expensive bioequivalent generic alternatives are manufactured and sold.

Pharmacies, as a matter of business routine and federal law, receive prescriber–identifying information when processing prescriptions. [ ] Many pharmacies sell this information to "data miners," firms that analyze prescriber–identifying information and produce reports on prescriber behavior. Data miners lease these reports to pharmaceutical manufacturers subject to nondisclosure agreements. Detailers, who represent the manufacturers, then use the reports to refine their marketing tactics and increase sales.

The legislature further found that detailing increases the cost of health care and health insurance; encourages hasty and excessive reliance on brand–name drugs, before the profession has observed their effectiveness as compared with older and less expensive generic alternatives; and fosters disruptive and repeated marketing visits tantamount to harassment. The legislative findings further noted that use of prescriber–identifying information "increase[s] the effect of detailing programs" by allowing detailers to target their visits to particular doctors. [ ]. Use of prescriber–identifying data also helps detailers shape their messages by "tailoring" their "presentations to individual prescriber styles, preferences, and attitudes." [ ].

The Court noted the content– and speaker–based restrictions on the sale, disclosure, and use of prescriber–identifying information:

> The statute thus disfavors marketing, that is, speech with a particular content. More than that, the statute disfavors specific speakers, namely pharmaceutical manufacturers. As a result of these content–and speaker–based rules, detailers cannot obtain prescriber–identifying information, even though the information may be purchased or acquired by other speakers with diverse purposes and viewpoints. Detailers are likewise barred from using the information for marketing, even though the information may be used by a wide range of other speakers.

After a careful analysis of the legislative language, the court found that the Act aimed to impose a specific, content–based burden on protected expression, and as such warranted heightened judicial scrutiny. According to the majority, commercial speech is no different from political speech, and may even be more important for the consumer. The court observed that "that reality has great relevance in the fields of medicine and public health, where information can save lives."

Vermont argued that some physicians have been harassed by the sales behavior of drug representatives. The Court responded that physicians could simply refuse to see the salespeople, noting that

> [p]hysicians can, and often do, simply decline to meet with detailers, including detailers who use prescriber–identifying information. [ ]. Doctors who wish to forgo detailing altogether are free to give "No Solicitation" or "No Detailing" instructions to their office managers or to receptionists at their places of work.

Vermont also contended that "detailers' use of prescriber–identifying information undermines the doctor–patient relationship by allowing detailers to influence treatment decisions." The Court counters that "[s]peech remains protected even when it may 'stir people to action,' 'move them to tears,' or 'inflict great pain'". And detailing speech can be useful to prescribers, giving them information about new products. The Court notes that it is the speaker and the audience, not the government, who judge the information and its value.

The Court concluded by rejecting Vermont's position:

> If Vermont's statute provided that prescriber–identifying information could not be sold or disclosed except in narrow circumstances then the State might have a stronger position. Here, however, the State gives possessors of the information broad discretion and wide latitude in disclosing the information, while at the same time restricting the information's use by some speakers and for some purposes, even while the State itself can use the information to counter the speech it seeks to suppress. Privacy is a concept too integral to the person and a right too essential to freedom to allow its manipulation to support just those ideas the government prefers.
>
> When it enacted § 4631(d), the Vermont Legislature found that the "marketplace for ideas on medicine safety and effectiveness is frequently one–sided in that brand–name companies invest in expensive pharmaceutical marketing campaigns to doctors." 2007 Vt. Laws No. 80, § 1(4). "The goals of marketing programs," the legislature said, "are often in conflict with the goals of the state." § 1(3). The text of § 4631(d), associated legislative findings, and the record developed in the District Court establish

that Vermont enacted its law for this end. The State has burdened a form of protected expression that it found too persuasive. At the same time, the State has left unburdened those speakers whose messages are in accord with its own views. This the State cannot do.

The Court affirmed the judgment of the Court of Appeals.

The dissenters, Justices Breyer, Ginsburg and Kagan, argued that the Vermont statute only deprives pharmaceutical and data–mining firms of data (collected under a government mandate) that could be used to improve their sales messages. In Breyer's words, "this effect on expression is inextricably related to a lawful governmental effort to regulate a commercial enterprise. The First Amendment does not require courts to apply a special "heightened" standard of review when reviewing such an effort. And, in any event, the statute meets the First Amendment standard this Court has previously applied when the government seeks to regulate commercial speech. For any or all of these reasons, the Court should uphold the statute as constitutional."

NOTES AND QUESTIONS

1. Why are states worried about pharmaceutical data mining of prescription records? The goal is not to market drugs directly to patients, but rather to physicians. Physicians are sophisticated agents. Are they not capable of choosing the best drugs for their patients? The Vermont statute is predicated on several state purposes: "It is the intent of the general assembly to advance the state's interest in protecting the public health of Vermonters, protecting the privacy of prescribers and prescribing information, and to ensure costs are contained in the private health care sector, as well as for state purchasers of prescription drugs, through the promotion of less costly drugs and ensuring prescribers receive unbiased information." The goal seems to be to reduce the costs of prescriptions by changing physician prescribing behavior, which Vermont assumes is highly susceptible to pressure from the drug companies through their marketing techniques, such as the use of detailers who push the higher cost drugs of the companies, rather than the identical generics.

2. The Vermont legislature concluded that detailing risked physician prescribing decisions based on "incomplete and biased information." Surely this addresses legitimate public health concerns of unnecessary prescriptions as well as policy concerns over high cost drugs, does it not? Or, as the dissent puts it, the statute merely deprives drug and data–mining companies of data that could help them "create better sales messages".

3. Studies show that such marketing to physicians works: interaction with drug company representatives is associated with changes in doctor's

prescribing patterns. Drug marketing pushes the newest and most expensive drugs whether or not they are the best according to medical evidence. The majority in *Sorrell* contends that "[i]f pharmaceutical marketing affects treatment decisions, it does so because doctors find it persuasive." Does this assume that physicians have thoughtfully and reflectively weighed their drug choices and adopted the drug recommendations of the drug companies? Vermont's approach assumes to the contrary that physicians are influenced unconsciously and inappropriately by the pressures and promises made by drug detail personnel. Marketing rather than objective and unbiased information raises the costs of prescription drugs for consumers, government and health insurers. See Consumers' Union, Prescription for Change: Safe, Effective, Affordable Prescription Drugs (2005).

Another metastudy of drug prescribing concludes:

> With rare exceptions, studies of exposure to information provided directly by pharmaceutical companies have found associations with higher prescribing frequency, higher costs, or lower prescribing quality or have not found significant associations. We did not find evidence of net improvements in prescribing, but the available literature does not exclude the possibility that prescribing may sometimes be improved. Still, we recommend that practitioners follow the precautionary principle and thus avoid exposure to information from pharmaceutical companies.

Geoffrey K. Spurling, et al., Information from Pharmaceutical Companies and the Quality, Quantity, and Cost of Physicians' Prescribing: A Systematic Review, 7 PLoS Medicine e1000352 (2010).

For an overview of the tension between free speech and regulation generally, see Lars Noah, Truth or Consequences? Commercial Free Speech vs. Public Health Promotion (At the FDA), 21 Health Matrix 1 (2011) (looking at thirty five years of commercial speech regulation and the marketing of medical device and drug information to patients, physicians, and public interest groups). For ACA requirement of disclosure of pharmaceutical and medical device manufacturer payments and gifts to physicians, see Note on Physician Payment Sunshine Act, above.

CHAPTER 5

LIABILITY OF HEALTH CARE PROFESSIONALS

■ ■ ■

This chapter will examine the framework for a malpractice suit against health care professionals and the doctrinal and evidentiary dimensions of such litigation. As you read the chapter, think about the cases and materials on three levels. First, how is the plaintiff's case proved and how does the defendant counter it? Second, how does tort doctrine respond to medical error? And third, how does malpractice litigation affect medical practice and the cost and quality of medical care?

I. THE STANDARD OF CARE

A. ESTABLISHING THE STANDARD OF CARE

HALL V. HILBUN

Supreme Court of Mississippi, 1985.
466 So.2d 856.

ROBERTSON, JUSTICE, for the Court:

I.

This matter is before the Court on Petition for Rehearing presenting primarily the question whether we should, as a necessary incident to a just adjudication of the case at bar, refine and elaborate upon our law regarding (a) the standard of care applicable to physicians in medical malpractice cases and (b) the matter of how expert witnesses may be qualified in such litigation.

* * *

When this matter was before the Court on direct appeal, we determined that the judgment below in favor of the surgeon, Dr. Glyn R. Hilbun, rendered following the granting of a motion for a directed verdict, had been correctly entered. * * *

For the reasons set forth below, we now regard that our original decision was incorrect. * * *

II.

Terry O. Hall was admitted to the Singing River Hospital in Jackson County, Mississippi, in the early morning hours of May 18, 1978, complaining of abdominal discomfort. Because he was of the opinion his patient had a surgical problem, Dr. R.D. Ward, her physician, requested Dr. Glyn R. Hilbun, a general surgeon, to enter the case for consultation. Examination suggested that the discomfort and illness were probably caused by an obstruction of the small bowel. Dr. Hilbun recommended an exploratory laparotomy [sic]. Consent being given, Dr. Hilbun performed the surgery about noon on May 20, 1978, with apparent success.

Following surgery Mrs. Hall was moved to a recovery room at 1:35 p.m., where Dr. Hilbun remained in attendance with her until about 2:50 p.m. At that time Mrs. Hall was alert and communicating with him. All vital signs were stable. Mrs. Hall was then moved to a private room where she expired some 14 hours later.

On May 19, 1980, Glenn Hall commenced this wrongful death action by the filing of his complaint * * *.

* * *

At trial Glenn Hall, plaintiff below and appellant here, described the fact of the surgery. He then testified that he remained with his wife in her hospital room from the time of her arrival from the recovery room at approximately 3:00 p.m. on May 20, 1978, until she ultimately expired at approximately 5:00 a.m. on the morning of May 21. Hall stated that his wife complained of pain at about 9:00 p.m. and was given morphine for relief, after which she fell asleep. Thereafter, Hall observed that his wife had difficulty in breathing which he reported to the nurses. He inquired if something was wrong and was told his wife was all right and that such breathing was not unusual following surgery. The labored breathing then subsided for an hour or more. Later, Mrs. Hall awakened and again complained of pain in her abdomen and requested a sedative, which was administered following which she fell asleep. Mrs. Hall experienced further difficulty in breathing, and her husband reported this, too. Again, a nurse told Hall that such was normal, that patients sometimes make a lot of noise after surgery.

After the nurse left the following occurred, according to Hall.

> [A]t this time I followed her [the nurse] into the hall and walked in the hall a minute. Then I walked back into the room, and walked back out in the hall. Then I walked into the room again and I walked over to my wife and put my hand on her arm because she had stopped making that noise. Then I bent over and flipped the light on and got closer to her where I could see her, and it looked like she was having a real hard problem breathing

and she was turning pale or a bluish color. And I went to screaming.

Dr. Hilbun was called and came to the hospital immediately only to find his patient had expired. The cause of the death of Terry O. Hall was subsequently determined to be adult respiratory distress syndrome (cardio–respiratory failure).

Dr. Hilbun was called as an adverse witness and gave testimony largely in accord with that above. * * *.

Dr. Hilbun stated the surgery was performed on a Saturday. Following the patient's removal to her room, he "went home and was on call that weekend for anything that might come up." Dr. Hilbun made no follow–up contacts with his patient, nor did he make any inquiry that evening regarding Mrs. Hall's post–operative progress. Moreover, he was *not* contacted by the nursing staff or others concerning Mrs. Hall's condition during the afternoon or evening of May 20 following surgery, or the early morning hours of May 21, although the exhibits introduced at trial disclose fluctuations in the vital signs late in the evening of May 20 and more so, in the early morning hours of May 21. Dr. Hilbun's next contact with his patient came when he was called by Glenn Hall about 4:55 or 5:00 that morning. By then it was too late.

* * *

The autopsy performed upon Mrs. Hall's body revealed the cause of death and, additionally, disclosed that a laparotomy [sic] sponge had been left in the patient's abdominal cavity. The evidence, however, without contradiction establishes that the sponge did not contribute to Mrs. Hall's death. Although the sponge may ultimately have caused illness, this possibility was foreclosed by the patient's untimely death.

Plaintiff's theory of the case centered around the post–operative care provided by Dr. Hilbun. Two areas of fault suggested were Dr. Hilbun's failure to make inquiry regarding his patient's post–operative course prior to his retiring on the night of May 20 and his alleged failure to give appropriate post–operative instructions to the hospital nursing staff.

When questioned at trial, Dr. Hilbun first stated that he had practiced for 16 years in the Singing River Hospital and was familiar with the routine of making surgical notes, i.e., a history of the surgery. He explained that the post–operative orders were noted on the record out of courtesy by Dr. Judy Fabian, the anesthesiologist on the case. He stated such orders were customarily approved by his signature or he would add or subtract from the record to reflect the exact situation.

[Dr. Hilbun testified as to the post–operative orders noted in the medical records as of May 20, 1978. Mrs. Hall had a nasogastric tube, an i.v., a catheter; she was receiving medications for pain, nausea, and infections. He testified that he checked on Mrs. Hall in the recovery room and stayed with her, took her vital signs, and discharged her to the floor. He confirmed on cross examination that he customarily followed his patient postoperatively, Until the patient left the hospital.]

* * *

Insofar as the record reflects, Dr. Hilbun gave the nursing staff no instructions regarding the post–operative monitoring and care of Mrs. Hall beyond those [summarized above]. Dr. Hilbun had no contact with Mrs. Hall after 3:00 p.m. on May 20. Fourteen hours later she was dead.

The plaintiff called Dr. S.O. Hoerr, a retired surgeon of Cleveland, Ohio, as an expert witness. The record reflects that Dr. Hoerr is a *cum laude* graduate of the Harvard Medical School, enjoys the respect of his peers, and has had many years of surgical practice. Through him the plaintiff sought to establish that there is a national standard of surgical practice and surgical care of patients in the United States to which all surgeons, including Dr. Hilbun, are obligated to adhere. Dr. Hoerr conceded that he did not know for a fact the standard of professional skill, including surgical skills and post–operative care, practiced by general surgeons in Pascagoula, Mississippi, but that he did know what the standard should have been.

* * * [T]he trial court ruled that Dr. Hoerr was not qualified to give an opinion as to whether Dr. Hilbun's post–operative regimen departed from the obligatory standard of care. * * *.

* * *

Parts of Dr. Hoerr's testimony excluded under the trial judge's ruling follow:

> A. My opinion is that she [Mrs. Hall] did not receive the type of care that she should have received from the general surgical specialist and that he [Dr. Hilbun] was negligent in not following this patient; contacting, checking on the condition of his patient sometime in the evening of May 20th. *It is important in the post–operative care of patients to remember that very serious complications can follow abdominal operations, in particular in the first few hours after a surgical procedure.* And this can be inward bleeding; it can be an explosive development in an infection; or *it can be the development of a serious pulmonary complication, as it was in this patient. As a result of her condition, it is my opinion that he lost the opportunity to diagnose a condition, which in all probability could have been diagnosed at the time by an experienced general surgeon, one with expertise in thoracic surgery. And then appropriate treatment could have been undertaken to abort the complications and save her life.*

> There are different ways that a surgeon can keep track of his patient—"follow her" as the expression goes—besides a bedside visit, which is the best way and which need not be very long at all, in which the vital signs are checked over. The surgeon gets a general impression of what's going on. He can delegate this responsibility to a competent physician, who need not be a surgeon but could be a knowledgeable family practitioner. He could call in and ask to speak to the registered nurse in charge of the patient and determine through her what the vital signs are, and if she is an experienced Registered Nurse what her evaluation of the patient is. *From my review of the record, none of these things took place, and there is no effort as far as I can see that Dr. Hilbun made any effort to find out what was going on with this patient during that period of time.* I might say or add an additional belief that I felt that the nursing responsibility which should have been exercised was not exercised, particularly at the 4:00 a.m. level when the pulse rate was recorded at 140 per minute without any effort as far as I can see to have any physician see the patient or to get in touch with the operating surgeon and so on.
>
> There is an additional thing that Dr. Hilbun could have done if he felt that the nursing services might be spotty—sometimes good, sometimes bad. This is commonly done in Columbus, Ohio, in Ashtabula, Pascagoula, etcetera. *He could put limits on the degree in which the vital signs can vary, expressing the order that he should be called if they exceeded that.* Examples would be: Call me if the pulse rate goes over 110; call me if the temperature exceeds 101; call me if the blood pressure drops below 100. There is a simple way of spelling out for the nursing services what the limits of discretion belong to them and the point at which the doctor should be called.

* * *

Dr. Hilbun did not place any orders on the chart for the nurses to call him in the event of a change in the vital signs of Mrs. Hall. He normally made afternoon rounds between 4:00 and 5:00 p.m. but didn't recall whether he went by to see her before going home. Dr. Hilbun was on call at the hospital that weekend for anything which might come up. Subsequent to the operation and previous to Mrs. Hall's death, he was called about one other person on the same ward, one door down, twice during the night. He made no inquiry concerning Mrs. Hall, nor did he see or communicate with her.

Dr. Donald Dohn, of expertise unquestioned by plaintiff and with years of practical experience, gave testimony for the defendant. He had practiced on the staff at the Cleveland Clinic Foundation in Cleveland,

How?

Ohio, beginning in 1958. Fortuitously, he had moved to Pascagoula, Mississippi, about one month before the trial. Dr. Dohn stated he had practiced in the Singing River Hospital for a short time and there was a great difference in the standard of care in medical procedures in Cleveland, Ohio, and those in Pascagoula, Mississippi. Although he had practiced three weeks in Pascagoula, he was still in the process of acquainting himself with the local conditions. He explained the differences as follows:

> Well, there are personnel differences. There are equipment differences. There are diagnostic differences. There are differences in staff responsibility and so on. For example, at the Cleveland Clinic on our service we had ten residents that we were training. They worked with us as our right hands. Here we have no staff. So it is up to us to do the things that our residents would have done there. There we had a team of five or six nurses and other personnel in the operating room to help us. Here we have nurses in the operating room, but there is no assigned team. You get the luck of the draw that day. I am finding out these things myself. Up there it is a big center; a thousand beds, and it is a regional center. We have tremendous advantages with technical systems, various types of x–ray equipment that is [sic] sophisticated. Also in terms of the intensive care unit, we had a Neurosurgical Intensive Care with people who were specially trained as a team to work there. From my standpoint personally, I seldom had to do much paperwork there as compared to what I have to do now. I have to dictate everything and take all my notes. So, as you can see, there is a difference.

Finally, he again stated the standard of care in Ohio and the standard of care in the Singing River Hospital are very different, although it is obvious to the careful reader of Dr. Dohn's testimony that in so doing he had reference to the differences in equipment, personnel and resources and not differences in the standards of skill, medical knowledge and general medical competence a physician could be expected to bring to bear upon the treatment of a patient.

At the conclusion of the plaintiff's case, defendant moved for a directed verdict on the obvious grounds that, the testimony of Drs. Hoerr and Sachs having been excluded, the Plaintiff had failed to present a legally sufficient quantum of evidence to establish a prima facie case. The Circuit Court granted the motion. * * *

III.

A. General Considerations

Medical malpractice is legal fault by a physician or surgeon. It arises from the failure of a physician to provide the quality of care required by law. When a physician undertakes to treat a patient, he takes on an obligation enforceable at law to use minimally sound medical judgment and render minimally competent care in the course of the services he provides. A physician does not guarantee recovery. If a patient sustains injury because of the physician's failure to perform the duty he has assumed under our law, the physician may be liable in damages. A competent physician is not liable *per se* for a mere error of judgment, mistaken diagnosis or the occurrence of an undesirable result.

The twin principles undergirding our stewardship of the law regulating professional liability of physicians have always been reason and fairness. For years in medical malpractice litigation we regarded as reasonable and fair what came to be known as the "locality rule" (but which has always consisted of at least two separate rules, one a rule of substantive law, the other a rule of evidence).

* * *

C. The Physician's Duty of Care: A primary rule of substantive law

1. The Backdrop

* * *

2. The Inevitable Ascendency of National Standards

* * *

We would have to put our heads in the sand to ignore the "nationalization" of medical education and training. Medical school admission standards are similar across the country. Curricula are substantially the same. Internship and residency programs for those entering medical specialties have substantially common components. Nationally uniform standards are enforced in the case of certification of specialists. Differences and changes in these areas occur temporally, not geographically.

Physicians are far more mobile than they once were. They frequently attend medical school in one state, do a residency in another, establish a practice in a third and after a period of time relocate to a fourth. All the while, they have ready access to professional and scientific journals and seminars for continuing medical education from across the country. Common sense and experience inform us that the laws of medicine do not vary from state to state in anything like the manner our public law does.

Medicine is a science, though its practice be an art (as distinguished from a business). Regarding the basic matter of the learning, skill and competence a physician may bring to bear in the treatment of a given patient, state lines are largely irrelevant. That a patient's temperature is 105 degrees means the same in New York as in Mississippi. Bones break and heal in Washington the same as in Florida, in Minnesota the same as in Texas. * * *

* * *

3. The Competence–Based National Standard of Care: Herein of the Limited Role of Local Custom

All of the above informs our understanding and articulation of the competence–based duty of care. Each physician may with reason and fairness be expected to possess or have reasonable access to such medical knowledge as is commonly possessed or reasonably available to minimally competent physicians in the same specialty or general field of practice throughout the United States, to have a realistic understanding of the limitations on his or her knowledge or competence, and, in general, to exercise minimally adequate medical judgment. Beyond that, each physician has a duty to have a practical working knowledge of the facilities, equipment, resources (including personnel in health related fields and their general level of knowledge and competence), and options (including what specialized services or facilities may be available in larger communities, e.g., Memphis, Birmingham, Jackson, New Orleans, etc.) reasonably available to him or her as well as the practical limitations on same.

In the care and treatment of each patient, each physician has a non–delegable duty to render professional services consistent with that objectively ascertained minimally acceptable level of competence he may be expected to apply given the qualifications and level of expertise he holds himself out as possessing and given the circumstances of the particular case. The professional services contemplated within this duty concern the entire caring process, including but not limited to examination, history, testing, diagnosis, course of treatment, medication, surgery, follow–up, after–care and the like.

* * *

Mention should be made in this context of the role of good medical judgment which, because medicine is not an exact science, must be brought to bear in diagnostic and treatment decisions daily. Some physicians are more reluctant to recommend radical surgery than are other equally competent physicians. There exist legitimate differences of opinion regarding medications to be employed in particular contexts. "Waiting periods" and their duration are the subject of bona fide medical controversy. * * *We repeat: a physician may incur civil liability only when the quality of care he renders (including his judgment calls) falls below minimally acceptable levels.

Different medical judgments are made by physicians whose offices are across the street from one another. Comparable differences in medical judgment or opinion exist among physicians geographically separated by much greater distances, and in this sense local custom does and must continue to play a role within our law, albeit a limited one.

We recognize that customs vary within given medical communities and from one medical community to another. Conformity with established medical custom practiced by minimally competent physicians in a given area, while evidence of performance of the duty of care, may never be conclusive of such compliance. [ ] The content of the duty of care must be objectively determined by reference to the availability of medical and practical knowledge which would be brought to bear in the treatment of like or similar patients under like or similar circumstances by minimally competent physicians in the same field, given the facilities, resources and options available. The content of the duty of care may be informed by local medical custom but never subsumed by it.

* * *

4. The Resources–Based Caveat to the National Standard of Care

The duty of care, as it thus emerges from considerations of reason and fairness, when applied to the facts of the world of medical science and practice, takes two forms: (a) a duty to render a quality of care consonant with the level of medical and practical knowledge the physician may reasonably be expected to possess and the medical judgment he may be expected to exercise, and (b) a duty based upon the adept use of such medical facilities, services, equipment and options as are reasonably available. With respect to this second form of the duty, we regard that there remains a core of validity to the premises of the old locality rule.

* * *

A physician practicing in Noxubee County, for example, may hardly be faulted for failure to perform a CAT scan when the necessary facilities and equipment are not reasonably available. In contradistinction, objectively reasonable expectations regarding the physician's knowledge, skill, capacity for sound medical judgment and general competence are, consistent with his field of practice and the facts and circumstances in which the patient may be found, *the same everywhere.*

* * *

As a result of its resources–based component, the physician's non–delegable duty of care is this: given the circumstances of each patient, each physician has a duty to use his or her knowledge and therewith treat through maximum reasonable medical recovery, each patient, with such reasonable diligence, skill, competence, and prudence as are practiced by minimally competent physicians in the same specialty or general field of practice throughout the United States, who have available to them the same general facilities, services, equipment and options.

* * *

As we deal with general principles, gray areas necessarily exist. One involves the case where needed specialized facilities and equipment are not available locally but are reasonably accessible in major medical centers—New Orleans, Jackson, Memphis. Here as elsewhere the local physician is held to minimally acceptable standards. In determining whether the physician's actions comport with his duty of care, consideration must always be given to the time factor—is the physician confronted with what reasonably appears to be a medical emergency, or does it appear likely that the patient may be transferred to an appropriate medical center without substantial risk to the health or life of the patient? Consideration must also be given to the economic factors—are the proposed transferee facilities sufficiently superior to justify the trouble and expense of transfer? Further discussion of these factors should await proper cases.

D. Who May Qualify As Expert Medical Witness In Malpractice Case: A rule of evidence

As a general rule, if scientific, technical or other specialized knowledge will assist the trier of fact to understand the evidence or to determine a fact in issue, a witness qualified as an expert by knowledge, skill, experience, training or education (or a combination thereof), coupled with independence and lack of bias, may testify thereto in the form of an opinion or otherwise. Medical malpractice cases generally require expert witnesses to assist the trier of fact to understand the evidence.[ ]

Generally, where the expert lives or where he or she practices his or her profession has no relevance *per se* with respect to whether a person may be qualified and accepted by the court as an expert witness. There is no reason on principle why these factors should have *per se* relevance in medical malpractice cases.

* * *

In view of the refinements in the physician's duty of care * * * we hold that a qualified medical expert witness may without more express an opinion regarding the meaning and import of the duty of care * * *, given the peculiar circumstances of the case. Based on the information reasonably available to the physician, i.e., symptoms, history, test results, results of the doctor's own physical examination, x-rays, vital signs, etc., a qualified medical expert may express an opinion regarding the conclusions (possible diagnoses or areas for further examination and testing) minimally knowledgeable and competent physicians in the same specialty or general field of practice would draw, or actions (not tied to the availability of specialized facilities or equipment not generally available) they would take.

Before the witness may go further, he must be familiarized with the facilities, resources, services and options available. This may be done in any number of ways. The witness may prior to trial have visited the facilities, etc. He may have sat in the courtroom and listened as other witnesses described the facilities. He may have known and over the years interacted with physicians in the area. There are no doubt many other ways in which this could be done, but, significantly, we should allow the witness to be made familiar with the facilities (and customs) of the medical community in question via a properly predicated and phrased hypothetical question.

Once he has become informed of the facilities, etc. available to the defendant physician, the qualified medical expert witness may express an opinion what the care duty of the defendant physician was and whether the acts or omissions of the defendant physician were in compliance with, or fell substantially short of compliance with, that duty.

* * *

V. Disposition of the Case at Bar

[The court reversed and remanded for a new trial, on the grounds that the testimony of Drs. Hoerr and Sachs was improperly excluded, and with their testimony, the plaintiff might have survived the defense motion for a directed verdict.]

NOTES AND QUESTIONS

1. How does the court in Hall v. Hilbun view the customary practice of the defendant's medical specialty? Why does it adopt this position? How much of a burden is it for a defendant to rebut the plaintiff's evidence on customary practice? Could a plaintiff use the studies cited in Chapter 1 to support a position that the efficacy of a standard practice is not proven? How would a court react to such studies?

2. The medical profession sets standards of practice and the courts have historically enforced these standards in tort suits. Defendants trying to prove a standard of care normally present expert testimony describing the actual pattern of medical practice, without any reference to the effectiveness of that practice. Courts have traditionally given professional medical standards conclusive weight, so that the trier of fact is not allowed to reject the practice as improper. See, e.g., Doe v. American Red Cross Blood Serv., 297 S.C. 430, 435, 377 S.E.2d 323, 326 (1989) (involving issue of blood bank failing to screening for HIV/AIDS at time when customary practice was not to screen). The court held "in a professional negligence cause of action, the standard of care that the plaintiff must prove is that the professional failed to conform to the generally recognized and accepted practices in his profession. If the plaintiff is unable to demonstrate that the professional failed to conform to the generally recognized and accepted practices in his profession, *then the professional cannot be found liable as a matter of law.*"[ ].

3. The evidence of medical practice variation, in Chapter 1, certainly supports the argument that customary practices are often little more than

habitual practices lacking evidence of efficacy. In tort litigation not involving professionals, courts are willing to reject customary practice if they find the practice dangerous or out of date. See Joseph King, In Search of a Standard of Care for the Medical Profession—the "Accepted Practice" Formula, 28 Vand.L.Rev. 1213, 1236 (1975). Critics such as King worry that standard practice may at times be little more than a routine into which physicians have drifted by default.

4. The customary or accepted practice standard measures physicians against the standard of their profession, not merely the standard of a reasonable and prudent person. Medical practices are always evolving as new developments and scientific studies alter the customary practice. Such evolution in medical practices often creates tensions for the physician who believes that the customary practice is dangerous but the new standard has not yet been generally accepted. Courts have however been unwilling generally to allow a plaintiff to present evidence to attack a customary practice that the defendant physician complied with, except under rare circumstances. See, e.g., Burton v. Brooklyn Doctors Hospital, 88 A.D.2d 217, 452 N.Y.S.2d 875 (1982), where the plaintiff was exposed while in the hospital as a newborn to a prolonged liberal application of oxygen and developed retrolental fibroplasia (RFL) as a result. At the time of his birth, a "significant segment of the medical community continued to believe that the liberal administration of oxygen to prematures was important in preventing death or brain damage. Yet, a respected body of medical opinion believed that oxygen contributed to RLF." He was part of a study at the hospital examining various level of oxygen and the effects of its withdrawal or curtailment; the study found in 1954 that prolonged liberal use led to the development of RLF, and cutting off oxygen to premature infants after 48 hours decreased the incidence of RLF without increasing the risk of either death or brain damage. The court allowed a jury instruction to the effect that adherence to acceptable practice is not a defense if the physician fails to use his best judgment. See also Toth v. Community Hospital at Glen Cove, 22 N.Y.2d 255, 292 N.Y.S.2d 440, 239 N.E.2d 368 (1968).

5. Physicians who hold themselves out as having specialized knowledge will be held to the standard of specialists with those enhanced qualifications. See Zaverl v. Hanley, 64 P.3d 809 (Alaska 2003) (affirmative steps to present himself or herself to public as specialist is sufficient to elevate the standard).

6. *Hall* provides an excellent discussion of the locality rule. Most states have moved from the locality rule to a similar locality or a national standard, in part due to worries about a "conspiracy of silence" that unfairly limits the pool of available experts. Doctors do not like to testify against one another. As the court noted in Mulder v. Parke Davis & Co., 288 Minn. 332, 181 N.W.2d 882 (1970), "All too frequently, and perhaps understandably, practicing physicians are reluctant to testify against one another. Unfortunately, the medical profession has been slow to fashion machinery for making

impartial and objective assessments of the performance of their fellow practitioners."

Legislatures enacting malpractice reform statutes on the other hand have often imposed modified locality rule tests in order to protect physicians from out–of–state witnesses testifying for plaintiffs. See e.g. Henry v. Southeastern Ob–Gyn Associates, 142 N.C.App. 561, 543 S.E.2d 911 (2001) ("similar locality" test of N.C.Gen.Stat. S. 90–21.12 was intended to avoid the adoption of a national standard for health care providers).

Many courts, like *Hall,* also allow evidence describing the practice limitations under which the defendant labors. *Hall's* "resource component" allows the trier of fact to consider the facilities, staff, and other equipment available to the practitioner in the institution, following the general rule that courts should take into account the locality, proximity of specialists, and special facilities for diagnosis and treatment. See, e.g., Primus v. Galgano, 329 F.3d 236 (1st Cir. 2003) ("permissible to consider the medical resources available to the physician as one circumstance in determining the skill and care required"); Restatement (Second) of Torts, § 299A, Comment g. ("Allowance must be made also for the type of community in which the actor carries on his practice. A country doctor cannot be expected to have the equipment, facilities, experience, knowledge or opportunity to obtain it, afforded him by a large city.")

NOTE: EXPERT TESTIMONY IN PROFESSIONAL LIABILITY CASES

The standard of practice in the defendant doctor's specialty or area of practice is normally established through the testimony of medical experts. *Hall* illustrates the burden that the plaintiff bears. In any jurisdiction, plaintiffs, to withstand a motion for a directed verdict, must 1) qualify their medical witnesses as experts; 2) satisfy the court that the expert's testimony will assist the trier of fact; and 3) have the witnesses testify based upon facts that support their expert opinions. The requirement that the expert be of the same specialty as the defendant typically governs the qualifying of the expert for testifying at trial. The standard of care may be based upon the expert's own practice and education. See Wallbank v. Rothenberg, M.D., 74 P.3d 413 (Colo.App. 2003) (personal practices of medical experts may be relevant to the standard of care).

The abolition of the locality rule has been one way to ease the plaintiff's burden of proof, broadening the plaintiff's choices of available experts. Many states still require that the expert at least be familiar with the standard of practice in a similar locality, and some testimony is required as to the similarities between the two localities. See, e.g., First Commercial Trust Company v. Rank, 323 Ark. 390, 915 S.W.2d 262 (1996) (family practitioner was sued for medical negligence and failure to report suspected child abuse; held that Florida emergency room physician should have been allowed to testify on the standard of care for diagnosing child abuse).

Plaintiff's experts normally must be in the same specialty as the defendant. Under some circumstances, however, courts have allowed physicians in other specialties to testify, so long as the alleged negligence involved matters within the knowledge of every physician. A general surgeon can testify as to the standard of care of a plastic surgeon performing elective surgery, as to general surgical issues as to whether nerves in the forehead should have been protected, Hauser v. Bhatnager, 537 A.2d 599 (Me.1988); a cardiologist can testify in a case involving a family practice physician, Fiedler v. Spoelhof, 483 N.W.2d 486 (Minn.App.1992); and a psychiatrist has been allowed to testify as to the standard of post–operative care for a breast implant procedure, Miller v. Silver, 181 Cal.App.3d 652, 226 Cal.Rptr. 479 (1986).

An expert need not be board certified in the subject of the suit, so long as he has the appropriate education and experience. Hanson v. Baker, 534 A.2d 665 (Me.1987). Some jurisdictions adopt a narrower view, requiring that the expert have practiced in the same area as the defendant. See Bell v. Hart, 516 So.2d 562 (Ala.1987) (pharmacist and toxicologist testimony disallowed).

Expert testimony is often based upon clinical literature, FDA statements, and other evidence of the standard of practice and of side–effects of treatments and drugs. Several sources of reliable and authoritative statements may be used by experts in professional liability cases, or relied upon by the trial judge as definitive.

a. *Practice guidelines or parameters.* Statements by medical societies as to good practice will provide a ready–made particularized standard that an expert can use as a benchmark against which to test a defendant's conduct. See section B. *infra*.

b. *Pharmaceutical package insert instructions and warnings.* Package inserts may be used to establish the standard of care for use of the particular drug. In Thompson v. Carter, 518 So.2d 609 (Miss.1987), the physician used Bactrim, a sulfonamide antibiotic, to treat the plaintiff's kidney infection. She developed Stevens Johnson Syndrome, a severe allergic reaction associated with use of Bactrim. The court allowed the admission of the package insert, holding that the package insert was prima facie proof of the proper method of use of Bactrim, an "authoritative published compilation by a pharmaceutical manufacturer."

c. *Physicians Desk Reference (PDR).* The PDR is allowed by most courts as some evidence of the standard of care, if an expert witness relies on it. See, e.g., Morlino v. Medical Center, 152 N.J. 563, 706 A.2d 721 (1998). Other courts allow the PDR as prima facie evidence of the standard of the standard of care under some circumstances. See Garvey v. O'Donoghue, 530 A.2d 1141 (D.C. 1987) (holding that " * * * in a medical malpractice case alleging improper administration, dosage, and monitoring of the drug, they are admissible as both *prima facie* evidence of the standard of care and physicians' notice of their contents.")

d. *Judicial notice.* When the defendant physician's clinical decisions violate a clearly articulated practice within the specialty, courts are sometimes even willing in rare cases to make a finding of per se negligence. See Deutsch v. Shein, 597 S.W.2d 141 (Ky.1980), where the defendant was negligent per se in ordering radiology and other tests on the pregnant plaintiff, injuring the fetus.

e. *Substantive use of a learned treatise*. At the common law, a treatise could be used only to impeach the opponent's experts during cross–examination. It could only undercut the expert's testimony, not build the plaintiff's case. The concern was hearsay, because the author of the treatise was not available for cross–examination as to statements contained in the treatise. Federal Rule of Evidence (FRE) 803(18) creates an exception to the hearsay rule so that the learned treatise can be used for substantive purposes, so long as the treatise is accepted as reliable. Jacober v. St. Peter's Med. Ctr., 128 N.J. 475, 608 A.2d 304 (1992). An expert must be on the stand to explain and assist in the application of the treatise. Tart v. McGann, 697 F.2d 75 (2d Cir.1982). The treatise must be declared reliable by the trial court after a motion by the moving lawyer to use the treatise substantively under FRE 803(18) or its state equivalent. Maggipinto v. Reichman, 481 F.Supp. 547 (E.D.Pa.1979).

f. *Expert reliance on research findings*. Experts in malpractice cases base their testimony on their knowledge, education, and experience. They may also rely on outside studies in the research literature. On rare occasions, courts have allowed such research material into evidence in a malpractice suit. In Young v. Horton, 259 Mont. 34, 855 P.2d 502 (1993), the court allowed into evidence four medical journal articles that had concluded that a majority of patients forget that they gave informed consent to their doctors prior to surgery. The medical expert then testified based both on his experience with informed consent and on the articles' conclusions.

The admissibility of "novel" scientific evidence is often a thorny issue in environmental and toxic tort cases, although rarely in malpractice cases. The standard for evaluating such evidence was established by the Court in Frye v. United States, 54 App.D.C. 46, 293 F. 1013 (1923), a case in which Supreme Court considered the polygraph test and its limitations. The Court held that expert opinion based on a scientific technique is inadmissible unless the technique is "generally accepted" as reliable in the relevant scientific community.

In Daubert v. Merrell Dow Pharmaceuticals, Inc., 509 U.S. 579, 113 S.Ct. 2786, 125 L.Ed.2d 469 (1993), the Court again considered the admissibility of scientific evidence, in this case epidemiological and other evidence of birth defects caused by mothers' ingestion of Bendectin. The Court rejected the *Frye* test of "general acceptability" as a threshold test of admissibility of novel scientific evidence, holding that the Federal Rules of Evidence, particularly Rule 702, make the trial judge the gatekeeper of such evidence, with the responsibility to assess the reliability of an expert's testimony, its relevance, and the underlying reasoning or methodology. Expert testimony must have a valid scientific connection to the issues in the case, and be based on "scientifically valid principles". The scientific evidence must pertain to scientific knowledge defined as falsifiable scientific theories capable of empirical testing.

The Supreme Court has extended the *Daubert* factors to all expert testimony, not just scientific testimony. In Kumho Tire v. Carmichael, 526 U.S. 137, 119 S.Ct. 1167, 143 L.Ed.2d 238 (1999), the Court held that *Daubert's* gatekeeping role for federal courts, requiring an inquiry into both relevance and reliability, applies not only to scientific testimony but to all expert testimony. The Court noted that this was a flexible test, not a checklist, and it is tied to the particular facts of the case. But "some of these factors may be helpful in evaluating the reliability even of experience–based expert testimony . . . " Id. At 1176. The use of the *Daubert* test is to "make certain that an expert, whether basing testimony upon professional studies or personal experience, employs in the courtroom the same level of intellectual rigor that characterizes the practice of an expert in the relevant field." Id. This would seem to impose a higher level of scrutiny on the typical malpractice expert, particularly in cases involving institutional liability, where the expert may testify about a system design in a hospital or a salary incentive system in a managed care system.

Courts have usually found that a qualified expert is reliable without going into the underlying scientific qualities of the opinion. See, e.g. Potter ex rel. Potter v. Bowman, 2006 WL 3760267 (D.Colo.2006) ("the touchstone of reliability is 'whether the reasoning or methodology underlying the testimony is scientifically valid'". * * *; [t]he party proffering the expert opinion must demonstrate both that the expert has employed a method that is scientifically sound and that the opinion is "based on facts which enable [the expert] to express a reasonably accurate conclusion as opposed to conjecture or speculation." The court allowed all three of plaintiff's witnesses to testify). But see Carlen v. Minnesota Comprehensive Epilepsy Program, 2001 WL 1078633 (D. Minn. 2001) (rejecting expert testimony for failing to satisfy *Daubert* factors.). The court concluded that the expert's opinion on causation was not based on a proper differential diagnosis; while he reviewed several studies, there was no evidence as to the known or potential rate of error for his methodology of evaluating causation, or whether it was generally accepted within the medical community.

B. PRACTICE GUIDELINES AS STANDARDS OF CARE

CONN V. UNITED STATES

U.S. District Court, Southern District of Mississippi, 2012.
880 F.Supp.2d 741, 2012 WL 3064111.

CARLTON W. REEVES, DISTRICT JUDGE.

In Mississippi, "[t]he success of a plaintiff in establishing a case of medical malpractice rests heavily on the shoulders of the plaintiffs selected medical expert," because "[t]he expert must articulate an *objective* standard of care." If that expert fails to do so, then summary judgment

must be granted in favor of the defendant. That is the situation that finds itself before this Court today.

FACTS

Conn's Heart Attack. On February 10, 2009, John Conn was suffering from chest pains. He first visited the Stone County Hospital but soon transferred to the G.V. "Sonny" Montgomery V.A. Medical Center in Jackson, Mississippi (hereinafter "the V.A."). By the time he arrived at the V.A., Conn's chest pains had subsided, but he "had a troponin I value of 0.17 and some nonspecific EKG changes."

That afternoon, an EKG showed an "[i]ncomplete [r]ight bundle branch block." The V.A.'s records noted to "[c]onsider ECHO in the AM."

The V.A. kept Conn overnight for observation, and during the night, his "[t]roponin I began to trend down[,] and Conn had no episodes overnight on telemetry monitoring." Conn related to the V.A. that he had undergone a stress test the prior year, and he "was placed on omeprazole 40 mg po for possible GERD." The V.A. discharged Conn after a one–night stay and recorded that he was "asymptomatic." He never underwent an ECHO test.

Unbeknownst to Conn or the V.A., Conn had a 90–percent blockage in his left descending artery. Two days later, Conn returned to the Stone County Hospital with chest pains. He suffered a massive heart attack and had "to be shocked back to life after flat lining in the emergency room."

Conn's Expert Report. In time, Conn and his wife filed suit against the United States government for medical malpractice. As part of that suit, Conn submitted his medical records to Dr. Mark Strong, who reviewed the records and submitted an expert report. According to Dr. Strong, Conn's elevated troponin levels and irregular EKG readings leave "no question that Mr. Conn suffered an acute myocardial infarcation the morning of 2/10/09."

In light of that condition, Dr. Strong wrote that the V.A.'s course of treatment was "not appropriate." In particular, Dr. Strong took note that Conn "did not receive any type of beta–blocker therapy, anti–platelet therapy or thrombin inhibitor" at the V.A., nor did Conn "receive any type of vasodilator therapy/nitrate therapy." Even after the V.A. confirmed Conn's elevated troponin level, Dr. Strong contends that Conn "was not treated with what the American College of Cardiology, American Heart Association recommend for an acute myocardial infarcation."

According to Dr. Strong, the "most concerning aspect" of Conn's stay at the V.A. was the nature of his discharge from the facility. Dr. Strong wrote:

> The discharge diagnosis and discharge medications fail to address, account for or treat what is clearly documented by EKG,

> lab value and clinical history to be an acute myocardial infarcation. *My professional recommendation* given his documented medical course would have been to proceed with diagnostic coronary angiography. At the least, there should be been some type of pre–discharge risk stratification to assess Mr. Conn's risk of suffering recurrent angina, a second myocardial infarcation or further complications from his acute myocardial infarcation.

Ultimately, Dr. Strong opined that "the failure of the medical staff at the [V.A.] to appropriately diagnose, treat and risk stratify Mr. Conn following his admission for an acute myocardial infarcation on 2/10/09 left him with an unacceptably high risk of recurrent symptoms and complications of angina/myocardial infarcation and death." Dr. Strong concluded that Conn's "underlying coronary artery disease . . . was clearly evident and should have been diagnosed on 2/10/09."

ANALYSIS

Controlling Law. The Government moved for summary judgment on June 15, 2012. Specifically, the Government argues that Dr. Strong's report fails in three respects: that it offers no standard of care, that it does not show that the V.A. breached the standard of care, and that it does not establish that the breach caused Conn's injuries. The first point is dispositive, and therefore, this opinion does not reach the second and third arguments.

Negligence suits against the federal government are controlled by the Federal Tort Claims Act, and they are evaluated "in accordance with the law of the place where the act or omission occurred." Therefore, this suit is governed by Mississippi law's view of medical malpractice.

In Mississippi, a plaintiff in a medical malpractice case must prove, among other things, that a standard of care governed his physician's actions. The standard of care must be "specific," and at its core, it is a requirement that a physician be "minimally competent" in his practice.

According to the Government, Dr. Strong's report attempts but fails to establish a standard of care at three separate points. First, in the Government's view, Dr. Strong's reliance on "what the American College of Cardiology, American Heart Association recommend for an acute myocardial infarcation" merely represents "the standard suggested by one group of cardiologists" and does not state an objective standard of care. Second, the Government argues that Dr. Strong's report mistakenly attempts to delineate a standard of care by explaining "what his personal treatment choices may have been." And third, the Government contends that Dr. Strong's report is vague.

Conn disagrees. Conn recounts the portions of Dr. Strong's report that discuss the V.A.'s decision not to use beta–blocker therapy, its failure to order a diagnostic coronary angiography, and its failure to adhere to the recommendations of the American College of Cardiology and the American Heart Association.

[The Court concluded that Dr. Strong's Reports failed to state that the V.A. physician's decisions were not those of a minimally competent physician, rather listing them only as actions not taken. Strong's personal recommendations did not establish the standard of care with particularity.]

Dr. Strong's Reliance on Clinical Practice Guidelines. Casting aside these portions of Dr. Strong's report leaves only his contention that Conn "was not treated with what the American College of Cardiology, American Heart Association recommend for an acute myocardial infarcation." The Government claims that this statement does not establish a national standard of care; Conn disagrees. Neither party offers any authority in support of its position.

Research reveals that the American Heart Association and the American College of Cardiology Foundation jointly publish a series of Guidelines for different aspects of cardiac medicine. For example, the two groups recently published a set of performance measures for adults with heart failure. The series also contains Guidelines regarding percutaneous coronary intervention, coronary artery bypass graft surgery, management of patients with atrial fibrillation, and a host of other topics. These publications are not simple "how–to" checklists regarding the practice of medicine; in length and scope, they resemble law review articles. For example, the 2011 ACCF/AHA Guideline for Coronary Artery Bypass Graft Surgery is 83 pages long.

The breadth of the Guidelines series and the depth of each publication raise two obvious problems with Dr. Strong's claim that Conn "was not treated with what the American College of Cardiology, American Heart Association recommend for an acute myocardial infarcation." First, Dr. Strong does not identify a specific publication within the Guidelines series. Therefore, it is impossible to tell which set of recommendations he claims the V.A. failed to live up to. Second, even if Dr. Strong had identified one particular publication, it is doubtful that he would satisfy Mississippi law: an enunciated standard of care must be "specific," and each Guidelines publication probably contains dozens, if not hundreds, of recommendations.

But more fundamentally, Conn's reliance on the Guidelines implicates an issue arising more and more often in the nation's courts: whether the ACCF/AHA Guidelines, or any other set of published clinical practice guidelines, can establish a national standard of care in a medical malpractice lawsuit. To put it mildly, the question does not enjoy a consensus answer.[41]

On one hand, several courts have considered clinical practice guidelines in favorable lights, and not solely for the purpose of establishing a standard of care. In 2006, a federal court in New York permitted a defendant to offer clinical practice guidelines to establish the appropriate standard of care. In 2010, another New York district judge favorably mentioned the Guidelines within a discussion of the standard of care. And in 2001, a federal judge in New Jersey considered an expert report that relied on guidelines published by the American Heart Association.

Other courts, including one district judge in this Circuit, view these publications as "just guidelines" and have held that they do not establish a standard of care.[ ] Similarly, the New York Court of Appeals wrote in 2002 that clinical practice guidelines "merely recommend" certain actions and "are not rules." [ ] And some 20 years ago, the Pennsylvania Supreme Court deduced that the volume of clinical practice guidelines circulating throughout the medical community demonstrated that guidelines could not, in and of themselves, establish a standard of care because their conflicts showed "two schools of thought" in the medical community. [ ]

So far as research indicates, neither the Mississippi Court of Appeals nor the Mississippi Supreme Court has explored this subject.[ ] But a 1997 concurring opinion on the subject by a Tennessee Court of Appeals judge is particularly compelling. In *Frakes v. Cardiology Consultants, P.C.*, then–Judge Koch wrote separately to describe clinical practice guidelines as "consensus standards of conduct that are both clearer and more rational than those currently used to identify professional negligence." [ ] The guidelines, Judge Koch wrote, "should not necessarily be viewed as conclusive evidence of the standard of care," but he conceded that "[t]hey can be extremely helpful in cases calling into question whether a physician chose the wrong course of diagnosis or treatment or should have gone further in attempting to understand or correct the situation."[ ] At the very least, Judge Koch observed, these guidelines "are relevant to the question of the proper standard of care and should be admitted as substantive evidence if introduced through a witness who can lay a proper foundation."[ ]

The only guidance gleanable from Mississippi caselaw suggests that Mississippi courts are, under some circumstances, open to the idea of permitting expert witnesses to rely on clinical practice guidelines when enunciating a standard of care. Therefore, were this Court to hazard an

---

[41] *See generally* Arnold J. Rosoff, *The Role of Clinical Practice Guidelines in Healthcare Reform: An Update,* 21 ANNALS HEALTH L. 21 (2012); Carter L. Williams, *Evidence–Based Medicine in the Law Beyond Clinical Practice Guidelines: What Effect Will EBM Have on the Standard of Care?,* 61 Wash. & Lee L.Rev. 479 (Winter 2004); Michelle M. Mello, *Of Swords and Shields: The Role of Clinical Practice Guidelines in Medical Malpractice Litigation,* 149 U. Pa. L.Rev. 645 (Jan.2001).

Erie guess on the subject, it would follow Judge Koch's suggestions and find that Mississippi law permits expert witnesses to rely on clinical practice guidelines if the conduct prescribed by those guidelines does indeed describe the specific actions that would be taken by a minimally competent physician.

However, even under that standard, Conn could not defeat the Government's motion for summary judgment. Even if Dr. Strong had not failed to identify a specific Guidelines publication, and even if he had not failed to identify a specific suggestion contained within such a publication, he still would have failed to state that the conduct recommended by the Guidelines marked the standard of care of a minimally competent physician. Therefore, this final piece of Dr. Strong's report, like all other aspects of the report, fails to establish the objective standard of care that the V.A. should have followed in treating Conn.

CONCLUSION

Because Conn has failed to produce an expert report that establishes an objective standard of care to which the V.A. should have adhered, he has failed to establish a *prima facie* case for medical malpractice. Therefore, the Government's motion for summary judgment is granted. A Final Judgment will be entered to memorialize this decision.

NOTES AND QUESTIONS

1. The Institute of Medicine has defined clinical guidelines as "systematically developed statements to assist practitioner and patient decisions about appropriate health care for specific clinical circumstances." They are standardized specifications for using a procedure or managing a particular clinical problem. Such guidelines may be quality–oriented, reducing variations in practice with improving patient care; they may also be cost–reducing, promoting a lower cost approach to care. The Agency for Health Care Policy and Research (AHCPR) within the Public Health Service, a subdivision of the Department of Health and Human Services (DHHS), has the responsibility for the Department's Medical Treatment Effectiveness Program. This program supports research, data development, and other activities to develop and review clinically relevant guidelines, standards of quality, performance measures, and medical review criteria, in order to improve the quality and effectiveness of health care services.

2. Courts are cautious about the use of clinical practice guidelines as evidence of the standard of care. The court in *Conn* refers to Frakes v. Cardiology Consultants, P.C., 1997 WL 536949 (Tenn.Ct.App. 1997), a case in which the issue was the effect of a Table, "Exercise Test Parameters Associated With Poor Prognosis and/or Increased Severity of CAD" (CAD=coronary heart disease), contained in a brochure produced by the American College of Cardiology and the American Heart Association as a consensus statement on the interpretation of exercise treadmill tests. The court held that "all the ex-

perts had adopted the document as a correct statement of the standard of care, and that it would serve as a useful tool for the jury." By contrast, in Liberatore v. Kaufman et al., 835 So.2d 404 (C.A. Fla. 2003), the Court of Appeals held that the trial court had abused its discretion in allowing defendants to use a bulletin published by the American College of Obstetricians and Gynecologists (ACOG) to bolster the testimony of their expert witnesses.

3. Are government–generated practice guidelines and best practices a needed improvement over medical specialty–created guidelines? Consider *Trowbridge v. U.S.*, 703 F.Supp.2d 1129 (D.C. Idaho 2010). The daughter of the plaintiffs suffered cerebral palsy allegedly as a result of the negligence of the defendant in treating the mother during her labor and delivery. Plaintiffs argued that their daughter's cerebral palsy was the result of defendant Dr. Ogden's negligence in failing to monitor the contraction pattern of fetal contractions using the fetal monitor, and to reduce or turn off the Pitocin because the baby was not tolerating excessive uterine contractions caused by the drug. The court noted the complexity of the case, particularly the "landscape of the labor and delivery ward of the hospital, where modern diagnostic and monitoring tools allow more opportunities for physicians to predict and protect against dangers to the mother and the baby, and perhaps more opportunities for their judgments in doing so to be criticized and second–guessed in the cases that turn out badly."

The case turned on expert testimony based on medical treatises and journal articles, and work of the ACOG committee on standards for the interpretation of FHR strips. One witness, Dr. Richard Depp, was a long–time medical legal consultant, then working for defendants about 95% of the time. He also participated in ACOG committees, helping to develop so–called "consensus guidelines."

The court made the following observations about ACOG practice guidelines:

> The Court understands from the testimony at trial that these guidelines have a purpose of identifying common ground and uniform clinical practices across the country. However, the Court was also left with a concern that the motivation of some who would press for such "consensus guidelines" is to revise terminology and set practice standards in a manner intended to provide litigation safe–harbors for delivery physicians.
>
> * * * [I]n a setting where Dr. Depp is living handsomely and almost entirely at this time from the fruits of his work as an expert witness on behalf of defendants in medical malpractice cases, his involvement in setting clinical standards and then pointing to such standards in support of his expert opinions inevitably implicates concerns about credibility. For such reasons, the Court has not wholly accepted Dr. Depp's testimony as beyond reproach.

What is the Court worried about? Can guidelines ever be trusted to be applied rigidly without clinical insight and variation by the treating physicians? See Bond v. U.S., 2008 WL 655609 (D.C.Oregon 2008) (plaintiff, a veteran, died allegedly as the result of his treatment at a VA hospital. The court considered a set of guidelines relied on by the plaintiff's expert, and noted that either course of treatment could be justified by them. " * * *The ultimate judgment regarding the care of a particular patient must be made by the physician and patient in light of all of the available information and the circumstances presented by that patient." [*emphasis the court's*])

Is the language above just typical guideline boilerplate language intended to avoid binding physicians to best practices and avoid holding them to a standard of care? Does it exalt what Gawande calls "expert audacity", individualist clinical heroism that medical professionals admire? Or is the tension between expert audacity and regimentation one that must be recognized? See Atul Gawande, Annals of Medicine: The Checklist, The New Yorker (December 10, 2007).

4. The development of practice guidelines is riddled with problems in too many cases, as the judge in *Trowbridge* notes. Guidelines may suffer from lack of sufficient scientific evidence to justify a consensus standard; the authors may be biased due to financial conflicts of interest; and disagreements in the drafting of a guidelines may be downplayed or concealed. See Maxwell J. Mehlman, Professional Power and the Standard of Care in Medicine, 44 Ariz. St. L. J. 1165, 1212–1215 (2012).

5. Clinical guidelines raise difficult legal questions because they potentially offer an authoritative and settled statement of what the standard of care should be for a given treatment or illness. A court has several choices when such guidelines are offered in evidence.

First, such a guideline might be evidence of the customary practice in the medical profession. A doctor practicing in conformity with a guideline would be shielded from liability to the same extent as one who can establish that she or he followed professional custom. The guideline acts as an authoritative expert witness or a well–accepted review article. A widely accepted clinical standard may be presumptive evidence of due care, but expert testimony will still be required to introduce the standard and establish its sources and its relevancy.

Second, clinical practice guidelines can be used to impeach the opinion of an expert witness. In Roper v. Blumenfeld, 309 N.J.Super. 219, 706 A.2d 1151, 1156 (A.D.1998), the defendant used 1992 Parameters of Care for Oral and Maxillofacial Surgery: A Guide of Practice, Monitoring and Evaluation in order to cross examine plaintiff's expert and to examine his expert. As used to impeach, it was permissible to counter the doctor's opinion that because plaintiff was injured during defendant's failed attempt at extraction, defendant must have deviated from the standard of care because the injury is not a medically accepted risk of the procedures he performed.

Third, such guidelines might be used as an affirmative defense by physicians in a malpractice suit to show compliance with accepted practice. Kentucky allows the use of practice parameters by physicians as an affirmative defense. See Ky. Rev. Stat. Ann. § 342.035(8)(b). Maryland, by contrast, under Md. Code Ann., [Health–Gen.] § 19–1606 (1995), has mandated that practice parameters are not admissible into evidence in any legal proceeding under the statute.

6. Professional societies often attach disclaimers to their guidelines, thereby undercutting their defensive use in litigation. The American Medical Association, for instance, calls its guidelines "parameters" instead of protocols to indicate a large sphere of physician discretion, and further suggests that all guidelines contain disclaimers stating that they are not intended to displace physician discretion. Such guidelines therefore cannot be treated as conclusive. See for example Missan v. Dillon, 12 Misc.3d 1153(A), 819 N.Y.S.2d 211 (N.Y.Sup. 2006), where the plaintiff sought to use the American Brachytherapy Society (ABS) Recommendations for Transperineal Permanent Brachytherapy of Prostate Cancer to set the standard of care. The court rejected the expert testimony as to the standard of care, based only on the ABS Guidelines; the Guidelines specifically stated: "these broad recommendations are meant to be technical and *advisory* in nature; however, the responsibility for medical decisions ultimately rests with the treating physician."

7. *The Role of the National Guideline Clearinghouse.* The Internet enables a doctor to stay current through bulletin boards, physician–directed online services, and both commercial and government–sponsored websites. Doctors are increasingly expected to seek and use the data. Web–based databases have proliferated to promote access by physicians to the newest clinical practice guidelines and other medical developments.

The National Guideline Clearinghouse offers free access by physicians and others to the current clinical practice guidelines, with instantaneous searches of the database. A search produces all guidelines on a given subject, along with an appropriateness analysis of each guideline. The Clearinghouse provides a standardized abstract of each guideline, and grades the scientific basis of its recommendations and the development process for each. Full text or links to sites with the guidelines are provided. Readers are given synopses to produce a side–by–side comparison of guidelines, outlining where they agree and disagree, and physicians can access electronic mail groups to discuss development and implementation. These guidelines must pass certain entry criteria to be included: they must be current, contain systematically developed statements to guide physician decisions, have been produced by a medical or other professional group, government agency, health care organization or other private or public organization; and they must show that they were developed through systematic search of peer–reviewed scientific evidence. Easy search features, database comprehensiveness and Internet location make this the most powerful tool to date.

Janabeth Fleming Taylor, Utilizing the Power of the Web: Medical Resources for Attorneys, gives a full list of medical sites useful to physicians (and to lawyers researching medical questions).

8. For a thorough treatment of the problems of practice guidelines, including their limitations as a possible "safe harbor" for defendant physicians, see generally Maxwell J. Mehlman, Professional Power and the Standard of Care in Medicine, 44 Ariz. St. L. J. 1165, 1230 (2012) (Mehlman skillfully traces the political history of physician control over the standards of practice, and the gradual dethronement of custom as a shield in malpractice litigation. He concludes: "The realization that medicine is less expert and more self–interested than it would like to believe is a major reason why the medical profession has lost a substantial degree of control over the standard of care, as reflected in the abandonment of the locality and customary care standards."). See also Michelle M. Mello, Of Swords and Shields: The Role of Clinical Practice Guidelines in Medical Malpractice Litigation, 149 U.Pa. L. Rev. 645 (2001).

NOTE: OUTCOMES, PRACTICE GUIDELINES, BEST PRACTICES, AND THE AFFORDABLE CARE ACT

The ACA has several sections that affect the potential tort liability of physicians, even though nothing in the Act deals explicitly with tort issues except the tort demonstration project section, Section 10607, *State Demonstration Programs to Evaluate Alternatives to Current Medical Tort Litigation*. What the ACA does, however, is to create four streams of pressure that converge toward measurable and specific standards of care in practice. (See generally the discussion in Chapter 1 for a fuller treatment of the quality and safety features of the ACA.)

First, outcome measures will be researched, developed, and disseminated. Section 10303 of the ACA instructs the Secretary of HHS to develop provider–level outcome measures for both hospitals and physicians, as well as other providers, in Section 10303. Such measures will include at least ten outcome measurements for acute and chronic diseases.

Second, best practices will be researched and disseminated. Section 10303 inserts a new Subpart II—Health Care Quality Improvement Programs. It mandates the Director to "identify, develop, evaluate, disseminate, and provide training in innovative methodologies and strategies for quality improvement practices in the delivery of health care services that represent best practices in health care quality, safety, and value" in collaboration with other Federal agencies.

Third, clinical practice guidelines will be developed in light of the research on outcome measures and best practice. Section 10303 (c) requires the Secretary of HHS to identify existing and new clinical practice guidelines.

Fourth, outcomes, best practices and guidelines will be disseminated rapidly to practice settings. The Center for Quality Improvement and Patient Safety will support research on system improvements and the development of tools "to facilitate adoption of best practices that improve the quality, safety, and efficiency of health care delivery services. Such support may include establishing a *Quality Improvement Network Research Program* for the purpose of testing, scaling, and disseminating of interventions to improve quality and efficiency in health care." Findings will be disseminated through multiple media and linked with the Office of the National Coordinator of Health Information Technology and used to "inform the activities of the health information technology extension program under Section 3012, as well as any relevant standards, certification criteria, or implementation specifications."

A Patient–Centered Outcomes Research Institute (PCORI) is created by Section 6301, Patient–Centered Outcomes Research. This institute is to "* * * assist patients, clinicians, purchasers, and policy–makers in making informed health decisions by advancing the quality and relevance of evidence concerning the manner in which diseases, disorders, and other health conditions can effectively and appropriately be prevented, diagnosed, treated, monitored, and managed through research and evidence synthesis." The PCORI must release its findings within 90 days of receipt and make them available to clinicians, patients, and the general public.

NOTES AND QUESTIONS

1. Judges and academics have written about the diffusion of new medical technologies and standards of practice through social and cultural forces aided by medical specialty societies—a slow evolutionary process. The effect of the cumulative ACA requirements—with money allocated for research on practice guidelines, best practices and outcome measures—will be to accelerate the diffusion of these new standards for best practice. First, federal research dollars under the American Recovery and Reinvestment Act of 2009 are supporting research to analyze what the practice–outcome linkage and what best practices should be.

Second, the ACA mandates dissemination in a variety of ways, including websites, pay–for–performance reforms, and models of integrated practice. New payment reforms in particular will tie physician performance to these measures, particularly in ACOs, medical homes, and other new integrated modes of practice. Best practices, grounded in research and made accessible and transparent to providers, patients, and payers, will start to squeeze out medical practice variation in clinical practice. The tort effect of such narrowing of practice is clear: defenses under liability rules (e.g., respectable minority defenses, variations in practice, and proximate causation) will rapidly narrow as practice choices also narrow. The physician who doesn't keep up with new research will not only suffer income loss; she will also suffer a higher risk of liability for failing to conform to what becomes the new standard of care.

2. How will such practice guidelines and best practices be used in a malpractice suit? The section of the ACA that creates the *Patient–Centered Outcomes Research Institute* specifies that its findings must be rapidly disseminated to clinicians, presumably so that they can adopt them. However,

Section 1181 (8)(A)(iv) specifies that such research findings shall ". . . not be construed as mandates for practice guidelines, coverage recommendations, payment, or policy recommendations . . . "

How do you interpret this language? Does it mean only that dissemination is not a command to clinicians? Or that plaintiff lawyers cannot use the findings as evidence of a standard of care? Surely they can be some evidence of such a standard, and very powerful evidence at that. As a constitutional matter, could Congress limit the way state courts use the guidelines and data developed as a result of the ACA in state tort actions?

PROBLEM: THE BATTLE OF STANDARDS II

Robert Guido is recovering from a myocardial infarction (a heart attack, when blood vessels that supply blood to the heart are blocked, preventing enough oxygen from getting to the heart, so that the heart muscle dies or becomes permanently damaged.) The current practice guidelines for implantable cardioverterdefibrillator (ICD) therapy do not recommend use of an implantable cardioverterdefibrillator (ICD) for primary prevention in patients recovering from a myocardial infarction or coronary artery bypass graft surgery and those with severe heart failure symptoms or a recent diagnosis of heart failure.

Dr. Perry, Robert's cardiologist, recommends the implantation of an ICD and the procedure goes well for Robert without any immediate complications. Within six months of the angiogram, Robert suffers stent thrombosis (the stent closes off the blood vessel completely) and he suffers a major heart attack and dies. The risk of a stent thrombosis is 1% after a cardiac catheterization, carrying a 60% risk of death (with the risk of such thrombosis rising to 2.4% three years after the intervention).

You are retained by Robert's family to bring a malpractice suit against Dr. Guido. How will you develop evidence as to the standard of care and the defendant's failure to comply with it? What kinds of claims will you make in the complaint, based on what you know of the treatment choices and best practices? Can you use any of the provisions of the ACA to your advantage in this case?

See Epstein AE, DiMarco JP, Ellenbogen KA, et al., ACC/AHA/HRS 2008 Guidelines for Device–Based Therapy of Cardiac Rhythm Abnormalities: a Report of the American College of Cardiology/American Heart Association Task Force on Practice Guidelines (Writing Committee to Revise the ACC/AHA/NASPE 2002 Guideline Update for Implantation of Cardiac Pacemakers and Antiarrhythmia Devices): developed in collaboration with the American Association for Thoracic Surgery and Society of Thoracic Surgeons, 117 Circulation e350 (2008) (Guidelines emphasize limits on ICD therapy, specifying that ICDs apply only to patients whose left ventricular ejection fraction is low (30% or 35%) despite receiving optimal medical therapy.)

For a discussion of unnecessary implantations, see Sana M. Al–Khatib et al, Non–Evidence–Based ICD Implantations in the United States, 305 JAMA

43 (2011) (more than 40 percent of the total number of implanted ICDs are not based on evidence); Senate Finance Committee Staff Report on Cardiac Stent Usage at St. Joseph Medical Center(2010 (describing the overuse of stenting at one hospital and the cost to Medicare of such unnecessary procedures).

C. OTHER METHODS OF PROVING PHYSICIAN NEGLIGENCE

The plaintiff will usually use his own experts to establish a standard of care, defendant's deviation from it, and causation, as was done in *Hall.* As discussed above, practice guidelines may also provide evidence of the standard of care. A physician's negligence can also in rare cases be established in other ways.

1. *Examination of defendant's expert witnesses.* The plaintiff may establish the standard of care through defense witnesses, leaving the issue of breach within the province of the fact finder, not the trial court on summary disposition. Porter v. Henry Ford Hospital, 181 Mich.App. 706, 450 N.W.2d 37 (1989).

2. *An admission by the defendant that he or she was negligent.* In Grindstaff v. Tygett, 698 S.W.2d 33 (Mo.App.1985), the defendant described a delivery in the hospital records as a "tight midforceps rotation". In his deposition, when asked what this phrase meant, he described the rotation as "[o]ne in which you would have to apply excessive pressure to effect the maneuver." This was held to be sufficient to submit the case to the jury.

An implicit admission of culpability can be found through evidence of intimidation by defendant of plaintiff's expert witnesses, which a jury is allowed to consider as defendant's consciousness of the weakness of his case. See, e.g., Meyer v. McDonnell, 40 Md.App. 524, 392 A.2d 1129 (Md.App. 1978).

An extrajudicial statement by a physician that he would not provide necessary treatment because of financial constraints has been held by one court to be an implicit admission of liability, sufficient to relieve the plaintiff of the need for expert testimony on the standard of care. See Benson v. Tkach, 30 P.3d 402 (Okla. Civ. App. Div. 2 2001) (physician refused to perform additional surgery on patient's infected area to allow it to heal because "Medicare had his hands tied" and there was no money to pay for the surgery).

3. *Common knowledge in situations where a layperson could understand the negligence without the assistance of experts.* See Gannon v. Elliot, 19 Cal.App.4th 1, 23 Cal.Rptr.2d 86 (1993) (plastic cap from a surgical instrument left in plaintiff's hip socket after a hip joint replacement.)

4. *Use of "res ipsa loquitur".* In most states, res ipsa loquitur operates as an inference of negligence. That is, the jury may infer that the defendant was in some way negligent, but it is not compelled to conclude negligence. It can reject the inference as well as accepting it. A few states treat res ipsa as a presumption, so that a plaintiff who proves a res ipsa case should win unless the defendant comes forward with some evidence to rebut the presumed negligence. See generally Dan Dobbs, The Law of Torts § 249 (2000). The doctrine has three conditions: (1) the accident must be of a kind which ordinarily does not occur in the absence of someone's negligence; (2) it must be caused by an agency or instrumentality within the exclusive control of the defendant; (3) it must not have been due to any voluntary action or contribution on the part of the plaintiff. The classic case is Ybarra v. Spangard, 25 Cal.2d 486, 154 P.2d 687 (1944).

The doctrine continues to be applied in medical malpractice cases where the injury is to a part of the body outside the scope of an operation. See, e.g., Pacheco v. Ames, 149 Wash.2d 431, 69 P.3d 324 (2003) (dentist operated on wrong side of the patient's mouth).

The doctrine has been resisted by some courts, reluctant to apply the doctrine in medical malpractice cases out of concern that doctors might be held liable for rare bad outcomes, whether or not they were related to any negligence by the defendant. Siverson v. Weber, 57 Cal.2d 834, 22 Cal.Rptr. 337, 372 P.2d 97 (1962).

Many states have eliminated the availability of res ipsa loquitur by statute as part of malpractice reform packages. See Chapter 6, section IV, *infra*.

5. *Vicarious Liability*. Physicians who offer services directly to patients in outpatient settings, such as gastroenterologists, typically use nurses and anesthesiologists to assist when performing certain procedures. Many of the new delivery models supported by the Affordable Care Act, such as Accountable Care Organizations and Medical Homes, are likely to place physicians in the central treatment role, with other providers offering support. If the physician uses independent contractors, not fulltime employees, this risks expanding physician liability for mistakes of these independent contractors. See e.g. Parker v. Freilich, 803 A.2d 738, 2002 PA Super 188 (2002) (allowing ostensible agency to be considered by the jury as to the role of the independent contractor nurse). See generally the discussion of vicarious liability in Chapter 6, *supra*.

The Captain of the Ship doctrine is an older doctrine that imposes liability on the surgeon who manages a medical procedure in the hospital using a variety of medical professionals, including nurses. It has fallen out of favor with the courts. See, e.g., Lewis v. Physicians Ins. Co. of Wis., 243 Wis.2d 648, 627 N.W.2d 484, 492 (2001) (" '[C]aptain of the ship' has lost its vitality across the country as plaintiffs have been able to sustain actions against full–care modern hospitals for the negligence of their employees."). A few jurisdictions however still apply it. See e.g. Ochoa v. Vered,186 P.3d 107, 112 (Colo.Ct.App.2008) (a surgeon is responsible for the acts of those under his or her special supervision and control during an operation.).

PROBLEM: EVIDENTIARY HURDLES

You have been approached by Clinton Scott, whose wife Diane died of toxemia at the end of pregnancy. The facts are as follows. Clinton tells you that Diane had experienced symptoms of blurred vision, headaches, chest pains, and swelling in the second half of pregnancy, with worsening symptoms in early February. She had had long–standing severe hypertension, as her medical record indicated. Diane had described these symptoms to her obstetrician, Dr. Fowles, during her January examination. He had told her not to worry, that this was normal in first pregnancies, and that everything would be fine. He did not regularly test her urinary protein excretion or her platelet count, nor did he advise her to take low–dose aspirin daily. Early in February her symptoms got markedly worse. Dr. Fowles then tested her urinary protein excretion and her platelet count and concluded that she had pre–eclampsia (toxemia). He admitted her to the hospital and drugs were administered to control Diane's condition, but she went into convulsions a few hours later. Later that day the staff failed to detect fetal heart tones and a C–section was promptly performed. A stillborn baby girl was delivered. Six days later, Diane's brain had ceased to function. She was taken off life–support with Clinton's approval, and died.

In your preliminary discovery, you have had trouble finding a local obstetrician to testify against Dr. Fowles, who is the president of the local medical society and is quite well–respected among his peers. Your jurisdiction follows the *Hall* rule, so you could hire an expert from elsewhere in the state or region, but you would prefer to use someone who can claim familiarity with local practices and who would cost you less in discovery costs as well.

Consider the following evidence issues. Will you be successful in getting this evidence admitted? In getting the case to the jury? In winning a jury trial?

1. You took the deposition of Dr. Fowles, who was forthright and candid during the examination. The following questions and answers are particularly interesting.

> Q. Is the standard of care when managing a pregnant patient that where you have a condition of persistent headaches, blurred vision, fatigue, significant epigastric pain, and developing edema of the feet, that the physician managing the woman should suspect pre–eclampsia as a cause?
>
> A. Yes, those symptoms should put a doctor on notice of the potential of toxemia. When you suspect this, you should promptly treat

the patient, since immediate treatment increases the likelihood of a cure without the development of any adverse complications.

Q. Would earlier diagnosis and treatment of Diane have prevented her brain death and the loss of the infant?

A. That is impossible to say.

2. A review article in the New England Journal of Medicine stated as follows:

> Hypertensive disorders are the most common medical complications of pregnancy and are an important cause of maternal and perinatal morbidity and mortality worldwide. * * *
>
> * * *
>
> Pregnant women with chronic hypertension are at increased risk for superimposed preeclampsia and abruptio placentae, and their babies are at increased risk for perinatal morbidity and mortality. * * *
>
> Women with preeclampsia require close observation because the disorder may worsen suddenly. The presence of symptoms (such as headache, epigastric pain, and visual abnormalities) and proteinuria increase the risk of both eclampsia and abruptio placentae; women with these findings require close observation in the hospital. * * * The management should include close monitoring of the mother's blood pressure, weight, urinary protein excretion, and platelet count, as well as of fetal status. In addition, the woman must be informed about the symptoms of worsening preeclampsia. If there is evidence of disease progression, hospitalization is indicated.

Baha M. Sibai, Drug Therapy: Treatment of Hypertension in Pregnant Women, 335 New Eng. J. Med. 257 (1996).

3. You have interviewed a nurse–practitioner in obstetrics in the area, who examined the medical records and talked with Clinton. She is willing to testify that based upon her experience as an obstetric nurse for over 10 years, Dr. Fowles was negligent in failing to immediately treat Diane when her symptoms were first related to him in January.

4. **Williams Obstetrics (23rd edition)**, a leading textbook used in many medical schools, states the following:

> Since eclampsia is preceded in most cases by premonitory signs and symptoms, its prophylaxis is in many ways more important than its cure and is identical with the treatment of pre–eclampsia. Indeed, a major aim in treating of pre–eclampsia is to prevent convulsions. The necessity of regular and frequent blood pressure measurements thus becomes clear, as well as the importance of detection of rapid

gain of weight and of proteinuria, and the immediate institution of appropriate dietary and medical treatment as soon as the earliest signs and symptoms appear. By the employment of these precautionary measures and by prompt termination of pregnancy in those cases that do not improve or that become progressively worse under treatment, frequency of eclampsia will be greatly diminished and many lives will be saved. Prophylaxis, while valuable, is not invariably successful. * * *

You did an Internet search for preeclampsia and found, in the Medem Network website, www.medem.com, a news item from the American College of Obstetricians and Gynecologists in 2001 that discussed the benefits of treating high–risk women with daily low–dose aspirin to significantly reduce the incidence of preeclampsia.

5. You have learned during discovery that two hospital committees, the Morbidity Committee and the Obstetrics Committee, have investigated Dr. Fowles' past performance in dealing with patients with eclampsia. You would like to obtain hospital incident reports and committee minutes to find out whether the medical staff has described his performance as substandard. Your peer immunity statute is identical to the Minnesota statute discussed in Chapter 6, *infra*, in Larson v. Wasemiller.

6. You have decided to seek an out–of–state expert to testify about toxemia. You are considering hiring Dr. Matthew Berkle, an obstetrician in practice in Pennsylvania. Dr. Berkle has strong opinions on the importance of early and accurate diagnosis of toxemia, formed as the result of his delivery of over a thousand babies in his career and his own study of his patients, over fifty of whom manifested symptoms of toxemia during their pregnancies. He has kept careful records and has determined that several subtle warning signs can be detected by a properly trained physician who follows his methods. Dr. Berkle is not a trained researcher, but rather a highly intelligent and thoughtful physician who cares about his patients.

The relevant rules of evidence in your jurisdiction are identical to the Federal Rules of Evidence below. These rules were amended to reflect the scientific evidence concerns raised in *Daubert* and *Kumho* by the Supreme Court and were effective December 1, 2000.

Federal Rule of Evidence 701 (Opinion testimony by lay witnesses)

If the witness is not testifying as an expert, the witness' testimony in the form of opinions or inferences is limited to those opinions or inferences which are (a) rationally based on the perception of the witness, (b) helpful to a clear understanding of the witness' testimony or the determination of a fact in issue, and (c) not based on scientific, technical, or other specialized knowledge within the scope of Rule 702.

Federal Rule of Evidence 702 (Testimony by experts)

If scientific, technical, or other specialized knowledge will assist the trier of fact to understand the evidence or to determine a fact in issue, a witness qualified as an expert by knowledge, skill, experience, training, or education, may testify thereto in the form of an opinion or otherwise, if (1) the testimony is based upon sufficient facts or data, (2) the testimony is the product of reliable principles and methods, and (3) the witness has applied the principles and methods reliably to the facts of the case.

Federal Rule of Evidence 703 (Bases of opinion testimony by experts)

The facts or data in the particular case upon which an expert bases an opinion or inference may be those perceived by or made known to the expert at or before the hearing. If of a type reasonably relied upon by experts in the particular field in forming opinions or inferences upon the subject, the facts or data need not be admissible in evidence in order for the opinion or inference to be admitted. Facts or data that are otherwise inadmissible shall not be disclosed to the jury by the proponent of the opinion or inference unless the court determines that their probative value in assisting the jury to evaluate the expert's opinion substantially outweighs their prejudicial effect.

Federal Rule of Evidence 803(6) (Records of Regularly Conducted Activity)

A memorandum, report, record, or data compilation, in any form, of acts, events, conditions, opinions, or diagnoses, made at or near the time by, or from information transmitted by, a person with knowledge, if kept in the course of a regularly conducted business activity, and if it was the regular practice of that business activity to make the memorandum, report, record or data compilation, all as shown by the testimony of the custodian or other qualified witness, or by certification that complies with Rule 902(11), Rule 902(12), or a statute permitting certification, unless the source of information or the method or circumstances of preparation indicate lack of trustworthiness. The term "business" as used in this paragraph includes business, institution, association, profession, occupation, and calling of every kind, whether or not conducted for profit.

Federal Rule of Evidence 803(18) (Statements in Learned Treatises, Periodicals, or Pamphlets)

A statement contained in a treatise, periodical, or pamphlet if:

(A) the statement is called to the attention of an expert witness on cross–examination or relied on by the expert on direct examination; and

(B) the publication is established as a reliable authority by the expert's admission or testimony, by another expert's testimony, or by judicial notice.

If admitted, the statement may be read into evidence but not received as an exhibit.

II. JUDICIAL STANDARD SETTING

HELLING V. CAREY

Supreme Court of Washington, 1974.
83 Wash.2d 514, 519 P.2d 981.

HUNTER, ASSOC. JUSTICE.

The plaintiff suffers from primary open angle glaucoma. Primary open angle glaucoma is essentially a condition of the eye in which there is an interference in the ease with which the nourishing fluids can flow out of the eye. Such a condition results in pressure gradually rising above the normal level to such an extent that damage is produced to the optic nerve and its fibers with resultant loss in vision. The first loss usually occurs in the periphery of the field of vision. The disease usually has few symptoms and, in the absence of a pressure test, is often undetected until the damage has become extensive and irreversible.

The defendants (respondents), Dr. Thomas F. Carey and Dr. Robert C. Laughlin, are partners who practice the medical specialty of ophthalmology. Ophthalmology involves the diagnosis and treatment of defects and diseases of the eye.

The plaintiff first consulted the defendants for myopia, nearsightedness, in 1959. At that time she was fitted with contact lenses. She next consulted the defendants in September, 1963, concerning irritation caused by the contact lenses. Additional consultations occurred in October, 1963; February, 1967; September, 1967; October, 1967; May, 1968; July, 1968; August, 1968; September, 1968; and October, 1968. Until the October 1968 consultation, the defendants considered the plaintiff's visual problems to be related solely to complications associated with her contact lenses. On that occasion, the defendant, Dr. Carey, tested the plaintiff's eye pressure and field of vision for the first time. This test indicated that the plaintiff had glaucoma. The plaintiff, who was then 32 years of age, had essentially lost her peripheral vision and her central vision was reduced to approximately 5 degrees vertical by 10 degrees horizontal.

Thereafter, in August of 1969, after consulting other physicians, the plaintiff filed a complaint against the defendants alleging, among other things, that she sustained severe and permanent damage to her eyes as a proximate result of the defendants' negligence. During trial, the testimony of the medical experts for both the plaintiff and the defendants established that the standards of the profession for that specialty in the same or similar circumstances do not require routine pressure tests for glaucoma upon patients under 40 years of age. The reason the pressure test for glaucoma is not given as a regular practice to patients under the age of 40 is that the disease rarely occurs in this age group. Testimony indicated, however, that the standards of the profession do require pressure tests if the patient's complaints and symptoms reveal to the physician that glaucoma should be suspected.

The trial court entered judgment for the defendants following a defense verdict. The plaintiff thereupon appealed to the Court of Appeals, which affirmed the judgment of the trial court.[ ] The plaintiff then petitioned this Court for review, which we granted.

* * *

We find this to be a unique case. The testimony of the medical experts is undisputed concerning the standards of the profession for the specialty of ophthalmology. It is not a question in this case of the defendants having any greater special ability, knowledge and information than other ophthalmologists which would require the defendants to comply with a higher duty of care than that "degree of care and skill which is expected of the average practitioner in the class to which he belongs, acting in the same or similar circumstances."[ ] The issue is whether the defendants' compliance with the standard of the profession of ophthalmology, which does not require the giving of a routine pressure test to persons under 40 years of age, should insulate them from liability under the facts in this case where the plaintiff has lost a substantial amount of her vision due to the failure of the defendants to timely give the pressure test to the plaintiff.

The defendants argue that the standard of the profession, which does not require the giving of a routine pressure test to persons under the age of 40, is adequate to insulate the defendants from liability for negligence because the risk of glaucoma is so rare in this age group. * * *

The incidence of glaucoma in one out of 25,000 persons under the age of 40 may appear quite minimal. However, that one person, the plaintiff in this instance, is entitled to the same protection, as afforded persons over 40, essential for timely detection of the evidence of glaucoma where it can be arrested to avoid the grave and devastating result of this disease. The test is a simple pressure test, relatively inexpensive. There is no judgment factor involved, and there is no doubt that by giving the test the evidence of glaucoma can be detected. The giving of the test is harmless if the physical condition of the eye permits. The testimony indicates that although the condition of the plaintiff's eyes might have at times prevented the defendants from administering the pressure test, there is an absence of evidence in the record that the test could not have been timely given.

Justice Holmes stated[ ] in Texas & Pac.Ry. v. Behymer,[ ]:

> What usually is done may be evidence of what ought to be done, but what ought to be done is fixed by a standard of reasonable prudence, whether it usually is complied with or not.

In The T.J. Hooper, 60 F.2d 737 * * *, Justice Hand stated:

> [I]n most cases reasonable prudence is in fact common prudence; but strictly it is never its measure; a whole calling may have unduly lagged in the adoption of new and available devices. It never may set its own tests, however persuasive be its usages. *Courts must in the end say what is required; there are precautions so imperative that even their universal disregard will not excuse their omission.*

(Italics ours.)

Under the facts of this case reasonable prudence required the timely giving of the pressure test to this plaintiff. The precaution of giving this test to detect the incidence of glaucoma to patients under 40 years of age is so imperative that irrespective of its disregard by the standards of the ophthalmology profession, it is the duty of the courts to say what is required to protect patients under 40 from the damaging results of glaucoma.

We therefore hold, as a matter of law, that the reasonable standard that should have been followed under the undisputed facts of this case was the timely giving of this simple, harmless pressure test to this plaintiff and that, in failing to do so, the defendants were negligent, which proximately resulted in the blindness sustained by the plaintiff for which the defendants are liable.

NOTES AND QUESTIONS

1. Is the court correct in imposing its own risk–benefit conclusion on the specialty of ophthalmology? Certainly its view of the tradeoff between blindness and a low–cost test seems to lead inevitably to the *Helling* conclusion. A survey of Washington ophthalmologists subsequent to the *Helling* decision found that they did test for glaucoma with some regularity before *Helling,* with 20.3 percent reporting that they tested "quite often", and 30.1% testing "virtually always". Jerry Wiley, "The Impact of Judicial Decisions on Professional Conduct: An Empirical Study, 55 S.Cal.L.Rev. 345, 383 (1982). Yet the expert testimony in the case was that testing was not the customary practice for patients under forty.

2. What problems do you see with the Court's opinion? Should we be reluctant to encourage courts to move beyond the customary practice, given the complexity inherent in medical practice? Or should courts be aggressive in judging the community standard, so long as the parties present full evidence as to the pros and cons of the procedure at issue?

Helling v. Carey is one of a small number of cases rejecting a customary medical practice. See also Lundahl v. Rockford Memorial Hospital Association, 93 Ill.App.2d 461, 465, 235 N.E.2d 671, 674 (1968) ("what is usual or customary procedure might itself be negligence"); Favalora v. Aetna Casualty & Surety Company, 144 So.2d 544 (La.App.1962); Toth v. Community Hospital at Glen Cove, 22 N.Y.2d 255, 263, 292 N.Y.S.2d 440, 447–48, 239 N.E.2d 368, 373 (1968) ("evidence that the defendant followed customary practice is not the sole test of professional malpractice"). These cases involve a readily understandable therapy or diagnostic procedure, and the courts have allowed the trier of fact to weigh without expert testimony the relative risks of using the procedure or omitting it.

3. *Negligence per se*. If a statute is used by a court to set the standard of care, the court is judicially setting the standard based on a legislative mandate. The usual American practice in a tort case not involving health care is to treat violations of a statute as negligence per se, giving rise to a rebuttable presumption of negligence. If the defendant fails to rebut the presumption, the trier of fact must find against him on the negligence issue. The classic statement of the rule is found in Martin v. Herzog, 228 N.Y. 164, 126 N.E. 814 (1920). Negligence per se is usually applied in cases where a statute is used to show a standard of care.

Courts have proved resistant to the application of negligence per se to health care institutions, even to create an inference of negligence, unless the standard is specific and supported by expert testimony. In Van Iperen v. Van Bramer, 392 N.W.2d 480 (Iowa 1986), the court considered the effect of Joint Commission standards on a hospital. The plaintiff had argued that the hospital should have provided drug monitoring services, based on Joint Commission accreditation standards requiring that a hospital provide drug monitoring services through its pharmacy, including a medication record or drug profile and a review of the patient's drug regimen for potential problems. The court rejected the argument, holding that the standards were not sufficiently specific to justify a negligence per se standard. Such standards may however provide some evidence of a standard and its violation, through the testimony of experts.

4. The federal Medicare program in its Conditions of Participation (CoPs) also sets standards for hospitals, as do a range of other federal programs that condition receipt of federal funds on compliance with government requirements. 42 CFR § 482.21, Condition of Participation: Quality Assessment and Performance Improvement Program, applies to hospitals:

> The hospital must develop, implement, and maintain an effective, ongoing, hospital–wide, data–driven quality assessment and performance improvement program. The hospital's governing body must ensure that the program reflects the complexity of the hospital's organization and services; involves all hospital departments and services (including those services furnished under contract or arrangement); and focuses on indicators related to improved health outcomes and the prevention and reduction of medical errors. The hospital must maintain and demonstrate evidence of its QAPI program for review by CMS.

Do such requirements create the possibility of a negligence per se claim in a malpractice case?

5. *The Reasonable Practice Standard.* Many jurisdictions may be moving to a *reasonable practice standard* that allows the jury to consider evidence that a custom is no longer reasonable or acceptable. The Court in Nowatske v. Osterloh, 198 Wis.2d 419, 543 N.W.2d 265 (1996) stated:

> " * * *in most situations there will be no significant difference between customary and reasonable practices. In most situations physicians, like other professionals, will revise their customary practices so that the care they offer reflects a due regard for advances in the profession. An emphasis on reasonable rather than customary practices, however, insures that custom will not shelter physicians who fail to adopt advances in their respective fields and who consequently fail to conform to the standard of care which both the profession and its patients have a right to expect.".

See generally Philip G. Peters, Jr., The Role of the Jury in Modern Malpractice Law, 87 Iowa L. Rev. 909 (2002). Peters concludes that many state courts are reconsidering deference to medical custom in malpractice cases.

III. OTHER THEORIES

A. NEGLIGENT INFLICTION OF EMOTIONAL DISTRESS

Most medical malpractice suits are negligence suits for physical injury and lost wages suffered by the patient, or in a wrongful death action, for damages that include harm to the deceased's relatives. Plaintiffs may be able to sue a health care provider for the negligent infliction of emotional distress under particularly egregious circumstances, even without tangible physical injury or impact, and without the need for expert testimony on the standard of care and its violation.

STRASEL V. SEVEN HILLS OB–GYN ASSOCIATES, INC.

Court of Appeals of Ohio, 2007.
170 Ohio App.3d 98, 866 N.E.2d 48.

PER CURIAM.

On December 13, 2001, plaintiff–appellee and cross–appellant, Christina Strasel, went to defendants–appellants and cross–appellees, Seven Hills OB–GYN Associates, Inc., d.b.a. Seven Hills Women's Health Centers, and Seven Hills Obstetrics and Gynecology Associates, Inc. ("Seven Hills") for an initial pregnancy appointment. Strasel, who was obese, had a history of irregular menstrual cycles, and the date of her last cycle was undetermined. Strasel was the mother of two children, the oldest of which had been born with a birth defect.

The Seven Hills midwife scheduled Strasel for a sonogram on December 27, 2001, to confirm her due date. The sonogram showed a sac in

Strasel's uterus, but the sonographer could not detect a heart beat or a fetal pole. The sonographer's report stated that she suspected a blighted ovum, a condition in which an empty placental sac develops in the uterus without a fetus. The report also stated that because of Strasel's obesity, the sonographer's ability to see was "limited." The sonographer stated in her report, "I think a follow–up sonogram should be done." Seven Hills's midwife told Strasel that it appeared that she did not have a viable pregnancy. Strasel was told to go home and that she would be contacted later.

Defendant–appellant and cross–appellee Dr. Xavier G. Ortiz was given Strasel's medical file, including the sonographer's report and still photographs of the sonogram, to review. Dr. Ortiz saw an irregular tear–shaped gestational sac that apparently was without a fetal pole or a heartbeat. Dr. Ortiz diagnosed Strasel with a blighted ovum. Dr. Ortiz knew that Strasel was obese and that Strasel's body size had resulted in the sonographer's "limited ability to see." Dr. Ortiz knew that the sonographer had recommended a second sonogram. He also knew that there was a "great disparity" regarding the gestational age of Strasel's baby and that she had a history of irregular menstrual cycles. Dr. Ortiz did not examine Strasel.

Dr. Ortiz had the Seven Hills surgery scheduler reserve a time for Strasel to undergo a dilatation and curettage ("D & C") procedure the following morning. In a D & C procedure, the cervix is opened, a suction device is placed in the uterus, and the contents of the uterus are suctioned out. Any tissue adhering to the uterine wall is "combed out," and the uterus is aspirated to remove any remaining contents. A D & C procedure is essentially the same as an abortion procedure. Dr. Ortiz did not order a follow–up sonogram or blood tests to confirm whether Strasel was pregnant.

Strasel was contacted by the Seven Hills midwife, who told Strasel that she was not pregnant and that Dr. Ortiz wanted to talk to her about a D & C. Before Dr. Ortiz spoke to Strasel, she was contacted by an anesthesiologist from Mercy Hospital Anderson to discuss the surgery, which had been scheduled for the next day. Later that day, Strasel and her husband, plaintiff Daniel Strasel, met with Dr. Ortiz to discuss the D & C procedure. Strasel stated that when she questioned Dr. Ortiz about his diagnosis of a blighted ovum, he stated that he was certain of her condition. Dr. Ortiz never informed Strasel that the sonographer had recommended another sonogram or that other blood tests could confirm her pregnancy. Strasel stated that Dr. Ortiz told her it was difficult to schedule surgeries and that waiting could endanger her health. Strasel consented to a D & C, which Dr. Ortiz performed the next day.

For weeks after her surgery, Strasel experienced bleeding, discomfort, pain, cramping, and nausea. Strasel also began to suffer emotionally. Seven weeks after her surgery, Strasel still believed that she was pregnant, and she made an appointment at Seven Hills. After a positive blood test, Strasel was scheduled for a sonogram. The sonographer told Strasel that the sonogram revealed a 13–week–old fetus. Subsequently, Dr. Ortiz told Strasel that he had misdiagnosed her viable pregnancy as a blighted ovum. Strasel was told that the problems and complications that her baby might suffer as a result of the D & C procedure were unknown.

Strasel transferred her prenatal care to Dr. Patrick Marmion. Strasel consulted with a perinatologist to determine what problems her baby might have due to the D & C. Strasel underwent a series of 11 additional sonograms to monitor her baby's progress. Strasel learned that the D & C posed a serious risk of injury to her baby, and that it was impossible to determine what loss of limb or neurological problems the D & C might have caused until after the baby was born.

Throughout the balance of her pregnancy, Strasel suffered from panic attacks related to her unrelenting fear of the harm that the D & C might have caused to her baby. She had nightmares, and she was unable to function on a day–to–day basis. Strasel withdrew from her children, and she was unable to care for them as she had in the past. Strasel worried constantly about the condition of her unborn child. Strasel and her husband separated. She sought psychological treatment from a Dr. Reed and a Dr. Thompson.

Strasel delivered a healthy baby girl. But her fears for the baby's health did not subside. Strasel worried constantly about whether the baby would develop neurological problems. She had panic attacks. Strasel's anxiety caused her to fear that her baby might develop cystic fibrosis, and she continually licked the child's face to determine whether her skin was salty, because Strasel understood that salty skin was a symptom of cystic fibrosis.

Psychologist Dr. Paul Deardorff examined and tested Strasel. Dr. Deardorff opined that Strasel suffered from major depressive disorder and post–traumatic stress disorder, both of which had resulted from the D & C procedure and the uncertainty about how it would affect her child. Dr. Deardorff stated at trial that Strasel required six to nine months of additional psychological treatment.

Strasel and her husband filed suit for malpractice and negligent infliction of emotional distress. Strasel also requested punitive damages. The case was referred to arbitration, where Strasel was awarded $210,000. Dr. Ortiz and Seven Hills appealed the arbitration award. The trial court directed a verdict in favor of Dr. Ortiz and Seven Hills on Strasel's claim for punitive damages. Following a trial, the jury returned a verdict of $372,000 in Strasel's favor. The jury found against Strasel's husband on his claims. Dr. Ortiz and Seven Hills filed motions for a new trial, for judgment notwithstanding the verdict or, in the alternative, for remittitur, which the trial court denied. Strasel filed a motion for prejudgment interest, which the trial court denied after a hearing.

* * *

For their first assignment of error, Dr. Ortiz and Seven Hills allege that the trial court erred in allowing Strasel to file a claim for, present evidence of, and recover damages for psychological harm and emotional injuries that arose from the fear of a "non–existent peril." Dr. Ortiz and Seven Hills argue that because Strasel delivered a healthy baby, she could not recover for major depressive disorder and post–traumatic stress disorder based upon her fear for the baby's well–being.

[The Court discussed several cases where the Ohio Supreme Court held denied the plaintiff any recovery for negligent infliction of emotional distress "where the defendant's negligence produced no actual threat of physical harm to the plaintiff or any other person."]

* * *

We point out that none of the plaintiffs in any of the foregoing cases cited by Ortiz and Seven Hills were placed in any real danger by the alleged negligence of the defendants. Further, the alleged negligence of the defendants did not place any other person in real or impending physical danger. In this case, Strasel's baby was placed in actual physical peril by Ortiz's misdiagnosis and performance of the D & C.

* * *

In this case, Strasel was clearly present when the D & C was performed. It is uncontroverted that her baby was subjected to a real physical peril by the D & C, regardless of whether the peril led to an actual injury. Strasel's emotional distress resulted from the very real risk of injury to a seven–week–old fetus subjected to what was the equivalent of an abortion procedure. The fact that the baby was born without any apparent physical injury did not alter the fact that the D & C had subjected the baby to a very real danger. Strasel clearly appreciated the risk to her baby, and as a result of her recognition of the peril, she suffered psychological injuries that were compensable under *Paugh*. The first assignment of error is overruled.

The second assignment of error, which alleges that the trial court erred in allowing Strasel's expert psychologist, Dr. Deardorff, to give unqualified testimony about the presence of birth defects in Strasel's child, is overruled. Dr. Deardorff testified exclusively about Strasel's psychological injuries. The references to the health of the child and the numerous trips to the emergency room were clearly elicited to show how Strasel's psychological problems manifested themselves. The testimony was not offered to show that the baby might experience any problem in the future.

No claims were made for any future damages on behalf of the baby, and no such damages were awarded.

* * *

The judgment of the trial court denying Strasel's motion for prejudgment interest is reversed, and the cause is remanded for a determination of the amount of prejudgment interest to be awarded to Strasel. The trial court's judgment is affirmed in all other respects.

Judgment affirmed in part and reversed in part, and cause remanded.

NOTES AND QUESTIONS

1. Was the plaintiff required to introduce expert testimony as to the defendants' breach of the standard of care in performing a D & C? How was negligence established? Is it simply the kind of provider failure that is within the common knowledge and experience of a lay jury? Is this a straightforward application of the "bystander" rule in emotional distress cases?

2. In malpractice cases that have allowed an emotional distress claim without physical injury or expert testimony, the action of the defendant is easily evaluated by the lay trier of fact. Campbell v. Delbridge, 670 N.W.2d 108 (Iowa, 2003) (the plaintiff, a Jehovah's Witness, was tranfused with blood even though he had given explicit instructions, which were in his medical record, that he refused such transfusions.)

In another case, *Oswald*, the plaintiff gave birth to an apparent stillborn child, which turned out in fact to be alive, and which lived briefly. The court summarized the facts as follows:

> A nurse told her if the fetus miscarried it would not be a baby, only a "big blob of blood." One of her treating doctors said, within her hearing, that he did not want to treat her. At one point, the mother screamed in pain and yelled that she was in labor. The doctor did not do a pelvic exam. He suspected, but did not inform the parents, that the mother had a uterine infection. The doctor told the father to calm down his wife, and approximately one–half hour before the doctor's shift ended, he left for vacation. The baby soon began to be born, without medical attention, until the father kicked on a door and got the attention of the medical staff. A one–pound baby girl was delivered, but a nurse announced she was stillborn. One of the doctors examined her for gender but made no further examination. The father called family members to tell them of their loss and, on returning to the room, discovered the baby grasped his finger. The baby, who had been kept on a surgical tray for half an hour, was rushed to a neonatal unit but died twelve hours later.

The court found that expert testimony was not needed to evaluate whether the nurses and doctors' statements were "rude and uncaring" and thereby violated the standard of care expected of health care professionals.

What do these three cases have in common?

B. PHYSICIAN DUTIES TO CONTEST REIMBURSEMENT LIMITS

Physicians practice in a variety of settings—group practices, hospitals, and other outpatient settings such as urgent care facilities and surgicenters, where they share patients with other doctors. Physician office practices continue to grow, usually group practices with a range of employees to support recordkeeping and electronic health record mandates. The group setting gives doctors backup coverage, allows them more time off, and lets them coordinate care for their patients, but it also reduces their independence. The ACA provides incentives for physicians to be employed in new group settings, such as ACOs or Medical Homes, and by hospitals. See generally Bureau of Labor Statistics, U.S. Department of Labor, Occupational Outlook Handbook. See also Jeff Goldsmith, Health Care: An Alternate Economic Universe, Health Affairs Blog, August 23, 2012 (noting that key sectors, specifically hospitals and physician offices, have expanded their workforces despite declining admissions and office visit volume).

Institutions that provide health care—such as hospitals or nursing homes—and entities that pay for health care—including insurers and self–insured employers—now oversee the work of the medical professionals who practice within them or whose care they purchase. The emergence of managed care organizations that both pay for and provide care gives lay managers even greater control over medical practice, in the name of both cost containment and quality of care.

The prevalence of managed care as the dominant mode of financing health care has also imposed substantial constraints on the formerly open–ended fee–for–service system of American health care. Physicians in the past could order tests, referrals and hospitalization for patients with little resistance from either insurers or employers who may have footed the premium bill. Cost–constrained systems now create tensions between cost control and quality of care. Heavy pressure is put on physicians to reduce diagnostic tests, control lengths of stay in hospitals, and trim the fat out of medical practice. As physicians experience outside utilization review, limits in drug formularies as to what may be prescribed, and constraints on specialist and hospital referrals, they feel caught between duties to patients and duties to the institutions in which they now operate.

A physician may have an obligation to assist patients in obtaining payment for health care. At a minimum, this means that the doctor must be aware of reimbursement constraints, so that he can promptly advise the patient or direct him to an appropriate institutional office for further information. Must a physician actively assist a patient in obtaining funding for a procedure that the physician feels is necessary? No court would require a physician to pay out of his own pocket for a treatment that a patient needs; there is no "duty to rescue" in the sense of a physician's financial obligation to support his patient, although there may be ethical obligations to treat in a range of circumstances. However, the *Wickline* and *Murray* cases support the argument that a physician operating within a constrained reimbursement structure and an institutional bureaucracy is expected to be familiar with limits on payment.

WICKLINE V. STATE

Court of Appeal, Second District, Division 5, California, 1986.
192 Cal.App.3d 1630, 239 Cal.Rptr. 810.

ROWEN, ASSOCIATE JUSTICE.

This is an appeal from a judgment for plaintiff entered after a trial by jury. For the reasons discussed below, we reverse the judgment.

Principally, this matter concerns itself with the legal responsibility that a third party payor, in this case, the State of California, has for harm caused to a patient when a cost containment program is applied in a manner which is alleged to have affected the implementation of the treating physician's medical judgment.

The plaintiff, respondent herein, Lois J. Wickline (plaintiff or Wickline) sued defendant, appellant herein, State of California (State or Medi–Cal). The essence of the plaintiff's claim is found in paragraph 16 of her second amended complaint which alleges: "Between January 6, 1977, and January 21, 1977, Doe I an employee of the State of California, while acting within the scope of employment, negligently discontinued plaintiff's Medi–Cal eligibility, causing plaintiff to be discharged from Van Nuys Community Hospital prematurely and whil [sic] in need of continuing hospital care. As a result of said negligent act, plaintiff suffered a complete occlusion of the right infrarenal aorta, necessitating an amputation of plaintiff's right leg."

Responding to concerns about the escalating cost of health care, public and private payors have in recent years experimented with a variety of cost containment mechanisms. We deal here with one of those programs: The prospective utilization review process.

At the outset, this court recognizes that this case appears to be the first attempt to tie a health care payor into the medical malpractice causation chain and that it, therefore, deals with issues of profound importance to the health care community and to the general public. For those reasons we have permitted the filing of amicus curiae briefs in support of each of the respective parties in the matter to assure that due consideration is given to the broader issues raised before this court by this case.

Traditionally, quality assurance activities, including utilization review programs, were performed primarily within the hospital setting under the general control of the medical staff. * * * The principal focus of such quality assurance review schema was to prevent overutilization due to the recognized financial incentives to both hospitals and physicians to maximize revenue by increasing the amount of service provided and to insure that patients were not unnecessarily exposed to risks as a result of unnecessary surgery and/or hospitalization.

Early cost containment programs utilized the retrospective utilization review process. In that system the third party payor reviewed the patient's chart after the fact to determine whether the treatment provided was medically necessary. If, in the judgment of the utilization reviewer, it was not, the health care provider's claim for payment was denied.

In the cost containment program in issue in this case, prospective utilization review, authority for the rendering of health care services must be obtained before medical care is rendered. Its purpose is to promote the well recognized public interest in controlling health care costs by reducing unnecessary services while still intending to assure that appropriate medical and hospital services are provided to the patient in need. However, such a cost containment strategy creates new and added pressures on the quality assurance portion of the utilization review mechanism. The stakes, the risks at issue, are much higher when a prospective cost containment review process is utilized than when a retrospective review process is used.

A mistaken conclusion about medical necessity following retrospective review will result in the wrongful withholding of payment. An erroneous decision in a prospective review process, on the other hand, in practical consequences, results in the withholding of necessary care, potentially leading to a patient's permanent disability or death.

II

[Mrs. Wickline, a woman in her 40s, was treated in 1976 by Dr. Daniels, a physician in general family practice. She failed to respond to physical therapy and was admitted to Van Nuys Community Hospital and examined by Dr. Polonsky, a specialist in peripheral vascular surgery. He diagnosed Leriche's Syndrome, a condition caused by obstruction of the terminal aorta due to arteriosclerosis. He recommended surgery. Ms. Wickline was eligible for Medi–Cal, California's medical assistance program. Dr. Daniels submitted a treatment authorization request to Medi–Cal, which authorized the surgery and 10 days of hospitalization. Dr. Polonsky then performed the surgery, which involved removing a part of

Ms. Wickline's artery and substituting a synthetic artery. She then developed a clot and a second operation was required. Her recovery after these two procedures was described as "stormy".

Ms. Wickline was to leave the hospital on January 17, 1977. Dr. Polonsky decided on January 16 however that it was "medically necessary" for her to remain in the hospital for another eight days beyond the scheduled discharge date. He was worried about infection, and also about his ability to respond quickly to any emergency that might develop in her legs. He therefore filed a Medi–Cal form 180. The physician puts on this form the patient's diagnosis, significant history, clinical status and treatment plan, in order to permit the Medi–Cal representative—either an "on–site" nurse and/or the Medi–Cal physician consultant—to evaluate the request. The form as filled out by Dr. Polonsky was complete and accurate, and was signed off by Dr. Daniels and submitted to the nurse responsible for completing such forms. The nurse, Doris Futerman, felt that she should not approve the entire eight–day extension. She therefore telephoned the Medi–Cal consultant, Dr. Glassman, a board certified surgeon. Dr. Glassman rejected Wickline's physician's request and authorized only four days beyond the original discharge date.

Doctors Polonsky and Daniels each then wrote discharge orders based on the limited four day extension. As the court described their actions, "[w]hile all three doctors were aware that they could attempt to obtain a further extension of Wickline's hospital stay by telephoning the Medi–Cal Consultant to request such an extension, none of them did so."

Ms. Wickline was discharged. At the time of her departure from the hospital, her condition appeared stable, with no evidence that her leg was in danger. Dr. Polonsky testified that he felt his hands were tied as to further appeals on his part. In the words of the court,

> Dr. Polonsky testified that at the time in issue he felt that Medi–Cal Consultants had the State's interest more in mind than the patient's welfare and that that belief influenced his decision not to request a second extension of Wickline's hospital stay. In addition, he felt that Medi–Cal had the power to tell him, as a treating doctor, when a patient must be discharged from the hospital. Therefore, while still of the subjective, non–communicated, opinion that Wickline was seriously ill and that the danger to her was not over, Dr. Polonsky discharged her from the hospital on January 21, 1977. He testified that had Wickline's condition, in his medical judgment, been critical or in a deteriorating condition on January 21, he would have made some effort to keep her in the hospital beyond that day even if denied authority by Medi–Cal and even if he had to pay her hospital bill himself.

The medical experts in the case agreed that Dr. Polonsky was within the standard of practice in discharging Wickline on January 21. Within a few days of her arrival home, Ms. Wickline had problems with her right leg. She was ordered back to the hospital on January 30, nine days after her last discharge. Attempts to save the leg were unsuccessful, and on February 8 Dr. Polonsky amputated Wickline's leg below the knee, to save her life. On February 17, because of the failure to heal, her leg was amputated above the knee. Dr. Polonsky testified that if she had remained in the hospital, he would have observed the leg's change in color, realized that a clot had formed, and ordered her back into surgery to reopen the graft to remove the clot. He testified to a reasonable medical certainty that she would not have lost her leg if she had remained in the hospital. He further testified, in the court's words, that the "Medi–Cal Consultant's rejection of the requested eight–day extension of acute care hospitalization and his authorization of a four–day extension in its place did not conform to the usual medical standards as they existed in 1977. He stated that, in accordance with those standards, a physician would not be permitted to make decisions regarding the care of a patient without either first seeing the patient, reviewing the patient's chart or discussing the patient's condition with her treating physician or physicians."]

III

From the facts thus presented, appellant takes the position that it was not negligent as a matter of law. Appellant contends that the decision to discharge was made by each of the plaintiff's three doctors, was based upon the prevailing standards of practice, and was justified by her condition at the time of her discharge. It argues that Medi–Cal had no part in the plaintiff's hospital discharge and therefore was not liable even if the decision to do so was erroneously made by her doctors.

* * *

IV

[In this section the court examined the negligence liability rules in California, and concluded that Medi–Cal is absolved from liability in this case.]

Dr. Kaufman, the chief Medi–Cal Consultant for the Los Angeles field office, was called to testify on behalf of the defendant. He testified that in January 1977, the criteria, or standard, which governed a Medi–Cal Consultant in acting on a request to consider an extension of time was founded on title 22 of the California Administrative Code. That standard was "the medical necessity" for the length and level of care requested. That, Dr. Kaufman contended, was determined by the Medi–Cal Consultant from the information provided him in the 180 form. The Medi–Cal Consultant's decision required the exercise of medical judgment and, in doing so, the Medi–Cal Consultant would utilize the skill, knowledge, training and experience he had acquired in the medical field.

Dr. Kaufman supported Dr. Glassman's decision. He testified, based upon his examination of the MC–180 form in issue in this matter, that Dr. Glassman's four–day hospital stay extension authorization was ample to meet the plaintiff's medically necessary needs at that point in time. Further, in Dr. Kaufman's opinion, there was no need for Dr. Glassman to seek information beyond that which was contained in Wickline's 180 form.

Dr. Kaufman testified that it was the practice in the Los Angeles Medi–Cal office for Medi–Cal Consultants not to review other information that might be available, such as the TAR 160 form (request for authorization for initial hospitalization), unless called by the patient's physician and requested to do so and, instead, to rely only on the information contained in the MC–180 form. Dr. Kaufman also stated that Medi–Cal Consultants did not initiate telephone calls to patient's treating doctors because of the volume of work they already had in meeting their prescribed responsibilities. Dr. Kaufman testified that any facts relating to the patient's care and treatment that was not shown on the 180 form was of no significance.

As to the principal issue before this court, i.e., who bears responsibility for allowing a patient to be discharged from the hospital, her treating physicians or the health care payor, each side's medical expert witnesses agreed that, in accordance with the standards of medical practice as it existed in January 1977, it was for the patient's treating physician to decide the course of treatment that was medically necessary to treat the ailment. It was also that physician's responsibility to determine whether or not acute care hospitalization was required and for how long. Finally, it was agreed that the patient's physician is in a better position than the Medi–Cal Consultant to determine the number of days medically necessary for any required hospital care. The decision to discharge is, therefore, the responsibility of the patient's own treating doctor.

Dr. Kaufman testified that if, on January 21, the date of the plaintiff's discharge from Van Nuys, any one of her three treating doctors had decided that in his medical judgment it was necessary to keep Wickline in the hospital for a longer period of time, they, or any of them, should have filed another request for extension of stay in the hospital, that Medi–Cal would expect those physicians to make such a request if they felt it was indicated, and upon receipt of such a request further consideration of an additional extension of hospital time would have been given.

Title 22 of the California Administrative Code section 51110, provided, in pertinent part, at the relevant time in issue here, that: "The determination of need for acute care shall be made in accordance with the usual standards of medical practice in the community."

The patient who requires treatment and who is harmed when care which should have been provided is not provided should recover for the injuries suffered from all those responsible for the deprivation of such care, including, when appropriate, health care payors. Third party payors of health care services can be held legally accountable when medically inappropriate decisions result from defects in the design or implementation of cost containment mechanisms as, for example, when appeals made on a patient's behalf for medical or hospital care are arbitrarily ignored or unreasonably disregarded or overridden. However, the physician who complies without protest with the limitations imposed by a third party payor, when his medical judgment dictates otherwise, cannot avoid his ultimate responsibility for his patient's care. He cannot point to the health care payor as the liability scapegoat when the consequences of his own determinative medical decisions go sour.

There is little doubt that Dr. Polonsky was intimidated by the Medi–Cal program but he was not paralyzed by Dr. Glassman's response nor rendered powerless to act appropriately if other action was required under the circumstances. If, in his medical judgment, it was in his patient's best interest that she remain in the acute care hospital setting for an additional four days beyond the extended time period originally authorized by Medi–Cal, Dr. Polansky should have made some effort to keep Wickline there. He himself acknowledged that responsibility to his patient. It was his medical judgment, however, that Wickline could be discharged when she was. All the plaintiff's treating physicians concurred and all the doctors who testified at trial, for either plaintiff or defendant, agreed that Dr. Polonsky's medical decision to discharge Wickline met the standard of care applicable at the time. Medi–Cal was not a party to that medical decision and therefore cannot be held to share in the harm resulting if such decision was negligently made.

In addition thereto, while Medi–Cal played a part in the scenario before us in that it was the resource for the funds to pay for the treatment sought, and its input regarding the nature and length of hospital care to be provided was of paramount importance, Medi–Cal did not override the medical judgment of Wickline's treating physicians at the time of her discharge. It was given no opportunity to do so. Therefore, there can be no viable cause of action against it for the consequences of that discharge decision.

* * *

[The court, after discussing relevant California statutory law, concluded that " * * * the Medi–Cal Consultant's decision, vis–a–vis the request to extend Wickline's hospital stay, was in accord with then existing statutory law."]

V

This court appreciates that what is at issue here is the effect of cost containment programs upon the professional judgment of physicians to prescribe hospital treatment for patients requiring the same. While we recognize, realistically, that cost consciousness has become a permanent feature of the health care system, it is essential that cost limitation programs not be permitted to corrupt medical judgment. We have concluded, from the facts in issue here, that in this case it did not.

For the reasons expressed herein, this court finds that appellant is not liable for respondent's injuries as a matter of law. That makes unnecessary any discussion of the other contentions of the parties.

The judgment is reversed.

NOTES AND QUESTIONS

1. What are the limits of the duty? Does it require only that a physician engage in bureaucratic infighting, exhausting her procedural rights, when a utilization review process has rejected her recommendation? The Medi–Cal consultant took a rather casual approach to his review, and the treating physicians acted passively in the face of the initial Medi–Cal rejection. Medi–Cal had argued that the decision to discharge was made by each of the plaintiff's three doctors, and Medi–Cal had no part in the discharge. Both sides agreed that "the decision to discharge is . . . the responsibility of the patient's own treating doctor." The chief Medi–Cal consultant testified that if any of the three doctors had filed another request for an extension based upon their determination of medical necessity, such a request would have been granted. The system, in other words, was designed to generate initial denials, which could be reversed with further appeals.

2. California passed legislation in 1994 to protect physicians who "advocate for medically appropriate health care", following the Wickline decision. See Cal. Bus. & Prof. Code § 2056(a) (West Supp. 1998) (prohibiting termination of or retaliation against physicians as a result of patient advocacy). The law states: "It is the public policy of the State of California that a health care practitioner be encouraged to advocate for appropriate health care for his or her patients," and defines advocacy as "to appeal a payer's decision to deny payment for a service pursuant to the reasonable grievance or appeal procedure established by a [managed care organization] or to protest a decision, policy, or practice that the health care practitioner . . . reasonably believes impairs the . . . ability to provide appropriate health care. . . . " Id. § 2056(b); see also id. § 510(b).

3. Later cases have held that external utilization review bodies can be held liable for negligent review if a patient suffers harm through denial of care. In Wilson v. Blue Cross of Southern California, 271 Cal.Rptr. 876, 222 Cal.App.3d 660 (1990), the court limited *Wickline* but expanded potential liability of outside reviewers. Howard Wilson suffered from major depression, drug dependency, and anorexia. On March 3, 1983 he entered a hospital for treatment. His insurer contracted with Western Medical, a third party utilization review organization, to make determinations of medical necessity. On March 11, Western Medical decided that Wilson's hospital stay was "not jus-

tified or approved." The treating physician felt that Wilson needed 3–4 weeks of care, but did not appeal the utilization review determination. Wilson was discharged, and on March 31 he killed himself. His physician testified that he would have survived if he could have remained longer in the hospital for treatment. The court, in overturning summary judgment for the insurer, held that the test for joint liability for tortious conduct, Restatement (Second) of Torts, § 431:

> . . . actor's negligent conduct is legal cause of harm to another if (a) his conduct is a substantial factor in bringing about the harm, and (b) there is no rule of law relieving the actor from liability because of the manner in which his negligence has resulted in harm.

While the doctor had no obligation to appeal the negative decision in *Wilson*, the court clearly held that under the right facts, the doctor is jointly liable with the utilization reviewer for a denial that leads to a bad patient outcome.

For a good discussion of *Wickline* and *Wilson*, see Gail B. Agrawal and Mark Hall, What If You Could Sue Your HMO? Managed Care Liability Beyond the ERISA Shield, 47 St. Louis U. L.J. 235 (2003).

4. Some courts have allowed plaintiffs to plead a duty of a managed care plan to assist patients in finding other sources of funding for expensive procedures. In Wilson v. Chesapeake Health Plan, Inc., Circuit Court, Baltimore, Maryland 1988 (No. 88019032/CL76201), the plaintiff Hugh Wilson, a thirty one year old employee of the city of Baltimore, developed liver disease. He was a member of a prepaid health plan, the Chesapeake Health Plan, Inc. (Chesapeake). Dr. Cooper, a Maryland gastroenterologist to whom Wilson was referred by his primary care physician, diagnosed Wilson as having non–alcoholic cirrhosis of the liver. Mr. Wilson and his wife were informed that this condition would be fatal without a liver transplant. Cooper reassured Wilson that a liver transplant would be covered under his HMO coverage. Chesapeake however decided that such a transplant was not a covered service under the subscriber agreement. Dr. Cooper contacted Dr. Starzl, the head of the transplant service at Presbyterian University Hospital (PUH) in Pittsburgh, Pennsylvania. Despite Mr. Wilson's lack of insurance coverage, Dr. Starzl agreed to admit Mr. Wilson and told Dr. Cooper to have Mr. Wilson come to PUH the following Monday. The Wilsons arrived in Pittsburgh two days later.

Upon his arrival, Mr. Wilson was refused admittance to PUH because Mr. Edward Berkowitz, PUH's credit administrator, had informed the admitting office that coverage for Mr. Wilson's liver transplant had not been confirmed. Mr. Berkowitz participated in protracted discussions with Chesapeake and Mr. Wilson's union, the International Brotherhood of Electrical Workers' (IBEW), to discuss the possibility of providing coverage for Mr. Wilson's liver transplant.

Due to deteriorating health, Mr. Wilson was admitted to the emergency room at PUH under his insurance three days later. At Dr. Starzl's urging, Mrs. Wilson returned to Baltimore to work further on the financing problem, and she then learned that the Maryland Medical Assistance Program would pay for the procedure once the Wilsons had spent down their savings. During this period a second liver became available, but it was also thrown away. Mr. Wilson died before Mrs. Wilson could obtain Maryland MA coverage and despite the fact that two suitable livers had become available to PUH for transplant during the time Mr. Wilson was in Pittsburgh.

The plaintiff's complaint, Count 16, Negligence, alleged that Dr. Cooper and the health plan "knew or should have known that staff and resources existed . . . to assist the Wilsons in determining the scope of coverage provided by their HMO, other insurers, and alternative funding sources, but they failed to utilize such resources, alert plaintiffs to the existence of such resources or advise them of the need to identify a funding source." (Complaint, p. 33). The trial court refused to dismiss this count in the complaint. The plaintiff then settled with Dr. Cooper and the Chesapeake Health Plan, and the case went to trial against Presbyterian Hospital. The plaintiff obtained a multi–million dollar jury verdict in the case.

What are the limits of the duty pleaded by the plaintiff? Dr. Cooper certainly went out of his way to get Mr. Wilson into the hospital for a transplant. The problem was that he simply wasn't an expert on the Maryland Medical Assistance program and eligibility. Can we expect physicians to be reimbursement experts on their patients' behalf? Should we expect managed care organizations, even if they don't cover a procedure, to offer financial advice to subscribers as to reimbursement options? Why shouldn't we add such duties to the fiduciary relationship between physician and patient, insurer and subscriber?

Courts have generally been reluctant to find a hospital or physician negligent for failing to advise patients that they were eligible for government funding. See, e.g., Mraz v. Taft, 85 Ohio App.3d 200, 619 N.E.2d 483 (8th Dist. 1993) (neither hospital nor nursing home had any duty to advise husband that he qualified for Medicaid).

Reimbursement constraints may involve not only expensive hospitalization, but also expensive modern drug therapies. High–cost drugs may strand physicians between a patient's clinical needs and the limits of possible reimbursement.

MURRAY V. UNMC PHYSICIANS

Supreme Court of Nebraska, 2011.
282 Neb. 260, 806 N.W.2d 118.

GERRARD, J.

This case involves a failure to provide medical treatment. The treatment at issue is a very expensive drug that must be administered indefinitely. But it also may cause serious and even deadly symptoms if its administration is interrupted. In this case, the patient's treating physicians, wary of those health risks, decided not to administer the drug until the patient's insurer approved it or another source of payment could be found. But, regrettably, the patient died before either happened. The question presented in this appeal is whether under such circumstances, an expert medical witness is permitted to opine that under the customary standard of care, a physician should consider the health risks to a patient who may be unable to pay for continued treatment. We conclude that such testimony is admissible and, therefore, reverse the district court's order granting a new trial.

BACKGROUND

This is a medical malpractice case in which Robert Murray, individually and as special administrator of the estate of his wife, Mary K. Murray, alleges that the defendants caused the death of Mary by negligently failing to administer Flolan therapy to treat her pulmonary arterial hypertension. The defendants were the Nebraska Medical Center, the Board of Regents of the University of Nebraska, UNMC Physicians (UNMC), and several associated individual employees, although UNMC was the only defendant remaining by the time of trial.

Pulmonary arterial hypertension is a chronic medical condition in which the blood vessels in the lungs constrict, and the resulting pressure on the heart leads to heart failure. Flolan is a vasodilator that relaxes blood vessels and prevents blood clotting. It is administered by a pump, connected to a port and catheter usually inserted above the collarbone. Flolan is very expensive and shortacting, so patients on Flolan treatment need a constant supply of the drug, because if its administration stops, pulmonary blood pressure rebounds and can be life threatening. And because Flolan is a chronic treatment, patients who begin Flolan need to remain on it, essentially, for the rest of their lives—it must be administered 24 hours a day and costs approximately $100,000 a year. The parties do not seem to disagree that generally, Flolan therapy is the appropriate course of treatment for chronic pulmonary arterial hypertension. Nor do the parties seem to dispute that there are significant and potentially deadly risks associated with interrupting Flolan treatment. [ ]

The course of treatment relevant to this case began in late June 2006, as Mary's treating physician, Austin Thompson, M.D., was preparing to treat Mary's pulmonary arterial hypertension with Flolan. On June 29, Mary underwent a heart catheterization to confirm her diagnosis and eligibility for Flolan; in fact, Thompson had already written the Flolan order before the catheterization, pending the results of the catheterization and insurance approval. The catheterization showed pulmonary arterial hypertension, significant heart failure, and reduced blood flow.

On July 4, 2006, Mary reported to the medical center with swollen legs and fluid around her heart. She was given diuretics and hospitalized until July 8. She was discharged and was supposed to begin Flolan after port placement the following week. But on July 10, she reported to the emergency room with a rapid heartbeat and shortness of breath. She began to seize, then her heartbeat stopped, and medical efforts failed to resuscitate her.

At trial, the parties disputed both the cause of Mary's death and whether UNMC had breached the standard of care. Robert presented expert medical testimony that the proximate cause of Mary's death was pulmonary arterial hypertension. UNMC, on the other hand, presented expert medical testimony that myocarditis, an inflammation of the heart usually caused by viral or bacterial infection, was a contributing factor to Mary's death—a conclusion with which Robert's experts disagreed. And Robert presented expert medical testimony that immediate Flolan administration, even a day or two before Mary's death, would have prevented her death; UNMC, on the other hand, presented expert medical testimony that Flolan would have made no difference.

[The plaintiff's experts contended that "the standard of care for a patient as sick as Mary was to start Flolan and obtain insurance approval afterward." The hospital's witnesses argued that Flolan was not an effective emergency treatment as it did not work immediately. Because the drug is dangerous if treatment is started and then stopped, their practice is to wait for insurance approval.]

The UNMC attending physician during Mary's July 2006 hospitalization, James Murphy, M.D., explained that because Flolan treatment can last for years and require hundreds of thousands of dollars, it was important to make sure the treatment was sustainable before commencing. Thompson testified to "horror stories" about patients who had been forced to discontinue treatment, and he said it would be "irresponsible" not to have lifelong financial support for the drug, because it could be "devastating" if discontinued. Thompson said that the standard of care required such a process. And another of UNMC's experts, William Johnson, M.D., explained that the standard of care required finding some source of payment for a patient, but that if insurance was unavailable, it was still usually possible to find some other payment on a "compassionate need basis" within the 12–week timeframe that Johnson opined was appropriate for treatment of chronic pulmonary arterial hypertension.

Robert moved for a directed verdict on the standard of care, arguing that as a matter of law, insurance coverage cannot dictate what doctors do. UNMC replied that according to its experts, a continuing source for treatment is something that doctors should consider in determining how treatment is to be administered. Robert's motion was overruled. Robert also asked that the jury be instructed that if the standard of care requires prescription of a drug, it is not a defense to a claim the standard of care has been violated that the drug would not be provided until approved by an insurance carrier. That instruction was refused.

The jury returned a general verdict for UNMC. Robert filed a motion for new trial that the district court granted. The court explained:

> The evidence offered by [Robert's] expert on the issue of standard of care indicated that after the confirmation of [pulmonary arterial hypertension] by a right heart catheterization, the standard of care required the commencement of FLOLAN therapy. The evidence offered by [UNMC's] expert was basically the same with one major difference. [UNMC's] expert opined that the standard of care required the commencement of FLOLAN therapy after payment approval by the patient's insurance carrier. On cross–examination, [UNMC's] expert conceded that if no outside funds were available to subsidize the treatment to a patient who needed it, then treatment would be provided on a "humanitarian" basis. The substance of this concession was that the treatment was required by the standard of care regardless of how it was to be paid for.
>
> This Court is of the opinion that, as a matter of law, a medical standard of care cannot be tied to or controlled by an insurance company or the need for payment. The "bean counters" in an insurance office are not physicians. Medicine cannot reach the point where an insurance company determines the medical standard of care for the treatment of a patient. Nor, can we live in a society where the medical care required is not controlled by the physicians treating the patient. The position advanced by [UNMC's] expert tells us that the standard of care is different for those with money than for those without. This is neither moral nor just. It is wrong.
>
> This Court cannot determine the basis upon which the jury found in favor of [UNMC]. It could have been on the standard of care issue and it could have been on the causation issue. This Court erred in not directing the jury that the standard of care had not been met by [UNMC]. This error taints the entire verdict of the jury and requires a new trial.

UNMC appeals from the order granting Robert's motion for new trial. [ ]

* * *

ANALYSIS

It is important, from the outset, to carefully note what issues this appeal does *not* present. This appeal arises against a backdrop of increasing concern about the costs of health care, among health care providers, insurers, government officials, and consumers. That concern has prompted a great deal of discussion, among commentators and in the public arena, about what should be done to control health care costs or to allocate potentially limited resources. As we will explain below, the question presented in this appeal is narrow and does not require us to address the more sweeping issues that are the subject of greater public policy debate. But some discussion of the broader picture will help us clarify what this case is about—or, more precisely, what it is not about.

In Nebraska, in cases arising (like this one) under the Nebraska Hospital–Medical Liability Act,[ ] the standard of reasonable and ordinary care is defined as "that which health care providers, in the same community or in similar communities and engaged in the same or similar lines of work, would ordinarily exercise and devote to the benefit of their patients under like circumstances." [ ] That standard is consistent with the general common–law rule and is a so–called unitary, or wealthblind, standard of care.[ ]. In other words, the standard of care is found in the customary practices prevailing among reasonable and prudent physicians and must not be compromised simply because the patient cannot afford to pay.] That standard of care, however, developed in a world of fee–for–service medicine and persisted while health insurance still primarily provided first–dollar unlimited coverage.[ ]. Today, [h]ealth plans and self–insured corporations are placing increasingly stringent controls on health care resources, thereby limiting physicians' freedom to practice medicine as they see fit. Clinical guidelines have proliferated from a wide variety of sources: managed care organizations, medical subspecialty societies, malpractice insurers, entrepreneurial guideline–writing firms, and others. Each guideline purports to tell physicians the best way to practice. Yet often they conflict with each other, with traditional practice patterns, and with patients' expectations.[ ]

But "[b]ecause tort law expects physicians to provide the same standard of care regardless of patients' ability to pay, and because this standard sometimes encompasses costly technologies no longer readily available for the poorest citizens," physicians are "caught in a bind between legal expectations and economic realities."[ ] Courts have been accused of being "oblivious to the costs of care, essentially requiring physicians to commandeer resources that may belong to other parties, regardless of whether those other parties owe the patient these resources." [ ]

It has been suggested that at a fundamental level, a unitary, wealth–blind standard of care cannot be reconciled with the growth of technology and the stratification of available health care. Custom is increasingly difficult to identify in today's medical marketplace, as resource distinctions produce fragmentation and disintegration.[ ] It has also been suggested that maintaining a unitary standard of care disadvantages those who may not be able to pay for health care. Physicians remain free, for the most part, to decline to treat those who cannot pay, and "an outright refusal to treat an indigent patient, in contrast to a decision to treat in a manner inconsistent with the unitary malpractice standard, rarely creates the threat of liability."[ ] So, it has been argued that rather than assume the burden of paying for a patient's treatment, or the potential liability of providing some but not all possible care, the unitary standard makes it more likely that "providers will now sidestep the entire problem simply by refusing to accept some, or all, of such patients for treatment." [ ]

On the other hand, it has been argued that permitting physicians to make medical decisions based on resource scarcity would compromise the fiduciary relationship between patient and physician, creating a conflict of interest because the patient's well–being would no longer be the physician's focus.[ ] The question is how the value judgments inherent in the development of the standard of care might evolve in response to a societal interest in controlling health care costs. It has been explained that a physician's initial value judgment, in treating a patient, is made in light of conclusions reached about the likely benefits that services would have had for the plaintiff patient. It involves an evaluation as to whether the services should have been provided given their likely benefits, the risk of iatrogenic harm, and the gravity of the problem experienced by the patient. Normally the value judgment does not involve an explicit consideration of the costs of caring for a patient, although economics are implicitly considered. Physicians do not do everything conceivably possible in caring for a patient—they draw what they consider to be reasonable boundary lines. For example, physicians do not order every diagnostic test available for a patient that requests a physical examination, even though doing so might reveal interesting information. Instead, they order tests which are indicated given the age and physical characteristics of the patient.[ ]

A physician's initial value judgment, in other words, is constrained by reason but does not include a societal interest in conserving costs or resources, and certainly does not include weighing the physician's own economic interests.

In short, the traditional ethical norms of the medical profession and the legal demands of the customary standard of care impose significant restrictions on a physician's ability to consider the costs of treatment, despite significant and increasing pressure to contain those costs. Whether the legal standard of care should change to alleviate that conflict, and how it might change, has been the subject of considerable discussion. It has been suggested that the customary standard of care could evolve to permit the denial of marginally beneficial treatment—in other words, when high costs would not be justified by minor expected benefits.[ ] Others have suggested that the standard of care should evolve to consider two separate components: (1) a skill component, addressing the skill with which diagnoses are made and treatment is rendered, that would not vary by a patient's financial circumstances and (2) a resource component, addressing deliberate decisions about how much treatment to give a patient, that would vary so as to not demand more of physicians than is reasonable.[ ] It has been suggested that physicians should be permitted to rebut the presumption of a unitary standard of care when diminution of care arises by economic necessity instead of negligence.[ ] And many have suggested that custom should no longer be the benchmark for the standard of care; instead, practice standards or guidelines could be promulgated that would settle issues of resource allocation.

All of the concerns discussed above are serious, and they present difficult questions that courts will be required to confront in the future. But we do not confront them here, because under the unique facts of this case, they are not presented. Contrary to the district court's belief, this is not a case in which insurance company "bean counters" overrode the medical judgment of a patient's physicians[25] or in which those physicians allowed their medical judgment to be subordinated to a patient's ability to pay for treatment.[26] Nor is this a case in which the parties disputed the cost–effectiveness of the treatment at issue.[27] Rather, UNMC's evidence was that its decision to wait to begin Flolan treatment was not economic—it was a medical decision, based on the health consequences to the patient if the treatment is interrupted.

Whether a medical standard of care can appropriately be premised on such a consideration is a matter of first impression in Nebraska, and the parties have not directed us to (nor are we aware of) any other authority speaking directly to that issue. But as a general matter, we have said that while the identification of the applicable standard of care is a question of law, the ultimate determination of whether a party deviated from the standard of care and was therefore negligent is a question of fact.[ ] And it is for the finder of fact to resolve that issue by determining what conduct the standard of care would require under the particular circumstances presented by the evidence and whether the conduct of the alleged tort–feasor conformed with that standard.[ ]

Malpractice, as alluded to above, is defined as a health care provider's failure to use the ordinary and reasonable care, skill, and knowledge ordinarily possessed and used under like circumstances by members of his or her profession engaged in a similar practice in his or her or in similar localities.[ ] The district court granted a new trial based on its conclusion that UNMC's expert testimony was inconsistent with the standard of care. So the question is whether, as a matter of law, UNMC's expert opin-

[25] Compare *Long v. Great West Life & Annuity Ins.*, 957 P.2d 823 (Wyo.1998).

[26] Compare *Wickline v. State,* 192 Cal.App.3d 1630, 239 Cal.Rptr. 810 (1986).

[27] Compare *Helling v. Carey,* 83 Wash.2d 514, 519 P.2d 981 (1974).

ion testimony was inconsistent with the standard of care as defined above.

The district court determined that it was. But the district court's reasoning was erroneous in three respects. First, the district court understood Johnson's testimony to concede that "if no outside funds were available to subsidize the treatment to a patient who needed it, then treatment would be provided on a 'humanitarian' basis." The "substance of this concession," the court reasoned, "was that the treatment was required by the standard of care regardless of how it was to be paid for."

But that is not exactly what Johnson said. The import of Johnson's testimony, as revealed by the record, was that if a patient was unable to obtain insurance coverage for Flolan, it was Johnson's practice to try to work with the patient to find another way for the patient to get the drug on a "compassionate need" basis. Johnson's testimony in that regard was about his practice, not the general standard of care. Nor did Johnson testify that the drug would be started regardless—he simply said that if insurance was unavailable, he would try to find another way for the patient to obtain the medication. Nothing in Johnson's testimony is contrary to his basic opinion that the standard of care requires a doctor to make sure that a payment source is in place before beginning Flolan treatment, because of the risks associated with interruption of treatment.

Second, the customary standard of care in this case is defined by statute, and it is not a court's place to contradict the Legislature on a matter of public policy.[ ] UNMC's witnesses testified that UNMC's treatment of Mary was consistent with the statutory standard of care—in other words, that health care providers in the same community or in similar communities and engaged in the same or similar lines of work would ordinarily defer Flolan treatment until payment for a continuous supply had been secured. We cannot depart from the customary standard of care on policy grounds, even if it is subject to criticism, because the standard of care is defined by statute and public policy is declared by the Legislature.[ ] Robert was, of course, free to argue and present evidence that UNMC's experts were wrong when they opined about customary practice. But that was a jury question.

Finally, and more fundamentally, the district court's concerns about health care policy, while understandable, are misplaced in a situation in which the patient's ability to continue to pay for treatment is still a *medical* consideration. In other words, even when the standard of care is limited to medical considerations relevant to the welfare of the patient, and not economic considerations relevant to the welfare of the health care provider,[ ] the standard of care articulated by UNMC's witnesses in this case was still consistent with a medical standard of care.

This case does not involve a conflict of interest between the physician and patient—there was no evidence, for instance, of a financial incentive for UNMC's physicians to control costs.[ ] As explained by UNMC's witnesses, the decision to defer Flolan treatment was not based on its financial effect on UNMC, or subordinating Mary's well–being to the interests of other patients, or even considering Mary's own financial interest. Instead, when making its initial value judgment regarding Mary's treatment,[ ] UNMC's physicians were not weighing the risk to Mary's health against the risk to her pocketbook, or UNMC's budget, or even a general social interest in controlling health care costs. UNMC's physicians were weighing the *risk to Mary's health* of delaying treatment against the *risk to Mary's health* of potentially interrupted treatment. Stated another way, this was not a case in which a physician refused to provide beneficial care—it was a case in which the physicians determined that the care *would not be beneficial* if it was later interrupted. In fact, it could be deadly.

As explained by Murphy, Thompson, and Johnson, the reason for waiting to begin Flolan until after insurance approval had been obtained was out of concern for the health of the patient. That was not meaningfully different from any number of other circumstances in which a health care provider might have to base a treatment decision upon the individual circumstances of a patient. For instance, a physician with concerns about a particular patient's ability to follow instructions, or report for appropriate followup care, might treat the patient's condition differently in the first instance. And a health care provider who is told that a patient cannot afford a particular treatment may recommend a less expensive but still effective treatment, reasoning that a treatment that is actually used is better than one that is not. These are difficult decisions, and there may be room to disagree, but it is hard to say they are unreasonable as a matter of law, or that an expert cannot testify that such considerations are consistent with the customary standard of care.

And as noted above, Robert's witnesses were free to disagree with UNMC's witnesses; Robert could (and did) argue that the standard of care required more than UNMC's witnesses said it did. And the evidence might have supported the conclusion that given Mary's deteriorating condition, there was little risk in beginning Flolan even without a payment source in place. (Although we note, for the sake of completeness, that Johnson also testified that Mary's weakening condition militated against beginning Flolan on an emergent basis, because its side effects could have been deadly.)

In other words, the jury *could* have found that in this case, given the facts and testimony, the standard of care required Flolan to be administered immediately. But it was a question for the jury, and there was also competent evidence supporting a conclusion that the standard of care had not been breached. The court erred in concluding that it should have directed a verdict on the standard of care. And for that reason, the court abused its discretion in granting Robert's motion for new trial. UNMC's assignment of error has merit.

UNMC's evidence and opinion testimony reflect difficult medical decisions—but still *medical* decisions. Therefore, the scope of our holding is limited. We need not and do not decide whether the standard of care can or should incorporate considerations such as cost control or allocation of limited resources. Although the decision (or lack thereof) of a third–party payor contributed to the circumstances of this case, UNMC's decisions were still (according to its evidence) premised entirely upon the medical well–being of its patient. In a perfect world, difficult medical decisions like the one at issue in this case would be unnecessary. But we do not live in a perfect world, and we cannot say as a matter of law that UNMC's decisions in this case violated the standard of care.

CONCLUSION

For the foregoing reasons, the district court's order granting Robert's motion for new trial is reversed.

NOTES AND QUESTIONS

1. How does the Court handle the physician obligations in this case? The Court says at one point that "[a]lthough the decision (or lack thereof) of a third–party payor contributed to the circumstances of this case, UNMC's decisions were still (according to its evidence) premised entirely upon the medical well–being of its patient." Is this persuasive? The treating physician delayed necessary life–saving treatment while awaiting reimbursement confirmation, to avoid a start–and–stop treatment that had pernicious clinical effects. What does the Court mean by "medical well–being" in this case? Can you make an argument on the patient's behalf in a lawsuit alleging malpractice?

2. Is the future of medical care presented in this case? Why is Flolan so expensive? Orphan drugs for uncommon diseases are profitable for the manufacturer as long as Medicare or private insurers pay for their use, even when very few patients benefit. Incentives for the development of such drugs were spurred by the Orphan Drug Act, Pub. L. No. 97–414, 96 Stat. 2049 (1983) (codified as amended at 21 U.S.C. §§ 360aa—ee (1998)). See generally David Duffield, The Orphan Drug Act: An Engine of Innovation—At What Cost, 55 Food & Drug L.J. 125 (2000).

Drug cancer treatments are another example of drugs that are very expensive and often offer very little gain to patients. Lack of competition in these markets allows the drug companies to charge high prices. The tension between individualized medicine and reimbursement is likely to grow as the technologies evolve. See Matthew Herper, Health Care: The World's Most Expensive Drugs, Forbes, February 22, 2010.

PROBLEM: IS IT WORTH IT?

Jill Hanley has Guacher disease, a rare disorder in which a missing enzyme causes lumps of fat to build up in the spleen, heart, and even the brain. *Genzyme* sells *Cerezyme*, made from genetically engineered hamster cells, which replaces that enzyme at a cost of $200,000 per year. Jill's physician, Dr. Gavande, wants to begin treatment of Jill with the drug, but her insurer, *Golden Rule*, has told him they won't pay for the drug under her insurance policy coverage. What can Dr. Gavande do? If Jill ends up severely disabled because she can't be treated, can she sue *Golden Rule*? Dr. Gavande? *Genzyme*?

IV. DEFENSES TO A MALPRACTICE SUIT

A physician named as a defendant in a malpractice suit has a range of defenses available. Some are familiar affirmative defenses such as statutes of limitations. Most defense arguments however involve an argument that either the physician acted according to the standard of care of some subgroup of practitioners, or merely made an error of judgment not rising to the level of malpractice.

A. STANDARD OF CARE EXCEPTIONS

The most powerful defense to a malpractice suit is that the defendant physician acted in accordance with the prevailing medical standard of care as established by medical experts and clinical practice guidelines. However, in many areas of practice, there are several different approaches and lack of strong evidence of effectiveness of the current approach. When a physician acts according to a generally accepted practice, the courts have historically found that the physician acted properly. See, e.g., Chumbler v. Mcclure, 505 F.2d 489 (6th Circuit 1974).

The "respectable minority" or "two schools of thought" doctrine further protects the physician by expanding treatment leeway, acknowledging medical practice variation. States that instruct on "two schools of thought" often impose restrictions on the defense. Pennsylvania limits the doctrine to cases involving schools of thought followed by a "considerable number of physicians." Duckworth v. Bennett, 320 Pa. 47, 181 A. 558 (1935).

Where the critical issue is what the diagnosis is, as for example whether the patient had a localized or a generalized infection, then the "two schools of thought" or "alternative means of treatment" instruction may not be appropriate where there is only one agreed approach to each type of infection. See Hutchinson v. Broadlawns Medical Center, 459 N.W.2d 273 (Iowa 1990).

The "respectable minority" rule allows for variation in clinical judgment. Downer v. Veilleux, 322 A.2d 82, 87 (Me.1974). In the typical case, the minority approach is followed by at least a few doctors, and is often the "best available" for a certain problem. Leech v. Bralliar, 275 F.Supp. 897 (D.Ariz.1967) (prolotherapy for whiplash; 65 doctors in the country used this treatment, with a claimed 85% success rate; the defendant was held liable because he varied the treatment and therefore became a minority of one within the respectable minority.)

PROBLEM: TO MONITOR OR NOT?

You are general counsel for the Columbia Hospital for Women. The head obstetric resident has just walked into your office to get your advice regarding hospital policy. Jane Rudd, pregnant with her second child, has just been admitted to the Obstetrics Ward at term and in labor. The charts reveal that her first delivery of a healthy 7 1/2 pound baby boy had been uncomplicated. Upon admission, she asked not to be given intravenous fluids and stated that she does not want continuous fetal monitoring (EFM). Rather, she wished to be free to walk around with her husband during labor. The nurses told her that hospital policy requires electronic monitoring of all women in labor. The patient responded that she did not need EFM during her first labor, which went well, and expects the same experience again. She has appealed to the resident, who has discussed the request with the staff.

The staff split over the issue. One doctor argued that the policy is a wise measure intended to protect infants. Further, EFM shields staff from accusations that the best care was not provided, if a bad outcome occurs. Another doctor opposed routine EFM, arguing that unmonitored fetuses run an extremely small risk of fetal distress or intrapartum death. Without monitoring the intrapartum death rate was only 1.5 per 1,000 among all labors involving infants who weighed 5 1/2 pounds or more. The mother's risk status is altered, however, since the likelihood of a cesarean section is increased. This doctor pointed out that a careful British study of low–risk patients revealed that the rate of C–sections doubled, from 4.4 to 9%, when EFM was used. An American study found that the number of Caesareans performed on women hospitalized for delivery between 1980 and 1987 jumped 48%, much of this increase traceable to fetal monitoring.

If Ms. Rudd is allowed to labor with reasonable staff surveillance by auscultation, i.e. use of the stethoscope by staff on a regular basis, and if the obstetric unit can resuscitate her infant if the unexpected occurs, then, this doctor argued, the risks for both mother and child are very low.

You have done some further reading. The conclusions of Karin B. Nelson et al. are striking:

> Electronic fetal monitoring during labor was developed to detect fetal–heart–rate patterns thought to indicate hypoxia. The early recognition of hypoxia would, it was reasoned, alert clinicians to potential problems and enable them to intervene quickly to prevent fetal death or irreversible brain injury. . . . More than 20 years and 11 randomized trials later, electronic fetal monitoring appears to

> have little documented benefit over intermittent auscultation with respect to perinatal mortality or long–term neurologic outcome. Furthermore, probably in part because of the widespread use of fetal monitoring, the rate of cesarean section has increased, with a resulting increase in maternal morbidity and costs but without apparent decrease in the incidence of cerebral palsy.

Karin B. Nelson et al., Uncertain Value of Electronic Fetal Monitoring in Predicting Cerebral Palsy, 334 N.E.J.M. 334, 334 (1996). The authors found that cesarean sections did not prevent cerebral palsy in infants born at term, that monitoring did not correlate with reductions in perinatal mortality, nor were low Apgar scores, acidosis, neonatal apnea, or need for intubation less frequent among monitored infants.

A second study analyzed the neurologic development of premature infants. The authors compared the early development of children born prematurely whose heart rates were monitored electronically during delivery, compared to children born prematurely whose heart rates were monitored by auscultation. The authors found that not only had the infants' neurologic development not improved with monitoring, compared with auscultation, but there was a 2.9–fold increase in the odds of having cerebral palsy with the monitored infants. Shy et al., Effects of Electronic Fetal–Heart–Rate Monitoring, As Compared with Periodic Auscultation, on the Neurologic Development of Premature Infants, 322 N.Eng.J.Med. 588 (1990). The authors noted, however, that the trials for the study had dedicated nurses assigned to the auscultation group, "a circumstance that is not always possible in a busy clinical setting."

A third study looked at rehospitalizations in the first thirty days after giving birth. They were more likely in planned cesarean (19.2 in 1,000) when compared with planned vaginal births (7.5 in 1,000). Mothers with a planned primary cesarean were 2.3 times more likely to require a rehospitalization in the first 30 days postpartum. The leading causes of rehospitalization after a planned cesarean were wound complications (6.6 in 1,000) and infection (3.3 in 1,000). The average initial hospital cost of a planned primary cesarean of $4,372 was 76% higher than the average for planned vaginal births of $2,487, and length of stay was 77% longer. The authors concluded that "[c]linicians should be aware of the increased risk for maternal rehospitalization after cesarean deliveries to low–risk mothers when counseling women about their choices." Eugene Declercq, Mary Barger, Howard J. Cabral, Stephen R. Evans, Milton Kotelchuck, Carol Simon, Judith Weiss, and Linda J. Heffner, Maternal Outcomes Associated With Planned Primary Cesarean Births Compared With Planned Vaginal Births, 109 Obstetrics & Gynecology 669 (2007).

See generally Thomas P. Sartwelle, Electronic Fetal Monitoring: A Bridge Too Far, 33 J. Leg. Med. 313 (2012) (tracing the history of EFM, its problems, and explanations for its continued use in hospitals).

What policies will minimize the hospital's liability exposure while also respecting the patient's wishes whenever it is safe to do so? How do the tort doctrines we have discussed interact?

What policies should the Chief Medical Officer of the hospital consider?

B. CLINICAL INNOVATION

Much of medical practice requires taking standard tools and altering them to fit the needs of particular patients. Surgeons in particular are constantly innovating; physicians often prescribe drugs for off–label uses. The question is how to evaluate innovations in light of customary practices.

1. Procedure Innovations

BROOK V. ST. JOHN'S HICKEY MEMORIAL HOSPITAL

Supreme Court of Indiana, 1978.
269 Ind. 270, 380 N.E.2d 72.

HUNTER, JUSTICE.

This case began as an action by Tracy Lynn Brook and her father (Arthur) against St. John's Hickey Memorial Hospital, Guy E. Ross, M.D., Lawrence Allen, M.D., and Dr. Fischer. The record discloses that Tracy was diagnosed by a specialist as having a possible urological disorder and that X–rays taken with a contrast medium would be necessary to confirm the diagnosis. The Court of Appeals summarized Dr. Fischer's role in Tracy's treatment as follows:

> "Dr. Fischer, a radiologist, injected the contrast medium into the calves of both of Tracy's legs, because he was unable to find a vein which he could use. The package insert, which contained the manufacturer's directions for injecting the contrast medium, recommended that the contrast medium be injected into the gluteal muscles (buttocks). * * *
>
> "A short while [four months later] after being discharged from the hospital Tracy began to have trouble with her right leg. Her leg was stiff and her heel began to lift off the ground. Tracy's problem was later diagnosed as a shortening of the achilles tendon, which *may* have been precipitated by some kind of trauma to her ankle or calf muscle. After two operations and other expensive treatment, including the wearing of a leg brace, Tracy's problem was substantially corrected." 368 N.E.2d 264, 266, 267 [emphasis added].

* * *

* * * [T]he Brooks contended that the trial court erred in refusing to give to the jury plaintiffs' tendered instruction No. 4 which reads as follows:

> "You are instructed that a Radiologist is not limited to the most generally used of several modes of procedure and the use of another mode known and proved by the profession is proper, but every new method of procedure should pass through an experimental stage in its development and a Radiologist is not authorized in trying untested experiments on patients."

The Brooks alleged that Dr. Fischer was negligent in choosing an injection site which had not been specifically recommended by the medical community and that this choice of an unusual injection site was a medical experiment. The trial court refused to give this instruction on the basis that since no substantial evidence of a medical experiment had been introduced, it would be erroneous to give an instruction covering medical experiments. We agree.

The Court of Appeals found that since there was no evidence presented which showed that any other doctors had used the calf muscles as an injection site, Dr. Fischer's use of them may have been a medical experiment. We disagree. The record clearly shows that Dr. Fischer had several compelling, professional reasons for choosing the calf muscles as an injection site for the contrast medium in this case.

First, the record shows that Dr. Fischer had read medical journals which cautioned against the injection of the contrast medium into the buttocks (gluteal area) and thighs of infants and small children. * * *.

Tracy Brook was only twenty–three months old when the injection was given. Dr. Fischer testified that other articles had also warned against the use of the thighs in young children. Because Dr. Fischer was trying to avoid any damage to the sciatic nerve, he chose the next largest muscle mass "away from the trunk" as the site for the injection.

Second, Dr. Fischer had used this injection site successfully on children on prior occasions. He also testified that he had never read or heard anything that proscribed the selection of the calf muscles as an injection site.

Too often courts have confused judgmental decisions and experimentation. Therapeutic innovation has long been recognized as permissible to avoid serious consequences. The everyday practice of medicine involves constant judgmental decisions by physicians as they move from one patient to another in the conscious institution of procedures, special tests, trials and observations recognized generally by their profession as effective in treating the patient or providing a diagnosis of a diseased condition. Each patient presents a slightly different problem to the doctor. A physician is presumed to have the knowledge and skill necessary to use some innovation to fit the peculiar circumstances of each case.

Thus, the choice of the calf muscles as the site for the injection of a contrast medium in a two–year old child, based upon prior successful uses of this same injection site, is not a medical experiment where the use of more common sites had been warned against and where it was reasonably and prudently calculated by the physician [radiologist] to accomplish the intended purpose of diagnosis of the patient's condition.

* * *

The judgment of the trial court is in all respects affirmed.

NOTES AND QUESTIONS

1. If you disagree with the Supreme Court of Indiana, what do you think Dr. Fischer should have done? Should he have refused to treat Tracy? Should he have explained that his treatment was experimental? How would that have helped Tracy?

2. New surgical procedures and treatments, other than drugs and medical devices, fall into a regulatory gap. Drugs and medical devices are carefully regulated by the Food and Drug Administration through licensing. See the Federal Food, Drug, and Cosmetic Act, 21 U.S.C.A. § 301 et seq. Human experimentation generally, if the institution is funded by the federal government in whole or part, is governed by regulations of the Department of Health and Human Services. The regulations require the institution sponsoring the research to establish Institutional Review Boards (IRBs). These evaluate the research proposals before any experimentation begins, in order to determine whether human subjects might be "at risk" and if so, how to protect them. See 45 C.F.R. § 46.101(a).

3. Innovation in the clinical setting is common. It is closer to medical practice than to medical experimentation. Medical experimentation means that a physician treats his or her patient in conformity with a protocol crafted to test an hypothesis and to add to the body of medical knowledge. Medical practice, by contrast, assumes accepted therapies ". . . designed solely to enhance the well–being of an individual patient or client and that have a reasonable expectation of success." National Commission for the Protection of Human Subjects of Biomedical and Behavioral Research, The Belmont Report: Ethical Principles and Guidelines for the Protection of Human Subjects of Research 3 (1979).

Innovation falls somewhere in between, neither standard nor methodologically experimental: it aims to help the particular patient of the doctor but lacks sufficient evaluation to be able to say that there is "a reasonable expectation of success." The risks to the patient may be unknown and substantial; the therapy may be ineffective; and even if effective, lack of proper testing and recording of results means that such innovation may not advance the state of medical practice. Are clinicians likely to be trained scientists, keeping careful records and publishing their results for peer review? Medical researchers have criticized such clinical "experiments," calling instead for randomized scientifically valid trials. See Gordon Guyatt et al., Determining Optimal Therapy—Randomized Trials in Individual Patients, 314 N.Eng.J.Med. 889 (1986).

4. *Mini–IRBs and Innovation.* The line between "innovative therapy" and human subject research is clearer on paper than in practice. While there are strict guidelines for obtaining institutional research board (IRB) approval for research, innovative therapy does not require IRB approval. Innovative therapy is an intermediate step between clinical care and formal research. Innovative therapy is typically an unproven approach used on a limited number of patients to assist in clinical diagnosis or therapy.

Although innovative therapy does not require IRB , it could be harmful to patients. Some hospitals have therefore implemented a limited peer review process for clinical practices that are more experimental than traditional clinical practice but do not reach the level of research. These "mini IRBs" allow peer physicians to review and critique innovative therapy without hampering innovation by requiring the rigorous and time–consuming approval of an IRB. Such small–scale peer review is not legally required, but institutions often implement these procedures to ensure that physicians are making the best decisions. These peer review procedures help ensure patient safety, particularly when the consequences of using a new and unproven therapy are unknown. See for example the procedures for evaluating innovative therapies, as outlined by the Partners Human Research Committee, Innovative Therapy and Diagnosis.

For a thorough discussion of the problem, see Anna C. Mastroianni, Liability, Regulation and Policy in Surgical Innovation: The Cutting Edge of Research and Therapy, 16 Health Matrix 351 (2006); Nancy M. P. King, The Line Between Clinical Innovation and Human Experimentation, 32 Seton Hall L. Rev. 573 (2002).

5. Experiments may be acceptable to the courts when conventional treatments are largely ineffective or when the patient is terminally ill and has little to lose by experimentation with potentially useful treatments. Organ transplantation often involves therapeutic innovation. The classic case is Karp v. Cooley, 493 F.2d 408 (5th Cir.1974), where Dr. Denton Cooley was sued for the wrongful death of Haskell Karp. Dr. Cooley had implanted the first totally mechanical heart in Mr. Karp, who died some 32 hours after the transplant surgery. The court directed a verdict for Dr. Cooley on the issue of experimentation. It held:

> The record contains no evidence that Mr. Karp's treatment was other than therapeutic and we agree that in this context an action for experimentation must be measured by traditional malpractice evidentiary standards. Whether there was informed consent is necessarily linked to the charge of experimentation, and Mr. Karp's con-

sent was expressly to all three stages of the operation actually performed—each an alternative in the event of a preceding failure.

2. Drug Therapy Innovations: Off–Label Uses

Drug therapies also raise questions of clinical experimentation, both in off–label uses of drugs, and in the appropriate dosages for particular diseases and patients.

RICHARDSON V. MILLER

Court of Appeals, Tennessee, 2000.
44 S.W.3d 1.

KOCH, JR., J.

This appeal involves a medical malpractice action stemming from the use of an infusion pump to administer terbutaline sulphate subcutaneously to arrest a pregnant woman's labor. After suffering a heart attack shortly before giving birth to a healthy child, the woman and her husband filed suit in the Circuit Court for Davidson County against her attending physician, the supplier of the infusion pump, and others alleging that their negligence had caused her heart attack. * * * [W]e conclude that the trial court erred by excluding the evidence regarding the off–label use of terbutaline and by declining to give the requested instruction. * * * Accordingly, we vacate the judgment for the physician and manufacturer of the pump and remand the case for a new trial.

Cynthia Richardson married William Richardson in 1991. Ms. Richardson was a 26–year–old physical therapist, and Mr. Richardson was four years her junior. Ms. Richardson loved children, and the couple decided not to delay starting a family because Ms. Richardson, as she put it later, felt her "biological clock ticking." Ms. Richardson learned that she was pregnant with the couple's first child on Thanksgiving Day 1992. Her estimated due date was July 28, 1993.

Ms. Richardson sought her prenatal care from Dr. James Miller. In early January 1993, Ms. Richardson complained that she was experiencing periods of palpitations, rapid heartbeats, and shortness of breath. Dr. Miller referred her to Dr. James W. Ward, Jr., a cardiologist who had previously evaluated Ms. Richardson in 1987 for a similar complaint. Dr. Ward placed Ms. Richardson on a 24–hour heart monitor that showed only benign changes in her heart rhythm. Accordingly, Dr. Ward reported to Dr. Miller that he recommended no additions to Ms. Richardson's medical care. Ms. Richardson made no other cardiac complaints during subsequent office visits with Dr. Miller.

Ms. Richardson made her last prenatal office visit to Dr. Miller on June 23, 1993, when she was approximately thirty–five weeks pregnant. The checkup was routine and ended with the doctor's office scheduling her for a return visit the following week. Events, however, brought the parties together sooner. On the afternoon of the very next day, Ms. Richardson was admitted to Nashville Memorial Hospital in labor. Dr. Miller was immediately concerned that the labor was premature and that there could possibly be complications for the baby if born at thirty–five weeks. He ordered bed rest and hydration and tested Ms. Richardson to rule out mere uterine irritability. When the contractions showed no signs of abating, Dr. Miller opted to affirmatively retard Ms. Richardson's premature labor by tocolysis, *i.e.,* giving her medication to stop her contractions by relaxing her uterine muscles.

Dr. Miller first prescribed and administered magnesium sulfate with limited success. On June 24, 1993, when the frequency of Ms. Richardson's contractions did not decrease, Dr. Miller ordered a different tocolytic drug–terbutaline sulfate ("terbutaline"). While terbutaline had been approved by the FDA only for treating bronchial asthma, it was also being widely used as a tocolytic agent because it relaxes smooth muscles, including the muscles of the uterus.

Ms. Richardson received her first oral dose of terbutaline at approximately 8:30 p.m. on June 24 and her second dose, again by mouth, four hours later. Sometime during the early morning hours of June 25, she awoke with a "horrible pain" in her chest. Ms. Richardson had not gone back to sleep when a nurse came in at approximately 4:00 a.m. with a third oral dose of terbutaline. Ms. Richardson refused the drug, telling the nurse, as the nurse's notes reflect, that her chest hurt. Said Ms. Richardson, "I'm not taking that. . . . [M]y chest is killing me. I don't want any more of that stuff."

The next morning, the nursing staff informed Dr. Miller that Ms. Richardson had complained of chest pain and had refused to take the third dose of terbutaline. When Dr. Miller examined Ms. Richardson, he discovered that her chest pains had subsided but that she was still in labor. At that point, Dr. Miller suggested using an infusion pump to subcutaneously infuse smaller, timed doses of terbutaline into Ms. Richardson's system. * * *

Dr. Miller had little prior experience with terbutaline infusion pumps other than attending a 1989 seminar, conversing with a manufacturer's representative, and reading professional articles. After completing his examination of Ms. Richardson, Dr. Miller directed the attending nurses to contact Vanderbilt University Hospital about arranging for a terbutaline pump. Nurse Gail Harris was eventually directed to Tokos Medical Corporation ("Tokos"), a California–based medical services and drug provider, who arranged to supply a tocolytic pump designed and programmed to infuse terbutaline subcutaneously in set doses. Other than deciding to start Ms. Richardson on the pump, Dr. Miller was not directly involved with installing the pump or determining the dosage of terbutaline Ms. Richardson would receive while on the pump.

On the afternoon of June 25, Christine Evans, a nurse employed by Tokos, arrived at Memorial Hospital with the infusion pump ordered by Dr. Miller. She did not confer with Dr. Miller, but instead, she reviewed Ms. Richardson's medical records, talked with Ms. Richardson, and then gave Ms. Richardson and the hospital nursing staff instructions concerning the use of the pump. After conferring with one of Tokos's staff pharmacists, Ms. Evans also established the dosage of terbutaline that Ms. Richardson would receive. The hospital staff then obtained the terbutaline from the hospital pharmacy, filled the infusion pump, inserted the needle that would deliver the medication, and activated the pump. As Ms. Richardson remembers it, "[t]hey initially set it up, and the [hospital] nurse put the needle in. And I remember that every four hours the machine would give [me a] dose [of medicine]. And before [each] time I was to check my pulse rate to see if it was in the range—I don't remember the range that they gave me."

Ms. Richardson received regular subcutaneous doses of terbutaline for approximately the next forty–eight hours. Her labor contractions did not stop immediately; however, they eventually began to decrease. By around noon on June 27, three days after their onset, the contractions stopped. Although Ms. Richardson experienced shakiness and what she characterized as a "rapid heart rate," the nurses' notes stated that Ms. Richardson's vital signs were "stable" around the time her contractions stopped.

Ms. Richardson visited with her sister at approximately 3:00 p.m. on June 27. She became upset when her sister told her that their mother's dog had died. At that time, Ms. Richardson's chest, arm, jaw, and head began hurting. When a nurse arrived, Ms. Richardson exclaimed that she was having a heart attack and insisted that she be removed from the terbutaline pump. After some confusion and hesitation, the nurses disconnected Ms. Richardson from the pump, and she was subsequently transferred to a critical care unit where an electrocardiogram confirmed that she had, in fact, experienced a heart attack.

That night Ms. Richardson gave birth to a healthy, six–pound boy. A few days later, Ms. Richardson underwent open–heart by–pass surgery to repair a tear in her coronary artery associated with her heart attack. After recuperating for several days, Ms. Richardson and her baby were discharged from Memorial Hospital.

* * *

The remaining parties, the Richardsons, Dr. Miller, and Tokos, all requested a trial by jury. In anticipation of the trial, all sides moved in limine to exclude certain evidence. Dr. Miller moved to prevent the Richardsons from introducing or using any information from both terbutaline's drug package insert and the Physicians' Desk Reference ("PDR") indicating that the drug had not been approved by the federal Food and Drug Administration for use in stopping premature labor.[2] The trial court granted Dr. Miller's motion.

[By the time of trial, the Richardsons had narrowed their negligence claims against Dr. Miller and Tokos. They asserted against Dr. Miller that he was negligent by continuing tocolysis using terbutaline after Ms. Richardson began experiencing chest pain while taking terbutaline orally and by electing to administer the terbutaline subcutaneously using an infusion pump. The jury found for Dr. Miller, the trial court entered judgment on the verdict, and the Richardsons appealed. The Court on appeal concluded that the trial court committed reversible error by preventing the Richardsons "from introducing evidence regarding or cross–examining Dr. Miller's or Tokos's witnesses concerning the FDA–approved uses of terbutaline, Ciba–Geigy's directions for using terbutaline, or the off–label use of terbutaline as a tocolytic agent.]

Any discussion of the admissibility of evidence regarding the off–label use of a prescription drug must begin with a definition of the term "off–label use." The term is an essentially regulatory concept derived from the federal Food and Drug Administration's ("FDA") regulation of prescription drugs and their labeling. [ ] The term, as customarily used by health care providers, is medically neutral and refers to a circumstance in which a patient uses a prescribed drug or device in a manner that varies in some way from the drug's or device's FDA–approved labeling.[ ][3]

[The Court's exhaustive treatment of the FDA procedures for approving the promotion and sale of prescription drugs is omitted.]

* * *

Once the FDA has approved a prescription drug for a particular use or uses, the drug's manufacturer cannot market or promote the drug for an off–label use until it resubmits the drug for another series of clinical trials similar to those required for initial approval of a new drug applica-

[2] Ciba–Geigy's package insert and the parallel PDR reference state under "Usage" that terbutaline "is indicated for the prevention and reversal of bronchospasm in patients with bronchial asthma and reversible bronchospasm associated with bronchitis and emphysema." Both sources expressly warn that, "Terbutaline sulfate should not be used for tocolysis. Serious adverse reactions may occur after administration of terbutaline sulfate to women in labor. In the mother, these include increased heart rate, transient hyperglycemia, hypokalemia, cardiac arrhythmias, pulmonary edema, and myocardial ischemia."

[3] The director of the FDA's Center for Drug Evaluation and Research describes off-label use as "[u]se for indication, dosage form, dose regimen, population of other use parameter not mentioned in the approved labeling."[ ] As a general matter, off-label usage occurs in one of three circumstances: (1) off-label prescriptions where a physician orders a drug or device to be used in any manner that varies from the label's instructions; (2) off-label promotion or marketing where a manufacturer promotes a drug or device for purposes, to patient populations, or in combinations other than those approved by the FDA; and (3) off-label use by the patient that may take place without the knowledge of the manufacturer or prescribing physician.[ ]

tion.[ ] As new uses for an already approved drug become known, the drug's manufacturer may request the FDA's approval to add new approved uses to the drug's labeling.[ ] Because of the time and expense of obtaining FDA approval of new uses for an already approved drug, drug manufacturers frequently do not voluntarily request FDA approval for a new use unless the change in the labeling will pay for itself in increased profits.[ ]

The FDA's broad authority over prescription drugs and devices does not extend to a physician's decisions regarding the use of these products.[ ] To avoid limiting the ability of physicians to treat their patients, the lack of FDA approval of a drug or device for a particular use does not imply that using the drug or device for that use is either disapproved or improper.[9] [ ] Thus, physicians may use approved drugs or devices in any way that they, in their professional judgment, believe will best serve their patients, regardless of whether the FDA has approved the drug or device for that particular use.[ ] This prerogative includes (1) prescribing a drug for conditions other than those for which it has been approved, (2) prescribing a drug for patient groups other than those for which it was originally approved, and (3) varying the dosage or method of administering a drug from that contained in its labeling.[ ]

In the current regulatory environment, when the FDA authorizes a prescription drug or device to be marketed, it is well aware that the drug or device will likely be put to an off–label use.[ ] The FDA has acknowledged that once a drug or device is on the market, a "physician may, as part of the practice of medicine, lawfully prescribe a different dosage for his [or her] patient or may otherwise vary the conditions of use from those approved in the package insert, without informing or obtaining the approval of the Food and Drug Administration.[ ]" An FDA technical bulletin has recognized that the off–label use of an approved drug represents acceptable, and sometimes essential, clinical practice. *See Use of Unapproved Drugs for Unlabeled Indications,* 12 FDA Drug Bull., Apr. 1982, at 4–5,[ ] noting that ("[v]alid new uses for drugs already on the market are often first discovered through serendipitous observation and therapeutic innovation").[11] It is also possible that the off–label uses of a drug may exceed the uses for which the drug was originally approved. [ ]

Off–label prescriptions are now an integral part of the modern practice of medicine.[ ] While estimates concerning the prevalence of off–label use varies, there is a consensus that the practice is widespread.[ ] Off–

[9] Similarly, the off-label use of a drug or device by a physician seeking an optimal treatment for his or her patient is not necessarily considered to be research or an investigational or experimental treatment when the use is customarily followed by physicians.[ ]

[11] Because the pace of medical discovery runs ahead of the FDA's regulatory machinery, the off-label use of some drugs is frequently considered to be "state-of-the-art" treatment.[ ] In some circumstances, an off-label use of a particular drug or device may even define the standard of care.

label uses of approved drugs have become extremely important in specialities such as cancer, pediatric medicine, heart and circulatory disease, AIDS, and kidney disease.

* * *

The off–label use of approved drugs results in one significant complication for physicians. Because of the FDA's restrictions on the dissemination of information regarding off–label uses of approved drugs, physicians do not have readily available the same information concerning the use, dosage, and method of administration of the drug that is provided for approved uses. Neither the FDA–approved labeling nor the parallel PDR reference contain information about off–label uses.[ ][17]

When the off–label use of a drug becomes widespread, there is an increased possibility that a physician with inadequate knowledge will prescribe it.[ ] Accordingly, physicians prescribing a drug or device off–label have a responsibility to be well–informed about the drug or device.[ ] In the absence of the information found in the FDA–approved labeling, physicians must obtain reliable, up–to–date information from other sources. These sources may include: (1) discussion with professional colleagues, (2) continuing medical education programs, (3) case studies in professional journals, and (4) reports of the clinical results of the use of the drug in other countries.[ ]

The next issue to be addressed is whether a prescription drug's labeling or parallel PDR reference is admissible with regard to the standard of care for using and administering the drug. Virtually every court addressing this question has concluded that the drug's labeling and PDR reference are relevant to the standard of care issue. The primary dispute among the courts involves the weight to be given to this evidence. The great weight of authority is that a drug's labeling or its parallel PDR reference is admissible, as long as it is accompanied by other expert evidence regarding the standard of care.

[The Court stated that the conduct of providers must be judged by an objective community standard under Tennessee statutory law, and this professional standard of care requires expert testimony.]

Plaintiffs in other medical malpractice cases have argued that the instructions in a prescription drug's FDA–approved labeling or the parallel PDR reference should be sufficient, by themselves, to establish a physician's standard of care regarding the use of the drug. Several jurisdictions, believing drug manufacturers to be uniquely knowledgeable about the proper use of their products, have held that a drug's labeling or its

[17] The publisher of the PDR now publishes the "PDR Companion Guide," an 1,800 page reference augmenting the PDR. This guide includes an "Off–Label Treatment Guide" listing drugs routinely used, but never approved, for the treatment of nearly one thousand disorders. *See* Medical Economics Co., *Physicians' Desk Reference,* Foreword (54th ed.2000).

parallel PDR reference amounts to prima facie evidence of the standard of care as far as the use of that drug is concerned. However, a majority of jurisdictions have determined that a prescription drug's labeling or parallel PDR reference is admissible to prove the standard of care, but only if the plaintiff also introduces other expert testimony regarding the standard of care. These jurisdictions have concluded that while the labeling and PDR reference provide relevant and useful information regarding the standard of care, they are not the sole determinant of the standard of care because, in any particular case, adhering to the manufacturer's recommendations and warnings in the labeling or the PDR may or may not have been within the standard of care when the alleged negligent act occurred.

Four considerations support the majority view governing the admissibility of a prescription drug's labeling or parallel PDR reference in a medical malpractice case. First, permitting the labeling or the PDR reference alone to establish a physician's standard of care would be inconsistent with Tenn.Code Ann. § 29–26–115(a)(1) because it would permit the drug manufacturer, rather than the medical profession, to establish the standard of care.[ ] Second, the FDA–required labeling and parallel PDR reference may not be easily understood by the jury without expert assistance because these materials are written for the medical profession, not the general public.[ ] Third, the drug manufacturer and the FDA do not intend to establish the standard of care when they prepare a drug's labeling or PDR reference. These materials are intended to comply with the FDA's regulations, to provide advertising and promotional material, and to limit the manufacturer's liability.[ ] Finally, the labeling and PDR reference cannot be cross–examined.[ ]

We adopt the majority approach regarding the introduction and evidentiary weight to be given to FDA–approved drug labeling and the parallel PDR reference. Neither of these materials, by themselves, are prima facie evidence of the prescribing physician's standard of care. Thus, proof of a departure from the recommendations in a drug's labeling or PDR reference is not alone sufficient to prove a breach of the standard of care. However, the labeling and the PDR reference can provide significant assistance in identifying the standard of care. Accordingly, we find that a prescription drug's labeling or its PDR reference, when introduced along with other expert evidence on the standard of care, is admissible to assist the trier–of–fact to determine whether the drug presented an unacceptable risk to the patient.

At trial, the Richardsons claimed that Dr. Miller violated the standard of care by continuing Ms. Richardson on terbutaline after she complained of severe chest pains, and by deciding to administer terbutaline to Ms. Richardson subcutaneously using an infusion pump. A survey of the evidence and other information about the off–label use of drugs like terbutaline for tocolysis provides a helpful framework for determining whether the trial court properly excluded the evidence regarding the off–label use of terbutaline for tocolysis in light of the Richardsons' claims. This information indicates that the safety and efficacy of terbutaline administered with an infusion pump for tocolysis was being debated when it was administered to Ms. Richardson and continues to be debated today.

[The Court discussed at length the history of treatments of tocolysis, including ritrodrine and terbutaline. By 1997, the FDA issued a "Dear Colleague" letter warning physicians about the continuous subcutaneous administration of terbutaline. The letter stated that "it is clear that the demonstrated value of tocolytics in general is limited to an initial, brief period of treatment, probably no more than 48–72 hours" and that "[n]o benefit from prolonged treatment has been documented." Thus, the FDA letter alerted "practitioners, home health care agencies, insurance carriers, and others that continuous subcutaneous administration of terbutaline sulfate has not been demonstrated to be effective and is potentially dangerous."]

* * *

While the practice of using drugs off–label is widespread and not inherently inappropriate, there are well–documented instances where an accepted and popular off–label use of a drug has ultimately proved to be harmful.[ ] Physicians may be found negligent if their decision to use a drug off–label is sufficiently careless, imprudent, or unprofessional. The Richardsons' causes of action against Dr. Miller and Tokos are not based simply on the fact that tocolysis is an off–label use of terbutaline. Rather, their negligence claim rests on the following two theories: (1) Dr. Miller should have discontinued administering terbutaline for tocolysis when she began experiencing chest pain following the second oral dose and (2) Dr. Miller should not have ordered, and Tokos should not have provided, the subcutaneous administration of terbutaline using an infusion pump because the effect of using the pump was to maintain or even increase, rather than decrease, the level of terbutaline in her system.

[The Richardsons intended to call several witnesses to address the standard of care, the FDA–approved labeling, the lack of instructions on dosage or method of administration, and individual policies for use of terbutaline to retard preterm labor. The court noted that this testimony " * * * would have been sufficient to require Dr. Miller to explain why he continued administering terbutaline after Ms. Richardson began experiencing severe chest pains, as well as the basis for his decision to use an infusion pump and how the proper dosage was determined.[3]]

[3] If, for example, he asserted that using the infusion pump to administer terbutaline posed less of a danger to Ms. Richardson because lower doses were being administered, he would have been required to explain away the fact that using the infusion pump results in the same or higher levels of terbutaline in the patient's system.[ ]

* * *

[The court found that the trial court has misapplied Tenn.R.Evid. 403, which requires that the trial court first balance the probative value of the evidence sought to be excluded against the combined weight of the countervailing factors; and second, if the probative value is found, exercise its discretion to decide whether the evidence should be excluded notwithstanding its relevancy. The evidence as to terbutaline's off–label use was relevant as to the breach of the standard of care.]

* * *

[The court's discussion of an EKG protocol, licensing, and a missing evidence instruction is omitted.]

Based on the foregoing, we reverse the judgment dismissing the Richardsons' claims against Dr. Miller and Tokos and remand the case for a new trial consistent with this opinion. We tax the costs of this appeal in equal proportions to James Miller, M.D. and to Tokos Medical Corporation for which execution, if necessary, may issue.

NOTES AND QUESTIONS

1. Is the use of Terbutaline clearly inappropriate in this case? Consider how unfamiliar the doctor was with the pump. Were there other clinical options available to him in this case? What is the role of the trier of fact in a case like this? Will the practitioner always be at some risk of liability in the case of off–label uses, or is this a special case?

2. Physicians in all areas of medicine commonly prescribe prescription drugs for uses other than FDA–approved uses. Many drugs are prescribed more often off–label than on–label. Thalidomide has been approved for use in treating leprosy but is much more commonly used to treat multiple myeloma and AIDS. Most cancer and AIDS patients are given drugs that are not FDA–certified for the prescribed use. In a large number of fields, a majority of patients are prescribed at least one drug off–label. See Sandra Johnson, Polluting Medical Judgment? False Assumptions in the Pursuit of False Claims for Off–Label Prescribing, 9 Minn. J. Law, Science & Tech. 61 (2007).

Is such common prescribing a good thing? An analysis of reports from the 2001 National Disease and Therapeutic Index (tracking epidemiological trends and treatment patterns among private practice physicians) found that 73 percent of off–label uses lacked evidence of clinical efficacy, and only 27 percent were supported by strong scientific evidence.

Insurance companies, such as Blue Cross Blue Shield, typically have explicit policies as well on such uses of drugs. Blue Cross Blue Shield of California, for example, specifies that an off–label drug use may be defined as medically necessary when:

> 1. The drug is approved by the U.S. Food and Drug Administration (FDA).

AND

2. The drug is being prescribed to treat a medical condition not listed in the product label; and for which medical treatment is medically necessary.

AND

3. The prescribed drug use is supported in any one or more of the following:

- American Hospital Formulary Service Drug Information; or
- U.S. Pharmacopoeia Dispensing Information®, Vol. I; or
- Two articles from major scientific or medical peer–reviewed journals (excluding case reports, letters, posters, and abstracts), or published studies having validated and uncontested data, which support the proposed use for the specific medical condition as safe and effective.
    - Accepted journals include, but are not limited to, Journal of American Medical Association, New England Journal of Medicine, and Lancet.
    - Accepted study designs include, but are not limited to, randomized, double blind, placebo controlled clinical trials.

3. Off–label use of drugs and medical devices by physicians, while common, raises serious concerns about safety and efficacy. Should the law require a physician to disclose the off–label use of a drug to the patient? One author has recommended that patients be informed of off–label prescriptions and that such use of a drug or medical device should prompt research review by an institutional review board. See John D. Casler, Clinical Use of New Technologies Without Scientific Studies, 129 Archives Otolaryngology Head & Neck Surgery 674, 675 (2003); Margaret Z. Johns, Informed Consent: Requiring Doctors to Disclose Off–Label Prescriptions and Conflicts of Interest, 58 Hastings Law Journal 967 (2007).

Does this make sense? Even FDA–approved drugs risk unknown toxic effects when they enter the drug marketplace. Nearly 20 million patients took at least 1 of 5 drugs withdrawn from the market between September 1997 and September 1998. Three of these five drugs were new, having been on the market for less than 2 years. The authors of one study concluded that "[m]any serious ADRs [adverse drug reactions] are discovered only after a drug has been on the market for years." Only half of newly discovered serious ADRs are detected and documented in the Physicians' Desk Reference within 7 years after drug approval. See Karen E. Lasser et al., Timing of New Black

Box Warnings and Withdrawals for Prescription Medications, 287 JAMA 2215 (2002).

4. Use of experimental drugs lacking FDA approval for any use, is not allowed, even in situations of terminal illness. See Abigail Alliance v. von Eschenbach, 495 F.3d 695 (D.C.Cir. 2007) (holding that the Constitution does not provide terminally ill patients a right of access to experimental drugs that have passed limited safety trials but have not been proven safe and effective.)

5. *Freedom of Speech as a Liability Defense.* In U.S. v. Caronia, Slip Opinion, (Court of Appeals, 2nd Circuit 2012), Alfred Caronia was convicted of conspiracy to introduce a misbranded drug into interstate commerce in violation of the Federal Drug and Cosmetic Act. He had engaged in off–label promotion of Xyrem. Xyrem is a powerful central nervous system depressant manufactured and distributed by Orphan Medical (since acquired by Jazz Pharmaceuticals). The drug carries a "black box" warning because of serious side effects such as difficulty breathing while asleep, abnormal thinking and depression. If abused, Xyrem can lead to comas and even death.

Two of the three judges on the appeals court panel agreed with Caronia that the conviction violated his free speech rights, and they vacated it. The majority said it objected to "the government's theory of prosecution [that] identified Caronia's speech alone as the proscribed conduct," and concluded that a pharmaceutical sales representative's truthful off–label statements, which on their own do not violate the federal Food, Drug and Cosmetic Act (FDCA), are entitled to First Amendment protection as long as they are not misleading. The court's opinion also indicated that off–label promotional statements may be evidence of the manufacturer's "intended use" for a drug, and thus support prosecution for "misbranding" violations under the FDCA. Misbranding under the FDCA is couched in terms of whether the drug's label is adequate for its "intended use."

The *Caronia* case may have liability implications civilly as well as criminally, raising the possible of a First Amendment defense in a medical malpractice case.

C. AFFIRMATIVE DEFENSES

An affirmative defense is one that a defendant can raise by the pleadings, and may lead to a dismissal of the lawsuit after a judicial hearing on a defendant's motion to dismiss or summary judgment motion. Some affirmative defenses are ruled on by the trial court judge, and thus can resolve a case without letting the jury ever hear the plaintiff's case, while others may require factual determinations by the jury. A defendant asserting an affirmative defense may not contest negligence, but instead argue that other factors excuse his conduct as a matter of law or prevent the plaintiff from suing him at all. Consider a defense of conflicting legal duty. A doctor who releases information about a patient's medical condition normally violates the patient's right to confidentiality, but in some situations he is legally required to inform others of a patient's medical condition. If a patient suffers from a gunshot wound, the doctor treating him or her must inform the police; if he has a contagious disease the doctor must inform the department of health in the state; if child abuse is suspected, the authorities must be notified.

Consent is perhaps the most frequently asserted affirmative defense in medical malpractice cases. Doctors and hospitals have tried to protect themselves from malpractice suits by having patients sign consent forms before patients receive treatment. See discussion of informed consent in Chapter 4 *supra*.

Other less commonly asserted affirmative defenses are available under the right circumstances, such as the bar of statute of limitations and Good Samaritan laws.

1. Statute of Limitations

Malpractice litigation is subject in most states to its own statute of limitation, often shorter than other civil litigation. The complication in medical cases is often how and when the plaintiff becomes aware that her injury was caused by her physician.

ARROYO V. U.S.

Seventh Circuit Court of Appeals, 2011.
656 F. 3d 663.

CUDAHY, CIRCUIT JUDGE.

Christian Arroyo contracted a bacterial infection from his mother during his birth. The physicians involved in Christian's delivery and post–delivery care failed to diagnose and treat this infection in a timely manner, which caused the newborn to suffer severe brain injuries. Several years later, Christian's parents filed suit against the United States under the Federal Tort Claims Act. The district court found the United States liable for Christian's injuries, rejecting the United States' claim that the Arroyos' claims were untimely. We affirm.

I. Background

In 2002, Maria Solorzano Arroyo and Carlos Arroyo conceived a child (collectively referred to as the Arroyos). During the course of Solorzano Arroyo's pregnancy, she received low cost medical care at the Erie Family Health Center, Inc. (Erie Center), a health clinic that received federal funds for the purpose of treating low income, underinsured individuals. The Erie Center's doctors did not detect any problems with Solorzano Arroyo's pregnancy when providing her with prenatal care and forecasted her due date for June 12, 2003.

On May 16, 2003, Solorzano Arroyo went into labor. She went to Northwestern Memorial Hospital and gave birth to her son, Christian Arroyo in the early morning hours of May 17, 2003. Because Christian's birth was more than a month premature, Solorzano Arroyo had not undergone the battery of diagnostic tests, including a test for Group B Streptococcus (GBS), that women typically undergo in the month prior to delivery. These diagnostic tests are extremely important, as they indicate whether an infant will be at risk of contracting any diseases from his or her mother's blood during birth and allow health care practitioners to take steps to reduce the risks that such incidents will harm the infant.

When a mother has not had these diagnostic tests, medical professionals protect infants by utilizing a two–pronged approach. First, at the delivery stage, doctors are required to observe the presence or absence of four risk factors. Second, after the baby is born, doctors are required to be vigilant in looking for signs indicating the presence or absence of neonatal sepsis (a bacterial infection of the baby's bloodstream). If a medical professional finds any indications of infection, then she must immediately administer antibiotics to prevent the spread of infection. Because GBS is fairly benign in adults, mothers can carry it asymptomatically during pregnancy. Newborns can contract the disease during birth and, unless it is treated immediately, it can cause severe and permanent brain injuries.

Shortly after birth, Christian exhibited several symptoms indicating that exposure to his mother's blood had infected him with GBS. However, the obstetrician, Rahda B. Reddy, M.D. (Dr. Reddy), and pediatrician, Verlainna Callentine, M.D. (Dr. Callentine), responsible for taking care of Solorzano Arroyo failed to detect the infection and treat Christian with antibiotics. Because of this failure, Christian suffered severe and permanent brain injuries. If the doctors had promptly treated Christian, it is likely that the damage done to Christian's brain would have been significantly reduced.

On July 11, 2003, Christian was discharged from Northwestern Memorial hospital. At the time of discharge, doctors informed the Arroyos that Christian had suffered brain injuries and that the injuries were caused by his exposure to his mother's blood during birth. The Arroyos were not told that Christian's injuries could have been prevented if the GBS infection had been treated at an earlier point in time. As a result of the injuries to his brain, Christian suffers from cerebral palsy, spastic quadriplegia, a seizure disorder, an inability to swallow, a communications deficit, incontinence and permanent pain.

In July of 2004, Christian's mother gave birth to her second son and it was at this time that she first heard about the use of neonatal antibiotics. In approximately October of 2004, the Arroyos saw a lawyer's television commercial that indicated that Christian's injuries could have been caused by his doctors and that they might have grounds for a lawsuit. After seeing this commercial, the Arroyos contacted a law firm and began to investigate the cause of Christian's injuries.

On December 30, 2005, the Arroyos filed a state court lawsuit, naming Drs. Reddy and Callentine as defendants, alleging that both doctors failed to provide proper prenatal care at the Erie Center and during the time surrounding Christian's birth. At the time of Christian's injuries, both Dr. Reddy and Dr. Callentine were affiliated with the Erie Center and were on the Northwestern Memorial Hospital medical staff. * * * [T]he Federal Tort Claims Act (FTCA) shields the Erie Center's employees, which include Dr. Reddy and Dr. Callentine, from liability while acting within the scope of their duties, with the United States assuming liability for any negligent acts they commit. *See* 42 U.S.C. § 233(g)(1).

* * *

In January of 2010, the district court conducted a week–long bench trial. At the conclusion of trial, the court found in favor of the Arroyos. It held that both Drs. Reddy and Callentine negligently failed to recognize and act upon risk factors and signs indicating GBS infection, and as such, caused Christian's injuries by failing to administer antibiotics. Even though the court found that the government was liable for Christian's injuries, it ordered the parties to file post–trial briefs addressing the issues of damages and the government's statute of limitations defense.

On April 2, 2010, the district court issued a written opinion concluding that the Arroyos' claim was filed within the two year statute of limitations for claims filed pursuant to the FTCA. [ ] The court awarded the Arroyos over $29 million in damages for various past and future losses and expenses. The government filed a timely appeal from this decision and requests that we reverse the district court's statute of limitation finding.

II. Analysis

The only part of the district court's decision that the government challenges on appeal is the court's rejection of its statute of limitations defense. The government argues that the district court's decision should be reversed on two grounds: (1) the court failed to apply the proper test for determining when the Arroyos' FTCA claim accrued and (2) several of the court's factual determination were erroneous.

* * *

1. The FTCA's Statute of Limitations and FTCA Claim Accrual

[The court discussed the caselaw on when FTCA claims accrue and when the FTCA's statute of limitations bars a plaintiff's claim.]

Federal law governs when a claim accrues under the FTCA, [ ] and we, along with other circuits, have held that a plaintiff's claim accrues when: (A) the plaintiff discovers; or (B) a reasonable person in the plaintiff's position would have discovered that he has been injured by an act or omission attributable to the government. [ ] It is worth emphasizing that an individual's FTCA claim accrues only when the individual knows (or should have known) of the "cause that is in the government's control, not a concurrent but independent cause that would not lead anyone to suspect that the government had been responsible for the injury." [ ].

* * *

There are two final aspects of our FTCA claim accrual jurisprudence that warrant discussion. First, it is worth emphasizing the disjunctive nature of the claim accrual inquiry. An FTCA claim accrues when: (A) an individual actually knows enough to tip him off that a governmental act (or omission) may have caused his injury; *or* (B) a reasonable person in the individual's position would have known enough to prompt a deeper inquiry. Thus, the proper way to determine when the statute of limitations for FTCA claims begins to run is a two–part inquiry that incorporates subjective and objective components. [ ]. A plaintiff's claim accrues the first time the plaintiff knew, or a reasonably diligent person in the plaintiff's position, reacting to any suspicious circumstances of which he or she might have been aware, would have discovered that an act or omission attributable to the government could have caused his or her injury.

Second, we have held that accrual of an individual's FTCA claim is not postponed until the individual obtains complete knowledge of the cause of his injury. Rather, accrual occurs when an individual acquires information that would prompt a reasonable person to make "a deeper inquiry into a potential [government–related] cause" of his or her injury. [ ]. An individual does not need to have reason to believe that the relevant governmental conduct was negligent; mere knowledge of the potential existence of a governmental cause is sufficient to start the clock ticking. [ ]. In other words, the statute of limitations begins to run "either when the government cause is known or when a reasonably diligent person (in the tort claimant's position) reacting to *any suspicious circumstances* of which he might have been aware would have discovered the government cause—whichever comes first." [ ].

2. The District Court Applied the Proper Claim Accrual Test

* * *

We reject the government's argument and find that the district court applied the proper claim accrual rule. * * * It is clear that the district court considered whether the Arroyos had actual knowledge that Christian's injuries were attributable to an act or omission of a government doctor. [ ] It is similarly clear that the district court considered the objective component of the inquiry. [ ]

3. The District Court's Factual Determinations Regarding When the Arroyos' Claim Accrued Were Not Erroneous

* * *

* * * Hence, the only issues before us are whether the district court erred when it determined the date that: (A) the Arroyos knew; or (B) a reasonable person in the Arroyos' position would have known enough to suspect, that actions taken by Christian's doctors contributed to his injuries.

The district court did not err in finding that the Arroyos did not actually know that there was a doctor–related cause until 2004. As stated earlier, the only information that the hospital conveyed to the Arroyos was that Christian's injuries were due to a blood infection that his mother had transmitted to him at birth. The fact that the Arroyos knew about the biological cause of Christian's injuries, however, does nothing to establish that the Arroyos knew that there was also a malpractice–related cause. The record is devoid of evidence establishing that the Arroyos knew that the hospital's doctors should have given Christian and his mother antibiotics, that Christian's infection was left untreated following his birth or that prompt treatment of his infection would have reduced or prevented the infection's damage. In short, the government failed to present *any* evidence establishing that, at the time of Christian's discharge, the Arroyos possessed knowledge that was sufficient to cause their claim to accrue.

We also find that the district court did not err in finding that a reasonably diligent person in the Arroyos' position in 2003 would have lacked information sufficient to prompt a deeper inquiry into whether Christian's doctors caused his injuries. In order to prevail on its statute of limitations defense, the government needed to show that a reasonable person, when informed that his or her infant's injuries were caused by an infection that had been transmitted during birth, would have searched for potential iatrogenic causes for the injuries. The United States did not meet this burden. First, the government failed to present any evidence establishing that injuries caused by birth–transmitted infections are typically caused by doctors. Second, and even more significantly, the government neglected to argue that iatrogenic causes are frequent enough that a reasonably diligent person would have investigated whether there was a doctor–related cause for Christian's injuries. While these omissions, on their own, provide more than sufficient grounds for affirming the district court's decision, we also note that courts have found that it is reasonable for individuals presented with similar information about the etiology of birth–related injuries to assume that the hospital's staff did everything they could to prevent the injury. [ ].

* * *

* * * A rule that forces patients to scour their records whenever they receive medical treatment and to initiate preemptive litigation is inequitable, inefficient and—most importantly—contrary to the commonsensical intuitions that "reasonable man" tests are supposed to embody.

* * *

In closing, we take a moment to clarify an issue that many have seemed to find confusing—the distinction between (1) injuries that have a doctor–related cause and (2) injuries that are caused by a doctor's negligence. It is always the case that an injury that is caused by a doctor's negligence will have a doctor–related cause. The converse, however, is not true. There are many situations in which an individual's injury has a doctor–related cause, but is not the result of a doctor's negligence. When determining the accrual date of a plaintiff's FTCA malpractice claim, courts must decide when the plaintiff knew enough (or should have known enough) to suspect that their injury had a doctor–related cause. [ ] But, accrual does not wait until the plaintiff learns that their injury was caused by a doctor's negligence. [ ]

III. Conclusion

For the reasons stated above, the ruling of the district court is AFFIRMED.

POSNER, CIRCUIT JUDGE, concurring in the court's judgment and opinion.

I join the court's opinion without reservations, and write separately only to raise two general questions about limitations periods in medical malpractice litigation (specifically litigation under the Federal Tort Claims Act) that while presented by this case do not have to be answered in order to decide it. Both relate to the discovery rule: the rule that federal statutes of limitations don't begin to run until the prospective plaintiff discovers, or should have discovered, that he has been injured—and by whom. [ ]. The first question is the role of the tort concept of the "reasonable person" in deciding whether the plaintiff "should have" discovered the injury and by whom it was inflicted. The second question is the relation of an ethical duty of candor by medical staff to the "should have" question.

As a practical matter what used to be called the "reasonable man" concept in tort law, now unsexed to conform to modern sensibilities, means the *average* person; this is in recognition of the fact that "when men live in society, a certain average of conduct, a sacrifice of individual peculiarities going beyond a certain point, is necessary to the general welfare. . . . The law considers, in other words, what would be blameworthy in the average man, the man of ordinary intelligence and prudence, and determines liability by that." [ ] So negligence is failure to take the care that the average person would have taken in the defendant's position, and contributory or comparative negligence is failure to take the care that the average person in the plaintiff's position would have taken.

* * *

The goal of the average–person rule (to give it the more perspicuous name), in instrumental terms, is to provide an additional incentive, beyond that of moral duty or concern with personal safety, to avoid injuring people (or being injured). A driver who falls below the average of care, and as a result injures someone, is subject to tort liability; it is hoped that the threat will motivate drivers to be careful to avoid injuring others (or themselves). [ ] Similarly, a pedestrian who falls below the average of care, and would not have been injured had he not done so, cannot obtain damages (full damages, and in some states [ ] even if his injurer also failed to exercise the care of an average person.

But this motivational system works only if potential injurers and potential victims are *capable* of exercising the care of the average person, or if incapable can at least avoid situations in which they are likely to cause or suffer injury. Drivers have to be licensed, and this excludes, in principle anyway, the least competent persons. And persons licensed to drive but nonetheless unskilled can avoid accidents by driving slowly or avoiding night driving and dangerous roads, or by not driving at all. Similarly, financially unsophisticated persons don't have to buy financial instruments, so all buyers of such instruments can properly be held to the standard of care of the average buyer. Moreover, if the law held unsophisticated buyers to only a lower standard, it would in effect be subsidizing them and thus encouraging the entry of financially unsophisticated persons into those markets.

"Care" thus connotes both the level of performance that the law requires and the set of compensatory measures that persons who are clumsy or inexperienced can use to attain a level of care that the average person attains with less effort. But a blind person, no matter how careful he tries to be, cannot cross a street as safely as a sighted person unless he can afford to hire an escort. Holding him to the standard of care of a sighted person would just discourage him from going out of his house, and this is thought an excessive cost (in contrast to forbidding blind people to drive); it "could lead to levels of social isolation that are no longer found acceptable."[ ]

* * *

There is no way in which holding the Arroyos, who seem to be typical clients of the Erie Family Health Center, to the level of medical knowledge of the average person in American society could make them as knowledgeable as such a person. That would be almost as unrealistic as ruling that the statute of limitations in a medical malpractice suit begins to run whenever a patient who had been trained as a physician would have discovered that he had been injured as a result of a medical act or omission, though the actual plaintiff had no medical training. Which is not to say that contributory (or comparative) negligence has no role to play in medical malpractice cases. Drugs come with warnings; due care requires reading the warnings, provided they are intelligible to the average person. [ ] Everyone knows one should read warning labels, though, like the plaintiff in the *Robinson* case, many do not.

In applying the discovery rule, which governs when a federal claim accrues in the sense of starting the running of the period allowed by the statute of limitations for bringing suit, courts generally use the same average–person standard they use in determining negligence and contributory negligence. [ ] And typically they state the standard without qualification. But such statements should be treated as generalities open to exception, in conformity with Holmes's overstated but illuminating observation that "general propositions do not decide concrete cases. * * *

When knowing a fact depends on having technical knowledge, the incredible variance in such knowledge across American society can make the knowledge of the average person a perverse benchmark. Mrs. Arroyo had an infection (Group B Streptococcus), benign to her, when she entered the hospital to give birth. The birth seemed uneventful, but it was soon discovered that the infection had been communicated to her newborn during childbirth, causing the terrible injuries described in the court's opinion. Had she been a doctor, she would have suspected that the communication of her infection to the child during childbirth might have been preventable, and this suspicion in turn would have impelled her to investigate whether the failure of prevention had reflected a lack of due care and borne a causal relation to the child's injuries. See Centers for Disease Control and Prevention, "Prevention of Perinatal Group B Streptococcal Disease," *Morbidity and Mortality Weekly Report,* Nov. 19, 2010 [ ]. And similarly if her husband had been a doctor.

The Arroyos' baby was delivered at Northwestern Memorial Hospital by an obstetrician employed by the Erie Family Health Center in Chicago, and the baby's initial care was by a pediatrician also employed by the Center. The mother was a patient at Erie's West Town Health Center, which is located in a neighborhood that is 47 percent Hispanic. Erie's website explains that its goal is "to deliver quality health care to Chicago's medically underserved communities with compassion and respect." Erie Family Health Center, "About Erie," [ ]. Eighty–four percent of the Center's patients are Hispanic, 62 percent "are best served in Spanish," 34 percent are uninsured, and 86 percent "come from households with incomes that fall below the Federal Poverty Line." The Arroyos are Hispanic (Mrs. Arroyo does not speak English) and poor (her medical bills were paid for by "Public Aid"). Mr. Arroyo is a manual worker. Neither is college–educated.

As persons of limited education living we may assume at or near the poverty line, the Arroyos probably are deferential to medical staff. Told by the staff only that their child's injuries were the result of the mother's infection, they could not have been expected to suspect that another cause was that the staff hadn't administered antibiotics to her, and to conduct research into the risk and prevention of the transmission of a deadly infection from mother to child during childbirth. Suppose that, contrary to the court's opinion, a person of average medical sophistication would have conducted an investigation that would have enabled suit to be filed before the statute of limitations expired. That should not defeat the Arroyos' claim. When the question in applying the discovery rule in a malpractice case is what knowledge should be ascribed to the plaintiff, the court should either determine the knowledge of the particular plaintiff or make a judgment applicable to the subset of the population that has approximately the same educational background and socioeconomic status as the plaintiff.

Granted, this approach would require, though only in cases in which the statute of limitations was pleaded as a defense, that plaintiffs present evidence about their educational background and socioeconomic status, in lieu of a guess by judge or jury, based on no evidence, of the medical sophistication of the average American. [ ]. But why is that an objection rather than a confession that there is too much guesswork in American law and a clue that the traditional approach can produce absurd results when applied in a technical field—as in this case? For the government in its brief tells us—without references or other elaboration—that "from an objective standpoint, reasonably diligent persons are aware that infections can be prevented, particularly in hospital settings." On the contrary, knowledgeable persons, fearful of hospital–based infections—see R. Monina Klevens et al., "Estimating Health Care–Associated Infections and Deaths in U.S. Hospitals, 2002," 122 *Pub. Health Rep.* 160 (2007), [ ]; Andrew Pollack, "Rising Threat of Infections Unfazed by Antibiotics," *N.Y. Times,* Feb. 27, 2010, p. B1—strive to minimize the amount of time they spend in a hospital because they know, unlike the authors of the government's brief (if they believe what they wrote), that many infections in hospital settings *cannot* be prevented even with reasonable care. If "diligent" is a synonym for expert, as the government's brief implies, the government is not a diligent student of hospital infection. How can it demand that the Arroyos have a level of medical expertise that the Department of Justice appears to lack?

I need to make clear that I am discussing only the standard for determining when the statute of limitations begins to run, not the standard of care. *Kubrick* holds that the statute of limitations begins to run in a malpractice case when the plaintiff either discovers, or if diligent would have discovered, that he has been injured by the (at that point merely potential) defendant, and not when the plaintiff discovers or should have discovered that his injury was the result of negligence. This is not only the law; it is sensible. Even unsophisticated people, when they learn that they have been injured by a physician rather than (just) by the condition the physician was (or should have been) treating, should know that there may have been malpractice, and so should consult another physician, or other medical person, or a lawyer. * * * [Posner notes that Kubrick was informed by someone that it was "highly possible" that his condition was caused by negligence of the defendant physicians.]

Had someone informed the Arroyos that it was "highly possible" that the injuries to their child had been caused by the failure to administer antibiotics to Mrs. Arroyo, the statute of limitations would have begun to run then, just as in *Kubrick*. For they would have known, or in the exercise of reasonable diligence (reasonably understood in light of their socio-economic position) should have known, that a cause of their child's injuries might have been the failure of the doctors to administer antibiotics to Mrs. Arroyo; given that information, they would or should have known enough to consult a lawyer or other expert. That may be asking a lot of them; but to ask that they have suspected malpractice in the absence of any disclosure of the possibility of an iatrogenic injury would be to ask too much.

I anticipate the objection that the suggested approach would nullify the statute of limitations in many medical malpractice cases. The Arroyos missed the two-year statutory deadline by seven months; they might have missed it by a greater margin but for the happenstance of seeing a tort lawyer's television commercial. The obvious answer would be to add a statute of repose to the Federal Tort Claims Act * * * [ ] Statutes of repose are a common feature of medical malpractice law. [ ].

But if the Erie Family Health Center (or its backer, the United States) wants to avoid being hit by stale malpractice suits, it has only to level with patients (or in the case of a child, the patient's parents) concerning possible causes of a medical injury. When the Arroyos' child was discharged from the hospital with brain injuries two months after his birth, the Center's physicians told the parents only that their child's injuries had been caused by an infection that Mrs. Arroyo had transmitted to him during his birth. They said nothing that might have alerted the Arroyos to the possibility that a medical act or omission had contributed to the infection. The physicians did not have to confess liability; indeed, at the trial the defense presented respectable evidence that there had been no negligence. All the Center would have had to do was give the Arroyos a reasonably full account of the circumstances of the child's injuries—that antibiotics could have been administered to the mother before the birth and to the child immediately after and that had this been done the injuries might have been averted, or been less serious. [ ].

"According to recent codes and guidelines . . . individual clinicians and institutions have an ethical responsibility to disclose unanticipated negative outcomes. Respect for personal autonomy entails disclosure of what occurred—even if no further medical decisions are involved—and of options to take nonmedical actions, including legal actions, if appropriate." [ ] If a patient dies as a result of his physician's failure to diagnose a readily diagnosable, and if diagnosed readily curable, condition, such as appendicitis, it is a deceptive half–truth to tell the grieving spouse or parents that the patient died of appendicitis; the patient's death was jointly caused by appendicitis and medical negligence. Compliance with the ethical duty of disclosure of possible medical errors in simple, intelligible terms would give medically unsophisticated plaintiffs enough information to recognize that medical decisions might have contributed to their injuries.

I am not arguing that a breach of the ethical duty of disclosure is itself malpractice, although it could be if it prevented the patient from obtaining medical treatment that would mitigate the consequences of the original medical error. I am not arguing that the disclosure must go beyond an acknowledgment of the *possibility* of medical error and become a confession that there *was* a medical error; or that a doctor is required to explain that additional treatment might have avoided the patient's injury if failure to provide that treatment would not have been negligent, because of the expense, side effects, or uncertain benefits of the treatment, as when a patient suffers an injury that would have been prevented had the doctor performed a battery of painful and expensive experimental tests. But if a potential defendant in a medical malpractice suit wants to take advantage of the statute of limitations he should have to disclose information known to him that would alert the patient to the possibility of an error. By doing that he can be sure that the statute of limitations will begin to run immediately (for that is what *Kubrick* holds) and not years later, though even without that precaution the statute of limitations might begin to run upon injury if the average member of the plaintiff's socioeconomic stratum would have realized that his injury might have been caused by medical staff rather than by (or just by) an illness.

* * *

* * *The concealment in this case occurred before rather than after the statute of limitations began to run, because the concealment of the fact that the doctors had contributed to the child's injuries prevented the Arroyos from discovering the doctors' causal role. The statute of limitations does not begin to run until that discovery is made or should have been made by a reasonable person of the plaintiffs' educational and socioeconomic background. This is not a tolling case, so limitations on tolling are irrelevant.

NOTES AND QUESTIONS

1. The *Arroyo* rule, requiring plaintiff awareness that defendants "caused" their injury, raises complex problems of patient awareness of health care risks, as Posner notes; and also creates an environment in which providers are more inclined to conceal their actions that caused injury to protect themselves from litigation. The complexities of malpractice causation reveal the stress lines in an affirmative defense like the statute of limitations, and how injured patients may be disadvantaged.

Should Posner's discussion of the ethics of disclosure lead us to impose legal obligations of disclosure by providers of adverse events suffered by their patients? See discussion in Chapter 1 of adverse events and in Chapter 4 of physician disclosure obligations generally.

2. The usual rule in most state jurisdictions is based on statutes of repose, so called "discovery" rules: the statute begins to run once the plaintiff: (1) has some knowledge of the injury, (2) its cause in fact, and (3) some evidence of wrongdoing on the part of the person responsible. See Hardi v. Mezzanotte, 818 A.2d 974 (D.C. Court of Appeals, 2003). The federal rule, exemplified in *Arroy,* does not require evidence of negligence by the provider but only a suspected causal connection before the statute begins to run.

2. Good Samaritan Acts

Forty–nine states and the District of Columbia have adopted Good Samaritan legislation to protect health care professionals who render emergency aid from civil liability for damages for any injury they cause or enhance. The statutes take a variety of forms. West's Ann.Cal.Bus. & Prof.Code § 2395, for example, states, in relevant part:

> No licensee, who in good faith renders emergency care at the scene of an emergency, shall be liable for any civil damages as a result of any acts or omissions by such person in rendering the emergency care.
>
> "The scene of an emergency" as used in this section shall include, but not be limited to, the emergency rooms of hospitals in the event of a medical disaster. * * *

What kinds of situations do the Good Samaritan statutes cover? Suppose a physician walking down the street on Sunday morning to buy her New York Times sees a man fall to the pavement, gasping for breath and turning blue. The physician does not have her black bag, never met the victim before, and is aware of a gathering crowd. If she attempts to help the man and is negligent in administering aid, should she be sued for malpractice? Certainly physicians have worried about such situations. Good Samaritan statutes seem on their face to protect physicians in this kind of situation. See, e.g., McCain v. Batson, 233 Mont. 288, 760 P.2d 725 (1988), in which a physician on vacation sutured a hiker's wound at his condominium, using limited medical supplies on hand. The court held that this was an "emergency" within the meaning of statute.

Some states by statute or judicial interpretation have extended the Good Samaritan defense even to the hospital setting. Where a physician does not have a legal duty to respond, but rather acts as a "volunteer" in responding to an emergency, he or she is protected by the defense. See, e.g., McKenna v. Cedars of Lebanon Hospital, 93 Cal.App.3d 282, 155 Cal.Rptr. 631 (1979), in which the physician responded to an alert from his beeper after the plaintiff had a seizure after a therapeutic abortion and tubal ligation. The court held that he was a "medical volunteer", and "the legislative intent of encouraging emergency medical care by doctors who have no legal duty to treat a patient is carried out by applying Business and Professions Code section 2144 to Dr. Warner."

Hospital–based emergency assistance by a physician is often protected where the physician is not on duty at the time of the call for help. See Gordin v. William Beaumont Hospital, 180 Mich.App. 488, 447 N.W.2d 793 (1989), where the plaintiff's decedent was admitted to the emergency room after a car accident. The ER physician called for the on–call surgeon to assist, but the surgeon was unavailable. He then called Dr. Howard, who was not officially on call. The court held that the Good Samaritan Statute applied. The Michigan statute had been amended to include hospital settings and off–duty physicians. Accord, Kearns v. Superior Court, 204 Cal.App.3d 1325, 252 Cal.Rptr. 4 (2 Dist.1988).

Some statutes protect health care professionals, while others protect all Good Samaritans, without regard to their profession. Some states grant statutory immunity from suit to emergency medical personnel unless gross negligence is shown. Mallory v. City of Detroit, 181 Mich.App. 121, 449 N.W.2d 115 (1989). Physicians working in state institutions often are granted immunity. Verhoff v. Ohio State Univ. Medical Center, 125 Ohio Misc.2d 30, 797 N.E.2d 592 (Ct.Cl. 2003). See generally Anno., Construction of "Good Samaritan" Statutes Excusing from Civil Liability One Rendering Care in Emergency, 39 A.L.R.3d 222.

D. CONTRIBUTORY FAULT OF THE PATIENT

Patients through their own mistakes or lifestyle often enhance, or even cause, their injuries. People don't take their doctor's advice; they fall off their diets, stop exercising, start smoking, or act in a variety of ways counterproductive to their health. Very few tort cases have raised a patient's lifestyle choice as a defense to a malpractice claim. Consider the following case.

OSTROWSKI V. AZZARA

Supreme Court of New Jersey, 1988.
111 N.J. 429, 545 A.2d 148.

O'HERN, J.

This case primarily concerns the legal significance of a medical malpractice claimant's pre-treatment health habits. Although the parties agreed that such habits should not be regarded as evidencing comparative fault for the medical injury at issue, we find that the instructions to the jury failed to draw the line clearly between the normal mitigation of damages expected of any claimant and the concepts of comparative fault that can preclude recovery in a fault-based system of tort reparation. Accordingly, we reverse the judgment below that disallowed any recovery to the diabetic plaintiff who had bypass surgery to correct a loss of circulation in a leg. The need for this bypass was found by the jury to have been proximately caused by the physician's neglect in performing an improper surgical procedure on the already weakened plaintiff.

I

As noted, the parties do not dispute that a physician must exercise the degree of care commensurate with the needs of the patient as she presents herself. This is but another way of saying that a defendant takes the plaintiff as she finds her. The question here, however, is much more subtle and complex. The complication arose from the plaintiff's seemingly routine need for care of an irritated toe. The plaintiff had long suffered from diabetes attributable, in unfortunate part perhaps, to her smoking and to her failure to adhere closely to her diet. Diabetic patients often have circulatory problems. For purposes of this appeal, we shall accept the general version of the events that led up to the operation as they are set forth in defendant-physician's brief.

On May 17, 1983, plaintiff, a heavy smoker and an insulin-dependent diabetic for twenty years, first consulted with defendant, Lynn Azzara, a doctor of podiatric medicine, a specialist in the care of feet. Plaintiff had been referred to Dr. Azzara by her internist whom she had last seen in November 1982. Dr. Azzara's notes indicated that plaintiff presented a sore left big toe, which had troubled her for approximately one month, and calluses. She told Dr. Azzara that she often suffered leg cramps that caused a tightening of the leg muscles or burning in her feet and legs after walking and while lying in bed. She had had hypertension (abnormally high blood pressure) for three years and was taking a diuretic for this condition.

Physical examination revealed redness in the plaintiff's big toe and elongated and incurvated toenails. Incurvated toenails are not ingrown; rather, they press against the skin. Diminished pulses on her foot indicated decreased blood supply to that area, as well as decreased circulation and impaired vascular status. Dr. Azzara made a diagnosis of onychomycosis (a fungous disease of the nails) and formulated a plan of treatment to debride (trim) the incurvated nail. Since plaintiff had informed her of a high blood sugar level, Dr. Azzara ordered a fasting blood sugar test and a urinalysis; she also noted that a vascular examination should be considered for the following week if plaintiff showed no improvement.

Plaintiff next saw Dr. Azzara three days later, on May 20, 1983. The results of the fasting blood sugar test indicated plaintiff's blood sugar was high, with a reading of 306. The urinalysis results also indicated plaintiff's blood sugar was above normal. At this second visit, Dr. Azzara concluded that plaintiff had peripheral vascular disease, poor circulation, and diabetes with a very high sugar elevation. She discussed these conclusions with plaintiff and explained the importance of better sugar maintenance. She also explained that a complication of peripheral vascular disease and diabetes is an increased risk of losing a limb if the diabetes is not controlled. The lack of blood flow can lead to decaying tissue. The parties disagree on whether Dr. Azzara told plaintiff she had to return to her internist to treat her blood sugar and circulation problems, or whether, as plaintiff indicates, Dr. Azzara merely suggested to plaintiff that she see her internist.

In any event, plaintiff came back to Dr. Azzara on May 31, 1983, and, according to the doctor, reported that she had seen her internist and that the internist had increased her insulin and told her to return to Dr. Azzara for further treatment because of her continuing complaints of discomfort about her toe. However, plaintiff had not seen the internist. Dr. Azzara contends that she believed plaintiff's representations. A finger–stick glucose test administered to measure plaintiff's non–fasting blood sugar yielded a reading of 175. A physical examination of the toe revealed redness and drainage from the distal medial (outside front) border of the nail, and the toenail was painful to the touch. Dr. Azzara's proposed course of treatment was to avulse, or remove, all or a portion of the toenail to facilitate drainage.

Dr. Azzara says that prior to performing the removal procedure she reviewed with Mrs. Ostrowski both the risks and complications of the procedure, including nonhealing and loss of limb, as well as the risks involved with not treating the toe. Plaintiff executed a consent form authorizing Dr. Azzara to perform a total removal of her left big toenail. The nail was cut out. (Defendant testified that she cut out only a portion of the nail, although her records showed a total removal.)

Two days later, plaintiff saw her internist. He saw her four additional times in order to check the progress of the toe. As of June 30, 1983, the internist felt the toe was much improved. While plaintiff was seeing the internist, she continued to see Dr. Azzara, or her associate, Dr. Bergman.

During this period the toe was healing slowly, as Dr. Azzara said one would expect with a diabetic patient.

During the time plaintiff was being treated by her internist and by Dr. Azzara, she continued to smoke despite advice to the contrary. Her internist testified at the trial that smoking accelerates and aggravates peripheral vascular disease and that a diabetic patient with vascular disease can by smoking accelerate the severity of the vascular disease by as much as fifty percent. By mid–July, plaintiff's toe had become more painful and discolored.

At this point, all accord ceases. Plaintiff claims that it was the podiatrist's failure to consult with the patient's internist and defendant's failure to establish by vascular tests that the blood flow was sufficient to heal the wound, and to take less radical care, that left her with a non–healing, pre–gangrenous wound, that is, with decaying tissue. As a result, plaintiff had to undergo immediate bypass surgery to prevent the loss of the extremity. If left untreated, the pre–gangrenous toe condition resulting from the defendant's nail removal procedure would have spread, causing loss of the leg. The plaintiff's first bypass surgery did not arrest the condition, and she underwent two additional bypass surgeries which, in the opinion of her treating vascular surgeon, directly and proximately resulted from the unnecessary toenail removal procedure on May 31, 1983. In the third operation a vein from her right leg was transplanted to her left leg to increase the flow of blood to the toe.

At trial, defense counsel was permitted to show that during the pre–treatment period before May 17, 1983, the plaintiff had smoked cigarettes and had failed to maintain her weight, diet, and blood sugar at acceptable levels. The trial court allowed this evidence of the plaintiff's pre–treatment health habits to go to the jury on the issue of proximate cause. Defense counsel elicited admissions from plaintiff's internist and vascular surgeon that some doctors believe there is a relationship between poor self–care habits and increased vascular disease, perhaps by as much as fifty percent. But no medical expert for either side testified that the plaintiff's post–treatment health habits could have caused her need for bypass surgery six weeks after defendant's toenail removal. Nevertheless, plaintiff argues that defense counsel was permitted to interrogate the plaintiff extensively on her post–avulsion and post–bypass health habits, and that the court allowed such evidence of plaintiff's health habits during the six weeks after the operation to be considered as acts of comparative negligence that could bar recovery rather than reduce her damages. The jury found that the doctor had acted negligently in cutting out the plaintiff's toenail without adequate consideration of her condition, but found plaintiff's fault (fifty–one percent) to exceed that of the physician (forty–nine percent). She was therefore disallowed any recovery. On appeal the Appellate Division affirmed in an unreported decision. We granted certification to review plaintiff's claims.[ ] We are told that since the trial, the plaintiff's left leg has been amputated above the knee. This was foreseen, but not to a reasonable degree of medical probability at the time of trial.

II

Several strands of doctrine are interwoven in the resolution of this matter. The concepts of avoidable consequences, the particularly susceptible victim, aggravation of preexisting condition, comparative negligence, and proximate cause each play a part. It may be useful to unravel those strands of doctrine for separate consideration before considering them in the composite.

Comparative negligence is a legislative amelioration of the perceived harshness of the common–law doctrine of contributory negligence. * * *

Comparative negligence was intended to ameliorate the harshness of contributory negligence but should not blur its clarity. It was designed only to leave the door open to those plaintiffs whose fault was not greater than the defendant's, not to create an independent gate–keeping function. Comparative negligence, then, will qualify the doctrine of contributory negligence when that doctrine would otherwise be applicable as a limitation on recovery. * * *

* * * The doctrine [of avoidable consequences] proceeds on the theory that a plaintiff who has suffered an injury as the proximate result of a tort cannot recover for any portion of the harm that by the exercise of ordinary care he could have avoided.[ ] * * * Avoidable consequences, then, normally comes into action when the injured party's carelessness occurs *after* the defendant's legal wrong has been committed. Contributory negligence, however, comes into action when the injured party's carelessness occurs *before* defendant's wrong has been committed or concurrently with it.[ ]

A counterweight to the doctrine of avoidable consequences is the doctrine of the particularly susceptible victim. This doctrine is familiarly expressed in the maxim that "defendant 'must take plaintiff as he finds him.' "[ ] * * * It is ameliorated by the doctrine of aggravation of a preexisting condition. While it is not entirely possible to separate the doctrines of avoidable consequence and preexisting condition, perhaps the simplest way to distinguish them is to understand that the injured person's conduct is irrelevant to the consideration of the doctrine of aggravation of a preexisting condition. Negligence law generally calls for an apportionment of damages when a plaintiff's antecedent negligence is "found not to contribute in any way to the original accident or injury, but to be a substantial contributing factor in increasing the harm which ensues." *Restatement (Second) of Torts*, § 465 at 510–11, comment c. Courts recognize that a defendant whose acts aggravate a plaintiff's preexisting condition is liable only for the amount of harm actually caused by the negligence.[ ] * * *

Finally, underpinning all of this is that most fundamental of risk allocators in the tort reparation system, the doctrine of proximate cause. * * *

We have sometimes melded proximate cause with foreseeability of unreasonable risk. * * *

We have been candid in New Jersey to see this doctrine, not so much as an expression of the mechanics of causation, but as an expression of line–drawing by courts and juries, an instrument of "overall fairness and sound public policy."[ ] * * * [ ]

III

Each of these principles, then, has some application to this case.[3] Plaintiff obviously had a preexisting condition. It is alleged that she failed to minimize the damages that she might otherwise have sustained due to mistreatment. Such mistreatment may or may not have been the proximate cause of her ultimate condition.

But we must be careful in reassembling these strands of tort doctrine that none does double duty or obscures underlying threads. In particular, we must avoid the indiscriminate application of the doctrine of comparative negligence (with its fifty percent qualifier for recovery) when the doctrines of avoidable consequences or preexisting condition apply.

The doctrine of contributory negligence bars any recovery to the claimant whose negligent action or inaction *before* the defendant's wrongdoing has been completed has contributed to cause actual invasion of plaintiff's person or property. By contrast,

> "[t]he doctrine of avoidable consequences comes into play at a later stage. Where the defendant has already committed an actionable wrong, whether tort or breach of contract, then this doctrine [avoidable consequences] limits the plaintiff's recovery by disallowing only those items of damages which could reasonably have been averted * * * [.]" "[C]ontributory negligence is to be asserted as a complete defense, whereas the doctrine of avoidable consequences is not considered a defense at all, but merely a rule of damages by which certain particular items of loss may be excluded from consideration * * *."

Hence, it would be the bitterest irony if the rule of comparative negligence, designed to ameliorate the harshness of contributory negligence,

[3] Each principle, however, has limitations based on other policy considerations. For example, the doctrine of avoidable consequences, although of logical application to some instances of professional malpractice, is neutralized by countervailing policy. Thus, a physician who performed a faulty tubal litigation cannot suggest that the eventual consequences of an unwanted pregnancy could have been avoided by termination of the fetus.[ ]

should serve to shut out any recovery to one who would otherwise have recovered under the law of contributory negligence. Put the other way, absent a comparative negligence act, it would have never been thought that "avoidable consequences" or "mitigation of damages" attributable to post–accident conduct of any claimant would have included a shutout of apportionable damages proximately caused by another's negligence. * * *

* * *

In this context of post–injury conduct by a claimant, given the understandable complexity of concurrent causation, expressing mitigation of damages as a percentage of fault which reduces plaintiff's damages may aid juries in their just apportionment of damages, provided that the jury understands that neither mitigation of damages nor avoidable consequences will bar the plaintiff from recovery if the defendant's conduct was a substantial factor without which the ultimate condition would not have arisen.

* * * In the field of professional health care, given the difficulty of apportionment, sound public policy requires that the professional bear the burden of demonstrating the proper segregation of damages in the aggravation context.[ ] The same policy should apply to mitigation of damages.[ ] Hence, overall fairness requires that juries evaluating apportionment of damages attributable in substantial part to a faulty medical procedure be given understandable guidance about the use of evidence of post–treatment patient fault that will assist them in making a just apportionment of damages and the burden of persuasion on the issues. This is consistent with our general view that a defendant bear the burden of proving the causal link between a plaintiff's unreasonable conduct and the extent of damages.[ ] Once that is established, it should be the "defendant who also has the burden of carving out that portion of the damages which is to be attributed to the plaintiff."[ ]

IV

As noted, in this case the parties agree on certain fundamentals. The pre–treatment health habits of a patient are not to be considered as evidence of fault that would have otherwise been pled in bar to a claim of injury due to the professional misconduct of a health professional. This conclusion bespeaks the doctrine of the particularly susceptible victim or recognition that whatever the wisdom or folly of our life–styles, society, through its laws, has not yet imposed a normative life–style on its members; and, finally, it may reflect in part an aspect of that policy judgment that health care professionals have a special responsibility with respect to diseased patients.[ ]

This does not mean, however, that the patient's poor health is irrelevant to the analysis of a claim for reparation. While the doctor may well take the patient as she found her, she cannot reverse the frames to make it appear that she was presented with a robust vascular condition; likewise, the physician cannot be expected to provide a guarantee against a cardiovascular incident. All that the law expects is that she not mistreat such a patient so as to become a proximate contributing cause to the ultimate vascular injury.

However, once the patient comes under the physician's care, the law can justly expect the patient to cooperate with the health care provider in their mutual interests. Thus, it is not unfair to expect a patient to help avoid the consequences of the condition for which the physician is treating her. * * *

Hence, we approve in this context of post–treatment conduct submission to the jury of the question whether the just mitigation or apportionment of damages may be expressed in terms of the patient's fault. If used, the numerical allocation of fault should be explained to the jury as a method of achieving the just apportionment of the damages based on their relative evaluation of each actor's contribution to the end result—that the allocation is but an aspect of the doctrine of avoidable consequences or of mitigation of damages. In this context, plaintiff should not recover more than she could have reasonably avoided, but the patient's fault will not be a bar to recovery except to the extent that her fault caused the damages.

An important caveat to that statement would be the qualification that implicitly flows from the fact that health care professionals bear the burden of proving that their mistreatment did not aggravate a preexisting condition: that the health care professional bear the burden of proving the damages that were avoidable.

Finally, before submitting the issue to the jury, a court should carefully scrutinize the evidence to see if there is a sound basis in the proofs for the assertion that the post–treatment conduct of the patient was indeed a significant cause of the increased damages. Given the short onset between the contraindicated surgery and the vascular incident here, plaintiff asserts that defendant did not present proof, to a reasonable degree of medical probability, that the plaintiff's post–treatment conduct was a proximate cause of the resultant condition. Plaintiff asserts that the only evidence given to support the defense's theory of proximate cause between plaintiff's post–treatment health habits and her damages was her internist's testimony regarding generalized studies showing that smoking increases vascular disease by fifty percent, and her vascular surgeon's testimony that some physicians believe there is a relationship among diabetes, smoking, and vascular impairment. Such testimony did not address with any degree of medical probability a relationship between her smoking or not between May 17, 1983, and the plaintiff's need for bypass surgery in July 1983. Defendant points to plaintiff's failure to consult with her internist as a cause of her injury, but the instruction to the jury gave no guidance on whether this was to be considered as conduct that concurrently or subsequently caused her injuries.[ ]

V

We acknowledge that it is difficult to parse through these principles and policies in the course of an extended appeal. We can well imagine that in the ebb and flow of trial the lines are not easily drawn. There are regrettably no easy answers to these questions.

* * *

[The court noted the factual complexities of the case, and concluded that "the instructions to the jury in this case did not adequately separate or define the concepts that were relevant to the disposition of the plaintiff's case." The case was remanded for a new trial.]

NOTES AND QUESTIONS

1. Do you advocate applying contributory negligence, or comparative negligence (depending upon the jurisdiction), to situations such as that of *Ostrowski*? Such cases raise fundamental questions about the limits of medicine and the role of patients in their own illnesses. Can a smoker easily stop? Is it fair to bar his recovery when his smoking is not a simple, easily abandoned, choice? See Sawka v. Prokopowycz, 104 Mich.App. 829, 306 N.W.2d 354 (1981), where the plaintiff sued the defendant for his failure to diagnose lung cancer. The court rejected the claim that the plaintiff's continued smoking and failure to return for further examination as instructed were contributory negligence.

2. Should a doctor be able to argue that a patient's negligent pre–treatment conduct as contributory negligence? See for example Cavnes v. Zabrerdac, 849 N.E.2d 526 (Indiana 2006), where a patient being treated for severe asthma had an attack. She took several doses of her medication in the course of the morning before going to the hospital emergency room, where she went into cardiac arrest and died. Defendant argued that Peggy "improperly used her medications in excess of their prescribed doses, which probably aggravated her condition, and that Peggy unreasonably delayed seeking medical treatment and emergency room care, which decreased her chances of surviving." The Court rejected the defendant's arguments:

> It is people who are sick or injured that most often seek medical attention. Many of these infirmities result, at least in part, from the patients' own carelessness (e.g. negligent driving or other activities, failure to regularly exercise, unhealthy diet, smoking, etc.). To permit healthcare providers to assert their patients' pre–treatment negligent conduct to support a contributory negligence defense would absolve such providers from tort responsibility in the event of medical negligence and thus operate to undermine substantially such providers' duty of reasonable care.

3. If a patient continues to refuse to take steps to reduce his health care risks, over a period of time, he may be held liable in comparative negligence. In Striff v. Luke Medical Practitioners, 2010 WL 5296941 (Ohio App. 3 Dist. 2010), the plaintiff Striff had a fatal heart attack. He suffered from coronary artery disease, and the defendants claimed that they followed the standard of care, but that "Striff was completely responsible for his medical condition due to his life–style choices and, more importantly, his failure to follow through with the recommendations and follow–up treatments ordered by Appellees. Mr. Striff was overweight, smoked a pack of cigarettes a day, and drank several alcoholic beverages every day. Mr. Striff also failed to obtain a lipid profile to measure his cholesterol and did not see a cardiologist, as he was instructed to do on many occasions." The jury found that 100% of the negligence that caused Striff's death was attributable to him, and the verdict was upheld on appeal.

4. See the reporters' note on Restatement Torts, 3d, Apportionment of Liability, § 7, comment m, p. 83:

> . . . the best explanation of pre–presentment negligence is that the consequences of the plaintiff's negligence—the medical condition requiring medical treatment—caused the very condition the defendant doctor undertook to treat so it would be unfair to allow the doctor to complain about that negligence.

5. Would you treat an overzealous jogger who had cardiac arrest while running in the same way as a chain smoking or obese sedentary patient? How much of your decision is based on your desire to punish the smoker or glutton for immoral or irresponsible behavior which may be virtually impossible to control? Blaming the victim, or scapegoating, is a frequent argument used by employers, insurers and the government to reduce obligations to insure, pay benefits, or, as in *Ostrowski*, to pay damages for patient injury. See Robert Schwartz, Life Style, Health Status, and Distributive Justice, 3 Health Matrix 195, 198 (1993)("If all of those whose life style choices have health consequences were required to bear the full burden of those consequences, there would be few of us (and few diseases or injuries) that would not be implicated.")

6. Providers are expected to consider the needs and limitations of their patients. Bryant v. Calantone, 286 N.J.Super. 362, 669 A.2d 286 (A.D.1996). In Windisch v. Weiman, 161 A.D.2d 433, 555 N.Y.S.2d 731 (1990), the court held that the failure of a physician to properly follow–up a patient, resulting in a missed diagnosis of lung cancer, may provide the basis for imposing liability even when the patient is partially responsible for the delay in diagnosis.

7. Contributory fault is typically invoked when a patient failed to follow a physician's instructions after a procedure was performed, or while in the hospital. Musachia v. Rosman, 190 So.2d 47 (Fla.App.1966) (decedent left the hospital over the objections of, and contrary to the advice of, the defendants; and drank liquor and ignored instructions to eat only baby food. He

then died from fecal peritonitis due to small perforations in the bowel, and his recovery was barred)

8. Almost all American jurisdictions have adopted comparative fault, simplifying the issue by eliminating the harsh all–or–nothing effect of contributory negligence. Courts in comparative fault jurisdictions are likely to be more willing to allow evidence of plaintiffs' contributions to their injuries. See generally Victor Schwartz, Comparative Negligence (5th ed. 2010).

9. Assumption of the risk. The doctrine of assumption of the risk is a viable defense even in many comparative fault jurisdictions. In Schneider v. Revici, 817 F.2d 987, 995 (2d Cir.1987), the Second Circuit considered whether a patient undergoing unconventional treatment for breast cancer after signing a consent form had waived all her rights to sue or assumed the risk of injury from the treatment. The court held that the consent form was not clear and unequivocal as a covenant not to sue, but that the doctrine of assumption of risk was available:

> * * * we see no reason why a patient should not be allowed to make an informed decision to go outside currently approved medical methods in search of an unconventional treatment. While a patient should be encouraged to exercise care for his own safety, we believe that an informed decision to avoid surgery and conventional chemotherapy is within the patient's right to "determine what shall be done with his own body,"[ ]

The court held that the jury could consider assumption of the risk as a total bar to recovery, based on the language of the signed consent form and the patient's general awareness of the risks of treatment.

Assumption of the risk is rarely argued except in cases of obvious defects of which the patient should have been aware, such as hazards in the hospital room. See, e.g., Charrin v. Methodist Hospital, 432 S.W.2d 572 (Tex.Civ.App.1968) (plaintiff tripped over television cord in hospital room; she knew it was there, having previously pointed it out to the staff.) The problem of assumption of the risk, in the sense of a conscious explicit assumption of medical risks, blends into the issues of informed consent and waivers of liability, discussed in Chapter 4, *supra*.

PROBLEM: THE DIFFICULT PATIENT

Alice Frost is profoundly obese. She is a smoker and drinks a bottle of gin a day. She works for the State as a disability counselor and her state health insurance coverage is excellent. She sees Dr. Wilson regularly. He has admonished her to stop smoking and cut down on her drinking, and to begin a program of exercise. He has also set up a series of monthly appointments with her to monitor her health. She fails to obtain a lipid profile to measure her cholesterol and never sees a cardiologist, even though Dr. Wilson has instructed her to do so on many occasions. She continues to smoke and drink. She also begins to miss her monthly appointments. Dr. Wilson has his nurse call her to remind her several times, but Alice never calls back. After six months of missed appointments, Alice has a heart attack and dies.

Can her estate sue Dr. Wilson?

V. CAUSATION PROBLEMS

Causation is often a major stumbling block for plaintiffs in complex medical malpractice cases. Plaintiffs have preexisting conditions, and it is hard to tell whether the negligent acts of the physician "caused" the bad outcome, or it would have happened in any event. Robins v. Garg, 276 Mich.App. 351, 741 N.W.2d 49 (Court of Appeals, Michigan, 2007). Causation questions are usually left to the jury to decide. Causation is normally satisfied by a showing by substantial evidence that the injury of the plaintiff is a natural and probable consequence of the defendant's negligence. Causation may be inferred from the facts of the case. Williams v. Daus, 114 S.W.3d 351 (Mo. App. 2003).

Where a defendant's acts have increased the risk of harm that later materializes, courts often look to the "relative risk—the ratio of the risk with the negligent act to the risk without negligence—to decide whether the negligent acts or omissions constitute a cause in fact of the harm." Theofanis v. Sarrafi, 339 Ill.App.3d 460, 274 Ill.Dec. 242, 791 N.E.2d 38, 48 (1 Dist. 2003). A finding of causation rapidly becomes more complicated in the typical malpractice case due to the presence of multiple defendants, often treating a patient over time.

Joint Tortfeasors. In the typical malpractice case in which the parties acted together to commit the wrong, or the parties' acts, if independent, unite to cause a single injury, multiple defendants are considered joint rather than separate tortfeasors. In determining whether to assess liability jointly, the courts have considered factors such as whether each defendant has a similar duty; whether the same evidence will support an action against each; the indivisible nature of the plaintiff's injury; and identity of the facts as to time, place or result. See Riff v. Morgan Pharmacy, 353 Pa.Super. 21, 508 A.2d 1247 (1986).

The adoption of comparative fault in almost all American jurisdictions means that once a defendant is joined, the trier of fact will have the job of apportioning damages among defendants in conformity with the particular standards of that jurisdiction. Most negligence cases end up in the hands of the jury as a result of this move to comparative fault.

What if a doctor fails to diagnose a patient's problem, and subsequently another doctor is negligent in treating it? The first negligent treating doctor might be liable to the injured plaintiff for all foreseeable injuries resulting from the later negligent medical treatment of a second doctor. Two or more physicians who fail to make a proper diagnosis on successive occasions are joint tortfeasors under contribution statutes.

Harvey v. Washington, 95 S.W.3d 93 (Mo. Banc 2003) (two causes can satisfy "but for" causation: kidney specialist's failure to initiate dialysis treatment was sufficient to have caused patient's death, as was another doctor's failure to treat the patient's infection.). See, e.g., Gilson v. Mitchell, 131 Ga.App. 321, 205 S.E.2d 421 (1974) (" * * * if the separate and independent acts of negligence of several persons combine naturally and directly to produce a single indivisible injury, and a rational basis does not exist for an apportionment of damages, the actors are joint tortfeasors.")

Where an existing injury is aggravated by malpractice, the innocent plaintiffs are not required to establish that share of expenses, pain, suffering, disability or impairment attributable solely to malpractice. The burden of proof shifts to the culpable defendant, who is responsible for all damages unless he can demonstrate that the damages for which he is responsible are capable of some reasonable apportionment.

For the physician who knows that his patients see alternative practitioners, or who offers such treatments as an option, what are his or her liabilities? Joint and several liability is likely to hook the physician firmly if injury is the end result of a continuum of care that includes alternative practitioners. In Samuelson v. McMurtry, 962 S.W.2d 473 (Tenn.1998), the plaintiff was treated by physicians and a chiropractor. He died of pneumonia, which had not been diagnosed by any provider. The court held that "* * * the participation of all potentially responsible persons as parties in the original action would have resulted in a fuller and fairer presentation of the relevant evidence and would have enabled the jury to make a more informed and complete determination of liability."

For a critical look at alternative and complementary medicines generally, see Christopher Wanjek, Bad Medicine: Misconceptions and Misuses Revealed, From Distance Healing to Vitamin O (2002).

Where only one of several defendants could have caused the plaintiff's injuries, but the plaintiff cannot produce evidence as to which defendant is responsible, the courts have developed special rules to protect the obviously deserving plaintiff. Cases like Ybarra v. Spangard, *supra*, reflect judicial attempts to use doctrines like *res ipsa loquitur* to cover multiple defendant/uncertain proof situations. An equitable doctrine of burden shifting is derived from the exception in the Restatement (Second) of Torts, § 433B(3) (1965):

> Where the conduct of two or more actors is tortious, and it is proved that harm has been caused to the plaintiff by only one of them, but there is uncertainty as to which one has caused it, the burden is upon each actor to prove that he has not caused the harm.

The reason for this burden shift is " * * * the injustice of permitting proved wrongdoers, who among them have inflicted an injury upon the entirely innocent plaintiff, to escape liability merely because the nature of their conduct and the resulting harm has made it impossible to prove which of them has caused the harm." Id., comment f.

VI. DAMAGE INNOVATIONS

In the typical malpractice case, the available damages are the standard tort list: medical expenses, past and future; loss wages; diminished future earning capacity; loss of consortium; and noneconomic losses such as pain and suffering. In many health care settings, however, the alleged malpractice of the provider occurs to a patient who has a preexisting illness, such as a cancer patient. If the patient's chances of recovery are less than fifty percent, the old rule would deny recovery. The problem is one both of causation—did a provider's inaction increase the risk to the patient—and damage—exactly how should harm be quantified in such a situation.

A. THE "LOSS OF A CHANCE" DOCTRINE

HERSKOVITS V. GROUP HEALTH COOPERATIVE OF PUGET SOUND

Supreme Court of Washington, 1983.
99 Wash.2d 609, 664 P.2d 474.

DORE, JUSTICE.

This appeal raises the issue of whether an estate can maintain an action for professional negligence as a result of failure to timely diagnose lung cancer, where the estate can show probable reduction in statistical chance for survival but cannot show and/or prove that with timely diagnosis and treatment, decedent probably would have lived to normal life expectancy.

Both counsel advised that for the purpose of this appeal we are to *assume* that the respondent Group Health Cooperative of Puget Sound and Dr. William Spencer negligently failed to diagnose Herskovits' cancer on his first visit to the hospital and *proximately* caused a 14 percent reduction in his chances of survival. It is undisputed that Herskovits had less than a 50 percent chance of survival at all times herein.

The main issue we will address in this opinion is whether a patient, with less than a 50 percent chance of survival, has a cause of action against the hospital and its employees if they are negligent in diagnosing a lung cancer which reduces his chances of survival by 14 percent.

* * *

I

The complaint alleged that Herskovits came to Group Health Hospital in 1974 with complaints of pain and coughing. In early 1974, chest x–rays revealed infiltrate in the left lung. Rales and coughing were present. In mid–1974, there were chest pains and coughing, which became persistent and chronic by fall of 1974. A December 5, 1974 entry in the medical records confirms the cough problem. Plaintiff contends that Herskovits was treated thereafter only with cough medicine. No further effort or inquiry was made by Group Health concerning his symptoms, other than an occasional chest x–ray. In the early spring of 1975, Mr. and Mrs. Herskovits went south in the hope that the warm weather would help. Upon his return to the Seattle area with no improvement in his health, Herskovits visited Dr. Jonathan Ostrow on a private basis for another medical opinion. Within 3 weeks, Dr. Ostrow's evaluation and direction to Group Health led to the diagnosis of cancer. In July of 1975, Herskovits' lung was removed, but no radiation or chemotherapy treatments were instituted. Herskovits died 20 months later, on March 22, 1977, at the age of 60.

At hearing on the motion for summary judgment, plaintiff was unable to produce expert testimony that the delay in diagnosis "probably" or "more likely than not" caused her husband's death. The affidavit and deposition of plaintiff's expert witness, Dr. Jonathan Ostrow, construed in the most favorable light possible to plaintiff, indicated that had the diagnosis of lung cancer been made in December 1974, the patient's possibility of 5–year survival was 39 percent. At the time of initial diagnosis of cancer 6 months later, the possibility of a 5–year survival was reduced to 25 percent. Dr. Ostrow testified he felt a diagnosis perhaps could have been made as early as December 1974, or January 1975, about 6 months before the surgery to remove Mr. Herskovits' lung in June 1975.

Dr. Ostrow testified that if the tumor was a "stage 1" tumor in December 1974, Herskovits' chance of a 5–year survival would have been 39 percent. In June 1975, his chances of survival were 25 percent assuming the tumor had progressed to "stage 2". Thus, the delay in diagnosis may have reduced the chance of a 5–year survival by 14 percent.

Dr. William Spencer, the physician from Group Health Hospital who cared for the deceased Herskovits, testified that in his opinion, based upon a reasonable medical probability, earlier diagnosis of the lung cancer that afflicted Herskovits would not have prevented his death, nor would it have lengthened his life. He testified that nothing the doctors at Group Health could have done would have prevented Herskovits' death, as death within several years is a virtual certainty with this type of lung cancer regardless of how early the diagnosis is made.

Plaintiff contends that medical testimony of a reduction of chance of survival from 39 percent to 25 percent is sufficient evidence to allow the proximate cause issue to go to the jury. Defendant Group Health argues conversely that Washington law does not permit such testimony on the issue of medical causation and requires that medical testimony must be at least sufficiently definite to establish that the act complained of "probably" or "more likely than not" caused the subsequent disability. It is Group Health's contention that plaintiff must prove that Herskovits "probably" would have survived had the defendant not been allegedly negligent; that is, the plaintiff must prove there was at least a 51 percent chance of survival.

II

* * *

This court heretofore has not faced the issue of whether, under § 323(a), [of the Restatement (Second) of Torts (1965)] proof that the defendant's conduct increased the risk of death by decreasing the chances of survival is sufficient to take the issue of proximate cause to the jury. Some courts in other jurisdictions have allowed the proximate cause issue to go to the jury on this type of proof.[ ] These courts emphasized the fact that defendants' conduct deprived the decedents of a "significant" chance to survive or recover, rather than requiring proof that with absolute certainty the defendants' conduct caused the physical injury. The underlying reason is that it is not for the wrongdoer, who put the possibility of recovery beyond realization, to say afterward that the result was inevitable.[ ]

Other jurisdictions have rejected this approach, generally holding that unless the plaintiff is able to show that it was *more likely than not* that the harm was caused by the defendant's negligence, proof of a decreased chance of survival is not enough to take the proximate cause question to the jury.[ ] These courts have concluded that the defendant should not be liable where the decedent more than likely would have died anyway.

The ultimate question raised here is whether the relationship between the increased risk of harm and Herskovits' death is sufficient to hold Group Health responsible. Is a 36 percent (from 39 percent to 25 percent) reduction in the decedent's chance for survival sufficient evidence of causation to allow the jury to consider the possibility that the physician's failure to timely diagnose the illness was the proximate cause of his death? We answer in the affirmative. To decide otherwise would be a blanket release from liability for doctors and hospitals any time there was less than a 50 percent chance of survival, regardless of how flagrant the negligence.

III

[The court then discusses at length the case of *Hamil v. Bashline,* [ ], where the plaintiff's decedent, suffering from severe chest pains, was negligently treated in the emergency unit of the hospital. The wife, because of the lack of help, took her husband to a private physician's office, where he died. If the hospital had employed proper treatment, the decedent would have had a substantial chance of surviving the attack, stated by plaintiff's medical expert as a 75 percent chance of survival. The defendant's expert witness testified that the patient would have died regardless of any treatment provided by the defendant hospital.]

* * *

* * * In *Hamil* and the instant case, however, the defendant's act or omission failed in a *duty* to protect against harm from *another source*. Thus, as the *Hamil* court noted, the fact finder is put in the position of having to consider not only what *did* occur, but also what *might have* occurred.

* * *

The *Hamil* court held that once a plaintiff has demonstrated that the defendant's acts or omissions have increased the risk of harm to another, such evidence furnishes a basis for the jury to make a determination as to whether such increased risk was in turn a substantial factor in bringing about the resultant harm.

* * *

Under the *Hamil* decision, once a plaintiff has demonstrated that defendant's acts or omissions in a situation to which § 323(a) applies have increased the risk of harm to another, such evidence furnishes a basis for the fact finder to go further and find that such increased risk was in turn a substantial factor in bringing about the resultant harm. The necessary proximate cause will be established if the jury finds such cause. It is not necessary for a plaintiff to introduce evidence to establish that the negligence resulted in the injury or death, but simply that the negligence increased the *risk* of injury or death. The step from the increased risk to causation is one for the jury to make.

* * *

Where percentage probabilities and decreased probabilities are submitted into evidence, there is simply no danger of speculation on the part of the jury. More speculation is involved in requiring the medical expert to testify as to what would have happened had the defendant not been negligent.

Conclusion

* * * We reject Group Health's argument that plaintiffs *must show* that Herskovits "probably" would have had a 51 percent chance of survival if the hospital had not been negligent. We hold that medical testimony of a reduction of chance of survival from 39 percent to 25 percent is sufficient evidence to allow the proximate cause issue to go to the jury.

Causing reduction of the opportunity to recover (loss of chance) by one's negligence, however, does not necessitate a total recovery against the negligent party for all damages caused by the victim's death. Damages should be awarded to the injured party or his family based only on damages caused directly by premature death, such as lost earnings and additional medical expenses, etc.

We reverse the trial court and reinstate the cause of action.

PEARSON, J., concurring.

* * *

* * * I am persuaded * * * by the thoughtful discussion of a recent commentator. King, *Causation, Valuation, and Chance in Personal Injury Torts Involving Preexisting Conditions and Future Consequences,* 90 Yale L.J. 1353 (1981).

* * *

Under the all or nothing approach, typified by *Cooper v. Sisters of Charity of Cincinnati, Inc.,* 27 Ohio St.2d 242, 272 N.E.2d 97 (1971), a plaintiff who establishes that but for the defendant's negligence the decedent had a 51 percent chance of survival may maintain an action for that death. The defendant will be liable for all damages arising from the death, even though there was a 49 percent chance it would have occurred despite his negligence. On the other hand, a plaintiff who establishes that but for the defendant's negligence the decedent had a 49 percent chance of survival recovers nothing.

This all or nothing approach to recovery is criticized by King on several grounds, 90 Yale L.J. at 1376–78. First, the all or nothing approach is arbitrary. Second, it

> subverts the deterrence objectives of tort law by denying recovery for the effects of conduct that causes statistically demonstrable losses * * *. A failure to allocate the cost of these losses to their tortious sources * * * strikes at the integrity of the torts system of loss allocation.

90 Yale L.J. at 1377. Third, the all or nothing approach creates pressure to manipulate and distort other rules affecting causation and damages in an attempt to mitigate perceived injustices.[ ] Fourth, the all or nothing approach gives certain defendants the benefit of an uncertainty which, were it not for their tortious conduct, would not exist. * * * Finally, King argues that the loss of a less than even chance is a loss worthy of redress.

These reasons persuade me that the best resolution of the issue before us is to recognize the loss of a less than even chance as an actionable injury. Therefore, I would hold that plaintiff has established a prima facie issue of proximate cause by producing testimony that defendant probably caused a substantial reduction in Mr. Herskovits' chance of survival. * * *

Finally, it is necessary to consider the amount of damages recoverable in the event that a loss of a chance of recovery is established. Once again, King's discussion provides a useful illustration of the principles which should be applied.

> To illustrate, consider a patient who suffers a heart attack and dies as a result. Assume that the defendant–physician negligently misdiagnosed the patient's condition, but that the patient would have had only a 40% chance of survival even with a timely diagnosis and proper care. Regardless of whether it could be said that the defendant caused the decedent's death, he caused the loss of a chance, and that chance–interest should be completely redressed in its own right. Under the proposed rule, the plaintiff's compensation for the loss of the victim's chance of surviving the heart attack would be 40% of the compensable value of the victim's life had he survived (including what his earning capacity would otherwise have been in the years following death). The value placed on the patient's life would reflect such factors as his age, health, and earning potential, including the fact that he had suffered the heart attack and the assumption that he had survived it. The 40% computation would be applied to that base figure.

(Footnote omitted.) 90 Yale L.J. at 1382.

I would remand to the trial court for proceedings consistent with this opinion.

BRACHTENBACH, JUSTICE (dissenting).

I dissent because I find plaintiff did not meet her burden of proving proximate cause. While the statistical evidence introduced by the expert was relevant and admissible, it was not alone sufficient to maintain a cause of action.

Neither the majority nor Justice Dolliver's dissent focus on the key issue. Both opinions focus on the significance of the 14 percent differentiation in the patient's chance to survive for 5 years and question whether this statistical data is sufficient to sustain a malpractice action. The issue is not so limited. The question should be framed as whether all the evidence amounts to sufficient proof, rising above speculation, that the doctor's conduct was a proximate cause of the patient's death. While the relevancy and the significance of the statistical evidence is a subissue bearing on the sufficiency of the proof, such evidence alone neither proves nor disproves plaintiff's case.

II

Furthermore, the instant case does not present evidence of proximate cause that rises above speculation and conjecture. The majority asserts that evidence of a statistical reduction of the chance to survive for 5 years is sufficient to create a jury question on whether the doctor's conduct was a proximate cause of the death. I disagree that this statistical data can be interpreted in such a manner.

Use of statistical data in judicial proceedings is a hotly debated issue.[ ] Many fear that members of the jury will place too much emphasis on statistical evidence and the statistics will be misused and manipulated by expert witnesses and attorneys.[ ]

Such fears do not support a blanket exclusion of statistical data, however. Our court system is premised on confidence in the jury to understand complex concepts and confidence in the right of cross examination as protection against the misuse of evidence. Attorneys ought to be able to explain the true significance of statistical data to keep it in its proper perspective.

Statistical data should be admissible as evidence if they are relevant, that is, if they have

> any tendency to make the existence of any fact that is of consequence to * * * the action more probable or less probable than it would be without the evidence.

ER 401. The statistics here met that test; they have some tendency to show that those diagnosed at stage one of the disease may have a greater chance to survive 5 years than those diagnosed at stage two.

The problem is, however, that while this statistical fact is relevant, it is not sufficient to prove causation. There is an enormous difference between the "any tendency to prove" standard of ER 401 and the "more likely than not" standard for proximate cause.

* * *

Thus, I would not resolve the instant case simply by focusing on the 14 percent differentiation in the chance to survive 5 years for the different stages of cancer. Instead, I would accept this as an admissible fact, but not as proof of proximate cause. To meet the proximate cause burden, the record would need to reveal other facts about the patient that tended to show that he would have been a member of the 14 percent group whose chance of 5 years' survival could be increased by early diagnosis.

Such evidence is not in the record. Instead, the record reveals that Mr. Herskovits' cancer was located such that corrective surgery "would be more formidable". This would tend to show that his chance of survival may have been less than the statistical average. Moreover, the statistics relied on did not take into consideration the location of the tumor, therefore their relevance to Mr. Herskovits' case must be questioned. Clerk's Papers, at 41.

In addition, as the tumor was relatively small in size when removed (2 to 3 centimeters), the likelihood that it would have been detected in 1974, even if the proper test were performed, was less than average. This uncertainty further reduces the probability that the doctor's failure to perform the tests was a proximate cause of a reduced chance of survival.

Other statistics admitted into evidence also tend to show the inconclusiveness of the statistics relied on by the majority. One study showed the *two*–year survival rate for this type of cancer to be 46.6 percent for stage one and 39.8 percent for stage two. Mr. Herskovits lived for 20 months after surgery, which was 26 months after defendant allegedly should have discovered the cancer. Therefore, regardless of the stage of the cancer at the time Mr. Herskovits was examined by defendant, it cannot be concluded that he survived significantly less than the average survival time. Hence, it is pure speculation to suppose that the doctor's negligence "caused" Mr. Herskovits to die sooner than he would have otherwise. Such speculation does not rise to the level of a jury question on the issue of proximate cause. Therefore, the trial court correctly dismissed the case.[ ]

The apparent harshness of this conclusion cannot be overlooked. The combination of the loss of a loved one to cancer and a doctor's negligence in diagnosis seems to compel a finding of liability. Nonetheless, justice must be dealt with an even hand. To hold a defendant liable without proof that his actions *caused* plaintiff harm would open up untold abuses of the litigation system.

Cases alleging misdiagnosis of cancer are increasing in number, perhaps because of the increased awareness of the importance of early detection. These cases, however, illustrate no more than an inconsistency among courts in their treatment of the problems of proof. [ ]. Perhaps as medical science becomes more knowledgeable about this disease and more sophisticated in its detection and treatment of it, the balance may tip in favor of imposing liability on doctors who negligently fail to promptly diagnose the disease. But, until a formula is found that will protect doctors against liability imposed through speculation as well as afford truly aggrieved plaintiffs their just compensation, I cannot favor the wholesale abandonment of the principle of proximate cause. For these reasons, I dissent.

NOTES AND QUESTIONS

1. How would damages be figured under the majority's approach? Under the Pearson/King theory? What is the relationship between causation and damages in these cases? The majority and Pearson opinions would effectively

permit recovery but reduce damages as the causation link weakens. Is this a reasonable approach?

2. Judicial approaches to the loss of a chance can be grouped into four categories.

a. *All or nothing.* The traditional rule allows the plaintiff no recovery unless survival was more likely than not. A less than 51% chance of survival receives nothing. Plaintiff who proves a chance of survival greater than 50% can receive judgment with no discount for the chance that the loss would have occurred without negligence. This award is based on the physical injury suffered and not the lost chance to avoid it. See Smith v. Parrott, 175 Vt. 375, 833 A.2d 843 (2003) (rejecting the doctrine due to "fundamental questions about its potential impact on not only the cost, but the very practice of medicine in Vermont; about its effect on causation standards to other professions and the principles—if any—which might justify its application to medicine but not other fields such as law, architecture, or accounting; and ultimately about the overall societal cots which may result from awarding damages to an entirely new class of plaintiffs who formerly had no claim under the common law in this state.") See also Kramer v. Lewisville Memorial Hospital, 858 S.W.2d 397, 405 (Tex.1993).

b. *Loss of an appreciable or substantial chance of recovery.* Jeanes v. Milner, 428 F.2d 598 (8th Cir.1970). This approach does not give proportional recovery based on the percentage of harm attributable to the defendant, instead manipulating the burden of proof rather than acknowledging the lost chance as the real injury. See Hicks v. United States, 368 F.2d 626 (4th Cir.1966).

c. *Increased risk of harm.* This approach, found in the Restatement (Second) of Torts, § 323(a) and adopted by the majority in *Herskovits,* lowers causation requirements to allow causes of action for those who have a less than 50% chance of survival. Hamil v. Bashline, 481 Pa. 256, 392 A.2d 1280 (1978). Compensation is for the increased risk of harm rather than loss of a chance, and damage awards are not discounted for the percentage of harm caused by the physician, death is typically the compensable injury. Any percentage is enough to get to the jury. See Thompson v. Sun City Community Hospital, Inc., 141 Ariz. 597, 688 P.2d 605 (1984) (linking Restatement (Second) of Torts, § 323A to the interest seen as "the chance itself.")

d. *Compensation for the loss of a chance.* This looks at damages that include the value of the patient's life reduced in proportion to the lost chance. This approach was developed by Joseph King in his seminal article, Causation, Valuation and Chance in Personal Injury Torts Involving Pre–existing Conditions and Future Consequences, 90 Yale L.J. 1353 (1981). The approach requires a percentage probability test, with the value of the patient's life determined and damages decreased accordingly. This approach was considered in Pearson's concurring opinion in *Herskovits.* See generally Matsuyama v. Birnbaum, 452 Mass. 1, 890 N.E.2d 819 (Supreme Judicial Court of Massachusetts 2008) (adopting the lost of a chance doctrine, and providing an exhaustive treatment of the doctrine and the jurisdictions adopting and rejecting it).

3. What problems do you foresee with the application of the "loss of a chance" doctrine to medical practice? Note that the evidence as to risk must be put in probabilistic form for the jury to consider. What about Judge Brachtenbach's concerns about the weight to be given statistical evidence? Would his concerns always prevent the use of statistics in litigation? Or can you offer some solutions to his problems? In Drew v. William W. Backus Hospital, 77 Conn.App. 645, 825 A.2d 810 (2003), the court rejected the testimony of the plaintiff's expert, who failed to apply general statistical data as to survival to the particular patient, so that the requirement of proof of a causal link was not satisfied.

4. A judicial illustration of the calculation process for loss of a chance is found in McKellips v. St. Francis Hospital, Inc., 741 P.2d 467 (Okl.1987):

> "To illustrate the method in a case where the jury determines from the statistical findings combined with the specific facts relevant to the patient, the patient originally had a 40% chance of cure and the physician's negligence reduced the chance of cure to 25%, (40%—25%) 15% represents the patient's loss of survival. If the total amount of damages proved by the evidence is $500,000, the damages caused by defendant is 15% × $500,000 or $75,000 * * *."

This has come to be called the "proportional damages" approach. See Matsuyama v. Birnbaum, 452 Mass. 1, 890 N.E.2d 819 (Supreme Judicial Court, Massachusetts 2008). The court must measure the monetary value of the patient's full life expectancy and, if relevant, work life expectancy as it would in any wrongful death case. The defendant must then be held liable only for the portion of that value that the defendant's negligence destroyed.

PROBLEM: MISSING THE DIAGNOSIS

Jane Rogers was a fair complected woman in her early thirties. She had worked every summer during high school and college as a lifeguard at the beach. While she was in graduate school, one of her sisters was diagnosed as having melanoma, a deadly cancer that is often fatal if not detected and treated early. Melanoma is more prevalent in people who have fair complexions, and prolonged exposure to the sun over time, particularly severe sun burns, are a risk factor for the cancer.

Ms. Roger's sister died. The family physician, Dr. James, told the family members that they should all get a thorough physical to check for signs of skin tumors that might be precancerous. Ms. Rogers went to the University Student Clinic and requested a physical examination. She explained why she was worried. Dr. Gillespie, an older physician who had retired from active practice and now helped out part–time at the Clinic, examined her. He observed a nodule on her upper back, but incorrectly diagnosed it as a birthmark. He told her not to worry. She continued her lifeguarding and water safety instruction activities during the summer to pay for her graduate education.

At a party one Friday night, Ms. Rogers met a young physician who was a resident at the University hospital. She was wearing a strapless dress, and the resident, Dr. Wunch, noted a mole on her shoulder. He recognized it as a melanoma. He pointed it out to her, and told her that she really ought to get it checked. He gave her his card, with his phone number, and said he would be glad to set her up with an appointment with a good cancer specialist at the hospital. Ms. Rogers called, made an appointment, and filled out the forms required by the University Hospital, but then missed her appointment. She never went back.

A year later, during a routine physical as part of an employment application, the examining physician found several large growths on Ms. Roger's back. She was diagnosed as having melanoma, which had spread into her blood and had metastasized into her lymph nodes. She was dead within a year.

What problems do you see with the suit by her estate against the available defendants?

B. PUNITIVE DAMAGES

MARSH V. ARNOT OGDEN MEDICAL CENTER

Supreme Court, App. Div., New York, 2012.
91 A.D.3d 1070, 937 N.Y.S.2d 383.

GARRY, J.

Appeal from an order of the Supreme Court (O'Shea, J.), entered January 20, 2011 in Chemung County, which, among other things, granted a motion by defendants Arnot Ogden Medical Center and Jane Doe for partial summary judgment dismissing the claim for punitive damages.

In April 2009, Leslie E. Marshall (hereinafter decedent) was a patient in a hospital facility operated by defendant Arnot Ogden Medical Center (hereinafter AOMC) when defendant Jane Doe, a registered nurse employed by AOMC, mistakenly injected him with an insulin–reducing medication that had not been prescribed for him. When advised by telephone of the error, defendant Renee Abderhalden–Friend, the attending physician, directed Doe to monitor decedent's glucose level every two hours and call her at home if the level fell below 120. This testing revealed that decedent's glucose level was 132 at 8:15 P.M. and 107 at 10:15 P.M. After learning of the second test result, Abderhalden–Friend allegedly ordered the glucose testing to be discontinued until the next morning. When next tested at 6:15 A.M., decedent's glucose level was 15, and he died shortly thereafter. The cause of death was determined to be insulin overdose resulting from the medication error.

Plaintiff thereafter commenced this negligence and medical malpractice action against, among others, AOMC, Doe and Abderhalden–Friend seeking, among other things, punitive damages. Abderhalden–Friend moved pursuant to CPLR 3211(a)(7) for dismissal of the punitive damages claim against her, and AOMC and Doe moved for partial summary judgment dismissing the punitive damages claim against them. Supreme Court granted said defendants' motions. Plaintiff appeals.

In the context of medical malpractice, punitive damages may be recovered when a defendant's conduct evinces " 'a reckless indifference equivalent to willful or intentional misdoing' "[ ]), or a "wanton and reckless disregard of [a] plaintiff's rights" [ ]. A showing of malice or wrongful intent is not required.

As to Abderhalden–Friend, the complaint alleges that, despite her knowledge of the medication error, decedent's medical condition and the particular risks posed to him by the inappropriate medication, she did not come to the hospital to examine decedent, but thereafter directed AOMC staff by telephone to discontinue monitoring his glucose level until the next morning, without ordering any other actions to monitor his condition in the interim. In plaintiff's view, Abderhalden–Friend abandoned decedent when he was in need of emergency treatment, thereby justifying punitive damages [ ]. If these claims are proven, it is possible that her conduct may be found to have been "grossly inappropriate given [her] actual knowledge of decedent's condition"[ ]. Thus, viewing the allegations in the light most favorable to plaintiff, we find the stated claim to be legally sufficient to overcome the motion to dismiss [ ].

As to the motion for partial summary judgment by Doe and AOMC, the necessary inquiry is whether there are factual issues in controversy. "Only if it can be said, as a matter of law, that punitive damages are unavailable to a plaintiff in a medical malpractice action is a summary determination in favor of [a] defendant warranted on this issue" [ ]. Plaintiff alleges that, just before Doe administered the medication to decedent, his daughter specifically warned that decedent was not a diabetic and did not use insulin, and Doe nonetheless injected the medication without ascertaining decedent's identity and confirming that a physician had ordered the medication for this patient. Decedent's medical records and autopsy report were submitted upon this motion. These documents confirm that Doe administered the medication and that this error caused his death; Doe's answer denies that she was warned, but plaintiff's allegations stand otherwise unrefuted within the record. We find that there are factual issues presented as to whether Doe's conduct in administering the medication despite the alleged admonition by the daughter "transcend[ed] mere carelessness" and demonstrated the requisite reckless indifference to decedent's medical care to justify a punitive damages award [ ].

Further, plaintiff alleges—and the medical records confirm—that decedent's medical chart at AOMC was not updated to reflect Doe's mistaken administration of medicine until four months after his death. Willful failure to disclose pertinent medical information may be sufficient to support punitive damages when undertaken to evade a malpractice claim [ ]; no explanation of the delay has yet been offered by Doe or AOMC, and no pretrial discovery has taken place. Dismissal of a punitive damages claim is "premature where, as here, the party opposing the motion has not had an adequate opportunity to conduct discovery into issues within the knowledge of the moving party" [ ].

Finally, the record reveals that the federal Department of Health and Human Services conducted a medication error review after the incident and determined that Doe was responsible not only for the mistaken administration of medication that caused decedent's death, but also for another error two months earlier in which she mistakenly placed ear drops in a patient's eye. The Department found that AOMC had no methodology in place to identify patterns of repeated medication errors by specific staff members, had not discussed trends for medication errors at quarterly quality assurance meetings, and had thereby failed to ensure that its "residents [were] free of any significant medication errors" as required by 10 NYCRR 415.12(m)(2). A medical facility's failure to provide appropriate safety precautions and training may constitute a basis for a punitive damages award if shown to constitute conscious disregard for patient safety [ ]. Accordingly, plaintiff has established that there are triable issues of fact as to whether Doe and AOMC may be found liable for punitive damages, and their motion for partial summary judgment should have been denied.

ORDERED that the order is reversed, on the law, with costs, and motions denied.

NOTES AND QUESTIONS

1. What negligent acts did Dr. Doe commit? How should an institution deal with a physician so prone to mistakes? In the normal malpractice case, damages typically include special damages, such as costs of treating a condition and loss of earning capacity; and general damages, primarily pain and suffering. Punitive damages are extremely rare.

2. The case also raises the possibility of punitive damages against the defendant medical center for failing to update the patient's medical record to indicate the prescribing error, and failing to have a system in place to trace medication errors and institute educational programs for staff. Why would a hospital fail to develop such programs, given the financial risk they face if punitive damages are imposed? Did the regulatory system, state and federal, fail the plaintiff in this case? *Marsh* illustrates the complexities of medical

errors and the role of various responsible parties. See the discussion of institutional liability in Chapter 6.

CHAPTER 6

LIABILITY OF HEALTH CARE INSTITUTIONS

■ ■ ■

I. INTRODUCTION

The hospital is the classic health care "institution". The U.S. has over 5,700 hospitals—almost 3,000 are nonprofit, 1,000 for–profit, and 1,200 are local, state and federal government owned. The remainder are psychiatric and long term care hospitals. See American Hospital Association, Fast Facts on U.S. Hospitals (2013).

Hospitals are major providers of emergency care and highly complicated surgical and other procedures. They are therefore the largest sources of patient harms in the U.S. system. Hospitals provide acute care in severe health crises and, given the possibility of errors and serious adverse events, we also think of institutional liability for those injuries.

The Affordable Care Act has created pressure on hospitals to coordinate care and move patients safely from acute care situations to other institutions—assisted living, long term care, or home. Hospitals have also been acquiring physician practices in response to the incentives of the Affordable Care Act and the pressures for a better coordinated health care system.

Faced with the high cost of the HITECH Act's mandate for electronic health records and other regulatory mandates, many free standing hospitals are joining systems; and these systems are merging to achieve market share and necessary economies of scale in an increasingly competitive environment. As a result, 3,000 of these hospitals are now in systems, defined as either a multihospital or a diversified single hospital system. A multihospital system is two or more hospitals owned, leased, sponsored, or contract managed by a central organization. Single, freestanding hospitals may be categorized as a system by bringing into membership three or more, and at least 25 percent, of their owned or leased non–hospital preacute or postacute health care organizations. Hospitals in systems are likely to have more resources to devote to patient safety, and system pressures are likely to push hospitals toward the adoption of safety–based standards more rapidly.

Health care delivery also includes institutional forms such as managed care organizations that finance health care and contract with physicians and hospitals to provide care, as well as ambulatory care facilities such as surgicenters and physician offices. As more and more medicine is moved out of the hospital into less expensive settings, the liability of these institutional arrangements emerges as a new concern. Most caselaw has originated with hospitals as the predominant form of delivery of high technology high risk care—where the most severe patient harms can occur—and the courts are now adapting to changes in the delivery system.

See generally For an excellent extended discussion of the history of the hospital, see Paul Starr, The Social Transformation of American Medicine (1982), particularly Chapter 4.

II. AGENCY LAW AND THE TEST OF "CONTROL"

A. DEFINING "EMPLOYEE" IN THE HOSPITAL SETTING

Hospitals employ nurses, technicians, clerks, custodians, cooks, and others who are clearly employees of the hospital under agency principles. Their terms and conditions of employment are controlled by the hospital, which sets their hours, wages and working conditions. When employees are negligent, the hospital is vicariously liable for their acts as a result of the master–servant relationship of agency law. It is the relationship of physicians to the hospital that raises more complicated agency problems.

The hospital–physician relationship is an unusual one by corporate standards. A typical hospital may have several categories of practicing physicians, but the largest group is comprised of private physicians with staff privileges. Staff privileges include the right of the physicians to admit and discharge their private patients to and from the hospital and the right to use the hospital's facilities. See generally Chapter 9.

These physicians have typically been independent contractors rather than employees of the hospital. This legal status means that the hospital is therefore not easily targeted as a defendant in a malpractice suit. Only if the doctor whose negligence injured a patient is an employee could the hospital be reached through the doctrine of vicarious liability. The hospital is independently liable only if it is negligent in its administrative or housekeeping functions, for example causing a patient to slip and fall on a wet floor. Otherwise, the hospital has been immune in the past from liability. This has changed as the courts have confronted the evolution of the modern hospital and expanded vicarious liability doctrine in the health care setting.

SCOTT V. SSM HEALTHCARE ST. LOUIS

Mo.App. E.D., 2002.
70 S.W.3d 560.

* * *

Background

In 1994 Matthew Scott, then seventeen, sustained serious injuries as a result of a sinus infection that spread into his brain. Matthew was involved in a car accident and was taken to Hospital, where he was treated for minor injuries and released to his father. Two days later Matthew returned to Hospital's emergency room, complaining of a severe headache. Dr. Doumit was Hospital's emergency room physician who examined Matthew that day. Soon after Matthew arrived, a CT scan of his head was conducted. Dr. Richard Koch, a partner in RIC, read the CT film and concluded that the CT scan was normal. Matthew was diagnosed as having a mild concussion from the previous auto accident, was given medication for his headache and sent home.

The next day, Matthew's headache had not improved. His parents called Hospital three times and informed Dr. Doumit that Matthew was lethargic, nauseous and vomiting. Dr. Doumit told them that he was still exhibiting signs of a minor concussion, that he would probably improve within a few days, that they should continue to observe him, but that if they became very concerned about his condition they could bring him back to the emergency room.

Early the next morning, Matthew collapsed in the kitchen, unable to use the right side of his body. He was rushed by ambulance to Barnes Hospital in St. Peters, Missouri. A spinal tap and CT scan revealed an infection at the top of his brain, and his brain was swelling inside his skull. Matthew was taken to Barnes Hospital in St. Louis, where a number of surgeries were performed to remove infected brain tissue and portions of his skull. He remained in a coma for several weeks.

Eventually, after undergoing skull reconstructive surgery and an extensive program of rehabilitation, Matthew was able to achieve a considerable recovery. He also has sustained serious permanent injuries, however, including among others a significant degree of paralysis on the right side of his body, and the requirement of a permanent ventricular drainage tube in his brain.

Matthew and his mother filed this medical malpractice action against Hospital and others, alleging, *inter alia,* that the negligence of Dr. Doumit and Dr. Koch caused Matthew's injuries. Specifically, plaintiffs alleged that Dr. Koch had acted below the accepted standard of care in misreading the initial CT scan on September 24, and that Dr. Doumit had acted below the standard of care by failing to instruct Matthew's parents, when they called with their concerns, to bring him back to the emergency room. Plaintiffs' suit further alleged that at all relevant times Dr. Koch had been acting as an agent for Hospital, notwithstanding the fact that he was formally employed by RIC, which had contracted to provide radiology services at Hospital. Plaintiffs' action also named Dr. Koch and RIC as defendants. Before trial, plaintiffs settled their claims against Dr. Koch and RIC for the sum of $624,800 (hereinafter, "the Koch settlement"). The case then proceeded to trial against Hospital.

[The court first found that the evidence at trial supported the allegations of medical negligence by the treating physicians. The jury found for the plaintiffs, having found that Dr. Koch was the Hospital's agent.]

Discussion

1. *Sufficiency of Evidence on Issue of Dr. Koch's Agency*

[The Court considered the differences between independent contractor status and employee. It noted that the employer–employee relationship is a fact question for the jury.]

* * *

Two elements are required to establish an agency relationship: (1) the principal must consent, either expressly or impliedly, to the agent's acting on the principal's behalf, and (2) the agent must be subject to the principal's control.[ ] In the context of a hospital–physician relationship, the primary focus is on whether the hospital generally controlled, or had the right to control, the conduct of the doctor in his work performed at the hospital.[ ] Additionally, our courts have also cited with approval a list of ten factors set forth in the Restatement (Second) of Agency, § 220(2) (1958), as a helpful aid in "determining whether one acting for another is a servant or an independent contractor."[ ]

In the case at hand, Hospital cites a handful of facts from the record which, arguably, could support the conclusion that RIC and Dr. Koch were acting as independent contractors rather than as agents of Hospital. Among them are: the relationship between Dr. Koch and Hospital was based upon a written contract, in which RIC agreed to provide radiology services to Hospital; RIC was a partnership, of which Dr. Koch was a partner and signatory to the contract; Hospital did not employ or pay Dr. Koch (RIC did); Hospital did not directly set Dr. Koch's hours at the Hospital; and Hospital did not bill patients for the services of Dr. Koch or the other RIC radiologists.

However, a jury question is presented when the evidence is sufficiently conflicting that reasonable minds could differ as to whether agency existed.[ ] The following evidence, all of it from the contract and/or testimony in the record, supports finding a principal–agent relationship between Hospital and Dr. Koch: (1) Hospital establishes the medical standards for the provision of radiological services at Hospital; (2) Hospital determines the qualifications necessary for Dr. Koch; (3) Hospital has the right to require Dr. Koch to submit reports regarding radiological services rendered according to standards established by Hospital; (4) Hospital sets the prices for Dr. Koch's services, and those prices cannot be changed without prior approval of Hospital; (5) Hospital required that Dr. Koch be "an active member" of Hospital's medical staff; (6) Hospital required that Dr. Koch maintain liability insurance in specific amounts; (7) in the event that Dr. Koch fails to procure such insurance, Hospital has the right to procure it for him at his expense; (8) Hospital has the right to terminate Dr. Koch if dissatisfied with his performance; (9) Hospital provides all nurses and technicians for the radiology department; (10) Hospital owns and provides all of the office space for the radiology department, as well as providing all of the radiology equipment, films, supplies and fixtures; (11) Hospital decides what type of film, film boxes and view jackets will be used; (12) the contract between Hospital and RIC is of infinite duration; (13) RIC has provided the only radiologists working at Hospital for over 60 years; (14) RIC exclusively provides all of the radiologists for Hospital, including even the doctor who serves as the administrative director of the radiology department; and (15) the RIC radiologist who was the director of the radiology department testified that he considered himself and the other RIC radiologists at Hospital to in effect be "employees of the hospital."

Despite these facts, Hospital argues that the evidence at trial was insufficient to establish agency because there was nothing in the record to show that Hospital controlled Dr. Koch specifically "in the performance of the act at the heart of plaintiffs' claim—his alleged negligent reading of Matthew Scott's CT scan." However, Missouri courts have long recognized that physicians must be free to exercise independent medical judgment; the mere fact that a physician retains such independent judgment will not preclude a court, in an otherwise proper case, from finding the existence of an employer–employee or principal–agent relationship between a hospital and physician.[ ] Courts in other states, as well, have strongly rejected the notion that such a relationship cannot be found merely because the hospital does not have the right to stand over the doctor's shoulder and dictate to him or her how to diagnose and treat patients. [ ]

In view of the foregoing principles of law, the evidence in this case and our standard of review, the trial court did not err in finding the evidence sufficient to present a jury question on the issue of Dr. Koch's agency. Point I is denied.

NOTES AND QUESTIONS

1. ***Physicians as Employees.*** The general definition of the term "servant" in the Restatement (Second) of Agency § 2(2) (1957) refers to a per-

son whose work is "controlled or is subject to the right to control by the master." The Restatement's more specific definition of the term "servant" lists factors to be considered when distinguishing between servants and independent contractors, the first of which is "the extent of control" that one may exercise over the details of the work of the other. Id. The relevant factor for analyzing the hospital–physician relationship by agency tests is § 220(2)(a), which looks to "the extent of control which, by the agreement, the master may exercise over the details of the work." This becomes a fact–intensive analysis for the trier of fact.

Physicians need considerable autonomy in practice, given the complexity of their decisions and their relationship to particular patients. As a result, determining the degree of control necessary to create an employment relationship in a medical malpractice claim poses a unique set of difficulties. As the court writes in Lilly v. Fieldstone, 876 F.2d 857 (C.A. 10 Kan.),1989. " * * * [i]t is uncontroverted that a physician must have discretion to care for a patient and may not surrender control over certain medical details. Therefore, the 'control' test is subject to a doctor's medical and ethical obligations. . . . What we must do in the case of professionals is determine whether other evidence manifests an intent to make the professional an employee subject to other forms of control which are permissible. A myriad of doctors become employees by agreement without surrendering their professional responsibilities."

2. Hospitals employ approximately 212,000 physicians. Hospitals have a range of relationships with privileged physicians: 55.1 percent of physicians are not employed or under contract, while 20.3 percent are covered by a group contract; 17.3 percent are directly employed and 7.2 percent have individual contracts. See the 2012 edition of *AHA Hospital Statistics*. From 2003 to 2010, the proportion of hospitals with hospitalists on staff grew from 29.6 percent to 59.8 percent. From 2007–10, the proportion of hospitals employing intensivists grew from 20.7 percent to 29.7 percent. Many physicians are moving from practicing in small groups to some form of employee in a changing delivery system.

B. THE MEDICAL STAFF: VICARIOUS LIABILITY

Absent evidence of indicia of control sufficient to make a physician the employee of a hospital, courts have turned to traditional agency tests that evaluate whether the health care institution is vicariously liable for the negligence of its independent contractors.

BURLESS V. WEST VIRGINIA UNIVERSITY HOSPITALS, INC.

Supreme Court of West Virginia, 2004.
215 W.Va. 765, 601 S.E.2d 85.

DAVIS, JUSTICE:

In these two appeals from two orders of the Circuit Court of Monongalia County granting summary judgment to West Virginia University

Hospitals (hereinafter referred to as "WVUH"), the Appellants ask this Court to rule that the circuit courts erred in finding that no actual or apparent agency relationship existed between physicians employed by the West Virginia University Board of Trustees (hereinafter referred to as "the BOT") and WVUH. We find no error in the circuit courts' rulings that no actual agency existed. However, we find that the courts erred in granting summary judgment on the issue of apparent agency. In reaching this conclusion, we find that for a hospital to be held liable for a physician's negligence under an apparent agency theory, a plaintiff must establish that: (1) the hospital either committed an act that would cause a reasonable person to believe that the physician in question was an agent of the hospital, or, by failing to take an action, created a circumstance that would allow a reasonable person to hold such a belief, and (2) the plaintiff relied on the apparent agency relationship.

I. Factual Procedural History

Each of the two cases consolidated for purposes of this opinion involve a woman who gave birth to her child at WVUH under circumstances that she alleges resulted in severe birth defects to her child. The relevant facts of each case, as developed in the pleadings, depositions, affidavits, and exhibits, follow.

A. Jaclyn Burless

In July of 1998 Jaclyn Burless learned she was pregnant and sought prenatal care at the Cornerstone Care Clinic (hereinafter referred to as "the Cornerstone Clinic" or simply "the clinic") located in Greensboro, Pennsylvania. The Cornerstone Clinic was where Ms. Burless had routinely sought her primary medical care. Similarly, Ms. Burless elected to receive her prenatal care at the clinic. She received her prenatal care from Dr. Douglas Glover for approximately seven months.

In November, 1998, Dr. Glover sent Ms. Burless to WVUH for an ultrasound. At that time, Ms. Burless signed a WVUH consent form that stated: "I understand that the faculty physicians and resident physicians who provide treatment in the hospital are not employees of the hospital." Thereafter, in February of 1999 when she was at approximately 37 weeks of gestation, Ms. Burless experienced an elevated blood pressure and edema. On February 15, 1999, Dr. Glover advised Ms. Burless to report to the WVU Emergency Department for an evaluation. On February 17, 1999, Ms. Burless presented herself at the WVUH Emergency Department as instructed and, after an evaluation, was instructed to return to the High Risk Clinic, which is located on the WVUH premises, in two days with a urine sample for testing. Ms. Burless was also advised that she would receive the remainder of her prenatal care at the High Risk Clinic. She followed the instructions to return to the High Risk Clinic in two days. She was then instructed to return in one week for further evaluation. When she returned, on February 26, 1999, she was induced into labor at 7:50 p.m. Her labor was permitted to continue throughout the remainder of February 26 and until 4:00 p.m. on February 27. She alleges that during this time, doctors, residents, and nurses at WVUH noted variable decelerations in the fetal heart rate of her unborn daughter, Alexis Price. At 4:00 p.m. on February 27 the decision was made to deliver the baby via cesarean section, and such delivery was accomplished at 4:16 p.m. The child was born with an APGAR[2] score of two at one minute and six at five minutes. Soon after birth the child began to experience seizures and suffered a stroke. Ms. Burless has alleged that the doctors and hospital were negligent, *inter alia,* in failing to monitor her labor and delivery, which negligence caused severe and permanent mental, neurological, and psychological injuries to the infant, Alexis Price.

Ms. Burless later filed a negligence action, claiming breaches of the standard of care in connection with the management of her labor, against the BOT as the physicians' employer, and claiming vicarious liability on the part of WVUH based upon a theory of apparent agency between WVUH and the physicians who provided the allegedly negligent care. WVUH moved for summary judgment asserting, in relevant part, that there was no apparent agency relationship between it and the doctors and residents who provided care to Ms. Burless. Finding no just cause for delay, pursuant to Rule 54(b) of the West Virginia Rules of Civil Procedure, the circuit court granted summary judgment to WVUH by final order entered December 11, 2002. The circuit court found that there was nothing in the record demonstrating the creation of an apparent agency relationship between the physicians who treated Ms. Burless and WVUH. Ms. Burless appealed the order and this Court granted her petition for appeal. For purposes of rendering our decision, we consolidated her case with a similar appeal filed by Ms. Melony Pritt.

B. Melony Pritt

[Plaintiff Melony Pritt had an ovarian cyst, and scheduled a laparotomy and left ovarian cystectomy. She signed several consent forms, all of which contained the statement " "I understand that the faculty physicians and resident physicians who provide treatment in the hospital are not employees of the hospital." The surgery did not go well, and she suffered a massive abdominal infection, which infection caused premature labor. Her son was alleged therefore to have suffered severe permanent mental, neurological, and psychological injuries]

---

2 An APGAR Score is a newborn's first evaluation and serves as a predictive indicator of any potential problems. The infant is examined at one and five minutes after birth and ranked on a scale of zero to two on five characteristics: 1) skin color; 2) heart rate; 3) response to stimuli of inserting a catheter in the nose; 4) muscle tone; and 5) respiratory effort. Thus, the maximum score is 10 with most healthy newborns scoring an eight or nine. The five APGAR factors can be mnemonically summarized as *A*-ppearance, *P*-ulse, *G*-rimace, *A*-ctivity, *R*-espiration.[ ].

II.

[The court's discussion of the standard of review is omitted.]

III.

Discussion

Ms. Burless and Ms. Pritt assert that the circuit courts erred both in finding no actual agency relationship between the doctors who treated them and WVUH, and in finding no apparent agency relationship. We address each of these assignments of error in turn.

A. Actual Agency

[The court found no actual agency, since the hospital did not have "power of control" over the physicians who provided treatment to Ms. Burless and Ms. Pritt.]

B. Apparent Agency

Ms. Burless and Ms. Pritt next assert that the circuit courts erred in finding no apparent agency relationship between the doctors who treated them and WVUH. Because we have explained in the previous section that we find no *actual* agency relationship in these cases, we have concluded that the doctors were, in fact, independent contractors. Our cases have recognized that, as a general rule, "[i]f [a physician] is found to be an independent contractor, then the hospital is not liable for his [or her] negligence."[ ]

As with most general rules, there are exceptions to the independent contractor rule. We have previously recognized that

> One who by his acts or conduct has permitted another to act apparently or ostensibly as his agent, to the injury of a third person who has dealt with the apparent or ostensible agent in good faith and in the exercise of reasonable prudence, is estopped to deny the agency relationship.

[ ] In the instant cases, however, we are asked to determine the existence of an apparent agency relationship in the hospital/physician context. As explained in more detail below, modern hospitals and their relationships with the physicians who treat patients within their facilities are rather unique and complex. Thus, instead of relying on a general rule for apparent agency such as those quoted above, we believe a more particular rule is in order.

In the hospital/physician context, this Court has heretofore established that even where a physician charged with negligence is an independent contractor, the hospital may nevertheless be found vicariously liable where the complained of treatment was provided in an emergency room.[ ] Although we have addressed using a theory of apparent agency to overcome the physician/independent contractor rule in the context of emergency room treatment, we have never expressly defined such a rule for use outside of the emergency room setting. We do so now.

1. Hospital/Physician Apparent Agency Outside the Emergency Room Setting. The public's confidence in the modern hospital's portrayal of itself as a full service provider of health care appears to be at the foundation of the national trend toward adopting a rule of apparent agency to find hospitals liable, under the appropriate circumstances, for the negligence of physicians providing services within its walls. As one court observed:

> In an often cited passage, a New York court explained: "The conception that the hospital does not undertake to treat the patient, does not undertake to act through its doctors and nurses, but undertakes instead simply to procure them to act upon their own responsibility, no longer reflects the fact. Present–day hospitals, as their manner of operation plainly demonstrates, do far more than furnish facilities for treatment. They regularly employ on a salary basis a large staff of physicians, nurses and interns, as well as administrative and manual workers, and they charge patients for medical care and treatment, collecting for such services, if necessary, by legal action. Certainly, *the person who avails himself of 'hospital facilities' expects that the hospital will attempt to cure him, not that its nurses or other employees will act on their own responsibility*." . . . In light of this modern reality, the overwhelming majority of jurisdictions employed ostensible or apparent agency to impose liability on hospitals for the negligence of independent contractor physicians.

Mejia v. Community Hosp. of San Bernardino,[ ] (quoting Bing v. Thunig [ ] In fact), this Court has itself observed that

> "Modern hospitals have spent billions of dollars on marketing to nurture the image that they are full–care modern health facilities. Billboards, television commercials and newspaper advertisements tell the public to look to its local hospital for every manner of care, from the critical surgery and life–support required by a major accident to the minor tissue repairs resulting from a friendly game of softball. These efforts have helped bring the hospitals vastly increased revenue, a new role in daily health care and, ironically, a heightened exposure to lawsuits.[ ]"

[ ]

* * *

[ ] * * * [W]e now hold that for a hospital to be held liable for a physician's negligence under an apparent agency theory, a plaintiff must establish that: (1) the hospital either committed an act that would cause a reasona-

ble person to believe that the physician in question was an agent of the hospital, or, by failing to take an action, created a circumstance that would allow a reasonable person to hold such a belief, and (2) the plaintiff relied on the apparent agency relationship.

2. **Hospital's Actions or Inactions.** The first element of our test requires evidence that the hospital either committed an act that would cause a reasonable person to believe that the physician in question was an agent of the hospital, or, by failing to take an action, created a circumstance that would allow a reasonable person to hold such a belief. This portion of the test focuses on the acts of the hospital and is generally satisfied when "the hospital 'holds itself out' to the public as a provider of care."[ ] One court has explained that "[i]n order to prove this element, it is not necessary to show an express representation by the hospital. . . . Instead, a hospital is generally deemed to have held itself out as the provider of care, unless it gave the patient contrary notice."[ ]. The "contrary notice" referred to by the *Mejia* court generally manifests itself in the form of a disclaimer. As one court has acknowledged, "[a] hospital generally will be able to avoid liability by providing *meaningful written notice* to the patient, acknowledged at the time of admission."[ ]. It has been said that "[l]iability under apparent agency . . . will not attach against a hospital where the patient knows, or reasonably should have known, that the treating physician was an independent contractor."[ ] Thus, a hospital's failure to provide a meaningful written notice may constitute "failing to take an action" and thereby allowing a reasonable person to believe that a particular doctor is an agent of the hospital. Conversely, absent other overt acts by the hospital indicating an employer/employee relationship, an unambiguous disclaimer by a hospital explaining the independent contractor status of physicians will generally suffice to immunize the hospital from being vicariously liable for physician conduct.[14]

Turning to the cases before us, the circuit courts in both cases relied on the disclaimers signed by Ms. Pritt & Ms. Burless in granting summary judgment in favor of WVUH. In addition, the circuit court considering Ms. Pritt's case summarily concluded that WVUH had not "held the physicians out to be its employees." We disagree with these conclusions.

The disclaimer that WVUH required both Ms. Pritt and Ms. Burless to sign stated: "I understand that the faculty physicians and resident physicians who provide treatment in the hospital are not employees of the hospital." WVUH contends that this "disclaimer" was sufficient to une-

[14] Of course, "we do not hold that the existence of an [unambiguous] independent contractor disclaimer . . . is always dispositive on the issue [.]" [ ] A plaintiff may still be able to prove that, under the totality of the circumstances, an unambiguous disclaimer was insufficient to inform him or her of the employment status of a hospital's physicians.

quivocally inform Ms. Pritt and Ms. Burless that the physicians treating them were not employees of the hospital. We disagree.

We do not find the disclaimer language used by WVUH, which indicated that "faculty physicians and resident physicians who provide treatment in the hospital" are independent contractors, was sufficient to support a grant of summary judgment in their favor. The WVUH disclaimer provision presupposes that all patients can distinguish between "faculty physicians," "resident physicians" and any other type of physician having privileges at the hospital. In other words, for this disclaimer to be meaningful, a patient would literally have to inquire into the employment status of everyone treating him or her. Obviously, "[i]t would be absurd to require . . . a patient . . . to inquire of each person who treated him whether he is an employee of the hospital or an independent contractor."

Consequently, it was improper for the circuit court to grant summary judgment in favor of WVUH. Ms. Burless and Ms. Pritt have established a genuine question of material fact as to whether WVUH has either committed an act that would cause a reasonable person to believe that the physician in question was an agent of the hospital, or, by failing to take an action, created a circumstance that would allow a reasonable person to hold such a belief.

3. **Reliance.** The reliance prong of the apparent agency test is a subjective molehill. "Reliance . . . is established when the plaintiff 'looks to' the hospital for services, rather than to an individual physician."[ ] It is "sometimes characterized as an inquiry as to whether 'the plaintiff acted in reliance upon the conduct of the hospital or its agent, consistent with ordinary care and prudence.'[ ] This factor 'simply focuses on the "patient's belief that the hospital or its employees were rendering health care." ' " "[ ] However, this portion of the test also requires consideration of the 'reasonableness of the patient's [subjective] belief that the hospital or its employees were rendering health care.' " "This . . . determination is made by considering the totality of the circumstances, including . . . any special knowledge the patient[/plaintiff] may have about the hospital's arrangements with its physicians."[ ]

Mrs. Pritt and Ms. Burless provided evidence indicating that they believed that the physicians treating them were employees of WVUH.

In the deposition testimony of Ms. Burless she stated her belief that the people treating her at the hospital were employees, as follows: "Q. Did anyone do anything to make you believe that they were employees of WVU Hospital? A. They were all wearing their coats and name tags and in the building, so, you know, you know they're—they work there, they're employees." In the affidavit submitted by Ms. Pritt in opposition to WVUH's motion for summary judgment, the following was stated:

2. At the West Virginia University Hospitals, I was assigned doctors who treated me and consulted me through my prenatal care, surgery and delivery of my son Adam.

3. Throughout all of my treatment and consultations, I believed that the doctors and nurses who treated me and spoke to me were employees of the West Virginia University Hospitals.

Ms. Burless and Ms. Pritt have also established a genuine question of material fact on the issue of their reliance on the apparent agency relationship between WVUH and their treating physicians. Consequently, on the issue of apparent agency, it is clear that summary judgment should not have been granted in favor of WVUH.

NOTES AND QUESTIONS

1. *The Medical Staff.* The medical staff is a self–governing body charged with overseeing the quality of care, treatment, and services delivered by practitioners who are credentialed and privileged through the medical staff process. See Chapter 9. The medical staff must credential and privilege all licensed independent practitioners. The self–governing organized medical staff creates and maintains a set of bylaws that defines its role within the context of a hospital setting and clearly delineates its responsibilities in the oversight of care, treatment, and services. It elects its own officers, and appoints its own committees.

The organized medical staff is intimately involved in carrying out, and in providing leadership in, all patient care functions conducted by practitioners privileged through the medical staff process. The medical staff oversees the quality of patient care, treatment, and services provided by practitioners privileged through the medical staff process. It recommends practitioners for privileges to perform medical histories and physical examinations. The hospital governing body approves such privileges.

The organized medical staff is not simply another administrative component of the hospital, and it has typically been subject to only limited authority of the governing board of the hospital. While the hospital board must approve the staff's bylaws and can approve or disapprove particular staff actions, it cannot usually discipline individual physicians directly or appoint administrative officers to exercise direct authority. A hospital's medical staff is therefore a powerful body within the larger organization.

2. *Patient Reliance.* The patient in most cases relies on the reputation of the hospital, not any particular doctor, and for that reason selects that hospital. See e.g., White v. Methodist Hosp. South, 844 S.W.2d 642 (Tenn.App.1992). If the negligence results from emergency room care, most courts have held that a patient may justifiably rely on the physician as an agent unless the hospital explicitly disclaims an agency relationship. Ballard v. Advocate Health and Hospitals Corporations, 1999 WL 498702 (N.D.Ill. 1999). A promotional campaign or advertising can create such reliance. See

Clark v. Southview Hospital & Family Health Center, 68 Ohio St.3d 435, 628 N.E.2d 46 (1994) (promotional and marketing campaign stressed the emergency departments); Gragg v. Calandra, 297 Ill.App.3d 639, 231 Ill.Dec. 711, 696 N.E.2d 1282 (1998) (unless patient is put on notice of the independent status of the professionals in a hospital, he or she will reasonably assume they are employees).

3. What can a hospital do to avoid liability under the *Burless* court's analysis? Will explicit notice to the plaintiff at the time of admission be sufficient? How about a large sign in the admitting area of the hospital? A brochure handed to each patient? If the hospital advertises aggressively, will the reliance created by such advertising overwhelm all of the hospital's targeted attempts to inform patients about the intricacies of the physicians' employment relationships with the hospital?

To avoid liability, a hospital can try to avoid patient misunderstanding by its billing procedures, the letterhead used, signs, and other clues of the true nature of the relationship of the physician to the institution. Cantrell v. Northeast Georgia Medical Center, 235 Ga.App. 365, 508 S.E.2d 716 (1998) (sign over registration desk stated that the physicians in the emergency room were independent contracts; consent form repeated this). The court is likely however to cut through these devices if the reliance on reputation by the patient is strong enough.

Explicit language in a patient consent form is the clearest way to put a patient on notice of the physician's legal status. A few states allow a clear statement in a consent form—that physicians in the hospital are independent contractors and not agents—to put a patient on notice. See Pendley v. Southern Regional Health System, Inc., 307 Ga.App. 82, 704 S.E.2d 198 (2010) (hospital had bolded the independent contractor disclaimers in both the General Consent for Treatment and the Routine Consent, and the Routine Consent also cautioned readers in bold: **"Important: Do not sign this form without reading and understanding its contents."** The court also noted that the defendant physician had made no representations to the plaintiff as to his employment status.)

4. *Nondelegable Duty Analysis.* Emergency room physicians are most often the source of vicarious liability claims against the contracting hospitals. In spite of various forms of notice as to the independent contractor status of emergency room physicians, many state courts have refused to allow the hospital to escape liability. The reasons typically given are based on the nature of patient reliance when entering a hospital for emergency care. As the court stated in Simmons v. Tuomey Regional Medical Center, 341 S.C. 32, 533 S.E.2d 312 (South Carolina, 2000), "[t]he point often made in the cases and commentary, either implicitly or explicitly, is that expecting a patient in an emergency situation to debate or comprehend the meaning and extent of any representations by the hospital—which likely would be based on an opinion gradually formed over the years and not on any single representation—imposes an unfair and improper burden on the patient. Consequently, we believe the better solution, grounded primarily in public policy reasons we ex-

plain below, is to impose a nondelegable duty on hospitals." (holding that a hospital owes a common law nondelegable duty to render competent service to its emergency room patients).

The nondelegable duty doctrine is similar to the "inherent function" test used by some courts to describe emergency room, radiology, or anesthesia services. These courts refuse to allow the independent contractor defense in such cases. See, e.g., Dragotta v. Southampton Hosp., 39 A.D.3d 697, 833 N.Y.S.2d 638 (N.Y.A.D. 2 Dept.,2007).

5. Other courts reach the same result by characterizing the duty of a hospital that uses physician independent contractors as a contractual or fiduciary duty to patients. See for example Pope v. Winter Park Healthcare Group, Ltd., 939 So.2d 185 (D.C. App.Florida, Fifth District, 2006). The plaintiff gave birth to an infant suffering from fetal–maternal hemorrhage, and compression of the umbilical vein. Resuscitation was delayed, and permanent brain damage resulted; the plaintiffs contended that the on–call neonatologist was negligent in failing to be present, in failing to communicate, in failing to order necessary tests, and in failing to order the necessary means of resuscitation.

The court concluded that " * * *if a hospital does undertake by contract to provide medical care, it cannot throw off that obligation simply by hiring an independent contractor. The use by hospitals of independent–contractor physicians eliminates "respondeat superior" liability, but it will not relieve the hospital of any contractual duties it has undertaken. A hospital can, by contract, undertake different duties or greater duties than those imposed by the common law of tort." See also Barragan v. Providence Memorial Hospital, 2000 WL 1731286 (Tex.App.–El Paso) (Nov. 22, 2000).

What does this mean for hospital liability? If the test is that a hospital is obligated by contract simply by agreeing to care for a patient, is anything left of the defense?

PROBLEM: CREATING A SHIELD

You represent Bowsman Hospital, a small rural hospital in Iowa. The hospital has until now relied on Dr. Headley for radiology services. It provides him with space, equipment, and personnel for the radiology department, sends and collects bills on his behalf, and provides him with an office. It also pays him $300 a day in exchange for which Dr. Headley agrees to be at the hospital one day a week. Bowsman is one of several small hospitals in this part of Iowa that use Dr. Headley's services. Bowsman advertises in the local papers of several nearby communities. Its advertisements stress its ability to handle trauma injuries, common in farming areas. The ads say in part:

"Bowsman treats patient problems with big league medical talent. Our physicians and nurses have been trained for the special demands of farming accidents and injuries."

What advice can you give as to methods of shielding Bowsman from liability for the negligent acts of Dr. Headley? Must it insist that Dr. Headley operate his own outside laboratory? Or furnish his own equipment? Pay his own bills? Should the hospital hire its own radiologist?

The Chief Executive Officer asks you to develop guidelines to protect the hospital from liability for medical errors of the radiologist. Your research has uncovered the following cases.

Estates of Milliron v. Francke, 243 Mont. 200, 793 P.2d 824 (1990). The plaintiff was referred to the hospital and the radiologist who practiced there by his family physician, for evaluation of prostatis and uropathy. The radiologist used an intravenous pyelogram, to which the plaintiff had a reaction. The patient suffered brain damage. The hospital provided space, equipment and personnel for the radiology department, sent and collected bills on his behalf, and provided him with an office. The court granted summary judgment for the defendant on the ostensible agency claim. The court noted that this was a small hospital in a rural area, and the radiologist rotated between this and several other small hospitals. This was an ordinary practice in smaller communities in Montana. The court concluded that "[p]roviding these traveling physicians with offices at the hospital simply helps ensure that these smaller and more remote communities will be provided with adequate medical care and is not a sufficient factual basis to establish an agency relationship." Id. at 827.

III. HOSPITAL LIABILITY

Patients may suffer injury in hospitals in many ways: they may fall out of bed, they may slip on the way to the bathroom, they may be given the wrong drug or the wrong dosage in their IV, the MRI machine may not be working, etc.. If expert testimony is not needed, that is, if an ordinary person could evaluate the failure, then the case may not be considered malpractice but rather ordinary negligence. Negligence may have a different statute of limitations and may not be subject to restrictive legislative restrictions on malpractice recovery such as certificates of merit, caps on noneconomic loss, or other restrictions.

Most hospital cases that involve treatment or diagnosis will require expert testimony of some sort. If the case involves the standard of care applicable to a hospital rather than one of the medical staff physicians, then the courts will look at the standard applicable to hospitals of that type, and inquire into the professional judgment of providers or decisions of a hospital governing body or the administration of the hospital. Such breaches of duty are considered malpractice, are subject to the rules pertaining to such cases, and require expert testimony.

A. NEGLIGENCE

WASHINGTON v. WASHINGTON HOSPITAL CENTER

District of Columbia Court of Appeals, 1990.
579 A.2d 177.

[The Court considered two issues: whether the testimony of the plaintiff's expert was sufficient to create a issue for the jury; and whether the hospital's failure to request a finding of liability of the settling defendants or to file a cross claim for contribution against any of the defendants defeated the hospital's claim for a pro rata reduction in the jury verdict. The discussion of the first issue follows.]

FARRELL, ASSOCIATE JUDGE:

This appeal and cross–appeal arise from a jury verdict in a medical malpractice action against the Washington Hospital Center (WHC or the hospital) in favor of LaVerne Alice Thompson, a woman who suffered permanent catastrophic brain injury from oxygen deprivation in the course of general anesthesia for elective surgery * * *

* * *

I. The Facts

On the morning of November 7, 1987, LaVerne Alice Thompson, a healthy 36–year–old woman, underwent elective surgery at the Washington Hospital Center for an abortion and tubal ligation, procedures requiring general anesthesia. At about 10:45 a.m., nurse–anesthetist Elizabeth Adland, under the supervision of Dr. Sheryl Walker, the physician anesthesiologist, inserted an endotracheal tube into Ms. Thompson's throat for the purpose of conveying oxygen to, and removing carbon dioxide from, the anesthetized patient. The tube, properly inserted, goes into the patient's trachea just above the lungs. Plaintiffs alleged that instead Nurse Adland inserted the tube into Thompson's esophagus, above the stomach. After inserting the tube, Nurse Adland "ventilated" or pumped air into the patient while Dr. Walker, by observing physical reactions—including watching the rise and fall of the patient's chest and listening for breath sounds equally on the patient's right and left sides—sought to determine if the tube had been properly inserted.

At about 10:50 a.m., while the surgery was underway, surgeon Nathan Bobrow noticed that Thompson's blood was abnormally dark, which indicated that her tissues were not receiving sufficient oxygen, and reported the condition to Nurse Adland, who checked Thompson's vital signs and found them stable. As Dr. Bobrow began the tubal ligation part of the operation, Thompson's heart rate dropped. She suffered a cardiac arrest and was resuscitated, but eventually the lack of oxygen caused catastrophic brain injuries. Plaintiffs' expert testified that Ms. Thompson remains in a persistent vegetative state and is totally incapacitated; her cardiac, respiratory and digestive functions are normal and she is not "brain dead," but, according to the expert, she is "essentially awake but unaware" of her surroundings. Her condition is unlikely to improve, though she is expected to live from ten to twenty years.

* * *

The plaintiffs alleged that Adland and Walker had placed the tube in Thompson's esophagus rather than her trachea, and that they and Dr. Bobrow had failed to detect the improper intubation in time to prevent the oxygen deprivation that caused Thompson's catastrophic brain injury. WHC, they alleged, was negligent in failing to provide the anesthesiologists with a device known variously as a capnograph or end–tidal carbon dioxide monitor which allows early detection of insufficient oxygen in time to prevent brain injury.

* * *

II. Washington Hospital Center's Claims on Cross–Appeal

A. Standard of Care

On its cross–appeal, WHC first asserts that the plaintiffs failed to carry their burden of establishing the standard of care and that the trial court therefore erred in refusing to grant its motion for judgment notwithstanding the verdict.

* * *

In a negligence action predicated on medical malpractice, the plaintiff must carry a tripartite burden, and establish: (1) the applicable standard of care; (2) a deviation from that standard by the defendant; and (3) a causal relationship between that deviation and the plaintiff's injury. [ ] * * *

Generally, the "standard of care" is "the course of action that a reasonably prudent [professional] with the defendant's specialty would have taken under the same or similar circumstances." [ ] With respect to institutions such as hospitals, this court has rejected the "locality" rule, which refers to the standard of conduct expected of other similarly situated members of the profession in the same locality or community, [ ] in favor of a national standard. [ ] Thus, the question for decision is whether the evidence as a whole, and reasonable inferences therefrom, would allow a reasonable juror to find that a reasonably prudent tertiary care hospital,[3] at the time of Ms. Thompson's injury in November 1987, and according to national standards, would have supplied a carbon dioxide monitor to a patient undergoing general anesthesia for elective surgery.

[3] Plaintiffs' expert defined a tertiary care hospital as "a hospital which has the facilities to conduct clinical care management of patients in nearly all aspects of medicine and surgery."

WHC argues that the plaintiffs' expert, Dr. Stephen Steen, failed to demonstrate an adequate factual basis for his opinion that WHC should have made available a carbon dioxide monitor. The purpose of expert opinion testimony is to avoid jury findings based on mere speculation or conjecture. [ ] The sufficiency of the foundation for those opinions should be measured with this purpose in mind. * * *

* * *

* * * [WHC] asserts that * * * Steen gave no testimony on the number of hospitals having end–tidal carbon dioxide monitors in place in 1987, and that he never referred to any written standards or authorities as the basis of his opinion. We conclude that Steen's opinion * * * was sufficient to create an issue for the jury.

Dr. Steen testified that by 1985, the carbon dioxide monitors were available in his hospital (Los Angeles County—University of Southern California Medical Center (USC)), and "in many other hospitals." In response to a question whether, by 1986, "standards of care" required carbon dioxide monitors in operating rooms, he replied, "I would think that by that time, they would be [required]." As plaintiffs concede, this opinion was based in part on his own personal experience at USC, which * * * cannot itself provide an adequate foundation for an expert opinion on a national standard of care. But Steen also drew support from "what I've read where [the monitors were] available in other hospitals." He referred to two such publications: The American Association of Anesthesiology (AAA) Standards for Basic Intra–Operative Monitoring, approved by the AAA House of Delegates on October 21, 1986, which "encouraged" the use of monitors, and an article entitled *Standards for Patient Monitoring During Anesthesia at Harvard Medical School,* published in August 1986 in the Journal of American Medical Association, which stated that as of July 1985 the monitors were in use at Harvard, and that "monitoring end–tidal carbon dioxide is an emerging standard and is strongly preferred."

WHC makes much of Steen's concession on cross–examination that the AAA Standards were recommendations, strongly encouraged but not mandatory, and that the Harvard publication spoke of an "emerging" standard. In its brief WHC asserts, without citation, that "[p]alpable indicia of widespread *mandated* practices are necessary to establish a standard of care" (emphasis added), and that at most the evidence spoke of "recommended" or "encouraged" practices, and "emerging" or "developing" standards as of 1986–87. A standard of due care, however, necessarily embodies what a *reasonably prudent* hospital would do, [ ] and hence care and foresight exceeding the minimum required by law or mandatory professional regulation may be necessary to meet that standard. It certainly cannot be said that the 1986 recommendations of a professional association (which had no power to issue or enforce mandatory requirements), or an article speaking of an "emerging" standard in 1986, have no bearing on an expert opinion as to what the standard of patient monitoring equipment was fully one year later when Ms. Thompson's surgery took place.

Nevertheless, we need not decide whether Dr. Steen's testimony was sufficiently grounded in fact or adequate data to establish the standard of care. The record contains other evidence from which, in combination with Dr. Steen's testimony, a reasonable juror could fairly conclude that monitors were required of prudent hospitals similar to WHC in late 1987. The evidence showed that at least four other teaching hospitals in the United States used the monitors by that time. In addition to Dr. Steen's testimony that USC supplied them and the article reflecting that Harvard University had them, plaintiffs introduced into evidence an article entitled *Anesthesia at Penn,* from a 1986 alumni newsletter of the Department of Anesthesia at the University of Pennsylvania, indicating that the monitors were then in use at that institution's hospital, and that they allowed "instant recognition of esophageal intubation and other airway problems. * * * " Moreover, WHC's expert anesthesiologist, Dr. John Tinker of the University of Iowa, testified that his hospital had installed carbon dioxide monitors in every operating room by early 1986, and that "by 1987, it is certainly true that many hospitals were in the process of converting" to carbon dioxide monitors.[5]

Perhaps most probative was the testimony of WHC's own Chairman of the Department of Anesthesiology, Dr. Dermot A. Murray, and documentary evidence associated with his procurement request for carbon dioxide monitors. In December 1986 or January 1987, Dr. Murray submitted a requisition form to the hospital for end–tidal carbon dioxide units to monitor the administration of anesthesia in each of the hospital's operating rooms, stating that if the monitors were not provided, the hospital would "fail to meet the national standard of care." The monitors were to be "fully operational" in July of 1987.[6] Attempting to meet this evidence, WHC points out that at trial

---

[5] In its reply brief, WHC argues that

> the fact that four teaching hospitals used CO_2 monitors during the relevant time period is almost irrelevant. Institutions with significantly enhanced financial resources and/or government grants which accelerate their testing and implementation of new and improved technologies would naturally have available to them items which, inherently, were not yet required for the general populace of hospitals.

In fact, Dr. Steen, in voir dire examination on his qualification as an expert on the standard required of hospitals in WHC's position in regard to equipment, testified that his review of WHC's President's Report for 1986–87 led him to conclude that WHC was a teaching hospital. Counsel for the hospital could have identified and probed fully before the jury any differences between WHC and the hospitals relied on to establish the standard of care. To the extent the record was not so developed, the jury could credit Steen's testimony that WHC was required to adhere to the standard applicable to teaching hospitals.

[6] As supporting documentation for the requisition, Dr. Murray attached a copy of the Journal of the American Medical Association article on standards at Harvard University. The requisitions, with attachments, were exhibits admitted in evidence.

> Dr. Murray was *never asked to opine,* with a reasonable degree of medical certainty, that the applicable standard of care at the relevant time *required* the presence of CO_2 monitors. Indeed, his testimony was directly to the contrary. Moreover, the procurement process which he had initiated envisioned obtaining the equipment * * * over time, not even beginning until fiscal year 1988, a period ending June 30, 1988. [Emphasis by WHC.]

Dr. Murray opined that in November 1987 there was *no* standard of care relating to monitoring equipment. The jury heard this testimony and Dr. Murray's explanation of the procurement process, but apparently did not credit it, perhaps because the requisition form itself indicated that the equipment ordered was to be operational in July 1987, four months before Ms. Thompson's surgery, and not at some unspecified time in fiscal year 1988 as Dr. Murray testified at trial.

On the evidence recited above, a reasonable juror could find that the standard of care required WHC to supply monitors as of November 1987. The trial judge therefore did not err in denying the motion for judgment notwithstanding the verdict.

NOTES AND QUESTIONS

1. Does the plaintiff present sufficient evidence that the carbon dioxide monitor is now standard equipment for tertiary care hospitals? The court seems to say that expert testimony is not critical, that the evidence of use by other institutions is something a lay juror could evaluate even if expert testimony is deficient?

2. A companion device to the carbon dioxide monitor is the blood–monitoring pulse oximeter, which has become a mandatory device in hospital operating rooms. In 1984 no hospital had them; by 1990 all hospitals used oximeters in their operating rooms. The device beeps when a patient's blood oxygen drops due to breathing problems or overuse of anesthesia. That warning can give a vital three or four minute warning to physicians, allowing them to correct the problem before the patient suffers brain damage. These devices have so improved patient safety that malpractice insurers have lowered premiums for anesthesiologists. The Joint Commission requires hospitals to develop protocols for anesthesia care that mandate pulse oximetry equipment for measuring oxygen saturation. See Revisions to Anesthesia Care Standards Comprehensive Accreditation Manual for Hospitals Effective January 1, 2001 (Standards and Intents for Sedation and Anesthesia Care).

3. Joint Commission standards often provide the basis for jury instructions in hospital negligence cases. See for example Tavares v. Evergreen Hospital Medical Center, 2010 WL 1541475 (Wash.App.Div.1, Unpublished, 2010). The plaintiff had sought prenatal care, and was a high risk pregnancy, having had an emergency cesarean section with her first child. The couple debated the risks of a vaginal birth after cesarean delivery (VBAC) or another cesarean section. They wanted to try a VBAC, if possible, despite contrary

medical advice. The plaintiff began to experience contractions, and went to the hospital. She was put on a fetal monitor, decelerations were noted, and the baby was delivered by emergency cesarean section. The baby had significant brain damage including cerebral palsy. The parents sued for medical and corporate negligence. Claims against the doctors were settled, and the jury found Evergreen liable to the plaintiff.

The jury instructions were at issue. Instruction 14 was taken from a Joint Commission standard: "The hospital is required to provide an adequate number of staff members whose qualifications are consistent with job responsibilities." The court held, following *Pedroza v. Bryant,* [ ] "that because hospitals are members of national organizations and subject to accreditation, the JCAHO standards are particularly relevant to defining the proper standard of care."

4. A health care institution, whether hospital, nursing home, or clinic, is liable for negligence in maintaining its facilities; providing and maintaining medical equipment; hiring, supervising and retaining nurses and other staff; and failing to have in place procedures to protect patients. Basic negligence principles govern hospital liability for injuries caused by other sources than negligent acts of the medical staff. As *Washington* holds, hospitals are generally held to a national standard of care for hospitals in their treatment category. Reed v. Granbury Hospital Corporation, 117 S.W.3d 404 (2003). They must provide a safe environment for diagnosis, treatment, and recovery of patients. Bellamy v. Appellate Department, 50 Cal.App.4th 797, 57 Cal.Rptr.2d 894 (5 Dist.1996).

a. Hospitals must have minimum facility and support systems to treat the range of problems and side effects that accompany procedures they offer. In Hernandez v. Smith, 552 F.2d 142 (5th Cir.1977), for example, an obstetrical clinic that lacked surgical facilities for cesarean sections was found liable for " * * * the failure to provide proper and safe instrumentalities for the treatment of ailments it undertakes to treat * * *."

b. Staffing must be adequate. Staff shortages can be negligence. See Merritt v. Karcioglu, 668 So.2d 469 (La.App. 4th Cir.1996) (hospital ward understaffed in having only three critical care nurses for six patients). If, however, existing staff can be juggled to cover a difficult patient, short staffing is no defense. See Horton v. Niagara Falls Memorial Medical Center, 51 A.D.2d 152, 380 N.Y.S.2d 116 (1976).

c. Equipment must be adequate for the services offered, although it need not be the state of the art. See Emory University v. Porter, 103 Ga.App. 752, 120 S.E.2d 668, 670 (1961); Lauro v. Travelers Ins. Co., 261 So.2d 261 (La.App.1972). If a device such as an expensive CT scanner has come into common use, however, a smaller and less affluent hospital can argue that it should be judged by the standards of similar hospitals with similar resources. This variable standard, reflecting resource differences between hospitals, would then protect a hospital in a situation where its budget does not allow purchase of some expensive devices. If an institution lacks a piece of equipment that has come to be recognized as essential, particularly for diagnosis, it may have a duty to transfer the patient to an institution that has the equipment. In Blake v. D.C. General Hospital (discussed in Maxwell Mehlman, Rationing Expensive Lifesaving Medical Treatments, 1985 Wisc.L.Rev. 239) the trial court allowed a case to go to the jury where the plaintiff's estate claimed that she died because of the hospital's lack of a CT scanner to diagnose her condition. The court found a duty to transfer in such circumstances.

d. A hospital and its contracting physicians may be liable for damages caused by inadequate or defective systems they develop and implement, particularly where emergency care is involved. On–call systems in smaller hospitals are a recurring issue in the caselaw. Delays in contacting physicians may be negligent, without the need for expert testimony. In Partin v. North Mississippi Medical Center, Inc., 929 So.2d 924 (Miss.Ct.App.2005), the plaintiff became septic while in the hospital recovering from surgery; the nurses failed to notify the on–call physician for more than twenty hours, and the patient died.

5. An institution's own internal rules and safety regulations for medical procedures must be followed, and a failure to follow them may be offered as evidence of a breach of a standard of care for the trier of fact to consider. They are material and relevant on the issue of quality of care, but are usually not sufficient by themselves to establish the degree of care owed. Jackson v. Oklahoma Memorial Hospital, 909 P.2d 765 (Okl.1995). In Williams v. St. Claire Medical Center, 657 S.W.2d 590 (Ky.App.1983), the court held that a hospital owes a duty to all patients, including the private patients of staff physicians, to enforce its published rules and regulations pertaining to patient care. The nurse anesthetist was required under hospital rules to work under the direct supervision of a certified registered nurse anesthetist, and he was alone when he administered the anesthesia to the plaintiff. Because of problems with the administration, the plaintiff went into a coma. The court stated:

> * * * [W]hile the patient must accept all the rules and regulations of the hospital, he should be able to expect that the hospital will follow its rules established for his care. Whether a patient enters a hospital through the emergency room or is admitted as a private patient by a staff physician, the patient is entering the hospital for only one reason * * * "Indeed, the sick leave their homes and enter hospitals because of the superior treatment there promised them."

See also Adams v. Family Planning Associates Medical Group, Inc., 315 Ill.App.3d 533, 248 Ill.Dec. 91, 733 N.E.2d 766 (2000) (internal policies and procedures of family planning clinic admissible as evidence of standard of care).

B. DUTIES TO TREAT PATIENTS

The relationship of the medical staff to the hospital insulates the hospital from liability, while giving physicians substantial autonomy in their treating decisions. What happens when the patient's insurance or other resources are exhausted but the staff physician believes that the standard of care requires continued hospitalization? Must the hospital accede to the doctor's request?

MUSE V. CHARTER HOSPITAL OF WINSTON–SALEM, INC.

Court of Appeals of North Carolina, 1995.
117 N.C.App. 468, 452 S.E.2d 589.

LEWIS, JUDGE.

This appeal arises from a judgment in favor of plaintiffs in an action for the wrongful death of Delbert Joseph Muse, III (hereinafter "Joe"). Joe was the son of Delbert Joseph Muse, Jr. (hereinafter "Mr. Muse") and Jane K. Muse (hereinafter "Mrs. Muse"), plaintiffs. The jury found that defendant Charter Hospital of Winston–Salem, Inc. (hereinafter "Charter Hospital" or "the hospital") was negligent in that, inter alia, it had a policy or practice which required physicians to discharge patients when their insurance expired and that this policy interfered with the exercise of the medical judgment of Joe's treating physician, Dr. L. Jarrett Barnhill, Jr. The jury awarded plaintiffs compensatory damages of approximately $1,000,000. The jury found that Mr. and Mrs. Muse were contributorily negligent, but that Charter Hospital's conduct was willful or wanton, and awarded punitive damages of $2,000,000 against Charter Hospital. Further, the jury found that Charter Hospital was an instrumentality of defendant Charter Medical Corporation (hereinafter "Charter Medical") and awarded punitive damages of $4,000,000 against Charter Medical.

The facts on which this case arose may be summarized as follows. On 12 June 1986, Joe, who was sixteen years old at the time, was admitted to Charter Hospital for treatment related to his depression and suicidal thoughts. Joe's treatment team consisted of Dr. Barnhill, as treating physician, Fernando Garzon, as nursing therapist, and Betsey Willard, as social worker. During his hospitalization, Joe experienced auditory hallucinations, suicidal and homicidal thoughts, and major depression. Joe's insurance coverage was set to expire on 12 July 1986. As that date neared, Dr. Barnhill decided that a blood test was needed to determine the proper dosage of a drug he was administering to Joe. The blood test was scheduled for 13 July, the day after Joe's insurance was to expire. Dr. Barnhill requested that the hospital administrator allow Joe to stay at Charter Hospital two more days, until 14 July, with Mr. and Mrs. Muse signing a promissory note to pay for the two extra days. The test results did not come back from the lab until 15 July. Nevertheless, Joe was discharged on 14 July and was referred by Dr. Barnhill to the Guilford County Area Mental Health, Mental Retardation and Substance Abuse Authority (hereinafter "Mental Health Authority") for outpatient treatment. Plaintiffs' evidence tended to show that Joe's condition upon discharge was worse than when he entered the hospital. Defendants' evidence, however, tended to show that while his prognosis remained guarded, Joe's condition at discharge was improved. Upon his discharge, Joe went on a one–week family vacation. On 22 July he began outpatient treatment at the Mental Health Authority, where he was seen by Dr. David Slonaker, a clinical psychologist. Two days later, Joe again met with Dr. Slonaker. Joe failed to show up at his 30 July appointment, and the next day he took a fatal overdose of Desipramine, one of his prescribed drugs.

On appeal, defendants present numerous assignments of error. We find merit in one of defendants' arguments.

II.

Defendants next argue that the trial court submitted the case to the jury on an erroneous theory of hospital liability that does not exist under the law of North Carolina. As to the theory in question, the trial court instructed: "[A] hospital is under a duty not to have policies or practices which operate in a way that interferes with the ability of a physician to exercise his medical judgment. A violation of this duty would be negligence." The jury found that there existed "a policy or practice which required physicians to discharge patients when their insurance benefits expire and which interfered with the exercise of Dr. Barnhill's medical judgment." Defendants contend that this theory of liability does not fall within any theories previously accepted by our courts.

* * *

Our Supreme Court has recognized that hospitals in this state owe a duty of care to their patients. Id.In Burns v. Forsyth County Hospital Authority, Inc. [ ] this Court held that a hospital has a duty to the patient to obey the instructions of a doctor, absent the instructions being obviously negligent or dangerous. Another recognized duty is the duty to make a reasonable effort to monitor and oversee the treatment prescribed and administered by doctors practicing at the hospital. [ ] In light of these holdings, it seems axiomatic that the hospital has the duty not to institute policies or practices which interfere with the doctor's medical judgment. We hold that pursuant to the reasonable person standard, Charter Hospital had a duty not to institute a policy or practice which required that patients be discharged when their insurance expired and which interfered with the medical judgment of Dr. Barnhill.

III.

Defendants next argue that even if the theory of negligence submitted to the jury was proper, the jury's finding that Charter Hospital had such a practice was not supported by sufficient evidence. * * * We conclude that in the case at hand, the evidence was sufficient to go to the jury.

Plaintiffs' evidence included the testimony of Charter Hospital employees and outside experts. Fernando Garzon, Joe's nursing therapist at Charter Hospital, testified that the hospital had a policy of discharging patients when their insurance expired. Specifically, when the issue of insurance came up in treatment team meetings, plans were made to discharge the patient. When Dr. Barnhill and the other psychiatrists and therapists spoke of insurance, they seemed to lack autonomy. For example, Garzon testified, they would state, "So and so is to be discharged. We must do this." Finally, Garzon testified that when he returned from a vacation, and Joe was no longer at the hospital, he asked several employees why Joe had been discharged and they all responded that he was discharged because his insurance had expired. Jane Sims, a former staff member at the hospital, testified that several employees expressed alarm about Joe's impending discharge, and that a therapist explained that Joe could no longer stay at the hospital because his insurance had expired. Sims also testified that Dr. Barnhill had misgivings about discharging Joe, and that Dr. Barnhill's frustration was apparent to everyone. One of plaintiffs' experts testified that based on a study regarding the length of patient stays at Charter Hospital, it was his opinion that patients were discharged based on insurance, regardless of their medical condition. Other experts testified that based on Joe's serious condition on the date of discharge, the expiration of insurance coverage must have caused Dr. Barnhill to discharge Joe. The experts further testified as to the relevant standard of care, and concluded that Charter Hospital's practices were below the standard of care and caused Joe's death. We hold that this evidence was sufficient to go to the jury.

Defendants further argue that the evidence was insufficient to support the jury's finding that Charter Hospital engaged in conduct that was willful or wanton. An act is willful when it is done purposely and deliberately in violation of the law, or when it is done knowingly and of set purpose, or when the mere will has free play, without yielding to reason. [ ] * * * We conclude that the jury could have reasonably found from the above–stated evidence that Charter Hospital acted knowingly and of set purpose, and with reckless indifference to the rights of others. Therefore, we hold that the finding of willful or wanton conduct on the part of Charter Hospital was supported by sufficient evidence.

* * *

For the reasons stated, we find no error in the judgment of the trial court, except for that part of the judgment awarding punitive damages, which is reversed and remanded for proceedings consistent with this opinion.

No error in part, reversed in part and remanded.

NOTES AND QUESTIONS

1. Should the *Muse* duty extend to all situations in which the physician and the hospital administration are in conflict? If the physician always prevails, then how does a hospital control its costs and its bad debts? Why does the court treat health care as special in this case? Surely a grocery store does not have to give us free groceries if we are short of cash as the checkout counter, nor does our landlord have to allow us to stay for free if we cannot cover our next month's rent. Is it simply the advantage of hindsight here that impels the court's imposition of such a duty on hospitals?

A provision in many hospital admissions forms states:

> Legal Relationship Between Hospital and Physicians. All physicians and surgeons furnishing services to the patient, including the radiologist, pathologist, anesthesiologist, and the like, are not agents, servants, or employees of the above–named hospital, but are independent contractors, and as such are the agents, servants, or employees of the patient. The patient is under the care and supervision of his attending physician and it is the responsibility of the hospital and its nursing staff to carry out the instructions of such physician.

Could the *Muse* case have been brought as a breach of contract case by the plaintiff as third party beneficiary under the contract? Reconsider *Wickline* and *Murray* in Chapter 5 in this context.

2. Consider the medical staff relationship under the bylaws. It is a shared power arrangement between the hospital and its medical staff, and the hospital has independent duties under Joint Commission accreditation and federal law to supervise quality within its walls. Insurance payment, whether private or governmental, will cover most hospital treatment. What is the hospital obligated to do in such situations? Offer free care? Or is this analogous to the duty of physicians to not abandon their patients? Does this case impose a corporate fiduciary duty on hospitals to treat high risk patients when their money runs out? Is it the equivalent of the EMTALA mandate that requires hospitals to treat all patients in their emergency rooms without regard to their ability to pay or their insurance status?

3. Does such a duty extend as well to managed care organizations, whose very design is premised on mechanisms for containing health care costs? What would happen to the underlying premises of cost control in managed care organizations if the *Muse* doctrine were held to apply?

C. CORPORATE NEGLIGENCE

The stretching of vicarious liability doctrine to sweep in doctors as conduits to hospital liability led inevitably to the imposition of corporate negligence liability on the hospital. Courts had often been willing to hold hospitals liable for institutional failures, such as not using modern technologies (see *Washington*, above), but had not examined the broader range of functions that a hospital engaged in as part of managing the safety of its patients. It wasn't until the *Darling* case was decided in 1965 that hospital liability began to expand to encompass the problem of physician errors and medical system failures, and the hospital's responsibility for such failures. The focus on the functions of a modern hospital corporation moved the law from discussions of ordinary institutional negligence to a broader focus on corporate duties to manage a complex institution safely.

1. The Elements of Corporate Negligence

The next step was to hold the hospital directly liable for the failure of administrators and staff to properly monitor and supervise the delivery of health care within the hospital.

DARLING V. CHARLESTON COMMUNITY MEMORIAL HOSPITAL

Supreme Court of Illinois, 1965.
33 Ill.2d 326, 211 N.E.2d 253.

This action was brought on behalf of Dorrence Darling II, a minor (hereafter plaintiff), by his father and next friend, to recover damages for allegedly negligent medical and hospital treatment which necessitated the amputation of his right leg below the knee. The action was commenced against the Charleston Community Memorial Hospital and Dr. John R. Alexander, but prior to trial the action was dismissed as to Dr. Alexander, pursuant to a covenant not to sue. The jury returned a verdict against the hospital in the sum of $150,000. This amount was reduced by $40,000, the amount of the settlement with the doctor. The judgment in favor of the plaintiff in the sum of $110,000 was affirmed on appeal by the Appellate Court for the Fourth District, which granted a certificate of importance. 50 Ill.App.2d 253, 200 N.E.2d 149.

On November 5, 1960, the plaintiff, who was 18 years old, broke his leg while playing in a college football game. He was taken to the emergency room at the defendant hospital where Dr. Alexander, who was on emergency call that day, treated him. Dr. Alexander, with the assistance of hospital personnel, applied traction and placed the leg in a plaster cast. A heat cradle was applied to dry the cast. Not long after the application of the cast plaintiff was in great pain and his toes, which protruded from the cast, became swollen and dark in color. They eventually became cold and insensitive. On the evening of November 6, Dr. Alexander "notched" the cast around the toes, and on the afternoon of the next day he cut the cast approximately three inches up from the foot. On November 8 he split the sides of the cast with a Stryker saw; in the course of cutting the cast the plaintiff's leg was cut on both sides. Blood and other seepage were observed by the nurses and others, and there was a stench in the room, which one witness said was the worst he had smelled since World War II.

The plaintiff remained in Charleston Hospital until November 19, when he was transferred to Barnes Hospital in St. Louis and placed under the care of Dr. Fred Reynolds, head of orthopedic surgery at Washington University School of Medicine and Barnes Hospital. Dr. Reynolds found that the fractured leg contained a considerable amount of dead tissue which in his opinion resulted from interference with the circulation of blood in the limb caused by swelling or hemorrhaging of the leg against the construction of the cast. Dr. Reynolds performed several operations in a futile attempt to save the leg but ultimately it had to be amputated eight inches below the knee.

The evidence before the jury is set forth at length in the opinion of the Appellate Court and need not be stated in detail here. The plaintiff contends that it established that the defendant was negligent in permitting Dr. Alexander to do orthopedic work of the kind required in this case, and not requiring him to review his operative procedures to bring them up to date; in failing, through its medical staff, to exercise adequate supervision over the case, especially since Dr. Alexander had been placed on emergency duty by the hospital, and in not requiring consultation, particularly after complications had developed. Plaintiff contends also that in a case which developed as this one did, it was the duty of the nurses to watch the protruding toes constantly for changes of color, temperature and movement, and to check circulation every ten to twenty minutes, whereas the proof showed that these things were done only a few times a day. Plaintiff argues that it was the duty of the hospital staff to see that these procedures were followed, and that either the nurses were derelict in failing to report developments in the case to the hospital administrator, he was derelict in bringing them to the attention of the medical staff, or the staff was negligent in failing to take action. Defendant is a licensed and accredited hospital, and the plaintiff contends that the licensing regulations, accreditation standards, and its own bylaws define the hospital's duty, and that an infraction of them imposes liability for the resulting injury.

* * *

The basic dispute, as posed by the parties, centers upon the duty that rested upon the defendant hospital. That dispute involves the effect to be given to evidence concerning the community standard of care and diligence, and also the effect to be given to hospital regulations adopted by the State Department of Public Health under the Hospital Licensing Act [ ], to the Standards for Hospital Accreditation of the American Hospital Association, and to the bylaws of the defendant.

As has been seen, the defendant argues in this court that its duty is to be determined by the care customarily offered by hospitals generally in its community. Strictly speaking, the question is not one of duty, for "* * * in negligence cases, the duty is always the same, to conform to the legal standard of reasonable conduct in the light of the apparent risk. What the defendant must do, or must not do, is a question of the standard of conduct required to satisfy the duty." (Prosser on Torts, 3rd ed. at 331.) * * * Custom is relevant in determining the standard of care because it illustrates what is feasible, it suggests a body of knowledge of which the defendant should be aware, and it warns of the possibility of far–reaching consequences if a higher standard is required. [ ] But custom should never be conclusive.

In the present case the regulations, standards, and bylaws which the plaintiff introduced into evidence, performed much the same function as did evidence of custom. This evidence aided the jury in deciding what was feasible and what the defendant knew or should have known. It did not conclusively determine the standard of care and the jury was not instructed that it did.

* * * [ ] The Standards for Hospital Accreditation, the state licensing regulations and the defendant's bylaws demonstrate that the medical profession and other responsible authorities regard it as both desirable and feasible that a hospital assume certain responsibilities for the care of the patient.

* * * Therefore we need not analyze all of the issues submitted to the jury. Two of them were that the defendant had negligently: "5. Failed to have a sufficient number of trained nurses for bedside care of all patients at all times capable of recognizing the progressive gangrenous condition of the plaintiff's right leg, and of bringing the same to the attention of the hospital administration and to the medical staff so that adequate consultation could have been secured and such conditions rectified; * * * 7. Failed to require consultation with or examination by members of the hospital surgical staff skilled in such treatment; or to review the treatment rendered to the plaintiff and to require consultants to be called in as needed."

We believe that the jury verdict is supportable on either of these grounds. On the basis of the evidence before it the jury could reasonably have concluded that the nurses did not test for circulation in the leg as frequently as necessary, that skilled nurses would have promptly recognized the conditions that signalled a dangerous impairment of circulation in the plaintiff's leg, and would have known that the condition would become irreversible in a matter of hours. At that point it became the nurses' duty to inform the attending physician, and if he failed to act, to advise the hospital authorities so that appropriate action might be taken. As to consultation, there is no dispute that the hospital failed to review Dr. Alexander's work or require a consultation; the only issue is whether its failure to do so was negligence. On the evidence before it the jury could reasonably have found that it was.

[The remainder of the opinion, discussing expert testimony and damages, is omitted.]

NOTES AND QUESTIONS

1. Consider the issues submitted to the jury. It is alleged that both the nurses and the administrators were negligent in not taking steps to curtail Dr. Alexander's handling of the case. How can a nurse "blow the whistle" on a doctor without risking damage to her own career? How can a nurse exercise medical judgment in violation of Medical Practice statutes? See Chapter 2.

Nurses have independent obligations to care for patients. In Brandon HMA, Inc. v. Bradshaw, 809 So.2d 611 (Miss.2001), the plaintiff sued the hospital, alleging that while she was being treated for bacterial pneumonia she was treated negligently by the nursing staff leading to her permanent disability from brain damage. The staff failed to monitor her, report vital information to her doctor, and allowed her condition to deteriorate to a critical state before providing urgently needed care and life support. One nurse failed to take her vital signs on several visits to her room.

Nurses, as *Darling* indicates, have obligations to advocate for patients when care is substandard in a hospital. In Rowe v. Sisters of Pallottine Missionary Society, 211 W.Va. 16, 560 S.E.2d 491 (2001), a 17 year old boy presented to the hospital emergency room after a motorcycle accident. He had severe pain in his left knee and numbness in his foot, and no pulse in his foot. He was discharged and told to make an appointment to see an orthopedist several days later and come back to the hospital if the pain got worse. He got worse that night and was admitted to another hospital. He ended up with substantial impairment of his leg. The court held that the nurses had breached the standard of care by not adequately advocating for his interests when he was discharged with unexplained and unaddressed symptoms.

2. *Darling* disclosed the prevailing attitude of hospital administrators toward affiliated doctors, reflecting the earlier concept of the doctor as independent contractor. The hospital administrator was subjected to a prolonged cross–examination by the plaintiff's attorney exploring his obligations to evaluate doctor training and conduct. The administrator testified that he did nothing to review Dr. Alexander's techniques, ability, or other competence. He stated that " * * * I never made any effort to see that Dr. Alexander, or any other physician admitted to practice more than thirty years ago, read them." Darling v. Charleston Community Memorial Hosp., 50 Ill.App.2d 253, 295, 200 N.E.2d 149, 171 (1964).

How can a hospital administrator devise procedures to trigger an alarm when a physician is incompetent? Must the administrator himself be an M.D.? Can you think of methods that would have avoided the *Darling* tragedy? Consider the ideas developed by Leape in Chapter 1. What systems might you implement to prevent such errors? Consider the discussion of the Joint Commission credentialing triggers discussed in part B *infra*.

3. Some states have adopted corporate negligence for institutional providers. Florida, for example, has incorporated "institutional liability" or "corporate negligence" in its regulation of hospitals. Hospitals and other providers will be liable for injuries caused by inadequacies in the internal programs that are mandated by the statute. West's Fla.Stat.Ann. § 768.60.

It became increasingly clear that hospitals were often responsible for errors, and not only their physicians. One study found that the proportion of errors with interactive or administrative causes in the hospital was as high as 25 percent. *See* Lori B. Andrews et al., *An Alternative Strategy for Studying Adverse Events in Medical Care*, 349 Lancet 309, 312 (1997).

THOMPSON V. NASON HOSP.

Supreme Court of Pennsylvania, 1991.
527 Pa. 330, 591 A.2d 703.

ZAPPALA, JUSTICE.

Allocatur was granted to examine the novel issue of whether a theory of corporate liability with respect to hospitals should be recognized in this Commonwealth. For the reasons set forth below, we adopt today the theory of corporate liability as it relates to hospitals. * * *

* * *

Considering this predicate to our analysis, we now turn to the record which contains the facts underlying this personal injury action. At approximately 7 a.m. on March 16, 1978, Appellee, Linda A. Thompson, was involved in an automobile accident with a school bus. Mrs. Thompson was transported by ambulance from the accident scene to Nason Hospital's emergency room where she was admitted with head and leg injuries. The hospital's emergency room personnel were advised by Appellee, Donald A. Thompson, that his wife was taking the drug Coumadin, that she had a permanent pacemaker, and that she took other heart medications.

Subsequent to Mrs. Thompson's admission to Nason Hospital, Dr. Edward D. Schultz, a general practitioner who enjoyed staff privileges at Nason Hospital, entered the hospital via the emergency room to make his rounds. Although Dr. Schultz was not assigned duty in the emergency room, an on–duty hospital nurse asked him to attend Mrs. Thompson due to a prior physician–patient relationship. Dr. Schultz examined Mrs. Thompson and diagnosed her as suffering from multiple injuries including extensive lacerations over her left eye and the back of her scalp, constricted pupils, enlarged heart with a Grade III micro–systolic murmur, a brain concussion and amnesia. X–rays that were taken revealed fractures of the right tibia and right heel.

Following Dr. Schultz's examination and diagnosis, Dr. Larry Jones, an ophthalmologist, sutured the lacerations over Mrs. Thompson's left eye. It was during that time that Dr. Schultz consulted with Dr. Rao concerning orthopedic repairs. Dr. Rao advised conservative therapy until her critical medical condition improved.

Dr. Schultz knew Mrs. Thompson was suffering from rheumatic heart and mitral valve disease and was on anticoagulant therapy. Because he had no specific training in establishing dosages for such therapy, Dr. Schultz called Dr. Marvin H. Meisner, a cardiologist who was treating Mrs. Thompson with an anticoagulant therapy. Although Dr. Meisner was unavailable, Dr. Schultz did speak with Dr. Meisner's associate Dr. Steven P. Draskoczy.

Mrs. Thompson had remained in the emergency room during this time. Her condition, however, showed no sign of improvement. Due to both the multiple trauma received in the accident and her pre–existing heart disease, Dr. Schultz, as attending physician, admitted her to Nason Hospital's intensive care unit at 11:20 a.m.

The next morning at 8:30 a.m., Dr. Mark Paris, a general surgeon on staff at Nason Hospital, examined Mrs. Thompson. He found that she was unable to move her left foot and toes. It was also noted by Dr. Paris that the patient had a positive Babinski—a neurological sign of an intracerebral problem. Twelve hours later, Dr. Schultz examined Mrs. Thompson and found more bleeding in her eye. He also indicated in the progress notes that the problem with her left leg was that it was neurological.

On March 18, 1978, the third day of her hospitalization, Dr. Larry Jones, the ophthalmologist who treated her in the emergency room, examined her in the intensive care unit. He indicated in the progress notes an "increased hematuria secondary to anticoagulation. Right eye now involved". Dr. Schultz also examined Mrs. Thompson that day and noted the decreased movement of her left leg was neurologic. Dr. Paris's progress note that date approved the withholding of Coumadin and the continued use of Heparin.

The following day, Mrs. Thompson had complete paralysis of the left side. Upon examination by Dr. Schultz he questioned whether she needed to be under the care of a neurologist or needed to be watched there. At 10:30 a.m. that day, Dr. Schultz transferred her to the Hershey Medical Center because of her progressive neurological problem.

Linda Thompson underwent tests at the Hershey Medical Center. The results of the tests revealed that she had a large intracerebral hematoma in the right frontal temporal and parietal lobes of the brain. She was subsequently discharged on April 1, 1978, without regaining the motor function of her left side.

* * * The complaint alleged inter alia that Mrs. Thompson's injuries were the direct and proximate result of the negligence of Nason Hospital acting through its agents, servants and employees in failing to adequately examine and treat her, in failing to follow its rules relative to consultations and in failing to monitor her conditions during treatment. * * *

* * *

The first issue Nason Hospital raised is whether the Superior Court erred in adopting a theory of corporate liability with respect to a hospital. This issue had not heretofore been determined by the Court. Nason Hospital contends that it had no duty to observe, supervise or control the actual treatment of Linda Thompson.

Hospitals in the past enjoyed absolute immunity from tort liability. [ ] The basis of that immunity was the perception that hospitals functioned as charitable organizations. [ ] However, hospitals have evolved into highly sophisticated corporations operating primarily on a fee–for–service basis. The corporate hospital of today has assumed the role of a comprehensive health center with responsibility for arranging and coordinating the total health care of its patients. As a result of this metamorphosis, hospital immunity was eliminated. [ ]

Not surprisingly, the by–product of eliminating hospital immunity has been the filing of malpractice actions against hospitals. Courts have recognized several bases on which hospitals may be subject to liability including respondeat superior, ostensible agency and corporate negligence. [ ]

The development of hospital liability in this Commonwealth mirrored that which occurred in other jurisdictions. * * * We now turn our attention to the theory of corporate liability with respect to the hospital, which was first recognized in this Commonwealth by the court below.

Corporate negligence is a doctrine under which the hospital is liable if it fails to uphold the proper standard of care owed the patient, which is to ensure the patient's safety and well–being while at the hospital. This theory of liability creates a nondelegable duty which the hospital owes directly to a patient. Therefore, an injured party does not have to rely on and establish the negligence of a third party.

The hospital's duties have been classified into four general areas: (1) a duty to use reasonable care in the maintenance of safe and adequate facilities and equipment—Candler General Hospital Inc. v. Purvis, 123 Ga.App. 334, 181 S.E.2d 77 (1971); (2) a duty to select and retain only competent physicians—Johnson v. Misericordia Community Hospital, 99 Wis.2d 708, 301 N.W.2d 156 (1981); (3) a duty to oversee all persons who practice medicine within its walls as to patient care—Darling v. Charleston Community Memorial Hospital, *supra.*; and (4) a duty to formulate, adopt and enforce adequate rules and policies to ensure quality care for the patients—Wood v. Samaritan Institution, 26 Cal.2d 847, 161 P.2d 556 (Cal. Ct. App.1945). [ ]

Other jurisdictions have embraced this doctrine of corporate negligence or corporate liability such as to warrant it being called an "emerging trend". [ ]

* * *

Today, we take a step beyond the hospital's duty of care delineated in Riddle in full recognition of the corporate hospital's role in the total health care of its patients. In so doing, we adopt as a theory of hospital liability the doctrine of corporate negligence or corporate liability under which the hospital is liable if it fails to uphold the proper standard of care owed its patient. In addition, we fully embrace the aforementioned four categories of the hospital's duties. It is important to note that for a hospital to be charged with negligence, it is necessary to show that the hospital had actual or constructive knowledge of the defect or procedures which created the harm. [ ] Furthermore, the hospital's negligence must have been a substantial factor in bringing about the harm to the injured party. [ ].

The final question Nason Hospital raises is did Superior Court err in finding that there was a material issue of fact with respect to the hospital's duty to monitor and review medical services provided within its facilities. Nason Hospital contends that during Linda Thompson's hospitalization, it did not become aware of any exceptional circumstance which would require or justify its intervention into her treatment. The Hospital Association of Pennsylvania, as amicus curiae, argues that it is neither realistic nor appropriate to expect the hospital to conduct daily review and supervision of the independent medical judgment of each member of the medical staff of which it may have actual or constructive knowledge.

Conversely, Appellees argue that Nason Hospital was negligent in failing to monitor the medical services provided Mrs. Thompson. Specifically, Appellees claim that the hospital ignored its Rules and Regulations governing Medical Staff by failing to ensure the patient received adequate medical attention through physician consultations. Appellees also contend that Nason Hospital's medical staff members and personnel treating Mrs. Thompson were aware of her deteriorating condition, brought about by being over anticoagulated, yet did nothing.

It is well established that a hospital staff member or employee has a duty to recognize and report abnormalities in the treatment and condition of its patients. [ ] If the attending physician fails to act after being informed of such abnormalities, it is then incumbent upon the hospital staff member or employee to so advise the hospital authorities so that appropriate action might be taken. [ ] When there is a failure to report changes in a patient's condition and/or to question a physician's order which is not in accord with standard medical practice and the patient is injured as a result, the hospital will be liable for such negligence. [ ]

A thorough review of the record of this case convinces us that there is a sufficient question of material fact presented as to whether Nason Hospital was negligent in supervising the quality of the medical care Mrs. Thompson received, such that the trial court could not have properly granted summary judgment on the issue of corporate liability.

The order of Superior Court is affirmed. Jurisdiction is relinquished.

NOTES AND QUESTIONS

1. What does *Thompson* add to *Darling*'s discussion of the scope of corporate negligence? As you think about the typical hospital's complexity in both its administrative and operational structure, where do you think liability should best be focused? On its physicians? On the hospital? Joint liability? Or something different?

Thompson combines duties that can be found in isolation in the caselaw of other jurisdictions. Consider the nature of these hospital duties: (1) a duty to use reasonable care in the maintenance of safe and adequate facilities and equipment; (2) a duty to select and retain only competent physicians; (3) a duty to oversee all persons who practice medicine within its walls as to patient care; and (4) a duty to formulate, adopt, and enforce adequate rules and policies to ensure quality care for the patients.

2. Duty 2, Selection and Retention of Competent Doctors, is the core obligation of hospitals, and in many jurisdictions, it defines corporate negligence. Probably the most important function of a hospital is to select high quality physicians for its medical staff. We will discuss this duty in the next section.

3. Duty 1, Maintenance of Safe Facilities and Equipment, is really an extension of common law obligations of all institutions that invite the public onto their property. It encompasses slip–and–fall cases and all forms of injury that patients and visitors might suffer while in the hospital.

4. Duty 3, Supervision of All Who Practice Medicine in the Hospital, encompasses staff physicians and all other health professionals, acknowledging that modern medicine is a "team" operation. Courts increasingly recognize the team nature of medical practice in hospitals, and liability follows from this recognition. In Hoffman v. East Jefferson General Hospital, 778 So.2d 33 (La. App. 5 Cir. 2000), the plaintiff underwent two surgical procedures. Plaintiff suffered severe burns on her buttocks during the operation as the result of the use of a speculum that had been sterilized and was too hot. The hospital would sterilize the instruments and provide the means for cool down. It was the responsibility of hospital employees to communicate the status of the equipment—whether it was sufficiently cooled down—to the doctor, but that the final decision as to when to use the equipment was the doctor's. The court found that "the use of an instrument before it is sufficiently cooled

after sterilization is a breach of the standard of care both for hospital employees and the doctor performing the surgery."

Institutional complexity requires accountability—a person in charge—often the attending physician in situations where residents are part of the care. In Lownsbury v. VanBuren, 94 Ohio St.3d 231, 762 N.E.2d 354 (2002), the parents sued a teaching hospital's attending physician for the injury to their adopted daughter. The physician as supervising physician had a duty to be familiar with the patient's condition and to review a contract stress test by the end of his scheduled working day and formulate a plan of management.

5. Duty 4, To Formulate, Adopt and Enforce Adequate Rules and Policies to Ensure Quality Care for the Patients", moves well beyond monitoring staff, drawing our scrutiny to how the institution operates as a system, and allowing plaintiffs to search for negligence in the very design of the operating framework of the hospital.

The language of Continuous Quality Improvement and Total Quality Management, the Joint Commission rules for hospitals—all suggest that the good aspects of the industrial model are being applied to hospitals. The problem with health care delivery is not just that patient care is complicated; it is rather that institutional politics and the inertia that seizes hospitals as they struggle for revenue in tough health care markets makes change difficult. The malpractice cases are often striking for their description of the level of errors that providers have tolerated in poorly managed institutions. See generally Chapter 1 as to the causes of medical errors, *supra*.

6. Hospitals need strong policies to ensure coordination among providers as a patient undergoes complex procedures. In Jennison v. Providence St. Vincent Medical Center, 174 Or.App. 219, 25 P.3d 358 (C.A. Oregon 2001), the plaintiff sued the hospital and physicians after she suffered severe brain injury while recovering from surgery. The Court of Appeals held that evidence supported the claim that the hospital was negligent in failing to have policies and procedures controlling verification of placement and use of central venous lines in hospital's post–anesthesia care unit. The court wrote:

> The hospital had no policy or procedure regarding the followup on central lines placed in the OR when a patient is transferred to the PACU. The call from radiology could potentially go to one of five different people, depending on whom the radiologist decides to call. Furthermore, no written documentation was required once one of those people received the call from radiology, thus precluding other people from knowing whether the call was ever actually made. Hospital's policy and procedure required verification, but it did not control what happened thereafter.

7. Expert testimony is required to establish a corporate negligence claim, unless it involves simple issues such as structural defects within the common knowledge and experience of the jury. See generally Neff v. Johnson Memorial Hospital, 93 Conn.App. 534, 889 A.2d 921 (Conn.App. 2006) (noting the complexity of the staff credentialing process, and holding that plaintiff

needed an expert to determine what the standard of care was for a hospital in allowing a physician with three malpractice cases in his history to be recredentialed).

2. Negligent Credentialing

CARTER V. HUCKS–FOLLISS

North Carolina Court of Appeals, 1998.
131 N.C.App. 145, 505 S.E.2d 177.

GREENE, JUDGE.

Tommy and Tracy Carter (collectively, Plaintiffs) appeal from the granting of Moore Regional Hospital's (Defendant) motion for summary judgment entered 26 June 1997.

On 20 August 1993, Dr. Anthony Hucks–Folliss (Dr. Hucks–Folliss) performed neck surgery on plaintiff Tommy Carter at Defendant. Dr. Hucks–Folliss is a neurosurgeon on the medical staff of Defendant. He first was granted surgical privileges by Defendant in 1975, and has been reviewed every two years hence to renew those privileges. Though he has been on Defendant's staff for over twenty years, Dr. Hucks–Folliss never has been certified by the American Board of Neurological Surgery. Presently, Dr. Hucks–Folliss is ineligible for board certification because he has taken and failed the certification examination on three different occasions.

The credentialing and re–credentialing of physicians at Defendant is designed to comply with standards promulgated by the Joint Commission on Accreditation of Healthcare Organizations (JCAHO). In 1992, the time when Dr. Hucks–Folliss was last re–credentialed by Defendant prior to the neck surgery performed on Tommy Carter, the JCAHO provided that board certification "is an excellent benchmark and is [to be] considered when delineating clinical privileges."

On the application filed by Dr. Hucks–Folliss, seeking to renew his surgical privileges with Defendant, he specifically stated, in response to a question on the application, that he was not board certified. Dr. James Barnes (Dr. Barnes), one of Plaintiffs' experts, presented an affidavit wherein he states that Defendant "does not appear [to have] ever considered the fact that Dr. Hucks–Folliss was not board certified, or that he had failed board exams three times," when renewing Dr. Hucks–Folliss's surgical privileges. Jean Hill (Ms. Hill), the manager of Medical Staff Services for Defendant, stated in her deposition that board certification was not an issue in the re–credentialing of active staff physicians. There is no dispute that Dr. Hucks–Folliss was on active staff in 1992. Additionally, this record does not reveal any further inquiry by Defendant into Dr. Hucks–Folliss's board certification status (beyond the question on the application).

In the complaint, it is alleged that Defendant was negligent: (1) in granting clinical privileges to Dr. Hucks–Folliss; (2) in failing to ascertain whether Dr. Hucks–Folliss was qualified to perform neurological surgery; and (3) in failing to enforce the standards of the JCAHO. It is further alleged that as a proximate result of Defendant's negligence, Tommy Carter agreed to allow Dr. Hucks–Folliss to perform surgery on him in Defendant. As a consequence of that surgery, Tommy Carter sustained "serious, permanent and painful injuries to his person including quadraparesis, scarring and other disfigurement."

The issue is whether a genuine issue of fact is presented on this record as to the negligence of Defendant in re–credentialing Dr. Hucks–Folliss.

Hospitals owe a duty of care to its patients to ascertain that a physician is qualified to perform surgery before granting that physician the privilege of conducting surgery in that hospital.[ ] In determining whether a hospital, accredited by the JCAHO, has breached its duty of care in ascertaining the qualifications of the physician to practice in the hospital, it is appropriate to consider whether the hospital has complied with standards promulgated by the JCAHO. Failure to comply with these standards "is some evidence of negligence."[ ]

In this case, Defendant has agreed to be bound by the standards promulgated by JCAHO and those standards provided in part that board certification was a factor to be "considered" when determining hospital privileges. Defendant argues that the evidence reveals unequivocally that it "considered," in re–credentialing Dr. Hucks–Folliss, the fact that he was not board certified. It points to the application submitted by Dr. Hucks–Folliss, specifically stating that he was not board certified, to support this argument. We disagree. Although this evidence does reveal that Defendant was aware of Dr. Hucks–Folliss's lack of certification, it does not follow that his lack of certification was considered as a factor in the re–credentialing decision. In any event, there is evidence from Dr. Barnes and Ms. Hill that supports a finding that Defendant did not consider Dr. Hucks–Folliss's lack of certification, or his failure to pass the certification test on three occasions, in assessing his qualifications to practice medicine in the hospital. This evidence presents a genuine issue of material fact and thus precludes the issuance of a summary judgment.[ ]

We also reject the alternative argument of Defendant that summary judgment is proper because there is no evidence that any breach of duty (in failing to consider Dr. Hucks–Folliss's lack of board certification prior to re–credentialing) by it was a proximate cause of the injuries sustained by Tommy Carter. Genuine issues of material fact are raised on this point as well. [ ].

Reversed and remanded.

NOTES AND QUESTIONS

1. Does Dr. Hucks–Follis's lack of certification speak to his skill and qualifications? How should a doctor's experience be weighed against his testing abilities? The court considers Joint Commission (formerly JCAHO) standards as an important source of duties with regard to hospital credentialing, and failure to comply "some evidence of negligence." Would it be sufficient if the hospital had noted the deficiencies and made a finding that the doctor's experience and references were enough to outweigh any negative implications of lack of certification?

2. The core function of a hospital is to select high quality physicians for its medical staff. See generally Chapter 9. The hospital's governing board retains the ultimate responsibility for the quality of care provided, but their responsibility is normally delegated to the hospital staff, and discharged in practice by medical staff review committees. The organization and function of these committees in accredited hospitals are described in publications of the Joint Commission.

3. The requirement of staff self–governance under Joint Commission standards maintains and reinforces this physician authority within hospitals. Courts have found, however, that the chief executive officer of a hospital and the governing board have the "inherent authority to summarily suspend clinical privileges to prevent an imminent danger to patients". See Lo v. Provena Covenant Medical Center, 342 Ill.App.3d 975, 277 Ill.Dec. 521, 796 N.E.2d 607, 614 (4 Dist. 2003).

4. *Joint Commission Prospective Monitoring of Quality.* The Joint Commission issued new standards on medical staff governance in 2010 that prescribe the relationship between the medical staff, the medical staff's Executive Committee, and the hospital's Board. Joint Commission standards have intensified the institutional focus on prospective monitoring of physician quality. One of the Standards, for example, specifically provides that the hospital must establish a system for collecting, recording, and addressing individual reports of concerns about individual physicians. See Joint Commission, Focused Professional Practice Evaluation, October 13, 2008.

The Joint Commission now requires a period of focused review for all new privileges and all new privileges for existing practitioners, without any exemption for board certification, documented experience, or reputation. Professional practice evaluation includes several elements: periodic chart review; direct observation; monitoring of diagnostic and treatment techniques; and discussion with other individuals involved in the care of each patient including consulting physicians, assistants at surgery, nursing, and administrative personnel.

The duration of the period of review however can be varied for different levels of documented training and experience, e.g. practitioners coming directly from an outside residency program; practitioners coming directly from the organization's residency program; practitioners coming with a documented record of performance of the privilege and its associated outcomes; and practitioners coming with no record of performance of the privilege and its associated outcomes.

The standard requires the organized medical staff to develop criteria to be used for evaluating the performance of practitioners when issues affecting the provision of safe, high quality patient care are identified. Criteria for performance issues, according to the Joint Commission, might include several triggering events:

- small number of admissions or procedures over an extended period of time that raise the concern of continued competence
- a growing number of longer lengths of stay than other practitioners
- returns to surgery
- frequent or repeat readmission suggesting possibly poor or inadequate initial management/treatment
- patterns of unnecessary diagnostic testing/treatments
- failure to follow approved clinical practice guidelines—may or may not indicate care problems but why the variance
- frequent or repeat readmission suggesting possibly poor or inadequate initial management/treatment
- patterns of unnecessary diagnostic testing/treatments
- failure to follow approved clinical practice guidelines—may or may not indicate care problems but why the variance

5. *Medicare Conditions of Participation.* Federal law requires among other things that hospital bylaws reflect the hospital governing board's responsibility to ensure that ". . . the medical staff is accountable to the governing body for the quality of care provided to patients." 42 C.F.R. § 482.12(a)(5)(2001). The federal government is also involved in credentialing issues through the 2008 *Medicare Improvement for Providers and Patients Act*, which removed permanent deemed status from the Joint Commission for hospitals and required it to periodically reapply for deemed status. This mandate has allowed CMS to engage the Joint Commission on its standards for hospitals. 20 BNA Health Law Rptr. 886 (June 9, 2011). (See discussion of accreditation generally in Chapter 3).

6. Under the Health Care Quality Improvement Act of 1986 (HCQIA), hospitals must check a national database maintained under contract with the Department of Health and Human Services, before a new staff appointment is made. This National Practitioner Data Bank contains information on individual physicians who have been disciplined, had malpractice claims filed against them, or had privileges revoked or limited. If the hospital fails to check the registry, it is held constructively to have knowledge of any infor-

mation it might have gotten from the inquiry. See discussion of staff privileges in Chapter 9.

The Data Bank has been criticized by the Government Accountability Office as having unreliable and incomplete data. See U.S. Government Accountability Office (GAO), National Practitioner Data Bank: Major Improvements are Needed to Enhance Data Bank's Reliability. Some health policy researchers have even suggested that the Data Bank should be abolished. See William M. Sage et al., Bridging the Relational–Regulatory Gap: A Pragmatic Information Policy for Patient Safety and Medical Malpractice, 59 Vand. L. Rev. 1263, 1307 (2006).

7. *Liability of Boards of Directors of Hospitals.* Most American hospitals are incorporated as non–profits under Section 501(c)(3) of the Internal Revenue Code. As such, the duties of non–profit boards of directors have been limited by comparison to for–profit corporations. Compliance programs in the nonprofit health care context are usually for the purpose of detecting and preventing fraud in accordance with federal and state anti–fraud laws.

States typically also mandate that the governing board is responsible for the competence of the medical staff. See for example Lo v. Provena Covenant Medical Center, 342 Ill.App.3d 975, 277 Ill.Dec. 521, 796 N.E.2d 607, 614 (4 Dist. 2003) (holding that the hospital has an "inherent right to summarily suspend the clinical privileges of a physician whose continued practice poses an immediate danger to patients").

Corporate negligence might apply to boards of trustees of hospitals under the right set of circumstances. See e.g. Zambino v. Hospital of the University of Pennsylvania, Slip Copy, 2006 WL 2788217 (E.D.Pa.2006). The court noted that Pennsylvania courts ". . . have extended the doctrine of corporate liability to other entities in limited circumstances, such as when the patient is constrained in his or her choice of medical care options by the entity sued, and the entity controls the patient's total health care." See Shannon v. McNulty, 718 A.2d 828 (Pa.Super.1998) (extending doctrine to an HMO that provided health care services similar to a hospital).

The corporate negligence argument is based on the duty of a Board of Directors of a non–profit hospital not only to detect and prevent fraud, but to detect and prevent patient injury. The traditional board fiduciary duties of care and obedience can arguably include responsibility of nonprofit hospital directors to ensure that the hospital promotes health. This new interpretation blends the oversight obligations stemming from the duty of care with the duty of obedience requiring obedience with the laws.

For a general discussion of the obligations of nonprofit Boards of Directors, see Arianne N. Callender et al., Corporate Responsibility and Health Care Quality: A Resource for Health Care Boards of Directors (The Office of Inspector General of the U.S. Department of Health and Human Services and The American Health Lawyers Association, 2007).

PROBLEM: CASCADING ERRORS

Carolyn Gadner was driving her car on the highway when another car driven by Bob Sneed passed her, sideswiped her, ran her off the road, and drove off. Gadner caught up with Sneed and forced him to stop. She got out of her vehicle and started to walk to his car when he drove away. While Gadner was walking back to her car, Charles Otis struck her with his vehicle. Gadner was transported to Bay Hospital, a small rural hospital, where Dr. Dick Samson, a second–year pediatric resident, was the attending emergency room physician. Upon arriving at Bay, Gadner's skin was cool and clammy and her blood pressure was 95/55, indicative of shock. Gadner received 200 ccs per hour of fluid and was x–rayed. She actively requested a transfer because of vaginal bleeding. Nurse Gilbert voiced her own concerns about the need for a transfer to the other nurses in the emergency room. Dr. Samson did not order one.

Bay is a rural hospital and is not equipped to handle multiple trauma patients like Gadner. Bay had no protocol or procedure for making transfers to larger hospitals. Bay breached its own credentialing procedures in hiring a physician who lacked the necessary training, expertise, or demonstrated competence to work the ER. Dr. Bay, the hospital's chief of staff, had screened Samson, who was not properly evaluated before he was hired. A second–year pediatric resident is not normally assigned to an ER setting, give his lack of experience.

The nurses failed to notice that Gadner was in shock and that this failure was substandard. After they initially noted that she arrived with cool and clammy skin and a blood pressure of 95/55, they did not advise Dr. Samson that the patient was likely in shock; they failed to place her on IV fluids, elevate her feet above her head, and give oxygen as needed. Dr. Samson ordered the administration of 500 cc's of fluid per hour, but Gadner received only about 200 cc's per hour because the IV infiltrated, delivering the fluid to the surrounding tissue instead of the vein. The nursing staff normally would discover infiltration and correct it. Scanty nurses' notes revealed that vital signs were not taken regularly, depriving Dr. Samson of critical and ongoing information about Gadner's condition. Nurse Gilbert administered Valium and morphine to Gadner, following Dr. Samson's orders, a mixture of drugs counter–indicated for a patient with symptoms of shock. Nurse Gilbert did not notice or protest.

Three hours after arriving at Bay, Gadner "coded" and Dr. Samson tried unsuccessfully to revive her. After she coded, Dr. Samson attempted to use the laryngoscope, following standard practice, but the one provided was broken. He then ordered epinephrine, but there was none in the ER. An autopsy was performed, and Gadner died of treatable shock according to the coroner.

Consider the various theories of liability available to the plaintiff. Then develop a plan to improve the hospital from a patient safety perspective so that this kind of disaster will not happen again.

3. Peer Review Immunity and Corporate Negligence

Credentialing decisions may be the central feature of corporate negligence claims, but such decisions are often the most difficult to prove. Virtually all American jurisdictions have peer review immunity statutes that limit access to hospital decisionmaking about physician problems that have been discovered.

LARSON V. WASEMILLER

Supreme Court of Minnesota, 2007.
738 N.W.2d 300.

Opinion

HANSON, JUSTICE.

Appellants Mary and Michael Larson commenced this medical malpractice claim against respondent Dr. James Wasemiller, Dr. Paul Wasemiller and the Dakota Clinic for negligence in connection with the performance of gastric bypass surgery on Mary Larson. The Larsons also joined respondent St. Francis Medical Center as a defendant, claiming, among other things, that St. Francis was negligent in granting surgery privileges to Dr. James Wasemiller. St. Francis then moved to dismiss for failure to state a claim. The district court denied the motion to dismiss, holding that Minnesota does recognize a claim for negligent credentialing, but certified two questions to the court of appeals. The court of appeals reversed the district court's denial of the motion to dismiss, holding that Minnesota does not recognize a common–law cause of action for negligent credentialing. [ ] We reverse and remand to the district court for further proceedings.

In April 2002, Dr. James Wasemiller, with the assistance of his brother, Dr. Paul Wasemiller, performed gastric bypass surgery on Mary Larson at St. Francis Medical Center in Breckenridge, Minnesota. Larson experienced complications following the surgery, and Dr. Paul Wasemiller performed a second surgery on April 12, 2002 to address the complications. On April 22, 2002, after being moved to a long–term care facility, Larson was transferred to MeritCare Hospital for emergency surgery. Larson remained hospitalized until June 28, 2002.

The Larsons claim that St. Francis was negligent in credentialing Dr. James P. Wasemiller. Credentialing decisions determine which physicians are granted hospital privileges and what specific procedures they can perform in the hospital. *See* Craig W. Dallon, Understanding Judicial Review of Hospitals' Physician Credentialing and Peer Review Decisions, 73 Temp. L.Rev. 597, 598 (2000). The granting of hospital privileges normally does not create an employment relationship with the hospital, but it allows physicians access to the hospital's facilities and imposes certain professional standards. [ ]. The decision to grant hospital privileges to a physician is made by the hospital's governing body based on the recommendations of the credentials committee. A credentials committee is a type of peer review committee. Minnesota, like most other states, has a peer review statute that provides for the confidentiality of peer review proceedings and grants some immunity to those involved in the credentialing process. [ ].

The district court noted that the majority of courts in other jurisdictions have recognized a duty on the part of hospitals to exercise reasonable care in granting privileges to physicians to practice medicine at the hospital. The court also noted that the existence of such a duty is objectively reasonable and consistent with public policy. The court therefore held that Minnesota "will and does recognize, at common law, a professional tort against hospitals and review organizations for negligent credentialing/privileging."

After denying St. Francis' motion to dismiss, the district court certified the following two questions to the court of appeals:

A. Does the state of Minnesota recognize a common law cause of action of privileging of a physician against a hospital or other review organization?

B. Does Minn.Stat. §§ 145.63–145.64 grant immunity from or otherwise limit liability of a hospital or other review organization for a claim of negligent credentialing/privileging of a physician?

* * *

A. Does Minnesota's peer review statute create a cause of action for negligent credentialing?

[The court concludes that " * * * the tort of negligent credentialing is inherent in and the natural extension of well–established common law rights." It further noted that more than half of the state courts have adopted the tort, and it has support in Restatement (Second) Tort sections such as section 320 and 411.]

3. Would the tort of negligent credentialing conflict with Minnesota's peer review statute?

St. Francis argues that the fact that a majority of other jurisdictions have recognized a negligent–credentialing claim is not dispositive because such a claim would conflict with Minnesota's peer review statute. Minnesota's peer review statute contains both confidentiality and limited liability provisions. [ ].

The Confidentiality Provision

The confidentiality provision of the peer review statute provides in part that

> [D]ata and information acquired by a review organization, in the exercise of its duties and functions, or by an individual or other entity acting at the direction of a review organization, shall be held in confidence, shall not be disclosed to anyone except to the extent necessary to carry out one or more of the purposes of the review organization, and shall not be subject to subpoena or discovery. No person described in section 145.63 shall disclose what transpired at a meeting of a review organization except to the extent necessary to carry out one or more of the purposes of a review organization. The proceedings and records of a review organization shall not be subject to discovery or introduction into evidence in any civil action against a professional arising out of the matter or matters which are the subject of consideration by the review organization.

[ ]. Credentialing committees are "review organizations" under the statutory definition. [ ]. Any unauthorized disclosure of the above information is a misdemeanor.[ ].

St. Francis argues that the prohibition on disclosing what information a credentialing committee relied upon precludes a claim of negligent credentialing because the precise fact question to be tried in a negligent–credentialing case is whether the hospital was negligent in making the decision on the basis of what it *actually knew* at the time of the credentialing decision. It argues that the confidentiality provision therefore makes it impossible for a hospital to defend against such a claim.

St. Francis' interpretation of the common law claim is too narrow because negligence could be shown on the basis of what was actually known or what *should have been known* at the time of the credentialing decision. [ ]. And Minnesota's confidentiality provision recognizes this broader concept, and addresses the problems of proof, by providing that

> [i]nformation, documents or records otherwise available from original sources shall not be immune from discovery or use in any civil action merely because they were presented during proceedings of a review organization, nor shall any person who testified before a review organization or who is a member of it be prevented from testifying as to matters within the person's knowledge, but a witness cannot be asked about the witness' testimony before a review organization or opinions formed by the witness as a result of its hearings. [ ].

Thus, although section 145.64, subdivision 1 would prevent hospitals from disclosing the fact that certain information was considered by the credentials committee, it would not prevent hospitals from introducing the same information, as long as it could be obtained from original sources. **

* * *

Although the confidentiality provision of Minnesota's peer review statute may make the proof of a common law negligent–credentialing claim more complicated, we conclude that it does not preclude such a claim.

The Limited Liability Provision

Minn.Stat. § 145.63, subd. 1 (2006) provides some immunity from liability, both for individual credentials committee members and hospitals, for claims brought by either a physician or a patient. Section 145.63, subdivision 1 provides that

> No review organization and no person who is a member or employee, director, or officer of, who acts in an advisory capacity to, or who furnishes counsel or services to, a review organization shall be liable for damages or other relief in any action brought by a person or persons whose activities have been or are being scrutinized or reviewed by a review organization, by reason of the performance by the person of any duty, function, or activity of such review organization, unless the performance of such duty, function or activity was motivated by malice toward the person affected thereby. No review organization and no person shall be liable for damages or other relief in any action by reason of the performance of the review organization or person of any duty, function, or activity as a review organization or a member of a review committee or by reason of any recommendation or action of the review committee when the person acts in the reasonable belief that the action or recommendation is warranted by facts known to the person or the review organization after reasonable efforts to ascertain the facts upon which the review organization's action or recommendation is made.

* * *

We conclude that the liability provisions of section 145.63 do not materially alter the common law standard of care and that, although the confidentiality provisions of section 145.64 present some obstacles in both proving and defending a claim of negligent credentialing, they do not preclude such a claim.

> 4. Do the policy considerations in favor of the tort of negligent credentialing outweigh any tension caused by conflict with the peer review statute?

The function of peer review is to provide critical analysis of the competence and performance of physicians and other health care providers in order to decrease incidents of malpractice and to improve quality of patient care. [ ] This court has held that the purpose of Minnesota's peer review statute is to promote the strong public interest in improving health care by granting certain protections to medical review organizations,[ ] and to encourage the medical profession to police its own activities with minimal judicial interference,[ ]. This court has also recognized that "the quality of patient care could be compromised if fellow professionals are reluctant to participate fully in peer review activities."[ ].

* * *

We recognize that a claim of negligent credentialing raises questions about the necessity of a bifurcated trial and the scope of the confidentiality and immunity provisions of the peer review statute. We likewise recognize that there is an issue about whether a patient must first prove negligence on the part of a physician before a hospital can be liable for negligently credentialing the physician. But, in part, these are questions of trial management that are best left to the trial judge. [ ] Further, they cannot be effectively addressed in the context of this Rule 12 motion.

We conclude that the policy considerations underlying the tort of negligent credentialing outweigh the policy considerations reflected in the peer review statute because the latter policy considerations are adequately addressed by the preclusion of access to the confidential peer review materials. We therefore hold that a claim of negligent credentialing does exist in Minnesota, and is not precluded by Minnesota's peer review statute. We reverse the answer of the court of appeals to the first certified question, answer that question in the affirmative, and remand to the district court for further proceedings consistent with this opinion.

Reversed and remanded.

[Justice Barry, concurring, raised several concerns about the efficacy of negligent credentialing litigation generally. First, physicians are reluctant to participate in peer review: they receive no compensation for their time, face the tension of evaluating their peers, risk reprisals through lost patient referrals, and may face litigation for their decisions.

Second, peer review immunity statutes attempt to deal with these concerns, but "[i]t is open for debate, however, whether these measures actually promote effective peer review." Judge Barry notes that only documents created by the peer review process are off limits but not incident reports and information from the original sources. Physicians will be unwilling to create records if litigants can ultimately discover them.

Third, the qualified immunity of the statue requires evidence of reasonable efforts to ascertain the facts, and this means that a negligent credentialing case will proceed to the summary judgment state, requiring discovery and expert testimony.

Judge Barry suggested that legislative and executive action is required to collect data on these issues and to provide a better solution to peer review costs and benefits.]

NOTES AND QUESTIONS

1. *Hospital Committee Proceedings.* Plaintiffs in malpractice actions frequently seek discovery of the proceedings of hospital quality assurance committees, as the problem above illustrates. If the suit is against the hospital on a theory of corporate liability (i.e., claiming that the hospital itself was negligent in appointing or failing to supervise a professional), evidence of committee proceedings may prove vital to establishing the hospital's liability.

These discovery requests are usually met with a claim that information generated within or by hospital committees is not discoverable. In Coburn v. Seda, 101 Wash.2d 270, 677 P.2d 173 (1984), the court considered the plaintiff's discovery requests for the records of the hospital quality review committees.

> * * * The discovery protection granted hospital quality review committee records, like work product immunity, prevents the opposing party from taking advantage of a hospital's careful self–assessment. The opposing party must utilize his or her own experts to evaluate the facts underlying the incident which is the subject of suit and also use them to determine whether the hospital's care comported with proper quality standards.
>
> The discovery prohibition, like an evidentiary privilege, also seeks to protect certain communications and encourage the quality review process. As the court stated in Bredice v. Doctors Hosp., Inc., 50 F.R.D. 249, 250 (D.D.C.1970), aff'd, 479 F.2d 920 (D.C.Cir.1973):
>
> Confidentiality is essential to effective functioning of these staff meetings; and these meetings are essential to the continued improvement in the care and treatment of patients. Candid and conscientious evaluation of clinical practices is a *sine qua non* of adequate hospital care * * *. Constructive professional criticism cannot occur in an atmosphere of apprehension that one doctor's suggestion will be used as a denunciation of a colleague's conduct in a malpractice suit.

2. A number of statutes immunizing committee proceedings from discovery do not explicitly render information from those committees privileged from admission into evidence if the plaintiff can obtain it otherwise. But would such information be otherwise admissible? Would it be hearsay? If so, would it be subject to the business records exception? See Fed.R.Evid. 803(6). Might committee records indicating that a hospital was concerned about the performance of a physician be admissible as an admission in a subsequent corporate negligence action against the hospital? See Fed.R.Evid.

801(d)(2)(D). Might a plaintiff's expert be permitted to testify on the basis of information gleaned from committee records, even though those records were themselves hearsay? See Fed.R.Evid. 703. In a suit brought by one particular patient, would committee records documenting errors made by a physician in the treatment of other patients be relevant? Might opinions concerning a physician's negligence found in committee records or reports invade the province of the jury? See, addressing these questions, Robert F. Holbrook & Lee J. Dunn, Medical Malpractice Litigation: The Discoverability and Use of Hospitals' Quality Assurance Records, 16 Washburn L.J. 54, 68–70 (1976).

3. *Hospital Incident Reports.* When a plaintiff seeks discovery of incident reports rather than committee proceedings, policy considerations are somewhat different. Hospitals have greater incentives to investigate untoward events than they have to carry on continuing quality review, and are less dependent on voluntary participation. The incident report would usually be more directly relevant to a single claim for malpractice than would general committee investigations. Possibly for these reasons, immunity statutes that protect committee proceedings less often protect incident reports, and courts have been less willing to immunize incident reports from discovery. On the other hand, since incident reports are more directly related to litigation of specific mishaps, two privileges can be asserted to protect them that would seldom apply to committee proceedings: the work product immunity and attorney client privilege.

4. *Hospital Sentinel Event Investigations.* Root cause investigations in compliance with Joint Commission guidelines have been denied discovery and confidentiality protections. In Reyes v. Meadowlands Hospital Medical Center, 809 A.2d 875 (N.J.Super. 2001), the defendant hospital argued that its root cause analysis of a sentinel event under Joint Commission guidelines should be protected from discovery. The plaintiff alleged that Meadowlands Hospital deviated from accepted standards of care in failing to properly diagnose and treat decedent, Debbie Reyes. Ms. Reyes was admitted to Meadowlands Hospital on August 1, 1998, and in the course of an attempted laproscopic colosceptomy she went into cardiac arrest and died. The Hospital moved for a protective order to shield from discovery information gathered through a process of "self–critical analysis," a "voluntary" investigation regarding the circumstances of Ms. Reyes' unanticipated death that followed Joint Commission guidelines for a root cause analysis. The hospital described this process as "the creation of a blame–free, protective environment that encourages the systematic surfacing and reporting of serious adverse events" as part of claiming a discovery shield.

The Hospital offered a statement from the General Counsel for the Joint Commission and a "Sentinel Event Policy" statement outlining the protocol governing the investigation and subsequent remedial measures taken in response to the unanticipated death or serious injury of a patient. The court described the process: " * * * A critical element of the Policy centered on health care organizations engaging in root cause analyses of such events. The basis of a root cause analysis is an industrial engineering model, and involves a thorough systems analysis to determine what, if any, systems changes a [sic] organization could put in place to make an unwanted event less likely to occur in the future."

> A twelve step process is utilized to analyze the event and propose systemic changes to avoid recurrence. The list of potential Sentinel Events includes "unexpected iatrogenic injury (i.e., in the course of treatment) resulting or likely to result in death or major permanent loss of function (physical, psychological or reproductive)." Conspicuously missing from the policy statement, however, is any statement that participants enjoyed an expectation of confidentiality as to statements made during the process.

The court noted that parties may obtain discovery for any matter that is not privileged, relevant to the subject matter at issue; however, " * * *privileges, because they stifle the pursuit of the truth, are disfavored."

The court discussed New Jersey caselaw, which requires a "a showing of particularized need that outweighs the public interest in confidentiality of the investigative proceedings, taking into account (1) the extent to which the information may be available from other sources, (2) the degree of harm that the litigant will suffer from its unavailability, and (3) the possible prejudice to the agency's investigation."

The court was skeptical. It noted that the defendant's motion,

> * * *although couched in language promoting the advancement of medical knowledge and the improvement of medical services, also serves the litigation interests of the defendants by depriving plaintiff from reviewing what would otherwise be clearly discoverable materials. Nor is the medical profession unique in its self–ascribed role as promoters and guardians of the public's welfare. Other professions can make a similar claim, i.e., engineers, architects, scientists, ecologists, educators, even lawyers.

The court rejected the defendants' argument that production of these files would " * * * severely prejudice the ability of St. Clares Riverside and its doctors to evaluate and criticize medical procedures in accordance with the overall public policy for improving medical care." It continued:

> Implicit in such a finding is the assumption that without this cloak of confidentiality the medical professionals taking part in this "self–critical analysis" would not have fully and candidly expressed their points of view about a given case. There is not a scintilla of evidence before me to support such a wholesale indictment of the medical profession. In fact, the current state of the law in this area supports the opposite conclusion. *N.J.A.C.* 8:43G–27.5 mandates hospitals to conduct medical peer review programs. * * *
>
> The creation and maintenance of peer review quality assurance processes are a condition of licensure by the State Department of

> Health. [ ]. The Code makes no provision for the results of such a process to be privileged. Therefore, those participating do so without any expectation of confidentiality.

The court observed that the hospital's argument about the Sentinel Events " * * * reveals more a desire by the Hospital to control the dissemination of potentially embarrassing information rather than a genuine interest in the enhancement of patient care. In short, these "Sentinel Events," on their face, go far beyond the professed "advancement of medical knowledge" justification argued by defendants, and wander freely in the world of public relations. The court then held that " * * * the Sentinel Event Policy invoked by defendant Meadowlands Hospital does not create a self–critical analysis privilege, insulating any and all discussions and statements made and conclusions reached by the participants therein and actions taken by the Hospital pursuant thereto not subject to the Civil Rules of Discovery."

5. Most states have statutes affording hospital quality assurance proceedings some degree of protection from discovery. Statutes protecting committee proceedings from discovery are often subject to exceptions, either explicitly or through judicial interpretation. One common exception affords discovery to physicians challenging the results of committee action against them. Thus a physician whose staff privileges were revoked may discover information from the credentialing committee, Schulz v. Superior Court, 66 Cal.App.3d 440, 446, 136 Cal.Rptr. 67, 70 (1977).

The work product immunity protects materials prepared in anticipation of litigation. See Federal Rules of Civil Procedure 56. Courts look to the nature and purpose of incident reports. If they are regularly prepared and distributed for future loss prevention, they are not considered to be documents prepared in anticipation of litigation so as to invoke application of the work product exception to discovery. See St. Louis Little Rock Hospital, Inc. v. Gaertner, 682 S.W.2d 146, 150–51 (Mo.App.1984).

This attorney–client privilege protects communications, even if the attorney is not yet representing a client, provided that the communication was made between the client as an insured to his liability insurer during the course of an existing insured–insurer relationship. To be privileged, a communication between a client and his attorney, or between an insured and his insurer, must be within the context of the attorney–client relationship, with a purpose of securing legal advice from the client's attorney. See The St. Luke Hospitals, Inc. v. Kopowski, 160 S.W.3d 771 (Kentucky 2005) (Two nurses communicated about the post–delivery care of an infant who died at the hospital to the officer in charge of risk management, who had conducted the interviews of the nurses at the direction of the hospital's attorney. The court held that the communications were protected by the privilege.)

PROBLEM: PROCTORING PEERS

You have been asked by Hilldale Adventist Hospital to advise it on the implications of its use of proctors for assessing candidates for medical staff privileges. The hospital has used Dr. Hook, a surgeon certified by the American Board of Orthopedic Surgery, as a proctor during two different operations on the plaintiff at two different hospitals during the process of evaluation of Dr. Frank DiBianco for staff privileges. Dr. Hook had been asked to observe ten surgeries by Dr. DiBianco and then file a report. He observed an operation on the plaintiff during one of these observations. Two months later, he was again asked to proctor Dr. DiBianco at another hospital, and he again observed a procedure on the plaintiff. Prior to each procedure, Dr. Hook had reviewed the x–rays and discussed the operative plan, but he otherwise had taken no part in the care and treatment of the plaintiff. He did not participate in the operations, did not scrub in, and always observed from outside the "sterile field." He got no payment for his proctoring efforts, and he had never met the plaintiff nor had any other contact with her.

Can Hilldale be liable for its use of Dr. Hook as a proctor? Can Dr. Hook be directly liable for failing to stop negligent work by Dr. DiBianco?

What if the process by which a hospital evaluates the credentials of a physician for staff privileges fails?

KADLEC MEDICAL CENTER V. LAKEVIEW ANESTHESIA ASSOCIATES

Fifth Circuit Court of Appeals, 2008.
527 F.3d 412.

REAVLEY, CIRCUIT JUDGE:

Kadlec Medical Center and its insurer, Western Professional Insurance Company, filed this diversity action in Louisiana district court against Louisiana Anesthesia Associates (LAA), its shareholders, and Lakeview Regional Medical Center (Lakeview Medical). The LAA shareholders worked with Dr. Robert Berry–an anesthesiologist and former LAA shareholder–at Lakeview Medical, where the defendants discovered his on–duty use of narcotics. In referral letters written by the defendants and relied on by Kadlec, his future employer, the defendants did not disclose Dr. Berry's drug use.

While under the influence of Demerol at Kadlec, Dr. Berry's negligent performance led to the near–death of a patient, resulting in a lawsuit against Kadlec. Plaintiffs claim here that the defendants' misleading referral letters were a legal cause of plaintiffs' financial injury, i.e., having to pay over $8 million to defend and settle the lawsuit. The jury found in favor of the plaintiffs and judgment followed. We reverse the judgment against Lakeview Medical, vacate the remainder of the judgment, and remand.

I. Factual Background

Dr. Berry was a licensed anesthesiologist in Louisiana and practiced with Drs. William Preau, Mark Dennis, David Baldone, and Allan Parr at LAA. From November 2000 until his termination on March 13, 2001, Dr. Berry was a shareholder of LAA, the exclusive provider of anesthesia services to Lakeview Medical (a Louisiana hospital).

In November 2000, a small management team at Lakeview Medical investigated Dr. Berry after nurses expressed concern about his undocumented and suspicious withdrawals of Demerol. The investigative team found excessive Demerol withdrawals by Dr. Berry and a lack of documentation for the withdrawals.

Lakeview Medical CEO Max Lauderdale discussed the team's findings with Dr. Berry and Dr. Dennis. Dr. Dennis then discussed Dr. Berry's situation with his partners. They all agreed that Dr. Berry's use of Demerol had to be controlled and monitored. But Dr. Berry did not follow the agreement or account for his continued Demerol withdrawals. Three months later, Dr. Berry failed to answer a page while on–duty at Lakeview Medical. He was discovered in the call–room, asleep, groggy, and unfit to work. Personnel immediately called Dr. Dennis, who found Dr. Berry not communicating well and unable to work. Dr. Dennis had Dr. Berry taken away after Dr. Berry said that he had taken prescription medications.

Lauderdale, Lakeview Medical's CEO, decided that it was in the best interest of patient safety that Dr. Berry not practice at the hospital. Dr. Dennis and his three partners at LAA fired Dr. Berry and signed his termination letter on March 27, 2001, which explained that he was fired "for cause":

> [You have been fired for cause because] you have reported to work in an impaired physical, mental, and emotional state. Your impaired condition has prevented you from properly performing your duties and puts our patients at significant risk. . . . [P]lease consider your termination effective March 13, 2001.

At Lakeview Medical, Lauderdale ordered the Chief Nursing Officer to notify the administration if Dr. Berry returned.

Despite recognizing Dr. Berry's drug problem and the danger he posed to patients, neither Dr. Dennis nor Lauderdale reported Dr. Berry's impairment to the hospital's Medical Executive Committee, eventually noting only that Dr. Berry was "no longer employed by LAA." Neither one reported Dr. Berry's impairment to Lakeview Medical's Board of Trustees, and no one on behalf of Lakeview Medical reported Dr. Berry's impairment or discipline to the Louisiana Board of Medical Examiners or to the National Practitioner's Data Bank. In fact, at some point Lauderdale took the unusual step of locking away in his office all files, audits, plans, and notes concerning Dr. Berry and the investigation.

After leaving LAA and Lakeview Medical, Dr. Berry briefly obtained work as a *locum tenens* (traveling physician) at a hospital in Shreveport, Louisiana. In October 2001, he applied through Staff Care, a leading *locum tenens* staffing firm, for *locum tenens* privileges at Kadlec Medical Center in Washington State. After receiving his application, Kadlec began its credentialing process. Kadlec examined a variety of materials, including referral letters from LAA and Lakeview Medical.

LAA's Dr. Preau and Dr. Dennis, two months after firing Dr. Berry for his on–the–job drug use, submitted referral letters for Dr. Berry to Staff Care, with the intention that they be provided to future employers. The letter from Dr. Dennis stated that he had worked with Dr. Berry for four years, that he was an excellent clinician, and that he would be an asset to any anesthesia service. Dr. Preau's letter said that he worked with Berry at Lakeview Medical and that he recommended him highly as an anesthesiologist. Dr. Preau's and Dr. Dennis's letters were submitted on June 3, 2001, only sixty–eight days after they fired him for using narcotics while on–duty and stating in his termination letter that Dr. Berry's behavior put "patients at significant risk."

On October 17, 2001, Kadlec sent Lakeview Medical a request for credentialing information about Berry. The request included a detailed confidential questionnaire, a delineation of privileges, and a signed consent for release of information. The interrogatories on the questionnaire asked whether "[Dr. Berry] has been subject to any disciplinary action," if "[Dr. Berry has] the ability (health status) to perform the privileges requested," whether "[Dr. Berry has] shown any signs of behavior/personality problems or impairments," and whether Dr. Berry has satisfactory "judgement."

Nine days later, Lakeview Medical responded to the requests for credentialing information about fourteen different physicians. In thirteen cases, it responded fully and completely to the request, filling out forms with all the information asked for by the requesting health care provider. The fourteenth request, from Kadlec concerning Berry, was handled differently. Instead of completing the multi–part forms, Lakeview Medical staff drafted a short letter. In its entirety, it read:

> This letter is written in response to your inquiry regarding [Dr. Berry]. Due to the large volume of inquiries received in this office, the following information is provided.
>
> Our records indicate that Dr. Robert L. Berry was on the Active Medical Staff of Lakeview Regional Medical Center in the field of Anesthesiology from March 04, 1997 through September 04, 2001.
>
> If I can be of further assistance, you may contact me at (504) 867–4076.

The letter did not disclose LAA's termination of Dr. Berry; his on–duty drug use; the investigation into Dr. Berry's undocumented and suspicious withdrawals of Demerol that "violated the standard of care"; or any other negative information. The employee who drafted the letter said at trial that she just followed a form letter, which is one of many that Lakeview Medical used.

Kadlec then credentialed Dr. Berry, and he began working there. After working at Kadlec without incident for a number of months, he moved temporarily to Montana where he worked at Benefis Hospital. During his stay in Montana, he was in a car accident and suffered a back injury. Kadlec's head of anesthesiology and the credentialing department all knew of Dr. Berry's accident and back injury, but they did not investigate whether it would impair his work.

After Dr. Berry returned to Kadlec, some nurses thought that he appeared sick and exhibited mood swings. One nurse thought that Dr. Berry's entire demeanor had changed and that he should be watched closely. In mid–September 2002, Dr. Berry gave a patient too much morphine during surgery, and she had to be revived using Narcan. The neurosurgeon was irate about the incident.

On November 12, 2002, Dr. Berry was assigned to the operating room beginning at 6:30 a.m. He worked with three different surgeons and multiple nurses well into the afternoon. According to one nurse, Dr. Berry was "screwing up all day" and several of his patients suffered adverse affects from not being properly anesthetized. He had a hacking cough and multiple nurses thought he looked sick. During one procedure, he apparently almost passed out.

Kimberley Jones was Dr. Berry's fifth patient that morning. She was in for what should have been a routine, fifteen minute tubal ligation. When they moved her into the recovery room, one nurse noticed that her fingernails were blue, and she was not breathing. Dr. Berry failed to resuscitate her, and she is now in a permanent vegetative state.

Dr. Berry's nurse went directly to her supervisor the next morning and expressed concern that Dr. Berry had a narcotics problem. Dr. Berry later admitted to Kadlec staff that he had been diverting and using Demerol since his June car accident in Montana and that he had become addicted to Demerol. Dr. Berry wrote a confession, and he immediately admitted himself into a drug rehabilitation program.

Jones's family sued Dr. Berry and Kadlec in Washington. Dr. Berry's insurer settled the claim against him. After the Washington court ruled that Kadlec would be responsible for Dr. Berry's conduct under *respondeat superior,* Western, Kadlec's insurer, settled the claim against Kadlec.

II. Procedural History

Kadlec and Western filed this suit in Louisiana district court against LAA, Dr. Dennis, Dr. Preau, Dr. Baldone, Dr. Parr, and Lakeview Medical, asserting Louisiana state law claims for intentional misrepresentation, negligent misrepresentation, strict responsibility misrepresentation, and general negligence. Plaintiffs alleged that defendants' tortious activity led to Kadlec's hiring of Dr. Berry and the resulting millions of dollars it had to expend settling the Jones lawsuit. Plaintiffs' claim against LAA for negligence, based on a negligent monitoring and investigation theory, was dismissed before trial.

Plaintiffs' surviving claims for intentional and negligent misrepresentation arise out of the alleged misrepresentations in, and omissions from, the defendants' referral letters for Dr. Berry. These claims were tried to a jury, which returned a verdict in favor of the plaintiffs on both claims. The jury awarded plaintiffs $8.24 million, which is approximately equivalent to the amount Western spent settling the Jones lawsuit ($7.5 million) plus the amount it spent on attorneys fees, costs, and expenses (approximately $744,000) associated with the Jones lawsuit. The jury also found Kadlec and Dr. Berry negligent. The jury apportioned fault as follows: Dr. Dennis 20%; Dr. Preau 5%; Lakeview Medical 25%; Kadlec 17%; and Dr. Berry 33%. The judgments against Dr. Dennis and Dr. Preau were *in solido* with LAA. Because defendants were found liable for intentional misrepresentation, plaintiffs' recovery was not reduced by the percentage of fault ascribed to Kadlec. But the amount was reduced to $5.52 million to account for Dr. Berry's 33% of the fault. The district court entered judgment against Lakeview Medical and LAA.

III. Discussion

A. The Intentional and Negligent Misrepresentation Claims

The plaintiffs allege that the defendants committed two torts: intentional misrepresentation and negligent misrepresentation. The elements of a claim for *intentional* misrepresentation in Louisiana are: (1) a misrepresentation of a material fact; (2) made with intent to deceive; and (3) causing justifiable reliance with resultant injury. To establish a claim for intentional misrepresentation when it is by silence or inaction, plaintiffs also must show that the defendant owed a duty to the plaintiff to disclose the information. To make out a *negligent* misrepresentation claim in Louisiana: (1) there must be a legal duty on the part of the defendant to supply correct information; (2) there must be a breach of that duty, which can occur by omission as well as by affirmative misrepresentation; and (3) the breach must have caused damages to the plaintiff based on the plaintiff's reasonable reliance on the misrepresentation.

The defendants argue that any representations in, or omissions from, the referral letters cannot establish liability. We begin our analysis below by holding that after choosing to write referral letters, the defendants assumed a duty not to make affirmative misrepresentations in the letters. We next analyze whether the letters were misleading, and we conclude that the LAA defendants' letters were misleading, but the letter from Lakeview Medical was not. We also examine whether the defendants had an affirmative duty to disclose negative information about Dr. Berry in their referral letters, and we conclude that there was not an affirmative duty to disclose. Based on these holdings, Lakeview Medical did not breach any duty owed to Kadlec, and therefore the judgment against it is reversed. Finally, we examine other challenges to the LAA defendants' liability, and we conclude that they are without merit.

1. *The Affirmative Misrepresentations*

The defendants owed a duty to Kadlec to avoid affirmative misrepresentations in the referral letters. In Louisiana, "[a]lthough a party may keep absolute silence and violate no rule of law or equity, . . . if he volunteers to speak and to convey information which may influence the conduct of the other party, he is bound to [disclose] the whole truth." In negligent misrepresentation cases, Louisiana courts have held that even when there is no initial duty to disclose information, "once [a party] volunteer[s] information, it assume[s] a duty to insure that the information volunteered [is] correct.".

Consistent with these cases, the defendants had a legal duty not to make affirmative misrepresentations in their referral letters. A party does not incur liability every time it casually makes an incorrect statement. But if an employer makes a misleading statement in a referral letter about the performance of its former employee, the former employer may be liable for its statements if the facts and circumstances warrant. Here, defendants were recommending an anesthesiologist, who held the lives of patients in his hands every day. Policy considerations dictate that the defendants had a duty to avoid misrepresentations in their referral letters if they misled plaintiffs into thinking that Dr. Berry was an "excellent" anesthesiologist, when they had information that he was a drug addict. Indeed, if defendants' statements created a misapprehension about Dr. Berry's suitability to work as an anesthesiologist, then by "volunteer[ing] to speak and to convey information which . . . influence[d] the conduct of [Kadlec], [they were] bound to [disclose] the whole truth." In other words, if they created a misapprehension about Dr. Berry due to their own statements, they incurred a duty to disclose information about his drug use and for–cause firing to complete the whole picture.

We now review whether there is evidence that the defendants' letters were misleading. We start with the LAA defendants. The letter from Dr. Preau stated that Dr. Berry was an "excellent anesthesiologist" and that he "recommend[ed] him highly." Dr. Dennis's letter said that Dr. Berry was "an excellent physician" who "he is sure will be an asset to [his future employer's] anesthesia service." These letters are false on their face and materially misleading. Notably, these letters came only sixty–eight days after Drs. Dennis and Preau, on behalf of LAA, signed a letter terminating Dr. Berry for using narcotics while on–duty and stating that Dr. Berry's behavior put "patients at significant risk." Furthermore, because of the misleading statements in the letters, Dr. Dennis and Dr. Preau incurred a duty to cure these misleading statements by disclosing to Kadlec that Dr. Berry had been fired for on–the–job drug use.

The question as to whether Lakeview Medical's letter was misleading is more difficult. The letter does not comment on Dr. Berry's proficiency as an anesthesiologist, and it does not recommend him to Kadlec. Kadlec says that the letter is misleading because Lakeview Medical stated that it could not reply to Kadlec's detailed inquiry in full "[d]ue to the large volume of inquiries received." But whatever the real reason that Lakeview Medical did not respond in full to Kadlec's inquiry, Kadlec did not present evidence that this could have affirmatively misled it into thinking that Dr. Berry had an uncheckered history at Lakeview Medical.

Kadlec also says that the letter was misleading because it erroneously reported that Dr. Berry was on Lakeview Medical's active medical staff until September 4, 2001. Kadlec presented testimony that had it known that Dr. Berry never returned to Lakeview Medical after March 13, 2001, it would have been suspicious about the apparently large gap in his employment. While it is true that Dr. Berry did not return to Lakeview Medical after March 13, this did not terminate his privileges at the hospital, or mean that he was not on "active medical staff." In fact, it appears that Dr. Berry submitted a formal resignation letter on October 1, 2001, weeks *after* September 4. Therefore, while the September 4 date does not accurately reflect when Dr. Berry was no longer on Lakeview Medical's active medical staff, it did not mislead Kadlec into thinking that he had less of a gap in employment than he actually had.

In sum, we hold that the letters from the LAA defendants were affirmatively misleading, but the letter from Lakeview Medical was not. Therefore, Lakeview Medical cannot be held liable based on its alleged affirmative misrepresentations. It can only be liable if it had an affirmative duty to disclose information about Dr. Berry. We now examine the theory that, even assuming that there were no misleading statements in the referral letters, the defendants had an affirmative duty to disclose. We discuss this theory with regard to both defendants for reasons that will be clear by the end of the opinion.

2. *The Duty to Disclose*

In Louisiana, a duty to disclose does not exist absent special circumstances, such as a fiduciary or confidential relationship between the parties, which, under the circumstances, justifies the imposition of the duty. Louisiana cases suggest that before a duty to disclose is imposed the defendant must have had a pecuniary interest in the transaction. In Louisiana, the existence of a duty is a question of law, and we review the duty issue here *de novo.*

* * *

Despite these compelling policy arguments, we do not predict that courts in Louisiana–absent misleading statements such as those made by the LAA defendants–would impose an affirmative duty to disclose. The defendants did not have a fiduciary or contractual duty to disclose what it knew to Kadlec. And although the defendants might have had an ethical obligation to disclose their knowledge of Dr. Berry's drug problems, they were also rightly concerned about a possible defamation claim if they communicated negative information about Dr. Berry. As a general policy matter, even if an employer believes that its disclosure is protected because of the truth of the matter communicated, it would be burdensome to impose a duty on employers, upon receipt of a employment referral request, to investigate whether the negative information it has about an employee fits within the courts' description of *which* negative information must be disclosed to the future employer. Finally, concerns about protecting employee privacy weigh in favor of not mandating a potentially broad duty to disclose.

The Louisiana court in *Louviere* recognized that no court in Louisiana has imposed on an employer a duty to disclose information about a former employee to a future employer. [The court examined caselaw outside Louisiana, concluding that mere mondisclosure was never sufficient.] * * * These cases reinforce our conclusion that the defendants had a duty to avoid misleading statements in their referral letters, but they do not support plaintiffs' duty to disclose theory. * * *

3. Legal Cause

[LAA argued that legal causation could not be proven, on the grounds that "Kadlec's and Dr. Berry's intervening negligence precludes concluding that it is a legal cause of plaintiffs' injuries." The court found that "[t]he harm to Jones and the harm to plaintiffs that resulted from the LAA defendants' breaches are "easily associated" with Kadlec's liability. In fact, harm stemming from Dr. Berry's use of narcotic drugs while on–duty is the type of harm we would expect."

The Court then rejected LAA's argument that they should be absolved because of the superseding negligence of Kadlec and Berry. "Dr. Berry's hiring and his subsequent negligent use of narcotics while on–duty was foreseeable and "easily associated" with the LAA defendants' actions. He had used narcotics while on–duty in the past, and the LAA defendants could foresee that he would do so again if they misled a future employer about his drug problem." The court noted that while Kadlec had warning signs of Dr. Berry's erratic behavior, LAA had ". . . negligently *and intentionally* misled Kadlec about Dr. Berry's drug addiction. By intentionally covering up Dr. Berry's drug addiction in communications with a future employer, they should have foreseen that the future employer might miss the warning signs of Dr. Berry's addiction. This was within the scope of the risk they took."

The court concluded: "Indeed, both plaintiffs' and defendants' witnesses agreed at trial that narcotics addiction is a disease, that addicts try to hide their disease from their co–workers, and that particularly in the case of narcotics–addicted anesthesiologists, for whom livelihood and drug supply are in the same place, colleagues may be the last to know about their addiction and impairment. This is not a case where a future tortious act is so unforeseeable that it should relieve the earlier tortfeasor of liability. In fact, this case illustrates why the comparative fault system was developed–so, as here, multiple actors can share fault for an injury based on their respective degrees of responsibility."]

* * *

D. Negligent Monitoring and Investigation

[The Court upheld the district court's holding that any duties under the HCQIA and Louisiana regulations do not reach these plaintiffs.]

E. Summary and Remand Instructions

The district court properly instructed the jury to find for the plaintiffs on their intentional and negligent misrepresentation claims if the jury concluded that the defendants' letters to Kadlec were intentionally and negligently misleading in a manner that caused injury to the plaintiffs. * * * The letters from Dr. Dennis and Dr. Preau were false on their face and patently misleading. There is no question about the purpose or effect of the letters. Because no reasonable juror could find otherwise, we uphold the finding of liability against Dr. Dennis and Dr. Preau. But because Lakeview Medical's letter was not materially misleading, and because the hospital did not have a legal duty to disclose its investigation of Dr. Berry and its knowledge of his drug problems, the judgment against Lakeview Medical must be reversed.

* * *

The judgment of the district court is REVERSED in part, VACATED in part, and REMANDED for proceedings consistent with this opinion.

NOTES AND QUESTIONS

1. The Fifth Circuit treated the case as just another employment case, applying a simple "materially misleading" test to the letter sent by Lakeview Medical, and finding it did not meet the test. As to a duty to disclose, the court found that ". . . . [t]he defendants did not have a fiduciary or contractual duty to disclose what it knew to Kadlec."

Why didn't the court consider the special fiduciary nature of health care, and the harm that a substance–abusing anesthesiologist can cause his patients? Can you make a strong argument for a special rule for a wide range of severe health care risks that transcend normal employment risks?

For a criticism of the case, see Sallie Thieme Sanford, Candor After Kadlec: Why, Despite the Firth Circuit's Decision, Hospitals Should Anticipate an Expanded Obligation to Disclose Risky Physician Behavior, 1 Drexel L. Rev. 383(2009).

2. In Douglass v. Salem Community Hospital, 153 Ohio App.3d 350, 794 N.E.2d 107 (2003), the hospital hired Wagner, a pedophile, as the assistant director of social services. It appears that in 1987, the police informed Western Reserve, his earlier hospital employer, that Wagner had been accused of exposing himself and molesting children and those accusations were being investigated at that time. Wagner resigned his employment on the condition that Western Reserve would state to those conducting reference checks in the future that he had voluntarily resigned. He then later resigned from Salem Hospital. A boy who had received counseling was invited to spend the weekend with Wagner, and his mother checked with an employee of Salem whom she knew, Williams; Williams told her that Wagner "would be good". Wagner sexually assaulted the boy and his cousin at his house over the weekend.

The court accepted the plaintiff's argument that Restatement (Second) of Torts (1965), § 323, negligent performance of an undertaking to render service, would apply in this situation of a failure to warn:

> One who undertakes, gratuitously or for consideration, to render services to another which he should recognize as necessary for the protection of the other's person or things, is subject to liability to the other for physical harm resulting from his failure to exercise reasonable care to perform his undertaking, if * * * (b) the harm is suffered because of the other's reliance upon the undertaking.

The theory of recovery under § 323(b) is that "when one undertakes a duty voluntarily, and another reasonably relies on that undertaking, the volunteer is required to exercise ordinary care in completing the duty." [ ] In other words, "[a] voluntary act, gratuitously undertaken, must be * * * performed with the exercise of due care under the circumstances." [ ] This theory of negligence does not require proof of a special relationship between the plaintiff and the defendant, or proof of somewhat overwhelming circumstances. This type of negligence follows the general rules for finding negligence, with the addition of one extra element of proof, that of reasonable reliance by the plaintiff on the actions of the defendant.

Why were the various institutions so hypercautious, when the harm threatened was criminal in nature? Is this level of defensiveness something the law should tolerate?

3. Can you make an argument that a hospital should be responsible, under some circumstances, for the negligent acts of physicians in their private practice, so long as they have staff privileges? What if the hospital is on notice of a long history of malpractice claims against one of its staff, resulting from negligence in that physician's private practice? If the physician has performed adequately while treating patients within the hospital, should the hospital have any further responsibility?

Consider the case of Copithorne v. Framingham Union Hospital, 401 Mass. 860, 520 N.E.2d 139 (1988). The plaintiff, Copithorne, was a technologist at Framingham Union Hospital who was drugged and sexually assaulted by a physician with staff privileges at the hospital. The Massachusetts Supreme Judicial Court imposed liability on the hospital. Helfant was a practicing neurosurgeon and a visiting staff member of the hospital, having been reappointed for seventeen years to the medical staff. The plaintiff Copithorne was a hospital employee. In the course of her employment, she injured her back, and, aware of Helfant's reputation within the hospital as a good neurosurgeon and a specialist in back injuries, she sought his professional assistance. In the course of treating her, Helfant made a house call to Copithorne's apartment, where he committed the drugging and rape for which he was convicted and which caused the injuries for which Copithorne sought compensation. The hospital had actual notice, and " * * * owed a duty of care to Copithorne, as an employee who, in deciding to enter a doctor–patient relationship with Helfant, reasonably relied on Helfant's good standing and reputation within the hospital community, and that the hospital violated this duty by failing to take sufficient action in response to previous allegations of Helfant's wrongdoing."

IV. LIABILITY AND THE AFFORDABLE CARE ACT

The rules governing hospital liability are largely based on the role of physicians and physician groups as independent contractors, and the hospital medical staff as an independent decision making body. The previous material has indicated that the courts have been increasingly willing to reject agency defenses for independent contractors in the health care setting. The ACA has no provisions that directly address agency relationships or corporate negligence, nor does it explicitly alter the existing common law rules relating to vicarious liability and independent contractors. What the ACA does do, however, is create strong pressures—through centers, demonstration projects, and Medicare reimbursement incentives—for providers to integrate and coordinate their delivery of health care for Medicare recipients.

A. ACA COORDINATION REFORMS

The ACA offers coordination models to reduce fee–for–service medicine and decrease fragmentation in the U.S. health care system. Some of these are listed below.

1. *Centers.* Centers can fund research, disseminate findings, and create a powerful force for the diffusion of effective models. A *Center for Medicare and Medicaid Innovation* (CMI) will research, develop, test, and expand innovative payment and delivery arrangements to improve the quality and reduce the cost of care provided to patients in each program. Centers such as the CMI can channel millions of dollars toward research and expansion of payment and delivery reforms and are likely to be influential on the future of medical practice.

2. *Healthcare Innovation Zones.* Section 3210 (xviii) aims to create such zones, comprised of groups of providers that include a teaching hospital, physicians, and other clinical entities that can deliver a full spectrum of integrated and comprehensive health care services to applicable individuals.

3. *Accountable Care Organizations.* Section 3022, the *Medicare Shared Savings Program*, creates a program that "promotes accountability for a patient population and coordinates items and services under parts A and B, and encourages investment in infrastructure and redesigned care processes for high quality and efficient service delivery. These Accountable Care organizations will offer a much more integrated model of care, including providers and institution within a coordinated legal structure.

4. *Performance–based Care Coordination.* Other coordination innovations include, among others, patient–centered medical homes, direct contracting with groups of providers to promote new delivery models "through risk–based comprehensive payment or salary–based payment", and coordinated care models.

5. *Payment Bundling.* Similar services are grouped together and are compensated using a single or global payment. Services could be grouped according to the care provided by a single doctor or multiple doctors.

6. *Patient–centered medical homes.* Primary care physicians receive additional monthly payments for effectively using health information technology and other innovations to monitor, coordinate and manage care.

B. THE EFFECT OF COORDINATION REFORMS ON INSTITUTIONAL LIABLITY

Assume that within a few years ACOs and Medical Homes are successfully formed, comprehensive patient bundling is implemented in many hospitals, and salary–based payment systems proliferate. These reforms do several things at once: they move physicians from solo or small group practice into a salaried position in a group model or a hospital; they shift power toward enterprises that can buy and coordinate the technologies—from EHRs to case management strategies—to meet the demands of the federal government; and they therefore turn more providers into agents of institutional providers.

The liability result is clear if these various reforms, incentives and forces converge. First, institutional providers will become liable for patient injury, as well as the physicians causing patient injury directly, because agency law will carry liability upstream from agent to principal. Physicians will be much more integrated into the system, whether or not they are salaried, and any argument of independent contractor status will evaporate.

Second, even if ACOs and other entities operate without a hospital as part of the organization, they have become institutional health care providers, subject to liability just as a hospital or managed care organization is, on both vicarious liability and direct negligence principles.

Third, corporate negligence principles will likely apply to integrated organizations that manage care, whether a patient medical home, an ACO, or some other delivery form that the ACA creates. The courts are willing to look beyond the hospital form in deciding whether a health care entity might be liable for corporate negligence. For example, in Gianquitti v. Atwood Medical Associates, LTD., 973 A.2d 580 (R.I. 2009), the court held that a professional medical–group practice that provides on–call medical care to its patients if and when they are hospitalized could be liable for corporate negligence if it lacked a formal backup system. In another case, Davis v. Gish, 2007 WL 5007253 (Pa.Com. Pl. 2007), the court noted the kinds of activities that would turn a professional group or a physicians' practice group into an entity subject to corporate negligence. The entity would, like an HMO, "involve themselves daily in decisions affecting their subscriber's medical care. These decisions may, among others, limit the length of hospital stays, restrict the use of specialists, prohibit or limit post–hospital care, restrict access to therapy, or prevent rendering of emergency room care." *Id.* at 835. The entity must have general responsibility for "for arranging and coordinating the total health care of its patients" It must take "an active role in patients' care".

Today most physician groups or physician office–based practices would not be said to possess such responsibility. But the entities fostered by the ACA and its millions of dollars in demonstration grants and Medicare mandates are far more likely to coordinate care, taking on new responsibilities that will make them appropriate defendants in tort litigation.

PROBLEM: THE BIRTHING CENTER

You have been approached by Rosa Hernandez to handle a tort suit for damages for the death of her infant during delivery at the Hastings Birthing Center. Discovery reveals the following facts.

The death of the infant is attributable to the negligence of Dr. Jones, the physician who attended Ms. Hernandez at the Center during delivery. The death was caused in part by the infant's aspiration of meconium into the lungs. Although the Center is equipped to suction meconium and other material from a newborn's throat, it is not equipped to perform an intubation and attach the infant to a ventilator. To intubate the infant, it would have to be transferred to the hospital. Even if the infant had been transferred, it would probably have suffered brain damage due to oxygen deprivation before the procedure could have been undertaken.

Dr. Jones has a spotless record, but over the two weeks preceding the incident he had appeared at the hospital smelling of alcohol and evidencing other signs of intoxication. He was apparently having marital problems at the time. Nurses at the hospital had reported this behavior to their supervisor and had watched the physician's work very carefully, calling his attention to things he missed. The nurse supervisor had reported the situation to the head of OB/GYN, who said he would "look into it". Ms. Hernandez noticed the smell of liquor on Dr. Jones' breath during her labor, and was upset by his apparent intoxication. Dr. Jones has also dropped his malpractice insurance coverage, a fact of which the hospital is aware.

Further discovery has revealed that the nurse–midwife had observed that Dr. Jones' acts were questionable, but she had not intervened because she knew of his excellent reputation. She knew that doctors were resentful of the independence of nurse–midwives at the Center, and she believed she could "compensate" for his mistakes during the delivery. By the time she realized the extent of Dr. Jones' intoxication and took over the delivery, it was too late.

Your discovery reveals that there is a complicated relationship between the Birthing Center and the nearby Columbia Hospital. The hospital found that it had needed to increase its patient census, and that neonatology was one of its most profitable services. To increase its census in this area and to better serve the community, Columbia established the Hastings Birthing Center last year. The hospital receives a percentage of the profits of the Center.

The Center is located in a former convent one block from the hospital. The hospital owns the building and rents it to the Center. This particular birthing center, according to its promotional literature, offers "both a home–like setting for the delivery of your child and the security of the availability of back–up physicians and hospital care." The Center is separately incorporated and has its own Board of Directors. It is totally self–governing and is solely responsible for staff, provision of equipment, and policy.

The phone listing in the Yellow Pages describes the Hospital as a "cooperating hospital that will provide hospital care for mother and child if needed." Columbia has a contract with the Center requiring the Center to establish a screening program that will exclude high–risk patients and require that doctors attending patients at the Center have privileges at Columbia Hospital. The hospital allows the employees of the Center to participate in the hospital's group health and pension plans. Nurses from the hospital moonlight at the Center. When they do so, they receive a separate paycheck from the Center.

Although the Center's by–laws provide for a committee to review the qualifications of physicians who attend at the Center, it has in fact relied on the hospital's review of qualifications, since the hospital has a better opportunity to review credentials and performance. It is not clear that the hospital is aware of this; while it does notify the Center of the suspension, denial or revocation of privileges, it does not provide the Center with information used in investigations.

If you decide to litigate, should you sue both the Center and the hospital as well as Dr. Jones? Describe your theories, based on the information you have discovered to date, and consider what other facts you would like to know.

PROBLEM: SYSTEM REFORMS AND LIABILITY

Axis University Hospital (*Axis*) has decided that it needs to better coordinate its patient care from the moment patients enter the hospital until they leave and return to the care of their own physicians or specialists. Its CEO and CFO have scoured the ACA and have decided to adopt the following steps.

First, they have developed their own model of direct contracting with local physician groups, particularly cardiologists and oncologists, designed to promote risk–based comprehensive payments.

Second, for elderly patients with comorbidities, who often seem to move between home or nursing home and the hospital, they propose a coordinated care model in which gerontologists will be paid by salary rather than fee–for–service.

Third, for primary care physicians in their community catchment area, they propose patient–centered medical homes that entail the use of medical technologies of monitoring, along with extensive electronic medical recordkeeping. Physicians who agree to participate in such medical homes will receive bonus payments based on their adoption of a range of treatment measures.

You are the general counsel of *Axis*, and have been asked to make a presentation to the Board of Directors on any negatives that such new payment models might create for *Axis*. Consider in particular the liability consequences of each of the three approaches. Are traditional tort concepts undermined by moving to these delivery forms? Who is more at risk for liability with these reforms—physicians, hospitals and systems, other providers?

V. TORT LIABILITY OF MANAGED CARE

Managed care rapidly supplanted fee–for–service medicine during the 1990s and after. By 2012 employment–based insurance covered 155 million members. Fewer than 1 percent of the employees in all firms are enrolled in fee–for–service indemnity plans. Preferred Provider Plans (PPOs) now cover 56 percent of insured workers, and HMO plans cover 16 perent, Point Of Service (POS) plans 9 percent, and High Deductible Plans cover 19 percnt, having risen from just 8 percent in 2009. The shift away from the more intensively cost managed HMO model is apparent, as the tools of managed care—preapproval of specialists, capitation, and other features—managed to alienate both providers and subscribers during those decades. See Kaiser Family Foundation et al., Employer Benefits: 2012 Annual Survey (2012) particularly Exhibit E, page 4.

"Managed care" is a phrase often used to describe organizational groupings that attempt to control the utilization of health care services through a variety of techniques, including limiting enrollees to contracted provider networks, reviewing the utilization of various services, or using incentives such as per capita payments to encourage providers to limit the provision of services. The groups cover a wide variety of plans—from plans that require little more than preauthorization of patient hospitalization, to staff model HMOs—that focus on utilization and price of services. The goal is reduction of health care costs and maximization of value to both patient and payer. A Managed Care Organization (MCO) is a reimbursement framework combined with a health care delivery system, an approach to the delivery of health care services that contrasts with "fee–for–service" medicine. Managed care is usually distinguished from traditional indemnity plans by the existence of a single entity responsible for integrating and coordinating the financing and delivery of services that were once scattered between providers and payers.

Managed care plans can avoid liability for state law claims—including tort claims—if they are "qualified" ERISA plans. The Employee Retirement Income Security Act of 1974 (ERISA) preempts either explicitly, or by U.S. Supreme Court interpretation the vast majority of managed care plans that are employment based and ERISA–qualified. ERISA does not cover insurance plans that are not employment–based, including individual, Medicaid, workers' compensation, or auto medical plans. See generally Chapter 8 for a full discussion of ERISA preemption. The following discussion is therefore applicable to managed care plans that fall in the category of non–ERISA qualified plans for which federal preemption is not a defense to the defendant, or to the increasingly limited range of theories that the Supreme Court has left open to plaintiffs in state courts. Individual coverage will become much more widespread under the Affordable Care Act, thus this body of law is likely to become more important as the ACA is implemented. Moreover, the liability principles discussed below will apply to the new delivery models promoted by the ACA, such as Accountable Care Organizations and Medical Homes, among others, that are not protected by ERISA preemption from being sued.

A. VICARIOUS LIABILITY

Health maintenance organizations (HMOs) and Independent Practice Associations (IPAs) in theory face the same vicarious and corporate liability questions as hospitals because they provide services through physicians, whether the physicians are salaried employees or independent contractors. These medical services can injure patients/subscribers, leading to a malpractice suit for such injuries.

PETROVICH V. SHARE HEALTH PLAN OF ILLINOIS, INC.

Supreme Court of Illinois, 1999.
188 Ill.2d 17, 241 Ill.Dec. 627, 719 N.E.2d 756.

JUSTICE BILANDIC delivered the opinion of the court:

The plaintiff brought this medical malpractice action against a physician and others for their alleged negligence in failing to diagnose her oral cancer in a timely manner. The plaintiff also named her health maintenance organization (HMO) as a defendant. The central issue here is whether the plaintiff's HMO may be held vicariously liable for the negligence of its independent–contractor physicians under agency law. The plaintiff contends that the HMO is vicariously liable under both the doctrines of apparent authority and implied authority.

* * *

Facts

In 1989, plaintiff's employer, the Chicago Federation of Musicians, provided health care coverage to all of its employees by selecting Share and enrolling its employees therein. Share is an HMO and pays only for medical care that is obtained within its network of physicians. In order to qualify for benefits, a Share member must select from the network a primary care physician who will provide that member's overall care and authorize referrals when necessary. Share gives its members a list of participating physicians from which to choose. Share has about 500 primary care physicians covering Share's service area, which includes the counties of Cook, Du Page, Lake, McHenry and Will. Plaintiff selected Dr. Marie Kowalski from Share's list, and began seeing Dr. Kowalski as her primary care physician in August of 1989. Dr. Kowalski was employed at a satellite facility of Illinois Masonic Medical Center (Illinois Masonic), which had a contract with Share to provide medical services to Share members.

In September of 1990, plaintiff saw Dr. Kowalski because she was experiencing persistent pain in the right sides of her mouth, tongue, throat and face. Plaintiff also complained of a foul mucus in her mouth. Dr. Kowalski referred plaintiff to two other physicians who had contracts with Share: Dr. Slavick, a neurologist, and Dr. Friedman, an ear, nose and throat specialist.

Plaintiff informed Dr. Friedman of her pain. Dr. Friedman observed redness or marked erythema alongside plaintiff's gums on the right side of her mouth. He recommended that plaintiff have a magnetic resonance imaging (MRI) test or a computed tomography (CT) scan performed on the base of her skull. According to plaintiff's testimony at her evidence deposition, Dr. Kowalski informed her that Share would not allow new tests as recommended by Dr. Friedman. Plaintiff did not consult with Share about the test refusals because she was not aware of Share's grievance procedure. Dr. Kowalski gave Dr. Friedman a copy of an old MRI test result at that time. The record offers no further information about this old MRI test.

Nonetheless, Dr. Kowalski later ordered an updated MRI of plaintiff's brain, which was performed on October 31, 1990. Inconsistent with Dr. Friedman's directions, however, this MRI failed to image the right base of the tongue area where redness existed. Plaintiff and Dr. Kowalski discussed the results of this MRI test on November 19, 1990, during a follow–up visit. Plaintiff testified that Dr. Kowalski told her that the MRI revealed no abnormality.

Plaintiff's pain persisted. In April or May of 1991, Dr. Kowalski again referred plaintiff to Dr. Friedman. This was plaintiff's third visit to Dr. Friedman. Dr. Friedman examined plaintiff and observed that plaintiff's tongue was tender. Also, plaintiff reported that she had a foul odor in her mouth and was experiencing discomfort. On June 7, 1991, Dr. Friedman performed multiple biopsies on the right side of the base of plaintiff's tongue and surrounding tissues. The biopsy results revealed squamous cell carcinoma, a cancer, in the base of plaintiff's tongue and the surrounding tissues of the pharynx. Later that month, Dr. Friedman operated on plaintiff to remove the cancer. He removed part of the base of plaintiff's tongue, and portions of her palate, pharynx and jaw bone. After the surgery, plaintiff underwent radiation treatments and rehabilitation.

Plaintiff subsequently brought this medical malpractice action against Share, Dr. Kowalski and others. Dr. Friedman was not named a party defendant. Plaintiff's complaint, though, alleges that both Drs. Kowalski and Friedman were negligent in failing to diagnose plaintiff's cancer in a timely manner, and that Share is vicariously liable for their negligence under agency principles. Share filed a motion for summary judgment, arguing that it cannot be held liable for the negligence of Dr. Kowalski or Friedman because they were acting as independent contractors in their treatment of plaintiff, not as Share's agents. Plaintiff countered that Share is not entitled to summary judgment because Drs. Kowalski and Friedman were Share's agents. The parties submitted various depositions, affidavits and exhibits in support of their respective positions.

Share is a for–profit corporation. At all relevant times, Share was organized as an "independent practice association–model" HMO under the Illinois Health Maintenance Organization Act (Ill.Rev.Stat.1991, ch. 111 ½, par. 1401et seq.). This means that Share is a financing entity that arranges and pays for health care by contracting with independent medical groups and practitioners. [ ] Share does not employ physicians directly, nor does it own, operate, maintain or supervise the offices where medical care is provided to its members. Rather, Share contracts with independent medical groups and physicians that have the facilities, equipment and professional skills necessary to render medical care. Physicians desiring to join Share'snetwork are required to complete an application procedure and meet with Share's approval.

Share utilizes a method of compensation called "capitation" to pay its medical groups. Share also maintains a "quality assurance program." Share's capitation method of compensation and "quality assurance program" are more fully described later in this opinion.

Share provides a member handbook to each of its members, including plaintiff. The handbook states to its members that Share will provide "all your healthcare needs" and "comprehensive high quality services." The handbook also states that the primary care physician is "your health care manager" and "makes the decisions" about the member's care. The handbook further states that Share is a "good partner in sickness and in health." Unlike the master agreements and benefits contract discussed below, the member handbook which plaintiff received does not contain any provision that identifies Share physicians as independent contractors or nonemployees of Share. Rather, the handbook describes the physicians as "your Share physician," "Share physicians" and "our staff." Furthermore, Share refers to the physicians' offices as "Your Share physician's office" and states: "All of the Share staff and Medical Offices look forward to serving you * * *."

Plaintiff confirmed that she received the member handbook. Plaintiff did not read the handbook in its entirety, but read portions of it as she needed the information. She relied on the information contained in the handbook while Drs. Kowalski and Friedman treated her.

The record also contains a "Health Care Services Master Agreement," entered into by Share and Illinois Masonic. Dr. Kowalski is a signatory of this agreement. The agreement states, "It is understood and agreed that [Illinois Masonic] and [primary care physicians] are independent contractors and not employees or agents of SHARE." A separate agreement between Share and Dr. Friedman contains similar language. Plaintiff did not receive these agreements.

Share's primary care physicians, under their agreements with Share, are required to approve patients' medical requests and make referrals to specialists. These physicians use Share's standard referral forms to indicate their approval of the referral. Dr. Kowalski testified at an evidence deposition that she did not feel constrained by Share in making medical decisions regarding her patients, including whether to order tests or make referrals to specialists.

Another document in the record is Share's benefits contract. The benefits contract contains a subscriber certificate. The subscriber certificate sets forth a member's rights and obligations with respect to Share. Additionally, the subscriber certificate states that Share's physicians are independent contractors and that "SHARE Plan Providers and Enrolling Groups are not agents or employees of SHARE nor is SHARE or any employee of SHARE an agent or employee of SHARE Plan Providers or Enrolling Groups." The certificate elaborates: "The relationship between a SHARE Plan Provider and any Member is that of provider and patient. The SHARE Plan Physician is solely responsible for the medical services provided to any Member. The SHARE Plan Hospital is solely responsible for the Hospital services provided to any Member."

Plaintiff testified that she did not recall receiving the subscriber certificate. In response, Share stated that Share customarily provides members with this information. Share does not claim to know whether Share actually provided plaintiff with this information. Plaintiff acknowledged that she received a "whole stack" of information from Share upon her enrollment.

Plaintiff was not aware of the type of relationship that her physicians had with Share. At the time she received treatment, plaintiff believed that her physicians were employees of Share.

In the circuit court, Share argued that it was entitled to summary judgment because the independent–contractor provision in the benefits contract established, as a matter of law, that Drs. Kowalski and Friedman were not acting as Share's agents in their treatment of plaintiff. The circuit court agreed and entered summary judgment for Share.

The appellate court reversed, holding that a genuine issue of material fact is presented as to whether plaintiff's treating physicians are Share's apparent agents. 296 Ill.App.3d 849, 231 Ill.Dec. 364, 696 N.E.2d 356. The appellate court stated that a number of factors support plaintiff's apparent agency claim, including plaintiff's testimony, Share's member handbook, Share's quality assessment program and Share's capitation method of compensation. The appellate court therefore remanded the cause for trial. The appellate court did not address the theory of implied authority.

Analysis

This appeal comes before us amidst great changes to the relationships among physicians, patients and those entities paying for medical care. Traditionally, physicians treated patients on demand, while insurers merely paid the physicians their fee for the services provided. Today, managed care organizations (MCOs) have stepped into the insurer's shoes, and often attempt to reduce the price and quantity of health care services provided to patients through a system of health care cost containment. MCOs may, for example, use prearranged fee structures for compensating physicians. MCOs may also use utilization–review procedures, which are procedures designed to determine whether the use and volume of particular health care services are appropriate. MCOs have developed in response to rapid increases in health care costs.

HMOs, i.e., health maintenance organizations, are a type of MCO. HMOs are subject to both state and federal laws. [ ] Under Illinois law, an HMO is defined as "any organization formed under the laws of this or another state to provide or arrange for one or more health care plans under a system which causes any part of the risk of health care delivery to be borne by the organization or its providers." [ ]. Because HMOs may differ in their structures and the cost–containment practices that they employ, a court must discern the nature of the organization before it, where relevant to the issues. As earlier noted, Share is organized as an independent practice association (IPA)–model HMO. IPA–model HMOs are financing entities that arrange and pay for health care by contracting with independent medical groups and practitioners. [ ]

This court has never addressed a question of whether an HMO may be held liable for medical malpractice. Share asserts that holding HMOs liable for medical malpractice will cause health care costs to increase and make health care inaccessible to large numbers of people. Share suggests that, with this consideration in mind, this court should impose only narrow, or limited, forms of liability on HMOs. We disagree with Share that the cost–containment role of HMOs entitles them to special consideration. The principle that organizations are accountable for their tortious actions and those of their agents is fundamental to our justice system. There is no exception to this principle for HMOs. Moreover, HMO accountability is essential to counterbalance the HMO goal of cost–containment. To the extent that HMOs are profit–making entities, accountability is also needed to counterbalance the inherent drive to achieve a large and ever–increasing profit margin. Market forces alone "are insufficient to cure the deleterious [e]ffects of managed care on the health care industry." [ ] Courts, therefore, should not be hesitant to apply well–settled legal theories of liability to HMOs where the facts so warrant and where justice so requires.

Indeed, the national trend of courts is to hold HMOs accountable for medical malpractice under a variety of legal theories, including vicarious liability on the basis of apparent authority, vicarious liability on the basis of respondeat superior, direct corporate negligence, breach of contract and breach of warranty. [ ] * * * Share concedes that HMOs may be held liable for medical malpractice under these five theories.

This appeal concerns whether Share may be held vicariously liable under agency law for the negligence of its independent–contractor physicians. We must determine whether Share was properly awarded summary judgment on the ground that Drs. Kowalski and Friedman were not acting as Share's agents in their treatment of plaintiff. Plaintiff argues that Share is not entitled to summary judgment on this record. Plaintiff asserts that genuine issues of material fact exist as to whether Drs. Kowalski and Friedman were acting within Share'sapparent authority, implied authority or both.

* * *

As a general rule, no vicarious liability exists for the actions of independent contractors. Vicarious liability may nevertheless be imposed for the actions of independent contractors where an agency relationship is established under either the doctrine of apparent authority [ ] or the doctrine of implied authority [ ].

I. Apparent Authority

Apparent authority, also known as ostensible authority, has been a part of Illinois jurisprudence for more than 140 years. [ ] Under the doctrine, a principal will be bound not only by the authority that it actually gives to another, but also by the authority that it appears to give. [ ]. The doctrine functions like an estoppel. [ ]. Where the principal creates the appearance of authority, a court will not hear the principal's denials of agency to the prejudice of an innocent third party, who has been led to reasonably rely upon the agency and is harmed as a result.[ ]

* * *

We now hold that the apparent authority doctrine may also be used to impose vicarious liability on HMOs. * * * [ ]

To establish apparent authority against an HMO for physician malpractice, the patient must prove (1) that the HMO held itself out as the provider of health care, without informing the patient that the care is given by independent contractors, and (2) that the patient justifiably relied upon the conduct of the HMO by looking to the HMO to provide health care services, rather than to a specific physician. Apparent agency is a question of fact. [ ]

A. *Holding Out*

The element of "holding out" means that the HMO, or its agent, acted in a manner that would lead a reasonable person to conclude that the physician who was alleged to be negligent was an agent or employee of the HMO. [ ] Where the acts of the agent create the appearance of authority, a plaintiff must also prove that the HMO had knowledge of and acquiesced in those acts. [ ] The holding–out element does not require the HMO to make an express representation that the physician alleged to be negligent is its agent or employee. Rather, this element is met where the HMO holds itself out as the provider of health care without informing the patient that the care is given by independent contractors. [ ] Vicarious liability under the apparent authority doctrine will not attach, however, if the patient knew or should have known that the physician providing treatment is an independent contractor. [ ]

Here, Share contends that the independent–contractor provisions in the two master agreements and the benefits contract conclusively establish, as a matter of law, that Share did not hold out Drs. Kowalski and Friedman to be Share's agents. Although all three of these contracts clearly express that the physicians are independent contractors and not agents of Share, we disagree with Share's contention for the reasons explained below.

First, the two master agreements at issue are private contractual agreements between Share and Illinois Masonic, with Dr. Kowalski as a signatory, and between Share and Dr. Friedman. The record contains no indication that plaintiff knew or should have known of these private contractual agreements between Share and its physicians. Gilbert expressly rejected the notion that such private contractual agreements can control a claim of apparent agency. [ ] * * * We hold that this same rationale applies to private contractual agreements between physicians and an HMO. [ ] Because there is no dispute that the master agreements at bar were unknown to plaintiff, they cannot be used to defeat her apparent agency claim.

Share also relies on the benefits contract. Plaintiff was not a party or a signatory to this contract. The benefits contract contains a subscriber certificate, which states that Share physicians are independent contractors. Share claims that this language alone conclusively overcomes plaintiff's apparent agency claim. We do not agree.

Whether a person has notice of a physician's status as an independent contractor, or is put on notice by the circumstances, is a question of fact. [ ] In this case, plaintiff testified at her evidence deposition that she did not recall receiving the subscriber certificate. Share responded only that it customarily provides members with this information. Share has never claimed to know whether Share actually provided plaintiff with this information. Thus, a question of fact exists as to whether Share gave this information to plaintiff. If this information was not provided to plaintiff, it cannot be used to defeat her apparent agency claim.

* * *

Evidence in the record supports plaintiff's contentions that Share held itself out to its members as the provider of health care, and that plaintiff was not aware that her physicians were independent contractors. Notably, plaintiff stated that, at the time that she received treatment, plaintiff believed that Drs. Kowalski and Friedman were Share employees. Plaintiff was not aware of the type of relationship that her physicians had with Share.

Moreover, Share's member handbook contains evidence that Share held itself out to plaintiff as the provider of her health care. The handbook stated to Share members that Share will provide "all your healthcare needs" and "comprehensive high quality services." The handbook did not contain any provision that identified Share physicians as independent contractors or nonemployees of Share. Instead, the handbook referred to the physicians as "your Share physician," "Share physicians" and "our staff." Share also referred to the physicians' offices as "Your Share physician's office." The record shows that Share provided this handbook to each of its enrolled members, including plaintiff. Representations made in the handbook are thus directly attributable to Share and were intended by Share to be communicated to its members.

* * *

We hold that the above testimony by plaintiff and Share's member handbook support the conclusion that Share held itself out to plaintiff as the provider of her health care, without informing her that the care was actually provided by independent contractors. Therefore, a triable issue of fact exists as to the holding–out element. We need not resolve whether any other evidence in the record also supports plaintiff's claim. Our task here is to review whether Share is entitled to summary judgment on this element. We hold that Share is not.

B. Justifiable Reliance

A plaintiff must also prove the element of "justifiable reliance" to establish apparent authority against an HMO for physician malpractice. This means that the plaintiff acted in reliance upon the conduct of the HMO or its agent, consistent with ordinary care and prudence. [ ]

The element of justifiable reliance is met where the plaintiff relies upon the HMO to provide health care services, and does not rely upon a specific physician. This element is not met if the plaintiff selects his or her own personal physician and merely looks to the HMO as a conduit through which the plaintiff receives medical care. [ ]

Concerning the element of justifiable reliance in the hospital context, Gilbert explained that the critical distinction is whether the plaintiff sought care from the hospital itself or from a personal physician. * * *

This rationale applies even more forcefully in the context of an HMO that restricts its members to the HMO's chosen physicians. Accordingly, unless a person seeks care from a personal physician, that person is seeking care from the HMO itself. A person who seeks care from the HMO itself accepts that care in reliance upon the HMO's holding itself out as the provider of care.

Share maintains that plaintiff cannot establish the justifiable reliance element because she did not select Share. * * *

* * * We reject Share's argument. It is true that, where a person selects the HMO and does not rely upon a specific physician, then that person is relying upon the HMO to provide health care. This principle, derived directly from Gilbert, is set forth above. Equally true, however, is that where a person has no choice but to enroll with a single HMO and does not rely upon a specific physician, then that person is likewise relying upon the HMO to provide health care.

In the present case, the record discloses that plaintiff did not select Share. Plaintiff's employer selected Share for her. Plaintiff had no choice of health plans whatsoever. Once Share became plaintiff's health plan, Share required plaintiff to obtain her primary medical care from one of its primary care physicians. If plaintiff did not do so, Share did not cover plaintiff's medical costs. In accordance with Share's requirement, plaintiff selected Dr. Kowalski from a list of physicians that Share provided to her. Plaintiff had no prior relationship with Dr. Kowalski. As to Dr. Kowalski's selection of Dr. Friedman for plaintiff, Share required Dr. Kowalski to make referrals only to physicians approved by Share. Plaintiff had no prior relationship with Dr. Friedman. We hold that these facts are sufficient to raise the reasonable inference that plaintiff relied upon Share to provide her health care services.

Were we to conclude that plaintiff was not relying upon Share for health care, we would be denying the true nature of the relationship among plaintiff, her HMO and the physicians. Share, like many HMOs, contracted with plaintiff's employer to become plaintiff's sole provider of health care, to the exclusion of all other providers. Share then restricted plaintiff to its chosen physicians. Under these facts, plaintiff's reliance on Shareas the provider of her health care is shown not only to be compelling, but literally compelled. Plaintiff's reliance upon Share was inherent in Share's method of operation.

* * *

In conclusion, as set forth above, plaintiff has presented sufficient evidence to support justifiable reliance, as well as a holding out by Share.

Share, therefore, is not entitled to summary judgment against plaintiff's claim of apparent authority.

* * *

II. Implied Authority

Implied authority is actual authority, circumstantially proved. [ ] One context in which implied authority arises is where the facts and circumstances show that the defendant exerted sufficient control over the alleged agent so as to negate that person's status as an independent contractor, at least with respect to third parties. [ ] The cardinal consideration for determining the existence of implied authority is whether the alleged agent retains the right to control the manner of doing the work. [ ] Where a person's status as an independent contractor is negated, liability may result under the doctrine of respondeat superior.

Plaintiff contends that the facts and circumstances of this case show that Share exerted sufficient control over Drs. Kowalski and Friedman so as to negate their status as independent contractors. Share responds that the act of providing medical care is peculiarly within a physician's domain because it requires the exercise of independent medical judgment. Share thus maintains that, because it cannot control a physician's exercise of medical judgment, it cannot be subject to vicarious liability under the doctrine of implied authority.

* * *

We now address whether the implied authority doctrine may be used against HMOs to negate a physician's status as an independent contractor. Our appellate court in Raglin suggested that it can. [ ] Case law from other jurisdictions lends support to this view as well. [ ]

* * *

We do not find the above decisions rendered in the hospital context to be dispositive of whether an HMO may exert such control over its physicians so as to negate their status as independent contractors. We can readily discern that the relationships between physicians and HMOs are often much different than the traditional relationships between physicians and hospitals. * * *

Physicians, of course, should not allow the exercise of their medical judgment to be corrupted or controlled. Physicians have professional ethical, moral and legal obligations to provide appropriate medical care to their patients. These obligations on physicians, however, will not act to relieve an HMO of its own legal responsibilities. Where an HMO effectively controls a physician's exercise of medical judgment, and that judgment is exercised negligently, the HMO cannot be allowed to claim that the physician is solely responsible for the harm that results. In such a circumstance, both the physician and the HMO are liable for the harm that results. We therefore hold that the implied authority doctrine may be used against an HMO to negate a physician's status as an independent contractor. An implied agency exists where the facts and circumstances show that an HMO exerted such sufficient control over a participating physician so as to negate that physician's status as an independent contractor, at least with respect to third parties. [ ] No precise formula exists for deciding when a person's status as an independent contractor is negated. Rather, the determination of whether a person is an agent or an independent contractor rests upon the facts and circumstances of each case. [ ] As noted, the cardinal consideration is whether that person retains the right to control the manner of doing the work. [ ] * * *

With these established principles in mind, we turn to the present case. Plaintiff contends that her physicians' status as independent contractors should be negated. Plaintiff asserts that Share actively interfered with her physicians' medical decisionmaking by designing and executing its capitation method of compensation and "quality assurance" programs. Plaintiff also points to Share's referral system as evidence of control.

Plaintiff submits that Share's capitation method of compensating its medical groups is a form of control because it financially punishes physicians for ordering certain medical treatment. The record discloses that Share utilizes a method of compensation called "capitation."[ ]. Under capitation, Share prepays contracting medical groups a fixed amount of money for each member who enrolls with that group. In exchange, the medical groups agree to render health care to their enrolled Share members in accordance with the Share plan. Each medical group contracting with Share has its own capitation account. Deducted from that capitation account are the costs of any services provided by the primary care physician, the costs of medical procedures and tests, and the fees of all consulting physicians. The medical group then retains the surplus left in the capitation account. The costs for hospitalizations and other services are charged against a separate account. Reinsurance is provided for the capitation account and the separate account for certain high cost claims. Share pays Illinois Masonic in accordance with its capitation method of compensation. Dr. Kowalski testified that Illinois Masonic pays her the same salary every month. Plaintiff maintains that a reasonable inference to be drawn from Share's capitation method of compensation is that Share provides financial disincentives to its primary care physicians in order to discourage them from ordering the medical care that they deem appropriate. Plaintiff argues that this is an example of Share's influence and control over the medical judgment of its physicians.

Share counters that its capitation method of compensation cannot be used as evidence of control here because Dr. Kowalski is paid the same salary every month. We disagree with Share that this fact makes Share's capitation system irrelevant to our inquiry. Whether control was actually exercised is not dispositive in this context. Rather, the right to control the alleged agent is the proper query, even where that right is not exercised. [ ]

[The court rejects Share's "quality assurance program" as evidence of control, since it is done primarily to comply with state regulations of the Department of Public Health. The court however allows as evidence of control chart review by Share; control over referral to specialists; and use of primary care physicians as gatekeepers].

We conclude that plaintiff has presented adequate evidence to entitle her to a trial on the issue of implied authority. All the facts and circumstances before us, if proven at trial, raise the reasonable inference that Share exerted such sufficient control over Drs. Kowalski and Friedman so as to negate their status as independent contractors. As discussed above, plaintiff presents relevant evidence of Share's capitation method of compensation, Share's "quality assurance review," Share's referral system and Share's requirement that its primary care physicians act as gatekeepers for Share. These facts support plaintiff's argument that Share subjected its physicians to control over the manner in which they did their work. The facts surrounding treatment also support plaintiff's argument. According to plaintiff's evidence, Dr. Kowalski referred plaintiff to Dr. Friedman. Dr. Friedman evaluated plaintiff and recommended that plaintiff have either an MRI test or a CT scan performed on the base of her skull. Dr. Friedman, however, did not order the test that he recommended for plaintiff. Rather, he reported this information back to Dr. Kowalski in her role as plaintiff's primary care physician. Dr. Kowalski initially sent Dr. Friedman a copy of an old MRI test. Dr. Kowalski later ordered that an updated MRI be taken. In doing so, she directed that the MRI be taken of plaintiff's "brain." Hence, that MRI failed to image the base of plaintiff's skull as recommended by Dr. Friedman. Dr. Kowalski then reviewed the MRI test results herself and informed plaintiff that the results revealed no abnormality. From all the above facts and circumstances, a trier of fact could reasonably infer that Share promulgated such a system of control over its physicians that Share effectively negated the exercise of their independent medical judgment, to plaintiff's detriment.

We note that Dr. Kowalski testified at an evidence deposition that she did not feel constrained by Share in making medical decisions regarding her patients, including whether to order tests or make referrals to specialists. This testimony is not controlling at the summary judgment stage. The trier of fact is entitled to weigh all the conflicting evidence above against Dr. Kowalski's testimony.

In conclusion, plaintiff has presented adequate evidence to support a finding that Share exerted such sufficient control over its participating physicians so as to negate their status as independent contractors. Share, therefore, is not entitled to summary judgment against plaintiff's claim of implied authority.

* * *

Conclusion

An HMO may be held vicariously liable for the negligence of its independent–contractor physicians under both the doctrines of apparent authority and implied authority. Plaintiff here is entitled to a trial on both doctrines. The circuit court therefore erred in awarding summary judgment to Share. The appellate court's judgment, which reversed the circuit court's judgment and remanded the cause to the circuit court for further proceedings, is affirmed.

Affirmed.

NOTES AND QUESTIONS

1. Does a subscriber to an IPA–style managed care organization look to it for care rather than solely to the individual physicians? In an IPA, there is no central office, staffed by salaried physicians; the subscriber instead goes to the individual offices of the primary care physicians or the specialists. What justifies extending ostensible agency doctrine to this arrangement?

Managed care advertising often holds out the plan in words such as "total care program," or "an entire health care system." A reliance by the subscriber on the managed care organization (MCO) for his or her choice of physicians, and any holding out by the MCO as a provider, is sufficient. See McClellan v. Health Maintenance Organization of Pennsylvania, 413 Pa.Super. 128, 604 A.2d 1053 (1992) (ostensible agency based on advertisements by HMO claiming that it carefully screened in primary care physicians).

2. IPA–model HMOs that become "the institution," that "hold out" the independent contractor as an employee, and also restrict provider selection are vulnerable to ostensible agency arguments. Where the HMO exercises substantial control over the independent physicians by controlling the patients they must see and by paying on a per capita basis, an agency relationship has been found. See Dunn v. Praiss, 256 N.J.Super. 180, 606 A.2d 862 (App.Div.1992); Boyd v. Albert Einstein Medical Center, 377 Pa.Super. 609, 547 A.2d 1229 (1988).

3. A breach of contract suit can be brought against an MCO on the theory of a "contract" to provide quality health care. *Williams v. HealthAmerica*, 41 Ohio App.3d 245, 535 N.E.2d 717 (1987) (MCO contracts and literature may also contain provisions to the effect that "quality" health care will be provided or that the organization will promote or enhance subscriber health). The *Share* literature contained such language. Where such assurances are made in master contracts of HMO–physician agreements, subscrib-

ers may be able to bring a contract action under a third party beneficiary theory. In *Williams*, for example, the court suggested that the subscriber could be a third–party beneficiary of the HMO–physician contract that required the physician to "promote of the rights of enrollees as patients."

A claim for breach of an express contract or an implied contract may also be argued based on representations by an HMO as to quality of care. Express promises, if proven, can give rise to a separate claim.

MCOs also typically market themselves by describing the quality of the providers on the panel. An assertion of quality furnishes courts another reason to impose on the organization the duty to investigate the competency of participating physicians. Such assertions might even be viewed as a warranty that all panel members maintain a certain minimum competence.

4. MCOs can be held liable for contracting with substandard providers or imposing overly constraining contracts on those providers. See Pagarigan v. Aetna U.S. Healthcare of California, Inc., 2005 WL 2742807 (California Court of Appeal, 2005.) (holding that "the HMO owes a duty to avoid contracting with deficient providers or negotiating contract terms which require or unduly encourage denials of service or below–standard performance by its providers.").

B. CORPORATE NEGLIGENCE

SHANNON V. MCNULTY

Superior Court of Pennsylvania, 1998.
718 A.2d 828.

ORIE MELVIN, JUDGE:

Mario L. Shannon and his wife, Sheena Evans Shannon, in their own right and as co–administrators of the Estate of Evan Jon Shannon, appeal from an order entered in the Court of Common Pleas of Allegheny County denying their motion to remove a compulsory nonsuit. This appeal concerns the Shannons' claims of vicarious and corporate liability against HealthAmerica stemming from the premature delivery and subsequent death of their son. We reverse the order refusing to remove the compulsory nonsuit and remand for trial.

This medical malpractice action arises from the pre–natal care provided by appellees, Larry P. McNulty, M.D. and HealthAmerica, to Mrs. Shannon. The Shannons claimed Dr. McNulty was negligent for failing to timely diagnose and treat signs of pre–term labor, and HealthAmerica was vicariously liable for the negligence of its nursing staff in failing to respond to Mrs. Shannon's complaints by timely referring her to an appropriate physician or hospital for diagnosis and treatment of her pre–term labor. The Shannons also alleged HealthAmerica was corporately liable for its negligent supervision of Dr. McNulty's care and its lack of appropriate procedures and protocols when dispensing telephonic medical advice to subscribers.

[The trial court granted HealthAmerica's motion for compulsory non-suit, and the Shannons appealed.]

* * *

[Thompson v. Nason Hospital, 527 Pa. 330, 591 A.2d 703 (Pa.1991),set out four corporate negligence duties:

> (1) Use of "reasonable care in the maintenance of safe and adequate facilities and equipment;"
>
> (2) Selection and retention of competent physicians;
>
> (3) Oversight of "all persons who practice medicine within its walls as to patient care;" and
>
> (4) Formulation, adoption and enforcement of "adequate rules and policies to ensure quality care for patients," including upholding "the proper standard of care owed its patient." Id. at 708.]

* * *

The evidence introduced by the Shannons may be summarized in relevant part as follows. Mrs. Shannon testified during the trial of this case that she was a subscriber of the HealthAmerica HMO when this child was conceived. It was Mrs. Shannon's first pregnancy. When she advised HealthAmerica she was pregnant in June 1992, they gave her a list of six doctors from which she could select an OB/GYN. She chose Dr. McNulty from the list. [ ] Her HealthAmerica membership card instructed her to contact either her physician or HealthAmerica in the event she had any medical questions or emergent medical conditions. The card contained the HealthAmerica emergency phone number, which was manned by registered nurses. [ ] She testified it was confusing trying to figure out when to call Dr. McNulty and when to call HealthAmerica because she was receiving treatment from both for various medical conditions related to her pregnancy, including asthma and reflux.[ ]

She saw Dr. McNulty monthly but also called the HealthAmerica phone line a number of times for advice and to schedule appointments with their in–house doctors. [ ] She called Dr. McNulty on October 2, 1992 with complaints of abdominal pain. The doctor saw her on October 5, 1992 and examined her for five minutes. He told Mrs. Shannon her abdominal pain was the result of a fibroid uterus, he prescribed rest and took her off of work for one week. He did no testing to confirm his diagnosis and did not advise her of the symptoms of pre–term labor. [ ]

She next called Dr. McNulty's office twice on October 7 and again on October 8 and October 9, 1992, because her abdominal pain was continuing, she had back pain, was constipated and she could not sleep. She asked Dr. McNulty during the October 8th call if she could be in pre–term labor because her symptoms were similar to those described in a reference book she had on labor. [ ] She told Dr. McNulty her pains were irregular and about ten minutes apart, but she had never been in labor so she did not know what it felt like. He told her he had just checked her on October 5th, and she was not in labor.[ ] The October 9th call was at least her fourth call to Dr. McNulty about her abdominal pain, and she testified that Dr. McNulty was becoming impatient with her. [ ]

On October 10th, she called HealthAmerica's emergency phone line and told them about her severe irregular abdominal pain, back pain, that her pain was worse at night, that she thought she may be in pre–term labor, and about her prior calls to Dr. McNulty. The triage nurse advised her to call Dr. McNulty again. [ ] Mrs. Shannon did not immediately call Dr. McNulty because she did not feel there was anything new she could tell him to get him to pay attention to her condition. She called the HealthAmerica triage line again on October 11, 1992, said her symptoms were getting worse and Dr. McNulty was not responding. The triage nurse again advised her to call Dr. McNulty. [ ] Mrs. Shannon called Dr. McNulty and told him about her worsening symptoms, her legs beginning to go numb, and she thought that she was in pre–term labor. He was again short with her and angry and insisted that she was not in pre–term labor.[ ]

On October 12, 1992, she again called the HealthAmerica phone service and told the nurse about her symptoms, severe back pain and back spasms, legs going numb, more regular abdominal pain, and Dr. McNulty was not responding to her complaints. One of HealthAmerica's in–house orthopedic physicians spoke with her on the phone and directed her to go to West Penn Hospital to get her back examined. [ ] She followed the doctor's advice and drove an hour from her house to West Penn, passing three hospitals on the way. At West Penn she was processed as having a back complaint because those were HealthAmerica's instructions, but she was taken to the obstetrics wing as a formality because she was over five (5) months pregnant. She delivered a one and one–half pound baby that night. He survived only two days and then died due to his severe prematurity. [ ]

The Shannons' expert, Stanley M. Warner, M.D., testified he had experience in a setting where patients would call triage nurses. Dr. Warner opined that HealthAmerica, through its triage nurses, deviated from the standard of care following the phone calls to the triage line on October 10, 11 and 12, 1992, by not immediately referring Mrs. Shannon to a physician or hospital for a cervical exam and fetal stress test. As with Dr. McNulty, these precautions would have led to her labor being detected and increased the baby's chance of survival. [ ] Dr. Warner further testified on cross examination that Mrs. Shannon turned to HealthAmerica's triage nurses for medical advice on these three occasions when she communicated her symptoms. She did not receive appropriate advice, and further, if HealthAmerica's triage nurses intended for the referrals back to Dr. McNulty to be their solution, they had a duty to follow up Mrs. Shannon's calls by calling Dr. McNulty to insure Mrs. Shannon was actually receiving the proper care from him.[ ]

Corporate Liability

[The court concludes that the third duty of *Thompson*,the duty to oversee all those who deliver care, is applicable.] * * *

Similarly, in the present case Dr. Warner, on direct examination, offered the following opinion when asked whether or not HealthAmerica deviated from the standard of care:

> I believe they did deviate from the standard of care. I believe on each occasion of the calls on October 10th, 11th, and October 12th, that Mrs. Shannon should have been referred to the hospital, and the hospital notified that this woman was probably in preterm labor and needed to be handled immediately. They did have the alternative of calling for a physician, if they wanted to, for him to agree with it, but basically she needed to be evaluated in a placd [sic] where there was a fetal monitor and somebody to do a pelvic examination to see what was happening with her.

[ ]. When asked whether this deviation increased the risk of harm Dr. Warner stated that "it did increase the risk of harm to the baby, and definitely decreased the chance of [the baby] being born healthy." [ ]

[Dr. Warner further testified, in response to a series of hypothetical questions, that severe abdominal pain should have led the triage nurse either to call the doctor so he could instruct the patient to get to the hospital, or tell the patient to get to the hospital as soon as possible, and on each of the three days that Shannon called Health America, the standard of care dictated that she be sent to hospital to determine if she was in preterm labor.]

Viewing the evidence in the light most favorable to the Shannons as the non–moving party, our examination of the instant record leads us to the conclusion that the Shannons presented sufficient evidence to establish a prima facie case of corporate liability pursuant to the third duty set forth in Thompson, *supra*.However, due to the different entities involved, this determination does not end our inquiry. The Welsh case involved a suit against a hospital and thus Thompson was clearly applicable. Instantly, HealthAmerica, noting this Court's decision not to extend corporate liability under the facts in McClellan v. Health Maintenance Organization of Pennsylvania, [ ], argues that the Thompson duties are inapplicable to a health maintenance organization. We disagree.

In adopting the doctrine of corporate liability the Thompson court recognized "the corporate hospital's role in the total health care of its patients." [ ] Likewise, we recognize the central role played by HMOs in the total health care of its subscribers. A great deal of today's healthcare is channeled through HMOs with the subscribers being given little or no say so in the stewardship of their care. Specifically, while these providers do not practice medicine, they do involve themselves daily in decisions affecting their subscriber's medical care. These decisions may, among others, limit the length of hospital stays, restrict the use of specialists, prohibit or limit post hospital care, restrict access to therapy, or prevent rendering of emergency room care. While all of these efforts are for the laudatory purpose of containing health care costs, when decisions are made to limit a subscriber's access to treatment, that decision must pass the test of medical reasonableness. To hold otherwise would be to deny the true effect of the provider's actions, namely, dictating and directing the subscriber's medical care.

Where the HMO is providing health care services rather than merely providing money to pay for services their conduct should be subject to scrutiny. We see no reason why the duties applicable to hospitals should not be equally applied to an HMO when that HMO is performing the same or similar functions as a hospital. When a benefits provider, be it an insurer or a managed care organization, interjects itself into the rendering of medical decisions affecting a subscriber's care it must do so in a medically reasonable manner. Here, HealthAmerica provided a phone service for emergent care staffed by triage nurses. Hence, it was under a duty to oversee that the dispensing of advice by those nurses would be performed in a medically reasonable manner. Accordingly, we now make explicit that which was implicit in McClellanand find that HMOs may, under the right circumstances, be held corporately liable for a breach of any of the Thompson duties which causes harm to its subscribers.

[The court also held that HealthAmerican was vicariously liable for the negligent rendering of services by its triage nurses, under Section 323 of the Restatement (Second) of Torts.]

NOTES AND QUESTIONS

1. Consider the underlying failures of the system in *Shannon*. The treating physician was impatient and inattentive to warning signs, but it was the triage nurses staffing the phone lines who failed to properly direct Shannon to a physician or hospital. How should the system have been designed to avoid such an error? What would you suggest to avoid a repetition of this kind of disaster?

2. *Poor Plan Design*. Many of the ERISA preemption cases involve claims of negligent design of the managed care plan, including telephone call–in services staffed by nurses, as in *Shannon*. Other claims of negligent

design and administration of the delivery of health care services have been allowed. See McDonald v. Damian, 56 F.Supp.2d 574 (E.D.Pa.1999) (claim for inadequacies in the delivery of medical services). See Chapter 8, section V., *infra.*

3. *Negligent Selection of Providers.* The MCO, like the hospital, has been held to owe its subscribers a duty to properly select its panel members. Harrell v. Total Health Care, Inc., 1989 WL 153066 (Mo.App.1989), affirmed, 781 S.W.2d 58 (Mo.1989).

The logic of a direct duty imposed on MCOs to properly select providers is even stronger for an MCO than for a hospital. In the hospital setting, the patient has often selected the physician. He is then admitted to the hospital because his physician has admitting privileges at that hospital. By contrast, in a managed care program, the patient has chosen the particular program, but not the physicians who are provided. The patient must use the physicians on the panel. The patient thus explicitly relies on the MCO for its selection of health care providers.

A duty of proper selection will expose a managed care organization to liability both for failing to properly screen its physicians' competence, and also for failing to evaluate physicians for other problems. If the MCO selects a panel physician or dentist who has evidenced incompetence in her practice, it may risk liability. This is comparable to negligently granting staff privileges to an impaired physician with alcohol or other substance abuse problems, or one with sexual pathologies that might affect patients. See McClellan v. Health Maintenance Organization of Pennsylvania, 413 Pa.Super. 128, 604 A.2d 1053 (1992), in which the court allowed a suit against the HMO to proceed for negligence in selecting, retaining and evaluating primary care physician, misrepresenting the screening process for selecting its primary care physicians, and breach of contract.

4. *Failures to supervise and control staff.* Just as hospitals have duties to supervise and control staff, MCOs are likely to face similar duties to supervise. MCO liability for negligent control of its panel physicians derives from the same common law duty that underlies the negligent selection basis of liability as well as federal and state quality assurance regulations. As courts continue to characterize MCOs as health care providers, suits are likely to increase. Only PPOs with their reduced level of physician control might have an argument that liability should not be imposed for negligent supervision. However, statutes in some states require PPOs to implement quality assurance programs and others contemplate the use of such programs by PPOs. See e.g., Iowa Code Ann. § 514.21.

C. PHYSICIAN INCENTIVE SYSTEMS

Most managed care programs have three relevant features from a liability perspective. First, such programs select a restricted group of health care professionals who provide services to the program's participants. Second, such programs accept a fixed payment per subscriber, in exchange for provision of necessary care. This capitation system, discussed in *Petrovich, supra*, pressures MCOs to search for ways to minimize costs. Third, following from number two, MCOs use a variety of strategies to ensure cost effective care. Altering physician incentives is central to managed care, since physicians influence 70 percent of total health spending, while receiving only about 20 percent of each health care dollar. Such plans use utilization review techniques, incentives systems, and gatekeepers to control costs. The subscriber typically pays a fee to the MCO rather than the provider, relinquishing control over treatment and choice of treating physician. The payer in turn shifts some of its financial risk to its approved providers, who must also accept certain controls over their practice. See Chapter 8.

The argument that physician judgment might be "corrupted" by cost–conserving payment systems in managed care systems has been litigated over the years without much success. In an early case, Bush v. Dake, File No. 86–25767 NM–2, Saginaw Cty. Circuit Court, Michigan, 1989, the court allowed the case to proceed beyond summary judgment on the issue of the effect of an HMO payment system. The issue was whether Dr. Dake failed to timely diagnose and treat the plaintiff's uterine cancer, because of the incentive effects of how he was paid. He failed to make a referral to a specialist when the plaintiff's bleeding persisted. A pap smear would have detected the cancer at an earlier stage.

> GHS set aside a certain amount of money each year for a "referral pool" and a "hospital/ancillary pool" for the Network physicians. The money in these pools would be depleted with each referral to a specialist or hospitalization of a patient during the year. At the end of the year, any money left over in these pools would be divided between GHS and the individual physicians in Network. The result was that the fewer referrals a doctor made and the fewer hospitalizations he ordered for his patients, the more money he made.

The court held that such a payment system was a jury issue in the case. While on appeal the case settled. See also, Sweede v. Cigna Healthplan of Delaware, Inc., 1989 WL 12608 (Del.Super.1989) (claim that doctor withheld necessary care because of financial incentives rejected on facts of case).

Is it hard to prove what motivates physician decisionmaking? How would you establish that a particular HMO payment structure motivated physicians to forego needed care for their patients?

The incentives that HMOs create for providers to under–utilize health care for their patients raise the possibility that these incentives will "corrupt" the medical judgment of a physician, the same concern raised in the *Wickline* case in Chapter 5. The fear with managed care—and its goal of reducing expenditures by its physicians—is that some patients will be undertreated and suffer injury as a result. These concerns have led managed care plans to offer less restrictive plan operation and to ease constraints on providers.

The Supreme Court addressed the role of managed care design and incentives in Pegram v. Herdrich, 530 U.S. 211, 120 S.Ct. 2143, 147 L.Ed.2d 164 (2000). See Chapter 8, section V., *infra*.

PROBLEM: WANTING THE "BEST"

Cheryl Faber, 20 years old and newly married, joined a managed care organization, Freedom Plus [the Plan], one of several choices offered by her employer, Primerica Bank. Cheryl had examined the literature for the various plan choices during her open enrollment period. She chose the Plan because its literature talked of a "high quality" program with the "best doctors" in the area, and "no cost–cutting where subscriber health is concerned."

The Plan sets aside a certain amount of money each year for a "referral pool" and a "hospital/ancillary pool" for Plan physicians. The money in these pools is depleted with each referral to a specialist or hospitalization of a patient during the year. At the end of the year, any money left over in these pools is divided between the Plan and the individual physicians.

Cheryl went to her primary care physician in the Plan, Dr. Hanks, for her initial physical examination. Dr. Hanks found small lumps in her breasts, which he noted in the patient record as fibroid tumors. He talked briefly with Cheryl about the lumps, but stated that she shouldn't worry.

A year later Cheryl came back for another checkup. Dr. Hanks had left the Plan. It turned out Dr. Hanks had been the defendant in several malpractice suits filed against him in the five years he had worked for another HMO and he was terminated by that HMO. The Plan could have discovered this by accessing the National Practitioners Data Bank, or by calling up the previous employer.

Cheryl was then examined by another primary care physician, Dr. Wick. Dr. Wick was concerned about the lumps, and she prepared a referral to an oncologist, Dr. Scanem, who had recently joined the panel of specialists affiliated with the Plan. Cheryl went to Dr. Scanem, who ordered a biopsy and confirmed that the lumps were malignant Stage III cancer. Stage III cancers have about a 10% five year survival rate, Stage II a 40% five year survival, and Stage I almost 100% survival with prompt treatment.

Dr. Scanem recommended a treatment regime for Cheryl that included limited radical mastectomy and chemotherapy. He planned to use a new drug for breast cancers that had recently become available through a research protocol in which he was participating. This drug appeared to offer a slightly higher cure rate with young patients such as Cheryl with advanced breast cancer.

The Plan approved Dr. Scanem's recommendations, with the exception of the new drug. The Plan rejected his proposal for use of this drug, stating that it only reimbursed for chemotherapy using the standard drugs used generally by oncologists. The new drug was extremely expensive, and would have increased the cost of Cheryl's chemotherapy by about 200%. Dr. Scanem was angry about the refusal by the Plan to reimburse Cheryl's treatment in full, and told her so. He told her that there was nothing he could do about it, and so he said he would use the standard approach that most oncologists used. Cheryl was a very nervous patient, terrified of her cancer. Dr. Scanem was worried about upsetting her too much, given the other stresses created by the surgery and the side–effects from chemotherapy. She asked him what her chances were, and he said only that she had "a reasonable shot at beating it, with luck and prayer." He did not tell her anything more about the prognosis, nor did she ask.

Cheryl underwent the radical mastectomy and chemotherapy. Optimistic about her chances, Cheryl proceeded to get pregnant. She and her husband also bought a new house, assuming that she would recover and her salary would continue.

Cheryl's cancer proved to be too far advanced to respond to treatment. She died six months after the chemotherapy regime finished. Her fetus could not be saved, in spite of efforts by Plan obstetricians to do so. Her husband lost their new house since he could no longer afford the mortgage payments.

What advice will you give Mr. Faber about the merits of litigation against the Plan?

VI. REFORMING THE TORT SYSTEM FOR MEDICAL INJURIES

Malpractice crises come and go in the United States, driven by an apparent insurance cycle of competitive entry in the market, followed by rapid premium increases as the insurers' returns dropped. A new malpractice crisis resurfaced in 1999, precipitated by a rapid escalation in malpractice insurance premiums for most physicians and limited availability of coverage in some states—as carriers went bankrupt or left the malpractice line of insurance. A new round of legislative reform efforts, spearheaded by angry physician groups, emerged from this latest "crisis," as physicians faced increases in their insurance premiums and pockets of unavailability in some areas and for some specialties. The "crisis," following the cyclical pattern common to malpractice insurance, has abated, but the outpouring of research and writing on the topic continues.

The explanations for the current crises are as varied as their proponents

A. MEDICAL PROGRESS AND OTHER CHANGES IN THE HEALTH CARE ENVIRONMENT

The hazards of health care are substantial. As we learned in Chapter 1, error rates in medicine are surprisingly high. As the Harvard Medical

Practice study discovered in surveying medical iatrogenesis in New York hospitals, as many as 4 percent of hospitalized patients suffer an adverse medical event that results in disability or death. The Harvard Study projected that approximately one percent of all hospital patients suffer injury due to negligently provided care. Harvard Medical Practice Study, Patients, Doctors, and Lawyers: Medical Injury, Malpractice Litigation, and Patient Compensation in New York, Exec.Summ. 3–4 (1990). .

Medical progress has been one of the drivers of expanded tort liability; medicine has increased its power to treat and diagnose, and this power has created increased risks to patients along with it. William Sage writes: "[f]oremost, improvements in the clinical capabilities of medicine increase expectations of success, redefine success upwards, and foster the belief that failure is the result of negligence rather than misfortune. The first wave of malpractice suits in the late 19th century, involving nonunion of limb fractures, arose only because medical science had developed an alternative to amputation. Malpractice litigation has become as specialized as the medical care it attacks."

Second, industrialization in the health care industry has brought expanded liability, as Chapters 5 and 6 indicate. Health care is delivered in institutions and group practices. As a result, hospital actions are subject to increasingly intense scrutiny; long term care has become a new and growing target for malpractice litigation; managed care companies are less protected by ERISA preemption than a decade ago; even pharmacists are now exposed to substantial new risks. While malpractice crises historically have been driven by perceived litigation risks to physicians, this crisis includes increased exposure to malpractice suits by all the institutional players in the health care system.

Third, managed care and its cost containment mechanisms have had a strong effect on the system. Physicians are no longer able to pass increased malpractice premiums on to their patients or insurers, the result of tightened reimbursement by both private and public payers. At the same time, physicians have less time to talk to their patients, leaving an injured patient disgruntled and angry at the loss of personal relationship. Angry and injured patients are more likely to sue in such a situation.

Fourth, as a result of the above forces and others, the malpractice insurance market has become less profitable and less stable. See section B below.

Fifth, complexity in medicine—the combination of medical progress and industrialization—is producing more medical adverse events and errors. The Harvard Study discussed in Chapter 1, based on review of hospital records, may understate the problem. Lori Andrews conducted a study in a large Chicago area hospital, looking at the actual incidence of negligent events in hospital wards. She discovered that many injuries were not recorded on the records as required, especially when the main person responsible for the error was a senior physician. 17.7 percent of patients in her study experienced errors with a significant impact, many more than the 3.7 percent found in the Harvard Study. See Lori Andrews, Studying Medical Error In Situ: Implications for Malpractice Law and Policy, 54 DePaul L. Rev. 357 (2005).

See Robert I. Field, The Malpractice Crisis Turns 175: What Lessons Does History Hold for Reform? 4 Drexel L. Rev. 7 (2011); Medical Malpractice and the U.S. Health Care System (William M. Sage and Rogan Kersh, eds.2006); William M. Sage, Understanding the First Malpractice Crisis of the 21st Century, in The Health Law Handbook, 2003 Edition, Alice Gosfield, Editor.

For a review of the claims for and against the existence of a medical malpractice crisis, see Tom Baker, The Medical Malpractice Myth (2005); Barry R. Furrow, Reforming Medical Malpractice Liability, in Debates on U.S. Health Care 189 (Jennie Jacobs Kronenfeld, Wendy E. Parmet, and Mar A. Zezza, eds. 2012).

Review the cases in Chapters 4 and 5 and this chapter. Consider the reasons for new theories such as the "loss of a chance" doctrine and hospital corporate negligence.

B. INCENTIVE EFFECTS OF MALPRACTICE LITIGATION ON PROVIDER BEHAVIOR

Are tort suits likely to change potentially dangerous patterns of medical practice? Malpractice litigation in theory operates as a quality control mechanism. From the economist's perspective, tort doctrine should be designed to achieve an optimal prevention policy, reducing the sum total of the costs of medical accidents and the costs of preventing them. In theory, the tort system deters accident producing behavior. How? The existence of a liability rule and the resulting threat of a lawsuit and judgment encourage health care providers to reduce error and patient injury in circumstances where patients themselves lack the information (and ability) to monitor the quality of care they receive. Potential defendants will take precautions to avoid error and will buy insurance to cover any errors that injure patients. By finding fault and assessing damages against a defendant, a court sends a signal to health care providers that if they wish to avoid similar damages in the future they may need to change their behavior.

Malpractice claims have proved to provide useful evidence for discovering problematic physicians. Multiple malpractice claims are predictive of medical discipline, confirming the validity of such claims as predictors. One study of problems with state medical licensing boards concluded that "physicians with high numbers of medical malpractice reports in the NPDB [National Practitioner Data Bank] tend to have at least some adverse actions reports (e.g. hospital disciplinary report, medical board report) and Medicare/Medicaid exclusion reports and vice versa." Alan Levine et al., State Medical Boards Fail to Discipline Doctors With Hospital Actions Against Them, Pub. Citizen 9 (March. 2011). Ten or more payouts predict adverse action reports, and almost 9 percent of those were excluded from the Medicare and Medicaid programs. The NPBD data reveals that a few physicians account for most of the malpractice dollars paid: "[e]leven percent . . . of physicians [in the NPDB] with at least one malpractice payment were responsible for half of all malpractice dollars paid from September 1, 1990 through December 31, 2006." Health Resources & Servs. Admin. Bureau of Health Professions Div. of Prac. Data Banks, U.S. Dep't of Health & Hum. Servs., National Practitioner Data Bank 2006 Ann. Rep. 42.

Does the existence of malpractice insurance weaken deterrence? If the insurer does not employ experience rating to distinguish the litigation–prone providers from their colleagues, it is in effect causing an inaccurate signal to be sent, since all physicians in a practice area pay the same premiums regardless of their level of malpractice claims. This may dilute or eliminate the financial incentives for these physicians to change their behavior.

Liability insurers however use several mechanisms to assess physician insurance risks, and physicians are in fact likely to feel the effects of increased malpractice litigation in terms of insurance availability and pricing. Private insurance operates as a mode of regulation in liability insurance as well as other lines of insurance. See generally Omri Ben–Shahar and Kyle D. Logue, Outsourcing Regulation: How Insurance Reduces Moral Hazard, 111 Mich. L. Rev. 197 (2012); Tom Baker, Liability Insurance as Tort Regulation: Six Ways that Liability Insurance Shapes Tort Law in Action, 12 Conn. Ins. L.J. 1, 3–4 (2005). For a general discussion of the incentive effects of litigation on both individual physicians and health care institutions, see Barry R. Furrow, The Patient Injury Epidemic: Medical Malpractice Litigation as a Curative Tool, 4 Drexel L. Rev. 41 (2011).

Malpractice litigation does affect medical practice, making anxious providers either overestimate the risks of a suit or at least adjust their practice to a new assessment of the risk of suit, regardless of the incentive effects of judgments and premium increases. Physicians perceive a threat from the system, judging their risk of being sued as much higher than it actually is. See David M. Studdert et al., Defensive Medicine Among High–Risk Specialist Physicians in a Volatile Malpractice Environment, 293 JAMA 2609 (2005). Studies conclude that physicians who have been malpractice defendants often alter their practice as a reaction, even if they win the litigation. They also suffer chronic stress until the trial is over. See, for example, Charles, Wilbert, and Kennedy, Physicians'

Self–Reports of Reactions to Malpractice Litigation, 141 Am. J. Psychiatry 563, 565 (1984) ("A malpractice suit was considered a serious and often a devastating event in the personal and professional lives of the respondent physicians").

Physician stress is compounded by the length of time that it takes a malpractice case to either settle or reach a verdict. See Seth A. Seabury et al., On Average, Physicians Spend Nearly 11 Percent Of Their 40–Year Careers With An Open, Unresolved Malpractice Claim, 32 Health Affairs, 111 (2013) (The authors note:

The Harvard New York Study, surveying New York physicians, found that physicians who had been sued were more likely to explain risks to patients, to restrict their scope of practice, and to order more tests and procedures. Patients, Doctors, and Lawyers: Medical Injury, Malpractice Litigation, and Patient Compensation in New York 9–29 (1990). Physicians surveyed in the New York study also felt that the malpractice threat was important in maintaining standards of care. Id. at 9–24.

What other forces and incentives affect the quality of health care delivery by physicians, other professionals, and institutions? A technological innovation for example may reduce both the level of medical injury for a procedure and the risks of being sued. Consider the pulse oximeter, discussed in Washington v. Washington Medical Center, above. In 1984, no hospital operating room had such a device, but by 1990 all operating rooms did, and the incidence of patient injuries due to anesthesia errors has dropped precipitiously.

As Professors Hyman and Silver put it, "The main problem with the legal system is that it exerts too little pressure on health care providers to improve the quality of the services they deliver. * * * Safe health care is expensive, and the tort system forces providers to pay only pennies on the dollar for the injuries they inflict." David A. Hyman and Charles Silver, Medical Malpractice Litigation and Tort Reform: It's the Incentives, Stupid, 59 Vand. L. Rev. 1085, 1130 (2006).

For a thorough review of the evidence for and against malpractice litigation as an effective deterrent to bad medical practices, see Michelle M. Mello and Troyen A. Brennan, Deterrence of Medical Errors: Theory and Evidence for Malpractice Reform, 80 Texas L. Rev. 1595 (2002) (based on Harvard Study data, evidence for a deterrent effect of malpractice suits is lacking); David A. Hyman, Medical Malpractice and the Tort System: What Do We Know and What (If Anything) Should We Do About It? 80 Tex. L. Rev. 1639 (2002) (noting that other studies looking at single institutions have found more favorable deterrent effects.); Joanna C. Schwartz, A Dose of Reality for Medical Malpractice Reform, 88 N.Y.U. L. Rev. ___ (2013) (study of effect of litigation on hospital patient safety efforts, concluding that lawsuits effectively promote patient safety, providing data about weaknesses in hospital policy, practices, staff, and administration).

C. THE NATURE OF THE INSURANCE INDUSTRY

Any serious analysis of the malpractice "crisis" begins (and some say it ends) with the insurance industry. Health care providers buy medical malpractice insurance to protect themselves from medical malpractice claims. Under the insurance contract, the insurance company agrees to accept financial responsibility for payment of any claims up to a specific level of coverage during a fixed period in return for a fee. The insurer investigates the claim and defends the health care provider. This insurance is sold by commercial insurance companies, health care provider–owned companies, and joint underwriting associations. Some large hospitals also self–insure for medical malpractice losses rather than purchasing insurance, and a few physicians practice without insurance. Joint underwriting associations are nonprofit pooling arrangements created by state legislatures to provide medical malpractice insurance to health care providers in the states in which they are established.

Insurance rate setting uses actuarial techniques to set rates, to generate funds to cover (1) losses occurring during the period, (2) the administrative costs of running the company, and (3) an amount for unknown contingencies, which may become a profit if not used. The profit may be retained as capital surplus or returned to stockholders as dividends.

See generally U.S.General Accounting Office, Medical Malpractice: No Agreement on the Problems or Solutions 66–72 (1986), from which the above discussion was taken, describing the crises of the 1970s and mid–1980s.

The U.S. General Accounting Office has described the malpractice insurance cycle.

> * * * [A] variety of factors combined to explain the malpractice insurance cycle that produced several years of relatively stable premium rates in the 1990s followed by the severe premium rate increases of the past few years. To begin with, insurer losses anticipated in the late 1980s did not materialize as projected, so insurers went into the 1990s with reserves and premium rates that proved to be higher than the actual losses they would experience. At the same time, insurers began a decade of high investment returns. This emerging profitability encouraged insurers to expand their market share, as both the downward adjustment of loss reserves and high investment returns increased insurers' income. As a result, insurers were generally able to keep premium rates flat or even reduce them, although the medical malpractice market as a whole continued to experience modestly

> increasing underlying losses throughout the decade. Finally, by the mid–to late 1990s, as excess reserves were exhausted and investment income fell below expectations, insurers' profitability declined.

The GAO noted that some insurers became insolvent, others dropped their malpractice lines of insurance, others reduced their size, and these changes combined to reduce the availability of insurance. Remaining insurers therefore asked for and got large rate increases in many states. Such increases hit physicians hard, leading to a "crisis" of affordability.

U.S. General Accounting Office, Medical Malpractice Insurance: Multiple Factors Have Contributed to Increased Premium Rates (2003).

NOTES AND QUESTIONS

1. *The Flaws in the Malpractice Insurance Market.* The market for malpractice insurance fails to satisfy many of the economist's conditions for an ideal insurance market. The ideal market consists of a pooling by the insurer of a large number of homogeneous but independent random events. The auto accident insurance market is perhaps closest to fulfilling this condition. The large numbers of events involved make outcomes for the insurance pool actuarially predictable. Malpractice lacks these desirable qualities of ". . . large numbers, independence, and risk beyond the control of the insured." Patricia Danzon, Medical Malpractice: Theory, Evidence, and Public Policy 90 (1985) The pool of potential policyholders is small, as is the pool of claims, and a few states have most of the claims. The awards vary tremendously, with 50 percent of the dollars paid out on 3 percent of the claims. In small insurance programs, a single multimillion dollar claim can have a tremendous effect on total losses and therefore average loss per insured doctor.

Second, losses are not independent, since neither claims against an individual doctor nor against doctors as a group are independent; multiple claims against a doctor relate usually to some characteristic of his practice or his technique, and a lawyer can use knowledge gained in one suit in another. Claims and verdicts against doctors generally reflect social forces—shifts in jury attitudes and legal doctrine. Given the long tail, or time from medical intervention to the filing of a claim, the impact of these shifts is increased.

Finally, the problems of moral hazard and adverse selection distort the market. Moral hazard characterizes the effect of insurance in reducing an insured's incentives to prevent losses, since he is not financially responsible for losses. Adverse selection occurs when an insurer attracts policy holders of above–average risk, ending up with higher claim costs and lower profits as a result.

2. *Premium Increases and the Medical Rate of Inflation.* Studies in some states have confirmed that all increases in award sizes are accounted for by medical inflation, wage inflation (for lost earnings) and the increase in severity of the injury to the patient. Missouri Department of Insurance, Med-

ical Malpractice Insurance in Missouri: The Current Difficulties in Perspective 6 (February 2003).

3. *The Underwriting Cycle*. The malpractice crisis is more a product of the way the insurance industry does business than of changes in the frequency of medical malpractice litigation or the severity of judgments. The malpractice market is a "lumpy" market, prone to cycles of underpricing and catchup. What doctors and hospitals see as "sudden" price increases are actually deferred costs passed on when premiums no longer cover payments plus profit. Once premiums reach actuarially sound levels, profits rise, new insurers enter the market with lower rates, competitive pressures return, and the cycle starts all over again.

The cyclical nature of interest rates, as a measure of return on investments, plays a central role in insurers' pricing decisions. The insurance industry engages in cash–flow underwriting, in which insurers invest the premiums they collect in the bond market and to a lesser extent in the stock market. When interest rates and investment returns are high, insurance companies accept riskier exposures to acquire more investable premium and loss reserves. If underwriting and investment results are combined during these periods, investment gains more than offset losses. Malpractice insurance premiums charged by insurance companies do not relate to payouts, but rather rise and fall in concert with the state of the economy, reflecting gains and losses of invested reserves and the insurance industry's calculation of their rate of return on the investment "float" (the time between collecting premium dollars and paying out losses) provided by the physician premiums. See generally Mimi Marchev, The Medical Malpractice Insurance Crisis: Opportunity for State Action (National Academy for State Health Policy, July 2002).

4. *Price Wars*. Insurance carriers sometimes act like gasoline stations that enter into pricing wars to gain market share, inflicting wounds on themselves in an attempt to grab more of the market. Favorable operating results in the malpractice line of insurance led insurers to compete aggressively. The overall performance of the market is thus a major factor in medical malpractice insurance. Companies sacrificed underwriting gains to attract more business and enhance their investment gains. In some cases the prices charged were far below good actuarial levels. If insurance premiums are priced low in competitive markets, carriers expect to generate investment income to offset underwriting losses. If interest rates and investment yields drop, insurance companies must raise their premiums and drop some lines of insurance, in order to compete. See testimony of James Hurley, spokesman for the American Academy of Actuaries, testimony to the House Energy and Commerce Subcommittee on Health (July 17, 2002).

5. *Limitations on State Insurance Regulation*. Many states grant their insurance regulators limited authority to regulation medical malpractice insurance rates unless they are either excessive and the market is not competitive. States tend to rely on the marketplace to adjust rates instead of granting broader regulatory powers to their insurance commissioners. Some states

are considering allowing their insurance departments to reject malpractice rate filings that do not meet acceptable standards. See, e.g., Missouri Department of Insurance, Medical Malpractice Insurance in Missouri: The Current Difficulties in Perspective 4 (February 2003).

D. APPROACHES TO REFORMING THE MEDICAL MALPRACTICE SYSTEM

1. Improving Insurance Availability

The response to the perceived "crisis" in malpractice litigation and insurance availability over the past thirty years has been twofold. First, the availability of insurance has been enhanced by a variety of changes in the structure of the insurance industry. Second, physicians have lobbied with substantial success at the state level for legislation to impede the ability of plaintiffs to bring tort suits and to restrict the size of awards.

Malpractice reform proposals can be evaluated by three overall standards. First, do the reforms improve the operation of the tort system for compensating victims of medical injuries? Second, will the reforms create incentives for the reduction of medical error and resulting injury to patients? Third, are changes likely to encourage insurers to make malpractice insurance more available and affordable? Institute of Medicine, Beyond Malpractice: Compensation for Medical Injuries 29–30 (1978). For a federal study that builds upon the Institute of Medicine report, see U.S.General Accounting Office , Medical Malpractice: No Agreement on the Problems or Solutions (1986). (hereafter GAO Malpractice Report). Can you think of other goals by which we should test tort reform? As you read through these materials, ask yourself if the various reforms are likely to promote or impede particular goals, and at what cost.

a. ***New Sources of Insurance***. New sources of insurance were created in response to earlier crises, either by the states or by providers. Joint underwriting associations, reinsurance exchanges, hospital self–insurance programs, state funds, and provider owned insurance companies have sprung into being. Physician–owned companies now write as much as 60 percent of malpractice coverage nationally. Hospitals have begun to self–insure. Some states have adopted state programs, such as patient compensation funds, to limit doctor liability to individual patients.

b. ***Claims–Made Policies***. Medical malpractice insurers changed in the late seventies to writing policies on a claims–made rather than an occurrence basis. Before 1975, most policies had been occurrence policies, covering claims made at any time as long as the insured doctor was covered during the time the medical accident giving rise to the claim occurred. The increase in the frequency and severity of claims in the mid–70s revealed the long tail problem of this kind of insurance. Insurers struggled to reliably predict their future losses and set premium prices, and often failed. Most insurers therefore have shifted to a claims–made policy, allowing them to use more recent claims experience to set premium prices and reserve requirements. The claims–made policy covers claims made during the year of the policy coverage, avoiding the predictability problem of the occurrence policy. Such policies arguably have allowed companies to continue to carry malpractice insurance lines, serving the goal of availability by keeping premium costs lower than they would otherwise have been.

c. ***Selective Insurance Marketing***. Physician mutual companies, with physician–investors, have often ridden out the underwriting cycle with less distress than the commercial carriers. One example is *Healthcare Providers Insurance Exchange* (HPIX), formed in 2002. It promises an intensive commitment to risk management:

> Our primary focus is to partner with our members, to both manage their claims and reduce their risk. We do not disrupt this relationship simply because a member has reported an adverse outcome or been involved in a claim. We listen to the feedback from our Physicians and implement changes as needed. We seek to attract Physicians who are proactive and willing to participate in programs to reduce risk.

d. ***Hospital Complaint Profiling***. For hospitals, complaint profiling has been proposed, spotting litigation–prone staff physicians and intervening to retrain them to avoid risks. The Hickson study took six years worth of hospital patient advocacy files and concluded that unsolicited patient complaints about physicians are a highly reliable predictor of litigation–prone physicians. The study found that 9 percent of the physicians produced 50 percent of the complaints, and the study showed an 86 percent success rate in predicting physicians with multiple claims. See Gerald B. Hickson et al., Patient Complaints and Malpractice Risk, 287 J.A.M.A. 2951 (2002).

2. Altering the Litigation Process

Starting in the 1970s, states enacted tort reform legislation. The preamble to the California Medical Injury Compensation Reform Act, the current Holy Grail for tort reformers of the malpractice system, is typical of the legislative perceptions of the malpractice crisis:

> The Legislature finds and declares that there is a major health care crisis in the State of California attributable to skyrocketing malpractice premium costs and resulting in a potential breakdown of the health delivery system, severe hardships for the medically indigent, a denial of access for the economically mar-

ginal, and depletion of physicians such as to substantially worsen the quality of health care available to citizens of this state.

Tort reform measures were intended by their proponents to reduce either the frequency of malpractice litigation or the size of the settlement or judgment. The goal was not to improve the lot of the injured patient, but instead to satisfy both the medical profession and the insurance industry.

These measures were designed to restrict the operation of the tort system in several: (1) affecting the filing of malpractice claims; (2) limiting the award recoverable by the plaintiff; (3) altering the plaintiff's burden of proof through changes in evidence rules and legal doctrine; (4) reducing the plaintiff lawyer's contingency fee recovery; and (5) changing the role of the courts by substituting an alternative forum. These are characterized by Eleanor Kinney as "first generation" reforms. See generally Eleanor D. Kinney, Learning from Experience, Malpractice Reforms in the 1990s: Past Disappointments, Future Success?, 20 J. Health Pol. Pol'y & L. 99 (1995).

The most powerful reform in actually reducing the size of malpractice awards has been a dollar limit, or cap, on awards. Caps may take the form of a limit on the amount of recovery of general damages, typically pain and suffering; or a maximum recoverable per case, including all damages. See David A. Hyman, Bernard Black, Charles Silver, and William M. Sage, Estimating the Effect of Damage Caps in Medical Malpractice Cases: Evidence From Texas, 1 J. Legal Analysis 355 (2009).

E. ALTERNATIVE APPROACHES TO COMPENSATION OF PATIENT INJURY

Second–generation reform proposals aimed to eliminate or reduce some of these perceived flaws of the current system, without impairing consumer access to compensation. Such proposals can be categorized in light of several central attributes. They involve combining different reforms, choosing variables from a series of categories into a single package. The categories that are available include: (1) the compensable event, (2) the measure of compensation, (3) the payment mechanism, (4) the forum used to resolve disputes, and (5) the method of implementing the new rights and responsibilities. See generally Kenneth Abraham, Medical Liability Reform: A Conceptual Framework, 260 Journal of the American Medical Association 68–72 (1988).

Abraham summarizes the categories and reform choices in the following table:

Compensable Event	Measure of Compensation	Payment Mechanism	Forum for Resolution of Disputes	Method of Implementation
Fault Cause Loss	Full tort damages Full out-of-pocket losses Partial out-of- pocket losses Scheduled damages Lump-sum payment Periodic payment	First-party insurance Third-party insurance Taxation Hybrid Funding	Jury trial Expert review panels Bench trial Binding arbitration Administrative boards Insurance company decision	Legislation Mandatory reform Elective options Private contract

1. Alternative Dispute Resolution (ADR)

Arbitration is often proposed as a way to solve the problems of the tort system. It is pervasive in all consumer contracts, from brokerage agreements to telephone contracts. The expected advantages of arbitration include diminished complexity in fact–finding, lower cost, fairer results, greater access for smaller claims, and a reduced burden on the courts. No state requires compulsory arbitration. Like screening panels, the arbitration process uses a panel to resolve the dispute after an informal presentation of evidence. The panel typically consists of a doctor, a lawyer and a layperson or retired judge. The arbitration panel, however, uses members trained in dispute resolution and has the authority to make a final ruling as to both provider liability and damages. The process is initiated only when there is an agreement between the patient and the health care provider to arbitrate any claims.

Arbitration has distinct disadvantages from a consumer perspective. Lawyers can drive up the costs and length of arbitration to match litigation. Evidence is also emerging that the "repeat player" phenomenon means a much higher victory rate for employers and other institutional players who regularly engage in arbitration in contrast to one–shot players such as employees or consumers. In employment arbitration cases, one study found that the odds are 5–to–1 against the employee in a repeat–player case. Much of this imbalance may be due to the ability and incentive of repeat players to track the predisposition of arbitrators and bias the selection process in their favor. See generally Ann H. Nevers, Medical Malpractice Arbitration in the New Millennium: Much Ado About Nothing ?, 1 Pepperdine Dispute Resolution Law Journal 45 (2001); Thomas Metzloff, Alternative Dispute Resolution Strategies in Medical Malpractice, 9 Alaska L. Rev. 429 (1992).

Mediation has also been proposed as an attractive alternative to litigation. See generally Edward A. Dauer, Leonard J. Marcus, and Susan M. C. Payne, Prometheus and the Litigators: A Mediation Odyssey, 21 J. Leg. Med. 159 (2000).

2. No–Fault Systems

a. Provider–Based Early Payment

Under this approach providers would voluntarily agree to identify and promptly compensate patients for avoidable injuries. Damages would be limited under most proposals. This approach was first proposed by Clark Havighurst and Lawrence Tancredi, and has been recommended in Institute of Medicine, Fostering Rapid Advances in Health Care: Learning from System Demonstrations 82 (2002).

When the adverse outcome first occurred, the patient or provider would file the claim with the insurer, who would decide whether the injury was covered. If so, it would make prompt payment. Disputes would be resolved through the courts or arbitration. The plan as proposed would experience rate insurance premiums paid by providers, in order to create incentives for the providers to improve the quality of care, thereby reducing their exposure for the adverse outcomes listed. Provider experience under the plan would also be used to strengthen peer review within hospitals. See Clark Havighurst and Laurence Tancredi, "Medical Adversity Insurance"—A No–Fault Approach to Medical Malpractice and Quality Assurance, 51 Milbank Memorial Fund Quarterly 125 (1973).

One example of such a model has been pioneered by the University of Michigan Health System, a self–insured system. Michigan limits compensation to cases where the institution determines that the care was inappropriate, tendering an offer to the injured patient. The offer may include compensation for all elements of loss that are compensable in tort cases, including medical expenses, lost income, other economic losses, and "pain and suffering." A patient can only accept the tendered money after agreeing that it is a final settlement, foreclosing a lawsuit. See generally Richard C. Boothman et al., A Better Approach to Medical Malpractice Claims? The University of Michigan Experience, 2 J. Health & Life Sci. L. 125, 135 (2009) (summarizing the approach); Michelle M. Mello and Thomas H. Gallagher, Malpractice Reform—Opportunities for Leadership by Health Care Institutions and Liability Insurers (March 31, 2010 at NEJM.org.

b. Administrative Systems

The most recent administrative idea is the health court, a hybrid model based on earlier "early–settlement" models around since the seventies. See *Problem: Health Courts as a Solution? infra* for a description of such courts. Another proposal offered by the Institute of Medicine has been to create by legislation a state system loosely based on the Workers' Compensation model. Under this approach, providers would receive immunity from tort in exchange for "mandatory participation in a state–sponsored, administrative system established to provide compensation to patients who have suffered avoidable injuries." See Institute of Medicine, Fostering Rapid Advances in Health Care: Learning from System Demonstrations 82 (2002). The AMA also developed an elaborate proposal in the late 1980s, but to date such state–administered systems have been limited to special categories of injuries, such as brain–damaged infants.

NOTES AND QUESTIONS

1. If you represent a hospital, what problems would you see in a system like that of the University of Michigan, tendering an offer of settlement to a plaintiff? Why should a provider come forward to inform a patient that he has suffered a compensable injury? What is in it for the provider in an uncertain case? Is the doctor in charge of the case likely to admit error, so that the hospital can present its offer to the patient? How can the hospital encourage staff doctors to come forward? How might legal rules improve the possibilities of disclosure of errors?

2. One of the primary goals in a no–fault system is to reduce the cost of insurance to providers. The California study in the 1970s estimated that a no–fault system in California could increase malpractice premiums 300 percent higher than the tort system's insurance costs. California Medical and Hospital Associations, Report on the Medical Insurance Feasibility Study (1977).

If a compensation system rewards many more claimants, particularly small ones, in an evenhanded and more rapid fashion than does the current tort system, it may well be an improvement. But it is unlikely to be a cheaper system. And if it ends up offering plaintiffs considerably smaller awards that they would receive in a trial system, such a compensation system may trade speed and smaller payouts for defendants for inadequate compensation for plaintiffs. In considering tort reform, one always must ask who is proposing the reforms and what do they stand to gain from them.

3. Disclosure, Apology, and Resolution Systems

Disclosure–and–resolution programs are described in Chapter 1, particularly the program implemented by the Veteran's Administration. Such programs have become more common in hospitals, as risk managers search for ways to control their liability costs. For a detailed description of how to design such systems, see ECRI Institute, Disclosure of Unanticipated Outcomes (January 2008) (outlining the disclosure steps developed by the American Society for Healthcare Risk Management (ASHRM)).

A hospital using this approach typically adopts several steps. First, a representative discloses adverse events to affected patients and their families. Second, she apologizes on behalf of the institution for causing the adverse event and harms suffered by the patient. Third, she offers compensation where appropriate. The approach combines the "early offer" ideas described above with the strategy of full disclosure and apology. The

Michigan approach, above, uses elements of these ideas. The idea is to induce settlements more quickly by co–opting plaintiff lawyers with the promise of much quicker, less adversarial settlements that bring the injured plaintiffs into the conversation earlier.

Apology strategies have a real downside. From a defendant's perspective, such proposals offer a strategic tool to buy off plaintiffs by showing them how sorry the provider is, and to rush settlement by getting plaintiffs (and their lawyers) to buy into early settlement by the offer of money up front. The problem is that the provider and its insurer control the screening for potential adverse event claims, using the process as a filter for payouts. Strategic apologies may improve claims resolution, but at the cost of lower payments because conciliation has discounted the level of compensation that a plaintiff may really need. As O'Hara and Yarn write, "the apology scholars have focused on the role of apology evidence in establishing liability, but they have neglected the fact that apology evidence very often has the practical effect of reducing damages." Erin Ann O'Hara & Douglas Yarn, On Apology and Consilience, 77 Wash. L. Rev. 1121, 1186 (2002). For a look at the complex interplay between settlement offers and patient willingness not to sue, see Lindsey Murtagh, Thomas H. Gallagher, Penny Andrew, and Michelle M. Mello, Disclosure–And–Resolution Programs That Include Generous Compensation Offers May Prompt A Complex Patient Response, 31 Health Affairs 2681 (2012).

See generally Barry R. Furrow, The Patient Injury Epidemic: Medical Malpractice Litigation as a Curative Tool, 4 Drexel. L. Rev. 101 (2011); Jennifer K. Robbennolt, Attorneys, Apologies, and Settlement Negotiations, 13 Harv. Negot. L. Rev. 349, 359–60 (2008). See also Lee Taft, Apology Subverted: The Commodification of Apology, 109 Yale L.J. 1135, 1150–54 (2000); Erin Ann O'Hara, Apology and Thick Trust: What Spouse Abusers and Negligent Doctors Might Have in Common, 79 Chi.–Kent L. Rev. 1055, 1076–77 (2004); Catherine T. Struve, Expertise in Medical Malpractice Litigation: Special Courts, Screening Panels, and Other Options, The Project on Medical Liability in Pennsylvania, 1, 63–64 (2003).

F. THE AFFORDABLE CARE ACT AND TORT REFORM

The Affordable Care Act makes big changes to the Medicaid and Medicare programs and private insurance regulation. Its impact on medical liability reform is much more modest, promoting state demonstration programs that are limited in their scope by the terms of grants to the states. Tort reform was never seriously considered as a central part of health care reform, in part because cost savings from reform were not expected to be substantial, and because it is a Democratic bill. The Congressional Budget Office, in a letter to Senator Orrin Hatch (October 9, 2009), responded to his request for an updated analysis of the effects of proposals to limit costs related to medical malpractice ("tort reform"). The

CBO began with the assumption that "[t]ort reform could affect costs for health care both directly and indirectly: directly, by lowering premiums for medical liability insurance; and indirectly, by reducing the use of diagnostic tests and other health care services when providers recommend those services principally to reduce their potential exposure to lawsuits."

The CBO estimated costs savings from the such tort reforms as caps on noneconomic damages; caps on punitive damages; modification of the "collateral source" rule; more restrictive statute of limitation rules; and replacement of joint–and–several liability with a fair–share rule limiting a defendant's liability to the percentage of the final award that was equal to his or her share of responsibility for the injury. The CBO estimate was that such reforms would reduce medical malpractice premiums by about 10 percent. The CBO estimated that the direct costs to providers for liability, including premiums, awards, and settlements, and administrative costs, would in 2009 be around $35 billion, or about 2 percent of total health care expenditures. A savings of 10 percent in premium plus costs would therefore, in the CBO's words, ". . . reduce total national health care expenditures by about 0.2 percent." This is hardly a significant savings.

The CBO further noted the possibility of measurable indirect savings from reduced utilization of health care services, although particular reforms might have different effects on physician incentives. Adding these savings to the reform savings would reduce total national health care spending by about 0.5 percent (about $11 billion in 2009), still nothing to get excited about.

Finally, the CBO noted that there remains a large area of uncertainty about the possible negative effect on health outcomes of limiting the rights of injured patients to sue for injuries form medical errors. They noted that the studies are in conflict, ranging from an estimate that a 10 percent reduction in costs would increase the overall mortality rate by 0.2 percent, to an estimate of no serious adverse outcomes for patient health. The hope of tort reformers that extensive reforms could be sold as cost reduction, as part of the the ACA package, was limited by this CBO analysis.

> The Senate defined the parameters of tort reform as bounded by a search for effective alternative dispute resolution systems. Title I, Section 6801 states that
>
> [i]t is the sense of the Senate that—
>
> (1) health care reform presents an opportunity to address issues related to medical malpractice and medical liability insurance;
>
> (2) States should be encouraged to develop and test alternatives to the existing civil litigation system as a way of improving patient safety, reducing medical errors, encouraging the efficient

resolution of disputes, increasing the availability of prompt and fair resolution of disputes, and improving access to liability insurance, while preserving an individual's right to seek redress in court; and

(3) Congress should consider establishing a State demonstration program to evaluate alternatives to the existing civil litigation system with respect to the resolution of medical malpractice claims.

The primary liability reform provision in the ACA is Section 10607, *State Demonstration Programs to Evaluate Alternatives to Current Medical Tort Litigation.* The Secretary of the Department of Health and Human Services may award demonstration grants for a period not to exceed five years to the States "for the development, implementation, and evaluation of alternatives to current tort litigation for resolving disputes over injuries allegedly caused by health care providers or health care organizations."

The ACA in (1) A specifies that the models should resolve disputes over patient injuries and promote a reduction in medical errors "by encouraging the collection and analysis of patient safety data related to disputes resolved under subparagraph (A) by organizations that engage in efforts to improve patient safety and the quality of health care."

Subsection (2) requires the State grant seeker to demonstrate how their model:

(A) makes the medical liability system more reliable by increasing the availability of prompt and fair resolution of disputes;

(B) encourages the efficient resolution of disputes;

(C) encourages the disclosure of health care errors;

(D) enhances patient safety by detecting, analyzing, and helping to reduce medical errors and adverse events;

(E) improves access to liability insurance;

(F) fully informs patients about the differences in the alternative and current tort litigation;

(G) provides patients the ability to opt out of or voluntarily withdraw from participating in the alternative at any time and to pursue other options, including litigation, outside the alternative;

(H) would not conflict with State law at the time of the application in a way that would prohibit the adoption of an alternative to current tort litigation; and

(I) would not limit or curtail a patient's existing legal rights, ability to file a claim in or a access a State's legal system, or otherwise abrogate a patient's ability to file a medical malpractice claim.

* * *

(B) NOTIFICATION OF PATIENTS.—A State shall demonstrate how patients would be notified that they are receiving health care services that fall within such scope, and the process by which they may opt out of or voluntarily withdraw from participating in the alternative. The decision of the patient whether to participate or continue participating in the alternative process shall be made at any time and shall not be limited in any way.

NOTES AND QUESTIONS

What kinds of alternative dispute resolution models will be eligible for one of these demonstration grants? How about mandatory arbitration of the sort in every brokerage agreement, telephone contract, or publishing contract? Why does the Act so constrain the kinds of models that can be considered? Whose interests are represented?

G. CONCLUSION

First–generation reforms are now in place in most states. Second–generation reforms, ranging from enterprise liability to contractual arbitration models, are far less likely to be adopted by either Congress or the states. The American Medical Association and state medical societies continue to advocate for statutory caps on pain and suffering awards, using the California model of a $250,000 cap on noneconomic losses as the solution to the problem. It remains to be seen whether broader innovations in malpractice compensation systems will be tried at either the federal or state levels. The vested interests are entrenched at this point, and serious system reform seems unlikely, particularly as the latest malpractice crisis abates as insurance costs drop for providers.

PROBLEM: HEALTH COURTS AS A SOLUTION?

A *health court* is a system of administrative compensation for medical injuries. It has five core features. First, injury compensation decisions are made outside the regular court system by specially trained judges. Second, compensation decisions are based on a standard of care that is broader than the negligence standard (but does not approach strict liability). "Avoidability" or "preventability" of the injury is the touchstone. To obtain compensation, claimants must show that the injury would not have occurred if best practices had been followed or an optimal system of care had been in place, but they need not show that care fell below the standard expected of a reasonable practitioner. Third, compensation criteria are based on evidence; that is, they are grounded in experts' interpretations of the leading scientific literature. To the maximum extent feasible, compensation decisions are guided by *ex ante* determinations about the preventability of common medical adverse events. Fourth, this knowledge, coupled with precedent, is converted to decision aids that allow fast–track compensation decisions for certain types of injury. Fifth and finally, *ex ante* guidelines also inform decisions about how much for economic and noneconomic damages should be paid.

Patients are informed, at the time an injury is disclosed by the provider, that they can file a compensation claim with the provider or its insurer. A panel of experts, aided by decision guidelines, determines whether the injury was avoidable—would the injury ordinarily have occurred if the care had been provided by the best specialist or an optimal health care system? For avoidable injuries, the institution offers full compensation for economic losses plus a scheduled amount for pain and suffering based on injury severity.

A voluntary model would allow patients to reject the compensation offer and file a lawsuit, unless they had waived this right as a condition of receiving care.

The health courts proposal is presented in Michelle M. Mello, David M. Studdert, Allen B. Kachalia, and Troyen A. Brennan, "Health Courts" and Accountability for Patient Safety, 84 The Milbank Quarterly 459, 460–461 (2006).

What problems do you see with this proposal? Given what you know of the current liability system, what advantages does the health court offer to defendants? Plaintiffs? Insurers? Will this model be promising even if plaintiffs choose to litigate at any time?

CHAPTER 7

DUTIES TO TREAT

■ ■ ■

I. INTRODUCTION

This chapter examines the legal obligations of doctors and hospitals to treat patients needing medical care. Among the cases you will read in this chapter are cases in which patients were refused medical treatment because they couldn't pay; because of their race; or because of their particular medical condition. The traditional legal principle of freedom of contract governs the physician–patient relationship, which the physician may choose to enter or not. See Chapter 4. Legal obligations on the part of health care professionals to provide treatment, whether as a matter of common law doctrine or statute, operate as exceptions to this general rule. The resulting legal fabric is a patchwork rather than a universal right to care. As you review the materials in this chapter, consider how this approach responds to some of the systemic challenges described here.

Ability to Pay

Projections anticipate that the Affordable Care Act will reduce the number of uninsured in the United States from 54 million to 23 million—not immediately, but over the next ten years. The remaining 23 million people will be seeking care directly from health care professionals and hospitals, especially when the need is extreme.

Among the 23 million are approximately 11 million undocumented immigrants. The ACA excludes all U.S. residents not "lawfully present" in the U.S. from access to the health insurance exchanges and subsidies for insurance. Moreover, the Act continues Medicaid's exclusion of undocumented immigrants, although limited federal funds to hospitals for emergency care will probably continue. These exclusions leave the problem of caring for millions of people at the door of physicians and hospitals.

Although the ACA provides for federal insurance subsidies for legal immigrants purchasing insurance through an exchange, it is likely that a good proportion of legal immigrants will be relegated to Medicaid. Immigrants in the United States legally are eligible for the Medicaid program, but state Medicaid rules typically bar them from the program until they have resided in the United States for five years. Once eligible for Medicaid, state rules often exclude this group specifically from particular medical treatments and services. But see Finch v. Commonwealth Health Ins. Connector Auth., 959 N.E.2d 970 (Mass. 2012), holding that Massachusetts program applying Medicaid's five–year waiting period to eligibility for state–provided insurance subsidies violates state constitutional equal protection provision. In addition, subsidies for purchase of insurance may prove inadequate for smokers as the ACA permits insurers to charge premiums up to 50% higher for this group than for other insureds. See Chapter 1.

Even with the ACA's subsidies, elimination of lifetime caps, and no–co–pay preventive care, individuals relying on private health insurance will still be faced with significant out–of–pocket costs. For some persons and families, and not only the poor, these costs may place needed medical care out of their reach. Data on consumer bankruptcies, for example, demonstrated that study participants with private health insurance faced higher out–of–pocket costs for health care on average ($13,460) than those who were uninsured when they or a family member became ill ($10,893). These studies, which played a role in advocacy for the ACA, also revealed that nearly half of all consumer bankruptcies were the result of costs related to illness. Melissa B. Jacoby & Elizabeth Warren, 100 Nw. U. L. Rev. 535 (2006); Melissa Jacoby & Mirya Holman, Managing Medical Bills on the Brink of Bankruptcy, 10 Yale J. Health Pol'y, L. & Ethics 239 (2010).

Source of payment operates independently as a barrier to access to care. The ACA greatly expands Medicaid eligibility, but Medicaid beneficiaries already have significant problems in finding physicians who accept Medicaid payment. Advocates for access to care argue that Medicaid payment levels are an access issue, and the ACA includes funding to reduce the gap between Medicaid and Medicare payment rates for primary care physicians. See, e.g., Brietta Clark, Medicaid Access, Rate Setting and Payment Suits: How the Obama Administration is Undermining Its Own Health Reform Goals, 55 How. L. J. 771 (2012). Some, however, have expressed concern that expected reductions in Medicare physician payment levels will drive physicians away from accepting Medicare as well. David Orentlicher, Rights to Healthcare in the United States: Inherently Unstable, 38 Am. J. L. & Med. 326 (2012). See also, Frank Pasquale, Access to Medicine in an Era of Fractal Inequality, 19 Annals Health L. 269 (2010), discussing the move to concierge or retainer care.

Race–Based Barriers

The legacy of racial segregation is still engraved on the U.S. health care system. Hospitals and nursing homes, formally and openly racially segregated through the 1960s, to this day avoid predominantly African–American neighborhoods; only one–quarter of pharmacies in these neighborhoods carry necessary prescription medications; and health insurers market different and more limited health plans, if they market at all, than they do in predominantly Caucasion neighborhoods. Sidney Watson, Section 1557 of the Affordable Care Act: Civil Rights, Health Reform, Race, and Equity, 55 How. L. J. 855 (2012); David Barton Smith, Healthcare's Hidden Civil Rights Legacy, 48 St. Louis U. L.J. 37 (2003). Race–based residential patterns originally established as a matter of *de jure* segregation in housing produce continuing *de facto* segregation in health care facilities. Ruqaiijah Yearby, African Americans Can't Win, Break Even, or Get Out of the System: The Persistence of "Unequal Treatment" in Nursing Home Care, 82 Temple L. Rev. (2010). Racially segregated neighborhoods also produce higher incidences of chronic illness and shorter lifespan due to a number of environmental factors, including exposure to environmental hazards, unsafe housing, and lack of health care services. Thomas LaVeist, Segregated Spaces, Risky Places: The Effects of Racial Segregation on Health Inequalities (2011).

The story of persistent racial disparities in access to quality health care is not captured entirely in the story of geographic segregation. Nor does socioeconomic status explain these distinctions in access to care. One of the most influential early studies of disparities, for example, used videotaped interviews of patients who all used the same script and presented the same symptoms but differed only in race and gender. Physician recommendations for cardiac catheterization for the video patients depended significantly on those two factors alone. Kevin A. Schulman et al., The Effect of Race and Sex on Physicians' Recommendations for Cardiac Catheterization, 340 NEJM 618 (1999). Disparities in treatment decisions appear in a great variety of medical conditions. See also Rene Bowser, The Affordable Care Act and Beyond: Opportunities for Advancing Health Equity and Social Justice, 10 Hastings Race & Poverty L. J. 69 (2013), citing studies documenting that African–American and Latino patients are categorized as needing less urgent care by ER personnel than whites with the same cardiac symptoms; are less likely to receive aspirin upon discharge after heart attack; and are less likely to receive pain medication in the ER for long–bone fractures.

An Institute of Medicine report, reviewing all available empirical data, found serious "racial or ethnic differences in the quality of healthcare that are not due to access–related factors or clinical needs, preferences and appropriateness of intervention." Institute of Medicine, Unequal Treatment: Confronting Racial and Ethnic Disparities in Health Care (2002). See also, National Health Care Quality and Disparities Reports (2011), by the federal Agency on Healthcare Research and Quality, reporting that African Americans and Latinos receive lower quality care than do non–hispanic whites on approximately 40% of quality measures and that African Americans had worse access to care than non–hispanic whites on 32% of the access measures, and Latinos, on 63%.

Inequality in access to needed medical care is influenced by institutional issues, including decisions of health care organizations in determining their location, service area, and programs, and by interpersonal issues, including individual physician treatment decisions. Inequality also can be supported by structural design of public health payment programs and civil rights enforcement policy. The Affordable Care Act makes some advances toward addressing racial disparities in access to health care, just as it misses some opportunities to do so. Ruqaiijah Yearby, Breaking the Cycle of "Unequal Treatment" with Health Care Reform: Acknowledging and Addressing the Continuation of Racial Bias, 44 Conn. L. Rev. 1281 (2012).

Access Barriers by Medical Condition

Persons with particular medical or physical conditions face a variety of condition–related barriers to accessing care. Men and women with mobility disabilities, for example, may not be able to get the care they need because of a hospital's lack of accessible medical equipment. Persons with chronic pain, obesity, addiction, mental illness, HIV/AIDS, or other conditions may find their access to medical care and the quality of care they receive impeded by the stigma attached to their condition.

A great number of physicians, for example, refuse to treat patients with chronic pain, in part because the chronic pain patient is painted with stereotypes relating to addiction and malingering. Evan Anderson & Corey Davis, Breaking the Cycle of Preventable Suffering: Fulfilling the Principle of Balance, 24 Temp. Int'l & Comp. L.J. 329 (2010). For other examples of stigma–associated limitations on care, see Jeffrey Friedman, Modern Science versus the Stigma of Obesity, 10 Nature Medicine 563 (2004); Julie Greenberg, Health Care Issues Affecting People with an Intersex Condition or DSD: Sex or Disability Discrimination, 45 Loy. L.A. L. Rev. 849 (2012); Richard Boldt, Introduction: Obstacles to the Development and Use of Pharmacotherapies for Addiction, 13 J. Health Care L. & Pol'y 1 (2010); Pamela Das & Richard Horton, The Cultural Challenge of HIV/AIDS, 380 The Lancet 309 (2012).

Other factors intersect with medical condition and can exacerbate lack of care. For example, lack of accessible medical equipment for mobility–impaired women reflects stereotypes about sexuality. Elizabeth Pendo, Disability, Equipment Barriers, and Women's Health: Using the ADA to Provide Meaningful Access, 2 St. Louis U. J. Health L. & Pol'y 15 (2008). Denial of adequate treatment for pain intersects directly with race and gender. Vence Bonham, Race, Ethnicity, and The Disparities in Pain Treatment: Striving to Understand the Causes and Solutions to the Disparities in Pain Treatment, 29 J. L. Med. & Ethics 52 (2001); Diane E. Hoffmann & Anita J. Tarzian, The Girl Who Cried Pain: A Bias Against Women in the Treatment of Pain, 29 J. L. Med. & Ethics 13 (2001).

Chapter Roadmap

This chapter begins with a consideration of the common law, examining what sorts of interactions or commitments will support a finding that there is, indeed, a physician–patient relationship and, therefore, a duty to treat. The chapter then considers a selection of statutory duties to treat. The first, the Emergency Medical Treatment and Labor Act (EMTALA), responds to a systemic problem of "patient dumping" and also adopts a framework from the common law by requiring that certain actions occur to trigger the obligation to treat. The second is a set of statutes that apply nondiscrimination principles to the provision of health care and limit the right of providers to refuse to treat patients with particular characteristics. This section focuses on disability discrimination under the Americans with Disabilities Act and the Rehabilitation Act and on race discrimination under Title VI of the Civil Rights Act of 1964. The chapter concludes with two Review Problems that will ask you to apply the full range of claims of a duty to treat.

II. COMMON LAW APPROACHES

RICKS V. BUDGE

Supreme Court of Utah, 1937.
91 Utah 307, 64 P.2d 208.

EPHRAIM HANSON, JUSTICE.

This is an action for malpractice against the defendants who are physicians and surgeons at Logan, Utah, and are copartners doing business under the name and style of the "Budge Clinic." * * * [P]laintiff alleges that he was suffering from an infected right hand and was in immediate need of medical and surgical care and treatment, and there was danger of his dying unless he received such treatment; that defendants for the purpose of treating plaintiff sent him to the Budge Memorial Hospital [BMH] at Logan, Utah; that while at the hospital and while he was in need of medical and surgical treatment, defendants refused to treat or care for plaintiff and abandoned his case. * * *

* * *

[T]he evidence shows that when plaintiff left the hospital on March 15th, Dr. [S.M.] Budge advised him to continue the same treatment that had been given him at the hospital, and that if the finger showed any signs of getting worse at any time, plaintiff was to return at once to Dr. Budge for further treatment; that on the morning of March 17th, plaintiff telephoned Dr. Budge, and explained the condition of his hand; that he was told by the doctor to come to his office, and in pursuance of the doctor's request, plaintiff reported to the doctor's office at 2 p.m. of that day.

Dr. Budge again examined the hand, and told plaintiff the hand was worse; he called in Dr. D.C. Budge, another of the defendants, who examined the hand, scraped it some, and indicated thereon where the hand should be opened. Dr. S.M. Budge said to plaintiff: "You have got to go back to the hospital." * * * Within a short time after the arrival of plaintiff, Dr. S.M. Budge arrived at the hospital. Plaintiff testified: "He [meaning Dr. S.M. Budge] came into my room and said, 'You are owing us. I am not going to touch you until that account is taken care of.' " (The account referred to was, according to plaintiff, of some years' standing and did not relate to any charge for services being then rendered.) Plaintiff testified that he did not know what to say to the doctor, but that he finally asked the doctor if he was going to take care of him, and the doctor replied: "No, I am not going to take care of you. I would not take you to the operating table and operate on you and keep you here thirty days, and then there is another $30.00 at the office, until your account is taken care of." Plaintiff replied: "If that is the idea, if you will furnish me a little help, I will try to move."

[A]fter being dressed, he left [BMH] to seek other treatment. At that time it was raining. He walked to the Cache Valley Hospital [CVH], a few blocks away, and there met Dr. Randall, who examined the hand. Dr. Randall testified that when the plaintiff arrived at [CVH], the hand was swollen with considerable fluid oozing from it; that the lower two–thirds of the forearm was red and swollen from the infection which extended up in the arm, and that there was some fluid also oozing from the back of the hand, and that plaintiff required immediate surgical attention; that immediately after the arrival of plaintiff at the hospital he made an incision through the fingers and through the palm of the hand along the tendons that led from the palm, followed those tendons as far as there was any bulging, opened it up thoroughly all the way to the base of the hand, and put drain tubes in. * * * About two weeks after the plaintiff entered [CVH], it became necessary to amputate the middle finger and remove about an inch of the metacarpal bone.

* * *

Defendants contend: (1) That there was no contract of employment between plaintiff and defendants and that defendants in the absence of a valid contract were not obligated to proceed with any treatment; and (2) that if there was such a contract, there was no evidence that the refusal of Dr. S.M. Budge to operate or take care of plaintiff resulted in any damage to plaintiff.

* * *

Under this evidence, it cannot be said that the relation of physician and patient did not exist on March 17th. It had not been terminated after its commencement on March 11th. When the plaintiff left the hospital on

March 15th, he understood that he was to report to Dr. S.M. Budge if the occasion required and was so requested by the doctor. Plaintiff's return to the doctor's office was on the advice of the doctor. While at the doctor's office, both Dr. S.M. Budge and Dr. D.C. Budge examined plaintiff's hand and they ordered that he go at once to the hospital for further medical attention. That plaintiff was told by the doctor to come to the doctor's office and was there examined by him and directed to go to the hospital for further treatment would create the relationship of physician and patient. That the relationship existed at the time the plaintiff was sent to the hospital on March 17th cannot be seriously questioned.

We believe the law is well settled that a physician or surgeon, upon undertaking an operation or other case, is under the duty, in the absence of an agreement limiting the service, of continuing his attention, after the first operation or first treatment, so long as the case requires attention. The obligation of continuing attention can be terminated only by the cessation of the necessity which gave rise to the relationship, or by the discharge of the physician by the patient, or by the withdrawal from the case by the physician after giving the patient reasonable notice so as to enable the patient to secure other medical attention. A physician has the right to withdraw from a case, but if the case is such as to still require further medical or surgical attention, he must, before withdrawing from the case, give the patient sufficient notice so the patient can procure other medical attention if he desires.[ ]

* * *

We cannot say as a matter of law that plaintiff suffered no damages by reason of the refusal of Dr. S.M. Budge to further treat him. The evidence shows that from the time plaintiff left the office of the defendants up until the time that he arrived at [CVH] his hand continued to swell; that it was very painful; that when he left [BMH] he was in such condition that he did not know whether he was going to live or die. That both his mental and physical suffering must have been most acute cannot be questioned. While the law cannot measure with exactness such suffering and cannot determine with absolute certainty what damages, if any, plaintiff may be entitled to, still those are questions which a jury under proper instructions from the court must determine.

* * *

FOLLAND, JUSTICE (concurring in part, dissenting in part).

* * *

* * * The theory of plaintiff as evidenced in his complaint is that there was no continued relationship from the first employment but that a new relationship was entered into. He visited the clinic on March 17th; the Doctors Budge examined his hand and told him an immediate opera-

tion was necessary and for him to go to the hospital. I do not think a new contract was entered into at that time. There was no consideration for any implied promise that Dr. Budge or the Budge Clinic would assume the responsibility of another operation and the costs and expenses incident thereto. As soon as Dr. Budge reached the hospital he opened negotiations with the plaintiff which might have resulted in a contract, but before any contract arrangement was made the plaintiff decided to leave the hospital and seek attention elsewhere. As soon as he could dress himself he walked away. There is conflict in the evidence as to the conversation. Plaintiff testified in effect that Dr. Budge asked for something to be done about an old account. The doctor's testimony in effect was that he asked that some arrangement be made to take care of the doctor's bill and expenses for the ensuing operation and treatment at the hospital. The result, however, was negative. No arrangement was made. The plaintiff made no attempt whatsoever to suggest to the doctor any way by which either the old account might be taken care of or the expenses of the ensuing operation provided for. * * * Dr. Budge had a right to refuse to incur the obligation and responsibility incident to one or more operations and the treatment and attention which would be necessary. If it be assumed that the contract relationship of physician and patient existed prior to this conversation, either as resulting from the first employment or that there was an implied contract entered into at the clinic, yet Dr. Budge had the right with proper notice to discontinue the relationship. While plaintiff's condition was acute and needed immediate attention, he received such immediate attention at [CVH]. There was only a delay of an hour or two, and part of that delay is accounted for by reason of the fact that the doctor at [CVH] would not operate until some paper, which plaintiff says he did not read, was signed. Plaintiff said he could not sign it but that it was signed by his brother before the operation was performed. We are justified in believing that by means of this written obligation, provision was made for the expenses and fees about to be incurred. I am satisfied from my reading of the record that no injury or damage resulted from the delay occasioned by plaintiff leaving the Budge Hospital and going to [CVH]. He was not in such desperate condition but that he was able to walk the three or four blocks between the two hospitals. * * *

CHILDS V. WEIS

Court of Civil Appeals of Texas, 1969.
440 S.W.2d 104.

WILLIAMS, J.

On or about November 27, 1966 Daisy Childs, wife of J.C. Childs, a resident of Dallas County, was approximately seven months pregnant. On that date she was visiting in Lone Oak, Texas, and about two o'clock A.M. she presented herself to the Greenville Hospital emergency room. At that time she stated she was bleeding and had labor pains. She was examined by a nurse who identified herself as H. Beckham. According to Mrs. Childs, Nurse Beckham stated that she would call the doctor. She said the nurse returned and stated "that the Dr. said that I would have to go to my doctor in Dallas. I stated to Beckham that I'm not going to make it to Dallas. Beckham replied that yes, I would make it. She stated that I was just starting into labor and that I would make it. The weather was cold that night. About an hour after leaving the Greenville Hospital Authority I had the baby while in a car on the way to medical facilities in Sulphur Springs. The baby lived about 12 hours."

[Dr. Weis] said that he had never examined or treated Daisy Childs and in fact had never seen or spoken to either Daisy Childs or her husband, J.C. Childs, at any time in his life. He further stated that he had never at any time agreed or consented to the examination or treatment of either Daisy Childs or her husband. He said that on a day in November 1966 he recalled a telephone call received by him from a nurse in the emergency room at the Greenville Surgical Hospital; that the nurse told him that there was a negro girl in the emergency room having a "bloody show" and some "labor pains." He said the nurse advised him that this woman had been visiting in Lone Oak, and that her OB doctor lived in Garland, Texas, and that she also resided in Garland. The doctor said, "I told the nurse over the telephone to have the girl call her doctor in Garland and see what he wanted her to do. I knew nothing more about this incident until I was served with the citation and a copy of the petition in this lawsuit."

* * *

Since it is unquestionably the law that the relationship of physician and patient is dependent upon contract, either express or implied, a physician is not to be held liable for arbitrarily refusing to respond to a call of a person even urgently in need of medical or surgical assistance provided that the relation of physician and patient does not exist at the time the call is made or at the time the person presents himself for treatment.

* * *

Applying these principles of law to the factual situation here presented we find an entire absence of evidence of a contract, either express or implied, which would create the relationship of patient and physician as between Dr. Weis and Mrs. Childs. Dr. Weis, under these circumstances, was under no duty whatsoever to examine or treat Mrs. Childs. When advised by telephone that the lady was in the emergency room he did what seems to be a reasonable thing and inquired as to the identity of her doctor who had been treating her. Upon being told that the doctor was in Garland he stated that the patient should call the doctor and find out what should be done. This action on the part of Dr. Weis seems to be not only reasonable but within the bounds of professional ethics.

We cannot agree with appellant that Dr. Weis' statement to the nurse over the telephone amounted to an acceptance of the case and affirmative instructions which she was bound to follow. Rather than give instructions which could be construed to be in the nature of treatment, Dr. Weis told the nurse to have the woman call her physician in Garland and secure instructions from him.

The affidavit of Mrs. Childs would indicate that Nurse Beckham may not have relayed the exact words of Dr. Weis to Mrs. Childs. Instead, it would seem that Nurse Beckham told Mrs. Childs that the doctor said that she would "have to go" to her doctor in Dallas. Assuming this statement was made by Nurse Beckham, and further assuming that it contained the meaning as placed upon it by appellant, yet it is undisputed that such words were uttered by Nurse Beckham, and not by Dr. Weis. * * *

[The court affirmed summary judgment in favor of the defendant.]

WILLIAMS v. U.S.

United States Court of Appeals, Fourth Circuit, 2001.
242 F.3d 169.

NIEMEYER, CIRCUIT JUDGE:

* * *

The revised amended complaint in this case alleges that in October 1997, Berlie White, while at a restaurant in Cherokee, North Carolina, became short of breath, developing "various signs of respiratory distress." Asserting that he was suffering from a medical emergency, White presented himself at about 7:00 p.m. to the emergency room of the nearby Cherokee Indian Hospital [CIH], an Indian hospital operated on the Cherokee Reservation by the United States Public Health Service. Federal employees operating the hospital refused to treat White or to refill his oxygen tank because he was not Indian. [The hospital was funded under the federal Indian Health Care Improvement Act which prohibits the hospital from treating non–Indians, with the exception of emergency medical treatment which the hospital is permitted but not required to provide to non–Indians.] They referred him to the Swain County Hospital [SCH] * * *, approximately 10 miles away. When White arrived at [SCH], he was in extreme respiratory distress, and he died the next day. The complaint alleges that White's death was caused by CIH's "refusal to provide any treatment or assistance" and "the delay of his access to medical care."

The United States filed a motion to dismiss. * * * The district court agreed, dismissing the action. In doing so, it held that * * * North Carolina has no law creating a duty in favor of a private person to provide medical treatment or to recover for a discriminatory refusal to provide medical treatment. [The plaintiff, representing White's estate, brought several claims under federal law, all of which also were dismissed.]

* * *

The North Carolina Supreme Court has held that a physician has no duty to render services to every person seeking them. See Childers v. Frye, 201 N.C. 42, 158 S.E. 744 (1931). The *Childers* court based its decision on a contract theory, concluding that a physician's decision of whether to treat a person amounts to a decision of whether to enter into a contractual relationship. In the case of an unconscious patient, where a traditional contract relationship could not be formed, the court explained that liability would then be established only if "the physician actually accepted an injured person as a patient and undertook to treat him." Holding that the common law does not limit a medical provider's discretion to turn away potential patients, the court found it unobjectionable that the doctor had refused to treat the patient because he mistakenly believed the patient was drunk.

Despite the holding in *Childers,* Williams advances four theories as to why a healthcare provider in North Carolina has a duty not to discriminate in the provision of emergency medical care. First, [plaintiff] argues that N.C.G.S. § 58–65–85, which prohibits nonprofit hospitals from discriminating on the basis of race, color, and national origin, would provide her with a cause of action against a private hospital. This provision, however, is part of North Carolina's Insurance Code and applies only to nonprofit hospitals seeking reimbursement from the North Carolina Department of Insurance. Moreover, the statute does not apply to every private hospital. Most importantly, we have been unable to find any North Carolina case that interprets this statute to give rise to a private cause of action.

Second, [plaintiff] directs us to N.C.G.S. § 131A–8, a statute pertaining to hospitals receiving state financing, which states, "All health care facilities shall be operated to serve and benefit the public and there shall be no discrimination against any person based on race, creed, color or national origin." Again, this statute does not provide a private enforcement mechanism. Arguably, the North Carolina Medical Care Commission is authorized to enforce this nondiscrimination rule [ ] * * *. While § 131A–15 permits "[a]ny holder of bonds or notes issued under the provisions of this Chapter" to bring suit to enforce his contractual rights under the bond, this provision does not authorize a private enforcement action against a hospital that has discriminated in violation of § 131A–8.

Third, [plaintiff] relies on the Patients' Bill of Rights, § 3C.4103, a state agency rule promulgated pursuant to the Hospital Licensure Act, N.C.G.S. § 131E–75. Again, however, the legislature provided for enforcement of this Act only by the North Carolina Department of Health and Human Services.

Finally, [plaintiff], relying on a Georgia case, asserts a common law duty based on her theory that a hospital emergency room is a "public utility." See Williams v. Hosp. Auth., 119 Ga.App. 626, 168 S.E.2d 336, 337 (1969) ("To say that a public institution which has assumed this duty and held itself out as giving such aid can arbitrarily refuse to give emergency treatment to a member of the public who presents himself with 'a broken arm and in a state of traumatic injury, suffering mental and physical pain visible and obvious to the hospital employees' is repugnant to our entire system of government"). In *Williams,* however, the court "express[ed] no opinion on the [existence of a] duty of a *private* hospital in Georgia." (emphasis added). * * *

The scope of duties imposed by positive law is necessarily narrower than the reach of moral command, and this case presents a tragic circumstance, if the allegations of the complaint are true, that could have been avoided by simple obedience to a moral command. That individuals at [CIH] would deny Berlie White the most meager of medical assistance—that of refilling his oxygen tank when it had run out—at a time of extreme need is incomprehensible, particularly when these individuals were not prohibited by law from providing White with this assistance. If they did deny White this minimal care, the burden of their moral failure will surely remain with them.

AFFIRMED.

NOTES AND QUESTIONS

1. Why did the doctor refuse to treat Mr. Ricks? Ms. Childs? Should the courts distinguish among such cases on the basis of the reason for the refusal? If the court were willing to make a distinction, how would you go about proving the basis for the refusal in each of these cases? See, Section III.B, below.

2. Could you devise a claim for the plaintiff in *Williams* under the common law principle enunciated in *Ricks*? See, for example, New Biloxi Hospital, Inc. v. Frazier, 245 Miss. 185, 146 So.2d 882 (Miss. 1962), in which the court held a hospital liable for the death of a patient who remained untreated in the emergency room for over two hours and died twenty–five minutes after transfer to a Veterans Administration hospital. The court based its holding on the hospital's breach of the duty to exercise reasonable care once treatment had been "undertaken." The court described the scene in detail:

> Sam Frazier was a 42 year old Negro man, who had lost his left eye and his left arm, just below the elbow, during World War II. He and his wife had two young children. * * * [Mr. Frazier was brought to the ED after being shot.] The blast made two large holes in the up-

> per arm and tore away the brachial artery. * * * Ambulance attendants carried him into the emergency room, where one of the Hospital's nurses just looked at him and walked away. He was bleeding profusely at that time. There was blood all over the ambulance cot, and while waiting in the hospital, blood was streaming from his arm to the floor, forming a puddle with a diameter of 24–30 inches. After about twenty minutes, another Hospital nurse came, looked at Frazier and walked away. * * * Neither [the nurse] nor the doctor made any effort to stop the bleeding in any way. [The nurse] continued to come in and out of the emergency room on occasion, but simply looked at Frazier. He asked to see his little boy, and for water. His bleeding continued.* * * This summary of the evidence reflects that Frazier was permitted to bleed to death. * * *

See also Wilmington Gen. Hospital v. Manlove, 174 A.2d 135 (Del. 1961), holding that a hospital must provide emergency care to a person who relies on the presence of an emergency room in coming to the hospital. In *Millard*, in note 3 below, the court references that EMTs brought the patient to the ER relying on the hospital's holding itself out as having 24–hour trauma care.

3. Physicians often commit by contract to treat a certain group of patients, for example in contracts with health plans or in employment contracts with health care facilities or employers. Physician specialists often have a contractual relationship with the hospital to be on–call for essential services, either for compensation or as required in the medical staff by–laws as a condition of staff privileges. These commitments to an organization may be sufficient to create a physician–patient relationship and trigger a duty to provide treatment. For example, in Hiser v. Randolph, 126 Ariz. 608, 617 P.2d 774 (Ariz. 1980), the court held that the physician had an obligation to treat the patient under his on–call contract with the hospital. In *Hiser*, there was some evidence that the physician refused to treat the patient because she was the wife of an attorney, although the doctor claimed that he was not qualified to treat her condition. In Millard v. Carrado, 14 S.W.3d 42 (Mo. Ct. App. 1999), the court held that a surgeon's on–call commitment to the hospital created a physician–patient relationship with a trauma patient who had to be transferred to another hospital for surgery when the on–call surgeon failed to notify the hospital that he would be out–of–town attending a medical conference during his on–call time. But see, Seeber v. Ebeling, 36 Kan.App.2d 501, 141 P.3d 1180 (2006), holding no claim available against on–call specialist who refused to come to the hospital due to fatigue. See also, discussion of on–call physicians under EMTALA in Section III, below.

4. The regulations promulgated under the hospital licensure statute of North Carolina at issue in *Williams* provided that:

> [t]he patient has the right to expect emergency procedures to be implemented without unnecessary delay [and] the right to medical and nursing services without discrimination based upon race, color, reli-

gion, sex, sexual preference, national origin, or source of payment. 10A N.C.Admin. Code tit. 13B.3302(f) & (m).

The state licensing agency had authority to investigate violations of this provision, but *Williams* held that there was no private right of action under these regulations. In contrast, see Thompson v. Sun City Community Hospital, Inc., 141 Ariz. 597, 688 P.2d 605 (1984), where the court relied on state hospital regulations and private accreditation standards to find a duty to provide emergency care enforceable through private litigation. Creating a right devoid of the ability to privately enforce that right is not entirely uncommon. See Problem: Residents' Rights in Chapter 3. Which is the better public policy strategy and why?

5. *Williams* considers state law governing not–for–profit organizations. Federal tax–exempt status requires that hospitals provide some level of community benefit and meet certain standards relating to emergency care and financial assistance plans.

PROBLEM: CHERYL HANACHEK

Cheryl Hanachek, a law student residing in Boston, discovered she was pregnant during an "action" called by the city's obstetricians in protest against Medicaid and discounted private insurance payment rates. Ms. Hanachek first called Dr. Cunetto, who had been her obstetrician for the birth of her first child two years earlier. Dr. Cunetto's receptionist informed Ms. Hanachek that Dr. Cunetto wasn't taking any patients covered by Ms. Hanachek's health plan.

About two weeks later, Ms. Hanachek called Dr. Simms, who had been recommended by her sister. Dr. Simms' receptionist told Ms. Hanachek that Dr. Simms was not taking any new patients as his malpractice premiums were so high that he was even considering discontinuing his obstetrical practice. In fact, however, Dr. Simms actually did not accept lawyers as patients. Ms. Hanachek reported to the receptionist that she was having infrequent minor cramping, and the receptionist told her that this was "nothing to worry about at this stage." Later that night Ms. Hanachek was admitted to the hospital on an emergency basis. Ms. Hanachek was in shock from blood loss due to a ruptured ectopic pregnancy. As a result of the rupture and other complications, Ms. Hanachek underwent a hysterectomy.

Ms. Hanachek has brought suit against Dr. Cunetto and Dr. Simms. If you were representing Ms. Hanachek, how would you proceed in arguing and proving your case?

PROBLEM: ETHICS AND LAW: NEVER THE TWAIN SHALL MEET?

The American Medical Association has adopted the following ethical principles, among others, concerning a physician's ethical duty to provide treatment to patients:

> A physician shall, in the provision of appropriate patient care, except in emergencies, be free to choose whom to serve, with whom to associate, and the environment in which to provide medical care. AMA Principles of Medical Ethics VI.
>
> Each physician has an obligation to share in providing care to the indigent. * * *. Caring for the poor should be a regular part of the physician's practice schedule * * *. Physicians are meeting their obligation * * * in a number of ways [including] participating in government programs that provide health care to the poor * * *. Opinion 9.065, AMA Council on Ethical and Judicial Affairs (CEJA).
>
> * * * Physicians must strive to offer the same quality of care to all their patients irrespective of personal characteristics such as race or ethnicity. Physicians must learn to recognize racial and ethnic health care disparities and should examine their own practices to ensure that inappropriate considerations do not affect clinical judgment. Opinion 9.121, AMA CEJA.

The AMA holds that these are to be ethical principles and not legal principles. Are these ethical principles legally enforceable? Can they be used in a tort claim, for example, against a physician who refused to treat a particular patient or provided substandard care?

Would you recommend that the state adopt these standards, or perhaps some of them, as grounds for disciplinary action? See N.Y.Educ. Law § 6509(6), providing that "[r]efusing to provide professional service to a person because of such person's race, creed, color, or national origin" constitutes grounds for discipline; Cal.Bus. & Prof.Code § 125.6. Such specific provisions are quite uncommon. What challenges would the board face in enforcing these standards? See Chapter 2 on licensure and discipline.

For contrasting views of doctors' obligations to provide treatment, see Allan Brett, Physicians Have a Responsibility to Meet the Health Care Needs of Society, 40 J. L. Med. & Ethics 526 (2012) and Marshall Kapp, Conscripted Physician Services and the Public's Health, 39 J. L. Med. & Ethics 414 (2011).

III. STATUTORY EXCEPTIONS TO THE COMMON LAW

A. EMTALA

The federal Emergency Medical Treatment and Labor Act, 42 U.S.C.A. § 1395dd (EMTALA), was enacted in response to "patient dumping," a practice in which patients are transferred from one hospital's emergency room to another's for other than therapeutic reasons. Several empirical studies documented patient dumping as a widespread practice.

See, e.g., Robert L. Schiff et al., Transfers to a Public Hospital, 314 NEJM 552 (1986).

EMTALA applies *only* to hospitals that accept payment from Medicare *and* operate an emergency department; however, EMTALA applies to all patients of such a hospital and not just to Medicare beneficiaries. While EMTALA does not require a hospital to offer emergency room services, some state hospital licensure statutes do; federal tax law encourages tax–exempt hospitals to do so; and Medicare Conditions of Participation require that all hospitals be capable of providing initial treatment in emergency situations as well as arrange for referral or transfer to more comprehensive facilities.

EMTALA specifically empowers patients to bring civil suits for damages against participating hospitals, but does not provide a private right of action against a treating physician. The Office of the Inspector General (OIG) of HHS enforces EMTALA against both hospitals and physicians. Private EMTALA litigation has burgeoned, while government enforcement has been much less active. Administrative enforcement actions under EMTALA are few; monetary penalties are quite small; and exclusion from Medicare is almost unheard of. Despite the passage of EMTALA, and perhaps because of its lax enforcement by the agency, patient dumping continues. Sara Rosenbaum et al., Case Studies at Denver Health: "Patient Dumping" in the Emergency Department Despite EMTALA, the Law that Banned It, 31 Health Affairs 1749 (2012).

EMERGENCY MEDICAL TREATMENT AND LABOR ACT

42 U.S.C. § 1395dd.

(a) Medical screening requirement. In the case of a hospital that has a hospital emergency department, if any individual * * * comes to the emergency department and a request is made on the individual's behalf for examination or treatment for a medical condition, the hospital must provide for an appropriate medical screening examination within the capability of the hospital's emergency department, including ancillary services routinely available to the emergency department, to determine whether or not an emergency medical condition * * * exists.

(b) Necessary stabilizing treatment for emergency medical conditions and labor.

(1) In general. If any individual * * * comes to a hospital and the hospital determines that the individual has an emergency medical condition, the hospital must provide either—

(A) within the staff and facilities available at the hospital, for such further medical examination and such treatment as may be required to stabilize the medical condition, or

(B) for transfer of the individual to another medical facility in accordance with subsection (c).

* * *

(c) Restricting transfers until individual stabilized.

(1) Rule. If an individual at a hospital has an emergency medical condition which has not been stabilized * * *, the hospital may not transfer the individual unless—

(A)(i) the individual (or a legally responsible person acting on the individual's behalf) after being informed of the hospital's obligations under this section and of the risk of transfer, in writing requests transfer to another medical facility, [or]

(ii) a physician * * * has signed a certification that[,] based upon the information available at the time of transfer, the medical benefits reasonably expected from the provision of appropriate medical treatment at another medical facility outweigh the increased risks to the individual and, in the case of labor, to the unborn child from effecting the transfer.

* * *

(B) [and] the transfer is an appropriate transfer * * * to that facility * * *.

* * *

(2) Appropriate transfer. An appropriate transfer to a medical facility is a transfer—

(A) in which the transferring hospital provides the medical treatment within its capacity which minimizes the risks to the individual's health and, in the case of a woman in labor, the health of the unborn child;

(B) in which the receiving facility—

(i) has available space and qualified personnel for the treatment of the individual, and

(ii) has agreed to accept transfer of the individual and to provide appropriate medical treatment;

(C) in which the transferring hospital sends to the receiving facility all medical records * * * related to the emergency condition for which the individual has presented, available at the time of the transfer * * *; [and]

(D) in which the transfer is effected through qualified personnel and transportation equipment. . . .

(d) Enforcement.

(1) Civil monetary penalties.

(A) A participating hospital that negligently violates a requirement of this section is subject to a civil money penalty of not more than $50,000 for each such violation* * *.

(B) [A]ny physician who is responsible for the examination, treatment, or transfer of an individual in a participating hospital * * * and who negligently violates a requirement of this section, including a physician on–call for the care of such individual, is subject to a civil money penalty of not more than $50,000 for each such violation and, if the violation is gross and flagrant or is repeated, to exclusion from participation in [Medicare and Medicaid]* * *.

(2) Civil enforcement.

(A) Personal harm. Any individual who suffers personal harm as a direct result of a participating hospital's violation of a requirement of this section may, in a civil action against the participating hospital, obtain those damages available for personal injury under the law of the State in which the hospital is located, and such equitable relief as is appropriate.

(B) Financial loss to other medical facility. Any medical facility that suffers a financial loss as a direct result of a participating hospital's violation of a requirement of this section may, in a civil action against the participating hospital, obtain those damages available for financial loss, under the law of the State in which the hospital is located, and such equitable relief as is appropriate.* * *

(e) Definitions. In this section:

(1) The term "emergency medical condition" means—

(A) a medical condition manifesting itself by acute symptoms of sufficient severity (including severe pain) such that the absence of immediate medical attention could reasonably be expected to result in—

(i) placing the health of the individual (or, with respect to a pregnant woman, the health of the woman or her unborn child) in serious jeopardy,

(ii) serious impairment to bodily functions, or

(iii) serious dysfunction of any bodily organ or part; or

(B) with respect to a pregnant woman who is having contractions—

(i) that there is inadequate time to effect a safe transfer to another hospital before delivery, or

(ii) that transfer may pose a threat to the health or safety of the woman or the unborn child * * *.

* * *

(3)(A) The term "to stabilize" means * * * to provide such medical treatment of the condition as may be necessary to assure, within reasonable medical probability, that no material deterioration of the condition is likely to result from or occur during the transfer of the individual from a facility.* * *

(B) The term "stabilized" means * * * that no material deterioration of the condition is likely, within reasonable medical probability, to result from or occur during the transfer of the individual from a facility, or, with respect to an emergency medical condition described in paragraph (1)(B), that the woman has delivered (including the placenta) * * *.

(h) No delay in examination or treatment. A participating hospital may not delay provision of an appropriate medical screening examination required under subsection (a) * * * or further medical examination and treatment required under subsection (b) * * * in order to inquire about the individual's method of payment or insurance status.

BABER V. HOSPITAL CORPORATION OF AMERICA

United States Court of Appeals, Fourth Circuit, 1992.
977 F.2d 872.

WILLIAMS, CIRCUIT JUDGE:

Barry Baber, Administrator of the Estate of Brenda Baber, instituted this suit against * * * Raleigh General Hospital (RGH), Beckley Appalachian Regional Hospital (BARH), and the parent corporations of both hospitals. Mr. Baber alleged that the Defendants violated the Emergency Medical Treatment and Active Labor Act (EMTALA)[ ]. The Defendants moved to dismiss the EMTALA claim under Rule 12(b)(6) of the Federal Rules of Civil Procedure. Because the parties submitted affidavits and depositions, the district court treated the motion as one for summary judgment. See Fed.R.Civ.P. 12(b).

* * *

Mr. Baber's complaint charged the various defendants with violating EMTALA in several ways. Specifically, Mr. Baber contends that Dr. Kline, RGH, and its parent corporation violated EMTALA by:

(a) failing to provide his sister with an "appropriate medical screening examination;"

(b) failing to stabilize his sister's "emergency medical condition;" and

(c) transferring his sister to BARH without first providing stabilizing treatment.

* * *

After reviewing the parties' submissions, the district court granted summary judgment for the Defendants. * * * Finding no error, we affirm.

* * *

* * * Brenda Baber, accompanied by her brother, Barry, sought treatment at RGH's emergency department at 10:40 p.m. on August 5, 1987. When she entered the hospital, Ms. Baber was nauseated, agitated, and thought she might be pregnant. She was also tremulous and did not appear to have orderly thought patterns. She had stopped taking her anti–psychosis medications, * * * and had been drinking heavily. Dr. Kline, the attending physician, described her behavior and condition in the RGH Encounter Record as follows: Patient refuses to remain on stretcher and cannot be restrained verbally despite repeated requests by staff and by me. Brother has not assisted either verbally or physically in keeping patient from pacing throughout the Emergency Room. Restraints would place patient and staff at risk by increasing her agitation.

In response to Ms. Baber's initial complaints, Dr. Kline examined her central nervous system, lungs, cardiovascular system, and abdomen. He also ordered several laboratory tests, including a pregnancy test.

While awaiting the results of her laboratory tests, Ms. Baber began pacing about the emergency department. In an effort to calm Ms. Baber, Dr. Kline gave her [several medications]. The medication did not immediately control her agitation. Mr. Baber described his sister as becoming restless, "worse and more disoriented after she was given the medication," and wandering around the emergency department.

While roaming in the emergency department around midnight, Ms. Baber * * * convulsed and fell, striking her head upon a table and lacerating her scalp. [S]he quickly regained consciousness and emergency department personnel carried her by stretcher to the suturing room, [where] Dr. Kline examined her again. He obtained a blood gas study, which did not reveal any oxygen deprivation or acidosis. Ms. Baber was verbal and could move her head, eyes, and limbs without discomfort. * * * Dr. Kline closed the one–inch laceration with a couple of sutures. Although she became calmer and drowsy after the wound was sutured, Ms. Baber was easily arousable and easily disturbed. Ms. Baber experienced some anxiety, disorientation, restlessness, and some speech problems, which Dr. Kline concluded were caused by her pre–existing psychiatric problems of psychosis with paranoia and alcohol withdrawal.

Dr. Kline discussed Ms. Baber's condition with Dr. Whelan, the psychiatrist who had treated Ms. Baber for two years. * * * Dr. Whelan concluded that Ms. Baber's hyperactive and uncontrollable behavior during her evening at RGH was compatible with her behavior during a relapse of her serious psychotic and chronic mental illness. Both Dr. Whelan and Dr. Kline were concerned about the seizure she had while at RGH's emergency department because it was the first one she had experienced. * * * They also agreed Ms. Baber needed further treatment * * * and decided to transfer her to the psychiatric unit at BARH because RGH did not have a psychiatric ward, and both doctors believed it would be beneficial for her to be treated in a familiar setting. The decision to transfer Ms. Baber was further supported by the doctors' belief that any tests to diagnose the cause of her initial seizure, such as a computerized tomography scan (CT scan), could be performed at BARH once her psychiatric condition was under control. The transfer to BARH was discussed with Mr. Baber who neither expressly consented nor objected. His only request was that his sister be x–rayed because of the blow to her head when she fell.

* * *

Because Dr. Kline did not conclude Ms. Baber had a serious head injury, he believed that she could be transferred safely to BARH where she would be under the observation of the BARH psychiatric staff personnel. At 1:35 a.m. on August 6, Ms. Baber was admitted directly to the psychiatric department of BARH upon Dr. Whelan's orders. She was not processed through BARH's emergency department. Although Ms. Baber was restrained and regularly checked every fifteen minutes by the nursing staff while at BARH, no physician gave her an extensive neurological examination upon her arrival. Mr. Baber unsuccessfully repeated his request for an x–ray.

At the 3:45 a.m. check, the nurse found Ms. Baber having a grand mal seizure. At Dr. Whelan's direction, the psychiatric unit staff transported her to BARH's emergency department. Upon arrival in the emergency department, her pupils were unresponsive, and hospital personnel began CPR. The emergency department physician ordered a CT scan, which was performed around 6:30 a.m. The CT report revealed a fractured skull and a right subdural hematoma. BARH personnel immediately transferred Ms. Baber back to RGH because that hospital had a neurosurgeon on staff, and BARH did not have the facility or staff to treat serious neurological problems. When RGH received Ms. Baber for treatment around 7 a.m., she was comatose. She died later that day, apparently as a result of an intracerebrovascular rupture.

* * *

Mr. Baber * * * alleges that RGH, acting through its agent, Dr. Kline, violated several provisions of EMTALA. These allegations can be summarized into two general complaints: (1) RGH failed to provide an appropriate medical screening to discover that Ms. Baber had an emergency medical condition as required by 42 U.S.C.A. § 1395dd(a); and (2) RGH transferred Ms. Baber before her emergency medical condition had been stabilized, and the appropriate paperwork was not completed to transfer a non–stable patient as required by 42 U.S.C.A. § 1395dd(b) & (c). Because we find that RGH did not violate any of these EMTALA provisions, we affirm the district court's grant of summary judgment to RGH.

Mr. Baber first claims that RGH failed to provide his sister with an "appropriate medical screening". He makes two arguments. First, he contends that a medical screening is only "appropriate" if it satisfies a national standard of care. In other words, Mr. Baber urges that we construe EMTALA as a national medical malpractice statute, albeit limited to whether the medical screening was appropriate to identify an emergency medical condition. We conclude instead that EMTALA only requires hospitals to apply their standard screening procedure for identification of an emergency medical condition uniformly to all patients and that Mr. Baber has failed to proffer sufficient evidence showing that RGH did not do so. Second, Mr. Baber contends that EMTALA requires hospitals to provide some medical screening. We agree, but conclude that he has failed to show no screening was provided to his sister.

* * *

While [the Act] requires a hospital's emergency department to provide an "appropriate medical screening examination," it does not define that term other than to state its purpose is to identify an "emergency medical condition."

* * *

[T]he goal of "an appropriate medical screening examination" is to determine whether a patient with acute or severe symptoms has a life threatening or serious medical condition. The plain language of the statute requires a hospital to develop a screening procedure[6] designed to identify such critical conditions that exist in symptomatic patients and to apply that screening procedure uniformly to all patients with similar complaints.

---

[6] While a hospital emergency room may develop one general procedure for screening all patients, it may also tailor its screening procedure to the patient's complaints or exhibited symptoms. For example, it may have one screening procedure for a patient with a heart attack and another for women in labor. Under our interpretation of EMTALA, such varying screening procedures would not pose liability under EMTALA as long as all patients complaining of the same problem or exhibiting the same symptoms receive identical screening procedures. We also recognize that the hospital's screening procedure is not limited to personal observation and assessment but may include available ancillary services through departments such as radiology and laboratory.

[W]hile EMTALA requires a hospital emergency department to apply its standard screening examination uniformly, it does not guarantee that the emergency personnel will correctly diagnose a patient's condition as a result of this screening.[7] The statutory language clearly indicates that EMTALA does not impose on hospitals a national standard of care in screening patients. The screening requirement only requires a hospital to provide a screening examination that is "appropriate" and "within the capability of the hospital's emergency department," including "routinely available" ancillary services. 42 U.S.C.A. § 1395dd(a). This section establishes a standard, which will of necessity be individualized for each hospital, since hospital emergency departments have varying capabilities. Had Congress intended to require hospitals to provide a screening examination which comported with generally–accepted medical standards, it could have clearly specified a national standard. Nor do we believe Congress intended to create a negligence standard based on each hospital's capability. * * * EMTALA is no substitute for state law medical malpractice actions.

* * *

The Sixth Circuit has also held that an appropriate medical screening means "a screening that the hospital would have offered to any paying patient" or at least "not known by the provider to be insufficient or below their own standards."

* * *

Applying our interpretation of section (a) of EMTALA, we must next determine whether there is any genuine issue of material fact regarding whether RGH gave Ms. Baber a medical screening examination that differed from its standard screening procedure. Because Mr. Baber has offered no evidence of disparate treatment, we find that the district court did not err in granting summary judgment.

* * *

Mr. Baber does not allege that RGH's emergency department personnel treated Ms. Baber differently from its other patients. Instead, he merely claims Dr. Kline did not do enough accurately to diagnose her condition or treat her injury.[ ] The critical element of an EMTALA cause of action is not the adequacy of the screening examination but whether

[7] Some commentators have criticized defining "appropriate" in terms of the hospital's medical screening standard because hospitals could theoretically avoid liability by providing very cursory and substandard screenings to all patients, which might enable the doctor to ignore a medical condition. [ ] Even though we do not believe it is likely that a hospital would endanger all of its patients by establishing such a cursory standard, theoretically it is possible. Our holding, however, does not foreclose the possibility that a future court faced with such a situation may decide that the hospital's standard was so low that it amounted to no "appropriate medical screening." We do not decide that question in this case because Ms. Baber's screening was not so substandard as to amount to no screening at all.

the screening examination that was performed deviated from the hospital's evaluation procedures that would have been performed on any patient in a similar condition.

* * *

Dr. Kline testified that he performed a medical screening on Ms. Baber in accordance with standard procedures for examining patients with head injuries. He explained that generally, a patient is not scheduled for advanced tests such as a CT scan or x–rays unless the patient's signs and symptoms so warrant. While Ms. Baber did exhibit some of the signs and symptoms of patients who have severe head injuries, in Dr. Kline's medical judgment these signs were the result of her pre–existing psychiatric condition, not the result of her fall. He, therefore, determined that Ms. Baber's head injury was not serious and did not indicate the need at that time for a CT scan or x–rays. In his medical judgment, Ms. Baber's condition would be monitored adequately by the usual nursing checks performed every fifteen minutes by the psychiatric unit staff at BARH. Although Dr. Kline's assessment and judgment may have been erroneous and not within acceptable standards of medical care in West Virginia, he did perform a screening examination that was not so substandard as to amount to no examination. No testimony indicated that his procedure deviated from that which RGH would have provided to any other patient in Ms. Baber's condition.

* * *

The essence of Mr. Baber's argument is that the extent of the examination and treatment his sister received while at RGH was deficient. While Mr. Baber's testimony might be sufficient to survive a summary judgment motion in a medical malpractice case, it is clearly insufficient to survive a motion for summary judgment in an EMTALA case because at no point does Mr. Baber present any evidence that RGH deviated from its standard screening procedure in evaluating Ms. Baber's head injury. Therefore, the district court properly granted RGH summary judgment on the medical screening issue.

Mr. Baber also asserts that RGH inappropriately transferred his sister to BARH. EMTALA's transfer requirements do not apply unless the hospital actually determines that the patient suffers from an emergency medical condition. Accordingly, to recover for violations of EMTALA's transfer provisions, the plaintiff must present evidence that (1) the patient had an emergency medical condition; (2) the hospital actually knew of that condition; (3) the patient was not stabilized before being transferred; and (4) prior to transfer of an unstable patient, the transferring hospital did not obtain the proper consent or follow the appropriate certification and transfer procedures.

* * *

Mr. Baber argues that requiring a plaintiff to prove the hospital had actual knowledge of the patient's emergency medical condition would allow hospitals to circumvent the purpose of EMTALA by simply requiring their personnel to state in all hospital records that the patient did not suffer from an emergency medical condition. Because of this concern, Mr. Baber urges us to adopt a standard that would impose liability upon a hospital if it failed to provide stabilizing treatment prior to a transfer when the hospital knew or should have known that the patient suffered from an emergency medical condition.

The statute itself implicitly rejects this proposed standard. Section 1395dd(b)(1) states the stabilization requirement exists if "any individual . . . comes to a hospital and the hospital determines that the individual has an emergency medical condition." Thus, the plain language of the statute dictates a standard requiring actual knowledge of the emergency medical condition by the hospital staff.

Mr. Baber failed to present any evidence that RGH had actual knowledge that Ms. Baber suffered from an emergency medical condition. Dr. Kline stated in his affidavit that Ms. Baber's condition was stable prior to transfer and that he did not believe she was suffering from an emergency medical condition. While Mr. Baber testified that he believed his sister suffered from an emergency medical condition at transfer, he did not present any evidence beyond his own belief that she actually had an emergency medical condition or that anyone at RGH knew that she suffered from an emergency medical condition. In addition, we note that Mr. Baber's testimony is not competent to prove his sister actually had an emergency medical condition since he is not qualified to diagnose a serious internal brain injury.

* * * [W]e hold that the district court correctly granted RGH summary judgment on Mr. Baber's claim that it transferred Ms. Baber in violation of EMTALA.

* * *

Therefore, the district court's judgment is affirmed.

NOTES AND QUESTIONS

1. The Affordable Care Act left EMTALA intact, although it adopted other measures favorable to the provision of emergency care. Most significantly, the Act authorizes states to allow hospitals to make presumptive Medicaid eligibility determinations for individuals, which should reduce the volume of uncompensated care that is provided to individuals eligible for but not enrolled in Medicaid. 42 U.S.C. § 1396b. The ACA also requires insurers to pay for emergency care under a prudent layperson standard, a provision welcomed by hospitals that argued that insurers refused to pay for emergency services that the insurer deemed unnecessary even though the hospital was

obligated under EMTALA. 42 U.S.C. § 300gg–19a. The more significant anticipated impact of the ACA, of course, is that it will decrease patients' reliance on emergency room care as a safety net and will decrease preventable emergency conditions by providing greater access to primary care. Because of the anticipated reduction in uncompensated care, the ACA scales back the Medicare and Medicaid Disproportionate Share (DSH) payments that are made to hospitals carrying heavy loads of indigent care.

2. The Sixth Circuit, in an early EMTALA case, declared the word "appropriate" to be "one of the most wonderful weasel words in the dictionary, and a great aid to the resolution of disputed issues in the drafting of legislation." Cleland v. Bronson Health Care Group, 917 F.2d 266 (6th Cir. 1990). In contrast to the standard for medical screening, the standard applied to the question of whether the patient was unstable when discharged or transferred is an objective professional standard and not defined by the specific hospital's policy. How should plaintiff structure discovery to meet each of these two standards? What is the role for expert testimony, if any, in an "unstable transfer or discharge" claim? In an "inappropriate screening" claim?

3. The great majority of EMTALA claims are resolved through summary judgment. Nathan Richards, Judicial Resolution of EMTALA Screening Claims at Summary Judgment, 87 N.Y.U.L.Rev. 591 (2012). In the view of one judge:

> It was for the jury, not the district court or this court, to determine the relative credibility of the parties and what occurred in the emergency room that day. We should not assume that the doctor did not hear Summers or forgot about his complaints. Nor should we assume that it was the physician's medical judgment that prompted his failure to give Summers a chest x–ray. It is possible that the doctor heard Summers' complaints and, for no legitimate reason, failed to do anything about them. That alternative would establish the essentials of an EMTALA cause of action. Dissenting opinion (Judge Heaney), Summers v. Baptist Med. Ctr. Arkadelphia, 91 F.3d 1132 (8th Cir. 1995).

4. Improper motive is not required for a violation of the EMTALA requirement that the patient be *stabilized*. Roberts v. Galen of Va., Inc., 525 U.S. 249, 119 S.Ct. 685, 142 L.Ed.2d 648 (1999). The Court expressed no opinion as to whether proof of improper motive is essential for a claim of failure to provide an appropriate screening. The Circuits, except for the Sixth Circuit in *Cleland*, *supra* note 2, uniformly have held that EMTALA reaches beyond economically motivated decisions and that proof of motive is not required for either a screening or a stabilization claim. Could proof of improper motive be useful to the plaintiff in distinguishing negligent misdiagnosis from an EMTALA claim? How might such proof assist plaintiff in making his or her case? How would you go about proving motive once the physician and hospital claim medical judgment as the basis for discharge or transfer?

5. One of the sticky issues in EMTALA is whether a patient has "come to" the hospital's emergency room. In a rather notorious case, a hospital emergency department refused to aid a teenager who had been shot and lay dying 35 feet from the ER doors. Kristine M. Meece, The Future of Emergency Department Liability after the Ravenswood Hospital Incident: Redefining the Duty to Treat?, 3 DePaul J. Health Care L. 101 (1999). After years of court opinions with conflicting results, HHS promulgated regulations in 2003 included in the Problem, below.

6. For many years, courts reached conflicting results as well on the issue of whether a patient who had been admitted to the hospital would be covered by EMTALA or whether the EMTALA obligations of the hospital ceased upon admission. Finally, in 2003, HHS promulgated regulations resolving the issue to the satisfaction of hospitals. The conflict may not be over, however. See Moses v. Providence Hosp. & Med. Ctrs., 561 F.3d 573 (6th Cir. 2009), holding that the regulations are contrary to the plain language of the statute. In 2010, CMS asked for comments on its 2003 regulations and ultimately decided not to change them. 77 Fed. Reg. 5213 (Feb. 2, 2012). See the Problem, below.

7. Emergency treatment in the ED often will require the services of an on–call specialist as well. The hospital generally doesn't employ on–call specialists, but may contract with individual physicians to provide on–call services or may require on–call coverage by physicians as a condition of receiving admitting privileges. The division of labor inherent in the ED/on–call relationship can be contentious and raise EMTALA risks. Consider Cherukuri v. Shalala, 175 F.3d 446 (6th Cir. 1999):

> Dr. Cherukuri determined by 4:00 A.M. that it would be best to operate on both [accident victims] to stop the internal bleeding. * * * But he was unable to do so for the next three hours because Dr. Thambi, the anesthesiologist on call, advised strongly against operating and did not come to the hospital. [H]e advised Dr. Cherukuri that the patients should be immediately transferred. * * * He advised repeatedly and adamantly that administering anesthesia for the abdominal surgery was too risky because they had no equipment to monitor its effect on the pressure in the brain.
>
> Dr. Cherukuri testified that over the next two hours [he and a nurse] requested Dr. Thambi by phone several times to come to the hospital but he maintained that anesthesia was out of the question and did not come. They tried to locate other anesthesiologists during this period but were unsuccessful.
>
> While recognizing that Dr. Thambi had made his position very clear that he did not intend to provide anesthesiology because it might kill the brain injured patients, the ALJ concluded that EMTALA required the surgeon to force Dr. Thambi to perform by expressly ordering him to administer anesthesia. The ALJ states * * * that the

law "necessarily required" Dr. Cherukuri to stop the bleeding for the patients to be considered "stabilized" under the statute and that this required Dr. Cherukuri to force Dr. Thambi against his will to administer anesthesia. Nothing in EMTALA demands such a confrontation, and for good reasons.

The management of on–call services remains an intractable problem for hospitals. See Sarah Coyne et al., Using Deferred Compensation to Incent On–Call Coverage, 23 Health Law. 28/No4 (2011) and the following Problem.

PROBLEMS: EMTALA AND HHS REGULATIONS

Ms. Miller

On May 21, Ms. Nancy Miller, who was eight months pregnant, called her obstetrician, Dr. Jennifer Gibson, at 2:00 a.m. because she was experiencing severe pain which appeared to her to be labor contractions. Dr. Gibson advised Ms. Miller to go to the emergency department of the local hospital and promised to meet her there shortly. Ms. Miller was admitted to the emergency department of General Hospital at 2:30 a.m., and Dr. Gibson joined her there at 3:14 a.m. After examining Ms. Miller, Dr. Gibson concluded that Ms. Miller had begun labor and that, despite the fact that the pregnancy had not reached full–term, the labor should be continued to delivery. At that time, Dr. Gibson asked that the on–call anesthesiologist, Dr. Martig, see Ms. Miller to discuss anesthesia during the delivery. At the same time, the procedure to admit Ms. Miller to the hospital's maternity floor was begun. The nurse informed Ms. Miller that there would be a short wait because there was no space available at that point.

Dr. Martig saw Ms. Miller at 4:00 a.m. When asked, Dr. Martig informed Ms. Miller that he was not qualified to and would not be able to perform an epidural (a spinal nerve–block anesthesia, often used in childbirth). Instead, he gave her Demerol and left the emergency department.

At 4:30 a.m., Ms. Miller was admitted to the labor and delivery floor. At 4:45 a.m., the obstetrical nurse observed fetal distress and called Dr. Gibson. At 4:50 a.m., Dr. Gibson concluded that Ms. Miller had a prolapsed umbilical cord and ordered an emergency caesarean section. The OB nurse paged Dr. Martig, but he could not be located. (Dr. Martig later stated that his pager had malfunctioned.) Because Dr. Martig could not be located, Dr. Gibson and a resident performed the C–section without an anesthetic and delivered the child healthy and alive. (These facts are based on Miller v. Martig, 754 N.E.2d 41 (Ind. Ct. App. 2001).)

Assume that Ms. Miller has brought suit against the hospital and Dr. Martig. What federal and state claims might Ms. Miller make? Assume that Dr. Martig and the hospital have filed a motion for summary judgment on all claims. What result? What result if the hospital had transferred Ms. Miller? Include the applicable regulations, below, in your discussion.

Mr. Liles

Jesse Liles has no health insurance but went to a local hospital (NMC) complaining of fever and shortness of breath. He was admitted to the hospital with a diagnosis of severe dehydration, bilateral pneumonia, and adult respiratory distress syndrome. According to Mr. Liles, the hospital attempted to transfer him on eighteen separate occasions during the course of his stay between December 28, 2009, and January 24, 2010. Mr. Liles charges that two physicians at NMC falsely certified that he was stable for transfer from the hospital. At 3:35 a.m., on January 1, 2010, EMS from the local privately owned ambulance service came at the hospital's request to transfer Mr. Liles to another hospital. Liles went into cardiac arrest in the ambulance where he was resuscitated by EMS personnel and brought back inside NMC. He was placed on a ventilator in the ICU and stayed at the hospital until he was discharged to home on January 24.

On January 26, 2010, Liles called the same ambulance company because of his acute respiratory distress. The EMS personnel called NMC en route, , but NMC told them to take Mr. Liles to some other hospital because there was no pulmonologist available at NMC. The ambulance was already at the entry to the hospital grounds, and continued to be in contact with NMC to get further instructions. Staff at NMC made a number of calls to potential "receiving hospitals" to identify a facility willing to accept Mr. Liles. Ultimately, he was taken to another hospital where he was admitted to the ICU and underwent surgery for a collapsed lung. (These facts are based on Liles v. TH Healthcare, Ltd., 2012 WL 3930616 (E.D.Tex.).)

Assume that Mr. Liles has sued the hospital for EMTALA violations. You are the hospital's attorney. What arguments do you expect Mr. Liles to make? What are your best defenses to Liles' claims? Include the applicable regulations, below, in your discussion.

42 C.F.R. § 489.24(b)

[A patient has come to the emergency department who:]

(2) Has presented on hospital property * * * and requests examination or treatment for what may be an emergency medical condition, or has such a request made on his or her behalf. In the absence of such a request by or on behalf of the individual, a request on behalf of the individual will be considered to exist if a prudent layperson observer would believe, based on the individual's appearance or behavior, that the individual needs emergency examination or treatment;

(3) Is in a ground or air ambulance owned and operated by the hospital for purposes of examination and treatment for a medical condition at a hospital's dedicated emergency department, even if the ambulance is not on hospital grounds. However, an individual in an ambulance owned and operated by the hospital is not considered to have "come to the hospital's emergency department" if—

(i) The ambulance is operated under communitywide emergency medical service (EMS) that directs it to transport the individual to a hospital other than the hospital that owns the ambulance; for example, to the closest appropriate facility. In this case, the individual is considered to have come to the emergency department of the hospital to which the individual is transported, at the time the individual is brought onto hospital property;

(ii) The ambulance is operated at the direction of a physician who is not employed or otherwise affiliated with the hospital that owns the ambulance; or

(4) Is in a ground or air nonhospital–owned ambulance on hospital property for presentation for examination and treatment for a medical condition at a hospital's dedicated emergency department. However, an individual in a nonhospital–owned ambulance off hospital property is not considered to have come to the hospital's emergency department, even if a member of the ambulance staff contacts the hospital by telephone or telemetry communications and informs the hospital that they want to transport the individual to the hospital for examination and treatment. The hospital may direct the ambulance to another facility if it is in "diversionary status," that is, it does not have the staff or facilities to accept any additional emergency patients. If, however, the ambulance staff disregards the hospital's diversion instructions and transports the individual onto hospital property, the individual is considered to have come to the emergency department.

42 C.F.R. § 489.24(d)(2)

* * * Application [of screening, stabilization, and transfer obligations] to inpatients

(i) If a hospital has screened an individual * * * and found the individual to have an emergency medical condition, and admits that individual as an inpatient in good faith in order to stabilize the emergency medical condition, the hospital has satisfied its special responsibilities under this section with respect to that individual.

(ii) This section is not applicable to an inpatient who was admitted for elective (nonemergency) diagnosis or treatment.

[Note: The language of section (i) was altered from that in HHS's proposed regulations. The original proposed language provided: "If a hospital admits an individual with an unstable emergency medical condition for stabilizing treatment, as an inpatient, and stabilizes that individual's emergency medical condition, the period of stability would be required to be documented by relevant clinical data in the individual's medical record, before the hospital has satisfied its special responsibilities under this section with respect to that individual. * * * " 67 Fed.Reg. 314045, 31496 (Dec. 32, 2002).]

42 C.F.R. § 489.24(j)

[A] hospital must have written policies and procedures in place—

(1) To respond to situations in which a particular specialty is not available or the on–call physician cannot respond because of circumstances beyond the physician's control; and

(2) To provide that emergency services are available to meet the needs of individuals with emergency medical conditions if a hospital elects to—

> (i) Permit on–call physicians to schedule elective surgery during the time that they are on call;
>
> (ii) Permit on–call physicians to have simultaneous on–call duties; and
>
> (iii) Participate in a formal community call plan. Notwithstanding participation in a community call plan, hospitals are still required to perform medical screening examinations on individuals who present seeking treatment and to conduct appropriate transfers. * * *

42 C.F.R. § 489.20(r)(2)

[The hospital must maintain an] on–call list of physicians who are on the hospital's medical staff or who have privileges at the hospital, or who are on the staff or have privileges at another hospital participating in a formal community call plan * * * available to provide treatment necessary after the initial examination to stabilize individuals with emergency medical conditions who are receiving [emergency care] in accordance with the resources available to the hospital * * *.

B. OBLIGATIONS UNDER FEDERAL ANTI–DISCRIMINATION STATUTES

1. The Americans with Disabilities Act and Section 504 of the Rehabilitation Act

The Americans with Disabilities Act (ADA) prohibits discrimination against persons who have or are considered to have a disability as defined in the statute. Title I of the Act (42 U.S.C. § 12111), applies to employment; Title II (42 U.S.C. § 12131), applies to state and local government services; Title III (42 U.S.C. § 12181), applies to public accommodations; Title IV (42 U.S.C. § 12201) includes miscellaneous provisions, including important provisions regarding insurance.

Section 504 of the Rehabilitation Act of 1973 (29 U.S.C. § 749) also prohibits discrimination against the disabled. The ADA and § 504 are quite similar in most respects, and courts have used cases under the Rehabilitation Act to assist in interpreting the later ADA. There are some significant differences, however. See *Howe*, below, for differences in the elements of a claim under each statute. In addition, Section § 504, in contrast to the ADA, applies only to programs and services receiving federal funding. The Affordable Care Act, however, broadens the reach of § 504 significantly. See discussion in relation to Title VI in Section III.B.2, below

BRAGDON V. ABBOTT

Supreme Court of the United States, 1998.
524 U.S. 624, 118 S.Ct. 2196, 141 L.Ed.2d 540.

KENNEDY, J., delivered the opinion of the Court, in which STEVENS, SOUTER, GINSBERG, and BREYER, JJ., joined. STEVENS, J., filed a concurring opinion. REHNQUIST, C.J., filed an opinion concurring in the judgment in part and dissenting in part, in which SCALIA and THOMAS, JJ., joined, and in Part II of which O'CONNOR, J., joined. O'CONNOR, J., filed an opinion concurring in the judgment in part and dissenting in part.

* * * We granted certiorari to review * * * whether the Court of Appeals, in affirming a grant of summary judgment, cited sufficient material in the record to determine, as a matter of law, that respondent's infection with HIV posed no direct threat to the health and safety of her treating dentist.

I

Respondent Sidney Abbott has been infected with HIV since 1986. When the incidents we recite occurred, her infection had not manifested its most serious symptoms. On September 16, 1994, she went to the office of petitioner Randon Bragdon in Bangor, Maine, for a dental appointment. She disclosed her HIV infection on the patient registration form. Petitioner completed a dental examination, discovered a cavity, and informed respondent of his policy against filling cavities of HIV–infected patients. He offered to perform the work at a hospital with no added fee for his services, though respondent would be responsible for the cost of using the hospital's facilities. Respondent declined.

* * *

* * * Notwithstanding the protection given respondent by the ADA's definition of disability, petitioner could have refused to treat her if her infectious condition "posed a direct threat to the health or safety of others."[ ] The ADA defines a direct threat to be "a significant risk to the health or safety of others that cannot be eliminated by a modification of

policies, practices, procedures, or by the provision of auxiliary aids or services."[ ] * * *

The ADA's direct threat provision stems from the recognition in School Bd. of Nassau Cty. v. Arline[ ] of the importance of prohibiting discrimination against individuals with disabilities while protecting others from significant health and safety risks, resulting, for instance, from a contagious disease. In *Arline,* the Court reconciled these objectives by construing the Rehabilitation Act not to require the hiring of a person who posed "a significant risk of communicating an infectious disease to others."[ ] * * * [The ADA's] direct threat provision codifies *Arline*. Because few, if any, activities in life are risk free, *Arline* and the ADA do not ask whether a risk exists, but whether it is significant.[ ]

The existence, or nonexistence, of a significant risk must be determined from the standpoint of the person who refuses the treatment or accommodation, and the risk assessment must be based on medical or other objective evidence.[ ] As a health care professional, petitioner had the duty to assess the risk of infection based on the objective, scientific information available to him and others in his profession. His belief that a significant risk existed, even if maintained in good faith, would not relieve him from liability. To use the words of the question presented, petitioner receives no special deference simply because he is a health care professional. It is true that *Arline* reserved "the question whether courts should also defer to the reasonable medical judgments of private physicians on which an employer has relied."[ ] At most, this statement reserved the possibility that employers could consult with individual physicians as objective third–party experts. It did not suggest that an individual physician's state of mind could excuse discrimination without regard to the objective reasonableness of his actions.

* * * In assessing the reasonableness of petitioner's actions, the views of public health authorities, such as the U.S. Public Health Service, CDC, and the National Institutes of Health, are of special weight and authority.[ ] The views of these organizations are not conclusive, however. A health care professional who disagrees with the prevailing medical consensus may refute it by citing a credible scientific basis for deviating from the accepted norm.[ ]

[An] illustration of a correct application of the objective standard is the Court of Appeals' refusal to give weight to the petitioner's offer to treat respondent in a hospital.[ ] Petitioner testified that he believed hospitals had safety measures, such as air filtration, ultraviolet lights, and respirators, which would reduce the risk of HIV transmission.[ ] Petitioner made no showing, however, that any area hospital had these safeguards or even that he had hospital privileges.[ ] His expert also admitted the lack of any scientific basis for the conclusion that these measures would lower the risk of transmission.[ ] Petitioner failed to present any objective, medical evidence showing that treating respondent in a hospital would be safer or more efficient in preventing HIV transmission than treatment in a well–equipped dental office.

We are concerned, however, that the Court of Appeals might have placed mistaken reliance upon two other sources. In ruling no triable issue of fact existed on this point, the Court of Appeals relied on the CDC Dentistry Guidelines and the 1991 American Dental Association Policy on HIV.[ ] This evidence is not definitive. * * * [T]he CDC Guidelines recommended certain universal precautions which, in CDC's view, "should reduce the risk of disease transmission in the dental environment."[ ] The Court of Appeals determined that, "[w]hile the guidelines do not state explicitly that no further risk–reduction measures are desirable or that routine dental care for HIV–positive individuals is safe, those two conclusions seem to be implicit in the guidelines' detailed delineation of procedures for office treatment of HIV–positive patients."[ ] In our view, the Guidelines do not necessarily contain implicit assumptions conclusive of the point to be decided. The Guidelines set out CDC's recommendation that the universal precautions are the best way to combat the risk of HIV transmission. They do not assess the level of risk.

Nor can we be certain, on this record, whether the 1991 American Dental Association Policy on HIV carries the weight the Court of Appeals attributed to it. The Policy does provide some evidence of the medical community's objective assessment of the risks posed by treating people infected with HIV in dental offices. It indicates:

> "Current scientific and epidemiologic evidence indicates that there is little risk of transmission of infectious diseases through dental treatment if recommended infection control procedures are routinely followed. Patients with HIV infection may be safely treated in private dental offices when appropriate infection control procedures are employed. Such infection control procedures provide protection both for patients and dental personnel."[ ]

We note, however, that the Association is a professional organization, which, although a respected source of information on the dental profession, is not a public health authority. It is not clear the extent to which the Policy was based on the Association's assessment of dentists' ethical and professional duties in addition to its scientific assessment of the risk to which the ADA refers. Efforts to clarify dentists' ethical obligations and to encourage dentists to treat patients with HIV infection with compassion may be commendable, but the question under the statute is one of statistical likelihood, not professional responsibility. Without more information on the manner in which the American Dental Association formulated this Policy, we are unable to determine the Policy's value in evaluating whether petitioner's assessment of the risks was reasonable as a matter of law.

* * *

We acknowledge the presence of other evidence in the record before the Court of Appeals which, subject to further arguments and examination, might support affirmance of the trial court's ruling. For instance, the record contains substantial testimony from numerous health experts indicating that it is safe to treat patients infected with HIV in dental offices.[ ] We are unable to determine the import of this evidence, however. The record does not disclose whether the expert testimony submitted by respondent turned on evidence available in September 1994.[ ]

There are reasons to doubt whether petitioner advanced evidence sufficient to raise a triable issue of fact on the significance of the risk. Petitioner relied on two principal points: First, he asserted that the use of high–speed drills and surface cooling with water created a risk of airborne HIV transmission. The study on which petitioner relied was inconclusive, however, determining only that "further work is required to determine whether such a risk exists."[ ] Petitioner's expert witness conceded, moreover, that no evidence suggested the spray could transmit HIV. His opinion on airborne risk was based on the absence of contrary evidence, not on positive data. Scientific evidence and expert testimony must have a traceable, analytical basis in objective fact before it may be considered on summary judgment.[ ]

[P]etitioner argues that, as of September 1994, CDC had identified seven dental workers with possible occupational transmission of HIV.[ ] These dental workers were exposed to HIV in the course of their employment, but CDC could not determine whether HIV infection had resulted. [ ] It is now known that CDC could not ascertain whether the seven dental workers contracted the disease because they did not present themselves for HIV testing at an appropriate time after their initial exposure.[ ] It is not clear on this record, however, whether this information was available to petitioner in September 1994. If not, the seven cases might have provided some, albeit not necessarily sufficient, support for petitioner's position. Standing alone, we doubt it would meet the objective, scientific basis for finding a significant risk to the petitioner.

* * *

We conclude the proper course is to give the Court of Appeals the opportunity to determine whether our analysis of some of the studies cited by the parties would change its conclusion that petitioner presented neither objective evidence nor a triable issue of fact on the question of risk.

JUSTICE STEVENS, with whom JUSTICE BREYER joins, concurring.

. . . I do not believe petitioner has sustained his burden of adducing evidence sufficient to raise a triable issue of fact on the significance of the risk posed by treating respondent in his office. * * * I join the opinion even though I would prefer an outright affirmance.[ ]

CHIEF JUSTICE REHNQUIST, with whom JUSTICE SCALIA and JUSTICE THOMAS join, and with whom JUSTICE O'CONNOR joins as to Part II, concurring in the judgment in part and dissenting in part.

* * *

II

I agree with the Court that "the existence, or nonexistence, of a significant risk must be determined from the standpoint of the person who refuses the treatment or accommodation," as of the time that the decision refusing treatment is made.[ ] I disagree with the Court, however, that "in assessing the reasonableness of petitioner's actions, the views of public health authorities . . . are of special weight and authority."[ ] Those views are, of course, entitled to a presumption of validity when the actions of those authorities themselves are challenged in court, and even in disputes between private parties where Congress has committed that dispute to adjudication by a public health authority. But in litigation between private parties originating in the federal courts, I am aware of no provision of law or judicial practice that would require or permit courts to give some scientific views more credence than others simply because they have been endorsed by a politically appointed public health authority (such as the Surgeon General). In litigation of this latter sort, which is what we face here, the credentials of the scientists employed by the public health authority, and the soundness of their studies, must stand on their own. The Court cites no authority for its limitation upon the courts' truth–finding function, except the statement in School Bd. of Nassau Cty. v. Arline,[ ] that in making findings regarding the risk of contagion under the Rehabilitation Act, "courts normally should defer to the reasonable medical judgments of public health officials." But there is appended to that dictum the following footnote, which makes it very clear that the Court was urging respect for *medical* judgment, and not necessarily respect for "official" medical judgment over "private" medical judgment: "This case does not present, and we do not address, the question whether courts should also defer to the reasonable medical judgments of private physicians on which an employer has relied."[ ]

Applying these principles here, it is clear to me that petitioner has presented more than enough evidence to avoid summary judgment on the "direct threat" question * * *. Given the "severity of the risk" involved here, i.e., near certain death, and the fact that no public health authority had outlined a protocol for *eliminating* this risk in the context of routine dental treatment, it seems likely that petitioner can establish that it was objectively reasonable for him to conclude that treating respondent in his office posed a "direct threat" to his safety.

* * *

NOTES AND QUESTIONS

1. *Bragdon* established that the analysis of "direct threat" as a defense to a claim under the ADA must rely on scientific evidence rather than stereotyping or misconceptions. On remand, the Ninth Circuit upheld the District Court's grant of summary judgment in favor of the plaintiff:

> The [American Dental] Association formulates scientific and ethical policies by separate procedures, drawing on different member groups and different staff complements. The Association's Council on Scientific Affairs, comprised of 17 dentists (most of whom hold advanced dentistry degrees), together with a staff of over 20 professional experts and consultants, drafted the Policy at issue here. By contrast, ethical policies are drafted by the Council on Ethics, a wholly separate body. Although the Association's House of Delegates must approve policies drafted by either council, we think that the origins of the Policy satisfy any doubts regarding its scientific foundation.
>
> For these reasons, we are confident that we appropriately relied on the Guidelines and the Policy. * * * Thus, we again conclude, after due reevaluation, that Ms. Abbott served a properly documented motion for summary judgment.
>
> We next reconsider whether Dr. Bragdon offered sufficient proof of direct threat to create a genuine issue of material fact and thus avoid the entry of summary judgment * * *. The Supreme Court suggested that one such piece of evidence—the seven cases that the CDC considered "possible" HIV patient–to–dental worker transmissions—should be reexamined. Since an objective standard pertains here, the existence of the list of seven "possible" cases does not create a genuine issue of material fact as to direct threat. * * *Each piece of evidence to which [defendant directs] us is still "too speculative or too tangential (or, in some instances, both) to create a genuine issue of material fact."

Abbott v. Bragdon, 163 F.3d 87 (1st Cir. 1998), cert. denied, 526 U.S. 1131, 119 S.Ct. 1805, 143 L.Ed.2d 1009 (1999).

2. The CDC reports that there have been no confirmed cases of occupational transmission of HIV to health care workers since 1991. CDC, Occupational HIV Transmission and Prevention Among Health Care Workers (2011). The CDC recommends "universal precautions" (using barriers such as gloves; handwashing; and design and use of sharps to reduce accidental needle sticks) against transmission of infectious diseases (including hepatitis, which is much more prevalent than HIV) be taken. For HIV in particular, the CDC recommends a specific protocol of post–exposure treatment following

any exposure to prevent seroconversion in the exposed health care worker. The risk of transmission of disease from needle stick is 0.3% for needles contaminated with HIV; up to 7%, for hepatitis C; and up to 40%, for hepatitis B.

3. Empirical studies demonstrate that a significant number of health care professionals refuse to provide care for persons with HIV/AIDS. See Brad Sears et al., HIV Discrimination in Dental Care: Results of a Testing Study in Los Angeles County, 45 Loy. L.A.L.Rev. 909 (2012), including results of studies from 2003–2008 demonstrating that 46% of skilled nursing facilities, 55% of OB/GYNs, and 26% of plastic surgeons in Los Angeles County refused to treat persons with HIV. See also, Ronda Goldfein, From the Streets of Philadelphia: The AIDS Law Project of Pennsylvania's How–To Primer on Mitigating Health Disparities, 82 Temp. L. Rev. 1205 (2010). The Department of Justice has brought actions against several providers for explicit refusal to treat patients with HIV. 21 Health Law Rept'r (2012).

4. In 2006, the CDC significantly altered its policy on routine screening for HIV. Under the new policy, routine HIV screening is to be "a normal part of medical practice" for all adults unless the prevalence of HIV infection is documented to be less than 0.1% in a particular provider's patient population. In addition, informed consent, beyond a general consent to medical treatment, is not required. Instead, the health care professional need only notify the patient that an HIV test will be performed unless the patient declines. Finally, the CDC asserts that counseling need not be provided for HIV testing. CDC, Revised Recommendations for HIV Testing of Adults, Adolescents, and Pregnant Women in Health–Care Settings, Sept. 22, 2006. The aim of the CDC policy is to prevent AIDS transmission among the general public and to lead persons with HIV to get treatment by addressing the fact that 20–25% of persons with HIV don't know they have the virus. The new policy raises issues concerning access to treatment for those testing positive; confidentiality of results; and whether routinization of testing will lead to a practice of testing without notice. Studies documenting continuing discrimination against persons with HIV raise substantial concern over routine testing. The new screening recommendations may be barred by state law, but the CDC encourages states to revise their statutes. See generally Sarah Schalman–Bergen, CDC's Call for Routine HIV Testing Raises Implementation Concerns, 35 J. L. Med. & Ethics 223 (2007). The U.S. Preventive Services Task Force issued proposed guidelines that mirror the CDC guidelines making it likely that HIV testing will become part of the preventive care package that must be offered by insurers under the ACA at no cost to patients.

5. Only persons with disabilities are covered by the ADA and § 504. In *Bragdon*, a deeply divided Court concluded that asymptomatic HIV could be considered a disability under narrow circumstances. In a series of cases after *Bradgon*, however, the Court established a very narrow interpretation of the ADA statutory definition of disability. Congress enacted the Americans with Disabilities Act Amendment Act of 2008 (ADAAA) specifically to reject the Supreme Court's narrow interpretation of the ADA, stating that Congress expected that the courts would interpret the term as they had for § 504. The

ADAAA directs that regulations adopt a more expansive interpretation of the ADA definition of disability. A person is disabled if he or she has "a physical or mental impairment that substantially limits one or more major life activities of such individual; a record of such impairment; or [is] regarded as having such an impairment."

HOWE V. HULL

U.S. District Court, Northern District, Ohio, 1994.
874 F.Supp.779.

JOHN W. POTTER, SENIOR DISTRICT JUDGE.

* * *

Plaintiff brought suit in the current action alleging that on April 17, 1992, defendants refused to provide Charon medical treatment because he was infected with HIV. Plaintiff claims that defendants' actions violate the Americans with Disabilities Act (ADA) [and] the Federal Rehabilitation Act of 1973 (FRA). * * * The defendants vehemently dispute these claims and allegations and have moved for summary judgment on all of plaintiff's claims.

* * *

On April 17, 1992, Charon and plaintiff Howe were travelling through Ohio, on their way to vacation in Wisconsin. Charon was HIV positive. That morning Charon took a floxin tablet for the first time. Floxin is a prescription antibiotic drug. Within two hours of taking the drug, Charon began experiencing fever, headache, nausea, joint pain, and redness of the skin.

Due to Charon's condition, Charon and plaintiff checked into a motel and, after consulting with Charon's treating physician in Maine, sought medical care at the emergency room of Fremont Memorial Hospital. Charon was examined by the emergency room physician on duty, Dr. Mark Reardon. There is some dispute over what Dr. Reardon's initial diagnosis of Charon's condition was.

Dr. Reardon testified that Charon suffered from a severe drug reaction, and that it was his diagnosis that this reaction was probably Toxic Epidermal Necrolysis (TEN).[2] This diagnosis was also recorded in Charon's medical records. Dr. Reardon also testified regarding Charon's condition that "possibly it was an early stage of toxic epidermal necrolysis, although I had never seen one." Dr. Reardon had no prior experience with TEN, other than what he had read in medical school.

---

[2] TEN is a very serious, very rare, and often lethal skin condition that causes an individual's skin to slough off the body.

Plaintiff's medical expert Calabrese, however, testified that, after reviewing the medical records and Reardon's deposition, while Charon did appear to be suffering from a severe allergic drug reaction, Calabrese "did not believe that [TEN] was the likely or even probable diagnosis. * * * "

Prior to Charon's eventual transfer to the Medical College of Ohio, Dr. Reardon called Dr. Lynn at MCO and asked Lynn if he would accept the transfer of Charon. Dr. Lynn testified that at no time did Dr. Reardon mention that plaintiff had been diagnosed with the extremely rare and deadly TEN. Dr. Reardon also did not inform the ambulance emergency medical technicians that plaintiff was suffering from TEN.

Dr. Reardon determined that Charon "definitely needed to be admitted" to Memorial Hospital. Since Charon was from out of town, procedure required that Charon be admitted to the on–call physician, Dr. Hull. Dr. Reardon spoke with Dr. Hull on the telephone and informed Dr. Hull that he wanted to admit Charon, who was HIV–positive and suffering from a non–AIDS related severe drug reaction.

While Dr. Reardon and Dr. Hull discussed Charon's situation, the primary area of their discussion appears to have been whether Charon's condition had advanced from HIV to full–blown AIDS. Dr. Hull inquired neither into Charon's physical condition nor vital signs, nor did he ask Dr. Reardon about the possibility of TEN. During this conversation, it is undisputed that Dr. Hull told Dr. Reardon that "if you get an AIDS patient in the hospital, you will never get him out," and directed that plaintiff be sent to the "AIDS program" at MCO. When Dr. Hull arrived at the hospital after Dr. Reardon's shift but prior to Charon's transfer, he did not attempt to examine or meet with Charon.

* * *

Charon was transferred to the Medical College of Ohio some time after 8:45 P.M. on April 17. After his conversation with Dr. Hull and prior to the transfer, Dr. Reardon told Charon and plaintiff that "I'm sure you've dealt with this before. . . . " Howe asked, "What's that, discrimination?" Dr. Reardon replied, "You have to understand, this is a small community, and the admitting doctor does not feel comfortable admitting [Charon]."

* * *

Charon was admitted and treated at the Medical College of Ohio (MCO). Despite the TEN diagnosis, Charon was not diagnosed by MCO personnel as having TEN and, in fact, was never examined by a dermatologist. After several days, Charon recovered from the allergic drug reaction and was released from MCO.

* * *

Before examining the merits of defendants' contentions, the Court must look at and compare the applicable parameters of the ADA and FRA. There are three basic criteria plaintiff must meet in order to establish a prima facie case of discrimination under the ADA:

a) the plaintiff has a disability;

b) the defendants discriminated against the plaintiff; and

c) the discrimination was based on the disability.

42 U.S.C. § 12182(a); 42 U.S.C. § 12182(b). The discrimination can take the form of the denial of the opportunity to receive medical treatment, segregation unnecessary for the provision of effective medical treatment, unnecessary screening or eligibility requirements for treatment, or provision of unequal medical benefits based upon the disability. [ ] A defendant can avoid liability by establishing that it was unable to provide the medical care that a patient required. [ ]

Similarly, to establish a prima facie case under the FRA the plaintiff must show

a) the plaintiff has a disability;

b) plaintiff was otherwise qualified to participate in the program;

c) defendants discriminated against plaintiff solely on the basis of the disability; and

d) the program received federal funding.

29 U.S.C. § 794(a).

[A] reasonable jury could conclude that the TEN diagnosis was a pretext and that Charon was denied treatment solely because of his disability. Further, there is no evidence to support the conclusion that Memorial Hospital was unable to treat a severe allergic drug reaction. In fact, the evidence indicates that Dr. Reardon initially planned to admit Charon for treatment. Therefore, Charon was "otherwise qualified" for treatment within the meaning of the FRA. * * *

The FRA states that "no otherwise qualified individual with a disability . . . shall, solely by reason of his or her disability . . . be subjected to discrimination. . . ." 29 U.S.C. § 794(a). The equivalent portion of the ADA reads "No individual shall be discriminated against on the basis of disability. . . ." 42 U.S.C. § 12182(a). It is abundantly clear that the exclusion of the "solely by reason of . . . disability" language was a purposeful act by Congress and not a drafting error or oversight * * *.

The inquiry under the ADA, then, is whether the defendant, despite the articulated reasons for the transfer, improperly considered Charon's HIV status. More explicitly, was Charon transferred for the treatment of a non–AIDS related drug reaction because defendant unjustifiably did not wish to care for an HIV–positive patient? Viewing the evidence in the light most favorable to the plaintiff, the Court finds plaintiff has presented sufficient evidence to preclude a grant of summary judgment on these claims. Defendant Memorial Hospital's motion for summary judgment on the plaintiff's ADA and FRA claims will be denied.

NOTES AND QUESTIONS

1. Although persons with HIV/AIDS require very specialized treatment, most also need the same medical services as other generally healthy individuals and as other chronically or intermittently disabled persons. The AMA Code of Ethics provides that "a physician may not ethically refuse to treat a patient whose condition is within the physician's current realm of competence solely because the patient is seropositive for HIV." Code of Ethics, Opinion 9.131. What is the significance of the AMA's use of the word "solely?" Many state legislatures have amended their medical practice acts to provide that discrimination against persons with HIV is grounds for disciplinary action, and usually this is the only antidiscrimination provision in the medical practice act. See e.g., Wis. Stat. § 252.14.

2. Much of the current ADA and § 504 litigation concerning access to care involves the provision of sign language interpreters for deaf patients. See, e.g., Loeffler v. Staten Island University Hospital, 582 F.3d 268 (2d Cir. 2009), holding that an action for damages under § 504 could proceed where facts alleged by plaintiff husband (the patient) and wife, both deaf, could support a conclusion that hospital acted with deliberate indifference in refusing repeated requests for a sign language interpreter for the patient, forcing his minor children to interpret for him. The Department of Justice also has brought a number of suits against providers for failing to provide sign language interpreters leading to settlements with payment of damages and injunctive relief. Settlement agreements are available on the DOJ website. The Office of Civil Rights is also pursuing equitable remedies against health care facilities for violation of the ADA and § 504 for failure to provide services for deaf persons.

3. Access to medical care for persons with disabilities has been greatly compromised by providers' failure to choose medical equipment (such as examination tables, dental and eye examination chairs, weight scales, mammography equipment, and so on) that is accessible for persons with mobility limitations. For a thorough discussion, see Elizabeth Pendo, Reducing Disparities Through Health Reform: Disability and Accessible Medical Equipment, 2010 Utah L. Rev. 1057, including review of litigation approaches and provisions of the Affordable Care Act requiring promulgation of standards for accessible medical equipment. Class action litigation has targeted health care facilities for violation of the ADA regarding physical access. See, e.g., Federal Court Certifies Class in ADA Suit Alleging Hospital Barriers to Disabled Access, 21 Health L. Rept'r 239 (2012)

4. The Affordable Care Act establishes the Patient–Centered Outcomes Research Institute (PCORI) to focus on comparative clinical effectiveness and other outcomes research. See Chapter 1. Under the ACA, PCORI's research findings may be used in coverage determinations by the Secretary of HHS, but with some limitations, including one related directly to disability status. It provides that HHS may not use the Institute's findings

> in a manner that treats extending the life of an elderly, disabled, or terminally ill individual as of lower value than extending the life of an individual who is younger, nondisabled, or not terminally ill.

Comparative effectiveness findings can be used, however, in coverage determinations that compare "the difference in the effectiveness of alternative treatments in extending an individual's life due to the individual's age, disability, or terminal illness." The statute also prohibits the Institute from developing and the Secretary from using a "dollars–per–quality adjusted life year (or similar measure that discounts the value of a life because of an individual's disability)" in determining cost effectiveness. 42 U.S.C. § 1320e–1.

What policy, legal, political, or ethical issues are embedded in these limitations? How are these categories alike or different in relation to cost effectiveness? What definition of disability should the Secretary use? See, Symposium on Cost and End–of–Life Care, 39 J. L. Med. & Ethics 111 (2011), for an excellent set of articles on these issues.

5. *Howe* correctly notes that the ADA and § 504 differ significantly on what the plaintiff must prove as the reason for the defendant's action. For seventeen years, the Sixth Circuit applied the "solely" standard from § 504 to ADA cases. Finally, it held: "Our interpretation of the ADA not only is out of sync with the other circuits, but it also is wrong." Lewis v. Humboldt Acquisition Corp., 681 F.3d 312 (6th Cir. 2012). In the course of correcting itself, it provides a very good analysis of the difference in standards.

It may be difficult in a particular case to prove the reason for the refusal of treatment much less meeting the requirement that the disability be the "sole" reason for denial of adequate treatment. In Lesley v. Hee Man Chie, 250 F.3d 47 (1st Cir. 2001), the District Court adopted the following standard:

> The case requires us to determine how far courts should defer to a doctor's judgment as to the best course of treatment for a disabled patient in the context of discriminatory denial of treatment claims. We hold that the doctor's judgment is to be given deference absent a showing by the plaintiff that the judgment lacked any reasonable medical basis.

Is the court's deference appropriate? Consistent with the statute? How would you go about proving or defending against a claim that the medical judgment defense is a subterfuge? Haavi Morreim offers the following as indicators of discriminatory decisions to withhold treatment: where the medical judgment is based on "inaccurate facts" resulting from presumptions or prejudices against persons with the patient's medical condition; where the reasoning underlying the treatment decision is "irrational" as, for example, where a surgeon would decide not to perform surgery only because of the high risk of mortality even though the surgery would provide the patient's only hope of survival; or where the decision is based on "inappropriate values" such as a conclusion that certain persons are by race or gender inherently inferior. E. Haavi Morreim, Futilitarianism, Exoticare, and Coerced Altruism: The ADA Meets Its Limits, 25 Seton Hall L. Rev. 883 (1995). See also Mary A. Crossley, Of Diagnoses and Discrimination: Discriminatory Nontreatment of Infants with HIV Infection, 93 Colum. L. Rev. 1581 (1993).

Dr. Chie had been Ms. Lesley's OB/GYN for thirteen years when he discovered her HIV–positive status after testing as part of prenatal care. Lesley's pregnancy was high–risk before the diagnosis of HIV due to several factors. After making the diagnosis, Chie consulted with Lesley's psychiatrist and numerous community resources on the treatment of HIV and transmission reduction to the child and contacted the hospital and attempted to order a supply of AZT to administer during labor and delivery. Chie then recommended to Lesley that she obtain treatment at a nearby hospital that participated in NIH studies of treatment for HIV–positive women and infants and arranged for her enrollment in that protocol.

2. Title VI of the Civil Rights Act of 1964

Title VI of the Civil Rights Act of 1964 (42 U.S.C.A. § 2000d) prohibits discrimination on the basis of race, color, or national origin by any program receiving federal financial assistance. Even after enactment of Title VI, however, hospitals were allowed to meet the federal nondiscrimination standard even if physicians with admitting privileges refused to admit African Americans and if doctors who would admit more broadly were excluded from privileges. The federal government originally threatened enforcement against such hospitals, but then retreated. See David Barton Smith, Healthcare's Hidden Civil Rights Legacy, 48 St. Louis U. L.J. 37 (2003).

The advent of Medicare and Medicaid in 1965, provided federal payments to physicians, hospitals, nursing homes, and other health care organizations. This presented an opportunity for the enforcement of the nondiscrimination requirement of Title VI to reach into most parts of the then–segregated health care system. The precursor agency to HHS, however, declared that Title VI did not apply to physicians who received payment under Part B of Medicare, interpreting that program as a "contract of insurance" rather than payment of public funds. The Affordable Care Act displaces this narrow interpretation and extends the reach of Title VI (and other federal nondiscrimination statutes, including Section 504 of the Rehabilitation Act, discussed in the previous section):

42 U.S.C. § 18116

(a) * * * [A]n individual shall not, on the ground prohibited under title VI of the Civil Rights Act of 1964 (42 U.S.C. 2000d et seq.), title IX of the Education Amendments of 1972 (20 U.S.C. 1681 et seq.), the Age Discrimination Act of 1975 (42 U.S.C. 6101 et seq.), or section 504 of the Rehabilitation Act of 1973 (29 U.S.C. 794), * * * be excluded from participation in, be denied the benefits of, or be subjected to discrimination under, any health program or activity, any part of which is receiving Federal financial assistance, including credits, subsidies, or contracts of insurance, or under any program or activity that is administered by an Executive Agency or any entity established under this title (or amendments). The enforcement mechanisms provided for and available under title VI * * * shall apply for purposes of violations of this subsection.

(b)* * * Nothing in this title * * * shall be construed to invalidate or limit the rights, remedies, procedures, or legal standards available to individuals aggrieved under title VI of the Civil Rights Act of 1964 * * * or to supersede State laws that provide additional protections against discrimination on any basis described in subsection (a).

There are many questions of interpretation and implementation under this section but it is likely to increase scrutiny of practices that result in race and national origin discrimination in previously undisturbed corners of the health care system. For example, the section appears in Title I of the ACA which governs the health insurance exchanges and private health plans; and it would seem to definitively resolve the issue of whether Title VI applies to physician practices. See Sidney Watson, Section 1557 of the Affordable Care Act: Civil Rights, Health Reform, Race and Equity, 55 How. L.J. 855 (2012).

The ACA provision, above, incorporates the rights and remedies under Title VI as the enforcement mechanism. Current regulations under Title VI prohibit both intentional discrimination and discrimination through facially neutral activities that have a disparate impact. Individuals, however, may bring suit for violations under Title VI only in cases of intentional discrimination. Alexander v. Sandoval, 532 U.S. 275, 121 S.Ct. 1511, 149 L.Ed.2d 517 (2001). The ACA leaves the *Sandoval* limitation on private litigation intact. The Office of Civil Rights (OCR) enforces Title VI as well and can pursue both intentional and disparate impact cases. Recently, OCR has pursued actions against hospitals that fail to provide adequate language services for patients who do not speak English. Joel Teitelbaum et al., Translating Rights into Access: Language Access and the Affordable Care Act, 38 Am. J. L. & Med. 348 (2012).

Prior to *Sandoval*, the most successful of Title VI private litigation efforts relied on disparate impact to challenge Tennessee's Medicaid plan. Linton v. Commissioner of Health and Environment, 779 F.Supp. 925 (M.D. Tenn. 1990), aff'd, 65 F.3d 508 (6th Cir. 1995), cert. denied, 517 U.S. 1155, 116 S.Ct. 1542, 134 L.Ed.2d 646 (1996). The case illustrates the impact of payment programs and institutional organization upon access to health care.

Plaintiffs in *Linton* challenged state law that allowed nursing homes to limit the number of the facility's beds that would be certified for Medicaid and to decertify individual beds (i.e., accepting only private pay and excluding Medicaid beneficiaries) rather than foregoing Medicaid payments entirely. The trial court in *Linton* concluded:

> [T]he limited bed certification policy * * * leads to disruption of care and displacement of Medicaid patients after they have been admitted to a nursing home. Such displacement often occurs when a patient exhausts his or her financial resources and attempts transition from private pay to Medicaid. In this situation, a patient who already occupies a bed in a nursing home is told that his or her bed is no longer available to the patient because he or she is dependent upon Medicaid. * * *
>
> * * * The Court is persuaded by the depositions, affidavits and exhibits concerning the severe impact of the limited bed certification policy. Finally, the Court is mindful of the Medicaid eligibility rules which allow eligibility for relatively more affluent patients already residing in nursing homes than those seeking initial admission. This phenomenon combined with the limited bed certification policy often renders the poorest and most medically needy Medicaid applicants unable to obtain the proper nursing home care. * * *
>
> * * * Because of the higher incidence of poverty in the black population, and the concomitant increased dependence on Medicaid, a policy limiting the amount of nursing home beds available to Medicaid patients will disproportionately affect blacks.
>
> Indeed, while blacks comprise 39.4 percent of the Medicaid population, they account for only 15.4 percent of those Medicaid patients who have been able to gain access to Medicaid–covered nursing home services. In addition, testimony indicates that the health status of blacks is generally poorer than that of whites, and their need for nursing home services is correspondingly greater. Finally, such discrimination has caused a "dual system" of long term care for the frail elderly: a statewide system of licensed nursing homes, 70 percent funded by the Medicaid program, serves whites; while blacks are relegated to substandard boarding homes which receive no Medicaid subsidies. * * *

How might OCR use its authority under Title VI to challenge institutional decisions such as the decision to move from urban to suburban locations; to require pre–admission deposits or admission only by a physician with staff privileges; to place childbirth services at a suburban rather than urban hospital within an integrated delivery system; to acquire physician practices only in high income areas; or to limit a home–care agency's services to a particular geographic area? If a nursing home requires the resident or family to prove that they have resources adequate to support one or two years of care upon admission in order to be eligible for a Medicaid bed in the facility when it is needed later, is that nursing home acting in a racially discriminatory way if its Medicaid patient population is, in fact, 95% white in an area where the population is 40% minorities? On continuing segregation in nursing homes and its effect on quality of care, see Ruqaiijah Yearby, African Americans Can't Win, Break Even, or Get Out of the System: The Persistence of "Unequal Treatment" in Nursing Home Care in Post–Racial America, 82 Temp. L. Rev. 1177 (2010). On hospital closures, see Ruqaiijah Yearby, Breaking the Cycle of "Unequal Treatment" with Health Care Reform: Acknowledging and Addressing the Continuation of Racial Bias, 44 Conn. L. Rev. 1281 (2012), evaluating the performance of OCR under Title VI and the ACA, focusing on systemic issues. See also, HHS Press Release (Sept. 2, 2010), describing terms of settlement with University of Pittsburgh Medical Center requiring UPMC to provide door–to–door transportation to new outpatient and inpatient facilities upon movement of hospital from predominantly African–American to predominantly white area.

The ACA requires that federally supported or conducted health programs collect their data in a form that is arrayed by race, ethnicity, sex, primary language, and disability status. Advocates for effective access to health care have been arguing in favor of such data collection for some time. Professor Sidney Watson argues:

> [C]ivil rights litigation focuses on identifying blame. Plaintiffs in civil rights cases must prove that a health care provider either intentionally discriminated or used policies, practices, or procedures that had a statistically significant, adverse impact on minority patients. But disparity issues are complex and may be deeply embedded in providers' actions and patients' decisions, as well as in institutional policies and practices. Given this genesis, many disparities are unlikely to be suitable to the approach required by civil rights laws. The adoption of systems reform, which moves disparity–reduction efforts from the civil rights arena into the world of health care quality regulation, may ease this limitation. Implementing this kind of approach, however, requires performance data that stratify quality–of–care indicators according to patient race and ethnicity, and such data are generally not available. Equity Measures and Systems Reform as

Tools for Reducing Racial and Ethnic Disparities in Health Care, The Commonwealth Fund (August 2005).

Watson supports her claim with several illustrations. For example, she reports a study that analyzed a quality improvement intervention to improve treatment for depression. Overall, the results were quite disappointing, but once the data were organized by race, the intervention showed a significant 10–20% improvement in results for African–American patients.

CHAPTER REVIEW PROBLEMS

Emmaus House

You are a volunteer attorney for a nonprofit organization that provides services through a community center called Emmaus House. You and several other attorneys come to Emmaus House to offer legal services a couple of hours each week as part of a program organized by the local bar association. While you are there, the director of the center comes rushing into the room where you are conducting interviews and tells you there is an emergency.

Mr. Raoul Tejada, a man who comes frequently to the center for assistance with job applications, is complaining of chest pains and shortness of breath. He has had these episodes before and, in fact, went to the public hospital very early this morning because of them. The doctor at the public hospital examined Mr. Tejada and concluded that he was not having a heart attack but rather was suffering from influenza. You and the director get Mr. Tejada into your car and take him to the nearest hospital which happens to be Eastbrook Memorial, a private hospital. Mr. Tejada is guided to a cubicle where the emergency room physician examines him. The doctor then tells you that they are going to transfer Mr. Tejada to the public hospital, twenty minutes away. What do you do?

Assume that Mr. Tejada is admitted to the public hospital but dies within the week. If you brought suit against Eastbrook, what would you have to prove? How would you structure discovery? Do you have a claim against the doctor?

The Health Fair

Elaine Osborne lives in Springfield. She works in a minimum–wage job that provides no health insurance, but she does not qualify for Medicaid. There is no public hospital in Springfield.

Ms. Osborne attended a free public health fair, and an evaluation by a volunteer medical student revealed a site suspicious for melanoma (cancer) on her face and some swelling of her lymph nodes. The student recommended that Ms. Osborne have a dermatologist do a biopsy as a follow up to the screening. She called several doctors' offices but was told that they required insurance or payment in advance. Ms. Osborne then went to the emergency department of each of the three local hospitals but was told that she was not in need of emergency care. Does Ms. Osborne have a claim against the hospitals or the medical student or the public health fair?

Eight months later, Ms. Osborne went to Westhaven Hospital complaining of pain and shortness of breath. Physicians in the ED first suspected that she was having a heart attack. They eventually concluded, however, that her pain and shortness of breath were due to the spread of the cancer. Ms. Osborne was discharged from the hospital with a prescription for pain medication. Does she have a claim against Westhaven or the emergency physicians?

In your own community, where could Ms. Osborne go for treatment of the cancer? If Ms. Osborne had breast cancer rather than melanoma, she may qualify for Medicaid coverage for treatment of the cancer under the Breast and Cervical Cancer Prevention and Treatment Act of 2000, PL 106–354, which allowed states to add this particular group to their Medicaid programs. What, if anything, justifies the preferential status of breast/cervical cancer as compared to other medical conditions?

CHAPTER 8

PRIVATE HEALTH INSURANCE AND MANAGED CARE: LIABILITY

■ ■ ■

I. INSURANCE AND MANAGED CARE: SOME BASIC CONCEPTS

A. THE CONCEPT OF MANAGED CARE

The United States is unique among modern industrialized nations in the extent to which it relies on private payment for health care services. In 2011 Americans paid $308 billion out–of–pocket to health care providers for health care services, eleven percent of the $2,707 billion national health consumption expenditures in that year. Private health insurance, amounting to $896 billion, covered thirty–three percent of personal health care costs. The federal and state governments paid most of the rest, or forty–five percent of the total. The government, however, finances primarily health care for the elderly and disabled, and for lower–income pregnant women and children. Most working age Americans rely on private health insurance to cover the cost of their health care.

Today, of course, private health insurance is usually provided through some form of managed care. Until the early 1990s, it was possible, and indeed sensible, to make a distinction between insurance (meaning indemnity or service benefit insurance) and managed care as different approaches to financing health care. In fact, some state regulatory programs continue even now to treat traditional commercial insurance, Blue Cross and Blue Shield plans, and some forms of managed care organizations differently. But, in general, health insurance has become managed care, and it no longer makes sense to consider them as distinct approaches to health care finance, although it continues to be useful to distinguish between the insurance and care management function of managed care.

Health insurance in the United States is of quite recent origin. It did not become truly widespread until the Great Depression of the 1930s. Some employers and unions offered employee medical care programs earlier, often through their own contracted physicians or clinics. But prior to the 1930s, health insurance was very uncommon. Most Americans paid for health care services out of pocket. During the Depression, however, hospitals reacted to their extreme financial distress by forming hospital–sponsored health plans to ensure a more consistent flow of revenue. These plans became the Blue Cross plans. They were called "service benefit" plans because they paid hospitals for services directly, based on payment rates that were negotiated with participating hospitals. They charged the same "community–rated" premium to the whole community. The states created special incorporation statutes and regulatory programs for Blue Cross plans, and often exempted them from state taxes as well. In the late 1930s and 1940s, doctors followed on the success of the Blue Cross plans by creating their own Blue Shield plans, which operated in much the same way.

Commercial insurers also observed the success of the Blue Cross plans and began to offer health insurance themselves, providing "indemnity coverage." Commercial insurers, unlike the Blue Cross and Blue Shield plans, did not pay providers directly, but rather indemnified their enrollees for services the enrollee paid for based on a fixed fee schedule, beginning with coverage of hospital expenses and later adding coverage for surgery and medical services. Commercial insurers were often able to pick off less expensive groups by offering lower premiums based on the lower expected costs of these groups, i.e. by using "experience rating."

Originally, most employment–related group insurance plans were paid for through a payroll check–off system, under which employers simply took the premiums out of the employee's wages. After World War II, however, unions focused collective bargaining negotiations on getting employers to pick up the cost of health care. Provisions of the 1954 Internal Revenue Code that permitted employers to claim health insurance premiums as business expenses while not taxing the premiums to employees as income, encouraged the rapid spread of health insurance as an employee benefit. Commercial insurers encouraged employers to fund health insurance by offering employers "rebates" for a portion of the premiums they paid. The Employee Retirement Income Security Act of 1974 (ERISA) further encouraged employment–based insurance by freeing employers who self–insured from state insurance regulation. By the 1970s and 1980s the vast majority of Americans had health insurance through their jobs. See Timothy Stoltzfus Jost, Health Care at Risk, 42–69 (2007).

Throughout the second half of the twentieth century prepaid health plans were also available, such as the Kaiser Permanente group in California, the Group Health Association of Washington, D.C., and the Health Insurance Plan of Greater New York. Prepaid medical practice was vigorously opposed by organized medicine, however. Indeed, the AMA was convicted of criminal antitrust violations in 1942 for its efforts to suppress it. AMA v. United States, 130 F.2d 233 (D.C.Cir.1942), affirmed, 317 U.S. 519, 63 S.Ct. 326, 87 L.Ed. 434 (1943). In the 1970s, Paul Ellwood renamed prepaid health care "Health Maintenance Organizations" as part of President Nixon's health reform program, and federal legislation to encourage the growth of HMOs was adopted in 1973.

It was not federal law, however, but double–digit percentage increases in health insurance premiums in the late 1980s and early 1990s that led to the triumph of "managed care," a term that emerged to describe HMOs and other forms of health insurance that attempted not just to pay for, but also to control the price, utilization, and sometimes even quality of, health care services. Most of the surviving Blue Cross and Blue Shield plans (and indeed most state Medicaid programs and, to a lesser extent, Medicare) now predominantly offer managed care products. Private health care finance in the United States has become managed care. But what exactly is "managed care"?

JACOB S. HACKER AND THEODORE R. MARMOR, HOW NOT TO THINK ABOUT "MANAGED CARE"

32 U. Mich. J. L. Ref. 661 (1999).

* * * The very term "managed care"—much like that ubiquitous reform phrase of the early 1990s, "managed competition"—is a confused assemblage of sloganeering, aspirational rhetoric, and business school jargon that sadly reflects the general state of discourse about American medical institutions. Because "managed care" is an incoherent subject, most claims about it will suffer from incoherence as well. * * *

* * *

The expression "managed care" came into widespread use only in the past decade. * * * The term "managed care" does not appear once in Paul Starr's exhaustive 1982 history of American medical care, The Social Transformation of American Medicine, nor can it be found in other books on American health policy written before the early 1980s. * * *

From the beginning, "managed care" was a category with a strong ideological edge, employed to imply competence, concern, and, above all, control over a dangerously unfettered health insurance structure. "Managed care," * * * was an alternative "to the unbridled fee–for–service non–system" that sent "blank checks to hospitals, doctors, dentists, etc." and led to "referrals of dubious necessity" and "unmanaged and uncoordinated care . . . of poor or dubious quality." As these words indicate, managed care was portrayed less as a means to control patient behavior than as a way to bring doctors and hospitals in line with perceived economic realities. Moreover, managed care promised not only cost–control but also coordination and cooperation, not only better management but also better care. By imposing managerial authority on an anarchic "non–system," managed care would simultaneously restrain costs and rationalize an allegedly archaic structure of medical care finance and delivery.

What exactly constitutes "managed care," however, has never been made clear, even by its strongest proponents. To some, the crucial distinguishing feature is a shift in financing from indemnity–style fee–for–service, in which the insurer is little more than a bill–payer, to capitated payment, in which medical providers are paid a fixed amount to treat an individual patient regardless of the volume of services delivered. However, there is nothing intrinsic in fee–for–service payment that requires open–ended reimbursement or passive insurance behavior. Conversely, many, if not most, health insurance plans labeled "managed care" do not rely primarily on capitation. To other proponents, the distinctive characteristic is the creation of administrative protocols for reviewing and sometimes denying care demanded by patients or medical professionals. Such micro–level managerial controls are likewise not universal among so–called managed care health plans. In fact, such controls may be obviated by particular payment methods, like capitation or regulated fee–for–service reimbursement, that create more diffuse constraints on medical practice. Finally, to some, what distinguishes managed care is its reliance on "integrated" networks of health professionals from which patients are required to obtain care. Yet some self–styled managed care plans have no such networks, and what is called a network by many plans is little more than a list of providers willing to accept discounted fee–for–service payments—hardly the dense coordination and integration that industry insiders routinely celebrate.

Perhaps the most defensible interpretation of "managed care" is that it represents a fusion of two functions that once were regarded as largely separate: the financing of medical care and the delivery of medical services. This interpretation, at least, provides a reasonably accurate description of the most familiar organizational entity that marched under the managed care banner until the late 1980s: the health maintenance organization (HMO), a successor to the pre–paid group practice plans that began in the 1930s. Today, however, that is no longer the case. In 1997, * * * between eighty and ninety–eight percent of today's private health insurers appear to fall into the broad category of managed care. "Managed care" therefore does not offer any guidance as to how to distinguish among the vast majority of contemporary health plans.

The standard response to this problem has been to subdivide the managed care universe into a collage of competing acronyms, most coined by industry executives and marketers: HMOs, Preferred Provider Organizations (PPOs), and Exclusive Provider Organizations (EPOs). This is the approach taken by Jonathan Weiner and Gregory de Lissovoy in their frequently cited 1993 article, Razing a Tower of Babel: A Taxonomy for Managed Care and Health Insurance Plans. [18 J. Health Pol. Pol'y & L. 75 (1993).]

* * *

The central problem with Weiner and de Lissovoy's taxonomy—and, indeed, with most contemporary commentary about health insurance—is the tendency to confuse reimbursement methods, managerial techniques, and organizational forms. For example, fee–for–service, a payment method, is regularly contrasted with "managed care," presumably an organizational form.

* * *

The practice of conflating organization, technique, and incentives leads to unnecessary confusion. It means that when we contrast health plans we are often comparing them across incommensurable dimensions. * * * By conflating distinct characteristics, we also are tempted to presume necessary relationships between particular features of health plans (such as their payment method) and specific outcomes that are claimed to follow from these features (such as the degree of integration of medical finance and delivery). Finally, the desire to describe an assortment of disparate plan features with a few broad labels encourages a wild goose chase of efforts to come up with black–and–white standards for identifying plan types. * * *

* * *

In understanding the structure of health insurance, the crucial relationship is between those who deliver medical care and those who pay for it. Even a passive indemnity insurer stands between the patient and the medical provider as a financial intermediary and an underwriter of risk. Today, with risk shifting from insurers to employers, and with financial intermediaries playing more of an administrative role than in the past, the trilateral relationship is more complex. Nonetheless, it still remains the locus of the insurance contract. To characterize this trilateral relationship, we focus on three of its essential features: first, the degree of risk–sharing between providers and the primary bearer of risk (whether an insurer or a self–insured employer); second, the degree to which administrative oversight constrains clinical decisions; and, third, the degree to which enrollees in a plan are required to receive their care from a specified roster of providers. * * *

* * * Our argument is that health plans differ across at least [these] three principal dimensions * * *. Each dimension crucially affects the trilateral connections among provider, patient, and plan. We also wish to emphasize that there is no simple relationship between plan label and the placement of a plan along these axes. Staff–model HMOs may seem like the quintessence of "managed care," yet because they place financial constraints at the group level they do not necessarily concentrate as much risk on physicians as do other network–based health plans, nor do they necessarily entail as much clinical regulation at the micro–level. Microregulation may go hand in hand with restrictions on patient choice of pro-

vider, but it also may not. Indeed, management of individual clinical decisions and the creation of broad incentives for conservative practice patterns may very well be alternative mechanisms for lowering the cost of medical care. Finally, as recent developments in the health insurance market suggest, greater risk–sharing can co–exist with almost any set of arrangements. It does not require a closed network, much less strict utilization review. * * *

Notice, too, that [we make] no mention of those popular buzzwords "integration" and "coordination." Movement toward a closed network, toward greater utilization control, or toward increased risk–sharing can create the conditions under which integration or coordination may occur. They do not imply, however, that such integrative activities actually take place. Getting the right care to the right patient at the right time is a managerial accomplishment, not a product of labels.

Finally, the conventional fee–for–service versus capitation dichotomy does not remain a useful means of distinguishing among different health plans. Instead, the crucial issue is what incentives medical providers actually face. The particular mix of payment methods that create those incentives is less important and will undoubtedly change as health plans experiment with new reimbursement modalities in the future.

* * *

NOTE

Following the lead of Hacker and Marmor, we will not primarily examine the regulation of managed care in terms of traditional distinctions among various types of managed care organizations, but rather will focus on how the states, as well as the Affordable Care Act, regulate the various techniques described above for managing care: networks, utilization controls, and provider incentives. However, because the abbreviations Hacker and Marmor disparage are used so ubiquitously in the health law and policy literature, and because many states base their regulatory schemes on these concepts, we offer definitions of them here.

> *Health Maintenance Organizations (HMOs)* usually limit their members to an exclusive network of providers, permitting their members to go to non–network providers only in special circumstances, like medical emergencies. They have also historically emphasized preventive care, and usually use incentives such as capitation payments to direct the behavior of their professionals and providers. Some HMOs provide care through their own employees or the employees of affiliated foundations (staff model HMOs), while others contract with independent networks of providers to deliver care.

Point–of–service plans (POSs) resemble HMOs, but allow their members to obtain services outside the network with additional cost–sharing (deductibles, coinsurance, or copayments), and often subject to gatekeeper controls.

Preferred Provider Organizations (PPOs) are organized systems of health care providers who agree to provide services on a discounted basis to subscribers. PPO subscribers are not limited to preferred, in–plan, providers, but face financial disincentives, such as deductibles or larger copayment or coinsurance obligations, if they elect non–preferred providers. PPOs usually pay their providers on a fee–for–service basis, and often use utilization review controls for certain kinds of services, like hospital admissions or advanced imaging.

Finally, *provider–sponsored–organizations (PSOs),* also called, in their various guises, integrated delivery systems (IDSs), physician–hospital organizations (PHOs), and provider–sponsored networks (PSNs), are networks organized by providers that contract directly with employers or other purchasers of health benefits to provide their own services on a capitated basis.

Before we proceed to discuss how managed care entities are regulated, however, we must first learn a bit about health insurance regulation.

B. THE CONCEPT OF INSURANCE

Even though managed care has become pervasive in the United States, it continues to make analytic sense to consider separately the insurance and the health care management functions of private health care financing. Insurance involves, by definition, the transfer of risk from the insured (also called the beneficiary, recipient, member, or enrollee) to a financing entity (the insurer, carrier, issuer, managed care organization, or self–insured benefits plan). It is invariably the case in health care that a small proportion of all insureds account for a very high proportion of health care costs. One percent of the population accounts for twenty percent of health care costs; five percent for half. National Institute for Health Care Management, The Concentration of Health Care Spending (2012). Health insurance essentially involves transferring costs from high–cost insureds, who account for most of health care costs, to low–cost insureds, who pay most of the premiums, through the medium of the insurer.

Insurers deal with risk by pooling the risks of large numbers of insureds. Traditionally, however, the insurer, had to be prudent about the risk it assumed from these insureds, and assure that it had the resources to cover the risk. When judging a particular applicant, the insurer had to first assess the risk presented by an applicant, then determine whether or not to take that risk on (a process called "underwriting"), and finally set an appropriate premium.

When financing is provided through employment–related group insurance, of course, part of the premium is paid by the employer and the underwriting is of the group as a whole. When an employer self–insures its employee benefits plan, no premium exchanges hands (except insofar as the employee pays part of the cost of the plan or the employer purchases stop–loss reinsurance) and there is no underwriting, except insofar as a person's health status might affect an employer's willingness to take on the person as an employee, or when the employer purchases stop–loss reinsurance. (Stop–loss reinsurance provides a self–insured employer with coverage if the claims of a particular employee or of the aggregate group exceed a certain amount).

Although managed care plans typically include an insurance function, managed care plans have not always been regarded as insurers. Managed care entities that themselves provide care, such as the classic staff–model HMO or the more recent provider–based integrated delivery system (or provider–sponsored organization), have sometimes been regarded as sellers of services on a pre–paid basis (a bit like appliance service agreements) rather than insurers. But managed care organizations in fact do assume and spread risk, a fact finally settled by the Supreme Court in Rush Prudential HMO, Inc. v. Moran, 536 U.S. 355, 366–370, 122 S.Ct. 2151, 153 L.Ed.2d 375 (2002), and are often, although not always, regulated much like insurers.

There are a number of concepts that must be mastered to understand health insurance and health insurance law. The excerpt that follows discusses these:

CONGRESSIONAL RESEARCH SERVICE, INSURING THE UNINSURED: OPTIONS AND ANALYSIS

(House Comm. on Education & Labor, Comm. Print, 1988).

II. Principles of Health Insurance

* * *

For insurance to operate, there has to be a way to predict the likelihood or probability that a loss will occur as a result of a specific outcome. Such predictions in insurance are based upon probability theory and the law of large numbers. According to probability theory, "while some events appear to be a matter of chance, they actually occur with regularity over a large number of trials."[ ] By examining patterns of behavior over a large number of trials, it is therefore possible for the insurer to infer the likelihood of such behaviors in the future.

* * * Applied to insurance, probability allows the insurer to make predictions on the basis of historical data. In so doing, the insurer "... implicitly says, 'if things continue to happen in the future as they happened in the past, and if our estimate of what has happened in the past is accurate, this is what we may expect.' "[ ]

Losses seldom occur exactly as expected, so insurance companies have to make predictions about the extent to which actual experience might deviate from predicted results. For a small group of insured units, there is a high probability that losses will be much greater or smaller than was predicted. For a very large group, the range of probable error diminishes, especially if the insured group is similar in composition to the group upon which the prediction is based. Thus, to predict the probability of a loss, insurers seek to aggregate persons who are at a similar risk for that loss. * * *

In theory all probabilities of loss can be insured. Insurance could cover any risk for a price. As the probability of loss increases, however, the premium will increase to the point at which it approaches the actual potential pay–out.

To keep premiums competitive, there are in practice some risks that insurers will not accept. In general, insurable risks must meet the following criteria:

— There has to be uncertainty that the loss will occur, and that the loss must be beyond the control of the insured. Insurers will not sell hospital insurance to a person who is on his way to a hospital, nor fire insurance to someone holding a lit match. * * *

— The loss produced by the risk must be measurable. The insurer has to be able to determine that a loss has occurred and that it has a specific dollar value.

— There must be a sufficiently large number of similar insured units to make the losses predictable. * * *

— Generally, the loss must be significant, but there should be a low probability that a very high loss will occur. * * *

* * *

III. Ratemaking

Ratemaking is the "process of predicting future losses and future expenses and allocating those costs among the various classes of insureds." The outcome of the ratemaking process is a "premium" or price of policy. The premium is made up of expected claims against the insurer and the insurer's "administrative expenses." The term "administrative expenses" is used to mean any expense that the insurance company charges that is not for claims (including reserves for potential claims). * * * In the case of employer group coverage, a third part of the premium is set aside in a reserve held against unexpected claims. This reserve is often refundable to the employer if claims do not exceed expectations.

In the textbook descriptions of ratemaking for health insurance, insurers predict losses on the basis of predicted claims costs. This prediction involves an assessment of the likely morbidity (calculated in terms of the number of times the event insured against occurs) and severity (the average magnitude of each loss) of the policyholder or group of policyholders. * * *

* * *

There are different approaches to determining rates. In health insurance, the most frequently used approaches are "experience rating" and "community rating."

Under experience rating, the past experience of the group to be insured is used to determine the premium. For employer groups, experience rating would take into account the company's own history of claims and other expenses. * * *

* * *

The advantage of experience rating is that it adjusts the cost of insurance for a specific group in a manner more commensurate with the expected cost of that particular group than is possible through the exclusive use of manual rates. In addition, the increasingly competitive environment among insurers demands that each one "make every effort to retain groups with favorable experience. Unless an insurer can provide coverage to such groups at a reasonable cost, it runs the risk of losing such policyholders to another insurer which more closely reflects the expected costs of their programs in its rates."[ ]

Under community rating, premium rates are based on the allocation of total costs to all the individuals or groups to be insured, without regard to the past experience of any particular subgroup. * * * Community or class rating has the advantage of allowing an insurer to apply a single rate or set of rates to a large number of people, thus simplifying the process of determining premiums.

* * *

IV. Adverse and Favorable Selection

If everyone in the society purchased health insurance, and if everyone opted for an identical health insurance plan, then insurance companies could adhere strictly to the models of prediction and rate–setting described above. However, everyone does not buy insurance, nor do all the purchasers of insurance choose identical benefits. People who expect to need health services are more likely than others to purchase insurance, and are also likely to seek coverage for the specific services they expect to need. * * *

Insurers use the term "adverse selection" to describe this phenomenon. Adverse selection is defined by the health insurance industry as the "tendency of persons with poorer than average health expectations to apply for, or continue, insurance to a greater extent than do persons with average or better health expectations."[ ]

* * *

Adjusting premiums for adverse selection results in further adverse selection. As the price of insurance goes up, healthier people are less likely to want to purchase insurance. Each upward rate adjustment will leave a smaller and sicker group of potential purchasers. If there were only a single insurance company, it would serve a steadily shrinking market paying steadily increasing premiums. However, because multiple insurance companies are operating in the market, each company may strive to enroll the lower cost individuals or groups, leaving the higher cost cases for its competitors. In this market, adverse selection consists (from the insurer's point of view) of drawing the least desirable cases from within the pool of insurance purchasers. "Favorable" selection occurs if the insurer successfully enrolls lower risk clients than its competitors.

It is thus necessary to distinguish between the more traditional use of "adverse selection," as a term to describe the differences between people who do and do not buy insurance, and the sense in which the term is often used today, to describe the differences among purchasers choosing various insurers or types of coverage. This second type of adverse selection can occur within an insured group, if the individuals in that group are permitted to select from among different insurance options.

Insurers are still concerned about the more traditional type of adverse selection. They use underwriting rules, to exclude or limit the worst risks. Some insurers may also attempt to limit adverse selection by careful selection of where they market and to whom they sell a policy. For example, a company offering a Medicare supplement (Medigap) plan might be more likely to advertise its plan in senior citizen recreation centers, where the patrons tend to be relatively young and healthy, than in nursing homes, where the residents are probably older and have chronic health conditions. Thus, from the perspective of the individual or group applying for insurance, the insurer's attempts to avoid adverse selection may result in lack of availability of coverage, denial of coverage, incomplete coverage or above–average premiums.

* * *

NOTES AND QUESTIONS

1. Adverse selection is one of the two major problems with which insurers must contend. The other is moral hazard. Moral hazard is the tendency of insured persons to use excessively products and services for which they are insured. Absent significant cost–sharing, insurance greatly reduces the price of insured products and services as experienced by consumers, thus increasing consumer demand. Many purchasing decisions in health care, moreover, are made by professionals (the decision to prescribe a drug or to admit to a hospital), and these professionals are even less sensitive to cost. Consumers with first–dollar insurance coverage have little incentive to shop around for products and services to get lower prices. Although insurers attempt to use managed care tools to assure that health care in fact is "medically necessary," insurers still have to pay for many products and services that their insureds receive that are in fact of little value. Advocates of consumer–driven health care contend that moral hazard is the central problem of our health care system. .

2. The reading asserts that the purpose of insurance is to spread risk from individuals to all members of a group. This suggests a vision of distributive justice that distributes risk broadly. Indeed, social insurance, based on the principle of social solidarity, distributes risk among the broadest possible group, the entire citizenry. But insurance can also be based on an alternative vision of justice, that of actuarial fairness, under which every individual pays for insurance based on his own risks. See Deborah Stone, The Struggle for the Soul of Health Insurance, 18 J. Health Pol., Pol'y & L. 287 (1993) and the discussion above at Chapter 1.

Private health insurance in the United States has to date been largely based on the principle of actuarial fairness, although there has been considerable risk distribution within employment–related groups. As discussed further below, however, the Affordable Care Act (ACA) makes a decisive choice on the side of the mutual aid approach to health insurance as opposed to the actuarial fairness approach. Actuarial fairness is not totally rejected—older people and tobacco users can still pay more, as will people who live in higher cost areas or who have families—but underwriting based on health status is decisively rejected as of 2014. The statute creates neither a social insurance program like that of Germany and France nor a socialized health service like England or Sweden. It continues to rely on private insurers to pay for and private health care providers and professionals to deliver health care. But it rejects health status as a basis for determining access to or the cost of health insurance. Moreover, it embraces the goal, if not the reality, of providing universal access to health insurance for all American citizens and legal residents, regardless of ability to pay or medical condition.

3. The ACA contains a number of provisions intended to curb adverse selection by individuals and favorable selection by insurers, including the minimum coverage requirement, which is intended to encourage healthy as well as unhealthy individuals to purchase insurance and discourage adverse

selection, as well as the health status underwriting prohibition, a risk adjustment program to require insurers who have healthier enrollees to compensate those with less healthy enrollees, and other provisions discussed below to discourage favorable selection by insurers. The ACA does less to curb moral hazard, although the health plans sold under the ACA will tend to be high cost–sharing plans that should discourage excessive use of health services. As you read this chapter, consider which health reforms are directed at adverse selection and which at moral hazard, and what other purposes the reforms serve.

Having now introduced the basic concepts of insurance and managed care, we will proceed to examine relevant state law, first considering the liability of insurers and managed care organizations under state contract and tort law, and then look at state programs that regulate health insurers and managed care organizations.

II. CONTRACT LIABILITY OF PRIVATE INSURERS AND MANAGED CARE ORGANIZATIONS

Insurance companies and insurance contracts have historically been governed primarily by state law, and states continue to have the primary responsibility for regulating managed care. In the first instance, insurance and managed care contracts are governed by contract law, and the failure of an insurer or managed care plan to perform to the expectations of the insured may result in contract litigation in state court. Our discussion begins, therefore, with an examination of state insurance contract law.

LUBEZNIK V. HEALTHCHICAGO, INC.

Appellate Court of Illinois, 1994.
268 Ill.App.3d 953, 206 Ill.Dec. 9, 644 N.E.2d 777.

JUSTICE JOHNSON delivered the opinion of the court:

Plaintiff, Bonnie Lubeznik, filed this action in the Circuit Court of Cook County seeking a permanent injunction requiring defendant, HealthChicago, Inc., to pre–certify her for certain medical treatment. Following a hearing, the trial court granted the injunction. Defendant appeals, contending the trial court improperly (1) determined that the requested treatment was a covered benefit under plaintiff's insurance policy; * * * and (4) granted the injunction.

We affirm.

The record reveals that in November 1988 plaintiff was diagnosed with Stage III ovarian cancer. At the time of her diagnosis, the cancer had spread through plaintiff's abdomen and liver and she had a 20 percent survival rate over the next five years. * * *

In June 1991, plaintiff was referred to Dr. Patrick Stiff, the director of the bone marrow treatment program at Loyola University Medical Center (hereinafter Loyola). Dr. Stiff sought to determine the prospect of treating plaintiff with high dose chemotherapy with autologous bone marrow transplant (hereinafter HDCT/ABMT). HDCT/ABMT is a procedure where bone marrow stem cells are removed from the patient's body and frozen in storage until after the patient has been treated with high dose chemotherapy. Following chemotherapy, which destroys the cancer, the marrow previously extracted is reinfused to proliferate and replace marrow destroyed by the chemotherapy. HDCT/ABMT had been a state of the art treatment for leukemia and Hodgkin's disease for many years. It began to be used in the late 1980's for women who were in the late stages of breast cancer.

* * *

On October 28, 1991, Dr. Stiff contacted defendant requesting that it pre–certify plaintiff for the HDCT/ABMT, i.e., agree in advance to pay for the treatment. Plaintiff's insurance policy required her to get pre–certified before receiving elective treatment, procedures and therapies. Dr. Wayne Mathy, defendant's medical director, received Dr. Stiff's pre–certification request and telephoned him shortly thereafter. During his conversation with Dr. Stiff, Dr. Mathy stated that the ABMT/HDCT was not a covered benefit under plaintiff's insurance policy because the treatment was considered experimental.

On October 31, 1991, plaintiff filed a two–count complaint against defendant * * *. In count one, plaintiff sought a mandatory injunction against defendant to pre–certify her for the HDCT/ABMT. * * *

Following a hearing, the trial court denied defendant's motion to dismiss and defendant filed its answer instanter. Thereafter, a hearing on the complaint was held at which Dr. Stiff testified that the HDCT/ABMT was an effective treatment for plaintiff given that all conventional treatment for her had been exhausted. He stated that he had performed 21 HDCT/ABMT procedures on patients with Stage III ovarian cancer and as a result, 75 percent of those patients were in complete remission.

During further testimony, Dr. Stiff opined that the HDCT/ABMT was not experimental and presented documents and literature in support of his testimony. * * *

Dr. Mathy testified at the hearing that his responsibilities as defendant's medical director included determining whether a requested medical treatment is covered under an insurance policy issued by defendant. He stated that after he received plaintiff's request for pre–certification, a member of defendant's benefit analysis staff contacted the National Institutes of Health, the National Cancer Institute, and Medicare seeking an assessment as to whether the requested treatment was experimental. According to Dr. Mathy, defendant determined that the HDCT/ABMT was experimental based on information received from those medical assessment bodies. * * *

During cross–examination, Dr. Mathy testified that he first learned on October 29, 1991, that Dr. Stiff was contemplating treating plaintiff with HDCT/ABMT. Dr. Mathy admitted that immediately upon learning of the proposed treatment, he decided that the HDCT/ABMT was experimental and that plaintiff's pre–certification request should be denied. Dr. Mathy stated that he did not consult with the National Institutes of Health or the National Cancer Institute before making the decision to deny plaintiff's request.

At the conclusion of the testimony, the parties presented final arguments to the trial court. Subsequently, the trial court issued an injunction against defendant ruling that the ABMT/HDCT is [not] * * * an experimental therapy for ovarian cancer, * * *. Defendant then filed this appeal.

Defendant initially argues that the trial court erroneously determined that the HDCT/ABMT procedure is a covered benefit under plaintiff's insurance policy. Defendant claims it supported its determination that the procedure is experimental with similar conclusions by appropriate medical technology boards as required by plaintiff's insurance contract. Plaintiff's insurance policy provides that "[e]xperimental medical, surgical, or other procedures as determined by the [Insurance] Plan in conjunction with appropriate medical technology assessment bodies," are excluded from coverage. Defendant contends that the trial court improperly disregarded the terms of the insurance contract, which, defendant argues, were clear and unambiguous.

At the outset, we note that coverage provisions in an insurance contract are to be liberally construed in favor of the insured to provide the broadest possible coverage.[ ] In determining whether a certain provision in an insurance contract is applicable, a trial court must first determine whether the specific provision is ambiguous.[ ] A provision which is clear or unambiguous, i.e., fairly admits but of one interpretation, must be applied as written.[ ] However, where a provision is ambiguous, its language must be construed in favor of the insured.[ ]

Moreover, where an insurer seeks to deny insurance coverage based on an exclusionary clause contained in an insurance policy, the clause must be clear and free from doubt.[ ] This is so because all doubts with respect to coverage are resolved in favor of the insured. * * *

After carefully reviewing the evidence, we cannot agree with defendant that the trial court improperly determined the HDCT/ABMT to be a covered benefit under plaintiff's insurance policy. First, we disagree with defendant that the exclusionary language was clear and unambiguous. We note that the plaintiff's insurance policy does not define the phrase "appropriate medical technology boards." The plain language of the policy does not indicate who will determine whether a certain medical board is appropriate. Further, the policy fails to outline any standards for determining how a medical board is deemed appropriate. Thus, the phrase, without more, gives rise to a genuine uncertainty about which medical boards are considered appropriate and how and by whom the determination is made.

Second, [the court concluded that the defendant's determination was not justified by a state statute on organ transplantation coverage].

Third, we must note that even if the exclusionary language did apply, defendant failed to follow the terms of the insurance policy. Plaintiff's insurance policy excludes from coverage medical and surgical procedures that are considered experimental by defendant "in conjunction with appropriate technology assessment bodies." At the hearing, Dr. Mathy testified that upon learning of plaintiff's pre–certification request, he had already determined that the HDCT/ABMT was experimental prior to receiving or reviewing any information from the medical assessment boards. Given our careful review of the evidence, including defendant's admitted disregard for the terms of the insurance policy, we hold that the trial court did not err in ruling that the requested treatment was a covered benefit under the policy.

* * *

Lastly, defendant claims that the trial court improperly granted the mandatory injunction because plaintiff failed to meet the requirements for an injunction to issue. An injunction may be granted only after the plaintiff establishes that (1) a lawful right exists; (2) irreparable injury will result if the injunction is not granted; and (3) his or her remedy at law is inadequate.[ ] * * *

* * *

At the hearing, Dr. Stiff testified that given the steady development of plaintiff's disease, it was imperative to begin the HDCT/ABMT treatment as quickly as possible. He opined that delaying the HDCT/ABMT any further might have rendered plaintiff ineligible for such treatment due to further development of the disease. Based on our understanding of Dr. Stiff's testimony, we do not believe, as defendant now posits, that plaintiff was not eligible for the treatment.

Moreover, Dr. Stiff further testified that the HDCT/ABMT was an effective treatment for plaintiff and offered her a "very high chance of a complete disappearance of her disease." In addition, when asked during direct examination to give a prognosis of plaintiff's condition, Dr. Stiff gave the following response:

> "[Plaintiff] has a fatal illness with a zero percent to one percent chance of being alive at five years, let alone alive and disease free."

Given the evidence presented at the hearing, including Dr. Stiff's testimony, we do not agree with defendant that plaintiff failed to show she would suffer irreparable harm without the treatment.[ ] Therefore, we hold that the trial court did not abuse its discretion in granting the requested injunctive relief.

* * *

NOTES AND QUESTIONS

1. Courts have traditionally viewed insurance contracts as adhesion contracts and interpreted them against the drafter (the insurance company) under the doctrine of *contra proferentem*. This has made it difficult for insurance companies to control their exposure to risk through general clauses that refuse payment for care that is not "medically necessary" or that is "experimental." Usually when such clauses are litigated, as in the principal case, the treating physician testifies that care is standard and is urgently necessary, while the insurer's medical director testifies that the care is experimental or unnecessary. What conflicts of interest does each face? Whom should the court believe? Are there more appropriate ways of resolving these disputes? What are the ramifications of these disputes for the cost of medical care?

2. Litigation challenging the refusal of insurance companies to cover ABMT provides a fascinating case study of the use of the courts to determine access to health care services, which is described in detail in Peter D. Jacobson and Stefanie A. Doebler, "We Were All Sold a Bill of Goods:" Litigating the Science of Breast Cancer Treatment, 52 Wayne L. Rev. 43 (2006). Nearly one hundred cases were litigated from the late 1980s to the early 2000s by women with breast cancer seeking coverage of ABMT. Many insurers refused to cover the procedure, claiming that it was experimental. In most litigated cases, as in *Lubeznik*, the plaintiff's treating physician testified for the plaintiff, claiming that the procedure was not only standard treatment, but also necessary to save the plaintiff's life. The insurer's medical director (often supported by other expert witnesses), on the other hand, usually testified that the procedure was still experimental, and thus excluded by the language of the policy. Occasionally, the insurer was also able to introduce into evidence a consent form signed by the insured acknowledging that the procedure was experimental. Plaintiffs won about half of these cases, with the other half going for the insurers. In 1993, a California jury awarded $89 million in damages against an insurer that had refused to cover ABMT, including $77 million of punitive damages. Fox v. HealthNet (No. 219692 [Cal. Super. Ct. Riverside Cty. December 28, 1993]). After that point, the focus of litigation and settlement negotiations turned from whether insurers had improperly denied the treatment to whether they had done so in bad faith, although defendants still continued to win cases. (Was the denial in *Lubeznik* in bad

faith?) Coverage of the procedure also became much more common. In the year 2000, clinical trials of ABMT were finally published, demonstrating that in fact HDC/ABMT was not effective for treating breast cancer. By that time, however, 30,000 women had received ABMT at a cost of $3 billion. What can we learn from this about the nature of the development of medical knowledge? What can we learn about the nature of medical litigation? See also E. Haavi Morreim, From the Clinics to the Courts: The Role Evidence Should Play in Litigating Medical Care, 26 J. Health Pol., Pol'y & L. 409, 411–13 (2001); Karen Antman, et al., High Dose Chemotherapy for Breast Cancer, 282 JAMA 1701 (1999).

3. Another interesting empirical study of coverage disputes is described in Mark Hall, et al., Judicial Protection of Managed Care Consumers: An Empirical Study of Insurance Coverage Disputes, 26 Seton Hall L. Rev. 1055 (1996). Professor Hall found that patients win litigated coverage disputes over half of the time, and that the specificity of the language with which the insurer attempts to exclude coverage does not significantly affect its likelihood of winning. The issue of how medical necessity should be defined and who should determine it has become an important and controversial issue in managed care reform proposals. See Sara Rosenbaum, David M. Frankford, Brad More & Phyllis Borzi, Who Should Determine When Health Care is Medically Necessary? 340 JAMA 229 (1999) and the discussion of Utilization Controls in Section V below. See also, regarding experimental treatment exclusions, J. Gregory Lahr, What is the Method to Their "Madness?" Experimental Treatment Exclusions in Health Insurance Policies, 13 J. Contemp. Health L. & Pol'y 613 (1997).

4. The ACA does not explicitly change or limit state contract (or tort) claims. Under the ACA, however, "coverage determinations and claims" will be subject to an internal review process and to binding external review. Public Health Service Act (PHSA) § 2719, added by ACA §10101(g). The extent to which the determinations of external reviewers will be subject to review in the courts and the approach the courts will take to this review are discussed further below. Contract litigation with insurers will continue to exist, moreover, regarding premium obligations and the application and interpretation of contract language governing issues not subject to external review.

III. TORT LIABILITY OF MANAGED CARE

Insurance and managed care coverage disputes present not only contract interpretation issues, but also issues of tort law. See Chapter 6, *supra*, for a full discussion of managed care tort liability.

IV. STATE REGULATION OF MANAGED CARE

A. INTRODUCTION

Managed Care Organizations (MCOs) differ from traditional health insurers because they manage care. As Marmor and Hacker note above, they do this through restricting members to the use of particular providers, reviewing the utilization of services, or creating incentives for limiting the cost of care. Some MCOs also attempt to oversee the quality of care their members receive. Though managed care was generally welcomed at first as offering the potential to both restrain costs and to improve quality, beginning in the late 1990s a decided "backlash" against managed care gathered steam. See Alice A. Noble and Troyen A. Brennan, The Stages of Managed Care Regulation: Developing Better Rules, in John E. Billi and Gail B. Agrawal, The Challenge of Regulating Managed Care, 29 (2001). There was a general perception—encouraged by the media—that managed care controls had become excessive, threatening access to care. Almost every state adopted some form of legislation—nearly 1000 statutes in all—during the last half of the 1990s. While many of these statutes address fairly narrow problems, a number of states have adopted comprehensive legislation addressing a variety of issues.

In 2001, a federal managed care "patient bill of rights" became a political cause célèbre. Both the House and the Senate adopted bills of rights in 2001, but efforts to reconcile the bills failed and after the terrorist attacks of September 11, Congress lost interest. The main sticking point between the two bills was the issue of whether a federal law should impose managed care plan liability. After 2001, as managed care became less restrictive, political pressure for a federal bill of rights eased. The Affordable Care Act contains many, but not all, of the elements of the proposed patient bill of rights, but was not primarily presented as managed care regulation legislation. State laws regulating managed care, however, will continue to be in force following the ACA and will not be preempted if they do not "prevent the application" of the ACA.

The Hacker and Marmor excerpt at the beginning of this chapter identified strategies through which MCOs manage care. The sections that follow examine each of these strategies and the forms of state managed care legislation that address each of them. Later sections will describe the ACA response to these issues. The best source for keeping up with state managed care legislation is the National Conference of State Legislature's website and the Blue Cross and Blue Shield Association's annual State Legislative Healthcare and Insurance Issues, Survey of Plans, from which many of the statistics below have been drawn.

B. STATE LAW REGULATING MANAGED CARE NETWORKS

Virtually all MCOs either limit their members to a particular network of providers or impose disincentives to discourage their members from "going out of network." As noted earlier, the type of limitations on access to providers imposed by an MCO has historically been seen as a defining characteristic of some forms of MCO, separating PPOs from

HMOs from POSs. Network limitations are not discouraged by the ACA and will continue to exist even after it fully takes effect.

Why might MCOs want to limit their members to particular providers? Of course, if the providers have agreed to deliver services to MCO members at a discount, the answer is obvious, but more is at stake than this. MCOs are also interested in limiting participating professionals and providers to those who share their vision of cost and utilization control. They may additionally want to limit participating professionals and providers to those who offer high quality care, or at least to exclude providers who exhibit clear quality problems. Finally, MCOs also often try to control access to specialists through gatekeeper arrangements to assure that the problems that can be handled more cheaply by primary care physicians are not passed on to specialists, in effect creating separate networks of primary care and specialist physicians.

The earliest response of the states to network limitations was to enact "free choice of provider" laws, which limited the ability of MCOs/insurers to build provider networks. Free choice laws prohibit MCOs from restricting their members to particular providers or, more often, limit the size of the cost–sharing obligations that MCOs can impose on their members who go out of plan. About 23 states currently have free choice of provider laws, though most date from the 1990s and the vast majority apply only to pharmacies.

Another early regulatory response to networks has been "any willing provider" (AWP) laws, which required MCO/insurers to accept into their network any provider who is willing to accept the terms offered by the MCO. Although the Supreme Court affirmed in 2003 the ability of states to impose AWP laws on ERISA plans in Kentucky Association of Health Plans, Inc. v. Miller, 538 U.S. 329, 123 S.Ct. 1471, 155 L.Ed.2d 468 (2003), few have been adopted in recent years, and most of the laws on the books date from the late–1990s or earlier. About 22 states have AWP statutes, though in some states these apply only to pharmacies.

More recent legislative efforts to limit the ability of MCOs to restrict access of their members to providers have been more modest in their reach. Some laws focus on network adequacy, requiring MCOs to maintain an acceptable ratio of providers to enrollees. Other states require MCOs to allow members to go out of network if network coverage is inadequate. Yet other states simply require plans to disclose their provider selection criteria.

A number of states have adopted laws guaranteeing MCO members access to particular specialists, such as gynecologists or pediatricians. Forty–two states required MCOs to allow women direct access to obstetrical and gynecological providers before the ACA provision requiring direct access went into effect. Many states also require plans to allow specialists to serve as primary care providers, especially when a patient with a chronic condition is under the regular care of a specialist. A number of states require MCOs to offer "standing referrals" of persons with chronic conditions to specialists in lieu of requiring continual re–referrals from primary care physicians. Provisions of the ACA addressing network adequacy and direct access are discussed below.

Another common state reform is "continuity of care" requirements, which assure plan members continuing access to a particular health care provider for a period of time after the plan terminates the provider. Some continuity of care statutes permit new members to continue to see their previous, non–network, provider for a period of time if the patient has a serious condition or is pregnant. Thirty–seven states now have continuity of care provisions, with transitional care periods lasting from 30 to 120 days.

Finally, most of states have adopted laws that protect network providers. Almost all states, for example, have adopted "prompt payment" laws or regulations that require insurers to pay "clean" provider claims (claims that are complete and not disputed) within periods ranging from 15 to 60 days. A smaller number of states require notices of disputed claims within similar periods. Several states impose interest or fines for claims that are not paid promptly. A number of states have been quite aggressive in enforcing these laws. Some states have also adopted "due process" requirements, limiting the ability of MCOs to terminate providers from their networks or to deny providers access to their networks without permitting some form of appeal. Other statutes go further, prohibiting "without cause" terminations. MCO plan terminations of providers are discussed in Chapter 9 below. See, discussing the effectiveness of state managed care laws on provider autonomy, Karl Kronebusch, Mark Schlesinger, and Tracey Thomas, Managed Care Regulation in the States: The Impact on Physicians' Practices and Clinical Autonomy, 34 J. Health Pol, Pol'y & L 219 (2009).

C. STATE LAWS REGULATING UTILIZATION CONTROLS

Utilization review (UR) seems to be the approach to managing care that has most irritated consumers and providers. UR refers to case–by–case evaluations conducted by insurers, purchasers, or UR contractors to determine the necessity and appropriateness (and sometimes the quality) of medical care. It is based on the knowledge that there are wide variations in the use of many medical services, and the belief that considered review of medical care by payers can reduce wasteful and unnecessary care.

UR can take several forms. The oldest form is retrospective review, under which an insurer denies payment for care already provided, normally by judging it to be medically unnecessary, experimental, or cosmetic. Retrospective review is of limited value for containing costs since the cost of the care has already been incurred by the time the review takes place.

Contemporary UR programs stress prior or concurrent review and high–cost case or disease management. Prior and concurrent review techniques include preadmission review (before elective hospital admissions); admission review (within 24 to 72 hours of emergency or urgent admissions); continued stay review (to assess length of stay and sometimes accompanied by discharge planning); pre–procedure or pre–service review (to review specific proposed procedures); and voluntary or mandatory second–opinions. High–cost case management addresses the small number (one to seven percent) of very expensive cases that account for most benefit plan costs. Case managers create individualized treatment plans for high–cost beneficiaries. Compliance with the plan is usually voluntary, but may be rewarded by the plan paying for services not otherwise covered by the insurer (such as home health or nursing home care), but less costly than covered alternatives. Disease management programs are similar but are designed to assure appropriate care for particular chronic or recurring medical conditions and often focus on self–care, prevention, and appropriate use of pharmaceuticals.

UR seems to reduce inpatient hospital use and costs. One of the best (although now quite dated) studies found that it reduced hospital admissions by 12.3 percent, inpatient days by 8 percent, and hospital expenditures by 11.9 percent. In particular, it reduced patient days by 34 percent and hospital expenditures by 30 percent for groups that had previously had high admission rates. Paul Feldstein, *et al.*, Private Cost Containment, 318 New Eng.J.Med. 1310 (1988). It is less clear that UR reduces total health care costs, however, since it often moves care from inpatient to outpatient settings, increasing outpatient costs as it reduces inpatient costs. Moreover, UR is most effective in the short run and has less effect on long–term cost increases. See, on UR generally, Institute of Medicine, Controlling Costs and Changing Patient Care?: The Role of Utilization Management (1989).

At the margins, UR blends into other care management strategies. Many MCOs have, for example, retreated from individual case review, instead keeping track of the practice patterns of particular physicians and using the information to decide which physicians to decertify from plan participation. Primary care gatekeeper systems, on the other hand, delegate UR decisions to primary care physicians, but motivate them to control utilization through the use of financial incentives.

UR decisions are basically coverage determinations—UR denies payment for experimental and medically unnecessary care because such care is not covered under the plan contract. UR decisions are also, however, medical treatment determinations because in most instances they determine whether or not the insured will receive medical treatment. UR determinations can thus raise issues of medical practice regulation. Is the UR entity or its employees engaged in the unauthorized practice of medicine when it makes coverage decisions? Is a physician reviewer retained by a utilization review entity engaged in unauthorized practice of medicine if she reviews a case in a state in which she is not licensed? Might the acts of a utilization review entity violate a state's corporate practice of medicine statute or doctrine? Compare Murphy v. Board of Medical Examiners, 190 Ariz. 441, 949 P.2d 530 (Ct.App.1997) (utilization review physician practicing medicine); with Morris v. District of Columbia Board of Medicine, 701 A.2d 364 (D.C.1997) (Blue Cross medical director not practicing medicine in particular UR situation). Thirty–two states have adopted statutes or regulations requiring that HMO medical directors meet specific requirements, usually to be a licensed physician in the state where they do reviews. See also, E. Haavi Morreim, Playing Doctor: Corporate Medical Practice and Medical Malpractice, 32 Mich. J. L. Ref. 939 (1999); J. Scott Andresen, Is Utilization Review the Practice of Medicine: Implications for Managed Care Administrators, 19 J. Legal Med. 431 (1998); John Blum, An Analysis of Legal Liability in Health Care Utilization Review and Case Management, 26 Hous. L. Rev. 191 (1989). Do these provisions protect patients or doctors?

UR has, as was noted above, become perhaps the most unpopular approach to managing care. While plans in fact routinely approve most claims for services, coverage denial can have disastrous consequences for insureds. Also, the hassle involved in fulfilling UR requirements (the interminably busy fax, the voicemail messages that are never responded to, the endless arguing with reviewers) undoubtedly deters physicians from offering or ordering services that would otherwise have been given.

A variety of regulatory strategies have been adopted for addressing utilization review issues. Every state has now adopted a law requiring MCOs to offer their members internal consumer grievance and appeal procedures. These statutes often establish time frames for the appeals (again requiring expedited hearings for emergencies), specify who must decide the appeal (specifying, for example, the professional credentials of the decision maker, or requiring a decision maker not involved in the initial decision), and provide the format for the final decision (in writing, giving reasons, etc.).

Forty–seven states required external or independent reviews before the ACA made the requirement universal (see below). As discussed below, the ACA requires insured plans to use state external review procedures if those procedures meet the requirements of the NAIC model act. See, on the resolution of grievances, appeals, and other disputes in managed care, Nan D. Hunter, Managed Process, Due Care: Structures of Accountability in Health Care, 6 Yale J. Health Pol'y, L. & Ethics 93 (2006); Carole Roan Gresenz and David M. Studdert, External Review of Coverage Denials by Managed Care Organizations in California, 2(3) Journal Empirical Legal Studies 449 (2005); Eleanor Kinney, Protecting American Health Care Consumers (2002); and Gerard F. Anderson and Mark A. Hall, The Management of Conflict Over Health Insurance Coverage, in M. Gregg Bloche, ed., The Privatization of Health Care Reform (2003).

A key issue in UR decisions is the definition of medical necessity. About half of the states have adopted statutory definitions of medical necessity, though in some states the definition applies only to particular insurers (Medicaid, HMOs) or particular areas of care (mental health, long term care, inpatient care). A number of these statutes also require some level of deference to the decision of the treating physician on medical necessity issues.

With respect to some forms of care, state statutes have simply preempted coverage decisions by imposing mandates. Providers and consumer groups have for decades lobbied successfully for state insurance mandates that require insurance companies to provide certain benefits (mammography, mental health and substance abuse treatment); cover the services of certain providers (chiropractors, podiatrists); or cover certain insureds or their dependents (newborn infants, laid–off employees). In recent years, however, state statutes mandating particular benefits have also often limited the reach of utilization controls.

Among the most common examples of this are emergency care mandates, which have been adopted in all but four states. (See chapter 7 above discussing the Emergency Medical Treatment and Labor Act, which provides a federal right to emergency care). These laws usually require insurers to cover emergency department visits if a "prudent layperson" would have considered the situation an emergency. A study of the effects of these laws found that many insurers were already applying a prudent layperson standard before these laws were adopted, and that the laws do not seem to have led to a significant increase in costs, although many MCOs reacted by raising copayments for emergency care. Mark A. Hall, The Impact and Enforcement of Prudent Layperson Laws, 43 Annals of Emergency Medicine 558 (2004). See also on the motivation of mandate statutes, Amy Monahan, Fairness Versus Welfare in Health Insurance Content Regulation, 2012 U. Ill. L. Rev. 139 (2012).

Other statutes address length of stay issues, requiring at least 48 hours of hospitalization coverage for vaginal or 96 hours for Cesarean deliveries (the famous "drive through delivery" statutes of the mid–1990s, added as a federal law requirement in 1996) or hospitalization coverage for mastectomies. Still other statutes prohibit plans from denying access to particular benefits, such as off–formulary drugs (usually specifically for cancer or life–threatening diseases) or clinical trials. Popular benefit mandates in recent years include requirements of coverage for mental health care, cancer screenings, contraceptives, infertility treatment, osteoporosis prevention, newborn hearing treatments, autism interventions, and reconstructive surgery following mastectomy.

Finally, fourteen states have adopted laws providing for liability suits against plans for failure to exercise ordinary care in the provision of medical care. To the extent that UR decisions are in fact decisions with respect to plan provision of medical care, they would seem to be covered by these liability statutes. Though these statutes are not enforceable against ERISA plans (see below), they do apply to non–ERISA insurers.

D. STATE LAWS REGULATING PROVIDER INCENTIVES

The third strategy that MCOs have used to manage care is financial incentives for professionals and providers. The earliest form was capitation. Under capitation the provider gets paid a fixed fee for providing care for the MCO beneficiary for a fixed period of time. If the services the beneficiary receives cost more than this payment, the provider loses money; if the services cost less, the provider makes money. In other words, the provider becomes the true insurer—i.e. risk bearer—with respect to the patient.

Providers (e.g., primary care physicians) may be capitated their own services, but can also be paid on a capitated basis for other services the patient may need, such as specialist services, laboratory tests, hospitalization, or even drugs. Some of these services, however, cost far more than primary care services, and putting a single primary care physician, or even physician group, at risk for these services might in many instances impose unreasonable risks.

Instead, MCOs usually put the primary care provider only partially at risk. This is done through the use of bonuses or withholds. A pool is established either from money withheld from payments made directly to the physician (a withhold) or from funds provided in addition to regular payments (a bonus). Specified expenses—for specialists or hospitalization, for example—are paid out of this pool. Any money left over at the end of an accounting period (e.g., a year), is paid over to the physician. In addition, the physician may or may not be fully capitated for his or her own services.

Alternatively, the MCO can capitate physicians and hospitals separately, putting the hospital at risk for its expenses and physicians at risk for theirs. An HMO receives a premium, for example, and after subtracting its administrative costs and profits, gives part to a hospital and part to a physician group, which may provide multispecialty services or might provide primary care and be at risk for paying specialists on a fee–for–service basis.

Insurers are also developing alternatives to both fee–for–service and capitated payments, including episode–based payments, comprehensive care payments, and bundled payments to physicians and providers. Accountable Care Organizations are another example of shared risk. These approaches blend the positive features of both earlier approaches, but also bring their own problems. See Peter Hussey, et al, Episode–Based Performance Measurement and Payment: Making it a Reality, 28 Health Aff. 1406 (2009); Harold Miller, From Volume to Value: Better Ways to Pay for Health Care, 28 Health Aff. 1418 (2009).

While incentives are an effective way to hold down costs, they can also result in underservice if the responses they elicit from providers are excessive. It is more difficult to regulate incentives, however, than it is to regulate network or utilization controls because it is more difficult to identify discrete unacceptable practices or to address these practices through enforcement procedures.

Thirty states in fact currently have statutes purporting to ban the use of financial incentives, usually prohibiting incentives that "deny, reduce, limit or delay medically necessary care." The statutes, however, usually go on to say that they are not intended to prohibit MCOs from using capitation payments or other risk–sharing arrangements. As MCOs would generally insist that their incentives are intended to deter unnecessary, rather than necessary care, these statutes have little effect on MCO incentive programs. More useful are statutes or regulations that more explicitly limit excessive incentives, restricting, for example, the proportion of a provider's income that can be put at risk or the size of the pool of patients or providers over which the risk is spread, or requiring stop–loss insurance.

A rather different regulatory approach is simply to require disclosure of financial incentives. Not surprisingly, there are problems with this approach as well. First, the vast majority of insured Americans receive their health coverage through their place of employment, and four–fifths of all employees are offered a choice of only one (48 percent) or two (37 percent) types of plans. Even employees offered a choice of two or more plans, of course, may not have much of a choice among incentive plan structures. Second, it is not at all clear how most plan members can use information about incentive plans structures, i.e. whether their understanding of health care finance and delivery is sophisticated enough to evaluate incentive structures. Finally, requiring disclosure imposes costs both on regulators, who need to devise a meaningful form of disclosure and police compliance, and on MCOs, which need to compile and disseminate the information.

Even if requiring plan disclosure to allow consumer choice is problematic, there may be other reasons for requiring disclosure. In a thoughtful article, William Sage identifies three other reasons why we might want to require MCOs and providers to disclose information. First, disclosure increases the likelihood that providers and MCOs will act as honest agents for their patients and members, while it facilitates the ability of patients and members to monitor fiduciary loyalty. Second, requiring collection and disclosure of particular kinds of performance–related information might increase incentives to direct practice in certain directions deemed to be socially important. Requiring disclosure of immunization rates, for example, may promote immunization programs. Finally, disclosure of more information might facilitate public deliberation and provider and MCO accountability. William M. Sage, Regulating Through Information: Disclosure Laws and American Health Care, 99 Columb. L. Rev. 1701 (1999). See also Tracy E. Miller & William M. Sage, Disclosing Physician Financial Incentives, 281 JAMA 1424 (1999).

E. STATE LAWS REGULATING MANAGED CARE QUALITY

The final issue addressed by state managed care statutes is the quality of care provided by MCOs. One of the aspirations of managed care has always been to manage care to improve quality. The term "health maintenance organization" evidences a commitment to maintaining health, not simply to providing medical services, and MCO marketing materials often talk about coordination or integration of care.

In a sense, most of the statutory provisions discussed so far at least touch on quality issues. Assuring better access to care and accuracy in plan or provider decision making, for example, presumably improves the care received by the plan member. Quality of care is addressed more directly, however, by statutes or regulations requiring MCOs to have quality assurance or improvement programs or to take quality of care into consideration in provider credentialing. Other statutes require or encourage MCOs to seek accreditation in the hope that accreditation agencies will provide quality oversight. Finally, a number of statutes require disclosure of quality–related information through the use of report cards or other forms of disclosure. See Barry R. Furrow, Regulating the Managed Care Revolution: Private Accreditation and a New System Ethos, 43 Vill. L. Rev. 361 (1998)

PROBLEM: REGULATING MANAGED CARE

You are the legal staff for the Health Committee of a state that has in place a comprehensive managed care regulation statute containing most of the provisions discussed above. You are now considering repealing parts of the statute. Whom do the provisions regulating provider networks primarily benefit? What effect do these provisions have on the cost of coverage? To the extent that they increase costs, what effect might this have on access? Which of the provisions addressing UR issues are likely to be most strongly supported by plan members? Which are most likely in fact to be of use to them?

Which provisions also benefit providers? Which providers benefit from these provisions? Which provisions are likely to be opposed most strongly by managed care trade associations? How enforceable are limitations on plan incentive structures? How useful are they to plan members? Are provisions aimed at improving quality of care likely to be effective? Considering only the interest of the public, which provisions will you recommend keeping and which repealing? Finally, after studying the next section, consider which provisions are redundant with requirements of the Affordable Care Act, and which, if any, might be preempted as preventing its application?

V. THE EMPLOYEE RETIREMENT INCOME SECURITY ACT OF 1974: ERISA

Although regulation of health insurance has traditionally been the responsibility of the states, the ACA is not the first foray of Congress into regulating private health insurance. Since the 1970s, a series of federal laws have been enacted regulating private health insurance. The most important of these is the Employee Retirement Income Security Act of 1974, ERISA, which has already been alluded to several times in previous chapters. ERISA's primary role throughout the 1980s and 1990s was deregulatory, as its preemptive provisions repeatedly blocked state common law actions against health plans as well as state attempts at plan regulation. The Supreme Court seemed to relax its interpretation of ERISA preemption in the late 1990s, however, giving the states somewhat more flexibility for regulating insured health plans, although it has become clear that there are limits to this flexibility. Finally, ERISA itself provides employee health plan beneficiaries with a positive right to sue to recover denied benefits, while also imposing fiduciary obligations on plan fiduciaries.

ERISA is not the only pre–ACA federal statute to regulate health plans. The Americans with Disabilities Act places at least minimal constraints on the ability of employers and insurers to discriminate against the disabled in the provision of health insurance. The Health Insurance Portability and Accountability Act of 1996 (which amended ERISA, as well as other federal statutes) limited the use of pre–existing condition clauses while prohibiting discrimination in coverage and rates within employee groups. It also offered certain protections in the small group and individual insurance markets. Until the ACA becomes fully effective in 2014, HIPAA will continue to be the primary federal law governing health insurance underwriting. The Consolidated Omnibus Budget Reconciliation Act of 1985 provides some protection for some who lose employee coverage. Finally, Congress has adopted in the past few years a handful of coverage mandates, which will continue to be in effect until overtaken by the essential benefits requirements in 2014.

A. ERISA PREEMPTION OF STATE HEALTH INSURANCE REGULATION

Section 514 of ERISA (codified as 29 U.S.C.A. § 1144) expressly preempts state statutes and common law claims that "relate to" employee benefit plans. Section 514, however, also explicitly exempts state regulation of insurance from preemption, while also prohibiting state regulation of self–insured plans. Section 502 of ERISA (codified as 29 U.S.C.A. § 1132) has been interpreted by the Supreme Court as providing for exclusive federal court jurisdiction over and an exclusive federal cause of action for cases that could be brought as ERISA claims. The text of these provisions follows:

29 U.S.C.A. § 1132 (Section 502)

A civil action may be brought—

(1) by a participant or beneficiary—

* * *

(B) to recover benefits due to him under the terms of his plan, to enforce his rights under the terms of the plan, or to clarify his rights to future benefits under the terms of the plan;

(2) by the Secretary, or by a participant, beneficiary or fiduciary for appropriate relief under section 1109 of this title [which imposes on plan fiduciaries the obligation to "make good" to a plan any losses resulting from a breach of fiduciary duties, and authorizes "other equitable or remedial relief" for breaches of fiduciary obligations];

(3) by a participant, beneficiary, or fiduciary (A) to enjoin any act or practice which violates any provision of this subchapter or the terms of the plan, or (B) to obtain other appropriate equitable relief (i) to redress such violations or (ii) to enforce any provisions of this subchapter or the terms of the plan;

* * *

29 U.S.C.A. § 1144 (Section 514)

(a) Except as provided in subsection (b) of this section, the provisions of this subchapter and subchapter III of this chapter shall supersede any and all State laws insofar as they may now or hereafter relate to any employee benefit plan * * *

(b) Construction and application

* * *

(2)(A) Except as provided in subparagraph (B), nothing in this subchapter shall be construed to exempt or relieve any person from any law of any State which regulates insurance, banking, or securities.

(B) Neither an employee benefit plan * * * nor any trust established under such a plan, shall be deemed to be an insurance company * * * or to be engaged in the business of insurance or banking for purposes of any law of any State purporting to regulate insurance companies, insurance contracts, banks, trust companies, or investment companies.

The task of sorting out ERISA's complex preemption scheme has resulted in a tremendous volume of litigation, including, to date, over twenty Supreme Court decisions and hundreds of state and federal lower court decisions. In this subsection we will examine the effect of Section 502 and 514 preemption on state laws "relating to" health insurance. In this context we will also consider the effect of Section 514's "savings clause," (§ 514(b)(2)(A)), which saves from preemption state laws "which regulate insurance," as well as § 514's "deemer" clause (§ 514(b)(2)(B)), which exempts self–insured ERISA plans from state insurance regulation. In the second subsection of this section, we will consider the effect of ERISA preemption on state common law tort causes of action against managed care plans and insurers. We begin with one of the more recent Supreme Court cases, which sets out the basic framework of ERISA preemption and debates the policies that ground it.

RUSH PRUDENTIAL, INC. V. DEBRA C. MORAN, ET. AL.

Supreme Court of the United States, 2002.
536 U.S. 355, 122 S.Ct. 2151, 153 L.Ed.2d 375.

JUSTICE SOUTER delivered the opinion of the Court.

* * *

Petitioner, Rush Prudential HMO, Inc., is a health maintenance organization (HMO) that contracts to provide medical services for employee welfare benefit plans covered by ERISA. Respondent Debra Moran is a beneficiary under one such plan, sponsored by her husband's employer. Rush's "Certificate of Group Coverage," issued to employees who participate in employer–sponsored plans, promises that Rush will provide them with "medically necessary" services. The terms of the certificate give Rush the "broadest possible discretion" to determine whether a medical service claimed by a beneficiary is covered under the certificate. * * *

As the certificate explains, Rush contracts with physicians "to arrange for or provide services and supplies for medical care and treatment" of covered persons. Each covered person selects a primary care physician from those under contract to Rush, while Rush will pay for medical services by an unaffiliated physician only if the services have been "authorized" both by the primary care physician and Rush's medical director.[ ]

In 1996, when Moran began to have pain and numbness in her right shoulder, Dr. Arthur LaMarre, her primary care physician, unsuccessfully administered "conservative" treatments such as physiotherapy. In October 1997, Dr. LaMarre recommended that Rush approve surgery by an unaffiliated specialist, Dr. Julia Terzis, who had developed an unconventional treatment for Moran's condition. Although Dr. LaMarre said that Moran would be "best served" by that procedure, Rush denied the request and, after Moran's internal appeals, affirmed the denial on the ground that the procedure was not "medically necessary."[ ] Rush instead proposed that Moran undergo standard surgery, performed by a physician affiliated with Rush.

In January 1998, Moran made a written demand for an independent medical review of her claim, as guaranteed by § 4–10 of Illinois's HMO Act,[ ] which provides:

> Each Health Maintenance Organization shall provide a mechanism for the timely review by a physician * * * who is unaffiliated with the Health Maintenance Organization, jointly selected by the patient . . . , primary care physician and the Health Maintenance Organization in the event of a dispute between the primary care physician and the Health Maintenance Organization regarding the medical necessity of a covered service proposed by a primary care physician. In the event that the reviewing physician determines the covered service to be medically necessary, the Health Maintenance Organization shall provide the covered service. * * *

* * *

When Rush failed to provide the independent review, Moran sued in an Illinois state court to compel compliance with the state Act. Rush removed the suit to Federal District Court, arguing that the cause of action was "completely preempted" under ERISA.[ ]

While the suit was pending, Moran had surgery by Dr. Terzis at her own expense and submitted a $94,841.27 reimbursement claim to Rush. Rush treated the claim as a renewed request for benefits and began a new inquiry to determine coverage. The three doctors consulted by Rush said the surgery had been medically unnecessary.

Meanwhile, the federal court remanded the case back to state court on Moran's motion, concluding that because Moran's request for independent review under § 4–10 would not require interpretation of the terms of an ERISA plan, the claim was not "completely preempted" so as to permit removal * * * The state court enforced the state statute and ordered Rush to submit to review by an independent physician. * * * [The reviewer] decided that Dr. Terzis's treatment had been medically necessary, based on the definition of medical necessity in Rush's Certificate of

Group Coverage, as well as his own medical judgment. Rush's medical director, however, refused to concede that the surgery had been medically necessary, and denied Moran's claim in January 1999.

Moran amended her complaint in state court to seek reimbursement for the surgery as "medically necessary" under Illinois's HMO Act, and Rush again removed to federal court, arguing that Moran's amended complaint stated a claim for ERISA benefits and was thus completely preempted by ERISA's civil enforcement provisions, 29 U.S.C. § 1132(a) [§ 502], * * * The District Court treated Moran's claim as a suit under ERISA, and denied the claim on the ground that ERISA preempted Illinois's independent review statute.

The Court of Appeals for the Seventh Circuit reversed. * * *

* * *

To "safeguar[d] . . . the establishment, operation, and administration" of employee benefit plans, ERISA sets "minimum standards . . . assuring the equitable character of such plans and their financial soundness,"[ ] and contains an express preemption provision that ERISA "shall supersede any and all State laws insofar as they may now or hereafter relate to any employee benefit plan. . . . " § 1144(a)[§ 514(a)]. A saving clause then reclaims a substantial amount of ground with its provision that "nothing in this subchapter shall be construed to exempt or relieve any person from any law of any State which regulates insurance, banking, or securities." § 1144(b)(2)(A) [§ 514(b)(2)(A)]. The "unhelpful" drafting of these antiphonal clauses * * * occupies a substantial share of this Court's time. In trying to extrapolate congressional intent in a case like this, when congressional language seems simultaneously to preempt everything and hardly anything, we "have no choice" but to temper the assumption that " 'the ordinary meaning . . . accurately expresses the legislative purpose,' "[ ] with the qualification " 'that the historic police powers of the States were not [meant] to be superseded by the Federal Act unless that was the clear and manifest purpose of Congress.' "[ ]

It is beyond serious dispute that under existing precedent § 4–10 of the Illinois HMO Act "relates to" employee benefit plans within the meaning of § 1144(a). * * * As a law that "relates to" ERISA plans under § 1144(a), § 4–10 is saved from preemption only if it also "regulates insurance" under § 1144(b)(2)(A). * * *

[The Court then proceeded to apply the savings clause analysis method that it had developed in earlier cases, concluding that the Illinois external review law was saved from preemption. As this analysis was superseded by the Court's decision in *Kentucky Association of Health Plans v. Miller*, described below, this discussion is omitted here. Ed.]

* * *

Given that § 4–10 regulates insurance, ERISA's mandate that "nothing in this subchapter shall be construed to exempt or relieve any person from any law of any State which regulates insurance," 29 U.S.C. § 1144(b)(2)(A), ostensibly forecloses preemption. [ ] Rush, however, does not give up. It argues for preemption anyway, emphasizing that the question is ultimately one of congressional intent, which sometimes is so clear that it overrides a statutory provision designed to save state law from being preempted. * * *

In ERISA law, we have recognized one example of this sort of overpowering federal policy in the civil enforcement provisions, 29 U.S.C. § 1132(a), * * * In *Massachusetts Mut. Life Ins. Co. v. Russell,*[ ] we said those provisions amounted to an "interlocking, interrelated, and interdependent remedial scheme,"[ ] which *Pilot Life* described as "represent[ing] a careful balancing of the need for prompt and fair claims settlement procedures against the public interest in encouraging the formation of employee benefit plans"[ ]. So, we have held, the civil enforcement provisions are of such extraordinarily preemptive power that they override even the "well–pleaded complaint" rule for establishing the conditions under which a cause of action may be removed to a federal forum. *Metropolitan Life Ins. Co. v. Taylor*[ ].

Although we have yet to encounter a forced choice between the congressional policies of exclusively federal remedies and the "reservation of the business of insurance to the States,"[ ] we have anticipated such a conflict, with the state insurance regulation losing out if it allows plan participants "to obtain remedies . . . that Congress rejected in ERISA."

In *Pilot Life*, an ERISA plan participant who had been denied benefits sued in a state court on state tort and contract claims. He sought not merely damages for breach of contract, but also damages for emotional distress and punitive damages, both of which we had held unavailable under relevant ERISA provisions.[ ] We not only rejected the notion that these common–law contract claims "regulat[ed] insurance,"[ ] but went on to say that, regardless, Congress intended a "federal common law of rights and obligations" to develop under ERISA,[ ] without embellishment by independent state remedies.

Rush says that the day has come to turn dictum into holding by declaring that the state insurance regulation, § 4–10, is preempted for creating just the kind of "alternative remedy" we disparaged in *Pilot Life.* As Rush sees it, the independent review procedure is a form of binding arbitration that allows an ERISA beneficiary to submit claims to a new decisionmaker to examine Rush's determination *de novo,* supplanting judicial review under the "arbitrary and capricious" standard ordinarily applied when discretionary plan interpretations are challenged[ ]. * * *

We think, however, that Rush overstates the rule expressed in *Pilot Life*. * * *

* * *

[T]his case addresses a state regulatory scheme that provides no new cause of action under state law and authorizes no new form of ultimate relief. While independent review under § 4–10 may well settle the fate of a benefit claim under a particular contract, the state statute does not enlarge the claim beyond the benefits available in any action brought under § 1132(a). And although the reviewer's determination would presumably replace that of the HMO as to what is "medically necessary" under this contract, the relief ultimately available would still be what ERISA authorizes in a suit for benefits under § 1132(a). * * *

Rush still argues for going beyond *Pilot Life,* making the preemption issue here one of degree, whether the state procedural imposition interferes unreasonably with Congress's intention to provide a uniform federal regime of "rights and obligations" under ERISA. However, "[s]uch disuniformities . . . are the inevitable result of the congressional decision to 'save' local insurance regulation."[ ][11] Although we have recognized a limited exception from the saving clause for alternative causes of action and alternative remedies in the sense described above, we have never indicated that there might be additional justifications for qualifying the clause's application. * * *

To be sure, a State might provide for a type of "review" that would so resemble an adjudication as to fall within *Pilot Life's* categorical bar. Rush, and the dissent,[ ] contend that § 4–10 fills that bill by imposing an alternative scheme of arbitral adjudication at odds with the manifest congressional purpose to confine adjudication of disputes to the courts. * * *

In the classic sense, arbitration occurs when "parties in dispute choose a judge to render a final and binding decision on the merits of the controversy and on the basis of proofs presented by the parties."[ ] Arbitrators typically hold hearings at which parties may submit evidence and conduct cross–examinations.[ ]

Section 4–10 does resemble an arbitration provision, then, to the extent that the independent reviewer considers disputes about the meaning

[11] Thus, we do not believe that the mere fact that state independent review laws are likely to entail different procedures will impose burdens on plan administration that would threaten the object of 29 U.S.C. § 1132(a); it is the HMO contracting with a plan, and not the plan itself, that will be subject to these regulations, and every HMO will have to establish procedures for conforming with the local laws, regardless of what this Court may think ERISA forbids. This means that there will be no special burden of compliance upon an ERISA plan beyond what the HMO has already provided for. And although the added compliance cost to the HMO may ultimately be passed on to the ERISA plan, we have said that such " "indirect economic effect[s],"[ ], are not enough to preempt state regulation even outside of the insurance context. We recognize, of course, that a State might enact an independent review requirement with procedures so elaborate, and burdens so onerous, that they might undermine § 1132(a). No such system is before us.

of the HMO contract and receives "evidence" in the form of medical records, statements from physicians, and the like. But this is as far as the resemblance to arbitration goes, for the other features of review under § 4–10 give the proceeding a different character, one not at all at odds with the policy behind § 1132(a). The Act does not give the independent reviewer a free–ranging power to construe contract terms, but instead, confines review to a single term: the phrase "medical necessity," used to define the services covered under the contract.[ ] This limitation, in turn, implicates a feature of HMO benefit determinations that we described in *Pegram v. Herdrich,*[ ] We explained that when an HMO guarantees medically necessary care, determinations of coverage "cannot be untangled from physicians' judgments about reasonable medical treatment."[ ] This is just how the Illinois Act operates; the independent examiner must be a physician with credentials similar to those of the primary care physician,[ ] and is expected to exercise independent medical judgment in deciding what medical necessity requires. * * *

Once this process is set in motion, it does not resemble either contract interpretation or evidentiary litigation before a neutral arbiter, as much as it looks like a practice (having nothing to do with arbitration) of obtaining another medical opinion. * * *

The practice of obtaining a second opinion, however, is far removed from any notion of an enforcement scheme, and once § 4–10 is seen as something akin to a mandate for second–opinion practice in order to ensure sound medical judgments, the preemption argument that arbitration under § 4–10 supplants judicial enforcement runs out of steam.

Next, Rush argues that § 4–10 clashes with a substantive rule intended to be preserved by the system of uniform enforcement, stressing a feature of judicial review highly prized by benefit plans: a deferential standard for reviewing benefit denials. Whereas *Firestone Tire & Rubber Co. v. Bruch,*[ ] recognized that an ERISA plan could be designed to grant "discretion" to a plan fiduciary, deserving deference from a court reviewing a discretionary judgment, § 4–10 provides that when a plan purchases medical services and insurance from an HMO, benefit denials are subject to apparently *de novo* review. If a plan should continue to balk at providing a service the reviewer has found medically necessary, the reviewer's determination could carry great weight in a subsequent suit for benefits under § 1132(a), depriving the plan of the judicial deference a fiduciary's medical judgment might have obtained if judicial review of the plan's decision had been immediate.

Again, however, the significance of § 4–10 is not wholly captured by Rush's argument, which requires some perspective for evaluation. First, in determining whether state procedural requirements deprive plan administrators of any right to a uniform standard of review, it is worth recalling that ERISA itself provides nothing about the standard. It simply requires plans to afford a beneficiary some mechanism for internal review of a benefit denial, * * *.

Not only is there no ERISA provision directly providing a lenient standard for judicial review of benefit denials, but there is no requirement necessarily entailing such an effect even indirectly. When this Court dealt with the review standards on which the statute was silent, we held that a general or default rule of *de novo* review could be replaced by deferential review if the ERISA plan itself provided that the plan's benefit determinations were matters of high or unfettered discretion[ ]. Nothing in ERISA, however, requires that these kinds of decisions be so "discretionary" in the first place; whether they are is simply a matter of plan design or the drafting of an HMO contract. In this respect, then, § 4–10 prohibits designing an insurance contract so as to accord unfettered discretion to the insurer to interpret the contract's terms. As such, it does not implicate ERISA's enforcement scheme at all, and is no different from the types of substantive state regulation of insurance contracts we have in the past permitted to survive preemption, such as mandated–benefit statutes and statutes prohibiting the denial of claims solely on the ground of untimeliness.[ ] * * *

* * *

In deciding what to make of these facts and conclusions, it helps to go back to where we started and recall the ways States regulate insurance in looking out for the welfare of their citizens. Illinois has chosen to regulate insurance as one way to regulate the practice of medicine, which we have previously held to be permissible under ERISA[ ]. While the statute designed to do this undeniably eliminates whatever may have remained of a plan sponsor's option to minimize scrutiny of benefit denials, this effect of eliminating an insurer's autonomy to guarantee terms congenial to its own interests is the stuff of garden variety insurance regulation through the imposition of standard policy terms. * * * And any lingering doubt about the reasonableness of § 4–10 in affecting the application of § 1132(a) may be put to rest by recalling that regulating insurance tied to what is medically necessary is probably inseparable from enforcing the quintessentially state–law standards of reasonable medical care. See *Pegram v. Herdrich* [ ]. To the extent that benefits litigation in some federal courts may have to account for the effects of § 4–10, it would be an exaggeration to hold that the objectives of § 1132(a) are undermined. The savings clause is entitled to prevail here, and we affirm the judgment.

JUSTICE THOMAS, with whom THE CHIEF JUSTICE, JUSTICE SCALIA, and JUSTICE KENNEDY join, dissenting.

This Court has repeatedly recognized that ERISA's civil enforcement provision, § 502 of the Employee Retirement Income Security Act of 1974 (ERISA), 29 U.S.C. § 1132, provides the exclusive vehicle for actions asserting a claim for benefits under health plans governed by ERISA, and therefore that state laws that create additional remedies are pre-empted.[ ] Such exclusivity of remedies is necessary to further Congress' interest in establishing a uniform federal law of employee benefits so that employers are encouraged to provide benefits to their employees.[ ]

* * * Therefore, as the Court concedes,[ ] even a state law that "regulates insurance" may be pre-empted if it supplements the remedies provided by ERISA, despite ERISA's saving clause,[ ]. Today, however, the Court takes the unprecedented step of allowing respondent Debra Moran to short circuit ERISA's remedial scheme by allowing her claim for benefits to be determined in the first instance through an arbitral-like procedure provided under Illinois law, and by a decisionmaker other than a court.[ ] * * *

From the facts of this case one can readily understand why Moran sought recourse under § 4–10. * * *

In the course of its review, petitioner informed Moran that "there is no prevailing opinion within the appropriate specialty of the United States medical profession that the procedure proposed [by Moran] is safe and effective for its intended use and that the omission of the procedure would adversely affect [her] medical condition."[ ] Petitioner did agree to cover the standard treatment for Moran's ailment,[ ] concluding that peer-reviewed literature "demonstrates that [the standard surgery] is effective therapy in the treatment of [Moran's condition]."[ ]

Moran, however, was not satisfied with this option. * * * She invoked § 4–10 of the Illinois HMO Act, which requires HMOs to provide a mechanism for review by an independent physician when the patient's primary care physician and HMO disagree about the medical necessity of a treatment proposed by the primary care physician. * * *

Dr. A. Lee Dellon, an unaffiliated physician who served as the independent medical reviewer, concluded that the surgery for which petitioner denied coverage "was appropriate," that it was "the same type of surgery" he would have done, and that Moran "had all of the indications and therefore the medical necessity to carry out" the nonstandard surgery. * * * Under § 4–10, Dr. Dellon's determination conclusively established Moran's right to benefits under Illinois law.

* * *

Section 514(a)'s broad language provides that ERISA "shall supersede any and all State laws insofar as they . . . relate to any employee benefit plan," except as provided in § 514(b). 29 U.S.C. § 1144(a). This language demonstrates "Congress's intent to establish the regulation of employee welfare benefit plans 'as exclusively a federal concern.' "[ ] It was intended to "ensure that plans and plan sponsors would be subject to a uniform body of benefits law" so as to "minimize the administrative and financial burden of complying with conflicting directives among States or between States and the Federal Government" and to prevent "the potential for conflict in substantive law . . . requiring the tailoring of plans and employer conduct to the peculiarities of the law of each jurisdiction."[ ]

* * * [T]he Court until today had consistently held that state laws that seek to supplant or add to the exclusive remedies in § 502(a) of ERISA, 29 U.S.C. § 1132(a), are pre–empted because they conflict with Congress' objective that rights under ERISA plans are to be enforced under a uniform national system.[ ] The Court has explained that § 502(a) creates an "interlocking, interrelated, and interdependent remedial scheme," and that a beneficiary who claims that he was wrongfully denied benefits has "a panoply of remedial devices" at his disposal. * * *

* * *

Section 4–10 cannot be characterized as anything other than an alternative state–law remedy or vehicle for seeking benefits. In the first place, § 4–10 comes into play only if the HMO and the claimant dispute the claimant's entitlement to benefits; the purpose of the review is to determine whether a claimant is entitled to benefits. * * *

There is no question that arbitration constitutes an alternative remedy to litigation.[ ] Consequently, although a contractual agreement to arbitrate—which does not constitute a "State law" relating to "any employee benefit plan"—is outside § 514(a) of ERISA's pre–emptive scope, States may not circumvent ERISA preemption by mandating an alternative arbitral–like remedy as a plan term enforceable through an ERISA action.

To be sure, the majority is correct that § 4–10 does not mirror all procedural and evidentiary aspects of "common arbitration."[ ] But as a binding decision on the merits of the controversy the § 4–10 review resembles nothing so closely as arbitration. * * *

* * *

[I]t is troubling that the Court views the review under § 4–10 as nothing more than a practice "of obtaining a second [medical] opinion." * * * [W]hile a second medical opinion is nothing more than that—an opinion—a determination under § 4–10 is a conclusive determination with respect to the award of benefits. * * *

Section 4–10 constitutes an arbitral–like state remedy through which plan members may seek to resolve conclusively a disputed right to benefits. Some 40 other States have similar laws, though these vary as to applicability, procedures, standards, deadlines, and consequences of independent review. * * *

For the reasons noted by the Court, independent review provisions may sound very appealing. Efforts to expand the variety of remedies available to aggrieved beneficiaries beyond those set forth in ERISA are obviously designed to increase the chances that patients will be able to receive treatments they desire, and most of us are naturally sympathetic to those suffering from illness who seek further options. Nevertheless, the Court would do well to remember that no employer is required to provide any health benefit plan under ERISA and that the entire advent of managed care, and the genesis of HMOs, stemmed from spiraling health costs. To the extent that independent review provisions such as § 4–10 make it more likely that HMOs will have to subsidize beneficiaries' treatments of choice, they undermine the ability of HMOs to control costs, which, in turn, undermines the ability of employers to provide health care coverage for employees.

As a consequence, independent review provisions could create a disincentive to the formation of employee health benefit plans, a problem that Congress addressed by making ERISA's remedial scheme exclusive and uniform. While it may well be the case that the advantages of allowing States to implement independent review requirements as a supplement to the remedies currently provided under ERISA outweigh this drawback, this is a judgment that, pursuant to ERISA, must be made by Congress. I respectfully dissent.

NOTES AND QUESTIONS

1. ERISA only governs employee benefit plans, i.e. benefit plans established and maintained by employers to provide benefits to their employees. It does not reach health insurance purchased by individuals as individuals (including self–employed individuals) or health benefits not provided through employment–related group plans, such as uninsured motorist insurance policies or workers' compensation. Certain church and government–sponsored plans are also not covered. See Macro v. Independent Health Ass'n, Inc., 180 F. Supp.2d 427 (W.D.N.Y.2001). Finally, ERISA does not regulate group insurance offered by insurers to the employees of particular businesses without employer contributions or administrative involvement. See 29 C.F.R. § 2510.3–1(j); Taggart Corp. v. Life & Health Benefits Admin., Inc., 617 F.2d 1208 (5th Cir.1980), cert. denied, 450 U.S. 1030, 101 S.Ct. 1739, 68 L.Ed.2d 225 (1981). Despite these exceptions, ERISA govern the vast majority of private health insurance in America, which is provided through employment–related group plans.

2. Part of the confusion inherent in ERISA preemption decisions is attributable to the fact that there are three distinct forms of ERISA preemption. One of these is express preemption based on § 514(a) (29 U.S.C. § 1144(a)). Section 514(a), reproduced above, provides that ERISA "supersedes" any state law that "relates to" an employee benefits plan. Express

514(a) preemption, however, is subject to the "savings" clause, § 514(b)(2)(A), and thus does not reach state insurance regulation.

Just because a law is saved from 514(a) preemption, however, does not mean that it is not preempted, as the controversy in *Rush* illustrates. ERISA preemption can also be based on § 502(a) of ERISA (29 U.S.C. § 1132(a)) which provides for federal court jurisdiction over specified types of claims against ERISA plans. The Supreme Court has long held that ERISA plans may remove into federal court claims that were brought in state courts but that could have been brought under § 502(a) in federal court. Removal is permitted under the "complete preemption" exception to the well–pleaded complaint rule. The well–pleaded complaint rule normally limits removal of cases from state into federal court on the basis of federal question jurisdiction (under 28 U.S.C.A. § 1331) to cases in which federal claims are explicitly raised in the plaintiff's complaint. However, under the "complete preemption" exception to this rule (sometimes called "superpreemption"), federal jurisdiction is permitted when Congress has so completely preempted an area of law that any claim within it is brought under federal law, and thus is removable to federal court. "Complete preemption" is, in reality, not a preemption doctrine, but rather a rule of federal jurisdiction.

Third, Section 502(a) also plays another role in ERISA jurisprudence, ousting state claims and remedies that would take the place of § 502 claims. The federal courts have interpreted § 502 to indicate a Congressional intent to preempt comprehensively the "field" of judicial oversight of employee benefits plans. Thus state tort, contract, and even statutory claims that could have been brought as claims for benefits or for breach of fiduciary duty under § 502(a) have been held to be preempted by § 502(a). As *Moran* demonstrates, § 502(a) preemption, like § 514(a) explicit preemption, is not comprehensive. In particular, ERISA does not necessarily preempt state court malpractice cases brought against managed care plans that provide as well as pay for health care, as we will see in subsection D. Also claims brought by persons who are not proper plaintiffs under § 502(a) or against persons who are not ERISA fiduciaries are not preempted by ERISA § 502(a) preemption. *Moran* also holds that external review procedures imposed by the states prior to the onset of litigation also may be exempt from § 502 preemption.

Section 502(a) and § 514(a) preemption are not, however, coextensive. Just because a lawsuit invokes a law that might be preempted as relating to an employee benefits claim does not mean that the claim could be brought under § 502(a), and is thus subject to "complete preemption." Not infrequently federal courts remand cases that are not § 502(a) claims to state court for resolution of § 514(a) preemption issues. As we see below in *Aetna Health Insurance v. Davila*, moreover, laws that are saved from preemption by an exception to § 514(a), may still be preempted as inconsistent with § 502(a) field preemption.

3. Early cases interpreting § 514(a) read it very broadly. The Supreme Court's first consideration of § 514(a), Shaw v. Delta Air Lines, Inc., 463 U.S. 85, 103 S.Ct. 2890, 77 L.Ed.2d 490 (1983), adopted a very literal and liberal

reading of "relates to" as including any provisions having a "connection with or reference to" a benefits plan. The Court rejected narrower readings of ERISA preemption that would have limited its reach to state laws that explicitly attempted to regulate ERISA plans or that dealt with subjects explicitly addressed by ERISA. For over a decade following *Shaw*, the Court applied the § 514(a) tests developed in *Shaw* expansively in a variety of contexts, almost always finding preemption when it found an ERISA plan to exist. The Court repeatedly expressed allegiance to the opinion that ERISA § 514(a) preemption had a "broad scope," Metropolitan Life v. Massachusetts, 471 U.S. 724, 739, 105 S.Ct. 2380, 85 L.Ed.2d 728 (1985), and "an expansive sweep," Pilot Life Ins. Co. v. Dedeaux, 481 U.S. 41, 47, 107 S.Ct. 1549, 95 L.Ed.2d 39 (1987), and that it was "conspicuous for its breadth," FMC Corp. v. Holliday, 498 U.S. 52, 58, 111 S.Ct. 403, 112 L.Ed.2d 356 (1990).

Attending to these Supreme Court pronouncements, lower courts in the 1980s and 1990s held a wide range of state regulatory programs and common law claims that arguably "related to" the administration of an ERISA plan or imposed costs upon plans to be preempted. As the *Fiedler* case discussed below demonstrates, the "connection with or reference to" test continues to sweep broadly. The Supreme Court finally recognized the limits of ERISA preemption, however, in New York State Conference of Blue Cross and Blue Shield Plans v. Travelers Ins. Co., 514 U.S. 645, 115 S.Ct. 1671, 131 L.Ed.2d 695 (1995). *Travelers* held that a New York law that required hospitals to charge different rates to insured, HMO, and self–insured plans was not preempted by § 514(a). Retreating from earlier expansive readings of ERISA preemption, the Court reaffirmed the principle applied in other areas of the law that Congress is generally presumed not to intend to preempt state law. 514 U.S. at 654. The Court proceeded to note that in cases involving traditional areas of state regulation, such as health care, congressional intent to preempt state law should not be presumed unless it was "clear and manifest." Id. at 655. Recognizing that the term "relate to" was not self–limiting, the Court turned for assistance in defining the term to the purpose of ERISA, which it defined as freeing benefit plans from conflicting state and local regulation. Id. at 656–57. Preemption was intended, the Court held, to affect state laws that operated directly on the structure or administration of ERISA plans, id. at 657–58, not laws that only indirectly raised the cost of various benefit options, id. at 658–64. Accordingly, the Court held that the challenged rate–setting law was not "related to" an ERISA plan, and thus not preempted.

The Court's post–*Travelers* preemption cases suggest that the Court in fact turned a corner in *Travelers*. It has rejected ERISA 514 preemption in a number of cases, though it had almost never done so before *Travelers*. Post–*Travelers* lower court cases on the whole continued to apply ERISA preemption broadly, generally finding that state programs aimed at regulating insurance and managed care "relate to" an ERISA plan. Some, however, have limited ERISA preemption. See, for example, Louisiana Health Service & Indemnity Co. v. Rapides Healthcare System, 461 F.3d 529 (5th Cir.2006), holding that a Louisiana statute that required insurance companies to honor all assignments of benefits by patients to hospitals did not have an impermissible connection with ERISA. See, reviewing comprehensively federal and state court cases applying ERISA to managed care regulation, Robert F. Rich, Christopher T. Erb, and Louis J. Gale, Judicial Interpretation of Managed Care Policy, 13 Elder L.J. 85 (2005).

4. As *Moran* notes, a state law that is otherwise preempted under § 514(a) is saved from preemption if it regulates insurance under the "savings clause" found in § 514(b)(2)(A) (29 U.S.C.A. § 1144(b)(2)(A)). In its early cases interpreting this clause, the Court read the savings clause conservatively, applying both a "common sense" test as well as the three part test developed in antitrust cases applying the McCarran–Ferguson Act for determining whether a law regulated "the business of insurance" to determine whether the savings clause applied. Metropolitan Life Ins. Co. v. Massachusetts, 471 U.S. 724, 740–44, 105 S.Ct. 2380, 85 L.Ed.2d 728 (1985), Pilot Life Ins. Co. v. Dedeaux, 481 U.S. 41, 107 S.Ct. 1549, 95 L.Ed.2d 39 (1987).

In Kentucky Association of Health Plans, Inc. v. Miller, 538 U.S. 329, 123 S.Ct. 1471, 155 L.Ed.2d 468 (2003) the court abandoned its earlier precedents and crafted a new approach to interpreting the savings clause. This case involved the claim of an association of managed care plans that Kentucky's "any willing provider" law was preempted by ERISA. The Sixth Circuit had held that the regulatory provision was saved from preemption under ERISA's savings clause. In a brief and unanimous opinion written by Justice Scalia (who had dissented in *Moran*), the Court held that the law was saved from preemption, abandoning its previous savings clause jurisprudence. The Court acknowledged that use of the McCarran–Ferguson test had "misdirected attention, failed to provide clear guidance to lower federal courts, and * * * added little to relevant analysis." The Court also admitted that the McCarran–Ferguson tests had been developed for different purposes and interpreted different statutory language.

The Court concluded:

> Today we make a clean break from the McCarran–Ferguson factors and hold that for a state law to be deemed a 'law . . . which regulates insurance' under § 1144(b)(2)(A), it must satisfy two requirements. First, the state law must be specifically directed toward entities engaged in insurance.[ ] Second, * * * the state law must substantially affect the risk pooling arrangement between the insurer and the insured. Kentucky's law satisfies each of these requirements. 123 S.Ct. at 1479.

Earlier in the opinion it had interpreted the "risk pooling" requirement as follows:

> We have never held that state laws must alter or control the actual terms of insurance policies to be deemed 'laws . . . which regulat[e] insurance' under § 1144(b)(2)(A); it suffices that they substantially

> affect the risk pooling arrangement between insurer and insured. By expanding the number of providers from whom an insured may receive health services, AWP laws alter the scope of permissible bargains between insurers and insureds * * *. No longer may Kentucky insureds seek insurance from a closed network of health–care providers in exchange for a lower premium. The AWP prohibition substantially affects the type of risk pooling arrangements that insurers may offer. 123 S.Ct. at 1477–78.

Kentucky Association significantly clarifies, and expands, the coverage of ERISA's savings clause. Virtually any state law that requires insurers to provide particular benefits would seem to be covered. See Matthew O. Gatewood, The New Map: The Supreme Court's New Guide to Curing Thirty Years of Confusion in ERISA Savings Clause Analysis, 62 Wash. & Lee U. L. Rev. 643 (2005). What effect is this green light to state regulation of managed care and health insurance likely to have on the willingness of employers to offer health insurance plans to their workers, or to offer insured rather than self–insured plans? Might Justice Thomas' prediction on this matter prove true? See Haavi Morreim, ERISA Takes a Drubbing: Rush Prudential and Its Implications for Health Care, 38 Tort Trial and Ins. Practice J. 933 (2003). Does the adoption of the ACA change the calculus, as it addresses many of the regulatory issues formerly addressed by state law?

5. As *Moran* acknowledges, even a statute saved from § 514(a) preemption by the savings clause may nevertheless, under *Pilot Life*, be preempted by § 502(a) if it provides a state remedy that takes the place of § 502(a). Aetna Health Inc. v. Davila, 542 U.S. 200, 124 S.Ct. 2488, 159 L.Ed.2d 312 (2004), reproduced below, applied this exception, holding that the Texas Health Care Liability Act, which allowed lawsuits against managed care companies for failing to exercise ordinary care in making coverage decisions, was preempted. Section 502 preemption is not limited to tort cases, however, it also extends to state statutes that provide private actions for civil penalties to the extent that these cases could have been brought under § 502. See, for example, Prudential Insurance Co. v. National Park Medical Center, Inc., 413 F.3d 897 (8th Cir.2005), holding that the provisions of the Arkansas Patient Protection Act allowing private suits for injunctive relief, damages of at least $1,000, and attorney's fees were preempted by ERISA § 502 to the extent that the lawsuits could have been brought under § 502. Thus an action to recover payment denied by a plan for the services of a provider who should have been qualified for payment under a state's "any willing provider" law would be preempted. In Hawaii Management Alliance Assoc. v. Insurance Comm'r, 100 P.3d 952 (Hawai'i 2004), the Hawaiian Supreme Court held that Hawaii's external review statute was preempted by ERISA because it provided a remedy alternative to § 502.

6. ERISA's § 514(b)(2)(A) savings clause is subject to its own exception, the § 514(b)(2)(B) "deemer" clause. This subsection, reproduced above, provides that "neither an employee benefit * * * nor any trust established under such a plan, shall be deemed to be an insurance company or other insurer,

* * * or to be engaged in the business of insurance * * * for purposes of any law of any State purporting to regulate insurance companies, [or] insurance contracts, * * *." 29 U.S.C.A. § 1144(b)(2)(B). In FMC Corporation v. Holliday, 498 U.S. 52, 111 S.Ct. 403, 112 L.Ed.2d 356 (1990), the Supreme Court interpreted this clause broadly to exempt self–funded ERISA plans entirely from state regulation and state law claims.

The deemer clause offers a significant incentive for employers to become self–insured, as a self–insured plan can totally escape state regulation, and in particular, benefit mandates. Self–insurance, however, also has disadvantages—it imposes upon the employer the burden of administering the plan as well as open–ended liability for employee benefit claims made under the plan. To mitigate these problems, self–insured employers often contract with third–party administrators to administer claims and with stop–loss insurers to limit their claims exposure. The courts have overwhelmingly held that employer plans remain self–insured even though they are reinsured through stop–loss plans, and have prohibited states from attempting to impose requirements on self–insured plans through regulation of stop–loss coverage. See, e.g., Bill Gray Enterprises, Inc. Employee Health and Welfare Plan v. Gourley, 248 F.3d 206 (3rd Cir.2001) and Lincoln Mutual Casualty v. Lectron Products, Inc. 970 F.2d 206 (6th Cir.1992). Third–party administrators that administer self–insured plans are also protected from state insurance regulation. NGS American, Inc. v. Barnes, 805 F.Supp. 462, 473 (W.D.Texas 1992). Thus an employer who is willing to bear some risk can escape state regulation under the "deemer" clause, even though most of the risk of insuring the plan is borne by a stop–loss insurer and the burden of administering the plan is assumed by a third–party administrator.

States may, however, regulate stop–loss coverage itself as a form of insurance. Some states ban stop loss coverage for small group plans, while others prohibit stop–loss policies that cover losses below a certain level. See, e.g. N.Y. Ins. Law § 3231(h); 4317(a). See also Edstom Indus. v. Companion Life Ins. 516 U.S. 546, 551 (7th Cir. 2008).

The calculus that an employer faces in deciding whether or not to self–insure changes under the ACA. A number of the ACA requirements that apply to small group plans—including the essential benefits package and single risk pool requirements, the risk adjustment program, the medical loss ratio and unreasonable premium increase justification requirement—do not apply to self–insured plans. It is likely, therefore, that a significant number of small employers that currently cover their employees through insured plans will switch to self–insured plans. Under the proposed regulations governing the SHOP exchanges, however, a self–insured small employer may shift to exchange coverage at any time. This creates a serious potential adverse selection problem because healthy small groups can be self–insured, but then move to the exchange with a community rate if a member incurs high health care expenses. See, Timothy Stoltzfus Jost, Loopholes in the Affordable Care Act: Regulatory Gaps and Border Crossing Techniques and How to Address Them, 5 St. Louis J. Health L. & Pol'y 27 (2011).

7. One issue that arose occasionally in pre–*Moran* savings clause litigation is whether health maintenance organizations are in the business of insurance and thus subject to state regulation. Early cases tended to say no, often on very formalistic grounds, see, e.g., O'Reilly v. Ceuleers, 912 F.2d 1383 (11th Cir.1990). *Moran* seems to have settled this issue once and for all. The defendant, Rush, argued that an HMO was a health care provider rather than an insurer, and thus regulations affecting it would not be protected by the savings clause. The Court responded:

> The answer to Rush is, of course, that an HMO is both: it provides health care, and it does so as an insurer. Nothing in the saving clause requires an either–or choice between health care and insurance in deciding a preemption question, and as long as providing insurance fairly accounts for the application of state law, the saving clause may apply. * * *
>
> The defining feature of an HMO is receipt of a fixed fee for each patient enrolled under the terms of a contract to provide specified health care if needed. *Pegram v. Herdrich,*[ ]. "The HMO thus assumes the financial risk of providing the benefits promised: if a participant never gets sick, the HMO keeps the money regardless, and if a participant becomes expensively ill, the HMO is responsible for the treatment. . . . " *Id.,* * * *. 536 U.S. at 367.

8. Among the most litigated ERISA issues in the past decade has been the effect ERISA has on the rights of health plans to recover amounts they paid for health care when a beneficiary subsequently recovers a tort judgment for the injuries that necessitated the care. These cases are either brought by a plan trying to recover from the beneficiary or by a beneficiary trying to block recovery by the plan or to get money back that a plan has already obtained by exercising its rights of subrogation. Some cases involve state statutes limiting a plan's right of subrogation. The Supreme Court has decided thru recent cases involving the rights of plans to recover benefits under ERISA, U.S. Airways v. McCutchen, ___ S.Ct. ___ (2013), Sereboff v. Mid Atlantic Medical Services, Inc., 547 U.S. 356, 126 S.Ct. 1869, 164 L.Ed.2d 612 (2006) and Great–West Life & Annuity Ins. Co. v. Knudson, 534 U.S. 204, 122 S.Ct. 708, 151 L.Ed.2d 635 (2002). These decisions interpret provisions of ERISA authorizing equitable relief and turn on arcane interpretations of the historical distinction between law and equity. They are beyond the scope of this chapter.

NOTE: ERISA PREEMPTION AND THE AFFORDABLE CARE ACT

The ACA does not explicitly change ERISA's preemption provisions. Inevitably, however, it will change the nature of ERISA plan regulation in two important respects.

First, the ACA applies a whole new group of federal requirements to group health insurance plans through amendments to the Public Health Services Act and through section 1563, which adopts a new section 715 to ERISA and section 9815 to the Internal Revenue Code that apply most of the new ACA insurance regulation requirements to ERISA plans, including self–insured plans. As already noted, not all of the protections of the law apply to self–insured plans, however, and neither large group nor self–insured group plans have to provide the essential benefits. Also, the exchanges will, at least initially, not cover large group plans, so large group plans will not be required to meet the QHP requirements. But most of the ACA insurance reforms will apply to all non–grandfathered ERISA plans, and some of these requirements, such as the provisions relating to rescissions, dependent coverage, pre–existing condition exclusions, excessive waiting periods, uniform benefits, and coverage disclosure, medical loss ratios, and lifetime and annual limits will even apply to grandfathered ERISA plans. ERISA has until now imposed only minimal requirements on employment–related plans. That will change dramatically with this legislation. Federal regulation will look much more like state regulation.

Second, because of this, some of the issues that have caused conflict with respect to state regulation of insured ERISA plans will probably be less salient under the ACA. The ACA has its own preemption provision, mentioned at the outset of this chapter: "Nothing in this title shall be construed to preempt any State law that does not prevent the application of the provisions of this title." Section 1321(d). The implication, of course, is that where the ACA and state law are incompatible, the ACA will govern. Thus, section 2712 prohibiting rescissions except in cases of intentional misrepresentation will apply to group health plans even though state law would otherwise have permitted rescission for unintentional misrepresentations.

But the ACA also applies state law to group plans. As noted above, for example, Section 2719, which requires plans to offer external review of coverage and claims denials, generally requires insured group health plans to comply with state external review requirements, which in turn must at a minimum comply with the NAIC External Review Model Act, as described above. The precise issue raised by *Rush Prudential*, that is, would not come up today, as the ACA would determine whether or not a state external review law applied to a group health plan. Where the ACA does not address a particular issue, however, the preemption rules of ERISA section 514 still apply. Moreover, the ACA does nothing to change the jurisdictional or remedial preemption rules of ERISA section 502. See, Mallory Jensen, Is ERISA Preemption Superfluous in the New Age of Health Care Reform, 2011 Colum. Bus.L. Rev. 464 (2011).

B. ERISA PREEMPTION OF STATE TORT LITIGATION

Courts have struggled to determine the nature and extent of ERISA preemption in medical negligence cases. Managed care plans as defendants are subject to the same theories of liability as hospitals—vicarious liability, corporate negligence, ordinary negligence. Vicarious liability against managed care organizations has been allowed by most courts that have considered the question. See Chapter 6, Part V, above. The Supreme Court, however, has severely limited the reach of state tort actions against ERISA–qualified health plans.

AETNA HEALTH INC. V. DAVILA

Supreme Court of the United States, 2004.
542 U.S. 200, 124 S.Ct. 2488, 159 L.Ed.2d 312.

JUSTICE THOMAS delivered the opinion of the Court.

In these consolidated cases, two individuals sued their respective health maintenance organizations (HMOs) for alleged failures to exercise ordinary care in the handling of coverage decisions, in violation of a duty imposed by the Texas Health Care Liability Act (THCLA)[ ]. We granted certiorari to decide whether the individuals' causes of action are completely pre–empted by the "interlocking, interrelated, and interdependent remedial scheme,"[ ] found at § 502(a) of the Employee Retirement Income Security Act of 1974 (ERISA)[ ]. We hold that the causes of action are completely pre–empted and hence removable from state to federal court. The Court of Appeals, having reached a contrary conclusion, is reversed.

Respondent Juan Davila is a participant, and respondent Ruby Calad is a beneficiary, in ERISA–regulated employee benefit plans. Their respective plan sponsors had entered into agreements with petitioners, Aetna Health Inc. and CIGNA HealthCare of Texas, Inc., to administer the plans. Under Davila's plan, for instance, Aetna reviews requests for coverage and pays providers, such as doctors, hospitals, and nursing homes, which perform covered services for members; under Calad's plan sponsor's agreement, CIGNA is responsible for plan benefits and coverage decisions.

Respondents both suffered injuries allegedly arising from Aetna's and CIGNA's decisions not to provide coverage for certain treatment and services recommended by respondents' treating physicians. Davila's treating physician prescribed Vioxx to remedy Davila's arthritis pain, but Aetna refused to pay for it. Davila did not appeal or contest this decision, nor did he purchase Vioxx with his own resources and seek reimbursement. Instead, Davila began taking Naprosyn, from which he allegedly suffered a severe reaction that required extensive treatment and hospitalization. Calad underwent surgery, and although her treating physician recommended an extended hospital stay, a CIGNA discharge nurse determined that Calad did not meet the plan's criteria for a continued hospital stay. CIGNA consequently denied coverage for the extended hospital stay. Calad experienced postsurgery complications forcing her to return to the hospital. She alleges that these complications would not have occurred had CIGNA approved coverage for a longer hospital stay.

Respondents brought separate suits in Texas state court against petitioners. Invoking THCLA § 88.002(a), respondents argued that petitioners' refusal to cover the requested services violated their "duty to exercise ordinary care when making health care treatment decisions," and that these refusals "proximately caused" their injuries. Ibid. Petitioners removed the cases to Federal District Courts, arguing that respondents' causes of action fit within the scope of, and were therefore completely pre–empted by, ERISA § 502(a). The respective District Courts agreed, and declined to remand the cases to state court. Because respondents refused to amend their complaints to bring explicit ERISA claims, the District Courts dismissed the complaints with prejudice.

Both Davila and Calad appealed the refusals to remand to state court. The United States Court of Appeals for the Fifth Circuit consolidated their cases with several others raising similar issues. The Court of Appeals recognized that state causes of action that "duplicat[e] or fal[l] within the scope of an ERISA § 502(a) remedy" are completely pre–empted and hence removable to federal court.[ ]. After examining the causes of action available under § 502(a), the Court of Appeals determined that respondents' claims could possibly fall under only two: § 502(a)(1)(B), which provides a cause of action for the recovery of wrongfully denied benefits, and § 502(a)(2), which allows suit against a plan fiduciary for breaches of fiduciary duty to the plan.

Analyzing § 502(a)(2) first, the Court of Appeals concluded that, under *Pegram v. Herdrich*,[ ], the decisions for which petitioners were being sued were "mixed eligibility and treatment decisions" and hence were not fiduciary in nature.[4] The Court of Appeals next determined that respondents' claims did not fall within § 502(a)(1)(B)'s scope. It found significant that respondents "assert tort claims," while § 502(a)(1)(B) "creates a cause of action for breach of contract,"[ ], and also that respondents "are not seeking reimbursement for benefits denied them," but rather request "tort damages" arising from "an external, statutorily imposed duty of 'ordinary care,' "[ ]. From *Rush Prudential HMO, Inc. v. Moran*,[ ], the Court of Appeals derived the principle that complete pre–emption is limited to situations in which "States . . . duplicate the causes of action listed in ERISA § 502(a)," and concluded that "[b]ecause the THCLA does not provide an action for collecting benefits," it fell outside the scope of § 502(a)(1)(B). 307 F.3d, at 310–311.

Under the removal statute, "any civil action brought in a State court of which the district courts of the United States have original jurisdiction, may be removed by the defendant" to federal court.[ ] One category of cases of which district courts have original jurisdiction is "[f]ederal question"

[4] In this Court, petitioners do not claim or argue that respondents' causes of action fall under ERISA § 502(a)(2). Because petitioners do not argue this point, and since we can resolve these cases entirely by reference to ERISA § 502(a)(1)(B), we do not address ERISA § 502(a)(2).

cases: cases "arising under the Constitution, laws, or treaties of the United States." § 1331. We face in these cases the issue whether respondents' causes of action arise under federal law.

Ordinarily, determining whether a particular case arises under federal law turns on the " 'well–pleaded complaint' " rule.[ ] The Court has explained that

> "whether a case is one arising under the Constitution or a law or treaty of the United States, in the sense of the jurisdictional statute[,] . . . must be determined from what necessarily appears in the plaintiff's statement of his own claim in the bill or declaration, unaided by anything alleged in anticipation of avoidance of defenses which it is thought the defendant may interpose."[ ].

In particular, the existence of a federal defense normally does not create statutory "arising under" jurisdiction,[ ], and "a defendant may not [generally] remove a case to federal court unless the *plaintiff's* complaint establishes that the case 'arises under' federal law,"[ ]. There is an exception, however, to the well–pleaded complaint rule. "[W]hen a federal statute wholly displaces the state–law cause of action through complete pre–emption," the state claim can be removed.[ ] This is so because "[w]hen the federal statute completely pre–empts the state–law cause of action, a claim which comes within the scope of that cause of action, even if pleaded in terms of state law, is in reality based on federal law."[ ] ERISA is one of these statutes.

Congress enacted ERISA to "protect . . . the interests of participants in employee benefit plans and their beneficiaries" by setting out substantive regulatory requirements for employee benefit plans and to "provid[e] for appropriate remedies, sanctions, and ready access to the Federal courts."[ ]. The purpose of ERISA is to provide a uniform regulatory regime over employee benefit plans. To this end, ERISA includes expansive pre–emption provisions, see ERISA § 514,[ ], which are intended to ensure that employee benefit plan regulation would be "exclusively a federal concern."[ ]

ERISA's "comprehensive legislative scheme" includes "an integrated system of procedures for enforcement."[ ] This integrated enforcement mechanism, ERISA § 502(a),[ ] is a distinctive feature of ERISA, and essential to accomplish Congress' purpose of creating a comprehensive statute for the regulation of employee benefit plans. As the Court said in *Pilot Life Ins. Co. v. Dedeaux,*[ ]:

> "[T]he detailed provisions of § 502(a) set forth a comprehensive civil enforcement scheme that represents a careful balancing of the need for prompt and fair claims settlement procedures against the public interest in encouraging the formation of employee benefit plans. The policy choices reflected in the inclusion

> of certain remedies and the exclusion of others under the federal scheme would be completely undermined if ERISA–plan participants and beneficiaries were free to obtain remedies under state law that Congress rejected in ERISA. 'The six carefully integrated civil enforcement provisions found in § 502(a) of the statute as finally enacted . . . provide strong evidence that Congress did *not* intend to authorize other remedies that it simply forgot to incorporate expressly.' "[ ]

Therefore, any state–law cause of action that duplicates, supplements, or supplants the ERISA civil enforcement remedy conflicts with the clear congressional intent to make the ERISA remedy exclusive and is therefore pre–empted.[ ]

The pre–emptive force of ERISA § 502(a) is still stronger. In *Metropolitan Life Ins. Co. v. Taylor,*[ ] the Court determined that the similarity of the language used in the Labor Management Relations Act, 1947 (LMRA), and ERISA, combined with the "clear intention" of Congress "to make § 502(a)(1)(B) suits brought by participants or beneficiaries federal questions for the purposes of federal court jurisdiction in like manner as § 301 of the LMRA," established that ERISA § 502(a)(1)(B)'s pre–emptive force mirrored the pre–emptive force of LMRA § 301. Since LMRA § 301 converts state causes of action into federal ones for purposes of determining the propriety of removal,[ ] so too does ERISA § 502(a)(1)(B). Thus, the ERISA civil enforcement mechanism is one of those provisions with such "extraordinary pre–emptive power" that it "converts an ordinary state common law complaint into one stating a federal claim for purposes of the well–pleaded complaint rule."[ ] Hence, "causes of action within the scope of the civil enforcement provisions of § 502(a) [are] removable to federal court."[ ]

ERISA § 502(a)(1)(B) provides:

> "A civil action may be brought—(1) by a participant or beneficiary—. . . (B) to recover benefits due to him under the terms of his plan, to enforce his rights under the terms of the plan, or to clarify his rights to future benefits under the terms of the plan."[ ]

This provision is relatively straightforward. If a participant or beneficiary believes that benefits promised to him under the terms of the plan are not provided, he can bring suit seeking provision of those benefits. A participant or beneficiary can also bring suit generically to "enforce his rights" under the plan, or to clarify any of his rights to future benefits. Any dispute over the precise terms of the plan is resolved by a court under a *de novo* review standard, unless the terms of the plan "giv[e] the administrator or fiduciary discretionary authority to determine eligibility for benefits or to construe the terms of the plan."[ ]

It follows that if an individual brings suit complaining of a denial of coverage for medical care, where the individual is entitled to such coverage only because of the terms of an ERISA–regulated employee benefit plan, and where no legal duty (state or federal) independent of ERISA or the plan terms is violated, then the suit falls "within the scope of" ERISA § 502(a)(1)(B)[ ]. In other words, if an individual, at some point in time, could have brought his claim under ERISA § 502(a)(1)(B), and where there is no other independent legal duty that is implicated by a defendant's actions, then the individual's cause of action is completely pre–empted by ERISA § 502(a)(1)(B).

To determine whether respondents' causes of action fall "within the scope" of ERISA § 502(a)(1)(B), we must examine respondents' complaints, the statute on which their claims are based (the THCLA), and the various plan documents. Davila alleges that Aetna provides health coverage under his employer's health benefits plan.[ ]. Davila also alleges that after his primary care physician prescribed Vioxx, Aetna refused to pay for it.[ ]. The only action complained of was Aetna's refusal to approve payment for Davila's Vioxx prescription. Further, the only relationship Aetna had with Davila was its partial administration of Davila's employer's benefit plan.[ ].

Similarly, Calad alleges that she receives, as her husband's beneficiary under an ERISA–regulated benefit plan, health coverage from CIGNA.[ ]. She alleges that she was informed by CIGNA, upon admittance into a hospital for major surgery, that she would be authorized to stay for only one day.[ ] She also alleges that CIGNA, acting through a discharge nurse, refused to authorize more than a single day despite the advice and recommendation of her treating physician.[ ] Calad contests only CIGNA's decision to refuse coverage for her hospital stay.[ ] And, as in Davila's case, the only connection between Calad and CIGNA is CIGNA's administration of portions of Calad's ERISA–regulated benefit plan.[ ].

It is clear, then, that respondents complain only about denials of coverage promised under the terms of ERISA–regulated employee benefit plans. Upon the denial of benefits, respondents could have paid for the treatment themselves and then sought reimbursement through a § 502(a)(1)(B) action, or sought a preliminary injunction,[ ].

Respondents contend, however, that the complained–of actions violate legal duties that arise independently of ERISA or the terms of the employee benefit plans at issue in these cases. Both respondents brought suit specifically under the THCLA, alleging that petitioners "controlled, influenced, participated in and made decisions which affected the quality of the diagnosis, care, and treatment provided" in a manner that violated "the duty of ordinary care set forth in §§ 88.001 and 88.002."[ ] Respondents contend that this duty of ordinary care is an independent legal duty.

They analogize to this Court's decisions interpreting LMRA § 301,[ ] with particular focus on *Caterpillar Inc. v. Williams,* (suit for breach of individual employment contract, even if defendant's action also constituted a breach of an entirely separate collective–bargaining agreement, not pre–empted by LMRA § 301). Because this duty of ordinary care arises independently of any duty imposed by ERISA or the plan terms, the argument goes, any civil action to enforce this duty is not within the scope of the ERISA civil enforcement mechanism.

The duties imposed by the THCLA in the context of these cases, however, do not arise independently of ERISA or the plan terms. The THCLA does impose a duty on managed care entities to "exercise ordinary care when making health care treatment decisions," and makes them liable for damages proximately caused by failures to abide by that duty.[ ] However, if a managed care entity correctly concluded that, under the terms of the relevant plan, a particular treatment was not covered, the managed care entity's denial of coverage would not be a proximate cause of any injuries arising from the denial. Rather, the failure of the plan itself to cover the requested treatment would be the proximate cause.[3] More significantly, the THCLA clearly states that "[t]he standards in Subsections (a) and (b) create no obligation on the part of the health insurance carrier, health maintenance organization, or other managed care entity to provide to an insured or enrollee treatment which is not covered by the health care plan of the entity."[ ] Hence, a managed care entity could not be subject to liability under the THCLA if it denied coverage for any treatment not covered by the health care plan that it was administering.

Thus, interpretation of the terms of respondents' benefit plans forms an essential part of their THCLA claim, and THCLA liability would exist here only because of petitioners' administration of ERISA–regulated benefit plans. Petitioners' potential liability under the THCLA in these cases, then, derives entirely from the particular rights and obligations established by the benefit plans. So, unlike the state–law claims in *Caterpillar, supra,* respondents' THCLA causes of action are not entirely independent of the federally regulated contract itself.[ ].

Hence, respondents bring suit only to rectify a wrongful denial of benefits promised under ERISA–regulated plans, and do not attempt to remedy any violation of a legal duty independent of ERISA. We hold that respondents' state causes of action fall "within the scope of" ERISA § 502(a)(1)(B),[ ] and are therefore completely pre–empted by ERISA § 502 and removable to federal district court.[4]

---

[3] To take a clear example, if the terms of the health care plan specifically exclude from coverage the cost of an appendectomy, then any injuries caused by the refusal to cover the appendectomy are properly attributed to the terms of the plan itself, not the managed care entity that applied those terms.

[4] Respondents also argue that ERISA § 502(a) completely pre-empts a state cause of action only if the cause of action would be pre-empted under ERISA § 514(a); respondents then argue

The Court of Appeals came to a contrary conclusion for several reasons, all of them erroneous. First, the Court of Appeals found significant that respondents "assert a tort claim for tort damages" rather than "a contract claim for contract damages," and that respondents "are not seeking reimbursement for benefits denied them."[ ] But, distinguishing between pre–empted and non–pre–empted claims based on the particular label affixed to them would "elevate form over substance and allow parties to evade" the pre–emptive scope of ERISA simply "by relabeling their contract claims as claims for tortious breach of contract." * * *[ ]. Nor can the mere fact that the state cause of action attempts to authorize remedies beyond those authorized by ERISA § 502(a) put the cause of action outside the scope of the ERISA civil enforcement mechanism. In *Pilot Life, Metropolitan Life,* and *Ingersoll–Rand,* the plaintiffs all brought state claims that were labeled either tort or tort–like.[ ] And, the plaintiffs in these three cases all sought remedies beyond those authorized under ERISA.[ ] And, in all these cases, the plaintiffs' claims were pre–empted. The limited remedies available under ERISA are an inherent part of the "careful balancing" between ensuring fair and prompt enforcement of rights under a plan and the encouragement of the creation of such plans. [ ].

Second, the Court of Appeals believed that "the wording of [respondents'] plans is immaterial" to their claims, as "they invoke an external, statutorily imposed duty of 'ordinary care.' "[ ] But as we have already discussed, the wording of the plans is certainly material to their state causes of action, and the duty of "ordinary care" that the THCLA creates is not external to their rights under their respective plans.

Ultimately, the Court of Appeals rested its decision on one line from *Rush Prudential.* * * * Nowhere in *Rush Prudential* did we suggest that the pre–emptive force of ERISA § 502(a) is limited to the situation in which a state cause of action precisely duplicates a cause of action under ERISA § 502(a).

Nor would it be consistent with our precedent to conclude that only strictly duplicative state causes of action are pre–empted. Frequently, in order to receive exemplary damages on a state claim, a plaintiff must prove facts beyond the bare minimum necessary to establish entitlement to an award.[ ]. In order to recover for mental anguish, for instance, the plaintiffs in *Ingersoll–Rand* and *Metropolitan Life* would presumably have had to prove the existence of mental anguish; there is no such element in an ordinary suit brought under ERISA § 502(a)(1)(B).[ ] This did not save these state causes of action from pre–emption. Congress' intent

that their causes of action do not fall under the terms of § 514(a). But a state cause of action that provides an alternative remedy to those provided by the ERISA civil enforcement mechanism conflicts with Congress' clear intent to make the ERISA mechanism exclusive.[ ].

to make the ERISA civil enforcement mechanism exclusive would be undermined if state causes of action that supplement the ERISA § 502(a) remedies were permitted, even if the elements of the state cause of action did not precisely duplicate the elements of an ERISA claim.

Respondents also argue—for the first time in their brief to this Court—that the THCLA is a law that regulates insurance, and hence that ERISA § 514(b)(2)(A) saves their causes of action from pre–emption (and thereby from complete pre–emption).[5] This argument is unavailing. The existence of a comprehensive remedial scheme can demonstrate an "overpowering federal policy" that determines the interpretation of a statutory provision designed to save state law from being pre–empted.[ ] ERISA's civil enforcement provision is one such example.[ ]

As this Court stated in *Pilot Life,* "our understanding of [§ 514(b)(2)(A)] must be informed by the legislative intent concerning the civil enforcement provisions provided by ERISA § 502(a).[ ]" The Court concluded that "[t]he policy choices reflected in the inclusion of certain remedies and the exclusion of others under the federal scheme would be completely undermined if ERISA–plan participants and beneficiaries were free to obtain remedies under state law that Congress rejected in ERISA."[ ] The Court then held, based on

> "the common–sense understanding of the saving clause, the McCarran–Ferguson Act factors defining the business of insurance, and, *most importantly,* the clear expression of congressional intent that ERISA's civil enforcement scheme be exclusive, . . . that [the plaintiff's] state law suit asserting improper processing of a claim for benefits under an ERISA–regulated plan is not saved by § 514(b)(2)(A)."[ ]

Pilot Life's reasoning applies here with full force. Allowing respondents to proceed with their state–law suits would "pose an obstacle to the purposes and objectives of Congress."[ ] As this Court has recognized in both *Rush Prudential* and *Pilot Life,* ERISA § 514(b)(2)(A) must be interpreted in light of the congressional intent to create an exclusive federal remedy in ERISA § 502(a). Under ordinary principles of conflict pre–emption, then, even a state law that can arguably be characterized as "regulating insurance" will be pre–empted if it provides a separate vehicle to assert a claim for benefits outside of, or in addition to, ERISA's remedial scheme.

Respondents, their *amici,* and some Courts of Appeals have relied heavily upon *Pegram v. Herdrich,*[ ], in arguing that ERISA does not pre–empt or completely pre–empt state suits such as respondents'. They con-

---

[5] ERISA § 514(b)(2)(A)[ ] reads, as relevant: "["[N]othing in this subchapter shall be construed to exempt or relieve any person from any law of any State which regulates insurance, banking, or securities."."

tend that *Pegram* makes it clear that causes of action such as respondents' do not "relate to [an] employee benefit plan," ERISA § 514(a),[ ] and hence are not pre–empted.[ ]

Pegram cannot be read so broadly. In *Pegram,* the plaintiff sued her physician–owned–and–operated HMO (which provided medical coverage through plaintiff's employer pursuant to an ERISA–regulated benefit plan) and her treating physician, both for medical malpractice and for a breach of an ERISA fiduciary duty.[ ] The plaintiff's treating physician was also the person charged with administering plaintiff's benefits; it was she who decided whether certain treatments were covered.[ ] We reasoned that the physician's "eligibility decision and the treatment decision were inextricably mixed."[ ] We concluded that "Congress did not intend [the defendant HMO] or any other HMO to be treated as a fiduciary to the extent that it makes mixed eligibility decisions acting through its physicians."[ ]

A benefit determination under ERISA, though, is generally a fiduciary act.[ ] "At common law, fiduciary duties characteristically attach to decisions about managing assets and distributing property to beneficiaries."[ ] Hence, a benefit determination is part and parcel of the ordinary fiduciary responsibilities connected to the administration of a plan.[ ] The fact that a benefits determination is infused with medical judgments does not alter this result.

Pegram itself recognized this principle. *Pegram,* in highlighting its conclusion that "mixed eligibility decisions" were not fiduciary in nature, contrasted the operation of "[t]raditional trustees administer[ing] a medical trust" and "physicians through whom HMOs act."[ ] A traditional medical trust is administered by "paying out money to buy medical care, whereas physicians making mixed eligibility decisions consume the money as well."[ ] And, significantly, the Court stated that "[p]rivate trustees do not make treatment judgments."[ ] But a trustee managing a medical trust undoubtedly must make administrative decisions that require the exercise of medical judgment. Petitioners are not the employers of respondents' treating physicians and are therefore in a somewhat analogous position to that of a trustee for a traditional medical trust.

ERISA itself and its implementing regulations confirm this interpretation. ERISA defines a fiduciary as any person "to the extent . . . he has any discretionary authority or discretionary responsibility in the administration of [an employee benefit] plan.[ ]. When administering employee benefit plans, HMOs must make discretionary decisions regarding eligibility for plan benefits, and, in this regard, must be treated as plan fiduciaries.[ ]" Also, ERISA § 503, which specifies minimum requirements for a plan's claim procedure, requires plans to "afford a reasonable opportunity to any participant whose claim for benefits has been denied for a full and fair review by the appropriate named fiduciary of the decision denying the claim."[ ] This strongly suggests that the ultimate decisionmaker in a plan regarding an award of benefits must be a fiduciary and must be acting as a fiduciary when determining a participant's or beneficiary's claim. The relevant regulations also establish extensive requirements to ensure full and fair review of benefit denials.[ ] These regulations, on their face, apply equally to health benefit plans and other plans, and do not draw distinctions between medical and nonmedical benefits determinations. Indeed, the regulations strongly imply that benefits determinations involving medical judgments are, just as much as any other benefits determinations, actions by plan fiduciaries.[ ] Classifying any entity with discretionary authority over benefits determinations as anything but a plan fiduciary would thus conflict with ERISA's statutory and regulatory scheme.

Since administrators making benefits determinations, even determinations based extensively on medical judgments, are ordinarily acting as plan fiduciaries, it was essential to *Pegram*'s conclusion that the decisions challenged there were truly "mixed eligibility and treatment decisions,"[ ], i.e., medical necessity decisions made by the plaintiff's treating physician *qua* treating physician and *qua* benefits administrator. Put another way, the reasoning of *Pegram* "only make[s] sense where the underlying negligence also plausibly constitutes medical maltreatment by a party who can be deemed to be a treating physician or such a physician's employer."[ ] Here, however, petitioners are neither respondents' treating physicians nor the employers of respondents' treating physicians. Petitioners' coverage decisions, then, are pure eligibility decisions, and *Pegram* is not implicated.

We hold that respondents' causes of action, brought to remedy only the denial of benefits under ERISA–regulated benefit plans, fall within the scope of, and are completely pre–empted by, ERISA § 502(a)(1)(B), and thus removable to federal district court. The judgment of the Court of Appeals is reversed, and the cases are remanded for further proceedings consistent with this opinion.[7]

It is so ordered.

NOTES AND QUESTIONS

1. What state law claims are left to plaintiff employee benefit plan subscribers after *Davila*? In general, *Davila* leaves a "regulatory vacuum" in

[7] The United States, as *amicus,* suggests that some individuals in respondents' positions could possibly receive some form of "make-whole" " relief under ERISA § 502(a)(3).[ ] However, after their respective District Courts denied their motions for remand, respondents had the opportunity to amend their complaints to bring expressly a claim under ERISA § 502(a). Respondents declined to do so; the District Courts therefore dismissed their complaints with prejudice.[ ] Respondents have thus chosen not to pursue any ERISA claim, including any claim arising under ERISA § 502(a)(3). The scope of this provision, then, is not before us, and we do not address it.

which consumer have no remedies if they are injured as the result of health care provided through ERISA plans. It would seem to allow tort actions for direct or vicarious liability only for physician–owned and operated managed care plans. And these are not the norm. The typical health plan today is an insurance vehicle that imposes coverage constraints on providers in its network, and would not be subject to tort liability. *Davila* does state that ERISA plan administrators are fiduciaries as to coverage decisions. But it does not explicitly recognize a cause of action for damages for breach of fiduciary duty, which earlier cases would seem to have foreclosed.

See, on ERISA preemption of managed care liability after *Davila*, Timothy S. Jost, The Supreme Court Limits Lawsuits Against Managed Care Organizations, Health Affairs Web Exclusive 4–417 (11 August 2004). See also Theodore W. Ruger, The Supreme Court Federalizes Managed Care Liability, 32 J.L. Med. & Ethics 528, 529 (2004) (criticizing the current ERISA enforcement scheme as crabbed and penurious, failing to serve remedial goals of either tort or contract.) For a full discussion of litigation leading up to *Davila*, see generally Margaret Cyr–Provost, Aetna v. Davila: From Patient–Centered Care to Plan–Centered Care, A Signpost or the End of the Road? 6 Hous. J. Health L. & Pol'y 171 (2005); M.Gregg Bloche and David Studdert, A Quiet Revolution: Law as an Agent of Health System Change, 23 Health Affairs 2942 (2004). See also Peter Jacobson, Strangers in the Night (New York: Oxford, 2002).

2. Tort cases against managed care plans are not entirely dead after *Davila,* however. Consider Smelik v. Mann, Texas Dist. Ct. (224th Jud. Dist., Bexar Co. No. 03–CI–06936 2006), where a Texas jury awarded $7.4 million in actual damages to the family of an HMO participant who died from complications of acute renal failure. The jury found Humana liable for 35 percent of the $7.4 million in actual damages for negligence, but found no evidence that Humana committed fraud. The jury also determined that Humana's behavior was consistent with gross negligence, and the company stipulated to $1.6 million in punitive damages pursuant to an out–of–court agreement. Humana was found to be responsible for a total of $4.2 million.

The plaintiff in *Smelik* argued that Humana was liable for "mismanaged managed care," or negligence in the coordination of medical care, rather than for a denial of medical care, as in *Davila*, and thus ERISA did not apply. Plaintiffs convinced the jury that Humana failed to follow its own utilization management policies, failing to refer Smelik to a kidney specialist or to its disease management program. Plaintiffs also established that Humana negligently approved payment for a combination of drugs considered dangerous for patients with kidney problems.

Vicarious liability also remains a viable theory post *Davila.* In Badal v. Hinsdale Memorial Hospital, 2007 WL 1424205 (N.D.Ill.2007), plaintiff's injured ankle was misdiagnosed by a plan physician as only a "sprain," causing serious injury. The court analyzed ERISA preemption arguments in light of *Davila*. The court noted that the plaintiff's claims under *Davila* were brought under THCLA, the Texas Health Care Liability Act, and asserted duties that did not arise independently of ERISA or the plan terms. *Davila* was about wrongful denial of benefits. In *Badal,* by contrast, the plaintiff alleged that "[w]hile committing the above acts and omissions, Dr. Lofthouse failed to apply, use or exercise the standard of care ordinarily exercised by reasonably well qualified or competent medical doctors." The court noted that the plaintiff was not complaining of the wrongful denial of benefits, quoting the plaintiff: "Plaintiff is asking for damages for the injuries caused, and does not give one iota if it was covered under the plan, or whether it should in the future be covered under some plan[ ]. In short, whether or not it was a violation of ERISA is of no concern to plaintiff."

It may also be possible to sue insurance brokers and agents for negligent misrepresentation or insurers for simple clerical errors where the misrepresentation or error results in loss of coverage. In McMurtry v. Wiseman, 445 F. Supp.2d 756 (2006), the U.S. District Court for the Western District of Kentucky held that negligent misrepresentations by an insurance broker that induced the plaintiff to buy disability insurance coverage were not ERISA preempted. The plaintiff claimed that agent Botts' duty was independent of any duty related to ERISA, and that he, like any insurance agent, had a duty not to negligently misrepresent the terms of the policy and/or fraudulently induce the Plaintiff to purchase the coverage. The court quoted with approval the language of Morstein v. National Ins. Services, Inc., 93 F.3d 715, 723 (11th Cir.1996), "[a]llowing preemption of a fraud claim against an individual insurance agent will not serve Congress's purpose for ERISA. As we have discussed, Congress enacted ERISA to protect the interests of employees and other beneficiaries of employee benefit plans. To immunize insurance agents from personal liability for fraudulent misrepresentation regarding ERISA plans would not promote this objective." The court held that the plaintiff's claims for "fraud and negligent misrepresentation did not arise directly from the plan, but rather from Botts' inducement to have the Plaintiff join the plan. The legal duty not to misrepresent the plan did not arise from the plan itself, but from an independent source of law; state tort law within Tennessee."

In Duchesne–Baker v. Extendicare Health Services, Inc., 2004 WL 2414070 (E.D. La. Oct. 28, 2004), the district court concluded that, while Aetna was a defendant in both this action and in *Davila,* and each case was removed to federal court, there was no other similarity between these two cases. The court noted that *Davila* fell within the scope of ERISA Section 502(a)(1)(B) because an essential part of the plaintiffs' state law claim in *Davila* required an examination and interpretation of the relevant plan documents. By contrast, the allegation in *Duchesne–Baker* was that the insurance coverage was wrongly terminated due to a clerical error and Aetna failed to exercise due care to correct this error. Thus, the court concluded that, because the allegation did not involve improper processing of a benefit claim and did not otherwise seek enforcement of the plaintiff's rights under the plan or to clarify future right under the plan, the claim in *Duchesne–*

Baker was distinguishable from *Davila* and, therefore, required remand back to the state court.

3. ERISA was interpreted by the federal courts in the first wave of litigation as totally preempting common law tort claims. See, e.g., Ricci v. Gooberman, 840 F.Supp. 316 (D.N.J.1993). It appeared from this caselaw that any managed care plan that was ERISA–qualified would receive virtually complete tort immunity.

In the 1990s, however, the federal courts began to split as to the limits of such preemption. The result was a litigation explosion against managed care as theories were imported from hospital liability case law, fiduciary law, and contract law to use against managed care organizations. See, e.g., Prihoda v. Shpritz, 914 F.Supp. 113 (D.Md.1996) (ERISA does not preempt an action against physicians and an HMO for physicians' failure to diagnose a cancerous tumor, allowing a vicarious liability action to proceed). See also Independence HMO, Inc. v. Smith, 733 F.Supp. 983 (E.D.Pa.1990) (ERISA does not preempt medical malpractice–type claims brought against HMOs under a vicarious liability theory); Elsesser v. Hospital of the Philadelphia College of Osteopathic Medicine, 802 F.Supp. 1286 (E.D.Pa.1992) (ERISA does not preeempt a claim against an HMO for the HMO's negligence in selecting, retaining, and evaluating plaintiff's primary–care physician); Kearney v. U.S. Healthcare, Inc., 859 F.Supp. 182 (E.D.Pa.1994) (ERISA preempts plaintiff's direct negligence claim, but not vicarious liability claim). See generally Barry Furrow, Managed Care Organizations and Patient Injury: Rethinking Liability, 31 Ga. L. Rev. 419 (1997).

Dukes v. U.S. Healthcare, Inc., 57 F.3d 350 (3d Cir.1995) was the watershed case that opened up a major crack in ERISA preemption of common law tort claims. In *Dukes*, the Third Circuit found that Congress intended in passing ERISA to insure that promised benefits would be available to plan participants, and that section 502 was "intended to provide each individual participant with a remedy in the event that promises made by the plan were not kept." The court was unwilling, however, to stretch the remedies of 502 to "control the quality of the benefits received by plan participants." The court concluded that " * * * [q]uality control of benefits, such as the health care benefits provided here, is a field traditionally occupied by state regulation and we interpret the silence of Congress as reflecting an intent that it remain such." The court developed the distinction between a right to benefits under a plan and a right to good quality care, holding that " * * * patients enjoy the right to be free from medical malpractice regardless of whether or not their medical care is provided through an ERISA plan." Quality of care could be so poor that it is essentially a denial of benefits. Or the plan could describe a benefit in terms that are quality–based, such as a commitment that all x–rays will be analyzed by radiologists with a certain level of training. But absent either of these extremes, poor medical care—malpractice—is not a benefits issue under ERISA.

Theories of liability based on the organizational structure of health plans were used by most courts to determine what is preempted and what is allowed under ERISA. While some meaningful functional distinctions can be made on this basis, the courts have not been consistent, and liability was often variable, depending on the court's attitude toward managed care. See Peter J. Hammer, Pegram v. Herdrich: On Peritonitis, Preemption, and the Elusive Goal of Managed Care Accountability, 26 J. Health Pol. Pol'y & L. 767, 768 n.2 (2001). The federal courts were often hostile to managed care plans, and struggled mightily to work around ERISA preemption and allow a common law tort action to go forward.

For an excellent overview of the interaction of ERISA preemption and MCO malpractice liability, see generally Gail B. Agrawal and Mark A. Hall, What If You Could Sue Your HMO? Managed Care Liability Beyond the ERISA Shield, 47 St. Louis U. L.J. 235 (2003). See also Wendy K. Mariner, Slouching Toward Managed Care Liability: Reflections on Doctrinal Boundaries, Paradigm Shifts, and Incremental Reform, 29 J.L. Med. & Ethics 253 (2001) (favoring enhanced liability); David Orentlicher, The Rise and Fall of Managed Care: A Predictable "Tragic Choices" Phenomenon, 47 St. Louis U. L.J. 411 (2003) (analyzing managed care as a device for concealing and avoiding tragic choices in a public forum).

4. The Affordable Care Act does not address the issue of health plan negligence liability. It does not, therefore, change ERISA preemption law with respect to health plan negligence.

NOTES AND QUESTIONS ON ERISA FIDUCIARY DUTY CLAIMS

1. The Supreme Court in *Davila* discusses at some length its earlier decision in Pegram v. Herdrich, 530 U.S. 211 (2000). In *Pegram*, an ERISA plan beneficiary, Louise Herdrich, sued the HMO administering her husband's employee benefit plans, claiming (among other theories) breach of fiduciary duty under ERISA when she suffered an undiagnosed ruptured appendix that caused peritonitis. She alleged:

> " * * * that provision of medical services under the terms of the Carle HMO organization, rewarding its physician owners for limiting medical care, entailed an inherent or anticipatory breach of an ERISA fiduciary duty, since these terms created an incentive to make decisions in the physicians' self–interest, rather than the exclusive interests of plan participants."

She claimed:

> " * * * that provision of medical services under the terms of the Carle HMO organization, rewarding its physician owners for limiting medical care, entailed an inherent or anticipatory breach of an ERISA fiduciary duty, since these terms created an incentive to make decisions in the physicians' self–interest, rather than the exclusive interests of plan participants."

The court noted that:

> Although it is true that the relationship between sparing medical treatment and physician reward is not a subtle one under the Carle scheme, no HMO organization could survive without some incentive connecting physician reward with treatment rationing. The essence of an HMO is that salaries and profits are limited by the HMO's fixed membership fees.[ ] This is not to suggest that the Carle provisions are as socially desirable as some other HMO organizational schemes; they may not be.[ ] But whatever the HMO, there must be rationing and inducement to ration.

The Court observed, however, that Congress had not intended to outlaw HMOs when it enacted ERISA (federal legislation encouraging HMOs had been adopted three years earlier), and that the Court was not in a position to distinguish between good and bad HMOs.

The Court stated:

> [ERISA] provides that fiduciaries shall discharge their duties with respect to a plan "solely in the interest of the participants and beneficiaries," § 1104(a)(1), that is, "for the exclusive purpose of (i) providing benefits to participants and their beneficiaries; and (ii) defraying reasonable expenses of administering the plan," § 1104(a)(1)(A).

The Court further compared ERISA fiduciary obligations to fiduciary obligations at the common law, but then observed:

> Beyond the threshold statement of responsibility, however, the analogy between ERISA fiduciary and common law trustee becomes problematic. This is so because the trustee at common law characteristically wears only his fiduciary hat when he takes action to affect a beneficiary, whereas the trustee under ERISA may wear different hats.
>
> * * * Under ERISA, however, a fiduciary may have financial interests adverse to beneficiaries. Employers, for example, can be ERISA fiduciaries and still take actions to the disadvantage of employee beneficiaries, when they act as employers (e.g., firing a beneficiary for reasons unrelated to the ERISA plan), or even as plan sponsors (e.g., modifying the terms of a plan as allowed by ERISA to provide less generous benefits). * * *
>
> ERISA does require, however, that the fiduciary with two hats wear only one at a time, and wear the fiduciary hat when making fiduciary decisions. * * * In every case charging breach of ERISA fiduciary duty, then, the threshold question is not whether the actions of some person employed to provide services under a plan adversely affected a plan beneficiary's interest, but whether that person was acting as a fiduciary (that is, was performing a fiduciary function) when taking the action subject to complaint.

The Court proceeded to say:

> The nub of the claim, then, is that when State Farm contracted with Carle, Carle became a fiduciary under the plan, acting through its physicians. At once, Carle as fiduciary administrator was subject to such influence from the year–end payout provision that its fiduciary capacity was necessarily compromised, and its readiness to act amounted to anticipatory breach of fiduciary obligation.
>
> The pleadings must also be parsed very carefully to understand what acts by physician owners acting on Carle's behalf are alleged to be fiduciary in nature. It will help to keep two sorts of arguably administrative acts in mind. Cf. Dukes v. U.S. Healthcare, Inc., 57 F.3d 350, 361 (C.A.3 1995) (discussing dual medical/administrative roles of HMOs). What we will call pure "eligibility decisions" turn on the plan's coverage of a particular condition or medical procedure for its treatment. "Treatment decisions," by contrast, are choices about how to go about diagnosing and treating a patient's condition: given a patient's constellation of symptoms, what is the appropriate medical response?
>
> These decisions are often practically inextricable from one another, as amici on both sides agree.[ ] This is so not merely because, under a scheme like Carle's, treatment and eligibility decisions are made by the same person, the treating physician. It is so because a great many and possibly most coverage questions are not simple yes–or–no questions, like whether appendicitis is a covered condition (when there is no dispute that a patient has appendicitis), or whether acupuncture is a covered procedure for pain relief (when the claim of pain is unchallenged). The more common coverage question is a when–and–how question. Although coverage for many conditions will be clear and various treatment options will be indisputably compensable, physicians still must decide what to do in particular cases. The issue may be, say, whether one treatment option is so superior to another under the circumstances, and needed so promptly, that a decision to proceed with it would meet the medical necessity requirement that conditions the HMO's obligation to provide or pay for that particular procedure at that time in that case. * * * In practical terms, these eligibility decisions cannot be untangled from physicians' judgments about reasonable medical treatment, and in the case before us, Dr. Pegram's decision was one of that sort. She decided (wrongly, as it turned out) that Herdrich's condition did not warrant immediate action; the consequence of that medical determination was that Carle would not cover immediate care, whereas it would have done so if Dr. Pegram had made the proper diagnosis and judgment to treat. The eligibility decision and the treatment decision were inextricably mixed, as they are in countless medical administrative decisions every day.

> The kinds of decisions mentioned in Herdrich's ERISA count and claimed to be fiduciary in character are just such mixed eligibility and treatment decisions: physicians' conclusions about when to use diagnostic tests; about seeking consultations and making referrals to physicians and facilities other than Carle's; about proper standards of care, the experimental character of a proposed course of treatment, the reasonableness of a certain treatment, and the emergency character of a medical condition.
>
> We do not read the ERISA count, however, as alleging fiduciary breach with reference to a different variety of administrative decisions, those we have called pure eligibility determinations, such as whether a plan covers an undisputed case of appendicitis. Nor do we read it as claiming breach by reference to discrete administrative decisions separate from medical judgments; say, rejecting a claim for no other reason than the HMO's financial condition. * * *
>
> Based on our understanding of the matters just discussed, we think Congress did not intend Carle or any other HMO to be treated as a fiduciary to the extent that it makes mixed eligibility decisions acting through its physicians. * * *

The Court held that such mixed decisions were not fiduciary decisions, but were rather questions of reasonable medical judgment. It suggested that poor decisions were better addressed by state malpractice law, and there was nothing to be gained by challenging them through ERISA fiduciary litigation. It is this language that the plaintiffs invoked in *Davila.*

Does *Davila* close the door to malpractice claims against HMOs potentially opened by *Pegram*? Does it reopen the door to fiduciary duty claims?

2. One of the underlying puzzles of *Pegram* is the question of remedy. The law was clear at the time *Pegram* was brought that breach of the fiduciary obligations imposed by ERISA could only result in recoveries for the benefit of the plan, not for individual participants. Ms. Herdrich herself did not stand to benefit individually from her lawsuit. Massachusetts Mut. Life Ins. Co. v. Russell, 473 U.S. 134, 105 S.Ct. 3085, 87 L.Ed.2d 96 (1985). In LaRue v. DeWolff, Boberg & Associates, Inc., 552 U.S. 248, 128 S.Ct. 1020, 169 L.Ed.2d 847 (2008), however, the Supreme Court held that a member of a defined contribution pension plan could sue under ERISA for individual relief for a breach of fiduciary duty affecting his individual account. If employee health benefits move from a defined benefit to a defined contribution model (for example, though increased use of health reimbursement accounts), claims for individual relief for breach of ERISA fiduciary duties might become more common.

3. In other contexts, cases continue to be brought claiming that ERISA plan administrators have breached their fiduciary obligations. Occasionally such cases succeed, or at least survive motions to dismiss or for summary

judgment. See, e.g., Bannistor v. Ullman, 287 F.3d 394 (5th Cir.2002) (suit against officers and parent corporation of bankrupt employer for failing to have forwarded employees' premiums to insurer prior to bankruptcy); Vescom Corp. v. American Heartland Health Admin., Inc., 251 F.Supp. 2d 950 (D.Me.2003) (suit by self–insured employer against reinsurer for breach of fiduciary obligations in management of funds). Most, however, fail, either because the court holds that the plan administrator has no fiduciary obligation under ERISA (see, e.g., Alves v. Harvard Pilgrim Health Care, Inc., 204 F.Supp.2d 198 (D.Mass.2002), aff'd, 316 F.3d 290 (1st Cir.2003) (no fiduciary breach for health plan to charge flat copayment amount in excess of cost of prescription drugs) or because a claim for equitable relief for breach of fiduciary duty under § 502(a)(3) is not available if a plan beneficiary can instead sue under § 502(a)(1). See, e.g., Lefler v. United Healthcare of Utah, 72 Fed. Appx. 818 (10th Cir.2003). See, on fiduciary duties under ERISA, Jillian Redding, ERISA: Remedies, Preemption, and the Need for More State Regulatory Oversight 18 Conn. Ins. L. J. 169 (2011–12).

4. Among other fiduciary obligations imposed on ERISA administrators is the duty to disclose information to ERISA plan beneficiaries. In a number of cases, beneficiaries have sued ERISA managed care organizations for failing to disclose information about the financial incentive structure of the plan. Plaintiffs in these cases have argued that the financial incentive structures of plans encourage physicians to deny care to beneficiaries, and that beneficiaries should be informed of these incentives.

One of the few cases that has been receptive to such claims is Shea v. Esensten, 107 F.3d 625 (8th Cir.1997). Mr. Shea's physician failed to give him a referral to a cardiologist in spite of warning signs of a cardiac condition. Mr. Shea's widow contended that, had her husband's ERISA benefits plan disclosed that his doctor could earn a bonus for providing less treatment, he would have sought out his own cardiologist. The Seventh Circuit found that a financial incentive system aimed at influencing a physician's referral patterns is "a material piece of information," Id. at 628, and that a subscriber has a right to know that his physician's judgment could be "colored" by such incentives. The court rested its conclusion on the obligation of an ERISA fiduciary to speak out if it "knows that silence might be harmful." The court held that information about a plan's financial incentives must be disclosed when the incentives might lead a treating physician to deny necessary referrals for conditions covered by the plan.

Most courts that have heard such claims, however, have rejected them, at least in the absence of facts suggesting that the lack of disclosure actually made a difference in a beneficiary's health or treatment options. In Horvath v. Keystone Health Plan East, Inc., 333 F.3d 450 (3d Cir.2003), for example, the Third Circuit affirmed a district court decision holding that the plaintiff "failed to create any issues of material fact with respect to her claim because (1) she failed to request the information Keystone offered to make available regarding its methods of physician compensation,[ ] (2) there was no set of circumstances pursuant to which Keystone should have known that such information was necessary to prevent Horvath from making a harmful decision regarding her healthcare coverage,[ ] and (3) she failed to explain how the information at issue was material in light of the fact that her employer offers no other options for healthcare coverage[ ].” 333 F.3d at 463. See also, Ehlmann v. Kaiser Found. Health Plan of Tex., 198 F.3d 552 (5th Cir.), cert. dismissed, 530 U.S. 1291, 121 S.Ct. 12, 147 L.Ed.2d 1036 (2000).

For excellent discussions of the general issue of disclosure of compensation arrangements, see Tracy E. Miller and William M. Sage, Disclosing Physician Financial Incentives, 281 JAMA 1424 (1999); William M. Sage, Physicians as Advocates, 35 Houston L.Rev. 1529 (1999); Kim Johnston, Patient Advocates or Patient Adversaries? Using Fiduciary Law to Compel Disclosure of Managed Care Financial Incentives, 35 San Diego L.Rev. 951 (1998); Bethany J. Spielman, Managed Care Regulation and the Physician–Advocate, 47 Drake L.Rev. 713 (1999).

5. The most important of ERISA disclosure obligations is the obligation to provide plan beneficiaries with a “summary plan description” that includes specific information about the rights and obligations of plan beneficiaries and which, “shall be written in a manner calculated to be understood by the average plan participant, and shall be sufficiently accurate and comprehensive to reasonably apprise such participants and beneficiaries of their rights and obligations under the plan.” 29 U.S.C. § 1022. The courts have reached varying positions on whether summary plan descriptions are binding or not and on whether plan participants must rely on the summary plan description for the plan to be bound by it. See Washington v. Murphy Oil USA, Inc., 497 F.3d 453, 458 n. 1 (5th Cir. 2007); Megan Rose Bosau, Defining the Parameters: When an ERISA Summary Plan Description Trumps the Corresponding Plan Document, 7 DePaul Bus. & Com. L.J. 521–553 (2009).

In Cigna Corp. v. Amara, 131 S.Ct. 1866 (2011), the Supreme Court held that the disclosures found in a summary plan description are not in fact enforceable against the plan under 29 U.S.C. § 1132(a)(1) in a suit for recovery under the “terms of the plan,” since the summary plan description does not include the terms of the plan. In a complex opinion written by Justice Breyer, however, the court held that a recovery might be possible under 29 U.S.C. § 1132(a)(3), which permits courts to enter “other appropriate equitable relief.” He suggested that equitable remedies like reformation, estoppel, or surcharge might be applicable. While injury would need to be shown for any remedy to be available, detrimental reliance is only necessary if estoppel is claimed. In sum, the Court indicated a willingness to interpret “appropriate equitable relief” more broadly than it has in past cases, and may have opened the door to more effective relief for injured plaintiffs in ERISA cases. See David Pratt, Summary Plan Descriptions After Amara, 45 J. Marshall L. Rev. 811 (2012).

An important question that arises under the ACA is the relationship between the summary plan description and the summary of benefits and coverage (SBC) required under ACA section 2715. The SBC requirement is independent of the SPD requirement. The SBC can be provided either as a stand–alone document or as part of the SPD, but if it is included in the SPD it must be intact in accordance with the prescribed format and prominently displayed at the beginning of the SPD.

6. Should ERISA plans be considered to be fiduciaries with respect to their beneficiaries, or should they rather be considered to be arms–length contractors? If plan administrators are considered to be fiduciaries, should fiduciary obligations only extend to management of trust funds, or should they also extend to provision of medical treatment? Should employment–related plans have obligations beyond those imposed on non–group insurance plans? Should employers have fiduciary obligations to their employees in the selection of health insurers, benefit plans, and benefits, and how should these obligations be reconciled with obligations to shareholders/owners?

C. BENEFICIARY REMEDIES PROVIDED BY ERISA

ERISA takes away, but ERISA has also given. ERISA obligates employee benefit plans to fulfill their commitments to their beneficiaries, and provides a federal cause of action under § 502 when they fail to do so. But the vision of health insurance that undergirds ERISA is very different from that which has traditionally undergirded state insurance regulation and, for that matter, the vision underlying the ACA.

State insurance regulation has generally been driven by a concern for access rights: e.g., the right of employees to have continued access to insurance coverage when they lose their jobs; the right of insureds to obtain mental health or mammography screening coverage; the right of chiropractors to have their services paid for by insurance; the right of "any willing provider" to participate in a PPO or pharmacy benefits plan; the right of small businesses to purchase insurance at affordable rates; the right of beneficiaries to ensure compliance with the insurance contract; and the right of beneficiaries to fair procedure. This body of state law looks to public utility regulation, and, more recently, civil rights laws, for its models. The ACA builds on this model. ,It requires insurers to offer insurance regardless of pre–existing conditions and require all insurers in the individual and small group market to cover "essential benefits" with limited out–of–pocket exposure and without annual or lifetime limits.

The categories of law that define ERISA, on the other hand, are trust law and classical contract law. ERISA does not compel employers to provide health insurance and prohibits the states from imposing such a requirement. If, however, employers choose voluntarily (or under collective bargaining agreements) to establish health benefit plans, any contributions made by employers (or employees) to such plans are held in trust for all of the participants (employee plan members) and beneficiaries (dependents and others covered under a participant's policy) of the plan and must be paid out according to the contract that defines its terms. If the plan fiduciary or administrator wrongfully withholds benefits, a participant or beneficiary is entitled to sue in federal or state court. Prior to the

ACA, if a fiduciary or administrator exercised properly delegated discretion to withhold benefits that were not expressly granted or denied by the plan, the court had to defer to the judgment of the administrator or fiduciary. When the fiduciary or administrator wrongfully withheld benefits, moreover, no matter how egregious its conduct in doing so, the court would merely order the plan to pay the beneficiary the amount due. ERISA does not, as interpreted by the Supreme Court, authorize tort relief or punitive damages.

While the limited rights that beneficiaries enjoyed under ERISA have troubled courts and commentators, they are consistent with ERISA's underlying theory. State insurance laws—be they the common law of *contra proferentem* or statutory mandates enacted by the legislature—focus on the absolute claim of a beneficiary whose life or health is in jeopardy to the assets held by the insurer: your money or my life. They also honor the political claims of providers who demand their turn at the insurance trough. The health insurance pot is, apparently, infinitely elastic and must be expanded to fulfill the demands of many claimants, each of whom, considered individually, makes a compelling case. Although the ACA is less driven by the concerns of providers, it too is based on the belief that all lawful residents of the United States should have access to health insurance coverage for essential medical care.

ERISA, by contrast, sees a zero sum game. The pot is only so big, and when it is empty, it is empty. To fudge the rules in favor of one beneficiary may result in the plan not being able to honor the legitimate claims of other beneficiaries. If one claimant who has been treated egregiously by the plan is permitted to recover extracontractual damages from its administrator, these damages will ultimately come out of the pockets of the other beneficiaries, who have themselves done nothing wrong. As long as health insurance coverage was dependent on the generosity of employers, employees had to make do with what employers were willing to offer. In a world of scarce resources, not everyone can be taken care of. But the administrator, nevertheless, is also a fiduciary, and there are some limits to its discretion.

Reconciling ERISA with the ACA in this respect will not be easy. As stated at the outset, the ACA amends ERISA and many of the ACA's requirements apply to ERISA plans. Employers are no longer completely unconstrained in their decision whether or not to provide employee benefits. The ACA does not require them to do so, but if employers fail to do so and their employees draw on the premium tax credits, the employer will owe a penalty. If an employer chooses to offer health benefits, it must comply with many ACA requirements, such as providing preventive care without cost–sharing (including contraceptives) or covering adult children up to age 26 (although many employer plans will remain grandfathered for some time and thus free from a number of these requirements). Most importantly, however, the ACA provides de novo, binding external review for ERISA plans. No longer will ERISA plan administrators have unbridled discretion to deny coverage. But what effect will this have in reality?

Section 502(a) of ERISA, reproduced above permits a plan participant or beneficiary to sue to "recover benefits due to him under the terms of the plan * * * " in federal or state court. 29 U.S.C.A. § 1132(a)(1). Although on its face this provision permits a suit against a plan for benefits denied, the courts have treated it historically as authorizing a review of the decision of the ERISA plan with respect to a benefit claim. That is, the ERISA administrator is treated as an independent decisionmaker whose decision is subject to judicial review, much like an administrative agency, rather than as a defendant who has allegedly breached a contract. See Semien v. Life Insurance Co. of North America, 436 F.3d 805, 814 (7th Cir. 2006); Jay Conison, Suits for Benefits Under ERISA, 54 U. Pitt. L. Rev. 1 (1992).

The Supreme Court's primary decision interpreting this provision, Firestone Tire & Rubber Co. v. Bruch, 489 U.S. 101, 109 S.Ct. 948, 103 L.Ed.2d 80 (1989), held that the courts should apply de novo review in reviewing ERISA plan decisions. The Court rejected the "arbitrary and capricious" standard of review generally applied in earlier lower federal court ERISA review cases. The Court went on to observe, however, that arbitrary and capricious review, rather than de novo review, would apply if "the benefit plan gives the administrator or fiduciary discretionary authority to determine eligibility for benefits or to construe the terms of the plan." 489 U.S. at 115, 109 S.Ct. at 957.

In doing so, the Court created an exception that swallowed the rule, since post–*Firestone* plans are almost always drafted to give plan administrators discretionary authority. Even where de novo review is available, moreover, some appellate courts have cabined it by limiting judicial review to consideration of the evidence considered by the plan administrator, Perry v. Simplicity Engineering, 900 F.2d 963 (6th Cir.1990); or by retaining deferential review for factual determinations of plan administrators and limiting de novo review to plan interpretations. Pierre v. Connecticut General Life Ins. Co., 932 F.2d 1552 (5th Cir.1991).

Although *Firestone* authorized arbitrary and capricious review where a plan fiduciary is granted decisionmaking discretion as the general exception to the de novo review rule, in true ERISA form, it also recognized an exception to the exception. It observed that if "an administrator or fiduciary * * * is operating under a conflict of interest, that conflict must be weighed as a 'facto[r] in determining whether there is an abuse of discretion.' " 489 U.S. at 114. The various circuits divided badly in their approaches to determining whether an administrator faces a conflict of interest in making the benefit determination, and what effect a conflict should have on the level of review if a conflict is found. Some courts permitted the plaintiff to demonstrate the presence of a conflict of interest in particular cases, then applying heightened review; others courts concluded that conflicts were not a serious problem; while yet other courts took conflicts of interest into account in determining whether a decision was arbitrary and capricious or not. See Kathryn J. Kennedy, Judicial Standard of Review in ERISA Benefit Claim Cases, 50 Am.U.L.Rev. 1083 (2001); Judith C. Brostron, The Conflict of Interest Standard in ERISA Cases: Can it be Avoided in the Denial of High Dose Chemotherapy Treatment for Breast Cancer?, 3 DePaul J. Health Care L. 1 (1999); Haavi Morreim, Benefits Decisions in ERISA Plans: Diminishing Deference to Fiduciaries and an Emerging Problem for Provider–Sponsored Organizations, 65 Tenn. L. Rev. 511 (1998).

The Supreme Court finally weighed in on the subject of conflicts of interest in Metropolitan Life Insurance Company v. Glenn, 554 U.S. 105, 128 S.Ct. 2343 (2008). The case recognized that conflicts of interest were present when an employer or insurer made a benefit decision:

> That answer is clear where it is the employer that both funds the plan and evaluates the claims. In such a circumstance, "every dollar provided in benefits is a dollar spent by . . . the employer; and every dollar saved . . . is a dollar in [the employer's] pocket."[ ] The employer's fiduciary interest may counsel in favor of granting a borderline claim while its immediate financial interest counsels to the contrary. Thus, the employer has an "interest . . . conflicting with that of the beneficiaries," the type of conflict that judges must take into account when they review the discretionary acts of a trustee of a common–law trust.[ ]
>
> * * *
>
> The answer to the conflict question is less clear where (as here) the plan administrator is not the employer itself but rather a professional insurance company. Such a company, MetLife would argue, likely has a much greater incentive than a self–insuring employer to provide accurate claims processing. That is because the insurance company typically charges a fee that attempts to account for the cost of claims payouts, with the result that paying an individual claim does not come to the same extent from the company's own pocket. It is also because the marketplace (and regulators) may well punish an insurance company when its products, or ingredients of its products, fall below par. And claims processing, an ingredient of the insurance company's product, falls below par when it seeks a biased result, rather than an accurate one. Why, MetLife might ask, should one consider an insurance company *inherently* more conflicted than any other market participant, say, a manufacturer who might earn

more money in the short run by producing a product with poor quality steel or a lawyer with an incentive to work more slowly than necessary, thereby accumulating more billable hours?

Conceding these differences, we nonetheless continue to believe that for ERISA purposes a conflict exists. For one thing, the employer's own conflict may extend to its selection of an insurance company to administer its plan. An employer choosing an administrator in effect buys insurance for others and consequently (when compared to the marketplace customer who buys for himself) may be more interested in an insurance company with low rates than in one with accurate claims processing.[ ]

For another, ERISA imposes higher–than–marketplace quality standards on insurers. It sets forth a special standard of care upon a plan administrator, namely, that the administrator "discharge [its] duties" in respect to discretionary claims processing "solely in the interests of the participants and beneficiaries" of the plan, *§ 1104(a)(1)*; it simultaneously underscores the particular importance of accurate claims processing by insisting that administrators "provide a 'full and fair review' of claim denials," [ ]; and it supplements marketplace and regulatory controls with judicial review of individual claim denials, see *§ 1132(a)(1)(B)*.

Finally, a legal rule that treats insurance company administrators and employers alike in respect to the *existence* of a conflict can nonetheless take account of the circumstances to which MetLife points so far as it treats those, or similar, circumstances as diminishing the *significance* or *severity* of the conflict in individual cases. [ ]

The Court turned then to the significance of a conflict of interest finding for judicial review:

We do not believe that *Firestone's* statement implies a change in the *standard* of review, say, from deferential to *de novo* review. Trust law continues to apply a deferential standard of review to the discretionary decisionmaking of a conflicted trustee, while at the same time requiring the reviewing judge to take account of the conflict when determining whether the trustee, substantively or procedurally, has abused his discretion. [ ] We see no reason to forsake *Firestone's* reliance upon trust law in this respect.

Nor would we overturn *Firestone* by adopting a rule that in practice could bring about near universal review by judges *de novo*—*i.e.*, without deference—of the lion's share of ERISA plan claims denials.[ ] Had Congress intended such a system of review, we believe it would not have left to the courts the development of review standards but would have said more on the subject.[ ] compare, *e.g.*, C. Gresenz et al., A Flood of Litigation? 8 (1999), [ ] (estimating that 1.9 million beneficiaries of ERISA plans have health care claims denied each year), with Caseload of Federal Courts Remains Steady Overall (Mar. 11, 2008),[ ] (257,507 total civil filings in federal court in 2007).[ ]

Neither do we believe it necessary or desirable for courts to create special burden–of–proof rules, or other special procedural or evidentiary rules, focused narrowly upon the evaluator/payor conflict. In principle, as we have said, conflicts are but one factor among many that a reviewing judge must take into account. Benefits decisions arise in too many contexts, concern too many circumstances, and can relate in too many different ways to conflicts—which themselves vary in kind and in degree of seriousness—for us to come up with a one–size–fits–all procedural system that is likely to promote fair and accurate review. Indeed, special procedural rules would create further complexity, adding time and expense to a process that may already be too costly for many of those who seek redress.

We believe that *Firestone* means what the word "factor" implies, namely, that when judges review the lawfulness of benefit denials, they will often take account of several different considerations of which a conflict of interest is one. This kind of review is no stranger to the judicial system. Not only trust law, but also administrative law, can ask judges to determine lawfulness by taking account of several different, often case–specific, factors, reaching a result by weighing all together.[ ]

In such instances, any one factor will act as a tiebreaker when the other factors are closely balanced, the degree of closeness necessary depending upon the tiebreaking factor's inherent or case–specific importance. The conflict of interest at issue here, for example, should prove more important (perhaps of great importance) where circumstances suggest a higher likelihood that it affected the benefits decision, including, but not limited to, cases where an insurance company administrator has a history of biased claims administration.[ ] It should prove less important (perhaps to the vanishing point) where the administrator has taken active steps to reduce potential bias and to promote accuracy, for example, by walling off claims administrators from those interested in firm finances, or by imposing management checks that penalize inaccurate decisionmaking irrespective of whom the inaccuracy benefits.[ ]

* * *

> Finally, we note that our elucidation of *Firestone's* standard does not consist of a detailed set of instructions. In this respect, we find pertinent this Court's comments made in a somewhat different context, the context of court review of agency fact finding. [ ] In explaining how a reviewing court should take account of the agency's reversal of its own examiner's factual findings, this Court did not lay down a detailed set of instructions. It simply held that the reviewing judge should take account of that circumstance as a factor in determining the ultimate adequacy of the record's support for the agency's own factual conclusion.[ ] In so holding, the Court noted that it had not enunciated a precise standard. [ ] But it warned against creating formulas that will "falsif[y] the actual process of judging" or serve as "instrument[s] of futile casuistry."[ ] The Court added that there "are no talismanic words that can avoid the process of judgment." [ ]. It concluded then, as we do now, that the "[w]ant of certainty" in judicial standards "partly reflects the intractability of any formula to furnish definiteness of content for all the impalpable factors involved in judicial review."[ ]

Metlife had an immediate and dramatic effect on the law. In the first four and a half years following the decision, it was cited in over 1450 cases, including cases from every circuit court of appeals except for the Federal circuit. It will continue to have an effect on ERISA disability and life benefit cases, which are more often litigated than health benefits cases because they involve much larger sums of money. But what effect will it have on health benefits cases?

As noted above, the ACA requires ERISA plans, like all other health plans, to offer binding, de novo, external review. The reviewer can consider new evidence not considered by the plan decisionmaker below, and need not defer to the plan administrator's decision. The decision of the external reviewer is, under ACA section 2719 binding on the plan, and under the external review interim regulations, "binding on the plan or issuer, as well as the claimant, except to the extent other remedies are available under State or Federal law." 29 C.F.R. § 2590.715–2719(c)(xi).

The ACA does not amend section 502 of ERISA, however, and judicial review of ERISA plan decisions will continue to be available. Pre–ACA ERISA cases involving external review decisions generally considered the decision of an external reviewer that confirmed a plan's determination to justify deference to the plan's original decision, as an external reviewer would clearly not face a conflict of interest. See Jon N. v. Blue Cross Blue Shield of Massachusetts, 684 F.Supp.2d 190 (D. Mass. 2010), Ransteck v. Aetna Life Ins. Co., 2009 WL 1796999 (E.D.N.Y. 2009); Smith v. Blue Cross Blue Shield of Massachusetts, 597 F.Supp.2d 214 (D. Mass. 2009). Other ERISA cases held that an external reviewer's rejection of a plan determination is additional evidence supporting a court's decision that the plan determination was arbitrary and capricious. Summers v. Touchpoint Health Plan, 749 N.W.2d 182 (2008). One court held, ingeniously, that the contractual possibility of external review justified de novo review by a court because the provision in the plan for external review negated the discretion of the plan administrator. Fry v. Regence Blueshield, 2008 WL 4223613 (W.D. Wash. 2008). Finally, one court has held that a claimant does not need to exhaust the external review remedy before filing a 502 action. Goldman v. BCBSM Foundation, 841 F.Supp.2d 1021 (E.D. Mich. 2012).

Whether the courts will actually treat external review decisions as binding; review the decision of the external reviewer under an administrative review, substantial evidence, arbitrary and capricious review standard; or review the underlying plan decision itself, treating the external review decision only as a factor that mitigates the possibility of a conflict of interest, remains to be seen. See, discussing external review under the ACA, David Goldin, External Review Process Options for Self–Funded Health Insurance Plans, 2011 Colum. Bus. L. Rev. 429 (2011); Roy F. Harmon, An Assessment of the New Appeals and External Review Processes—ERISA Claimants Get "Some Kind of Hearing," 56 S.D.L. Rev. 408 (2011).

NOTES AND QUESTIONS

1. ERISA requires health plans to provide an internal appeal procedure. 29 U.S.C.A. § 1133 (ERISA § 503). Rules implementing this statute are currently found at 29 C.F.R. § 2560.503–1. Under the ACA, these rules now apply to all health insurance plans. They are discussed above.

2. Some states have attempted to address the issue of deference to plan decisions by banning discretionary clauses in health plan contracts, thus leaving all of their decisions subject to judicial review. In 2002, the National Association of Insurance Commissioners drafted a model rule prohibiting the use of discretionary clauses in health insurance plans. More than a dozen states have adopted laws or regulations to implement this rule. These prohibitions have been challenged as preempted by ERISA. The Sixth and Ninth Circuit have held that these laws are saved from preemption as applied to insured plans. Standard Insurance v. Morrison, 584 F.3d. 837 (9th Cir. 2009); American Council of Life Insurers v. Ross, 558 F.3d 600 (6th Cir. 2009). The Tenth Circuit, however, held that Utah's rule prohibiting discretionary clauses was preempted. Hancock v. Metropolitan Life Ins. Co., 590 F.3d. 1141 (10th Cir. 2009). The Supreme Court has denied certiorari in the *Standard Insurance* case. The prohibitions do not, of course, affect self–insured plans. These statutes may be superfluous with binding de novo external review under the ACA. If, on the other hand, courts treat external review as merely one factor affecting an ERISA plan's conflict of interest, discretionary clause bans will continue to play a role in reducing the deference paid by the courts to the

underlying plan decision. See Maria O'Brien Hylton, Post–Firestone Skirmishes: The Patient Protection and Affordable Care Act, Discretionary Clauses and Judicial Review of ERISA Plan Administrator Decisions, 2 William & Mary Pol'y Rev. 1 (2010).

3. The Supreme Court's latest word on review of plan administrator decisions under ERISA is Conkright v. Frommert, 130 S.Ct. 1640 (2010), in which the Court held that in a situation where a plan administrator reaches an erroneous decision through an "honest mistake" decision, a reviewing court may not simply substitute its judgment for that of the administrator, but must rather defer to the administrator's subsequent attempt to reach a correct decision.

4. Whether or not extracontractual damages can ever be available under ERISA is a question that has provoked considerable controversy. The answer seems to be no, though a good argument can be made that this is not the result Congress intended. George Flint, ERISA: Extracontractual Damages Mandated for Benefit Claims Actions, 36 Ariz. L. Rev. 611 (1994); Note, Available Remedies Under ERISA Section 502(a), 45 Ala. L. Rev. 631 (1994). In Massachusetts Mutual Life Insurance Co. v. Russell, 473 U.S. 134, 105 S.Ct. 3085, 87 L.Ed.2d 96 (1985), the Supreme Court held that ERISA does not authorize recovery of extracontractual damages by plan participants for breach of fiduciary duty. In Mertens v. Hewitt Associates, 508 U.S. 248, 113 S.Ct. 2063, 124 L.Ed.2d 161 (1993), the Court read provisions of ERISA permitting plan participants and beneficiaries "to obtain other appropriate equitable relief to redress such violations 29 U.S.C.A. § 1132(a)(3), to not authorize damage actions, as damages are not equitable in nature.

The effect of these cases is that an ERISA participant or beneficiary denied benefits can only recover the value of the claim itself and cannot recover damages caused by the claim denial. Punitive damages are also unavailable against plan administrators and fiduciaries under even the most egregious circumstances. What effect might the lack of this relief have on ERISA fiduciaries and administrators? To what extent might the fact that ERISA permits courts to award attorneys' fees in some cases ameliorate this effect? 29 U.S.C.A. § 1132(g). Would state tort cases against ERISA plan managed care organizations be necessary if more comprehensive remedies were available under ERISA? See, arguing that many of the problems that the courts have encountered in dealing with state claims against ERISA plans could have been avoided had the Court interpreted ERISA's remedial provisions to include broader remedies, John H. Langbein, What ERISA Means by "Equitable": The Supreme Court's Trail of Error in Russell, Mertens and Great–West, 103 Colum. L. Rev. 1317 (2003).

Some members of the Court seem to be open to reconsidering this jurisprudence. In *Davila*, Justice Ginsberg, joined by Justice Breyer, suggested in concurrence that the Court should revisit the question:

> The Court today holds that the claims respondents asserted under Texas law are totally preempted by § 502(a) of [ ] ERISA [ ]. That

decision is consistent with our governing case law on ERISA's preemptive scope. I therefore join the Court's opinion. But, with greater enthusiasm, as indicated by my dissenting opinion in Great–West Life & Annuity Ins. Co. v. Knudson,[ ], I also join "the rising judicial chorus urging that Congress and [this] Court revisit what is an unjust and increasingly tangled ERISA regime." DiFelice v. Aetna U.S. Healthcare, 346 F.3d 442, 453 (C.A.3 2003) (Becker, J., concurring).

Because the Court has coupled an encompassing interpretation of ERISA's preemptive force with a cramped construction of the "equitable relief" allowable under § 502(a)(3), a "regulatory vacuum" exists: "[V]irtually all state law remedies are preempted but very few federal substitutes are provided."[ ]

A series of the Court's decisions has yielded a host of situations in which persons adversely affected by ERISA–proscribed wrongdoing cannot gain make–whole relief. First, in Massachusetts Mut. Life Ins. Co. v. Russell,[ ], the Court stated, in dicta: "[T]here is a stark absence—in [ERISA] itself and in its legislative history—of any reference to an intention to authorize the recovery of extracontractual damages" for consequential injuries.[ ] Then, in Mertens v. Hewitt Associates,[ ], the Court held that § 502(a)(3)'s term "equitable relief" . . . refer[s] to those categories of relief that were typically available in equity (such as injunction, mandamus, and restitution, but not compensatory damages).[ ] Most recently, in Great–West, the Court ruled that, as "§ 502(a)(3), by its terms, only allows for equitable relief," the provision excludes "the imposition of personal liability . . . for a contractual obligation to pay money."[ ]

As the array of lower court cases and opinions documents,[ ] fresh consideration of the availability of consequential damages under § 502(a)(3) is plainly in order.[ ]

The Government notes a potential amelioration. Recognizing that "this Court has construed Section 502(a)(3) not to authorize an award of money damages against a non–fiduciary," the Government suggests that the Act, as currently written and interpreted, may "allo[w] at least some forms of 'make–whole' relief against a breaching fiduciary in light of the general availability of such relief in equity at the time of the divided bench." Brief for United States as Amicus Curiae[ ]. * * * "Congress . . . intended ERISA to replicate the core principles of trust remedy law, including the make–whole standard of relief."[ ] I anticipate that Congress, or this Court, will one day so confirm.

Seven other justices, of course, were silent on this question, although remedies under ERISA were not at issue in the case. To date, attempts to obtain monetary relief in ERISA actions through traditional equitable remedies such as restitution or surcharge have failed. See Knieriem v. Group Health Plan, Inc. 434 F.3d 1058 (8th Cir.2006).

5. While ERISA preempts state common law, federal courts have, with some hesitancy, developed federal common law (such as the law of unconscionability) or applied traditional equity principles in ERISA cases to protect ERISA participants or beneficiaries. See Jayne Zanglein, Closing the Gap: Safeguarding Participants' Rights by Expanding the Federal Common Law of ERISA, 72 Wash. U.L Q. 671 (1994); William Carr & Robert Liebross, Wrongs Without Rights: The Need for a Strong Federal Common Law of ERISA, 4 Stanford L & Pol'y Rev. 221 (1993). Under what circumstances might federal common law or equitable doctrine apply? See Kane v. Aetna Life Insurance, 893 F.2d 1283 (11th Cir.1990) (court can apply equitable estoppel to interpret but not to change the terms of an ERISA plan); Nash v. Trustees of Boston Univ., 946 F.2d 960 (1st Cir.1991) (fraud in the inducement can be raised as an affirmative defense in ERISA case); but see Watkins v. Westinghouse Hanford Co., 12 F.3d 1517 (9th Cir.1993) (equitable doctrines may not be relied on to provide remedies not available under ERISA).

Should the federal courts adopt state insurance common law in interpreting ERISA policies, or do different considerations govern in ERISA cases? In particular, should courts apply the contract interpretation principle of *contra proferentem* (applied in *HealthChicago*) in an ERISA case? Several appellate courts have held that *contra proferentem* is not appropriate in cases where the plan administrator is granted discretion to interpret the plan. Kimber v. Thiokol Corp., 196 F.3d 1092 (10th Cir.1999); Morton v. Smith, 91 F.3d 867 (7th Cir.1996), while others have held that it is appropriate when reviewing plan interpretation decisions when the court is applying de novo review, Fay v. Oxford Health Plan, 287 F.3d 96, 104 (2nd Cir.2002). Yet other courts have recognized another general principal of insurance law—that ambiguous plan terms must be construed to accord with the reasonable expectations of the insured. Bynum v. Cigna Healthcare of N.C., Inc., 287 F.3d 305, 313–14 (4th Cir.2002).

6. Although the courts often act as though they were applying contract law in interpreting and enforcing ERISA plan provisions, ERISA plans are based on very unusual contracts. First, the insurance contract itself is between the employer and insurer, and the beneficiary rarely knows fully, or even has immediate access to, its terms. Second, the employer–insurer agreement tends to evolve over time, yet the beneficiary may be bound by terms that were far from clear at the time the claim was made. See, e.g., Mizzell v. Paul Revere Ins. Co., 278 F.Supp.2d 1146 (D.C.Cal.2003), in which the court deferred to the discretion of the insurer even though the provision granting discretion to the insurer was not finalized until after the claim was submitted. Despite this, courts seem usually to have little trouble binding beneficiaries by the terms of ERISA contracts.

7. ERISA does not by its terms permit providers to sue plans to collect payments due them for providing services to beneficiaries. Courts have gen-

erally rejected the argument that providers are "beneficiaries" under ERISA plans. Pritt v. Blue Cross & Blue Shield of West Virginia, Inc., 699 F.Supp. 81 (S.D.W.Va.1988). Providers have been more successful in asserting their rights as assignees of participants or beneficiaries, City of Hope Nat. Med. Ctr. v. HealthPlus, Inc., 156 F.3d 223 (1st Cir.1998); Hermann Hosp. v. MEBA Med. & Benefits Plan, 845 F.2d 1286 (5th Cir.1988), though a few courts have held that assignees have no standing to sue as they are not mentioned as protected parties within the statute. Other courts have upheld anti–assignment clauses in plan contracts.

Courts have split on whether providers can recover from insurers when the insurer leads the provider to believe that the insured or the service is covered, and then subsequently refuses payment and claims ERISA protection. Several courts have held that ERISA is intended to control relationships between employers and employees and should not preempt common law or statutory misrepresentation claims brought by providers. Transitional Hospitals Corp. v. Blue Cross & Blue Shield of Texas, Inc., 164 F.3d 952 (5th Cir.1999); Hospice of Metro Denver, Inc. v. Group Health Ins. of Okla., Inc., 944 F.2d 752 (10th Cir.1991). Other courts have held that misrepresentation claims are claims for benefits that are preempted by ERISA. Cromwell v. Equicor–Equitable HCA Corp., 944 F.2d 1272 (6th Cir.1991). Finally, several courts have allowed a provider to sue an ERISA plan on a contract or state statutory claim, stating that the claim was not preempted by ERISA because the provider had no standing to sue under ERISA. See Medical and Chirurgical Faculty v. Aetna U.S. Healthcare, Inc., 221 F.Supp.2d 618 (D.Md.2002), Foley v. Southwest Texas HMO, Inc., 226 F.Supp.2d 886 (E.D.Tex.2002). See, generally, Scott C. Walton, Note, ERISA Preemption of Third–Party Provider Claims: A Coherent Misrepresentation of Coverage Exception, 88 Iowa L. Rev. 969 (2003); Kevin Wiggins, Medical Provider Claims: Standing, Assignments, and ERISA Preemption, 45 J. Marshall L. Rev. 861 (2012).

8. ERISA requires health benefit plans to acknowledge and effectuate "qualified medical child support orders." These are state court orders that require a group health plan that covers dependents to extend group medical coverage to the children of a plan participant, even though the participant does not have legal custody of the children. 29 U.S.C.A. § 1169. Under this law, adopted in 1993, a plan participant can be required under court order to pay for family coverage to cover a dependent child not in the parent's custody, even though the parent might have otherwise chosen not to purchase coverage. Who benefits from this law, other than the children it protects?

PROBLEM: ERISA LITIGATION

John Mendez is in the advanced stages of a condition that results in degeneration of his nervous system. His doctor believes that he would be helped by a new gene therapy. John is covered under his employer's self–insured employee benefits plan. The plan has denied coverage for the therapy, claiming that it is experimental. The terms of the plan give the administrator discretion to decide whether or not to cover experimental procedures, but the plan does not define "experimental." John's doctor claims that the procedure is still quite new, but has advanced beyond the experimental stage. What standard will a court apply in reviewing the administrator's decision if John sues under § 502? How does this standard differ from that which a court would have applied had John sued an insurer under an individual health insurance policy under standard state insurance contract law?

VI. FEDERAL ANTI–DISCRIMINATION STATUTES

A. THE AMERICANS WITH DISABILITIES ACT

Title I of the ADA prohibits discrimination "against a qualified individual with a disability because of the disability of such individual in regard to * * * [the] terms, conditions, and privileges of employment." 42 U.S.C.A. § 12112. Discrimination prohibited by the statute extends to "fringe benefits." 42 U.S.C.A. § 12112(b)(4); 29 C.F.R. § 1630.4(f). Title II similarly prohibits discrimination by public entities. 42 U.S.C.A. § 12132. Title III proscribes discrimination "on the basis of disability in the full and equal enjoyment of the goods, services, facilities, privileges, advantages, or accommodations of any place of public accommodation * * *." 42 U.S.C.A. § 12182. "Public accommodation" is specifically defined to include an "insurance office." 42 U.S.C.A. § 12181(7)(F). Finally, Title V of the ADA contains a specific "safe harbor" providing that the ADA is not to be construed to restrict insurers, HMOs, employers, plans or administrators from "underwriting risks, classifying risks, or administering such risks that are based on or not inconsistent with State law," as long as the entity does not use this provision "as a subterfuge to evade the purposes" of the ADA. 42 U.S.C.A. § 12201(c).

The ADA would on its face seem to prohibit insurers and employers administering benefit plans from imposing coverage terms and conditions that discriminate against persons with particular disabilities. Cases have been brought under the ADA, therefore, challenging policies that provided less coverage for treatment of mental illnesses than for treatment of physical conditions, Rogers v. Department of Health and Envtl. Control, 174 F.3d 431 (4th Cir.1999); Ford v. Schering–Plough Corp., 145 F.3d 601 (3d Cir.1998); Fletcher v. Tufts University, 367 F.Supp.2d 99 (D.Mass.2005); that capped coverage for AIDS but not for other conditions, Doe v. Mutual of Omaha Ins. Co., 179 F.3d 557 (7th Cir.1999); or that excluded coverage for particular services, like heart transplants, Lenox v. Healthwise of Kentucky, Ltd., 149 F.3d 453 (6th Cir.1998); or infertility, Krauel v. Iowa Methodist Medical Center, 95 F.3d 674 (8th Cir.1996).

Although some of these cases have succeeded, they have encountered increasingly serious obstacles. First, most courts have held that the ADA does not require employers or insurers to offer any particular form of coverage, but merely prohibits them from offering different terms and conditions of coverage to disabled persons than those offered to nondisabled persons. EEOC v. Staten Island Sav. Bank, 207 F.3d 144 (2nd Cir.2000); Weyer v. Twentieth Century Fox Film Corp., 198 F.3d 1104 (9th Cir.2000); Doe v. Mut. of Omaha Ins. Co., 179 F.3d 557 (7th Cir.1999); Ford v. Schering–Plough Corp., 145 F.3d 601 (3d Cir.1998). These courts hold that the ADA does not demand that all disabilities be treated similarly, but only that disabled persons not be disfavored in comparison to nondisabled persons. Providing different coverage for different conditions, moreover, is not even necessarily prohibited unless the condition itself is a disability or unless discrimination in coverage of a particular condition disproportionately affects disabled persons.

Second, there is considerable debate as to when and whether the ADA applies to insurance policies. Though Title III clearly covers insurance offices, several courts have held that Title III only applies to physical places, i.e. the physical accessibility of insurance offices, and does not extend to the terms and conditions of the products the insurers offer independent of these places. Weyer v. Twentieth Century Fox Film Corp., 198 F.3d 1104 (9th Cir.2000); McNeil v. Time Ins., Co., 205 F.3d 179 (5th Cir.2000); Ford v. Schering–Plough Corp., 145 F.3d 601 (3d Cir.1998); Lenox v. Healthwise of Ky., Ltd., 149 F.3d 453 (6th Cir.1998); Parker v. Metro. Life Ins. Co., 121 F.3d 1006 (6th Cir.1997) (en banc). The EEOC Guidelines and a number of other courts, on the other hand, have held that Title III might extend to the contents of insurance policies as well. Doe v. Mut. of Omaha Ins. Co. 179 F.3d 557, 558–59 (7th Cir.1999); Pallozzi v. Allstate Life Ins. Co., 198 F.3d 28 (2d Cir.1999); Carparts Distribution Ctr., Inc. v. Automotive Wholesaler's Ass'n of New England, 37 F.3d 12 (1st Cir.1994); Fletcher v. Tufts Univ., 367 F.Supp.2d 99, 114–115 (D.Mass.2005). See Jeffrey S. Manning, Are Insurance Companies Liable Under the Americans With Disabilities Act? 88 Cal.L.Rev. 607 (2000); Jill L. Schultz, Note: The Impact of Title III of the Americans with Disabilities Act on Employer–Provided Insurance Plans: Is the Insurance Company Subject to Liability? 56 Wash. & Lee L. Rev 343 (1999). Of course, if insurance is offered through an employer, discrimination is prohibited under Title I even if the insurer's practices are not covered by Title III, although the employer, not the insurer, would be the proper defendant.

Third, several courts have read Title V's insurance "safe harbor" broadly to protect insurer practices that are not intentional stratagems to effectuate discrimination, following Supreme Court precedent in interpreting the term "subterfuge" in the ADEA in Public Employees Retirement System of Ohio v. Betts, 492 U.S. 158, 109 S.Ct. 2854, 106 L.Ed.2d 134 (1989). See Ford v. Schering–Plough Corp., 145 F.3d 601 (3d Cir.1998) and Krauel v. Iowa Methodist Med. Ctr., 95 F.3d 674, 678–9 (8th Cir.1996). Other courts, however, have required actuarial support for treating different conditions differently, particularly when the insurance practice is also suspect under state law. Morgenthal v. American Tel. and Tel. Co., 1999 WL 187055 (S.D.N.Y.1999); Chabner v. United of Omaha Life Ins. Co., 994 F.Supp. 1185 (N.D.Cal.1998).

Fourth, a number of courts have limited Title I ADA actions to current employees, contending that former employees, such as retirees, have no rights under the statute. See, e.g. EEOC v. CNA Ins. Cos., 96 F.3d 1039, 1045 (7th Cir.1996). But see, Castellano v. City of N.Y., 142 F.3d 58 (2d Cir.1998).

Of course, since the ACA bans health status underwriting and requires plans to cover essential benefits, the ADA should diminish in importance as a factor in health insurance disputes. Nonetheless, it may continue to be of some significance. The ADA limits, for example, the questions that employers can ask their employees about health issues, which might have an effect on wellness programs. Michelle M. Mello and Meredith B. Rosenthal, Wellness Programs and Lifestyle Discrimination—The Legal Limits, 359 New Eng. J. Med. 192 (2008). In any event, the ACA has proven a disappointment for advocates who had hoped that it would lead to more equitable and rational insurance coverage, and true protection against health status discrimination has had to wait for the ACA.

B. OTHER ANTI–DISCRIMINATION LAWS

A number of other federal laws prohibit discrimination in health insurance on other bases, though their impact is relatively modest. First, an employer covered by Title VII of the Civil Rights Act cannot treat medical costs associated with pregnancy or childbirth different than other medical costs covered by its health insurance plan. Title VII prohibits sex discrimination, and the Pregnancy Discrimination Act of 1978 (PDA) defines sex discrimination to include treatment of pregnancy, childbirth, or related medical conditions differently from other medical conditions under fringe benefit programs. 42 U.S.C.A. § 2000e(k). Maternity–related medical conditions must, therefore, be treated the same as other medical conditions under group health insurance with respect to terms of reimbursement (including payment maximums); deductibles, copayments, coinsurance, and out–of–pocket maximums; pre–existing condition limitations; extension of benefits following termination of employment; and limitations on freedom of choice. See 29 C.F.R. App. to Pt. 1604, Questions 25–29. The Eighth Circuit, however, has held that the PDA does not require coverage of fertility services. Saks v. Franklin Covey Co., 316 F.3d 337 (2d Cir.2003); Krauel v. Iowa Methodist Med. Ctr., 95 F.3d 674 (8th Cir.1996). The Eighth Circuit has also rejected the position of the EEOC and held that neither the PDA nor Title VII require employee benefit plans to cover contraceptives. In re Union Pacific Railroad Employment Practices Litigation, 479 F.3d 936 (8th Cir.2007). The definition of essential benefits under the ACA will, no doubt, determine the extent to which these services are offered in the future.

Second, the Age Discrimination in Employment Act (ADEA) 29 U.S.C.A. §§ 621–630, limits the ability of covered employers to discriminate among employees with respect to the provision of health insurance benefits. The Older Workers Benefit Protection Act of 1990 amended the ADEA to clarify that discrimination in the provision of benefits, including health insurance benefits is prohibited. 29 U.S.C.A. § 630(*l*). In 2000, the Third Circuit held that an employer who offers Medicare–eligible retirees inferior benefits compared to retirees who are not eligible for Medicare was in violation of the ADEA unless its practice was protected by a safe harbor in the Act, which permits employers offering bona fide benefit plans to offer older workers fewer benefits or to charge older workers more for benefits in voluntary contributory plans (as long as the proportion of total premium charged the employee does not change with age), if the distinctions are justified by cost data and the employer does not pay less than it does for benefit plans for younger workers. Erie County Retirees Assoc. v. County of Erie, 220 F.3d 193 (3d Cir.2000), applying 29 U.S.C.A. § 623(f)(2)(B)(1); 29 C.F.R. § 1625.10. In April of 2004, the EEOC issued a rule stating that employers could reduce or eliminate health benefits for Medicare–eligible beneficiaries without violating the ADEA. 68 Fed. Reg. 41542 (2003). The EEOC rule was upheld by American Ass'n of Retired Persons v. EEOC, 489 F.3d 558 (3d Cir. 2007).

Third, § 105 of the Internal Revenue Code limits the ability of self–insured employer health plans to discriminate in favor of highly–compensated individuals. 26 U.S.C.A. § 105(h), 26 C.F.R. §§ 1–105–1 through 1–105–11(c), while § 125 proscribes discrimination in favor of highly–compensated individuals by tax–subsidized cafeteria plans. 26 U.S.C.A. § 125(b) & (c). Section 2716 of the PHSA, added by the ACA, prohibits discrimination in favor of highly–compensated individuals by insured group plans.

Do any of these laws limit significantly the ability of insurers to discriminate against the unhealthy? See Mary Crossley, Discrimination Against the Unhealthy in Health Insurance, 54 U. Kan. L. Rev. 73 (2005). Will the antidiscrimination laws described in this section play any continuing role after the ACA is fully in effect? With the elimination of health status as a factor in underwriting, is the ADA still relevant at all? The ACA does not require that all medical conditions receive identical coverage. In particular, the law states at section 10101, amending section 2711 of the PHSA:

> (b) PER BENEFICIARY LIMITS.—Subsection (a) shall not be construed to prevent a group health plan or health insurance coverage from placing annual or lifetime per beneficiary limits on specific covered benefits that are not essential health benefits

under section 1302(b) of the Patient Protection and Affordable Care Act, to the extent that such limits are otherwise permitted under Federal or State law.

Will this provision continue to allow discrimination on the basis of health conditions? See, generally, Sara Rosenbaum, Insurance Discrimination on the Basis of Health Status: An Overview of Discrimination Practices, Federal Law, and Federal Reform Options, 37 Journal of Law, Medicine and Ethics 3 (2009).

How will the provisions of the ACA allowing premiums to vary by a ratio of 1 to 3 based on age interact with the Age Discrimination in Employment Act? Under the regulations implementing the Age Discrimination in Employment Act, an employer cannot require an employee to pay a higher percentage of the premium of employment–related coverage based on age alone (29 C.F.R. 1625.10(d)(4)(ii)). This would seem to mean that if an employer voluntarily contributes toward the purchase of insurance by employees through the exchange, the employer will have to pay more for older employees who face higher premiums, even though the percentage of the premium the employer pays will stay the same. This may complicate the use of the exchanges by employers.

CHAPTER 9

PROFESSIONAL RELATIONSHIPS IN HEALTH CARE ENTERPRISES

■ ■ ■

I. CREDENTIALING AND STAFF PRIVILEGES

SOKOL V. AKRON GENERAL MEDICAL CENTER

United States Court of Appeals for the Sixth Circuit, 1999.
173 F.3d 1026.

NORRIS, CIRCUIT JUDGE.

Plaintiff is a cardiac surgeon on staff at Akron General. The Medical Council at Akron General received information in the mid–1990's indicating that plaintiff's patients had an excessively high mortality rate. Concerned about plaintiff's performance of coronary artery bypass surgery ("CABG"), the Medical Council created the CABG Surgery Quality Task Force in 1994 to conduct a review of the entire cardiac surgery program at Akron General. The Task Force hired Michael Pine, M.D., a former practicing cardiologist who performs statistical risk assessments for evaluating the performance of hospitals. At a presentation in 1994 attended by plaintiff, Dr. Pine identified plaintiff as having a mortality rate of 12.09%, a "high risk–adjusted rate." Risk adjustment analyzes the likelihood that a particular patient or group of patients will die, as compared to another patient or group of patients. Dr. Pine stated in a summary of his findings that the predicted mortality rate for plaintiff's CABG patients was 3.65%, and plaintiff's "high mortality rate was of great concern and warrants immediate action."

James Hodsden, M.D., Chief of Staff at Akron General, requested that the Medical Council consider plaintiff for possible corrective action. Pursuant to the Medical Staff Bylaws, the Medical Council forwarded the complaint to the chairman of plaintiff's department, who appointed an Ad Hoc Investigatory Committee to review plaintiff's CABG surgery performance. The Medical Staff Bylaws require the Investigatory Committee to interview the staff member being reviewed and provide the Medical Council with a record of the interview and a report. The Investigatory Committee met with plaintiff three times. At the first meeting, the Investigatory Committee identified the issues before it to include addressing questions raised by plaintiff about the Pine study and determining the cause of plaintiff's excessive mortality rate. At the second meeting, the Investigatory Committee examined the mortality rate of plaintiff's patients using the Society of Thoracic Surgeons ("STS") methodology. Under STS methodology, the Investigatory Committee, like Dr. Pine, determined that plaintiff's CABG risk–adjusted mortality rate was roughly three times higher than the predicted mortality rate. The Investigatory Committee discussed the results of this analysis with plaintiff at the meeting.

At the third meeting, the Investigatory Committee reviewed with plaintiff various records of his twenty–six CABG patients who died either during or around the time of surgery. The Investigatory Committee determined that one factor leading to the deaths of these patients was poor case selection, meaning plaintiff did not adequately screen out those patients for whom CABG surgery was too risky. The Investigatory Committee also found that the excessive number of deaths may have been due to insufficient myocardial protection, which led to heart attacks.

The Investigatory Committee ultimately reported to the Medical Council that plaintiff's mortality rate was excessively high and that the two principal causes for this high mortality rate were poor case selection and "improper myocardial protection." The Investigatory Committee recommended that all cases referred to plaintiff for CABG surgery undergo a separate evaluation by another cardiologist who could cancel surgery felt to be too risky. It also recommended that plaintiff not be permitted to do emergency surgery or serve on "cathlab standby" and that there be an ongoing review of his CABG patients by a committee reporting to the Medical Council. Finally, it recommended that a standardized myocardial protection protocol be developed, and that all cardiac surgeons should be required to comply with the protocol.

Plaintiff appeared before the Medical Council on November 21, 1996, and the Medical Council voted to implement the recommendations. Under the Akron General Medical Staff Bylaws, when the Medical Council makes a decision adverse to the clinical privileges of a staff member, the staff member must be given notice of the decision of the Medical Council, and the notice shall specify "what action was taken or proposed to be taken and the reasons for it." This notice allows the staff member to prepare for a hearing to review the Medical Council's decision. * * *

Plaintiff and representatives from the Medical Council appeared before an Ad Hoc Hearing Committee on March 27, 1997. Plaintiff was represented by legal counsel, submitted exhibits, and testified on his own behalf. Dr. Gardner, a member of the Investigatory Committee, testified that although the Pine study and the STS methodology tended to underestimate the actual risk in some of plaintiff's cases, the Investigatory Committee concluded that the STS risk stratification tended to corroborate the Pine analysis. When asked about the Medical Council's determination that plaintiff engaged in poor case selection, Dr. Gardner had difficulty identifying specific cases that should not have had CABG surgery, yet he stated that "in the aggregate" there was poor case selection.

The Hearing Committee recommended that the Medical Council restore all plaintiff's CABG privileges. The Medical Council rejected the recommendation of the Hearing Committee and reaffirmed its original decision. In accordance with the Bylaws, plaintiff appealed the Medical Council's determination to the Executive Committee of the Board of Trustees of Akron General. This Committee affirmed the Medical Council's decision. Plaintiff then asked the district court for injunctive relief against Akron General.

* * *

Under Ohio law, private hospitals are accorded broad discretion in determining who will enjoy medical staff privileges at their facilities, and courts should not interfere with this discretion "unless the hospital has acted in an arbitrary, capricious or unreasonable manner or, in other words, has abused its discretion." [ ] However, hospitals must provide "procedural due process . . . in adopting and applying" "reasonable, nondiscriminatory criteria for the privilege of practicing" surgery in the hospital. [ ]

A. Insufficient notice

This appeal requires us to examine the extent of the procedural protections afforded plaintiff under Ohio law. In addition to an appeals process, "[f]air procedure requires meaningful notice of adverse actions and the grounds or reasons for such actions" when a hospital makes an adverse decision regarding medical staff privileges. [ ] Akron General's Medical Staff Bylaws require that notice of an adverse decision by the Medical Council state "what action was taken or proposed to be taken and the reasons for it" and thus do not contractually provide for a quality of notice exceeding that required by Ohio law.

The President of Akron General sent plaintiff a letter notifying him of the Medical Council's initial decision. The letter refers plaintiff to the minutes of the Medical Council's meeting which set out the reasons for the Council's decision. These minutes, provided to plaintiff, indicate that the findings and recommendations of the Investigatory Committee were presented. The Investigatory Committee found that "[t]he number and percentage of deaths in Dr. Sokol's population was excessively high compared to the published national statistics and other local surgeons." Two reasons for this high percentage were offered—poor case selection and problems with protecting against myocardial infarctions. * * *

According to the magistrate judge, the notice provided plaintiff was insufficient because [it failed] to provide Dr. Sokol with specific cases where he engaged in poor case selection and where he failed to provide appropriate myocardial protection.

The sort of notice demanded by the magistrate judge was not required by the circumstances of this case. Had Akron General restricted plaintiff's rights because the Medical Council determined that he had poor case selection or provided insufficient protections against myocardial infarctions, then perhaps specific patient charts should have been indicated, along with specific problems with each of those charts. However, Akron General had a more fundamental concern with plaintiff's performance: too many of his patients, in the aggregate, were dying, even after accounting for risk adjustment. Poor case selection and problems in preventing myocardial infarction were just two reasons suggested by the Investigatory Committee for the high mortality rate.

Plaintiff takes issue with the Pine study and the STS algorithm, claiming that they do not present an accurate picture of his performance as a surgeon because he is the "surgeon of last resort." In other words, so many of his patients die because so many of his patients are already at death's door. Perhaps plaintiff is correct about that. However, it is not for us to decide whether he has been inaccurately judged by the Investigatory Committee and the Medical Council. Instead, we are to determine whether plaintiff had sufficient notice of the charges against him to adequately present a defense before the Hearing Committee. He knew that the Medical Council's decision was based upon the results of the Pine study and the STS analysis, knew the identity of his patients and which ones had died, and had access to the autopsy reports and medical records of these patients. * * * Manifestly, he had notice and materials sufficient to demonstrate to the Hearing Committee's satisfaction that limiting his privileges was inappropriate.

It was well within Akron General's broad discretion to base its decision upon a statistical overview of a surgeon's cases. We are in no position to say that one sort of evidence of a surgeon's performance—a statistical overview—is medically or scientifically less accurate than another sort of evidence—the case–by–case study plaintiff suggests we require of Akron General.

B. Arbitrary decision

The magistrate judge also ruled that the Medical Council's decision was arbitrary. She reasoned that because Akron General did not have a fixed mortality rate by which to judge its surgeons before it limited plaintiff's privileges, it was arbitrary to take action against him based upon his mortality rate. We cannot agree. Surely, if plaintiff's mortality rate were 100%, the Medical Council would not be arbitrary in limiting his medical staff privileges, despite not having an established mortality rate. The magistrate judge's reasoning would prevent the Medical Council from instituting corrective action unless there were a preexisting standard by which to judge its staff. It is true that surgeons must be judged by "nondiscriminatory criteria." [ ]. However, in this context, that means, for example, that if it came to the attention of the Medical Council that another surgeon had a mortality rate as high as plaintiff's, the latter surgeon's medical privileges would be similarly limited. * * *

On appeal, plaintiff argues that the Medical Council's decision was so wrong that it was arbitrary, capricious, or unreasonable. He points to evidence tending to show that the Medical Council's case against him was assailable. Indeed, the Hearing Committee recommended that plaintiff's full privileges be restored. But as the Ohio Supreme Court has recognized, "[t]he board of trustees of a private hospital has broad discretion in determining who shall be permitted to have staff privileges." [ ] The board of trustees will not have abused its discretion so long as its decision is supported by any evidence. Here, the Medical Council had both the Pine Study and the STS analysis. While it is conceivable that these are inaccurate measurements of plaintiff's performance, they are evidence that the hospital was entitled to rely upon, and accordingly, we are unable to say that Akron General abused its discretion in limiting plaintiff's privileges.

MERRITT, CIRCUIT JUDGE, dissenting.

* * *

The heart surgeon has been treated unfairly by his hospital. The Hearing Committee was the only group composed of experts independent of the hospital administration. * * * The Committee completely exonerated Dr. Sokol. No one has cited a single operation or a single instance in which Dr. Sokol has made a mistake, not one.

* * *

NOTES AND QUESTIONS

1. Are the public's interests well served by statutory or common law procedural protections for actions against a doctor's staff privileges, or do these efforts create an obstacle to the removal of incompetent physicians? The court in *Sokol* examines the fairness of the procedures used by the hospital. The basis for this requirement is the common law doctrine of "fundamental fairness" applied to private associations generally. The requirements of fundamental fairness have been established on a case–by–case basis, and so its minimum requirements are not always clear. See *Potvin* in the next section, for example. The majority of states supplement common law requirements by imposing specific substantive and procedural requirements by statute. See, e.g., N.Y. Public Health Law § 2801–b, which requires that the hospital provide a written statement of reasons and provides for review by the state's Public Health Council of any denial or diminution of privileges. The federal Health Care Quality Improvement Act, discussed below, also establishes minimum procedures for hospitals desiring HCQIA immunity. The procedures for

credentialing in public hospitals must meet constitutional due process requirements. See, e.g., Osuagwu v. Gila Reg. Med. Ctr. 850 F.Supp. 1216 (D.N.M. 2012); Ripley v. Wyoming Med. Ctr., Inc. 559 F.3d 1119 (10th Cir. 2009), cert. den. 130 S.Ct. 287 (2009).

2. In *Sokol*, the court, applying Ohio law, limits its scope of review over the merits of the hospital's decision, testing only whether the hospital's decision was arbitrary, whether there was "any evidence" supporting its decision. A few other states also allow limited judicial review of the merits of staff privileges decisions. For example, California allows courts to reject denial or revocation of privileges if those decisions are not supported by substantial evidence. Ellison v. Sequoia Health Services, 183 Cal. App.4th 1486, 108 Cal. Rptr.3d 728 (Cal. App. 2010). (*Cf.* Sadler v. Dimensions Healthcare Corp., 378 Md. 509, 836 A.2d 655 (2003), holding that substantial evidence review is inappropriate under Maryland law.) Would a substantial evidence standard change the result in *Sokol*?

3. Only the minority of states allow substantive review of privileges decisions, whether under the arbitrariness criterion applied in *Sokol* or the substantial evidence standard described in note 2. In contrast to *Sokol*, the law in most states does not allow the courts to review the merits of privileges decisions at all. Instead, most states restrict judicial review to the question of whether the hospital followed its own by–laws; and for most of these states, the question is limited to compliance with the by–laws' procedural requirements only. See, e.g., Som v. Bd. of Trustees of Natchez Regional Med. Ctr., 98 So.3d 500 (Miss. App. 2012). What policy and practical considerations support broader and narrower judicial review? Why is the staff privileges system generally considered protective of physicians if judicial review is so limited in the majority of states? Do the procedures described in *Sokol* provide any insight here?

4. The Joint Commission (described in Chapter 3) has had extraordinary influence on credentialing procedures through its hospital accreditation standards. Joint Commission standards for the credentialing and privileges process set the following core expectations: that privileging and re–privileging assess physician performance against several competencies including patient care, medical/clinical knowledge, interpersonal and communication skills, and professionalism, among others; that there be continuous evaluation of practitioners rather than annual or biennial reviews alone; and that a separate standardized process be established to flag practitioners when there are competency concerns, including a process for newly credentialed physicians. Recently, the Joint Commission successfully resisted an effort by the Centers for Medicare & Medicaid Services (CMS) to force the Commission to adopt a streamlined credentialing process for professionals providing services through telemedicine, such as through remote review of images and biopsies. 20 Health Law Rptr. 886 (2011).

5. Joint Commission standards on credentialing are increasing the focus on the prospective monitoring of physician quality. One of the newer standards, for example, specifically provides that the hospital must establish

a system for collecting, recording, and addressing reports of concerns about individual physicians. These standards are intended to accelerate the use of data such as that relied upon in *Sokol.* See also Lo v. Provena Covenant Med. Ctr., 342 Ill.App.3d 975, 277 Ill.Dec. 521, 796 N.E.2d 607 (2003), considering a privileges action based on review of patient data revealing physician's mortality and return–to–surgery rates were about double the national average. Greater capacity for aggregating and analyzing patient data and an emphasis on outcomes for payment are making such actions more common. See, e.g., Barry R. Furrow, Data Mining and Substandard Medical Practice: The Difference between Privacy, Secrets and Hidden Defects, 51 Vill. L. Rev. 803 (2006) arguing that a hospital that fails to use available data effectively in peer review is negligent in credentialing.

6. In 2009, the Joint Commission adopted a standard that requires hospitals to establish a code of conduct that specifically defines what constitutes disruptive behavior and how that behavior will be addressed. Shortly after the Commission issued its standard, the AMA issued its own Model Medical Staff Code of Conduct. In comparison with the Joint Commission's standards on disruptive behavior, the AMA Code adopts a narrower definition of disruptive conduct, more procedural protections for the physician, and a greater emphasis on rehabilitation. The AMA Code also protects "any reasonable conduct to advocate for patients, to recommend improvements in patient care, to participate in the operations, leadership or activities of the organized medical staff, or to engage in . . . professional practice that may be in competition with the hospital."

The Joint Commission standard on disruptive health care professionals appears to have stimulated a wave of privileges actions against physicians for disruptive conduct, if judicial opinions are any indication. Courts have been quite supportive of hospitals in these circumstances. See, e.g., Poirier v. Our Lady of Bellefonte Hosp. 2006 W: 358241 (Ky. App.), holding that by–laws provision requiring doctors to "use a generally recognized level of quality" would reach a doctor engaging in a "recurring pattern of unacceptable and unprofessional behavior." What appears to be inappropriately disruptive behavior when viewed from one perspective, however, may be viewed by another as advocacy for quality of care. See Clark v. Columbia/HCA Information Services, Inc., 117 Nev. 468, 25 P.3d 215 (2001); Freilich v. Upper Chesapeake Health Systems, 33 A.3d 932 (Md. 2011). Adverse actions related to complaining behavior can trigger claims of unfair labor practice under the National Labor Relations Act in certain narrow circumstances.

7. The generally deferential posture of the courts toward hospitals' privileges decisions and the application of state and federal immunity statutes greatly reduce the likelihood of success for suits challenging such decisions. What factors might explain this deference? There has been a notable increase, however, in physicians claiming that an adverse action violated federal and state antidiscrimination statutes or was taken in retaliation for protected activity.

8. Hospitals can reduce the risk of litigation over credentialing decisions considerably by including clauses in their physician contracts or medical staff by–laws in which physicians waive their right to sue over adverse actions. See, e.g., Sadler v. Dimensions Healthcare Corp., 378 Md. 509, 836 A.2d 655 (2003), suggesting that hospitals pursue this option; Sternberg v. Nanticoke Mem.Hosp., 2012 WL 5830150 (Del Super.), for an example of language waiving procedural rights and obligating physicians to pay the hospital's attorney's fees. See also, the discussion of "clean sweep" clauses in the notes following *Mateo–Woodburn*, below.

NOTE: THE HEALTH CARE QUALITY IMPROVEMENT ACT (HCQIA)

The federal Health Care Quality Improvement Act, 42 U.S.C. § 11101, affords hospitals immunity from damages actions, except for civil rights claims. The HCQIA provides immunity to hospitals (and other entities) only if their credentialing decisions meet substantive and procedural statutory standards. Several states have also enacted local variations on the HCQIA, as the Act does not override or preempt state laws which provide "incentives, immunities, or protection for those engaged in a professional review action that is in addition or greater than that provided" in the federal statute. See, e.g., DeKalb Med. Ctr. v. Obekpa, 728 S.E.2d 265 (Ga. App. 2012), applying a state statute that reaches beyond the HCQIA in providing immunity from equitable relief.

The HCQIA creates a presumption that the credentialing decision (termed a "professional review action" in the Act) complies with the standards of the Act. To rebut this presumption, the plaintiff must prove by a preponderance of the evidence that the health care entity: (1) did not act in the reasonable belief that the action was in furtherance of quality health care; (2) did not make a reasonable effort to obtain the facts of the matter; (3) did not afford the physician adequate notice and hearing procedures and such other procedures required by fairness under the circumstances; or (4) did not act in the reasonable belief that the action was warranted by the facts known after such reasonable effort to determine the facts and after meeting the Act's procedural requirements. For a case that clearly lays out the plaintiff's burden, see Van v. Anderson, 199 F.Supp.2d 550 (N.D. Tex. 2002).

In testing these "four reasonables," courts use an objective standard of reasonableness. Neither the ultimate accuracy of the hospital's conclusions nor direct evidence of improper motive or bad faith is considered relevant to the objective reasonableness of the hospital's actions. See Cowell v. Good Samaritan Community Health Care, 225 P.3d 294 (Wash. App. 2009); Austin v. McNamara, 979 F.2d 728 (9th Cir. 1992), first establishing the objective standard so that immunity would be decided at an early stage of litigation. The courts have been generous with HCQIA immunity, ordinarily resolving cases through summary judgment in favor of the hospital. In fact, physicians only rarely succeed in overturning the rebuttable presumption of immunity. But see Granger v. Christus Health Ctr. Louisiana, 97 So.3d 604 (La. App.

2012), for a notable exception resulting in a damages award of nearly $3,000,000. Although evidence of improper motive or bad faith is not relevant under the HCQIA, such evidence may be used to prove violation of civil rights or discrimination laws. See Zawislak v. Mem. Hermann Hosp. System, 2011 WL 5082422 (S.D.Tex. 2011), denying hospital's motion to dismiss where physician produced facts supportive of a claim of retaliation.

Hospitals have generally been successful in claiming HCQIA immunity for actions based on disruptive conduct (see note 6, above) without evidence of substandard medical treatment or specific harm to patients. See, e.g., Sternberg v. Nanticoke Mem. Hosp., 15 A.3d 1225 (Del. 2011), in which the court held that the HCQIA provided immunity for summary suspension of a physician engaging repeatedly in verbally aggressive behavior against staff, even when patients were not in imminent danger; Guier v. Teton County Hosp. Dist., 248 P.3d 623 (Wyo. 2011), affirming termination of privileges for disruptive behavior with no evidence of deficiencies in quality of medical treatment.

The HCQIA provides that physicians who bring frivolous or bad faith suits challenging credentialing decisions may be ordered to pay defendant's attorney's fees and costs. See, e.g., Cohlmia v. St. John Med. Ctr., 2012 WL 5334724 (N.D. Okla.), accepting award of over $700,000 in attorneys' fees to hospital. But see, *Sternberg*, above, denying attorney's fees to hospital defendant.

The HCQIA also established the National Practitioner Data Bank (NPDB). (See Note on the National Practitioner Data Bank in Chapter 2.) To earn HCQIA immunity, hospitals must report certain adverse credentialing decisions to the NPDB and must check Data Bank records on the individual physician when considering an application for privileges and every two years for physicians who hold privileges. The HCQIA also provides hospitals limited immunity for their reports to the Data Bank, with the physician bearing the burden of proving that the hospital did not meet statutory standards in its reporting.

The hospital's obligation to report to the NPDB extends to situations where the physician has resigned once an investigation into quality of care issues has begun but before an adverse action has been taken. This has created a small window where a physician may resign prior to the beginning of an "investigation." Some argue that this allows hospitals and doctors too great an opportunity to bypass reporting, and that hospitals use this for leverage in pushing physicians out "voluntarily" with the result that there is no evidence in the Data Bank that the doctor has had problems. In any case, it is not entirely clear when the opportunity to resign without report has passed. See, e.g., Hooper v. Columbus Reg'l Healthcare System, 956 So.2d 1135 (Ala. 2006); *Sternberg*, above, describing use of leave of absence instead of precautionary suspension to avoid NPDB reporting. See also, Haavi Morreim, Moral Hazard: The Pros and Cons of Avoiding Data Bank Reports, 4 Drexel L. Rev. 265 (2011).

MATEO–WOODBURN V. FRESNO COMMUNITY HOSPITAL

Court of Appeal, Fifth District, 1990.
221 Cal.App.3d 1169, 270 Cal.Rptr. 894

BROWN, J.

* * *

Prior to August 1, 1985, and as early as 1970, the FCH department of anesthesiology operated as an open staff. The department was composed of anesthesiologists who were independently competing entrepreneurs with medical staff privileges in anesthesiology. Collectively, the anesthesiologists were responsible for scheduling themselves for the coverage of regularly scheduled, urgent and emergency surgeries.

[E]ach anesthesiologist was rotated, on a daily basis, through a first–pick, second–pick, etc., sequence whereby each anesthesiologist chose a particular operating room for that particular date. Usually no work was available for one or more anesthesiologists at the end of the rotation schedule. Once an anesthesiologist rotated through first–pick, he or she went to the end of the line. In scheduling themselves, the anesthesiologists established a system that permitted each anesthesiologist on a rotating basis to have the "pick" of the cases. This usually resulted in the "first–pick" physician taking what appeared to be the most lucrative cases available for that day.

The rotation system encouraged many inherent and chronic vices. For example, even though members of the department varied in their individual abilities, interests, skills, qualifications and experience, often "first–picks" were more consistent with economic advantage than with the individual abilities of the physician exercising his or her "first–pick" option. At times, anesthesiologists refused to provide care for government subsidized patients, allegedly due to economic motivations.

The department chairman had the authority to suggest to fellow physicians that they only take cases for which they were well qualified. However, the chairman was powerless to override the rotation system in order to enforce these recommendations.

Under the open–staff rotation system, anesthesiologists rotated into an "on call" position and handled emergencies arising during off hours. This led to situations where the "on–call" anesthesiologist was not qualified to handle a particular emergency and no formal mechanism was in place to ensure that alternative qualified anesthesiologists would become promptly available when needed. * * *

* * *

These chronic defects in the system led to delays in scheduling urgent cases because the first call anesthesiologists in charge of such scheduling at times refused to speak to each other. Often, anesthesiologists, without informing the nursing staff, left the hospital or made rounds while one or more of their patients were in post–anesthesia recovery. This situation caused delays as the nurses searched for the missing anesthesiologist.

The trial court found these conditions resulted in breaches of professional efficiency, severely affected the morale of the department and support staff, and impaired the safety and health of the patients. As a result of these conditions, the medical staff (not the board of trustees) initiated action resulting ultimately in the change from an "open" to a "closed" system. We recite the highlights of the processes through which this change took place.

* * *

[Mr.] Helzer, President and Chief Executive Officer of FCH, established an "Anesthesia Task Force" to study the proposed closure. In a subsequent memo to Helzer, dated April 6, 1984, the task force indicated it had considered four alternative methods of dealing with problems in the department of anesthesiology: (1) continuation of the status quo, i.e., independent practitioners with elected department chairman, (2) competitive groups of anesthesiologists with an elected department chairman, (3) an appointed director of anesthesia with independent practitioners and (4) an appointed director with subcontracted anesthesiologists, i.e., a closed staff.

The memo noted that under the third alternative—a director with independent practitioners—the director would have no power to determine who would work in the department of anesthesiology. "Any restriction or disciplinary action recommended by the director would need to go through the usual hospital staff procedure, which can be protracted." It was also noted in the memo that a director with subcontracted practitioners "would have the ability to direct their activities without following usual hospital staff procedures." The committee recommended a director with subcontracted practitioners.

[The board accepted the committee's recommendation and formed a search committee to recruit a director for the department.]

* * *

Mateo–Woodburn was offered the position of interim director on June 13, 1984, which position she accepted. Mateo–Woodburn was interviewed for the position of director on September 25, 1984. Hass was interviewed for the position on March 7, 1985.

At a special meeting of the board of trustees held on April 10, 1985, the anesthesia search committee recommended to the board that Hass be hired as director of the department of anesthesiology, and the recommendation was accepted by the board.

At the same April 10 meeting, the board authorized its executive committee to close the department of anesthesiology. On the same day, the executive committee met and ordered the department closed.

* * *

An agreement between FCH and the Hass corporation was entered into on June 7, 1985. On June 18, 1985, Helzer sent a letter to all members of the department of anesthesiology which states in relevant part:

* * *

"The Board of Trustees has now entered into an agreement with William H. Hass, M.D., a professional corporation, to provide anesthesiology services for all hospital patients effective July 1, 1985. The corporation will operate the Department of Anesthesia under the direction of a Medical Director who will schedule and assign all medical personnel. The corporation has appointed Dr. Hass as Medical Director, and the hospital has concurred with the appointment. The agreement grants to the corporation the exclusive right to provide anesthesia services to all hospital patients at all times."

"To provide the services called for by the agreement, it is contemplated that the Hass Corporation will enter into contractual arrangements with individual physician associates who must obtain Medical Staff membership and privileges as required by the staff bylaws. The negotiations with such associates are presently ongoing, and the hospital does not participate in them."

"Effective August 1, 1985, if you have not entered into an approved contractual agreement, with the Hass Corporation, you will not be permitted to engage in direct patient anesthesia care in this hospital. However, at your option, you may retain your staff membership and may render professional evaluation and assessment of a patient's medical condition at the express request of the attending physician."

The contract between the Hass corporation and FCH provided that the corporation was the exclusive provider of clinical anesthesiology services at the hospital; the corporation was required to provide an adequate number of qualified physicians for this purpose; physicians were to meet specific qualifications of licensure, medical staff membership and clinical privileges at FCH, and to have obtained at least board eligibility in anesthesiology; and the hospital had the right to review and approve the form of any contract between the corporation and any physician–associate prior to its execution.

Subject to the terms of the master contract between the Hass corporation and FCH, the corporation had the authority to select physicians with whom it would contract on terms chosen by the corporation subject to the approval of FCH. The contract offered to the anesthesiologists, among many other details, required that a contracting physician be a member of the hospital staff and be board certified or board eligible. The Hass corporation was contractually responsible for all scheduling, billing and collections. Under the contract, the corporation was to pay the contracting physician in accordance with a standard fee arrangement. The contracting physician was required to limit his or her professional practice to FCH except as otherwise approved by the FCH board of trustees.

[The contract also provided:] "... Provider shall not be entitled to any of the hearing rights provided in the Medical Staff Bylaws of the Hospital and Provider hereby waives any such hearing rights that Provider may have. However, the termination of this Agreement shall not affect Provider's Medical Staff membership or clinical privileges at the Hospital other than the privilege to provide anesthesiology services at the Hospital."

Seven of the thirteen anesthesiologists on rotation during July 1985 signed the contract. Of the six plaintiffs in this case, five refused to sign the contract offered to them. The sixth plaintiff, Dr. Woodburn, was not offered a contract but testified that he would not have signed it, had one been offered.

* * *

Some of the reasons given for refusal to sign the contract were: (1) the contract required the plaintiffs to give up their vested and fundamental rights to practice at FCH; (2) the 60–day termination clause contained no provisions for due process review; (3) the contract failed to specify amounts to be taken out of pooled income for administrative costs; (4) the contract required plaintiffs to change medical malpractice carriers; (5) the contract required plaintiffs to obtain permission to practice any place other than FCH; (6) the contract imposed an unreasonable control over plaintiffs' financial and professional lives; (7) the contract failed to provide tenure of employment. The Hass corporation refused to negotiate any of the terms of the contract with plaintiffs.

* * *

* * * Numerous cases recognize that the governing body of a hospital, private or public, may make a rational policy decision or adopt a rule of general application to the effect that a department under its jurisdiction shall be operated by the hospital itself through a contractual arrangement with one or more doctors to the exclusion of all other members of the medical staff except those who may be hired by the contracting doctor or doctors. * * *

* * *

[The position] of a staff doctor in an adjudicatory one–on–one setting, wherein the doctor's professional or ethical qualifications for staff privileges is in question, take[s] on a different quality and character when considered in light of a rational, justified policy decision by a hospital to reorganize the method of delivery of certain medical services, even though the structural change results in the exclusion of certain doctors from the operating rooms. If the justification is sufficient, the doctor's vested rights must give way to public and patient interest in improving the quality of medical services.

It is also noted, where a doctor loses or does not attain staff privileges because of professional inadequacy or misconduct, the professional reputation of that doctor is at stake. In that circumstance, his or her ability to become a member of the staff at other hospitals is severely impaired. On the other hand, a doctor's elimination by reason of a departmental reorganization and his failure to sign a contract does not reflect upon the doctor's professional qualifications and should not affect his opportunities to obtain other employment. The trial court correctly found the decision to close the department of anesthesiology and contract with Hass did not reflect upon the character, competency or qualifications of any particular anesthesiologist.

* * *

[I]f the hospital's policy decision to make the change is lawful, and we hold it is, then the terms of the contracts offered to the doctors was part of the administrative decision and will not be interfered with by this court unless those terms bear no rational relationship to the objects to be accomplished, i.e., if they are substantially irrational or they illegally discriminate among the various doctors.

Given the conditions existing under the open rotation method of delivering anesthesia services, including among others the lack of control of scheduling and the absence of proper discipline, we cannot say the terms of the contract were irrational, unreasonable or failed to bear a proper relationship to the object of correcting those conditions. Considered in this light, the terms are not arbitrary, capricious or irrational.

* * *

As to the contract provision which required waiver of hearing rights set forth in the staff bylaws, * * * those rights do not exist under the circumstances of a quasi–legislative reorganization of a department by the board of trustees. This quasi–legislative situation is to be distinguished from a quasi–judicial proceeding against an individual doctor grounded on unethical or unprofessional conduct or incompetency. Accordingly, the waiver did not further detract from or diminish plaintiffs' rights.

* * *

Plaintiffs contend the department of anesthesiology could not be reorganized without amending the bylaws of the medical staff in accordance with the procedure for amendment set forth therein. Closely allied to this argument is the assertion the hospital unlawfully delegated to Hass the medical staff's authority to make staff appointments.

* * * The hospital's action did not change the manner or procedure by which the medical staff passes upon the qualifications, competency or skills of particular doctors in accordance with medical staff bylaws. * * * In fact, plaintiffs remain members of the staff and the contract requires contracting anesthesiologists to be members of the staff. Moreover, it is clear the medical staff does not appoint medical staff members—it makes recommendations to the board of trustees who then makes the final medical staff membership decision. Hass was never given authority to appoint physicians to medical staff and never did so. Hass was merely hired to provide anesthesiology services to the hospital. His decision to contract with various anesthesiologists in order to provide those services was irrelevant to medical staff appointments except that all persons contracting with Hass were required to qualify as members of the medical staff.

We conclude the trial court's determination that the defendants' "actions were proper under the circumstance and that plaintiffs' Medical Staff privileges were not unlawfully terminated, modified or curtailed" is fully supported by the evidence and is legally correct.

NOTES AND QUESTIONS

1. *Mateo–Woodburn* considers two issues related to exclusive contracting. In addition to resolving the question of the procedural rights of the physician who held privileges prior to the institution of the exclusive contract, it reviews the termination provision in the exclusive contract itself. What contractual provision is made for termination of the contract and termination of staff privileges between Hass, P.C., and the anesthesiologists at Fresno Community Hospital? Some court opinions have separated "staff" privileges from "clinical" privileges with the result that hospitals are not required to use procedures required for revocation of staff privileges when they have revoked or limited only the physician's clinical privileges, which allow the physician to admit or treat patients. See, e.g., Plummer v. Community Gen'l Hosp. of Thomasville, Inc., 155 N.C.App. 574, 573 S.E.2d 596 (2002); Ripley v. Wyoming Med. Ctr., Inc., 2008 WL 5875551 (D.Wyo. 2008). What is the rationale for this approach?

2. Would a contract clause that provides that termination of the contract will result automatically in termination of staff privileges without benefit of the by–laws' procedures (known as a "clean sweep" clause) be enforceable? See, for example, Madsen v. Audrain Health Care, 297 F.3d 694 (8th Cir. 2002) which, like most cases, upholds clean sweep agreements. Contracts

such as those in *Mateo–Woodburn* allocate power and control differently than does the traditional staff privileges relationship. Which situation is more compatible with a goal of cost containment? With a goal of assuring quality? Do the policy concerns underlying the procedural protections for credentialing decisions dissipate when the physician has a contract allowing no–cause termination?

3. FCH positioned the closing of its staff as an action to improve quality. What if the goal had been to reduce costs? See, e.g., St. Mary's Hosp. of Athens, Inc. v. Radiology Prof'l Corp., 205 Ga.App. 121, 421 S.E.2d 731 (1992) (but holding that hospital must follow by–laws provisions). But see Ray v. St. John's Health Care Corp., 582 N.E.2d 464 (Ind. Ct. App.1991). Public hospitals may be required to maintain an open staff and precluded from entering into an exclusive contract as closing the staff may implicate due process concerns. In addition, some states have extended the same restriction on exclusive contracting to hospitals that are considered to be "quasi–public." See, e.g., Kessel v. Monongalia County Gen'l Hosp., 215 W.Va. 609, 600 S.E.2d 321 (2004). But see Gaalla v. Brown, 2012 WL 512687 (5th Cir. 2012), holding that public hospital's entering into exclusive contract for cardiology services and terminating existing privileges of excluded physician did not violate procedural due process.

4. If cost control is a legitimate concern for hospitals, payers, and patients, one might argue that hospitals should monitor physician practices related to utilization. Others would be concerned that such controls threaten patients with inadequate diagnostic or medical care. "Economic credentialing," a term that that the AMA coined to describe certain standards for determining staff status, occurs when a hospital makes privileges decisions based on financial factors unrelated to quality. Is it clear that utilization—for example, in terms of surgery, scans, biopsies—relates only to cost? For an excellent analysis of economic credentialing, see John D. Blum, Beyond the ByLaws: Hospital–Physician Relationships, Economics, and Conflicting Agendas, 53 Buff. L. Rev. 459 (2005). Conflicts over financial considerations in credentialing have intensified as hospitals use their credentialing process to exclude physicians who have business interests, such as ambulatory surgical centers, which compete directly with those of the hospital itself.

5. In *Mateo–Woodburn* there was no implication of any performance or quality problems in any single physician's practice. If there had been, would the doctors have been entitled to a hearing? In Major v. Memorial Hosps. Assn., 71 Cal.App.4th 1380, 84 Cal.Rptr.2d 510 (1999), the court considered a case in which a hospital entered into an exclusive contract for anesthesiology after repeated scheduling problems, altercations among the doctors, and quality problems attributed specifically to the plaintiff doctors. The plaintiffs claimed that they were entitled to a hearing under *Mateo–Woodburn* because, unlike the facts in *Mateo–Woodburn*, the revocation of their privileges required by the closing of the anesthesiology staff reflected on their personal character and competency and so required the by–laws' procedures. The court rejected this argument.

6. The court in *Mateo–Woodburn* issued its opinion more than twenty years ago, and it now appears to represent the majority view of cases considering a hospital's authority to restructure its medical staff without recourse to the hearings provisions of the medical staff by–laws. See, for example, Van Valkenburg v. Paracelsus Healthcare Corp., 606 N.W.2d 908 (N.D.2000); Stears v. Sheridan County Memorial Hosp. Bd. of Trustees, 491 F.3d 1160 (10th Cir. 2007). But see, Madonna v. Satilla Health Services, Inc., 658 S.E.2d 858 (Ga. App. 2008). Some hospitals in contracting situations employ a version of their fair hearing procedures as a way of processing their contracting decision. See, e.g., Radiation Therapy Oncology, P.C. v. Providence Hosp., 906 So.2d 904 (Ala. 2005), affirming summary judgment in favor of hospital that transferred its hospital–based radiation oncology service to an office–based practice related to the hospital.

7. Many states have enacted legislation relevant to economic credentialing, some restrictive and some permissive. See Beverly Cohen, An Examination of the Right of Hospitals to Engage in Economic Credentialing, 77 Temp. L. Rev. 705 (2004).

II. MANAGED CARE CONTRACTING

POTVIN V. METROPOLITAN LIFE INS. CO.

California Supreme Court, 2000.
22 Cal.4th 1060, 95 Cal.Rptr.2d 496, 997 P.2d 1153.

KENNARD, J.

* * *

On September 10, 1990, Metropolitan Life Insurance (MetLife) entered into an agreement with Dr. Louis E. Potvin, an obstetrician and gynecologist, to include him as one of 16,000 participants on two of its preferred provider lists. Potvin had practiced medicine for more than 35 years; he was a past president of the Orange County Medical Association; and he held full staff privileges at Mission Regional Hospital, where he had served as Chairman of the Obstetrics and Gynecology Department for nine years. Under the contract, Potvin was to provide medical services to MetLife's insureds in return for agreed–upon payment by MetLife. The agreement created no employment or agency relationship, and it allowed Potvin to also "contract with other preferred provider organizations, health maintenance organizations or other participating provider arrangements." It provided for termination by either party "at any time, with or without cause, by giving thirty (30) days prior written notice to the other party."

On July 22, 1992, MetLife notified Potvin in writing that effective August 31, 1992, it was terminating his preferred provider status. Potvin asked for clarification; MetLife replied that the termination, which the parties here also refer to as "delistment," was consistent with the contract, which allowed termination "without cause." When Potvin insisted on a further explanation, MetLife reiterated its right to terminate without cause. MetLife then stated that even though it did not have to give a reason, Potvin's "delistment from the provider network was related to the fact that [he] did not meet [MetLife's] current selection and retention standard for malpractice history." At the time, MetLife would not include or retain on its preferred provider lists any physician who had more than two malpractice lawsuits, or who had paid an aggregate sum of $50,000 in judgment or settlement of such actions. Potvin's patients had sued him for malpractice on four separate occasions, all predating his 1990 agreement with MetLife. In three of these actions, the plaintiffs had abandoned their claims, while the fourth case had settled for $713,000.

After MetLife failed to respond to Potvin's request for a hearing, Potvin filed this lawsuit. * * * Potvin alleged that MetLife's termination of his preferred provider status devastated his practice, reducing it to "a small fraction" of his former patients. He asserted that he was required to reveal his termination to other insurers and managed care entities, which then removed him from their preferred provider lists, and that he suffered rejection by "physician groups . . . dependent upon credentialing by MetLife" and by current MetLife preferred provider physicians, who ceased referring patients to him.

The trial court granted MetLife's motion for summary judgment. * * *

The Court of Appeal reversed. It disagreed with the trial court that Potvin's complaint failed to allege a claim for violation of the common law right to fair procedure. It also held that, before removing Potvin from its preferred provider lists, MetLife should have given him notice of the grounds for its action and a reasonable opportunity to be heard. With respect to Potvin's assertion that the removal violated [the California statute] setting forth procedures for physician peer review, the Court of Appeal agreed with the trial court that those provisions did not apply to the preferred provider contract involved here.

* * * We affirm the Court of Appeal's reversal of the trial court's grant of summary judgment for MetLife, but we disagree with the Court of Appeal that MetLife necessarily must comply with the common law doctrine of fair procedure before removing physicians from its preferred provider lists. In this case, that issue needs to be resolved by further proceedings in the trial court under the standards set forth below.

* * *

Plaintiff here points out that when an insurance company with fiduciary obligations to its insureds maintains a list of preferred provider physicians to render medical services to the insureds, a significant public interest is affected. One practical effect of the health care revolution, which has made quality care more widely available and affordable through health maintenance organizations and other managed care entities, is that patients are less free to choose their own doctors for they must obtain medical services from providers approved by their health plan. The Managed Care Health Improvement Task Force stressed in its 1997 report to the California Legislature that the provision of health care "has a special moral status and therefore a particular public interest." [ ] But an even greater public interest is at stake when those medical services are provided through the unique tripartite relationship among an insurance company, its insureds, and the physicians who participate in the preferred provider network. * * *

Our conclusion that the relationship between insurers and their preferred provider physicians significantly affects the public interest does not necessarily mean that every insurer wishing to remove a doctor from one of its preferred provider lists must comply with the common law right to fair procedure. The obligation to do so arises only when the insurer possesses power so substantial that the removal significantly impairs the ability of an ordinary, competent physician to practice medicine or a medical specialty in a particular geographic area, thereby affecting an important, substantial economic interest.[5]

* * *

Here, plaintiff's amici curiae, the American Medical Association and the California Medical Association, assert in their joint brief that "the managed care organizations operating in California hold substantial economic power over physicians and their patients." They also contend that "the control exercised by managed care organizations makes access to provider panels a 'practical prerequisite' to any effective practice as a health care provider." * * * If participation in managed care arrangements is a practical necessity for physicians generally and if only a handful of health care entities have a virtual monopoly on managed care, removing individual physicians from preferred provider networks controlled by these entities could significantly impair those physicians' practice of medicine.

Potvin alleged that among the adverse effects of removal from MetLife's preferred provider lists were rejection by "physician groups which were dependent upon credentialing by MetLife" and devastation of his practice, which was reduced to "a small fraction" of his former patients. Proof of these allegations might establish that, in terminating a physician's preferred provider status, MetLife wields power so substantial as to significantly impair an ordinary, competent physician's ability to practice

[5] Our decision here does not apply to employer-employee contractual relations. Rather, it applies only to an insurer's decision to remove individual physicians from its preferred providers lists. We express no view on whether the factors giving rise to the common law right of fair procedure would be present when an insurer, acting to limit its service in a geographic area or medical field, reduces the total number of physicians on its preferred provider lists.

medicine or a medical specialty in a particular geographic area, thereby affecting an important, substantial economic interest.

* * *

Our holding does not prevent an insurer subject to obligations of common law fair procedure from exercising its sound business judgment when establishing standards for removal of physicians from its preferred provider lists. We simply hold that, under principles recognized by the common law of this state for over a century, such removal must be "both substantively rational and procedurally fair."

* * *

MetLife contends that even if removal of a physician from its preferred provider lists is subject to the common law right to fair procedure, here Potvin waived that right by agreeing that MetLife could terminate the provider arrangement without cause. Potvin responds that the public policy considerations supporting the common law right to fair procedure render the "without cause" clause in the MetLife preferred provider agreement unenforceable. * * * California courts are loathe to enforce contract provisions offensive to public policy. [ ] We therefore agree with Potvin that the "without cause" termination clause is unenforceable to the extent it purports to limit an otherwise existing right to fair procedure under the common law.

The judgment of the Court of Appeal is affirmed.

GEORGE, C.J., MOSK, J., and WERDEGAR, J., concur.

Dissenting Opinion by BROWN, J.

* * * With its decision today, the majority, in effect, declares that it is the public policy of this state that physicians are entitled to a minimum income and, therefore, if removal of a physician from an insurer's preferred provider list would reduce the physician's income below that guaranteed minimum, the physician is entitled to a hearing and to the judicial review that would inevitably follow upon an adverse decision. * * *

* * *

* * * According to Dr. Potvin, the average physician who practices his specialty, obstetrics/gynecology, has been sued for malpractice 2.3 times. MetLife wishes to restrict its preferred provider lists to physicians with a slightly better than average malpractice history, to those who have not been sued more than twice. Potvin, by contrast, has been sued 4 times—nearly twice the average. Now the majority's public policy antennae may be more sensitive than mine, but I suspect the jury is still out on the question of whether an insurer should be able to control its costs by restricting its preferred provider lists to physicians with slightly better than average malpractice histories. That, surely, is a business judgment,

and if the insurer makes the wrong judgment by depriving itself of doctors that patients insist upon, then the market will punish the insurer and force it to retreat from the impracticable standard.

* * *

Moreover, despite the majority's effort to cloak it in the public interest, this case has never been about Dr. Potvin's ability to practice medicine. It has been about money. * * * As far as we can tell from this record, during the three and a half years that passed between his initial correspondence with MetLife and the filing of his motion for summary adjudication, Potvin's ability to practice medicine and his medical specialty was unaffected. He just wasn't making as much money at it.

* * *

BAXTER, J., and CHIN, J., concur.

NOTES AND QUESTIONS

1. While *Potvin* addresses only the situation of managed care contracting, should the same concerns be applied to no–cause terminations in physician contracting generally? Accountable care organizations are likely to exert control over utilization of particular medical services, perhaps very much as managed care does. Should physicians or nurse practitioners who participate in an accountable care organization have any procedural or substantive rights regarding termination? Is *Potvin* consistent with *Mateo–Woodburn*, also a California case, in its treatment of no–cause termination clauses? Should the decisions be consistent? The California Court of Appeals, in an unpublished decision, declined to extend *Potvin* in Siegel v. CHW West Bay, 2002 WL 31599012 (Cal. Ct. App. 2002). The Court held that even if *Potvin* were extended to hospitals, the facts did not meet the *Potvin* requirement that the decision maker hold economic power substantial enough to impair the physician's ability to practice. See also Edson v. Valleycare Health System, 2001 WL 1345981 (9th Cir. 2001).

2. Is Dr. Potvin entitled to a hearing prior to being delisted by MetLife? If he is entitled to a hearing, the Court indicates that he is also entitled to have MetLife's decision reviewed on the basis of whether it is "rational." How would each of the following reasons fare under a standard that considers "rationality" or "good faith:" a Caesarean section rate in excess of the norm for plan physicians or in excess of the plan's target rate; specialist referrals or hospital stays in excess of the average of all plan physicians; disclosure to patients of physician incentive compensation relating to practice patterns?

3. *Potvin* was eagerly awaited (taking nearly three years for the court to issue its decision), but its actual impact on case law nationally has been minimal. Several state courts have addressed the issues in *Potvin* with varying results. See, for example, Mayer v. Pierce County Med. Bureau, 80 Wash.App. 416, 909 P.2d 1323 (1995), holding that a no–cause termination

clause was enforceable; Grossman v. Columbine Med. Group, 12 P.3d 269 (Colo. Ct. App. 1999, as modified Jan. 14, 2000), holding that a state statute established public policy supporting no–cause terminations; Harper v. Healthsource New Hampshire, 140 N.H. 770, 674 A.2d 962 (1996), prohibiting bad faith use of no–cause termination clause.

4. Many states enacted legislation in the early 1990s in response to physician claims that managed care organizations threatened to terminate them if they advocated on behalf of their patients or if they told patients about the financial controls and incentives imposed by the MCO. Massachusetts enacted one of the more comprehensive legislative packages, establishing a Bureau of Managed Care within the Division of Insurance. Health Insurance Consumer Protections. M.G.L.A. ch. 1760 § 1. See also Colo.Stat. § 10–16–705, providing that no–cause terminations simply require 60 days' notice, but that physicians cannot be delisted for reporting quality concerns to federal or state agencies, for disclosing financial incentives to patients, or for giving patients "standing referrals" to specialists; Cal. Bus. & Prof. Code § 2056, providing that a physician may not be terminated or penalized for advocating for "medically appropriate health care" within an appeal of a denial for payment or in protesting a policy that "consistent with that degree of learning and skill ordinarily possessed by reputable physicians practicing according to the applicable legal standard of care, reasonably believes impairs the physician's ability to provide medically appropriate health care." See discussion of state regulation of managed care in Chapter 8. Should the state legislature extend these protections to physicians contracting with practice groups or with ACOs?

INDEX

References are to Pages